The Ghetto and Beyond

PETER I. ROSE / Editor

The
Ghetto
and
Beyond

Essays on Jewish Life in America

RANDOM HOUSE / NEW YORK

*This book is dedicated to
the memory of my grandparents
(and the millions of grandparents)
who came to America
in quest of a dream.*

ACKNOWLEDGMENTS

To my friends Dan Aaron, Milton Gordon, Milton Konvitz, Sy Leventman, Marty Lipset, Sol Poll, Philip Roth, Lou Ruchames, Mel Tumin, and Dennis Wrong, I can only say that I hope the wait was worth it. I am truly indebted to you and to all whose works, new and old, appear in these pages. This is not my book— it is ours.

For all of us, I would like to acknowledge the encouragement and support of Jess Stein, Ted Caris, and Leona Huberman of Random House who helped to see this *megillah* through.

PETER I. ROSE

Northampton, Massachusetts

Contents

Jews and Other Americans

Outsiders Within

Epilogue

Introduction

THE GHETTO AND BEYOND

PETER I. ROSE

> The Jewish quarter is generally supposed to be a place of poverty, dirt, ignorance and immorality—the seat of the sweat-shop, the tenement house, where "red lights" sparkle at night, where the people are queer and repulsive. Well-to-do persons visit the ghetto merely from motives of curiosity or philanthropy; writers treat of it sociologically, as of a place in crying need of improvement.[1]

THE SUMMARY of popular images of New York's lower East Side, written almost seventy years ago, sounds strikingly similar to what one might read of Harlem, Hough, or Central Newark today. But the echo has a hollow ring. Regardless of what outsiders say, today's ghetto is not the same. It has a different character.

When the Lower East Side teemed with Jewish immigrants trying to eke out a meager living in the overcrowded buildings of a worn out slum, they, too, were often poor, hungry, bewildered, and bedraggled. But they knew what "soul brother" meant long before that expression was to enter the American vernacular. Their word was *landsmann* and, in many ways, the fellow-feeling that it stood for made the old poverty tolerable. The modus vivendi of the poor Jew's existence was dominated by mutual assistance and a sense of community. It was also pervaded with a belief, an underlying faith, that "America is different."

And for them America *was* different. In an Afterword to a reissue of Michael Gold's *Jews Without Money*, Michael Harrington summed it up rather succinctly.

> The "old" poverty was the experience of an adventurous poor who sought, like the characters in [*Jews Without Money*], a mythical America where the streets were paved with gold. They became disillusioned, to be sure, yet they shared the solidarity of a language, a religion, a national memory. If there were countless human tragedies and terrible cycles of unemployment and want, there was still an expand-

3

ing economy and the possibility of battling one's way out of the ghetto, either individually or as part of a community, as in the labor movement.[2]

Indeed, the demonstrable successes of those who had arrived but a few years (and sometimes mere months) before kept the faith alive. Despite the repeated mutterings of *a klug tzu Columbus* (a curse on Columbus), one could make it here—and many did. The Jews' ghetto, unlike the Negroes', was a gateway. It served to help them get in rather than to keep them locked out.

Of course, the Jews of the Lower East Side, the "Jews without money," were not the first to settle in America. Merchant traders from Recife in Brazil arrived on the island of Manhattan in 1654. By the time of the Revolution there were nearly 3,000 Jews in America and established congregations were to be found in Newport, Savannah, Philadelphia, and Richmond, as well as New York. Their numbers were to increase a hundredfold by 1870 as economic conditions and political unrest prompted the emigration of Jews from Germany. When they arrived some stayed in the east. Others went south or west. German-Jewish immigrants followed the wagon trains plying their soft goods and hardware to the pioneers and, eventually, settled among them. Backpacks were replaced by wagons, which were replaced in turn by little shops, some of which became great emporia with names like Levy's, Goldwater's, Neiman-Marcus, I. Magnin, and Miller Stockman. By 1870 a quarter of a million Jews were residing— and often prospering—in this country.

Although not always welcomed with total equanimity, most did find acceptance as they settled in cities, towns, and hamlets across the land. In fact, anti-Jewish barriers were rarely constructed against the social or physical mobility of these American Hebrews (as they were sometimes called). The ghetto as a place of ascription or solace was hardly in evidence on this side of the Atlantic in the antebellum period. It "appeared" as East European immigrants began to arrive on the eastern shore in increasing numbers during the late 1870s.

Within ten years the number of Jews increased to five hundred thousand and within twenty years it exceeded a million. By 1924 when the "Golden Door" was shut for good, more than three and a half million Jews had come to the United States.

These poor "greenhorns," with their sallow faces and their strange clothes, with their few belongings and their many children, with their curious dialects and mysterious religious rites, were to change the character of Jewish life in America—and America's characterization of the Jew. From their ranks (and not from the earlier German group) came the poets and the painters, the polemicists and the provocateurs. This is not to deny that stereotypes already existed. They did. Shakespeare was widely read and the image of Shylock was not unknown (nor were Jewish peddlers spared the comparison). Moreover, as many social novelists of the Gilded Age pointed out, wealthy German Jews were often seen as its quintessential parvenus.[3] Still, prior to the "new immigration," Jews as a group had made but a slight dent on the consciousness of the average American and had even less of an impact on American culture (save, perhaps, for Levi Strauss's dungarees). All this was to change dramatically with the arrival and settlement of the "Russian" immigrants on the American scene.

The immigrants themselves (from Warsaw and Lublin, from Vilna and Kovno, from Bialystok, from Kiev, from a hundred little villages in the Pale of Settlement, Austria-Hungary, and Rumania) came to find in the United States what seemed eternally elusive in Europe—the privilege of being a part of society rather than mere parasites on the body politic. America was seen as offering something more as well. Not only could one belong; one could also be oneself. And once here, the immigrants began to recreate an urban equivalent of the *shtetl* they had left behind. It came to be called a ghetto, not by those who lived and worked and played out life's dramas there, but by the outsiders who peered into these "exotic" and "oriental" enclaves.

The American ghetto was from its inception a combined product of communal assistance and societal denial. Realities quickly intruded upon the optimistic visions of the "open society" and Jews found that, while they could join the society, the price of membership was high. Mounting fear over the "wretched refuse" of Europe had led to a growing anti-foreign sentiment throughout the country. And none decried the influx more quickly than those who had so recently been immigrants themselves. Such tensions exacerbated a tendency that already existed among most groups of newcomers and certainly among Jews. This was the tendency to seek one another out and develop institutions (or remodel existing ones) to aid their kith and kin. Perhaps the most striking characteristic of the Jews was the extent to which they felt united by membership in a single, if greatly extended, family.

To be asked whether one is a "member of the tribe" was (and remains) more than a facetious question. It is a request for identification, for placement in a meaningful social category. As Erich Kahler has pointed out, such a feeling of kinship with fellow Jews may have little to do with personal relations. One may be much closer to gentile friends than to Jews. One may even be the sort of Jew who is uneasy in the presence of those displaying "Jewish peculiarities" (which in its extreme form may take on the character of intense self-hatred).[4]

For the Sephardic and German Jews who had come to America prior to the great migrations for example, Jewish identity was a relevant part of personal existence and few denied their lineage or their heritage. Still, they tried to minimize their "differences" from the social world into which they sought admission. They wanted to be seen by their gentile peers as bankers, not "Jewish bankers," as lawyers, not "Jewish lawyers." And they tried to model their lives accordingly. Being a Jew was important; being Jewish was often quite distasteful.

With the entry of millions of East European Jews (many reflecting those "Jewish peculiarities"), emotions were stirred and conflicts arose. The German Jews, both elite and parvenu, came to be grouped willy nilly with their "cousins" from Russia, often to their profound dismay. They who had organized Reform temples with choirs, organs, and Sunday services, who belonged to the best clubs and traveled in the highest circles, who had eschewed all traces of the "ghetto mentality" (or thought they had), were chagrined at what the migration might and, indeed, did portend. Some sought to dissociate themselves from their less reputable "relatives," but because the uncouth newcomers *were* relatives, they could never be completely abandoned.

One way of reconciling desired social distance with social responsibility deeply (though often painfully) felt was to employ these new people in their own shops and factories or help them find employment in those of Christian friends. Another way was to aid in the organization of societies such as the ubiquitous free loan associations to assist poor Jews. There are many explanations for the motivation of German-Jewish philanthropists (including the obvious notion of charity beginning at home), but one that is too frequently overlooked is the desire to alter the stereotype of the ghetto dweller by helping the newer immigrants to help themselves.

Growing anti-foreign and, especially, anti-Semitic sentiment throughout the country touched all American Jews—oldtimers and newcomers alike. By the turn of the century many strange and sometimes strained alliances had developed between the German Jews and the "Russians," between the bosses (for many worked in the Jewish dominated needle trade) and the workers. The deepening cleavages between Jews and gentiles intensified the feeling of Jewish interdependence, whether one lived on Central Park West or in Brownsville. If exclusion inhibited the ease with which Jews could overcome the caste lines of privilege, it served to coalesce an ethnic community which could then mobilize its varied resources for mutual assistance.

More Jews, of course, were apt to be found in Brownsville than on Central Park West.

> We were the end of the line. We were the children of the immigrants who had camped at city's back door, in New York's rawest, remotest, cheapest ghetto, enclosed on one side by the Canarsie flats and on the other by the hallowed middleclass districts that showed the way to New York. "New York" was what we put last on our address, but first in thinking of the others around us. *They* were New York, the Gentiles . . .; we were Brownsville—*Brunzvil*, as the old folks said . . .[5]

Other immigrants also felt the sense of separateness. The Jews were not entirely unique. But the Jews were bound and determined not to let any barrier divert their quest for a respected place in American society. For one thing, Jewish immigrants, unlike, say, their contemporary sojourners from Italy, had almost all taken one-way tickets to America. One in five of the Italians went back home after they had made their nest egg (or after they had repeatedly failed to do so). The Jews had no homes to return to.

In yet another way their difference from other European immigrants is significant. Unlike the Italians (or the Irish or Poles) they were not former members of the lower levels of peasant societies. If they had come from societies that still showed the marks of a feudal social structure, *they* had never been in peonage. Rather, they had lived metaphorically as "eternal strangers" in the eastern countries where for centuries they had been relegated to marginal occupations and where in more recent times they had been left to practice their own traditions, periodically disrupted by acts of terror wrought by the Czar's officials or their loyal subjects.

The "Russian" Jews, unlike almost every other ethnic group to come to this country brought skills and values that were more in keeping with the society into which they hoped to move than those from which they had come. The skills they possessed were often entrepreneurial; and the values, aspiringly bourgeois (though few would admit it).

Although many were religious (if they kept the faith, they were Orthodox—at least in the beginning), they felt no allegiance to a dogma imposed by a dominating church and enforced by a bureaucratic hierarchy. Each *shul* was a world of its own; each congregation was a circle of close friends and relatives. What united the disparate groups was a tradition that encouraged searching inquiry and constant questioning. As the Protestant ethic had once been secularized into a social one for the early settlers, the Talmudic tradition in the early 1900s became transformed from a part of the central core of spiritual life into a *modus operandi* in the streets and workshops of urban America.

Finally, the well-known belief in the sanctity of the family, the respect for law and justice, and the faith that education could lead to both aesthetic and material benefits, all strengthened Jewish ambition to catch up with and eventually to overtake the Joneses of America.

Although few American Jews played out their lives as if Horatio Alger Jr. had written the scenario, their successes came to represent the clearest case of the American Dream becoming a reality. It seldom happened overnight, but, conquering the obstacles of language and culture and social discrimination, many East European Jewish families moved from rags to riches in three generations.

These generations—best seen as phases in process of acculturation rather than strictly chronological periods—varied rather markedly. What is usually referred to as the first generation pertains to that phase dominated by the immigrants and those old enough to have been affected directly by life in an East European culture. While the immigrants faced the upheaval of uprooting themselves, or being uprooted, traveled in steerage across a forbidding ocean, experienced the culture shock of arriving in a strange land, and the debilitating effects of life and work under the most adverse conditions, they proved amazingly resilient. Paradoxically, because they tried to reconstruct so much of the world they had left behind, the problem of culture-conflict may have seemed less acute for them than for their immediate descendants. They seldom wandered far—geographically or psychologically—from their "quarter."

Their children, most of whom grew up in Phase Two, lived their early lives scurrying between two worlds. For most, the centripetal attraction of the wider society often transmitted by public school teachers was too compelling to resist. They were to learn, often through bitter experience, that the accent, dress, and manners learned in their neighborhoods precluded easy access into the American mainstream. Some, disillusioned by both anti-foreign and anti-Jewish attitudes, withdrew to their territory. Others became actively engaged in radical activities that stressed universal brotherhood and rejected parochialism in all guises— save its own. Most continued to press for admission or, at least, tried to adjust their style of life to fit more readily into that toward which they aspired. Old ways were modified (the new, American "denomination," *Conservative* Judaism, was a case in point) and others were cast aside. For those of the second generation, Jewish-gentile stories and jokes abounded—many self-denigrating; but the lore of the *shtetl* and the sayings of the rabbis were left behind. As the oldtimers died, the Yiddish theaters lost their patrons, and the Yiddish newspapers, their readers.

What remained was the sense of community and the desire to maintain familial ties. As individuals became more successful they moved farther and farther away from the old ghetto area; but, as they went out from the Lower East Side of New York or the South Side of Chicago and moved uptown or, as in Boston, downtown, they settled in what came to be labeled "Jewish neighborhoods." This pattern of sticking together continued right out into the suburbs where homogeneous ethnic enclaves became countrified versions of the American ghetto—now adorned with million dollar synagogues.

Often members of the second generation were the first of their families to enjoy the benefit of what their hardworking parents had longed for: a living wage. And some became very wealthy. Newly rich, they could lavish upon themselves and their children what had for so long been denied. Homes, automobiles, and manners of dress were often ostentatiously garish. With these manifestly *nouveau riche* characteristics came a growing awareness that money could be used as well as spent. Increasingly, these parvenus (a twentieth-century version of their German-Jewish predecessors) began to use their money to give their children superior educations in elite universities. In time, these children often would find themselves embarrassed by the crude, uncultured ways of their elders. (More often, the second generation had to struggle and for every Jewish boy who went to Harvard, a hundred went to City College and *then* on to better things.)

The children who grew up in old-law tenements or in the gilded ghettoes built by the immigrants or their sons and daughters formed the third generation. This generation has now reached maturity and is raising and struggling to understand an even more ungrateful fourth. The grandchildren of the immigrants, and their children, too, live in a very different world. Everything has changed, or better stated, almost everything. Despite the phenomenal rate of acculturation, the rate of assimilation, as measured by intermarriage and even by interfaith socializing, has remained exceedingly low.[6] Or, to use Milton Gordon's terms, there has been a good deal of cultural adaptation but little structural assimilation.[7] Jews may no longer be very Jewish, but they are still Jews. And most not only want to remain so but wish their children to remain so, too.

Socialist grandparents lived in slums and yearned (and often campaigned) for better working conditions, better wages, and better times for their children. By and large, they were to get them. The second generation saw their fortunes rise and fall and rise again as the economy expanded, depressed precipitously, and was rejuvenated through New Deal innovations and, especially, the wartime boom. (Said one, "I started life as a Communist, then I became a Social Democrat, then a New Deal Democrat, then just a plain Democrat. Now I'm a full professor.") Jewish grand-children enjoyed the fruits of parental successes and the oppor-tunities offered in a society noticeably free from anti-Jewish bar-riers. The last point is extremely relevant.

During the first half of the century attitudes toward Jews varied markedly. In the early days Jewish workers had to con-tend with a good deal of prejudice and discrimination, which was exacerbated by involvement in radical causes and by an old but unfounded belief that Jews threatened unfair competition in the marketplace. Anti-Semitism rose and fell during the immediate post World War I years only to rise again during the days of the Depression. In the late 1930s and the early 1940s active Bundist groups sought to exclude the Jews from various spheres of life, and many unaffiliated Americans sympathized with their views. Most, of course, did not and discrimination against Jews in the United States even during the Depression tended to be of the social variety: quota systems on college and professional school enrollment, restrictions on buying into certain neighborhoods or working in certain industries. Perhaps the most pervasive view in those days was that Jews were all right as long as they didn't get "too pushy." Moreover, Americans displayed little sympathy for the plight of European Jews during the early days of the Nazi regime in Germany. Reluctance to offer sanctuary to the millions who were displaced and who eventually died in the gas chambers extended to the highest reaches of society.

Today it is argued that the desperate plight of European Jewry was simply not understood at home. The argument has more than a kernel of truth; few Jews and far fewer gentiles knew the true story of Nazi atrocities. But the horrors revealed as the camps were opened sent a shockwave through the country and, perhaps in a spirit of expiation, led to a rather changed view of the American Jew. Revelations about the depth of German calumny brought forth concern for the fate of those who survived. When the United Nations granted statehood to Israel, America vied with the Soviet Union to be the first to ratify, and Americans in general felt the need to offer a homeland for Jewish displaced persons. Moreover, the caricature of the Jew ingrained in the mind of Americans was soon to become seriously modified by the notion of the heroic fighter. Israel's victory over the Arabs in 1948 (and in 1956 and 1967) evoked admiration even from those who were not otherwise disposed kindly toward Jews. (One recent commentator has suggested wryly that figures such as Moshe Dayan represented the penultimate portrait of "the Jew as goy.")

For the majority of Jewish young people, things looked bright in the late 1940s and the future even brighter. In many ways, they had made it *into* American Society and, in this sense, they "had it made," or, at least, thought they did.

Yet few anticipated the day when Christian Americans or, at least, some middle-class Christian Americans would begin to want to "think Jewish"—or, at least, think "thinking Jewish" was in.

Some have argued that television provided the first wedge in opening the door to a Jewish era. Perhaps. Ethnic humor, especially Jewish humor, made its first nationwide appearance as old-time vaudevillians from the borscht circuit found the new media receptive to the public recounting of their very personal *tsoris*. Soon many Americans were larding their language with choice Yiddish phrases and the homely philosophy of Jewish mothers.

The turnabout probably came out of something somewhat more significant than the birth of the television age. It was part of a mood of frustration, anxiety, and for many bitterness. The generation raised on depression and war and unconditional surrender, on *Pax Americanus* and the world-is-our-oyster imagery, the silent generation (which included many young American Jews in college fraternities, in medical schools, in law offices, in universities, in executive training programs) was shaken from its apolitical lethargy by cold war realities, Korea, and McCarthyism. The aura of detached optimism was darkened by a realization that the end of the war did not signal the beginning of a new era of world peace maintained by American largesse and good intentions, but a time of upheaval and change—first abroad and, eventually, at home.

Among the first to "tell it like it was" were Jewish "sick" comedians who, while speaking from inside the box, or more often from the nightclub stage, vented not only their personal frustrations, but the general irritations of hundreds of thousands of Americans. To these iconoclasts nothing was too sacred to examine or decry. The sickniks were attacked as ghouls, as desecrators of the pantheon of America's most revered heroes, as ingrates for lampooning living legends such as President Eisenhower, J. Edgar Hoover, and Mom. Whatever their views, they were listened to and imitated. A whole new genre of "ethnocidic" humor was born, humor that was associated with Jews even when Jews had nothing to do with it (as in the case of Tom Lehrer). "Listen to this record . . . Listen," they were saying in Boston and Boise and Des Moines. "Those Jews sure got a lot of nerve. . . ." And they listened and laughed (often at themselves though they may not have known it).

Most Jews, now fairly prosperous and middle class, were embarrassed by the sickniks with whom they were fearful of being identified. What they feared was that once again they would be singled out as being different. (Of course, they still were different. Even as they listened to the same programs and records as other Americans they took special pride in *really understanding* the subtleties projected and the sources from which the allusions sprang.)

But the fears might have been allayed, for America—at least literate America—was about to enter its most philo-Semitic phase. The poignant stories of growing up in the ghetto told by standup comics from the Catskills had warmed the hearts of many gentiles who, themselves, were not so far removed from Shantytown, Little Italy, or even Winesburg. The *chutzpah* of the iconoclasts pricked the social consciences of their children, or, at least, made them laugh. But what had even greater appeal was the Jewish novel, or rather, the new American novel with Jew as protagonist.

Jews were no longer being portrayed simply as suffering philosophers out of touch with the real world, as conspirators in some radical campaign to overturn the social order, as tintypic shyster lawyers, grasping merchants, or unloved physicians. In place of the old caricatures were people who happened to be Jewish. For perhaps the first time in American literary history, the Jew became everyman and, through a curious transposition, everyman became the Jew.

Characters in the widely read fiction of Salinger, Bellow, Malamud, and Roth—the "Frannys" and "Herzogs" meant something to most literate Americans, not to Jews alone.

The latest generation, then, began growing up in a new kind of milieu, at least for American Jews: troubled on the outside but, for them, quite tranquil within. The grandchildren of Jews from

Russia, Rumania, or Austria-Hungary knew little of first-hand anti–Semitism and even less of deprivation. They entered a world in which Jews were not only tolerated but also accepted.

Melvin Tumin implies that some, perhaps many, Jews (at least those over thirty) have become too complacent, enjoying their acceptance and their success and internalizing the spirit of a sort of "cult of gratitude." They have become too far removed from radical grandparents who manned the battlements for the rights of workingmen or from anarchist uncles who mounted the soap-boxes to harangue their audiences for freedoms great and small. They hardly remember. And many shrink from thoughts of being considered too outlandish in their political views, if they think about such matters very deeply at all. For good or ill, most American Jews are part of the big wide—and white—Establishment. And some of their children (although far from all) have discovered with chagrin the soft, rather passive nature of their parents' liberalism. Many have come to resent the bourgeois views of parents who seek to prevent them from "going where the action is," or who fail to understand why they want to go at all.

This is not to say that the Jewish parents of college age children are not concerned with the fate of others. They have, for example, long been supporters of the civil rights movement. Many have contributed and petitioned. Some have marched. A few have died. But many of their children are claiming that when it comes to such matters as civil rights for Negroes one feels the Jew "doth protest too much." What may not be understood is the difference between naïveté and gentility.

The vast majority of America's Jews are committed to seeing Negroes accepted as genuinely free men and full citizens. Indeed, most go farther and support the idea of offering compensatory services to overcome the inequities of the past. But like many other middle-class Americans, there are those—especially the ones so recently out of the ghettoes themselves—who are fearful of what they see as the disruption of their communities and the disturbance of their children's education and growth by a rapid influx of lower-class Negroes into neighborhoods or school districts. For all the involvement in "the movement," there remains, at least in some Jewish circles, a paternalistic aura of *noblesse oblige* toward the Negro cause ("They should be grateful for what is being done for them"). Much of this is said only in the confines of the home or neighborhood because of what might be called "Jewish gentility" ("How can you say that Harry? People won't understand"), but it exists just the same.

For many Jews, confrontation is still a way off and those who say that liberalism increases the farther one gets from the problem may well be right. However, some Jews remain, or their property remains, back in the old "quarter." They are the special targets of verbal and, increasingly, physical abuse by Negroes who live there and upon whom they depend for a living. They live in fear of these neighbors as their Old Country parents and grandparents had once feared Russia's landless peasants. Milton Himmelfarb sees this estrangement as an irreconcilable conflict in which, once again, poor Jews face even poorer "Muzhiks." (This is not to discount the fact that there are Jewish "merchants" and "slumlords" in the ghettoes who do exploit the black residents. But most Jews living there are not rich, nor are they oppressors. They would dearly love to get out, leaving to others—perhaps the City itself—the thankless task of trying to salvage something from the ruins of their old neighborhoods.)

Recently, Jews in Harlem, in Brooklyn, and in the suburbs have become targets of anti-Semitic attacks by certain black power groups who claim they are not really interested in the cause of black people but only in their own security. As the tempo of demands increases, an even greater rift between Jewish liberals and black militants may be expected. Still, the remnants of the established civil rights movement look to Jews for continued support and for participation. As the late Martin Luther King stated: "It would be impossible to record the contribution that Jewish people have made toward the Negro's struggle for freedom—it has been so great."

As the nation awaits the next phase of the struggle, its Jewish citizens wonder which view shall prevail. It is no idle matter for, like most white liberals, the Jews (at least those middle-aged and older) will wait warily and react rather than take the initiative on civil rights in the future.

The children are not as skeptical, but they also seem deeply troubled and confused. In the early 1960s many militant young Jews walked hand-in-hand with their "black brothers." Indeed, half of the "visiting" white people in Mississippi during the fateful summer of 1964 were reported reliably to have been Jewish. Now these Jewish youngsters are not at all sure where to turn. They are no longer wanted by many of their old friends,

who tell them to go back to Westchester and work with prejudiced whites. Some have done so (though not without difficulty
for it is often hard to go home again). Some have opted out
altogether and become hippies. And some have found a new
outlet for radical passions on the campuses and in the peace movement.

The now-and-future war in Southeast Asia has also affected the
parents of these draft-age youngsters. On this issue, the majority
of Jews find themselves with their liberal friends: not pacifists,
but opponents of the government's war policy. While not all
doves are Jewish, most Jews are dovish.

Despite the fact that advertisements opposing the war in
Vietnam in the *New York Times* and other newspapers contained a very high percentage of Jewish-sounding names, few anti-
antiwar spokesmen singled out Jews as being a disloyal group.
Jewish defense agencies and many Jews feared a backlash, especially from conservative groups that viewed any protest against
the war as an affront to America's fighting men and who tended
to view dissent as tantamount to treason. Aside from rightwing
pamphlets, however, it was only after the first week of June 1967
that the issue was raised at all.

The barely concealed elation of American Jews (including
most Vietnam doves) over Israeli military successes caused some
to question why they have been unwilling to support America's
fight against communist aggression in Vietnam while they
eagerly endorsed Israel's war. Following the Israeli victories, neo-
Nazi polemicists wrote Streicher-like tracts on the "genocidal
policies of Israel" and of "American-Jewish complicity" in these
"atrocities." And others, too, began to raise troubling questions
about whose side the Jews were on. The questioners were robbed
of the one strong point that usually accompanies such diatribes:
alleged collusion between the Zionists and the Communists. The
Soviet line (which, in certain ways, was very much like that of
the American Right) gave little ammunition to *that* sort of
propaganda campaign. It may well be that the television coverage
of the Security Council debates served to reduce the amount of
potential tension that might have been created by the seemingly
inconsistent position of American Jews. And not a few Jews were
aware of this. They were also relieved that the desert war had
been swift and decisive for they feared the questions that would
have been raised had the Israelis found themselves at the mercy of

the Arabs with the United States reluctant to intervene—as well might have been the case.

American Jews delighted at Israeli victory in the Six Day War have evinced much less enthusiasm for their own country's protracted conflict in Southeast Asia and its stalemated war against poverty at home. Other groups in American life share the sense of frustration. In the search for scapegoats that may soon ensue, Jews may find themselves most vulnerable to attack from right, left, and below. By seeking reform and compromise on most issues instead of radical change, they may come increasingly to appear too white for the black militants, too red for the white conservatives, and too yellow for their own children.

Jews are not unaware of such possibilities. They know that latent anti-Semitism can be revived in America as it has been in the past. But they do not seem worried. They feel they can ride out the coming storms. Like their forebears who came to settle on the Lower East Side, the majority of Jews still believe in America and in the American people.

As for their dissident children: they feel (rightly or wrongly) that they've heard it all before. New Left protest, at least when voiced by Jewish youth, sounds strikingly familiar. Irving Howe sums up the sentiment in one succinct sentence. In writing about dissent in the thirties, Howe says:

> You might be shouting at the top of your lungs against reformism or Stalin's betrayal, but for the middle-aged garment worker strolling along Southern Boulevard you were just a bright and cocky Jewish boy, a talkative little *pisher*.[8]

The same is being said today—though the cause, the occupation of the listener, and the boulevard are different. The sentiment remains: today's young Jewish activists will grow up, too. When they do, they will probably find themselves radical in thought, reformist in action, bourgeois in manner—and Jewish. Just like the rest.

NOTES

1. Hutchins Hapgood, Foreword to *The Spirit of the Ghetto: Studies of the Jewish Quarter of New York* (New York: Funk and Wagnalls, 1902).

2. Michael Harrington, "Afterword" in Michael Gold, *Jews Without Money* (New York: Avon Books, 1965), p. 232. See also, Moses Rischin, *The Promised City: New York's Jews, 1870–1914* (Cambridge: Harvard University Press, 1962).

3. See John Higham, "Social Discrimination Against Jews in America," *American Jewish Historical Society*, 47 (September 1957), 9.

4. Erich Kahler, *The Jews Among the Nations* (New York: Frederick Ungar, 1967), pp. 5–6.

5. Alfred Kazin, *A Walker in the City* (New York: Grove Press, 1951), p. 12.

6. Marshall Sklare, "Survivalism or Assimilation; Changing Patterns in American Jewish Life," *Proceedings of the Jewish Orientation and Training Seminar for Social Workers* (New York, 1958), mimeographed.

7. See Milton M. Gordon, *Assimilation in American Life* (New York: Oxford University Press), 1964.

8. Irving Howe, *Steady Work* (New York: Harcourt, Brace & World, 1966), p. 353.

Jews,
Gentiles
and the
American
Dream

THE AMERICAN JEWISH COM\
IN A COMPARATIVE CONTEXT

SEYMOUR MARTIN LIPSET

MOST RESEARCH on Jewish communities around the world tends to investigate the 'Jewishness' of such communities, and to ask to what extent given communities are assimilating or retaining their 'Jewishness'.[1] Such a point of view may be justified from a religious orientation; that is, one may ask to what extent certain basic tenets and practices of a given form of Judaism are being followed in any community. But from an intellectual perspective it is difficult to defend the position that the study of the Jews should be organized around the maintenance or decline of 'Jewishness'. Rather, I would urge that any effort to develop a systematic study of Jewish communities must be organized in a comparative context. It is impossible to study the sources of variation in the beliefs and practices of comparable sub-groups in different countries without a conceptual framework and methodology which dictates a systematic comparison of the larger societies to which these groups belong.

Some years ago in a comparative discussion of Jewish communities published in *Commentary*, Milton Himmelfarb attempted to revive Heine's Law as a methodological guide to such investigations. Heinrich Heine suggested over a century ago that the only way one could understand the variations in the behaviour of Jews in different countries was by seeing these differences as adaptations to the dominant behaviour patterns within the Gentile community. There is much evidence for this view. Thus British Jewry has a structure somewhat like that of the dominant, high status Church of England; the Chief Rabbi roughly corre-

This article is reprinted by permission of the editors of *The Jewish Journal of Sociology*. Originally published as, "The Study of Jewish Communities in a Comparative Context," *The Jewish Journal of Sociology*, 5 (December 1963), pp. 157–66.

21

.nds to the Archbishop of Canterbury. Upper-class Gentile Englishmen are formally, at least, orthodox; they adhere to the traditional Anglican Creed and practice; nonconformist Protestantism has been lower-status in England. In the United States the dominant form of Christianity is congregationalist in organization and 'liberal' in theology. And American Jewry, including orthodox, is also congregationalist in its religious structure. It is true that American Jews attend synagogue less than the entirety of American Protestants attends church. However, well-educated Protestants do not go to church as frequently as less-educated ones. I would guess that a comparison of American Jews with socially and intellectually comparable Protestants would reveal that the Jews are, in fact, similar in their religious involvement. Similar logic may be applied to the situation in France. There, the Jewish religious organization resembles that of the Catholic Church; it is 'Episcopal'. However, the French Gentile community has been divided historically between a clerical segment, traditionally anti-semitic, and an anti-clerical part, favourable towards Jewish rights. The Jews have been placed by French history in the anti-clerical, or, if you will, non-Catholic community, a community which regards all religious adherence as outmoded. Hence, French Jewry also has been extremely irreligious; in effect, most native-born French Jews have behaved religiously like the rest of the non-Catholic half of France. (The large Argentinian Jewish community closely resembles the French in these respects.) Rather than give further general impressionistic comparisons of this type, I would like to illustrate my general methodological thesis with a discussion of the Americanism of the American Jewish community, for which there is ample evidence.

Many have pointed to the lack of centralized organization within the American Jewish community as a source of weakness. Rabbi Mordecai Kaplan has presented the Reconstructionist proposal for the creation of a *kehilla*, a formal community structure such as once existed in eastern Europe, which would be built around the community centres. The eminent sociologist Robert MacIver, in his famous Report on Jewish organizations made at their behest, also called for more community integration, for greater co-operation, for the merger of organizations performing similar functions, and other integrative measures. Both Kaplan and MacIver, however, were thereby asking American Jews to do something which other Americans refuse to do. The emphasis on achievement, on competition, on individualism, stressed by foreign observers from Tocqueville and Martineau in the first half of the nineteenth century down to recent visitors, affects organizations as it does individuals. Competitive pluralism has characterized associational life within many 'communities' in America. Competition and lack of systematic co-operation is also typical of the American Negro community. More than two decades ago the sociologists Edward Shils and Morris Janowitz concluded their analysis of American fascist groups with the comment that these groups did not constitute an effective threat because of the inability to get together. The factionalism and lack of party discipline of American political parties which so astonishes Europeans is but another example of the same general phenomenon. In a sense, these behaviour patterns may be considered as examples of one of the dominant value emphases in American culture, that of self-orientation as distinct from and stronger than collectivity orientation, to use one of Talcott Parsons's pattern-variables which serve to differentiate societies. And the American emphases on self-orientation and achievement are in turn related to the stress on equality. As Tocqueville well noted, when one thoroughly destroys aristocratic privileges and values, one opens 'the door to universal competition'. To urge the American Jewish community to return to, or to adopt, a community structure derivative from the much more elitist society of Europe is to ignore the interrelationships between sub-group systems and the social system of the larger society.

The various religions in America also reflect the values and pattern of organization of the larger society. Even the Catholic Church with its centralization of theological authority in Rome has been unable to avoid conforming. In the late nineteenth century Pope Leo XIII publicly complained about heretical tendencies within the American Church. He was concerned about the preoccupation with materialistic and Puritanical values. Most recently, the French Dominican R. L. Bruckberger has contended that American Catholics resemble American Baptists or Presbyterians more than they do Mexican or Italian Catholics.[2] In my book (*The First New Nation: The United States in Historical and Comparative Perspective*) I report in some detail on the similarities in descriptions and analyses of American religion made from the early nineteenth century down to the present by foreign visitors, both lay and clerical. Almost without exception, such commentators have noted that every American with whom they talked had a religious affiliation, belonged to or supported some denomination. But almost as common is the observation that Americans were reluctant to discuss the content of their own religion or to recommend its advantages to others. The standard American attitude for over a century and a half seems to have been that all religious affiliations and beliefs are good.

Fundamentalist or orthodox true believers have argued that such an attitude reflects a basic secularization of religion, that American religion has no effect on behaviour, that it is merely a weekly conventional ritual. I question this conclusion. In a multi-religious nation, in which no denomination comes close to having a majority of the population among its members, and in which many social situations—school, work, politics—bring together men of differing religions, a general consensus that religious affiliations are irrelevant to other relationships is essential. Even when men believe strongly in their own faith—and there is much evidence that most Americans do so believe—they must be willing to accept the convention that the secular and religious spheres of life are separate, for the sake of an integrated society. This does not, however, conflict with the generally accepted and broadly asserted value, for man and society, of religion in general. One may even urge Americans to fulfil those moral obligations based on religious tenets. But such obligations must necessarily be restricted to the limited area of 'Golden Rule' morality in which all agree. The alternatives to such a public and common religious creed are limited to those of a national religion with almost universal adherence, intense religious controversy, or a large, often majority, segment of non-believers, the situation most common in present-day Europe. Compared to Jews in most of present-day Europe, American Jews are much more likely to belong to and attend a synagogue, much as American Protestants and Catholics have a higher rate of church attendance than their European co-religionists. It should also be noted that despite greater freedom and opportunity to join the majority culture, American Jewry has had a lower rate of inter-marriage than western European Jews. Thus, American religious communities are properly described as irreligious only in contrast to the orthodoxy inherited by Christians and Jews alike from medieval Europe.

The pattern of shearing away ancient rituals characteristic of various religions in the process of their adaptation to modern America is not a recent phenomenon. In *American Judaism* Nathan Glazer recalls[3] that at the founding of Hebrew Union College in 1883 (perceived at that time not as the theological seminary of a distinct Reform movement but simply as an academy to train rabbis), shrimp was served at an opening ceremonial dinner. Almost all the rabbis present remained and only two or three objected and walked out. The tendency to ignore ritual, already dominant in the large community (over a quarter of a million Jews) of the 1880s, was reversed as a result of the mass migration of orthodox Jews from eastern Europe between 1890 and the First World War. The renewed power of orthodox religion simply reflected the export of the religious culture of the Pale to America. It is thus not surprising that with the emergence of an American Jewry, composed increasingly of the native-born, the forces which modified religious ritual before the mass immigration have reasserted themselves.

If we turn to the widely observed tendency of American Jews, as individuals, to obtain higher education and to shift from self-employed business occupations to the more intellectually prestigious though financially less rewarding salaried professions, especially academic and non-academic scientific and culturally creative positions, we see here also a reflection of the predominant national value pattern. An increasing proportion of Americans, currently close to forty per cent of the college-age population, enter institutions of higher learning. Almost ninety per cent of those from higher-status professional and business managerial families do so. Studies of the backgrounds of college students majoring in different subjects reveal that the liberal arts, the more intellectually oriented areas of university education, tend to recruit students from higher-status background, while the more vocational subjects, such as engineering, business, and education (for elementary and secondary school teaching), draw heavily from the upwardly mobile, those of working-class or lower-status ethnic background. The propensity of American Jews to send their children to universities, and the increasing trend of the offspring of well-to-do business men and independent professionals to study subjects leading to a creative intellectual or scientific career, rather than to enter the family business, reflects a pattern common among non-Jews as well. Recently, a study by

Fortune magazine of the way of life of the leading executives in the automobile industry, reported that this group of highly paid leaders of a major American industry, many of whom were of relatively lowly origin, typically boasted to one another about the intellectual accomplishments of their children as nuclear physicists, writers, and academics. The group, almost totally non-Jewish, included many who reported to the *Fortune* interviewer that they were proud of their earning enough to help their $8,000-a-year academic or research scientist son make his way in the world. Thus the children of the well-to-do New York Jewish clothing manufacturer and the Protestant mid-western vice-president of General Motors appear to have similar aspirations and attainments.

The intellectual achievements of American Jews in the university and elsewhere have sometimes been contrasted with the lesser achievements of English Jewry. Here again, the reduced academic orientation of Jews in Britain reflects the values of the larger society. In the late 1950s only four per cent of university-age English youth entered a university. If one includes, as one should, the various other non-university institutions and types of training in Britain which are contained within universities and colleges in the U.S., the total proportion entering higher education would still be under ten per cent in contrast to close to forty per cent in America. In 1957, only thirteen per cent of the children of men in professional and managerial positions entered British universities, a great contrast with the nearly unanimous pursuit of higher education among those from the same strata in America. And while the large majority of leading English business executives have not attended a university, a 1957 study indicates that 87 per cent of top executives in 287 major American companies have a Bachelor's degree, and 32 per cent have attained one or more advanced graduate degrees.[4] A study of the most important leaders in American business and governmental life reports that as a group they have much more formal education than the average college graduate. (See W. Bell et al., *Public Leadership*, San Francisco, 1941.) The differences in British and American values and attitude towards education affect not only the Jews of both countries, the bulk of whom are but two generations away from Jewish communities in eastern Europe; they also have sharply affected educational orientations in the liberated colonies of Britain and America. Few have noticed that the two major former American colonies, the Philippines and Puerto Rico, have a much larger college population proportionate to the relevant age group than any country in western Europe. About fourteen per cent of Filipinos and eleven per cent of Puerto Ricans of college age are in colleges or universities. Former British colonies, including Jamaica, a Caribbean island somewhat comparable in population to Puerto Rico, and Malaya, whose indigenous population is of similar ethnic stock to the Philippines, have fewer than one per cent of the college age group in institutions of higher learning. America's Jews, like the residents of America's former colonies, reflect in their behaviour the national belief that everyone should attend college. And, conversely, groups in Britain or those outside who have absorbed British educational values behave correspondingly. (Of course, in rough comparisons of this kind, one must ignore differences of standard: a British-type undergraduate education differs markedly from one on the American model. But here I am concerned less with quality than with aspirations and social consequences.) It should be noted, of course, that Britain is gradually changing in its educational structure in the process of becoming more equalitarian, and that English Jews like English Gentiles are showing increasing interest in higher education and in thus widening the base of support of creative intellectual and scientific endeavours.

While I have stressed the extent to which the American Jew reflects American society, some sociologists, such as Robert Park and Nathan Glazer, have even argued that the Jews are the *most* American of all groups in the nation, that they exhibit the predominant American traits in a more integrated fashion than any other group. Park, who is one of the major founding figures in American sociology, urged more than forty years ago that courses on the history, culture, and behaviour of the American Jews should be included as a *required* part of the curriculum of all American high schools, that by studying the American Jews in detail, Americans of all backgrounds could learn to understand their nation and themselves. Glazer has argued that Jews everywhere are more sensitive to trends in the larger society than are others, and, being completely free in America to choose their modes of behaviour, they often anticipate the general patterns of the future. Robert Park, who I think would have agreed with Glazer, urged, too, that American social scientists should take as a major topic for research the study of the Jews.

(See his reprinted essays, *Race and Culture*, Glencoe, Illinois, 1950.)

Park's two recommendations, courses on Jewish culture and history and intensive social science analysis of Jewish behaviour, were not adopted. The first, of course, was never seriously discussed, while the failure of the second is worthy of detailed investigation as part of the sociology of knowledge. Gentile social scientists, while revealing a considerable fascination with Jewish life, have, I think, avoided studying the Jews precisely because of the large number of Jews in their fields. Sustained contact with Jews suggests to them, I suspect, that Jewish social scientists would do a better job of understanding the Jewish community than an outsider. But, in fact, with relatively few exceptions, Jewish social scientists with a general reputation in their discipline have also abstained from writing about American Jews. Ely Ginsberg and Daniel Bell of Columbia and Nathan Glazer of the University of California at Berkeley are the major exceptions which come to mind, and only the latter has actually engaged in a major scholarly work on the subject.[5] (Parenthetically, it may be noted that as far as I know, David Mandelbaum of Berkeley is the only Jewish American anthropologist who has ever written professionally about Jewish communities abroad— other than those in Israel.) The failure of Jewish social scientists to engage in research on the Jews reflects their desire to be perceived as American rather than Jewish intellectuals. To write in depth about the Jewish community would seemingly expose them to being identified as 'Jewish Jews', as individuals who are too preoccupied with an ethnic identity, and who lack the universalistic orientation prized by social scientists and American intellectuals generally. The strength of this attitude among Jewish intellectuals as a group is demonstrated by the comments in a *Commentary* symposium published in 1961.[6] The editors of *Commentary* asked about fifty young Jewish intellectuals (almost all under thirty-five), many of whom were already prominent, to comment on their attitudes towards being a Jew and to things Jewish. The standard reply of almost all who answered was that they did not see what there was to comment about. They were American Jews, but they felt that the fact of their ethnic or religious background had little to do with their roles as creative intellectuals. It is fairly obvious that these men and women must have little insight into themselves if they really believe this. The fact that they espouse such a conception is, however, what is significant for the purposes of this discussion. American Jewish intellectuals want to receive recognition as individuals, and thus far the larger society has encouraged them in this aspiration. How much this behaviour reflects a capitulation to assimilationist pressures, to a desire to escape from Jewishness in any form, and how much it is an adaptation to the general American convention that each person can and should remain identified with his religious background, with the stricture that such differences should not affect relations in secular roles, remain a topic for future investigation (if anyone is interested in such a study).

To understand the American Jew, it is necessary to be sensitized to factors in American life which used to be discussed in Marxist circles as the problem of 'American exceptionalism'. Given the absence of a socialist movement in America, the limited character of working-class consciousness, the equalitarian social relationships, and the gap in living standards between the American lower strata and those elsewhere, a frequent topic of discussion was whether the analyses and political tactics fostered by Marxists in other capitalist nations were appropriate to the United States. And, of course, most American Jews, including a majority of those belonging to Zionist organizations, seem to believe that the conditions which bred major antisemitic movements in other nations do not exist in the United States, that 'American exceptionalism' applies to antisemitism as well as to socialism. I have dealt with the sources of various special American characteristics in *The First New Nation*, and I cannot detail my analysis here. I should like, however, to mention two key factors which are particularly relevant to any understanding of the way in which America responds to Jews. Most visible as a special variable is the role of immigration in forming the United States. No other nation has as many religions and ethnic groups whose presence is accepted as a permanent part of the society. In contrast, the Latin American countries have been predominantly Catholic; the English-speaking parts of the Commonwealth are composed largely of descendants of immigrants from the British Isles. For well over a century the United States has sustained a national ideology which defined efforts to emphasize ethnic-religious differences as 'un-American'. The frequent 'nativist' and anti-Catholic movements, which derived much of their strength from the Protestant rural and urban poor, had to be put down by the authority structure. Thus, unlike the situation of Jews else-where, those in America were never defined as the largest visible out-group, as one which differed in basic traits from the over-whelming majority. In the United States Jews have been but one of a very large number of religious-ethnic groups, many of whom were subject to some antagonism and discrimination from those who arrived earlier. In Poland, in France, in Germany, and in other parts of Europe, antisemitism has traditionally been the one most important, often almost the only, historic source of internal group prejudice. It has existed in the United States, but as one of many competing prejudices, much less salient on the whole than prejudice against Negroes, Orientals, Catholics, and whichever is the most recent group of impoverished slum-dwelling immigrants, such as Puerto Ricans in New York. Studies of the major post-war right-wing extremist leaders and move-ments indicate no propensity among their supporters to be anti-semitic. Those who believe in conspiratorial theories of politics, such as the belief that Communists control key segments of the American government, do not appear to translate their paranoid beliefs into generalizations about the Jews.[7]

From a long-run perspective on the situation of the Jew, perhaps a more important factor than the impact of diverse immigrant groups is the predominant value system. As many commentators on American values (Louis Hartz, Clinton Ros-siter, and others) have urged, the predominant political tradition with which America, as a nation, is identified is a liberal or left-wing one. This stems from the fact that the United States was formed out of an anti-colonial revolution, that the Declaration of Independence, its founding document and *raison d'être* as a state, proclaimed the equality of all men, the rights of all to total citizenship and access to power. An American Socialist writer, Leon Samson, seeking during the depths of the Great Depression of the 1930s to explain why efforts to build socialist movements made such little headway, argued convincingly that socialism as an ideology faced the problem of competing with Americanism, a political ideology whose *values* concerning the good society were similar to those of socialism. Samson compared the writings of prominent American conservatives and business men on the nature of preferred social relations with those of leading Marx-ists, from Marx on down. And he reported that, property rela-tions excepted (the economic content of socialism), the Marxists and the American conservatives agreed in describing the good society as one which stresses equality of interpersonal relations and of opportunity, which urges the necessity for hard efficient work, and which judges each man by his work, not his origins.[8]

The orientations towards men and groups stemming from equalitarian values and the structure of a society composed of many ethnic-religious groups, have given American Jews opportunities for acceptance as individuals such as have never existed in any predominantly Gentile society in history. The Jew can be part of American society in a way that has never been true elsewhere. And this real access, combined with the sensitivity to others resulting from a long history as an out-group minority in other societies, enables the Jew to become, as Park and Glazer suggested, the most American of Americans. I do not want to imply, of course, that there are no basic differences between Jews and other groups, since these persist even when one compares Jews and non-Jews with similar sociological characteristics. A variety of evidence suggests that the intellectual orientation of Jews is greater than that of non-Jews. No other American ethnic-religious group has been as successfully upward-mobile as the Jews. Sociological studies have indicated that Jews differ from various Christian groups on a variety of morality issues, from a relatively low rate of divorce to attitudes towards different types of law violations.[9] All studies of Jewish political attitudes and behaviour agree that they are far more liberal and even radical on most issues than are others with comparable socio-economic status.[10]

The one group of social scientists who have studied Jews systematically are those working on the problem of alcoholism. They are fascinated by the fact that Jews have a much lower rate of alcoholism than any other major ethnic-religious group.[11] Jews show different patterns of spending than others at the same level of income. They contribute more to charitable causes; they spend more on the 'good life' for themselves and their families than do Protestants at the same income level.[12] The combination of a positive attitude towards intellectual activities, relatively greater wealth, and propensity to contribute to worthy causes means that in many cities Jews play a disproportionately important role in supporting major cultural institutions, both as contributors and consumers.[13]

If these comments have any theme, it is that the comparative study of the Jew must be linked inseparably with the comparative study of the Gentile. To focus on the study of the Jews alone is to commit the moral sin of ethnocentrism, but it is also wrong methodologically and will result in erroneous conclusions about the nature of specific Jewish communities and customs. In other words, the renewed efforts to study the Jews in the Diaspora, stimulated by Israeli institutions, should be defined as a special part of comparative sociology, and must be based on the theoretical and methodological procedures of that discipline if they are to prove fruitful, either as a contribution to scholarly knowledge or to political action.

NOTES

1. This paper in its original version was read at the Third World Congress of Jewish Studies, held in Jerusalem, July–August 1961, in the section 'Contemporary Jewry'.
2. See R. L. Bruckberger, trans. C. G. Paulding and V. Peterson, *Image of America*, N.Y., 1959.
3. Chicago, 1957, p. 57.
4. See F. C. Pierson et al., *Education of American Businessmen: A Study of University–College Problems in Business Administration*, N.Y., 1959.
5. I am ignoring the excellent work done by men employed by Jewish institutions, and by those with specific appointments to posts on Jewish topics, e.g. Jewish History, Near Eastern Languages, Yiddish Literature, etc.
6. 'Jewishness and the Younger Intellectuals: A Symposium', *Commentary*, vol. 31, no. 4, April 1961.
7. See Daniel Bell, ed., *The Radical Right*, N.Y., 1963.
8. See L. Samson, *Toward a United Front: A Philosophy for American Workers*, N.Y., 1933.
9. See G. Lenski, *The Religious Factor*, N.Y., 1961, pp. 148ff.
10. See Lawrence Fuchs, *The Political Behavior of American Jews*, Glencoe, Illinois, 1954.
11. See C. R. Snyder, *Alcohol and the Jews, a Cultural Study of Drinking and Sobriety*, Glencoe, Illinois, 1958.
12. See Marshall Sklare, ed., *The Jews: Social Patterns of an American Group*, Glencoe, Illinois, 1958.
13. John Gunther, *Inside U.S.A.*, rev. ed., N.Y., 1951.

FROM SHTETL TO SUBURB

SEYMOUR LEVENTMAN

THE PROBLEM OF THE JEWISH COMMUNITY

A YOUNG JEWISH MAN of humble origins struck it rich in a business venture and suddenly became quite wealthy. Among his newly acquired possessions was a yacht. Proudly sporting a captain's uniform, he invited his parents aboard for a tour. As they were about to leave, the young man turned to his mother and said, "Well Mamma, what do you think of my yacht and captain's uniform?" His mother replied, "Well son, by me you're a captain, by Papa you're a captain, but tell me, what are you by the captains?"

This anecdote provides clues to a major feature of Jewish life in America, preoccupation with position in two social worlds, Jewish and non-Jewish. Regardless of his special circumstances, there is hardly a Jew who is not concerned with how he "rates" with both Jews and non-Jews, that is, with ethnic peers and with captains. Indeed, at one time or another most Jews in America have probably wondered if they could be "in" with the captains, or even a real captain. Yet what gives Jewish life in America its unique dual character of ingroup solidarity combined with intense desire for outgroup approval is that Jews discovered they didn't have to become real captains to enjoy the advantages of this position; they could and did become Jewish captains. The phenomenon of the formation by minority groups of institutions parallel to those of the dominant group will be discussed later. Suffice it to note here an observation by that most astute student of minority groups, Everett Hughes, who once wrote, "The Jews spend millions to reform the Christians, the reform wanted is that the Christians should think better of the Jews."[1]

Original for this volume.

33

Because Jews "had it so good" in an open class society, they never had to assimilate or convert *en masse* to achieve greater participation in the general society. They could reach this goal, however cautiously and selectively, from within the protective confines of the highly acculturated but separate community. Still Jews have not yet molded a completely successful formula for living an American middle class but Jewish life. Undoubtedly, a major dilemma for American Jews is how to participate as widely as possible in the general society and be as much like everyone else as possible while preserving a distinctive and separate ingroup life.

This essay examines how this dilemma is embodied in the structure of the Jewish community and how this structure in turn creates tensions requiring resolution. Special features of much behavior characteristic of Jews are seen as responses to these tensions, which are often inherent in minority status itself. In fact, the basic tension for all minority groups results from their exclusion from full participation in the general society. But for Jews the problem is intensified and made more complex by continued communal tradition and ingroup institutions. An important consideration then, is that, perhaps more than for any other minority group, most American Jews share a communal life that is identifiable socially, culturally, and even ecologically.

Recognizing that minority status is critically linked to the stratification system of a society, one might say that tensions emerge for Jews as they experience social closure[2] within their own community and lowered class and status opportunities in the wider community. These class and ethnic tensions derive from the conflicting principals of organization on which the Jewish community is based—societal inclusiveness and ethnic exclusiveness. These principals become competing demands made by the overlapping institutional structures and stratification systems of the Jewish and the general community. Much Jewish social insecurity and behavioral contradictions are therefore due to the availability of both Jewish and non-Jewish values. This is increasingly true as acculturation produces a mixture of newly acquired general values with persisting ethnic values.

THE BACKGROUND

The Jewish population in America dates from the first settlement of Jews in 1654, but the Jewish community as we know it today started almost two and a half centuries later with the great Eastern European migration. In 1880 the population in the United States of 250,000 Jews[3] was predominantly German. Beginning in 1881 the torrent of immigrants from Eastern Europe so swelled the Jewish ranks that by 1917 Jews in the United States numbered about 3,300,000,[4] and by 1927 the Jewish population numbered about 4,000,000 at least 80 percent of which[5] was of Eastern European origin. It was this group whose culture became virtually synonymous with that of American Jewry and that eventually formed the Jewish community in the United States. Recognizing the existence and contributions of various Western European Jewish groups, such as the Spanish, the Portuguese, and the Germans, the generalizations about American Jewry contained in this essay pertain mainly to the Eastern European group. It is their community, their culture and values, their class, status structures, and ethnic tensions that we will be discussing.

By 1926 over half of the Jews in the United States lived in New York, Chicago, and Philadelphia;[6] by 1957, 96 percent lived in urban areas[7] with almost four out of five living in the metropolitan areas of seven cities, New York, Los Angeles, Philadelphia, Chicago, Boston, Cleveland, and Detroit.[8] These important demographic facts help explain how Jewish immigrants who originally settled in ethnic islands in cities could at the same time gain the necessary knowledge and experience for achieving mobility in a rapidly changing society. As strangers or guest people, they were near to the hub of society though far removed socially and culturally.

Still, their success in a society that discouraged traditional social forms seems rather remarkable considering their strong ingroup traditions of cohesion and the fact that most Eastern European Jews came from small villages and towns. Indeed, one of the most amazing aspects of modern American society has been the speed with which Jews moved from the lower and working class to the middle and upper class, not by mass assimilation or conversion but by adapting their community to the requirements of a secular non-ethnic world.

THE SHTETL

Eastern European Jews have powerful traditions of communal life. "They came from a milieu in which they formed a very large part of the population and in which in all-Jewish villages and towns, they had created a Jewish culture almost wholly unaffected by the cultures of the people around them."[9]

Life in the village, or *shtetl*, has been poignantly and insightfully portrayed in Mark Zborowski's and Elizabeth Herzog's *Life Is with People*,[10] perhaps the single best reference on the Old World Jewish ethnic community. The authors describe a community where the sacred and secular were woven together, where the members shared a common cultural heritage, language, values, religion, feelings of belonging, and a common fate. Indeed, identification was derived from mergence (not submergence) with the community, which was seen by Jews as the family at large. The institutional structure of the Eastern European Jewish community could be characterized as religiofamilistic, with powerful cultural traditions, psychic sanctions, and sentimental attachments operating as critical behavioral influences. Ironically, Eastern European Jews had originally fled from persecution in medieval Germany and Central Europe and migrated to Eastern Europe to live their ethnically and ritually pure lives relatively free of outside interference. This area included Poland, Galicia, Lithuania, White Russia, the Ukraine, Bessarabia, Slovakia, and northeast regions of Hungary. They carried with them their version of Orthodox Judaism, intense familism, and a medieval German dialect (mixed with some words of Hebrew), which was to become Yiddish. Most Jews knew enough Hebrew to say their prayers and scholars knew it better, but Yiddish was the colloquial tongue expressing their deepest sacred and secular values, ideals, sentiments, and shared experiences and aspirations. Religious services were often conducted in Yiddish, and the *shtetl* produced an indigenous school of Yiddish literature and philosophy. Some Jews knew the language of the country in which they lived. But Yiddish was their vernacular.

An important clue to the social organization of the *shtetl* is provided by the comparative distribution of *yikhus*. This is a Hebrew term referring to high status based chiefly on a constellation of scholarship, family lineage, and wealth. Status can either be achieved by one's own efforts (*yikhus atsmo*) or ascribed by virtue of genealogy (*yikhus avos*).[11] In general, a life devoted to sacred learning (in Bible, Talmud, or the Law) conferred the highest status, but one could also derive status from being descended from a family of scholars. Wealth in itself was important only if used to fulfill the divine commandment of *tsdokeh*, charity or philanthropy. Similarly, occupation conferred status only in its relation to education, so one could compensate for lowly occupations such as butcher or shoemaker "if he has the manners and the learning to entitle him to a different rating."[12]

The closure of the *shtetl* was also guaranteed by the family whose role was to create "good Jews," that is, Jews who would remain loyal to the values of the *shtetl* and Judaism, and bring honor to the family. This was accomplished through various social and psychological mechanisms that instilled anxiety levels (particularly in children) appropriate to controlling behavior in desired directions. One of the most powerful sanctions exerted by the family was in mate selection. Naturally, marriage with gentiles was strictly forbidden. The acceptable Jewish prospects were evaluated essentially in terms of sacred learning, *yikhus* or family lineage, and money.[13] Marriages were not matters of individual choice, but were carefully calculated and arranged. Only *prosteh yidn* (lower class people) could marry for love—this was one of the privileges of poverty.[14]

Religion also promoted and protected social closure, although the *shtetl* was by no means a sacred community. Religion was as much a reflection of culture as of Judaic theological principles. Certainly there was respect for sacred learning, observance of the law and the 613 commandments of God including the kosher dietary laws. But so closely linked were religion and cultural tradition that it was difficult to distinguish between the spheres of the sacred and the secular. "To the man of the shtetl, Jewishness is 'my way of life,' in which religion, values, social structure, individual behavior are inextricably blended. It means the way life is lived among us and us means the shtetl."[15] This rather complete identification of religion and ethnicity reflects the deep anchorage of Jews in a separate social world which was justified and glorified in spite of the price paid for ghettoization in limited outside opportunities.

In America what was once virtually an "ethnic ecclesia" became a culturally and socially segregated minority group in a fluid open class society. In Eastern Europe religion and nationality were closely linked and, as Glazer puts it, "It was easier to envisage the (Eastern European) Jews abandoning their religion and becoming simply a people than to envisage them abandoning their ethnic character and becoming a denomination in Reform Jewish (German) style."[16]

It is significant that when asked their nationality upon arriving in the United States, most European Jews replied, "Jewish," whereas German Jews had replied, "German." The issue was really whether Judaism is a whole way of life or "simply" a religion. If one saw Judaism to be a whole way of life, mobility, achievement, and social interaction tended to be limited to the confines of the ghetto; but viewing Judaism as a religious denomination helped to free one to pursue values outside the ghetto, enhancing assimilation into the wider milieu.

Initially, Eastern European Jews saw Jewishness as stemming from total involvement in a rich culture of which religion was a part. This allowed Jews to be secularists, socialists, anarchists, and even atheists and still think of themselves as Jews.

In time, however, the Eastern European Jews seemingly "learned" from the German Jews, for with increased Americanization they too separated religion from the ethnic complex and utilized it as a vehicle for social mobility. However, this transformation also intensified conflicts between class and ethnic identity.

THE GHETTO TRANSPLANTED

In America Jews found that even though they might successfully recreate certain features of the *shtetl*, they could not (nor eventually did they want to) guarantee its persistence in its original form. In Eastern Europe the Jewish world was so complete and so isolated from the general society that Jews did not think of themselves as a segregated minority. The fact is that they lived a caste-like existence, with almost complete envelopment in a religious life, great occupational concentration, and a proscription of intimate social contacts with gentiles. Exclusion was so taken for granted that class and status positions in the general society were not even matters of concern to Jews.

In American society the situation was considerably different.

Eastern European Jews arrived in the United States during the peak years of immigration and at a time of great industrial and economic expansion, as well as population growth and movement to the cities. Most Jews settled in the low rent areas of the large Eastern cities adjacent to the central business districts. Wirth has pointed out a significant ecological difference in the settlement patterns of Jews in Europe and in America. Old World ghettoes were "homogeneous bodies concentrated in a single section of the city, with a common city-wide if not regional, cultural life. The American ghetto, on the other hand, is, as a rule, split up into various sections, containing various national groups of Jews and reflecting the influences of heterogeneous ways of immigration, as well as of successive generations of the same groups."[17]

Initially, efforts at recreating ghetto life in these sections were largely successful, particularly in the establishment of Orthodox synagogues. In 1890 there were 270 synagogues in the United States, by 1899 there were 533, and by 1916 almost two thousand.[18]

To perpetuate study of the Law, Jewish schools were formed to teach both Hebrew and Yiddish. In addition to the rabbi and religious teacher, the services of other sacred functionaries were made available, such as the *mohel* (circumciser), *shochet* (ritual slaughterer of animals), as well as the *mikveh* (ritual baths for women, now called *ritualariums*). To perpetuate old country ties, numerous *landsmanschaften* and *vereins* were founded, clubs or organizations consisting of persons coming from the same town or village. Burial and mutual aid societies came into being, as well as a full range of secular services, such as kosher butchers, bakeries, restaurants, Yiddish newspapers and theaters, and Turkish baths. In the streets of Jewish districts one could hear almost nothing but Yiddish being spoken by bearded men, many with side-curls, black frock coats, and broad brimmed hats. Life was meaningful and deeply emotionally involving, but also trying and difficult for poor immigrants uneducated and unskilled in Western, much less American, ways. Nevertheless, true to their ethnic traditions, Eastern European immigrants established a separate way of life that isolated them from the general community. Contacts with gentiles generally occurred only when economically necessary, intimate social relations were prohibited and avoided. Degree and frequency of such contacts were in fact determined by social differences resulting from time of arrival or degree of

Americanization. Class differences, which later critically influenced the nature of contact with gentiles, began to develop in the first generation, but did not really crystallize until the second generation community.

Conflicts eventually arose between the need to survive and earn a living and the desire to preserve the traditional ritually correct existence. One reason why so many Jewish men became peddlers, junkmen, or dealers in second hand goods was not just because these activities required relatively little skill and capital, but because in such independent occupations Jews could earn a living and still retain their freedom to observe Orthodox religious commandments. In fact, these requirements (plus, of course, exclusionary anti-Semitism) helped foster a pattern of self-employment among Jews that still persists. Furthermore, some Jews chose occupations regardless of their marginal or low status in the general community because of commitment to sacred values. For first generation Jews status among gentiles simply wasn't an issue.

Work versus ritual observance was especially a problem for Sabbath or daily prayers if one worked for a "goy." (Of course, Jews could and did work for other Jews.) A story is told that perhaps summarizes the problem. An Orthodox Jewish man who leaves early each morning to peddle his wares begins taking his oldest son to "break him in." But before leaving they must say their morning prayers, which necessitates awakening at 5 A.M. Sleepily, the son follows his father for several weeks but finally rebels saying, "Papa, you have got to make up your mind. Either we pray or we work." Religious ritual was apparently a luxury not everyone could afford and needless to say, work won out.

Enclosed as it was, the Jewish ghetto in America did not long remain impervious to the social and material attractions of an open class and highly mobile secular society. In taking advantage of opportunities, Jews transformed the traditional relationship between the social organization of the Jewish community and Judaism. The Jewish community became a secular minority group in which religion performed highly specialized functions instead of pervasive ones. Jews were then free to pursue the goals and values of the "good American life" while retaining some measure of social separateness.

Economic factors and forces of secularization were perhaps most important in these basic transformations. While many immigrants achieved self-employment, particularly in retail trades, more than half of the Jews from Russia entered the newly expanded garment industry. In 1900, 60 percent of the Russian Jews in the United States were garment workers and 15 percent were in trade.[19]

Sweatshop conditions were difficult and hazardous, but it was one of the few means of economic survival available for poor and unskilled immigrants. Adapting with amazing rapidity, Jews soon came to value economic over social survival, working long hours in hope of providing a better future for their children. Perhaps more than any other immigrant group, Jews insisted that their sons achieve a higher social and economic position than their fathers, even at the risk of becoming alienated from family and community. In the traditional Jewish family, identification by parents with children was so complete that the latter's successes were not only unthreatening to parents (unlike the situation in other groups), but were quite literally the parents' successes too. After all, one of the most hallowed traditions of the *shtetl*, *kest*, granted prestige to the father-in-law for supporting his son-in-law's scholarly pursuits.[20]

Perhaps relatively rapid secularization and acculturation was to be expected, considering the age-old skill of Jews, the perennial guest people, at adjusting successfully to new situations by first discovering how the system works and then working with it. In Eastern Europe, Jews had responded to the mixed indifference and outright hostility of the surrounding culture by isolating themselves and developing a vital and enclosed ingroup life.

In the United States, on the other hand, Jews responded to the promises of "the American Dream" by making the adjustments necessary to achieve social and economic success in the general society while maintaining a separate (though highly acculturated) ingroup life. Jews, for example, had always placed great value on education, but specifically on sacred learning. In American society they discovered sacred learning didn't "pay off" and shifted the emphasis to learning required by secular professions such as medicine, law, and dentistry.

Even in the first generation the ghetto began to reflect the effects of secularization; but it did not change dramatically until there was no longer a ready supply of immigrants to maintain the old ways intact. The Johnson Acts of 1921 and 1924 brought mass immigration to an end and with it one of the most unique periods in American history. The children of immigrants inherited certain salient values, including community traditions as well as the pragmatic tradition of working with the prevailing system; but much of the *Yiddishkeit* was to become an ever fading memory.

As a recent study of a Jewish community put it, "If tensions of the first generation were those of survival, the tensions of the second generation were those of success."[21] Having solved the problem of physical survival, focus was shifted to the more subtle goals of improving social status among Jews as well as among gentiles. This was achieved through rejection of many ghetto customs, accelerated acculturation, and intense striving for the values of the dominant society. But attachment to a communal life remained, and acculturation intensified the conflict already begun in the first generation between Jewish and non-Jewish values. Caught between the ghetto and the larger society, the community of the second generation emerged as an attempt to reconcile the dilemma of marginality, to live free of the stigma of Jewish identity while clinging to certain vestiges of ghetto life. The new community was sufficiently acculturated and adapted to American middle class life to suit the requirements for social mobility, but also sufficiently ethnic to preserve a shared ingroup life.

THE GILDING OF THE GHETTO

The first step in full acculturation was the mass exodus from the original ghetto to the better neighborhoods of the city. This was spurred by the economic successes achieved in the prosperous 1920s. In a single generation, Jews moved from working class to middle class status in American society, and it was this concentration in the middle class that laid the social foundations for the ethnic community of the second generation. The evidence on the occupational mobility of Jews indicates their successful participation in trade and commerce and in the independent professions.[22] These occupations provided the income necessary for new and more prestigeful styles of life. But it is important to recognize that many Jews achieved affluence in occupations that were (at least originally) marginal, risky, and even despised. Such was the case with credit and discount retailing, junk, salvage, pawnshops, and motion pictures. As the *Fortune* Magazine Survey of 1936 showed, Jews were relatively absent from heavy industry, banking, and finance, but were concentrated in the second hand goods business, light industry (textiles, clothing, and furniture) and in wholesaling merchandise, jobbing, and retailing.[23]

Even in the professions, Jews occupied the less important and less prestigeful positions. In 1948 Carey McWilliams pointed out, "The most important law offices in America such as the law businesses incidental to banking, insurance, trust company operations, investments, railroads, patents, admiralty and large corporation matters in general are in the hands of non-Jewish firms many of which, even though they have numerous Jewish clients, have no Jewish partners."[24] These observations were corroborated by a study of the status of the Jewish lawyer in New York City.[25]

Tensions resulting from this classic disparity between class and status positions were incorporated into the structure of the second generation community and became part of the third generation's heritage. Glazer observed that "While America in general became more markedly middle class in its occupational structure, Jews became even more so. The Jewish community today consists largely of well-to-do professionals, merchants, and white collar workers."[26]

The social legitimation of class position motivated a mass flight from the ghetto only to result in a re-concentration of Jews in the higher income areas of the city. This formed the physical basis for a new kind of ghetto, a closed community of middle class Jews whose social life was carried on exclusively with Jews of appropriate status. These were "gilded" ghettoes in which the institutions paralleled those of the American middle class, but whose participants were all Jews. Of course, not all Jews were equally successful economically and class and status differences began to develop among them. In general, adaptation of American ways and economic mobility were the keys to social mobility. This was a critical process because paradoxically achievement of majority values generated and actually reinforced the social foundations of the second generation Jewish community. Between the time of the first generation ghetto and the second generation gilded ghetto, there was a transition period in which the second generation community was more of an ecological than a social reality. Jews lived in close proximity to one another but "were too busy establishing themselves to establish a community. The impetus for a more organized social structure came from the economic advances of successful Jews eager for a social matrix in which to enjoy the fruits of their labors."[27]

Socially excluded from the general community, Jewish businessmen and professionals sought recognition and status among their fellow Jews. They emulated life styles of middle class gentiles and developed a complex structure of clubs and organizations paralleling those of the general society. Latent ethnic ties remained and were articulated and converted into a coherent social reality by professional community organizers, Jewish social workers, and fund raisers.

Traditional welfare activities became the basis of formalized secular organizations. Jewish Federations, for example, became not just central fund raising agencies, but forces regulating status activities as well, by influencing country club memberships to contribute to the Federation. Upwardly mobile and wealthy Jews needed community workers to guarantee them a status audience, while the latter needed successful Jews to provide a setting and the money for their professional activities. Thus, this persistent alliance between affluent Jews and Jewish community workers is a symbiotic one reaffirming mutual ethnic identity and strengthening communal bonds. The highly organized structure of the second generation community continues to "impose communal ties and sentiments on its members which in turn support the structure. It is no longer possible to determine whether the structure is the consequence of the sentiment or the sentiment is the consequence of the structure."[28]

This complex of sentiment, lingering ethnic traditions, and middle class American values were fused into that unique phenomenon, the second generation Jewish community. This was a minority community whose structure was based on conflicting principles of organization, those indigenous to Jewish life and the history of the ghetto and those emanating from the general society. Since acculturation as the necessary requirement for social mobility was unequally achieved by second generation Jews, the stratification system that emerged was perhaps the key to understanding the institutional structure of their community. It is generally the case, as it was in the Eastern European *shtetl*, that status competition is particularly intensified in socially closed and segregated communities. The second generation Jewish community was no different. With secularization, material factors replaced the sacred as criteria of evaluation. Furthermore, since Jews were concentrated in a narrow range of occupations, the distinctions between them were not as between laborers and business executives or between long established family fortunes and recently acquired ones. Rather invidious distinctions were made between poor junkmen and rich ones, the corner grocer and the chain store owner, the tailor and the garment manufacturer, and between rich lawyers or physicians and those of more moderate incomes. Unquestionably, money and what it could buy was the major source of status. Although professionals had more education than businessmen, they did not necessarily have more prestige in the second generation community unless they were also wealthy. Business values prevailed and businessmen were the elite. If professionals wanted to belong they had to accept these values and associate not just with other professionals, but with other Jews regardless of occupation. Thus, within the second generation Jewish community, class position rather than occupation *per se* determined status and the nature of one's associations.

Even religious patterns, once the center of Jewish life, came to reflect the social requirements of various strata. The orthodoxy of first generation Jews embodied the very cultural differences their children sought to eliminate because of their isolating effects from the mainstream of American life. Orthodoxy was too burdensome for those Jews who wished to achieve mobility unencumbered by restrictions and limiting patterns. Wishing to retain their Jewish identity, their choice was the Conservative synagogue,[29] which restructured Judaism according to majority group standards, reducing the scope and significance of religion until it became just another specialized institution. Once a place of worship and study, the synagogue became a center of various secular functions with the major task being to guarantee the social continuity of the Jewish community. One of the most important developments in American Judaism was the stratification of the synagogue in the manner of Protestant denominationalism. Reform Judaism, of German origin, eventually was taken over by socially and economically successful Eastern European Jews. Since theological differences between the denominations were underplayed, the real differences between them consisted mainly of the social and economic differences between their

respective congregations. Thus, although there are local variations, the general pattern is an association among the Orthodox,
Conservative, and Reform synagogues and lower, middle, and
upper class Jews respectively. As Jews become increasingly acculturated and continue to improve their social and economic
position, they do not necessarily assimilate. On the contrary, they
join synagogues in ever increasing numbers and the synagogues
themselves become increasingly Protestantized.

The social life in the second generation community also reflected its middle class as well as its continued ethnic character.
The many clubs, organizations, and lodges recruited their members from various class levels, which also differed in their affiliations with non-Jewish organizations. In general, the country club-
bers or high status Jews were more likely than low status Jews to
have contact with gentiles in some kind of organizational setting
outside the Jewish community.[30] The fact is that few second
generation Jews had any social contact with gentiles that could be
construed as "intimate" or friendly. The only exceptions were
those wealthy and highly acculturated Jews with especially high
status in the Jewish community.[31]

In the second generation community, there was no doubt that
wealth and appropriate life styles were the necessary pre-condi-
tions for cracking the ghetto walls and making social headway
with gentiles. But as many Jews discovered, much to their con-
sternation, having a certain income and living in certain neighborhoods, belonging to certain organizations, changing one's
name from Bernstein to Burns, sending one's children to certain
prep schools and Ivy League colleges, drinking certain brands of
whiskey, observing Christmas by having a tree in the house, or
even voting Republican, were not in themselves sufficient to
guarantee intimate social contact with gentiles.

A special and important type of organizational behavior is
philanthropic activity or fund raising. While philanthropy has
always been a legitimate way to consume wealth conspicuously,
among Jews there is the distinctive feature of "taking care of
one's own" sanctioned by Biblical and ethnic traditions. And although fund raising has become a highly technical and complex
activity, Jewish fund raisers have long been successful to an
extent rarely realized in the larger community. Fund raising became so highly institutionalized as to be a major principle of
organization in the Jewish community.[32]

Philanthropic contributions were of course greatest for wealthy Jews, thereby enhancing their status in the Jewish community. Regardless of Jewish traditions of charitable generosity, these contributions became something more than indices of traditional values. "Conspicuous charity is less a matter of religious or ideological commitment than a conventional social obligation serving as a source of status."[33] Furthermore, such contributions were critical for high status Jews in order to maintain their ties to the community that granted them their favorable social positions. Philanthropic activity, thus, was the one important link to the Jewish community that was not attenuated and in this area upwardly mobile and high status Jews vividly experienced the competing social forces exerted by the minority and majority communities. Their contributions to Jewish causes were a response to pressures exerted by the Jewish community for continued participation. And their participation in non-Jewish charitable activities was a response to the general community for desired social recognition by the gentiles.

The world of the second generation thus was highly stratified within a common minority situation. It was a world of paradox if not outright conflicts. Growing up and maturing in a society in which it was "tough to be a Jew," second generation Jews came to accept the anomalies of their life as being somehow inevitable. This generation achieved economic success but remained socially insecure; education remained highly prized but specifically secular education was a means to an occupational end; gentiles were suspect as being potential anti-Semites but their approval was eagerly sought; religious observance and synagogue attendance were minimal but religious identification was not totally rejected as it no longer bore the stigma of immigrant orthodoxy; in spite of acculturation, associations and social contacts were still based on shared Jewish birth rather than common achieved interests; children were urged to obtain an education and get ahead but also to maintain extended family ties through cousin clubs, family counsels, and the like.

And still guided by the ancient ghetto principle, "Is it good for the Jews or bad for the Jews," there was pride in Jewish accomplishment but fear lest these accomplishments support the belief that Jews really were different. In the 1930s and 1940s when Jews were socially ascending, Jewish organizations were anxious to publish records of Jewish accomplishment. But with the achievement of the new insecurity of middle class status after World War II, Jews became more anxious to conform to the respectable image of mass mediocrity than risk being excluded from American society. So intellectual, economic, and occupational accomplishments were played down and instead the attainment of mass produced suburban sameness and togetherness was played up. The trouble was that Jews continued to be nagged by the feeling that they really are better and superior to anyone else. Suppression of this "embarrassing" notion has required tremendous effort and discipline although no more than that required to carry on the dual life of "ingroup Jew" and "outgroup Joe."

THE JEWISH COMMUNITY IN MASS SOCIETY

There is reason to believe that with the third, fourth, and succeeding generations and the encroachment of mass society these two roles may be fused. Indeed, general societal forces now being exerted on the Jewish community are so powerful they have created a new kind of crisis. The crisis exists in trying to retain the "acculturated separatism" of the second generation in the face of threats, such as increasing rates of intermarriage and the defection of intellectuals, a new group of salaried professionals, and organizational men from a specifically Jewish life. In structural terms the problem is preserving the balance between the conflicting principals underlying the organization of the Jewish community. This does not necessarily mean that complete assimilation is imminent. On the contrary, there now seems to be a preoccupation with how to preserve Jewish identity. But with the decline of an *ethnic* basis for communal life, American Jewry ironically seems to be fulfilling the ideal of nineteenth century German Jewry, that of becoming just another religious denomination.

The changes are a part of general transformations in the structure of Western society, which sociologists have noted for some time. There has been a shift from a tradition-oriented sacred society to a rationally oriented secular society. In their dichotomous societal typologies, such thinkers as Henry Sumner Maine (status to contract), Emile Durkheim (mechanical to organic), Herbert Spencer (military to industrial), Max Weber (traditional to rational), Ferdinand Tönnies (community to society), Howard Becker (sacred to secular), and Robert Redfield (folk to urban), all recognized the same development. In recent years the concept of mass society has been applied to specific manifestations such as political apathy, alienation and anxiety, bureaucratic organization and personality, the decline of the small town, and presently, to the problem of the ethnic or minority community.

The American Jewish community, of course, has a historical connection with prior social forms such as the immigrant ghetto, the *shtetl*, the medieval ghetto, and the community formed by the exile of the ancient Hebrews from their nation. All of these were distinctive communities representing ways of life based on ethnic traditions. But these communities were all adapted to the minority status of Jews and so were culturally and socially isolated and not truly independent and self-sufficient. Religion and the family were the central community institutions while the political and economic institutions of the wider society were necessary for survival and livelihood. In this sense, Jewish communities have always been incomplete. Mass society threatens to "complete" the Jewish community by incorporating its members into the general religious and family institutions.

Thus, part of the status anxiety of contemporary American Jewry is attributable to the very social and economic advancements being made, which threaten the religio-familistic complex. Certainly not all Jews are feeling the effects equally nor are they all members of Jewish communities in the special organizational sense. But all Jews have some anchorage, attenuated or not, in a Jewish way of life of some kind. And these social forms do not die easily. On the contrary, they are self-perpetuating often by groups with vested interests in the maintenance of the community. Social life becomes inter-locally and more rationally organized, thus requiring shifts in loyalty and identification from local and non-rationally organized ethnic groups to national and impersonal organizations. In the past American Jews could obtain greater access to general social values and experiences from within the confines of the Jewish community. This is undoubtedly still the case with many Jews, but others, particularly in the third and succeeding generations, are not necessarily willing to limit their opportunities and experiences to those possible in an exclusively Jewish way of life.

The irony is that while many non-Jewish Americans are searching for a meaningful community experience,[34] Jews who have had it for so long apparently wish to give it up. The Jewish community is perhaps the last remaining instance of something approximating a whole way of life. Mass society threatens the ethnic community by extending institutional influences and displacing the formerly central institutions of religion and the family. This development undermines the original basis for a minority community's parallel institutions and forces its members to compete for positions in the general society, not just among ethnic peers.

The reactions of American Jews have varied according to class, status position, and generation. The concentration of first and second generation Jews in self-employed occupations and professions tied them to local communities. This of course made possible the vital and highly organized community life characteristic of those generations. Geographic immobility also sustained the influence of religion, family, and fund raising as critical forces of cohesion and stability. Subsequent generations, however, secure in their middle class American background, are not as likely to be motivated by economic necessity or by the desire to escape a stigmatized way of life. As college trained experts, young Jews can choose careers in the same fields as non-Jews impelled by similar desires for security and status. Reflecting general social developments, these careers increasingly lead to positions in large organizations as salaried professionals. Such occupations were characteristically considered non-Jewish in previous generations. Available evidence does reveal an increase in salaried employment among Jews, particularly in such professions as engineering, architecture, journalism, and college teaching.[35] These increases also indicate changes in fields of study traditionally chosen by Jews in college. Medical, dental, and law schools still attract large numbers of Jews, though research in those fields has now become a more respectable specialty. But there are many more Jewish students in graduate schools pursuing liberal arts and the various social and natural sciences. It took some time for families to grant the Ph.D. and the college professor as much status as the M.D. (the real doctor), but one suspects that the former may now have approached if not actually surpassed the latter in prestige among Jews.

The point is that with a much wider range of occupations now opened, Jews are increasingly choosing those that offer greater participation in the wider society. Tensions are often created as young Jews must choose between involvement in extended family and local ethnic affairs and involvement in the professional status community. Many seem to be choosing professional associations that often involve geographic as well as social mobility, thereby threatening the viability of traditional Jewish family and community life. And perhaps what makes these new occupations "better" in the long run is not necessarily their income but the increasing access they offer to social contacts with gentiles, which has eventually been accepted even by the second generation Jew as an important goal.

This is not to say all young Jews are entering these occupations. There are still many who continue to play more traditional occupational roles, entering the independent professions or taking over family businesses. The latter group often faces the special problem of inheriting lucrative businesses that bear the special stigma of identifiable ethnic specialization, e.g., retailing, wholesaling, salvage. Rather than spurn the profitable enterprise, young Jews will transform their role identity from "Jewish businessmen" to "business executives." Interesting changes in occupational titles also occur: a "shmata trader" becomes a "textile industrialist," a "junk dealer" becomes a "metallurgist," and a "plumbing supplier" becomes a "sanitary engineer."

Another problem is that along with the business these young Jews are likely to inherit the fathers' Jewish club and organizational affiliations, fund raising commitments, and predominantly Jewish friendships. But this "Jewishness" can be modified by developing appropriate taste patterns: foreign cars instead of Cadillacs or Buicks, Scotch or Bourbon whiskey instead of Canadian Club, camping out on vacations instead of going to expensive resort hotels, skiing or playing tennis instead of handball or pinochle, and adopting non-Jewish first names for children such as Kevin or Margery instead of Melvin or Marilyn. Of course, they are still Jews and commonly recognized as such, but in a society placing such great emphasis on appearance and style, it is possible to play a non-Jewish role without actually assimilating.

Religion and family life in particular feel the strains of these developments. American Judaism has become so attuned to middle class norms, young Jews have discovered they can be both Jewish and successful without feeling the need to reject their religious affiliation. Judaism seems to survive in American society only as it makes fewer religious demands and adapts itself to the social needs of a highly secular and mobile population. Reflecting dominant religious trends in American society, Judaism has come to embody the class and status interests of particular groups until the synagogue has become a kind of middle class settlement house. In the process, the status of the rabbi is often devalued to be replaced by the social director.

It is somewhat ironic that a people with so great a religious heritage should have become so a-religious that the rabbi can hardly be spoken of as a spiritual leader. At best, he is a pastoral psychologist, at worst, a sympathetic overseer. It is small wonder that theology students with deep scholarly interests and commitments are wary of leading congregations and instead consider careers in the seminary or the academy.

The recent boom in synagogue building and synagogue affiliation and apparent revived interest in Jewish education do not necessarily belie these remarks. These developments are part of the general religious revival in American society and reflect no revival of the spirit. Rather, they are products of the breakup of older communities where social identity was relatively fixed and reflect the mass movement into new communities (e.g., suburbs) where new sources of social identity had to be created. Religion was a likely basis for such identity since its most demanding precepts had already been emasculated making it nothing more imposing than a comfortable social habit. These same developments apply to Judaism with the added desire to perpetuate Jewish identity but in ways that would not lead to invidious identification. The usual rationale offered for synagogue affiliation and for providing Jewish education is group survival so the children "know what they are." Thus, being Jewish may mean nothing more than paying synagogue membership fees, sending children to Sunday School so they shouldn't feel "left out" when their gentile friends attend their Sunday School, or being able to answer "Jewish" instead of an embarrassing "nothing" when their teacher asks them their religion. Besides, with everyone desperately searching for a meaningful community experience, why not utilize the one built into the very nature of Jewish life?

Religion and the family have always been closely linked in Jewish life. With all the changes in Judaism, one would certainly expect changes in family life as well. Essentially, of course, the problem for the Jewish family is that its extended and familistic character could not withstand the desired and achieved social mobility of its members. And so, following general societal patterns, the extended family broke into conjugal units though not without much stress and strain. Parents made great investments to guarantee the success of their children but with the expectation they would eventually come home to live where the parents could at least bask in reflected glory. But with the geographic mobility required by new non-Jewish occupations, families can no longer guarantee the togetherness of their members. Furthermore, one of the most serious crises precipitated for the family by these new occupational choices is that the families no longer readily control mate selection. The available evidence is somewhat ambiguous[36] but there is good reason to believe that the rate of intermarriage is increasing, especially among salaried professionals. There are some patterns difficult to explain, such as the much higher rate of intermarriage among psychiatrists and among academicians. But part of the explanation involves the greater access to non-Jewish social circles and values and greater freedom from family and community control made possible by these occupational experiences where ethnic background is irrelevant as a criterion of evaluation and as a basis for social interaction.[37] As more Jews enter these occupations and as they meet gentiles in situations normally leading to mate selection, the intermarriage rate can be expected to increase. These developments will not necessarily be motivated by a desire to assimilate but to broaden social horizons outside the limitations of the ethnic community.

Suburbia has been the context in which many of these developments have occurred. Jews moved to the suburbs for the same reasons as everyone else, better housing, bigger backyards, and the like. But the move has special implications for Jews since for them the suburbs have the added boon of non-Jewish neighbors. While Jews in suburbs do congregate in enclaves, they usually constitute a minority of the general population. This is in contrast to the urban neighborhoods from which they came where they may have constituted over 50 percent of the population in the area. Suburban life can hardly be considered peculiarly Jewish and thus satisfies the desire of young Jews for social life based not on ethnic ties but on shared status and acquired styles of life. Social participation in the conventional patterns of suburban communities tends to create a kind of social invisibility rendering Jews indistinguishable from their non-Jewish neighbors. It is not that Jews are trying to disavow Jewish identity to avoid invidious social differentiation. "They reject the ideology of separateness that rationalizes the parallel institutions of the ethnic community and maximizes the value of togetherness in their suburban status communities. Almost convinced that there really are no differences between Jews and non-Jews, the third generation vigorously sets about eliminating any differences that remain to make a difference in the way it is treated socially."[38] This process of "becoming like everyone else" eventually broadens their status audience and subjects young Jews to the social judgments of the larger society rather than the Jewish community alone. Superficial emulation of gentiles is no longer sufficient and young Jews must now discover the subtleties and acquire the refinements that separate the pretenders from the holders of social honor.

Yet, in spite of this preoccupation with "Americanization," or perhaps because Jews have achieved such a measure of social security, there are signs of a re-glorification of certan "typical" Jewish ethnic characteristics. For example, consuming food in abundant quantities has always been a characteristic Jewish trait and Jews still seem to spend a greater proportion of their incomes on food than do other groups. So, the "gastronomic syndrome" lingers on in the passion for bagels and lox, knishes, blintzes, rye bread, kosher or kosher-style delicatessen, and for good food in general. (Has anyone ever explained the Jewish passion for Chinese food?) Paraphrasing Marcus Hansen's famous principle of the every-other-generational-alliance, what the son forgets it is safe for the grandson to remember. Hence, there is a revival, especially among college educated young Jewish housewives, of interest in traditional Jewish cooking evidenced by the successful sales of Jewish cookbooks. Yiddish folk music, humor, literature, and even theater all enjoy a kind of minor revival due to a curious fantasizing about a "close, meaningful way of life" that may never have existed, but for which there is a nostalgic longing in the decommunalized mass society. Not to be overlooked is a kind of reverse acculturation occurring in American society whereby gentiles from arid subcultural backgrounds attach special exotic value to ethnic traits and "Jewify" themselves in search of "true" meanings and values. But this is all delusionary play activity. Jews act like gentiles and gentiles act like Jews since only persons in comfortable middle class positions can afford to enjoy the cultural symbols of an existence that was as harsh, cold, and cruel as it was "emotionally gratifying."

NOTES

1. Everett and Helen Hughes, *When Peoples Meet* (Glencoe, Ill.: Free Press, 1951), p. 101.
2. See Max Weber, *Ancient Judaism*, pp. 336ff.; *The Religions of India*, pp. 100ff.; *Theory of Social and Economic Organization*, pp. 139–43.
3. Nathan Glazer, *American Judaism* (Chicago: University of Chicago Press, 1957), p. 23.
4. *American Jewish Yearbook* (Philadelphia, 1918).
5. Glazer, *op. cit.*, p. 83.
6. *American Jewish Yearbook* (Philadelphia, 1927), pp. 243–46.
7. *American Jewish Yearbook* (Philadelphia, 1964), pp. 6, 8–11.
8. *Ibid.*, pp. 7–11.
9. Louis Wirth, *The Ghetto* (Chicago: University of Chicago Press, 1955), p. 202.
10. Mark Zborowski and Elizabeth Herzog, *Life Is with People* (New York: International Universities Press, 1951).
11. *Ibid.*, p. 77.
12. *Ibid.*, p. 76.
13. *Ibid.*, p. 272.
14. *Ibid.*, pp. 269–77.
15. *Ibid.*, p. 428.
16. Glazer, *op. cit.*, p. 64.
17. Wirth, *op. cit.*, p. 204.
18. Glazer, *op. cit.*, p. 12.
19. Nathan Glazer, "Social Characteristics of American Jews, 1654–1954," *American Jewish Yearbook* (Philadelphia, 1955), pp. 11–12.
20. Zborowski and Herzog, *op. cit.*, p. 82.
21. Judith R. Kramer and Seymour Leventman, *Children of the Gilded Ghetto* (New Haven: Yale University Press, 1961), p. 8.
22. Nathan Goldberg, "Occupational Patterns of American Jews," *The Jewish Review*, Vol. III, pp. 262–90; William Kephart, "What is Known about the Occupations of American Jews," in *Race Prejudice and Dis-*

crimination, Arnold Rose, ed. (New York: Knopf, 1951), pp. 131–46; Nathan Glazer, "Social Characteristics of American Jews," *op. cit.,* pp. 20–24.

23. *Fortune Survey of American Jews* (New York, 1936), pp. 30–46.
24. Carey McWilliams, *A Mask for Privilege* (Boston: Little, Brown, 1948), p. 137.
25. Melvin Fagen, "The Status of Jewish Lawyers in New York," *Jewish Social Service,* 1939, pp. 73–104.
26. Glazer, "Social Characteristics of American Jews," *op. cit.,* p. 26.
27. Kramer and Leventman, *op. cit.,* p. 12.
28. *Ibid.,* p. 13.
29. See Marshall Sklare, *Conservative Judaism* (New York: Free Press, 1955).
30. Kramer and Leventman, *op. cit.,* pp. 94–96.
31. See E. Digby Baltzell, *The Protestant Establishment* (New York: Random House, 1964), for a brillant documentation of upper class Protestant anti-Semitism.
32. See Robert M. MacIver, *Report on Jewish Community Relations Agencies* (New York, 1951).
33. Kramer and Leventman, *op. cit.,* p. 101.
34. Robert A. Nisbet, *Community and Power* (New York: Oxford University Press, 1962), p. 30.
35. Glazer, "Social Characteristics of American Jews," *op. cit.,* pp. 26–27; Nathan Goldberg, *Occupational Patterns of American Jewry* (New York: Jewish Theological Seminary Press, 1947), pp. 42–43.
36. See Marshall Sklare, "Intermarriage and Jewish Life," *Commentary* (September, 1964); Erich Rosenthal, "Studies of Jewish Intermarriage in the United States," in *American Jewish Yearbook* (Philadelphia, 1963), pp. 3–56.
37. See Milton Gordon, *Assimilation and Acculturation in American Life* (New York: Oxford University Press, 1964), especially chapters 7 and 8.
38. Kramer and Leventman, *op. cit.,* p. 18.

IN DEFENSE OF THE JEWISH MOTHER

ZENA SMITH BLAU

A WIDESPREAD BELIEF in America shared by Jews as well as non-Jews, is that Jews are "smart but neurotic." The Jew's intellectual aptitudes are usually attributed to the cultural values transmitted by Jewish fathers for whom learning and study were traditionally a religious obligation. As for the neurosis, that of course is blamed on the Jewish mother.

That Jews are "smart" is confirmed by the available empirical evidence. Whatever indices have been employed to measure achievement—I.Q. scores, school grades, years of schooling, occupational level, and social mobility—Jews, on the average, exhibit higher levels of performance than the non-Jews to whom they have been compared.[1] But the proposition that neurosis is significantly more widespread among Jews than among non-Jews is not supported by the admittedly limited empirical studies of the subject. A study comparing the prevalence of emotional disorder among Protestants, Catholics, and Jews—based on a sample of 1660 respondents in midtown Manhattan[2]—found that neurotic symptoms were common in all three groups: respondents rated as "well" constituted only 20.2% of Protestants tested, 17.4% of the Catholics, and 14.5% of the Jews. And when the authors classified people according to the *severity* of their symptoms and the degree to which these interfered with their ability to carry on normal activities, they discovered that *impairing* forms of emotional disorder were significantly lower among Jews (17.2%) than among either Protestants (23.5%) or Catholics (24.7%). Further, Jews were concentrated in the mental health category of "mild symptom formation," exhibiting far fewer cases of incapacitating disorder than Protestants and Catho-

Reprinted by permission of the author and the editor of *Midstream*. First appeared in the February 1967 issue of *Midstream*.

lics. Interestingly, the Jewish immunity from psychological impairment was most pronounced among respondents from working-class families, where mental illness is generally most prevalent.

If Jewish mothers are to be blamed for their children's psychological problems, should they not also receive some credit for their relative strengths? Indeed this article will suggest that the child-rearing practices of immigrant Jewish mothers contributed significantly to the remarkable educational and occupational attainments of second generation Jews, and could provide an important model for scientific study and emulation.

I feel that I can speak with some authority on the subject of the Yiddishe Mameh, not only as a sociologist concerned with the comparative study of family structures and patterns of socialization, but also as a second generation Jew, who has known many Yiddishe Mamehs—my own mother, her friends, and the mothers of my friends—and who remembers well the social context of Jewish immigrant life in which my generation was raised. I do not suggest, of course, that all Jewish immigrant women exhibited identical maternal behavior, but there can be little question that the constellation of maternal traits commonly referred to as "the Yiddishe Mameh" was the modal maternal pattern among Jewish immigrants from Eastern Europe and that it was different from the typical maternal behavior found among non-Jews in America.[3]

Yiddishe Mamehs were active, responsible, stable, expressive and verbal women for whom *naches fun die kinder* represented the highest form of self-fulfillment and achievement for a woman. They perceived the child as a fragile creature whose body and spirit needed to be carefully and assiduously nurtured and protected not only in infancy but throughout childhood and even adolescence. They went to inordinate trouble and expense to provide their children with the "best and freshest" food, the best medical care, the warmest clothing, at considerable sacrifice of other needs and wants. That their high standards of child care were effective is attested to by the fact that infant and child mortality rates were lower among Jews than in the rest of the American population during the earlier decades of this century, despite the fact that the majority of Jewish immigrants were in the working class where the mortality risks are greatest.

Strong bonds of love and mutual dependency between mother and child are traditional among Jews. For most of their history they have occupied the position of a beleaguered minority exposed to hostility, as well as to the pressure to abandon their faith and take up the ways of the majority. Various practices evolved among diaspora Jews to strengthen and fortify the child to cope with these pressures. The responsibility for establishing the bulwark of this fortification system was assigned to the mother, and the task began at birth of building a healthy body, a strong ego and a strong primary identification with the mother which was perceived as the essential *motivating* force for learning the ways of Jews and for adhering to them, even under adverse conditions.

In America Yiddishe Mamehs appeared far more permissive, indulgent and self-sacrificing than the typical Anglo-Saxon mother, at least in the years prior to the nineteen-forties. For example, they were a good deal more tolerant of whining and crying, and of dependency behavior generally. They exerted little pressure on their children to control explosions of feeling and temper, and demanded only that they refrain from engaging in physical forms of aggression—*nit mit die hendt*, was a common admonishment in the Jewish home. Toward their fathers and other grown-ups Jewish children were expected to behave with respect, but toward their mothers they were allowed considerably more leeway to express negative as well as positive feelings. Yiddishe Mamehs erected no status distance between themselves and their children. They did not stand on ceremony; they did not protect their pride or their self-respect. With no other human being did the Jewish child develop as close, as trusting, as free and fearless a relationship as with his mother, and therein lay the secret of her power to gain his compliance ultimately in those areas of behavior in which she chose to exert pressure during the entire period of maturation.

Identification with the mother became the cornerstone of the entire socialization process, and Yiddishe Mamehs understood that once it was firmly established, but not before, it became possible to gain the *voluntary* compliance of their children to those basic social norms to which they as Jews were committed, and to which they were determined their children should also permanently adhere, whatever later pressures they might encounter to deny or violate them. That Jews as a rule retain their Jewish identity, and have done so over the centuries, however ambivalently, is largely due, although not entirely, of course, to the strength of the primary identification with the Yiddishe Mameh, and to the profound fear of the guilt that denial of her would engender. The well-known ambivalence of the Jew toward his mother, then, is part and parcel of his ambivalence about remaining a Jew.

Yiddishe Mamehs seemed singularly unconcerned with "discipline" and "independence training." They allowed their children a greater degree of liberty at home than was customary among Gentiles, and readily acknowledged that their children were *zelosen,* that is, pampered, demanding, spoiled, not well-behaved the way Gentile children seemed to be in the presence of their mothers. The Anglo-Saxon code of stoic endurance and suppressed emotion was alien to the Eastern European Jew. Of course, Yiddishe Mamehs had their boiling point, which varied a good deal depending on their individual temperament, but generally they preferred controlling their children *mit guten* that is, by explanation, reasoning, distraction, and admonishment. As a rule, they were naggers or screamers rather than disciplinarians. They gained compliance by entreaties repeated so often that finally the child would comply voluntarily, albeit wearily, to their requests. The Yiddishe Mameh avoided methods of control that aroused fear of herself in the child, and regarded such methods as morally wrong as well as inexpedient for cultivating inner controls in her children.

Not that Yiddishe Mamehs endured all misbehavior with perfect equanimity. They were volatile, expressive women, who, if other methods of control failed, would flare up, scream at their children, and occasionally slap them, usually taking care to avoid the region of face and head. But they didn't nurse their anger. The outbursts quickly subsided, the child was embraced and comforted, and peace was restored. Such scenes were commonplace in Jewish homes, and added to the liveliness of the atmosphere.

Jewish fathers as a rule were more controlled and reserved in their dealing with their children, but they were usually not any more harsh with them. However, their silence when they became angry with a child created more discomfort and readier compliance than the mother's outburst. But in both cases it was the discomfort—anxiety and guilt—that parental disapproval induced rather than fear of coercion that led Jewish children at a relatively tender age to internalize those norms of behavior which are of paramount importance to Jews.

But if the Yiddishe Mameh was permissive with respect to the acting out of willfulness, anger, tension, fearfulness in children—appreciating, perhaps, the cathartic uses of such behavior—she was not at all permissive on the question of moral training.

Teaching of the basic precepts of Judaism began virtually in infancy for Jewish children whether they were brought up in religious or in secular homes. The kind of appeal that Yiddishe Mamehs employed to motivate their children to eat, for example, was often couched in normative terms. They didn't simply impress on their children that eating was an act of self-interest—that by doing so they would grow up big and strong—but they also invested this mundane activity with moral significance and transformed it into an act of altruism by urging the child to eat *for others*—for mama, for poppa, for other members of the family, and inevitably, the appeal was made to eat for "the poor, starving children in Europe." Similarly, as their children grew older Mameh represented learning as not only being in the child's own self-interest but also as a means to fulfill his obligations to his parents, to his people, and to humanity.

For all their warmth and indulgence Yiddishe Mamehs were demanding, determined women who spared neither themselves nor their husbands and children. Their standards and expectations were extremely high, and they insisted on "the best" whether they were shopping for food or selecting a doctor. If you paid them a compliment on the excellence of their gefilte fish or chopped liver they would protest, for *they* could always find something wrong that a less discerning person would, of course, miss. Their ambition for the future achievements of their children was anything but modest. When her son began to make the first feeble sounds on his violin a Yiddishe Mameh already envisioned another Elman or Heifetz. If he showed scientific proficiency she foresaw another Einstein. At any signs of flagging effort or undue interest in activities that might divert their children from serious pursuits, Jewish mothers would inquire with withering contempt, "So what you want? To be a nothing?" In public, however, Jewish women shamelessly bragged about the achievements of their children, and took enormous pride in them.

The scholastic and occupational achievements of their children were, in fact, a major area of status competition among Jewish immigrant women, and there was no social activity that they carried on with more liveliness and zest than bragging about their children to each other. Even relatively diffident, quiet, modest women felt constrained to engage in this pattern of bragging: *Berimen sich mit die kinder.* To say nothing about the accomplishments of their own children when others did so was tantamount to admitting publicly that there was nothing extraordinary about them, which to a Yiddishe Mameh was unthinkable. This ubiquitous social pattern served two important functions in the Jewish immigrant community. First it was a highly effective mechanism for diffusing information and knowledge about paths of achievement and mobility open to Jewish youth. Immigrants had little knowledge initially about the American occupational structure and even those men who possessed extensive religious learning did not, as a rule, have the secular education necessary to enter professional and managerial positions. Fathers, therefore, could not draw on their own experience to prepare their children for occupational ascent. In this kind of a context the gossip that Jewish mothers exchanged about the educational achievements and career plans of their children became an important informational resource in the Jewish immigrant community. The mothers with older children transmitted information about career lines to the mothers with younger children, who, in turn, relayed it to their husbands and children. Every distinction that a Jewish child earned, every step that he traversed in his educational career, every career decision, and every advancement was duly reported by his mother to her circle of friends and acquaintances, and she, in turn, brought back their reports to her own family.

This vast information exchange, operated primarily by mothers in the Jewish immigrant community, not only bolstered parental ambitions and reinforced the pressure on their children to strive for high educational and occupational goals, but also served to disseminate concrete and realistic knowledge among both generations concerning the barriers, the costs, and the sacrifices involved in the achievement of these lofty goals. The triumphant accounts circulated by proud mothers of the rewards won by their sons through long, arduous educational preparation even in the face of widespread anti-Semitism, encouraged the spread of optimism tempered by realism among the Jewish masses. A Jew, parents would repeatedly remind their children, had to be twice as qualified as a Gentile in order to achieve the same rewards, and it was this kind of hard-headed realism that led them to stress educational attainment and excellence so heavily, and not simply their respect for learning.

Jewish immigrants were no better off economically when they settled in America than other immigrants; they lived in the same squalid neighborhoods; their children attended the same schools and learned from the same teachers but, as a rule, they exhibited a greater aptitude for learning and a greater will to learn than non-Jewish children. Learning, of course, has traditionally commanded respect even among the Jewish masses who, as a rule, had only a meagre amount of secular or religious education. Every indication of intellectual curiosity and verbal precocity in their children was received with pleasure and delight by Jewish parents and long before their formal schooling began Jewish youngsters understood that there was no more effective way to win approval and praise from adults. Even an impudent question or a naughty remark, if clever, was received with amused tolerance by parents and proudly relayed to friends and relatives as evidence of *chochma*, which is the Hebrew word for wisdom, but also is used colloquially to denote brightness, cleverness or wit.

Another stimulus to intellectual aptitude was the talkativeness of the Jewish home. It is now recognized that exposure to this factor in their early formative years increases the learning readiness of children, and it has long been known that verbal skill is an important component of I.Q. and achievement test performance. That Yiddishe Mamehs, in particular, were talkative, any Jewish male will ruefully confirm, but it is not generally recognized that this notorious attribute of theirs gave their children a head start in learning. Whatever Yiddishe Mamehs did for their children—and they did a great deal—was accompanied by a flow of language, consisting of rich, colorful, expressive words and phrases.

Their vocabulary of endearments alone could fill a modest sized paperback, but they also had a superb store of admonishments, curses, imprecations, explanations, songs and folksayings that they effortlessly invoked as they went about ministering to the needs of their children and their husbands. The freedom that they exhibited with the spoken word invited a similar response from their children and it carried over into school despite the fact that Yiddish, and not English, was their mother tongue. This helps account for the fact that learning aptitude was demonstrated not only by Jewish children whose fathers had extensive religious learning but also by those from homes where learning and cultivation were largely absent.

The determined struggle of Jewish mothers to delay the emotional emancipation of their children is well-known and often criticized but it was nevertheless a significant factor in the high educational attainment of second generation Jews in America. It is to their credit, I think, that they recognized that the basic conditions required to fashion a talmudic scholar are very much the same as those needed to achieve any other career requiring a high order of intellectual skill. In both cases, a prolonged period of time and arduous work must be spent in acquiring a complex body of knowledge, during which time the child must be provided encouragement and emotional support as well as protection from outside influence which might lure him into abandoning long-run plans for more immediate pleasures and rewards. Yiddishe Mamehs achieved this by denying the legitimacy of their children's declarations of independence. *Mainst as du bist shoin a ganzer mensch* (You only think you are a responsible human being), was their stock retort to youthful emancipation proclamations. They employed every stratagem to remain as indispensable to their children in later childhood and adolescence as they had been earlier in life. The concept of early independence training was foreign to their thinking. According to their view a child was a child whether he was five or fifteen and required much the same order of care, devotion and protection in adolescence as in childhood. With respect to learning and intellectual matters generally they encouraged the development of self-reliance and autonomy, but they were reluctant to grant their children other forms of independence or to impose any serious responsibility on them until they had completed their education and were ready to assume the obligations of marriage and a career.

A signal of their readiness to relinquish control was the application of pressure on their sons to find "a nice Jewish girl" and marry her. But until they saw their mission safely accomplished they doggedly resisted their children's perennial attempts to assert their independence. My generation learned to value independence not by being pressured to become self-reliant but by struggling against these formidable adversaries to loosen the bonds that tied us to them. We lost a good many skirmishes with our mothers, but we ultimately won the war, just as they intended.[4]

Perhaps further motivating the sustained protectiveness of Yiddishe Mamehs and their determination to delay the emotional emancipation of their children was their fear that the children would fall prey to the social influence of Gentile friends, particularly those from poor, immigrant families with rural origins in which parents did not value education. Non-Jewish immigrants generally wanted their children to grow up quickly, to get out and earn a living so that they might help relieve the family burden of poverty. In this setting, Jewish parents did not encourage their children to seek the companionship of these other children, preferring that their children pursue solitary pastimes at home rather than have the freedom of the streets.

There is some grim humor in the fact that these efforts by Jewish mothers to insulate their children from bad influences were aided and reinforced by the anti-Semitism that was so widespread in those days in Gentile society. The hostility of Gentiles and exclusion from their fun and games led Jewish youth, either as a matter of preference or because they had no other option, to seek the fellowship of other Jews, with whom they could feel at ease not only because they were Jews but because they shared the same aspirations, the same values and interests, and the same need to submerge the consciousness of the social rejection that each individually had experienced at the hands of the Gentiles. If their "clannishness" violated the democratic ideal it also operated to sustain and reinforce their mother's influence, which is to say their Jewish identification and commitment to learning. In alliance with the right friends, the Jewish mother could make successes, and Jews, of her children.

The unquestionable success of the Jewish mother in educating her children and immunizing them from severe emotional disorders warrants serious study by those interested in the way maternal strategies affect intellectual achievement. It is one thing for a parent to stress the importance of education as the means of escaping poverty; it is quite another, as the Jewish mother knew, to implement these objectives. Most lower class parents who stress the value of education (one thinks of many Negro parents today) must contend with the fact that their children's friends and associates undervalue education, so that a parent who a) values education and b) encourages early independence (as most lower class families do) is caught up in contradictory strategies. Children trained to be independent at an early age only become independent of parental influence and more dependent upon their peers.

Middle class families too could learn from the Jewish example. The trend here is toward more permissive, more love-oriented strategies of socialization, especially in the areas of weaning, toilet training, and sex behavior, but at the same time many parents fear that permissiveness will breed dependency and that dependency will hinder successful "adjustment." The child is pressured into doing things for himself and *also* "getting along" with other children. Thus a policy of encouraged early independence results in excessive dependence upon the peer group. This is one of the roots of conformism, the "other-directedness" so often observed in American character.

In the lower classes the tendency to encourage independence almost from birth is often a matter of economic necessity; in the middle-class it is more a matter of ideology. According to this view the prototype of the healthy, wholesome, normal child is one who is happy, extroverted, free of tension, sociable, athletic, and popular. Parents view with amused tolerance their children's preoccupation with keeping abreast of "the other kids" and their conformity to every fatuous fad of teenage culture. They are reluctant to impose limitations on their children's participation in these social rituals for fear that doing so might interfere with their social adjustment and their happiness. By the time their children reach adolescence and are confronted with decisions concerning school, career and marriage, many middle class parents discover that in their haste to establish early independence and good social adjustment they have abdicated to the culture of the young the power that was rightfully theirs. Mediocrity and conformism often ensue.[5]

There are no independent children—except autistic ones, perhaps—but the child whose dependency needs are met in the *home* has less need to turn to his *peers* for protection and emotional support. And, just because he needs his mother's approval, the young child will work harder to develop the skills *she* values and be more resistant to the influence of "the other kids." By the time he matures he will have internalized the motivation and goals that make autonomy and excellence possible. The cultivation of this kind of autonomy calls for a strategy of socialization not greatly different, I suspect, from that of the Jewish Mother.[6]

NOTES

1. See, for example, Gerald S. Lesser, Gordon Fifer and Donald Clark, "Mental Abilities of Children from Different Social-class and Cultural Groups," *Monographs of the Society For Research in Child Development*, Vol. 30, No. 4, 1965, pp. 82–3; also, Fred L. Strodtbeck, "Family Interaction, Values and Achievement," in David McClelland and Associates, *Talent and Society*, D. Van Nostrand Co. Inc., Princeton, 1958, pp. 135–94; and, Ben B. Seligman and Aaron Antonovsky, "Some Aspects of Jewish Demography," and S. Joseph Fauman, "Occupational Selection among Detroit Jews," in Marshall Sklare (editor), *The Jews: Social Patterns of an American Group*, Glencoe: Free Press, 1958, pp. 83–6 and pp. 119–137.

2. Leo Srole, Thomas Langner, et al., *Mental Health in the Metropolis*. New York: McGraw-Hill, 1962, Vol. 1, pp. 305–6. This study is of special interest because it sampled a *general* population, instead of only psychiatric patients as previous studies had done, and its findings are therefore unaffected by the fact that some groups, like the Jews, are more favorably disposed to psychiatry than others and more readily seek treatment even for problems of a relatively mild sort.

3. A striking similarity exists between the mode of maternal behavior of the Yiddishe Mameh and that found among women in the new middle class in contemporary Japan, who, like the Jews, are strongly committed to high educational attainment for their children. (Ezra Vogel, *Japan's New Middle Class*, Berkeley: University of California Press, 1963.)

4. A commonplace criticism of Jewish mothers is that they were over-protective, and overprotection, many people believe, has adverse effects on children, but the little empirical research that exists suggests that just the opposite may be the case. David Levy's well-known study, for example, of twenty "over-protected" children first seen at about the age of ten and followed up in late adolescence (*Maternal Overprotection*, New York: Columbia University Press, 1943) reports that they were better than average in their pattern of physical growth, their freedom from accidents, serious illness, eneuresis, and in their heterosexual development, classroom adjustment and scholastic ability, and that, almost without exception, they outgrew the behavior problems—acting out at home, eating problems, and difficulties in forming friendships—they had exhibited in childhood.

5. A number of studies indicate that high scholastic achievers exhibit less need for social affiliation and lower conformity to peer group standards than less successful students. (David E. Lavin, *The Prediction of Academic Performance*. New York: Russell Sage Foundation, 1965, pp. 64–121.)

6. Skepticism about the efficacy of independence training seems to be growing among behavioral scientists as the result of recent research. For example, Sears, Maccoby and Levin (*Patterns of Child Rearing*. Evanston: Row, Peterson, 1957) report that the more negatively mothers responded to dependency behavior in their five and six year old children, the more dependent they were likely to be; on the other hand, when mothers exhibited a sympathetic attitude or responded positively to dependency demands, dependency did *not* increase. Rosen and D'Andrade ("The Psychosocial Origins of Achievement Motivation," *Sociometry*, Vol. 22, 1959, pp. 185–218) report experimental evidence that high achievement motivation in boys is positively related to maternal warmth and pressure for high achievement but *negatively* related to independence training.

THE CULT OF GRATITUDE

MELVIN M. TUMIN

. . . As I WAS DRAFTING this paper I became quite convinced of one thing that seemed to me crucial here, namely, that leading Jewish thinkers or thinkers who are Jewish, and leading writers who are Jewish, and leading intellectuals, don't lead; that the main drift of the American Jewish community seems to be going much its own way with little or no regard to the urgings, the railings or the exhortations either of the Jewish religious leaders, or so-called intellectuals in the academies, or Jews in important political posts. I think that while this phenomenon may have been characteristic of earlier times it is distinctly characteristic of Jewish life in America today. What has happened to American Jewry seems not to have taken its direction from so-called Jewish leaders. Indeed, an assimilating Jewish leadership seems gradually to be co-opted into the drift of the community. If this is true, then while it might make an interesting exercise to examine the writings and thoughts of particular writers and intellectuals who are Jewish, either nominally or functionally or both, I would prefer to devote at least a substantial part of the paper to the brief analysis of the conservative *trends* in Jewish life *per se*, with little or no reference to particular Jewish "leaders."

Much of what I might here seem to be declaiming, by tone, as fact is not more than speculation and hypothesis. Especially when I infer and intuit the motivations behind the actions taken by Jews is this so, since there I am doubly speculative, both with regard to the motivations and to their hidden sources, on the one hand, and to whether in fact these are the majority actions, on the other. What is offered here then is offered as a set of observations which must be taken in this tentative spirit, though I stand responsibly behind them and willing to argue about their limita-

From Melvin M. Tumin, "Conservative Trends in American Jewish Life," *Judaism*, 13 (Spring 1964), pp. 131–142. Copyright 1964 by the American Jewish Congress. Reprinted by permission of the author and the publisher.

tions, and with the spirit that if they are true then what is concluded from them is also probably true. Even if they are not true to the extent implied here, the question at least ought to be raised whether it is likely that these are the dominantly *emerging* trends in Jewish life. If so, then again the conclusions I will draw seem to follow.

The need to be speculative about dominant trends in American Jewish life is due to the fact that we don't have any good surveys of that life, because, while we want very much to know what is going on in Jewish affairs, we are insistent that no one shall take a census of Jewish affairs, except privately. We don't have any good depth interviews by trained persons with selected samples of American Jewry to probe the hidden motivations of Jews. I don't *really* know what my fellow-Jews think about their participation in the community center, in the synagogue. I can only say what the matter *seems* like to me. And if I'm wrong, as I'm sure to be on at least some counts, then what I worry about is either not so worrisome as I claim, or it may be more worrisome.

Moreover, since I focus on only some trends in American Jewish life, I surely ignore others, that are perhaps just as important in shaping the course of American Jewish life, such as, for instance, the role of devoutly religious Jews. This is something I have not concerned myself with. . . .

The central fact about Jewish life in America today is that it has no definable center. There is no core of agreed upon meanings; no consensus on intentions; no community of connotations; no shared specifications of identity of what it means to be a Jew, or what it *should* mean. Every phase of ordinary life in which Jews are involved thus becomes a legitimate and natural focus for multiple and diverse kinds of affiliation, for differing interpretations of the relevance of that aspect of life for the Jews involved in it, and for dissent on the relevance of Jewishness for *it*.

It is also essentially characteristic of the Jews of the United States today that never before has any group of Jews had such an indeterminate identity, such amorphous boundaries, at the same time that there exists such an extraordinary opportunity to create for themselves virtually any identity they desire. Some historian of Jewish affairs will undoubtedly be able to cite some time and place when the Jewish situation resembled today's situation to some extent. But, necessarily, that other time and place will not be able to include, as central facts, the existence of a non-Jewish Jewish homeland; nor the great secular material success and advantaged social position of the Jew; nor the nominal widespread acceptance of the idea that Jews are admissible directly into the community as first-class citizens and not as representatives or non-representative exceptions to the majority of Jews. Nor could that other time and place include the astounding but evident militant assertion by Jews of their right to continued suspicion of non-Jews, based upon a prolongation of righteous indignation at the latest pogrom.

In sum, endowed with an extremely favorable material situation, capable of demanding and securing the highest level positions in the society; armed with a sense of their ordinary rights of citizenship and their extraordinary rights as compensation for the horrors of Nazism; emboldened in their self-images by the superlative achievements of Israel; facilitated, even if only for the moment, by the negative cultural norm on anti-Semitism; and by an extreme self-consciousness and caution by non-Jews about being offensive—Jewish people in the United States stumble and grope for a sense of being, for a possible set of common purposes, perhaps even for a way to pursue a mode of life without making common cause with other Jews.

In considering the Jewish situation one must also acknowledge the extent to which assimilation is a two-way street. For, just as surely as Jews have become American, often to the point of being virtually indistinguishable from non-Jews, so too, to some significant degree, American culture has become Jewish—at least wherever concentrations of Jews have dwelled in a community for any period of time.

Though numerically a tiny minority, the Jews in America have, nevertheless, managed to get themselves defined as one of the three major religions that are to be represented, wherever religious representation is relevant; they have infiltrated quasi-, pseudo- and contrived Jewish elements into numerous aspects of American culture: in food patterns, peculiarities of humor, metaphors and aphorisms, even something approaching a true irony in American thought and writing. It is no accident, therefore, that at the recent American Jewish Congress-sponsored "dialogue" in Israel between American Jewish and Israeli Jewish writers, various members of the American delegation should have found it necessary and apropos to speak of the new problems created by an emergent philo-Semitism which, of course, they do not trust.

Nor may we ignore the impressive fact that attached to the office of the President of the United States are various Jews who are there, one must suppose, both to counsel with the President on opinion among Jews and to serve as a liaison from the Jewish community to the President. Vague and nebulous and uncertain as it may be, a certain so-called Jewish point of view has become something to be reckoned with at the highest levels of political influence.

Leslie Fielder has suggested, partly, but only partly, with tongue in cheek, that as children Americans try to imitate and become like the American Indian, or the cowboy anti-Indian, and later, as adolescents, the Negro, with his coolness, his beatniktude, his detachment and alienation, becomes the model. With equal justification, one may say that one of the ideal models for adult deportment and conduct in America is the stern, self-consciously righteous, moral mentoring Jew. Suspicious of fun and flesh, relying desperately on the hope that rationality and democracy will commend themselves, at the same time recognizing the much greater natural force of anti-rationality and anti-democracy; self sacrificing on behalf of others (*vide:* our attitude toward underdeveloped countries), with a desperate hope that there may be gratitude, but ever expecting the laws of inverse reciprocity to prevail; quite privately certain of their own superiority to others, yet aware that it is very bad taste to claim the superiority, however unavoidable it is that one reveal his convictions about it—these are some characteristic elements of certain phases of Jewish life with which we are all familiar, and these too are some of the main dimensions of American domestic and international political and social life.

The openness of American society to which both the direct and inverse assimilation testify make it quite natural that there should emerge among Jews two quite contrasting demands on America. Put succinctly, these demands are that, on the one hand, Jews shall be allowed to behave as Jews—whoever that is—wherever and whenever they think it relevant; and, on the other hand, that their Jewishness shall not be given the slightest relevance in other contexts. In short, Jews are now asking the American community to respect their right to establish as full-bodied an identity as they care to contrive, and, at the same time, to act as though such an identified group did not exist.

For example, many Jews are obviously participating in the nominal reinvigoration of the rolls of Jewish community organizations and their affiliated bodies; day schools and synagogue lists have swollen; Jewish suburban neighborhoods have been established; Jewish country and city clubs have appeared; even Jewish universities have been brought into being, however much they are nominally non-denominational. These are examples of the first tendency toward increased Jewish identification.

By contrast, Jews have been vocal and effective in their insistence on the removal of discriminatory quotas at universities and in neighborhoods. They have insisted that their voting patterns not be identified as Jewish, but rather as independent judgments by Republicans, Democrats and others who just happen to be Jewish. If they give heavily to Jewish charities, they are always careful to give heavily to non-denominational charities. If, too, they have insisted on their right to be outward, voluble and generous in their support of and affection for Israel, they have been careful to insist in their words and deeds on their unstinted loyalty to the United States.

These two opposing moves in Jewish life—*toward* a Jewish center and *away* from it, simultaneously—might be interpreted, in the most favorable terms, as an attempt on the part of the Jewish community to institutionalize a genuine cultural pluralism. That is, the following challenge is laid down to the American non-Jewish community: Permit us to define ourselves as distinctly as we care to, and where we think it is relevant, but do not use our separateness, however self-contrived, as a basis of discrimination in terms of rights and citizenship. Viewed that way, it is simultaneously both sociologically extremely unrealistic and morally exemplar beyond cavil. After all, the test of genuine democratic living is whether we can sustain a fundamental unity and equality of all citizens at the same time that we maximize individuality.

Viewed this way, these opposing tendencies in modern Jewish life must be seen as together constituting a form of cultural radicalism, however much they may not be intended that way. Nor does it matter very much, in general, on this point that the Jewish community does not have very clear specifications at all, or at best has many differing specifications, of what it means to be Jewish. This may be a crucial matter for Jews, but it is not crucial for the non-Jewish community so long as the boundary lines of where Jewishness is and is not supposed to be relevant are kept fairly distinct. If they are fuzzed over, such as in the Catholic doctrine of obligations to Caesar and God, or infallibility in morals and dogma, without any clear definition of what is *not* morals or dogma, then there is bound to be both ideological and moral ambiguity in the position. Otherwise, one cannot fault a group in the process of creating an identity for not having clear lines of identity as yet.

I suppose it may be a Jewish peculiarity of my own—one, I am sure, that is shared by many of my non-Jewish colleagues—that makes me see this challenge to America's capacity for cultural pluralism as something morally noteworthy and politically salutary for our society. Yet I have deep doubts and regrets about it, based principally upon the realization that the sum total of this sociologically unrealistic set of demands is not intended by Jews as a radical cultural challenge. One is, therefore, placed in the peculiar position of having to applaud the net consequences of a set of actions, without at all being able to applaud the intentions of the actors themselves, indeed, often feeling the need to deplore those intentions. For, as I see both demands—that for the widest possible latitude in areas of open identification, and that for treating Jewish identity as otherwise irrelevant—they are both products of a conservative, security-seeking, status-minded, and apolitical set of intentions on the part of Jews.

I hasten to add that in this regard the Jewish situation is structurally identical with the new Negro demands on America. Claims for compensatory rights, to correct historical injustice, open propagation of a high degree of reactionary race consciousness and race antagonism, resulting in the formation of a solid bloc of Negro protest and voting power—all these radically shake up the American status quo, and represent a real challenge to anti-democratic tendencies in America. At the same time, from the point of view of the intentions of the actors, they are not premised on commitment to democracy and freedom in general, but on a conservative, security-seeking, protection-minded, status-anxious and apolitical orientation, and indeed, often indiscriminately include obviously reactionary forces and ideologies such as those of the Black Muslims.

Even the demands of the Black Bourgeoisie—to be allowed to become as middle-class, Babbitt-like, consumption-dominated and status-anxious as his white bourgeois neighbor—represents in its net *consequence* a kind of radical demand that if met will shake American social organization most effectively. At the same time, one can only deplore the kind of orientation to life which asks that one be allowed to be as silly and wasteful of life as one's foolish neighbors. But one returns to the realization that what America would have to do to arrive at the point where the Black Bourgeoisie would be allowed to be just like his white neighbor would be truly radical.

Returning to the Jewish scene, one is struck forcibly by the dominantly conservative character of the main dimensions of Jewish intentions in America. The return to the Jewish community and its center and its synagogue represents, as yet, nothing more—from the point of view of political structure and change—than a smooth fitting in of Jews into American life at its middle-class worst—and on precisely the same terms as the Presbyterians, Baptists, and all others. The Jewish support of Israel—again recognizing all its other intentions and consequences—must also be seen as, in certain ways, a kin and parallel form of assertion of naive vicarious nationalism of the kind earlier and today manifested by the Irish and Italians. Jewish representation at affairs of state and on public ritual occasions, along with Protestants and Catholics, is as politically worthy as the similar insistence by the latter two groups, and no more.

The demands that Jews make on each other to "return to the fold" and bear witness by joining in Jewish communal activities, most particularly the center and the synagogue, bear consequences of an unmistakably conservative nature. In effect, they tend to result in an increased ghettoization of Jews, self-induced for the most part, and invested with an undefined kind of pride that reinforces the original vague intentions by giving them an apparent positive emotional toning. This self-ghettoization is not simply in the religious sphere—but in the social and psychological spheres as well. From the simple aspect of increasing Jewish acquaintances and thereby decreasing non-Jewish acquaintances, to the terminal act of insuring a more steady flow of Jewish marriages, and thereby decreasing intermarriages, the center and the synagogue serve these ghettoizing functions—whatever else they provide by way of understandable comfort, cultural preservation and religious integration for the Jews involved.

In duplicating this 100-percent community-cum-church posture of the non-Jewish American, the Jew vouchsafes himself as an all-rightnik in the American host community. Operating with the morally dubious notion that one's neighbors will respect one more if one is religious, the Jew seeks to insure that acceptance—often without questioning whether acceptance at that price is worth it. Perhaps he does not question the moral premise and coloration because he fully believes in all its implications, and is involved consummately and not simply instrumentally. Whatever the intention or intentions, the consequences are the creation of a dual community, that is both inherently divisive at the outset and cumulatively divisive over time.

That is but one side of the Jewish ambivalent posture in America today. The other side—that of demanding the treatment of Jewish identity as irrelevant—is curiously just as conservative, however much at first blush it may seem to be quite the opposite.

For if we ask what the Jew is really asking in making this kind of demand, we are led to the supposition that, instead of asking that America accept him as he is and treat him as an equal in his full self-proclaimed identity, he is, in effect, asking that his separateness shall be forgotten and ignored. In short, the potentially culturally-pluralist and radical demand that insistence on full acceptance as we are might constitute, is converted, by Jewish fear of discrimination and oppression, into a form of ostrich-like make-believe "I don't exist." Instead of saying, "I am a Jew, of course; I have Jewish characteristics; I am a self-conscious and openly participating member in a Jewish community; I believe in cultural pluralities; know this of me and do not dare to forget it, but do not dare under any circumstances to fail to accord me the fullest of equality with all other people"—the Jews seem in effect to be saying, "However much I may be known elsewhere and otherwise as a Jew, however much I may insist on my right to some degree of cultural separation, in other contexts, in this one you are to forget I am Jewish, please, and make believe I am nothing."

Let me develop this just one more moment. What I am trying

to suggest here is that it would indeed be radical in American politics if there were an identifiable Jewish vote and if that Jewish vote stood for a morally radical position on the political spectrum. And it would be a beautiful challenge to America if the Jewish vote were known as such and worried about as such by all politicians, and known and responded to as such by all non-Jews. Then, you see, the Jews would stand for something, and something vital and alive on the American scene. Then Jewishness would constitute determinate identity. Then to be a Jew would be to be something definite and impressive, however much Jews might be joined in their political position by non-Jews. Short of that, what do Jews stand for in America? For a normal distribution of political opinions along the same spectrum and in the same proportions as non-Jews. However normal, self-protecting and expectable this may be, in effect, it is a phenomenon essentially preservative of the status quo. However much this may, in the long run, be the best strategy for self-preservation, it ducks—as it must—the essential question of what is the self that is being preserved. And however much finally—in view of their history—Jews have a right to find their way to life and safety by whatever means they discover or contrive—they ought not to confuse this right and this technique for self-preservation with either a determinate identity or with anything culturally valuable today.

In both areas then—where Jewish identity is insisted upon, and where Jewish non-identity is insisted upon—the net impact so far has been to end up exactly as much all right as other status-quo-minded, status-anxious, politically conservative, eye-on-the-main-chance, non-Jewish Americans.

The most distressing aspect of this move into the sphere of all-rightness is the ways in which it is manifested among Jewish intellectuals. In apparent total forgetfulness of the role which radical criticism of American society played in the first half of this century in helping make America less execrable than it might otherwise have been, Jewish intellectuals have increasingly come to play the role of gentlemen of the Establishment.

Beguiled by the chance to become influential—in government, education, industry, the mass media—many Jews have rushed in to take advantage of this opportunity to become insiders. Having established themselves within the mansions of the mighty, having achieved enviable positions at the best schools, magazines, publishing houses, government bureaus, and the like, many have become full-fledged members of the cult of gratitude, accepting fully the essentially conservative character of their enterprises, becoming ardent partisans of the "normal" way of life, and treating as enemies all those who stand outside and criticize, or who, worst of all, criticize from the inside out, and loudly.

If it has almost always been the fate of Jews—and a source of their distinctiveness—to be outsiders, no matter what the Establishment, then one can say that in America in the last three decades Jews have moved from that position of outside outsiders, to inside outsiders, where they served as counsellors to the king, but still as outsiders; and have today finally become inside insiders: not simply counsellors with a foot in the outside camp and an ear to outside councils, but full-fledged—so they think—institutionalized and bureaucratized defenders of the official faith, whatever it happens to be: the Republican or Democratic Party, the University, the Firm, or whatever. Their deepest anxieties and most vitriolic scorn are reserved for those other Jews, relatively small in number by comparison, who either remain totally outside or have come in only half way. They see them as capable of rocking this most luxurious boat enough to make terribly big waves. They are today's version of many Jews who just as wrongheadedly many years ago said that anti-Semitism could only be said to be the fault of Jews; that just as soon as Jews learned to dress and behave and talk and eat like non-Jews, then they would stop being discriminated against. Of course, they really meant they would therefore stop being identifiable as Jews and thereby eliminate anti-Semitism. But they were wrong then and their today's counterparts are wrong today. No one owes any gratitude to any institution for permitting him to live and to function decently. No one owes praise to a nation for conducting itself in minimally decent terms. No one should feel the need to be thankful for having available to him whatever one may reasonably expect as a normal right in a decent society. To be glad to be in such a society rather than another, less decent place is one thing. To wallow in gratitude to that society; to refrain from criticizing that society and its institutions; to consider critics as social enemies—these are quite other things, quite silly and self-defeating, quite conservatizing, quite destructful of the very conditions which made it possible for the society to be decent in the first place.

What is not well understood—neither by Jews nor non-Jews—is that any form of institutional loyalty must be suspected, since such loyalty can only be premised on some parochial conception of social life, one which tends to be structurally identical with Charles Wilson's famous claim that what is good for General Motors is good for the country. Such institutional loyalties are the obvious antipathies and antinomies of the forces which make social and cultural change possible. They narrow one's horizons of possibilities; they blind one to alternatives; they make one defensive against criticism; they naturally and inevitably tend toward self-encrustation.

To be institutionally loyal is to be an insider. To be an insider, therefore, is to be parochial, narrow-visioned, defensive, valuing expediency over principle, and the impersonal and overall view that destroys individuals over the personal and immediate view that is the life blood of a decent society. To be institutionally loyal is to be somebody else's man—no matter who—but somebody else's. And if you are somebody else's man, you are not your own. To the extent that Jews in America may be seen as striving to become allrightniks, to become insiders, it is their predictable fate that they too will end up becoming somebody else's man, but in no way their own.

These strictures apply not only to functioning bureaucrats in the major institutions of government, education, and the world of publications but to writers and painters and other artists who opt either for the happy solution, or the thin slice-of-life approach to their work, or who create fake non-tragedies for us to weep over with bathetic tears. Forcibly declaring themselves as against the tragic view of life—"life is so unhappy as it is, why must one write about it?"—or at best peering like voyeurs behind the first thin veil, and, at that, only through the eyes of adolescents, or insane captains of ships, such writers do not do the one thing which all writers must do, whatever their nominal background or religion, and that is to tell the truth. They fail to tell the truth from one or both of two possible grounds. Either they do not know what is the truth, or they know it, but out of expediency, whether of career or social group concern, or whatever, they refrain from saying what they know to be so.

The first failure, that of ignorance, is understandable and easily managed, since such books can be assigned to the limbo of non-books. The second failure, that of deliberate expedient refraining, is understandable but not so easily managed. For such writings are full of guile and pretended sophistication and cautious nudges at part-truths, that end up at being more damaging than full-bodied lies. The Jew who writes and who does not tell the truth as best he sees it again plays an essentially conservative role in that he simply makes it possible for all the lies about human existence to be perpetuated. So few people are charged by the very nature of their positions with telling the truth, one must take the artist who fails to do so especially to account, since he is among those very few.

Finally, one new trend toward a basically conservative line of thought in so-called intellectual circles must be mentioned. It is the reversion to a Germanic type of metaphysics of absolute essences and categories, with the real world seen only as ephemeral manifestations of these eternal essences. The German modality of capitalizing nouns lends itself admirably to this tendency. Thus, we get such terms as Work, Revolution, Labor, Morality, Humanity—all written in capital letters. And if the empirical facts of the real world do not correspond with what the metaphysical essences are intuited as demanding, so much the worse for the real world.

Starting with such assumptions, it becomes possible to call both the American and the French Revolutions failures, even though both succeeded extraordinarily by any reasonable criteria. With such premises, too, it becomes possible to blame Jews for Hitler's destruction of them; to make organization equal non-organization; to make culture into non-culture, and education into non-education. In view of the fact that the last fifty years in American social philosophizing had appeared finally to rid us of the intolerable burden of mystifying German metaphysics that we inherited from the nineteenth century, one can only deplore this return to essences, not only because it results in silly and evil books, but because it lends itself so admirably to an essentially conservative turn of mind and of politics, one that is the true ally of authoritarianism in social relations. Such an approach makes genuine intellectual exploration impossible. It leads to an anti-experimental attitude in human political affairs, precisely because it denies the validity of every single gain and move toward the left, such as when it leads to scoffing at voting rights, rights to jobs and to schooling, and the like, on the ground that, after all, these are not true equality, since they do not lead to intermarriage, and intermarriage is, after all, the only true test of equality. One may hope that because nothing follows from such thinking, it may find itself consigned to the rubble pile of meaninglessness in social thought, along with the equally pointless shaggy dog jokes.

Have we shown some of the major ways in which certain dimensions of Jewish life today are essentially conservative, perhaps more so than at any other time in the history of the American Jewish community? One may hope that at least some suggestions along this line have been made with sufficient clarity to bear argument. Now and only now it is possible to state the stand from which all this is written. What I shall say may seem incredible to many who have heard the foregoing remarks. And others may see this as an attempt to take the edge off these remarks. But these are not my problems.

I make these remarks primarily because I care and care deeply that Jews shall stand for something, something important, vital, progressive, democratic, truthful, and just in human affairs. I obviously care that all groups should stand for this. When that Messianic day arrives, distinctions among Jews and non-Jews will no longer be relevant. But we are, I am afraid, rapidly approaching the point where such a distinction is already irrelevant, but for the wrong reasons. It is no longer relevant, or is moving that way, because Jews don't stand for anything more valuable than anyone else stands for. The American Jewish community seems to be living on the rapidly shrinking psychic income from the capital investment of Jews of the last two thousand years—or the last thirty years. What can it mean, in all honesty, for the average Jew in America to claim he comes from a heritage and tradition of social justice, of respect for knowledge and learning, of concern for culture? He appears today to care for these things no more than anyone else around him. If one is not a religious Jew, there is not much point in calling himself a Jew, unless, in the non-religious conception and realization of the Jew's life, there is a dominant central focus upon that heritage and that tradition. If, as we know, that heritage and tradition are not distinctively and uniquely Jewish, as indeed they are not, this does not prevent the self-identifying and self-presenting Jew from participating in this fundamental human heritage, both as a general human and as a special Jewish human being. One's heritage need not be exclusive to be one's heritage. It is toward the achievement of this goal of investing Jewish identity with full meanings, with the meaning implicit in such a heritage and tradition, in which Jews can join hands with non-Jews in the celebration and full-bodied living-out of this tradition—it is toward that goal that these remarks are directed.

AMERICA IS DIFFERENT

STUART E. ROSENBERG

For Jews, America is different. . . . And yet, despite the obvious and often less than obvious patterns of their accommodation to the revolutionary environment of the New World, certain fundamental vestiges remain embedded in the depths of the Jewish psyche. In America, as elsewhere in the long history of their Diaspora, psychologically, Jews are still in exile. And as one wit has said, it is often more difficult to get the Exile out of the Jews than to get the Jews out of Exile.

A popular folktale told of Old-World Jews is no less incisive and relevant a description of their continuing marginality as men in America. A young Polish Jew, it is said, surfeited with his disabilities as a persecuted son of persecuted fathers, fled westward, determined to shed the last traces of his Jewish ties. He arrived in Berlin, changed his name and religion, worked hard, entered the university, and graduated as a physician. The years were as good to him as he had hoped: his fame spread wide about, and his worldly accumulations increased apace. Servants, coachmen, secretaries were his, in goodly number. His home was a palace, his friends regal and lordly. He indeed had arrived.

One day, after many years of longing for his "lost" son, the aged, pious, Jewish father came from Poland to search him out, to catch even one fleeting glimpse of his child, before he died. The son was pleasant enough, indeed proud to justify his achievements to his aged father. After listening to his son's glowing recitation of prowess and power, the old man ventured a single question. "But, son," he asked softly, "for all these wonderful things you have achieved, for all your present happiness, is there nothing at all that you have kept in sacred remembrance of your

...ul days at home? Has nothing remained to remind you
at you are a Jew?"

"No, nothing," the son began to reply, but quickly, bethinking
himself, added: "Well, perhaps there is one thing that I do still
remember, father."

"What is that, my son?" the aged one asked expectantly.

"Remember, father," he replied, "how, night after night, I
would trudge home in the dark from the Jewish school, in our
tiny village? On the way home, I had to pass by the houses of the
Christian farmers, and every night, as I passed, their dogs would
bark. Remember, father, how afraid I was of those barking dogs of
those Christian farmers? Well, father, even now, whenever dogs
bark, I am afraid."

Dogs still bark for the American Jew. And his fears are no
different from those of his ancestors in Poland, Russia, and other
parts of the Old World. They are often shielded from easy view,
covered over by the sophistications of a contrived modernism, and
the conceits of a nonpartisan universalism. But they are there.
And being there, they account for the undiminished sense of
estrangement, the unabated feelings of otherness that still pervade
the life and thought of the American Jew. Yet this American Jew
is different: different not only from the non-Jew in America, but
also from his own ancestors. At least his ancestors knew very well
that they were living as aliens on the margins of cultures other
than their own. "You know the heart of the stranger, for you
were strangers in the land of Egypt"; they read these Scriptural
words as a reminder of their own perennial condition. But much
of the ambivalence of the American Jew toward himself stems
from his pathetic confusion: he knows that in many non-Jewish
hearts he is regarded as a stranger, while in his own heart he
stubbornly refuses to be one. But a stranger who would not be a
stranger cannot easily "know the heart of the stranger."

When he has tried to forget that he is a Jew, the others have
remembered. But when he tries to remember that he is a Jew, he
often forgets how to be one. Middle-class Jews, in search of
adaptation and acceptance, often appropriate middle-class vices,
mistaking them for the virtues of America. On the other hand,
Jewish intellectuals who, like other intellectuals, glory in their
otherness, turn their backs on their middle-class Jewishness,
mistaking its aberrations for Judaism. Both remain alienated,
nevertheless: the middle-class Jew from his Anglo-Saxon neigh-

bors whom he is seeking to emulate; the intellectual Jew from his own fellow Jews, whom he is anxious to reject. The former compensates by returning to Jewishness, albeit often in strange ways. But the latter is the more pitiable. His "very awareness of an inheritance makes for him inexpressibly poignant the double sense of being tied to, and having broken from, the past. *He has inherited the agony of his people; its joy he knows only second hand.*"[1]

In 1944, two well-known American literary figures of Jewish descent were asked to express their personal views of "their" community, Jews in America. Said Clement Greenberg: "Jewish life in America has become for *reasons of security*, so solidly, so rigidly, restrictedly, and suffocatingly middle-class. . . . No people on earth are more correct, more staid, more provincial, more commonplace, more inexperienced; none observe more strictly the letter of every code that is respectable; none do so completely and habitually what is expected of them." And Alfred Kazin, with mock compassion, added the crushing coup: "What a stupendous moral pity, historically, that the Fascist cutthroats should have their eyes on him [the Jew] when he asks for so little—only to be safe, in all the Babbitt warrens."[2] Seventeen years later, *Commentary*, consistently brilliant, but consistently, too, a refuge for Jewish *literati* who enjoy bleeding in public, in dramatic and ostentatious display of the wounds joyfully sustained in their well-advertised flight from Jews and Judaism, sought out the new crop. What were the younger intellectuals, "these children of a neo-conservative age, the age of religious revival and the rediscovery of America," now thinking about their people and its heritage? Hardly anything pleasant at all, *Commentary* discovered. Notwithstanding all that had happened to both Jews and Judaism in the intervening years, nothing seems to have changed. Like those who preceded them, these angry young men were still angry, and still wilfully out of touch with the vital sources of Jewish life in America. They still disliked the middle class in general and the Jewish middle class in particular. These were, as ever before, hostile to religion, against "Jewish parochialism," but equally opposed to even the normal commitments normal people have, lest they be accused of "chauvinism."[3] *Plus ça change plus c'est la même chose.*

The exaggerated criticisms of such intellectuals, exaggerated by the self-hate of their alienation, cannot serve as an adequate guide to the true condition of the American Jewish community of today. Indeed, their views are published in a *Jewish* magazine, and, ironically, this very fact refutes their fundamental charge of "Jewish conformity." Thus, in a larger sense, even their rebellions and vituperations serve as a reminder of the wide range of opinion possible only in the midst of a free community, a Jewish community liberal enough to subsidize and sponsor such a magazine as *Commentary*, which fearlessly publishes what other religious groups might quickly suppress as heresy. Yet there are some truths to which these men do call attention that bear critical scrutiny. The American Jewish community of the future is already showing signs that it will consist almost entirely of college-trained men and women. What, then, are some of the danger points in current Jewish communal patterns that may adversely affect the Jewish loyalties of some of these future "intellectuals"?

In the older, traditional Jewish community, as enshrined in the *shtetl*, learning was considered even more important than prayer, and both were incomplete without *zedakah*, charity. In the *shtetl* it was customary to hear Jews say: "Praying three times a day does not make you a Jew. You have to be a Jew for the world. That means you have to do something for other people as well."[4] American Jews . . . have continued in this tradition of generosity. But often the methods they have chosen in pursuit of the ideal have been disturbing to the more sensitive among them, and seem to be a radical departure from the traditional style of Jewish life. Philanthropy often seems to be "industrialized" and geared to status-seeking, rather than as a mark of inner spirituality. The Jewish intellectual tends to recoil from association with the Jewish community on these accounts. But he would do well to plumb the deeper motivations at work. One observer has linked the new "fund-raising" to the malaise of many American Jews, and his objective but understanding description gives us sympathetic insight into the problem:

> The American Jew is not fully accustomed to his new security and alternately revels in it and doubts it. Similarly, he has not learned to live with his prosperity and to relax with it. He needs more and he wants more. . . .
> This ambition is different from that which plagued Western European Jewry in the post-Emancipation years. That ambition was a craving for recognition by the Gentile community. Since the American Jew knows . . . that his quest for status within the general community has pre-

defined limits, he intensifies his search within the Jewish group. Nowhere does this seem more clearly reflected than in Jewish community activities, both the pride of the American Jew and, in some degree, his shame. . . .

He has aided European Jewry in building new lives in new lands and shown his solidarity with them and with the downtrodden everywhere. At the same time, these examples of utter generosity often mirror Jewish unsettlement, aimless competitive flux and hence a loss of Jewish moral growth and vitality. It is paradoxical that the events which most symbolize positive Jewish thought and action also disclose *a dilution of moral substance for the sake of recognition, status and outer splendor.* . . .

The American Jew . . . works hard for Jewish groups, but much of his work seems prompted by considerations of conspicuous prestige. . . . He is both healthy and sick. The American Jew may be defined as a series of contradictions with the positive containing much that is negative and the negative, curiously, containing much that is positive.[5] (Italics mine.)

It has been said that there are really only two kinds of Jews: those who are consumed by Jewish anxiety but succeed in denying it even to themselves; those who are troubled by Jewish anxiety but would never dream of denying it. Most Jewish intellectuals cannot empathize with the malaise of the middle-class American Jew because they are themselves afflicted with their own unique brand of Jewish restlessness and unsettlement. But they play at the game of denying it, and thus do not understand those Jews who still hold on to their Jewishness or Judaism. In their case, the desire to avoid what they consider the Jewish community's extreme conformism to middle-class patterns succeeds in impelling them to adopt the extreme conformism of the nonconforming intellectual community. Both groups, however, seen in the perspective of historical Jewish experience, tend to emerge as *in*authentic Jews. "The authentic Jew," writes Will Herberg, "lives on two levels: as a responsible member of the historical community, and as a 'son of the covenant,' a member of the trans-historical community of faith with which his destiny is inextricably linked. The authentic Jew is *in* this world, but never quite *of* it, never fully conformed or adjusted to the world in which he lives."[6] Weighed in scales such as these, neither the middle-class Jew nor the Jewish intellectual measures up as authentic. The former too often adopts spurious adjustments that integrate him too glibly into a bland and unexciting cultural environment. The latter often seems to have a lot of heaven above him, but there is precious little earth beneath him: he belongs to everyone, therefore to no one. The middle-class Jew, at least, is in the Jewish community, but the cosmopolitan Jewish intellectual is neither in it nor of it.

"How are you connected to me as another man is not?"[7] Facing his "fellow Jew" with apparent disdain, Philip Roth poses this telltale question, as he proudly proclaims his disconnection from him. Since the God of Abraham, Isaac, and Jacob is not *his* God, what is Judaism to Roth, or he to Judaism? Multiply this one gifted writer several thousands of times and the result yields a group of Jewish intellectuals in America who have not only become estranged from Judaism, but who are equally estranged from Christianity as well. In the view of Jean-Paul Sartre, many of these do not realize that they continue, nevertheless, to exist as Jews, because as humans "they have in common the situation of a Jew." Yet, applying Sartre's views still further, because they are inauthentic Jews who refuse to accept their own situation, they will often spend a lifetime attempting to be what they are not, nor cannot ever become. The desire to avoid their Jewish situation does not, however, yield them a new identity.[8]

Thus, the clannishness of the average American Jew continues to strike their intellectual brethren as mere tribalism. They see in the Jewish desire to marry within the group a primitive fetish still at work. They are appalled by the seeming lack of universality in the contemporary Jewish spirit in America, when they contemplate the fact that of all other religious or ethnic groups the Jews still retain the highest proportion of in-marriage: while the national rate of "mixed marriages" among Catholics is 30 per cent, about 10 per cent of the American Jewish population marries out of the faith. As recently as thirty and forty years ago, in the relatively assimilated and highly acculturated west-European Jewish communities, the rate of intermarriage was much higher: from 25 to 50 per cent. Today, the prospects in the American Jewish community are that Jews will marry Jews, and this, despite the fact that doors continue to be opened wider for greater social intercourse between Jew and Gentile, and roads that could lead to intermarriage have been made smoother and smoother.[9]

Yet because they can attribute little intrinsic meaning to either

Jewishness or Judaism, many Jewish intellectuals see in this situation sinister rather than benign influences. And they buttress this view by accusing the American Jew of exploiting a neurotic fear of anti-Semitism as a justification for an exclusiveness that refuses to sanction intimate contact with the world of the non-Jew. To be sure, as an individual, "the over-anxious Jew may be as reluctant to give up his fear of anti-Semitism as the anti-Semite is reluctant to overcome his fear of the Jew."[10] But the intellectual refuses to recognize that despite a sometimes overstated ethnicity, the growing desire of American Jews to maintain their sense of historic continuity is, in many ways, the result of the unsuccessful attempts of an entire generation, in the 1920's and 1930's, to go beyond the limits of their Jewish situation. The third and fourth generations have learned lessons from the second generation that the intellectuals seem to wish not to remember.

No, their own sins of Jewish omission repeatedly invalidate the intellectuals' reproach of the American Jews for their sins of commission. True, some of the behavior of the American Jew, as we have pointed out, does produce strains of inauthenticity in him: in his too-easy adaptation to the environment, his assimilation of the baser rather than the nobler elements of contemporary middle-class practice. But these are, perhaps, passing phenomena in the American Jewish community, as they may be of American life itself. American Jews may be generous for the wrong reasons; but at least they are generous. They may sometimes band together for the wrong reasons; but, at least, they stand with one another, and do not seek to run away from themselves or their responsibility to one another. But what the intellectuals are not saying—perhaps because they are preoccupied with hypercriticism—remains to be said, however. The situation to which we refer is directly related to the amazing statistics revealed by a recent study at the Center for Human Relations of the University of Pennsylvania. Dr. Joshua Fishman, director of the study, reported that 61 per cent of the Jewish heads of households in the United States today are high school graduates, and 22 per cent are college graduates. Among Protestants, only 39 per cent are high school graduates and but 8 per cent are college graduates. In Catholic households, 38 per cent of the family heads have graduated from high school, and only 7 per cent from college.

On the one hand, these figures go a long way to explain the

group pride that Jews continue to take in education and the values of learning. And this helps to highlight why Jews have bulked so large as a group, despite their minority status in America, in the intellectual and scientific advancement of the nation. The first American to win a Nobel Prize was a Jew, Dr. Albert Abraham Michelson, whose work in physics earned America this award in 1907. Since his time, forty Jews, in various countries, have been awarded the Nobel Prize, and seven of these have been Americans, including the father of the "wonder drug," streptomycin, Dr. Selman Abraham Waksman. In scientific fields, other Jewish names in America have become national by-words: Dr. Charles P. Steinmetz, the engineering wizard of General Electric; Dr. Abraham Flexner, the developer of modern American medical school education; Dr. Albert Einstein, Dr. J. Robert Oppenheimer, Dr. Edward Teller, and Dr. Isidor Rabi, internationally known physicists; Dr. Jonas Salk of polio vaccine fame; David Sarnoff of R.C.A., the electronics expert. In the musical arts, the achievements of Yehudi Menuhin, Jascha Heifetz, Vladimir Horowitz, Leonard Bernstein, George Gershwin, Richard Tucker, Jan Peerce, and scores of others are part of the cultural history of America. Jurists and philosophers such as Morris Raphael Cohen, Louis D. Brandeis, and Felix Frankfurter have made an indelible mark on the intellectual development of the law. Journalists of the stature of Adolph Ochs of the *New York Times* and Joseph Pulitzer of St. Louis, plus many other first-rate writers and dramatists of the Jewish faith, have imprinted their names in the lists of the American unforgettable; not to mention less known but no less significant Jewish contributors to America on the university campuses, in the scientific research laboratories, the publishing houses, and the like. When, a few years ago, the President of Notre Dame University asked a conference of Catholic educators, "Where are *our* Einsteins, Oppenheimers, and Salks?" he was, in effect, doing something many Jewish intellectuals have refused to do: paying tribute to what the Jews in America had achieved for America.

And in even more subtle ways, many in the Protestant religious communities were aware of the creative contributions which "Jewish otherness" had made to the literary life—even more aware as observers than the participants themselves. The irony was great: Jewish artists and writers were leveling their critical shafts against "middle-class Jewishness" in America, when, in fact, all that seemed to remain of the earlier Protestant dynamic here was a twentieth-century "middle-class American way of life." Sensitive Protestant thinkers were, in fact, somewhat envious of Jewish otherness—it seemed to keep creative Jews alive, prevented them from becoming, as they felt most Protestants had become, part of the unexciting, unimaginative wallpaper of the American social setting. "Protestant is what one is if he does not take the pains to disassociate himself from the established background," sighed Martin E. Marty. "The Jewish novelist (of the Saul Bellow era)," his lament continues, "as the uprooted, alienated, displaced urbanite formed the parables of dislocation of the time. . . . But the Protestant writer is too much at home to speak with interest of an emerging world."[11]

Seen from this angle of vision, the alienations of the Jewish intellectuals were, indeed, more to be admired than the "cozy" attitudes to America which most Protestants held—attitudes and platitudes which served only to shore up a cultural monolith that was rapidly eroding. Perhaps their alienation from Jewishness was really more a symptom of their cultural aliveness and openness than these Jewish intellectuals knew—perhaps more a recoiling from the boredom of Anglo-Saxon sameness than from their own Jewish particularity. Perhaps, in fact, in their antibourgeois stance, Kazin, Greenberg, and their friends were more in keeping with Jewishness and Judaism, than they, or their Jewish critics would allow. And perhaps in the newer unfolding of a pluralist America theirs would be the prophetic voice of a new spirituality—the historic voice of the alienated outsider.

Paradoxically, however, while the educational statistics quoted earlier reflect the massive contribution of Jews to *American* cultural life, they also highlight a glaring failure in the *Jewish* cultural achievement of American Jews. In the European past the situation was reversed: many Jews had the benefit of higher Jewish learning, but were denied the possibilities of a general university education. In such circumstances, their cultural loyalties to Jewish life were firmly grounded in the roots of Jewish knowledge. While there has been a new and growing emphasis in the contemporary American Jewish community upon a more intensive elementary education, very few Jewish college graduates can boast of having received a higher Jewish education. It is already apparent that even their intensive elementary Jewish education cannot stand up to their new sophistication as college graduates; they rarely unlearn or relearn the Jewish materials they have been taught as children, in childish ways. Indeed, the more general learning they achieve, the more critical and secularized their thinking process grows. And if they have not complemented their new knowledge with an approach to Judaism equally adult and equally sophisticated, it is likely that they will forever identify its teachings only with the naïve and "primitive" meanings they were taught as children. Thus, the fact that American Jews will soon comprise a community consisting almost completely of college graduates poses new threats to their creative survival as a vital cultural group. Clearly, more strenuous efforts at developing programs to strengthen secondary and higher Jewish education are called for.

There are some signs on the horizon that do indicate a new orientation in this direction. Jewish students on the college campuses are turning in increasing numbers to the Hillel Foundations, the collegiate religious organizations sponsored by B'nai B'rith since 1925. There are today over 70 such full-time Foundations in addition to almost 150 part-time Hillel Counselorships. These groups offer Jewish students on the American campus a wide variety of cultural, religious, and academic opportunities. The lectures, discussion groups, seminars, and classes they provide make Judaism available to the college student, on a level more proximate to his own intellectual status. Hillel also publishes high-caliber books on Judaism, which further serve to advance the Jewish cultural level of the college student. The growing popularity of its program is attested to in the remarkable fact that, as of 1963, almost 200 American colleges were on Hillel's "waiting list," looking forward to the future establishment of its service on their own campuses. The Hillel Foundation has thus become an integral part of the landscape of American higher education, by the side of Wesley, the Methodist student organization, and Newman, the organization of Catholic college students.

The myriad of secular Jewish organizations on the American scene have been moving away from their earlier preoccupations with programs of community relations, political action, or civic defense, and are recognizing the need to expand their efforts in the direction of cultural enterprises. The American Jewish Committee, organized in 1906 to "prevent infraction of the civil and religious rights of Jews in any part of the world" continues to promote creative research into American Jewish life on a broad scale and sponsors the widely respected monthly magazine, *Commentary*. The American Jewish Congress, established by Dr. Stephen S. Wise in 1917 as a Zionist-oriented community-relations organization, is not only involved in activities seeking to eliminate racial and religious bigotry, but publishes the thoughtful journal *Judaism,* as well as the *Congress Bi-Weekly.* So, too, the B'nai B'rith, the oldest of all the national Jewish organizations, founded in 1843, continues to promote the work of its Anti-Defamation League, and in addition to its cultural involvement in the work of the Hillel Foundation, has recently embarked upon a full-scale effort to popularize adult education among hundreds of thousands of its members in local lodges and regional districts across the country. In 1960, the local units federated nationally in the Council of Jewish Federations and Welfare Funds helped to establish a significant, new undertaking, The National Foundation for Jewish Culture, to assist, guide and inform the American Jewish community in matters pertaining to the advancement of Jewish culture. Clearly, in all of these quarters, interest in the development of greater Jewish intellectual achievement was moving to new and higher ground.

Still another striking cultural development has occurred in recent years. The Hebrew Union College, the Jewish Theological Seminary of America, and the Yeshiva University, in addition to their own denominational theological programs, have widened the scope of their academic interests and, in effect, have come to serve as universities of Judaism. Increasing numbers of lay Jewish students are attracted to their courses in the pursuit of higher Jewish education. Although it was established in 1948 as a secular, nonsectarian university under Jewish auspices, Brandeis University in Waltham, Massachusetts, is now developing a full-scale Institute of Jewish Studies on a high academic plane. The Hebrew Teacher's Colleges of Boston and Baltimore, the Herzliah Teacher's Seminary in New York, and the College of Jewish Studies in Chicago are also doing effective work in these areas. And, of course, since 1907 the Dropsie College in Philadelphia, a postgraduate school of Jewish studies, has been an important center for advanced research in Judaic learning.

One of the most promising new areas, however, is the new interest on the part of a growing number of American universities in the field of Jewish studies, on a higher academic and cultural level. To be sure, the third oldest chair at Harvard University is the Hancock Professorship of Hebrew and other Oriental Languages established as early as 1764, and other universities in America, too, have long offered courses in Hebrew language and literature. For the most part, however, these were made available as part of a general theological grounding for future members of the Christian ministry. But with the growing use of Hebrew as a modern tongue, a number of secondary school systems in the East began to offer it as a language course that was acceptable for college entrance, alongside other modern foreign languages. Then, with the dynamic cultural rebirth in the State of Israel, this new American academic tendency became more widespread. Room was now made for Jewish studies, not as an aspect of pretheological Christian training but as a self-justified academic discipline. Already twenty-one universities and colleges in the United States have established either undergraduate or graduate departments of Jewish studies as an integral part of their American program for higher education. And the movement in this direction seems to be only the beginning of a trend.

Such educational activities as these make it possible for Jewish college students, and non-Jews as well, to gain deeper insights into the history and culture of Judaism as an ancient and venerable intellectual tradition. But on the psychological side they achieve something much more subtle and perhaps even more important. By placing higher Jewish study on a footing of equality with other academic disciplines offered on the campus, future Jewish intellectuals now at the colleges may come to regard Jewishness and Judaism as valid for and relevant to their own intellectual concerns. Ironically, as Jewish culture is taught and analyzed as a modern phenomenon, and not merely as a field for antiquarian or theological inquiry, Judaism may no longer appear to them to be nothing more than a fossilized religious tradition. And if they see purpose and meaning in *Judaism*, they may ultimately come to regard their relationship to the Jewish people—their *Jewishness*—with new and more hopeful eyes.

These efforts and the many other new experiments in adult Jewish education may yet burgeon into fuller flowering. If they do, then what today appears to be mainly a conforming, middle-class American community, powered principally by forces external to itself, may yet take its place by the side of the great Jewish communities of the past. If it does, it will be a testimony to the spiritual resources inherent in America whose liberating influences will call forth a creative spiritual response from the Jews of America. If it does, moreover, then important and creative changes must inevitably take place in the institutional life of the American Jewish community: the rabbi may again become the scholar-teacher (if not the saint); the synagogue an intellectual center rather than a house of social meeting; the educational system may shift its emphasis to a deepening and heightening of outreach instead of concentrating on elementals alone; and the fund-raising apparatus, while retaining its "American efficiency," may come closer to the spiritual values of *zedakah*, to which it is now only superficially related. Paul Tillich has said that he does not believe "that a free society can be derived from any religion unless the religion has been profoundly influenced by the Jewish tradition."[12] The converse is equally true: when Jews are themselves spiritually free, they can free the Jewish tradition to help make it speak again in its historic and authentic accents.

As early as 1907, Dr. Israel Friedlaender, an east-European professor at the Jewish Theological Seminary of America, discussing the "problem of Judaism in America," offered his fellow American Jews a vision:

> And when we thus try to penetrate the mist that encircles the horizon of the present, a vision unfolds itself before our mind's eye, presenting a picture of the future American Israel. We perceive a community great in numbers, mighty in power, enjoying life, liberty and the pursuit of happiness: true life, not mere breathing space; full liberty, not mere elbow room; real happiness, not that of pasture beasts; actively participating in the civic, social and economic progress of the country, fully sharing and increasing its spiritual possessions and acquisitions, doubling its joys, halving its sorrows; yet deeply rooted in the soil of Judaism, clinging to its past, working for its future, true to its traditions, faithful to its aspirations, one in sentiment with their brethren wherever they are, attached to the land of their fathers as the cradle and resting place of the Jewish spirit; men with straight backs and raised heads, with big hearts and strong minds, with no conviction crippled, with no emotion stifled, with souls harmoniously developed, self-centered and self-reliant; receiving and resisting, not yielding like wax to every impress from the outside, but blending the best they possess with the best they encounter; not a horde of individuals, but a set of individualities, adding a new note to the richness of American life, leading a new current into the stream of

American civilization; not a formless crowd of taxpayers and voters, but a sharply marked community, distinct and distinguished, trusted for its loyalty, respected for its dignity, esteemed for its traditions, valued for its aspiration, a community such as the Prophet of the Exile saw it in his vision: "And marked will be their seed among the nations, and their offspring among the peoples. Everyone that will see them will point to them as a community blessed by the Lord."[13]

America *is* different, and for Jews it can yet be magnificently different. If America forgets the hates, the hostilities, and the hurts, and if, in the midst of freedom and relative affluence, Jews can remember their spiritual integrity and their need to contribute creatively as religious co-equals, then this modern vision and prophecy may yet come true.

NOTES

1. Irving Howe, "The Lost Young Intellectual," in *Commentary*, October, 1946, p. 362; see also his "Spruceton Jewry Adjusts Itself," in *Commentary*, June, 1948, pp. 552–558.
2. Quoted in Norman Podhoretz, "Jewishness and the Younger Intellectuals" (Introduction), in *Commentary*, April, 1961, p. 307.
3. *Ibid.*, p. 309.
4. Mark Zborowski and Elizabeth Herzog, *Life Is With People* (New York: International Universities Press, 1952), p. 230.
5. Lothar Kahn, "Another Decade: The American Jew in the Sixties," in *Judaism*, 10, Spring, 1961, pp. 104–105; p. 111. Used by permission.
6. Will Herberg, "The Integration of the Jew in Contemporary America," in *Conservative Judaism*, Vol. XV, No. 3, Spring, 1961, p. 9.
7. Philip Roth in "Jewishness and the Younger Intellectuals: A Symposium," in *Commentary*, April, 1961, p. 351.
8. See Jean-Paul Sartre, *Anti-Semite and Jew* (New York: Schocken Books, 1948), pp. 67 f.
9. See Hershel Shanks, "Jewish-Gentile Intermarriage: Facts and Trends," in *Commentary*, October, 1953, pp. 370–375. Shanks believes that "the American Jewish intermarriage rate can now be reliably estimated at between 5 and 10 per cent." He goes on to point out that "This figure is, of course, higher than the proportion of the *individual* intermarried Jews in the total number of spouses. That proportion would be between 2.6 and 5.6 per cent." Almost all reports, too, "show Jewish men intermarrying more than Jewish women."
    . . . Erich Rosenthal's provocative essay, "Studies in Jewish Intermarriage in the United States" (see *American Jewish Year Book, 1963*, Vol. 64 [Philadelphia: Jewish Publication Society, 1963], pp. 3–53) is in many

ways a pioneering study and for the first time appears to document the view that "the ethnic and religious bonds that welded the immigrant generations into a highly organized community are becoming progressively weaker" (pp. 52–53).

His study of Jewish intermarriage in Greater Washington, D.C. (for 1956) shows that the total rate of intermarriage was 13.1 per cent—a somewhat higher figure than most previous students had assumed to be true of American Jewry as a whole. But of even greater significance is the fact that Rosenthal was able "to demonstrate empirically the relation between generation and intermarriage." "The level of intermarriage in the first generation (the foreign-born) was 1.4 per cent, the second generation (native-born of foreign parentage) had a level of 10.2 per cent, and the native-born of native parentage (the third and subsequent generations) had a level of 17.9 per cent" (pp. 18–19).

Rosenthal claims (p. 53) that these data "cast doubt on the doctrine of the persistence of religious endogamy in American life and on the idea of the 'return of the third generation.'" To be sure, an intermarriage rate of 17.9 per cent in the third generation seems to represent a significant and irreversible tendency towards growing assimilation as the generations continue. However, the newer trends in Jewish education are likely to check this spiralling. Some Jews will always opt non-Judaism, publicly or privately, but those who do remain within the community will probably have deeper loyalties than those who stayed on as alienated and alienating members of the second generation. In the larger metropolitan centers where there are greater opportunities for religious education, future generations are likely to demonstrate a greater tendency towards in-marriage than seems evident from Rosenthal's data. Indeed, his own statistics (despite their inconclusiveness—since Washington is not yet America!) point to the fact that "for the third generation . . . Jewish education was significant." It is no small matter that his findings indicate that for those men who had no religious education, the rate of intermarriage was almost twice as high!

See also Werner Cahnman (ed.), *Intermarriage and Jewish Life: A Symposium* (New York: The Herzl Press, 1963).

10. See Bruno Bettelheim, "How to Arm Our Children Against Anti-Semitism," in *Commentary*, September 1951, p. 218.
11. Martin E. Marty, *Second Chance for American Protestants* (New York: Harper and Row, 1963), pp. 58; 64–65.
12. Paul Tillich, "Freedom and Ultimate Concern," in *Religion in America*, ed. John Cogley (New York: Meridian Books, 1958), p. 282.
13. Israel Friedlaender, *Past and Present: A Collection of Jewish Essays* (Cincinnati: Ark Publishing Company, 1919), pp. 277–278.

Once
a Jew . . . .

THE ETHNIC CHURCH AND
THE DESIRE FOR SURVIVAL

MARSHALL SKLARE

FOR AMERICAN ETHNIC GROUPS the rate of their acculturation appears to depend to a considerable degree upon the *tempo of their social mobility*. Such a relationship may, however, be absent in less dynamic societies.

Comparing the Jews* with their sociological counterparts—ethnics who arrived at the same time and in about the same numbers—we find that the Jews have been more mobile than any of their fellows. What type of evidence exists to substantiate this assertion? Since the Federal Census does not include questions about ancestry or religious preference, it is necessary to rely chiefly upon (1) polls, and (2) community studies.

Although no special polls have been conducted on the problem of Jewish mobility, in some of the studies which include questions on socio-economic status respondents have also been asked to designate the religious group with which they affiliate. Community studies might be expected to yield even richer data than could be obtained by polling, but in terms of our purposes such studies have produced only limited results. Because an area must be chosen that can be fully covered with the resources at hand, most investigators prefer to study rather small communities. Important ethnic groups like the Jews are frequently missing from communities of this type, particularly if they are located outside of the Eastern part of the United States. In addition, most opinion and community studies do not differentiate between East-European and other types of Jews. Furthermore, since Jews

Reprinted with permission of the author and The Macmillan Company from *Conservative Judaism* by Marshall Sklare. Copyright © The Free Press, a Corporation 1955.

* From this point on, except where the content specifically indicates otherwise, "Jews" will mean East-European Jews.

lacked a peasant class in Europe, their mobility may seem deceptively high in comparison with peasant-descended ethnic groups. The absence of a sizable number of Jewish farmers in the United States also makes it more complicated to draw significant comparisons. Because of these considerations, it is necessary to handle the data with caution. But the main facts about Jewish mobility are hardly in doubt. . . .

Since rapid mobility has been characteristic of an entire segment of the Jewish population, a *larger* middle class was created here than in any other comparable ethnic group. In the others slow mobility has characterized the group as a whole; this has been coupled with rapid mobility on the part of exceptional individuals. The fact that among Jews rapid mobility has been a group rather than an individual phenomenon has resulted in the creation of a public whose level of acculturation was such as to make them feel strongly alienated from Orthodoxy. If mobility had been very gradual, it is conceivable that Orthodoxy might have adjusted itself. However, where mobility is *so* rapid, the tendency is for an institution to be outstripped in its adjustive efforts by its public. The constituency develops new needs to which the old institution cannot adapt itself without making too great a break with the past.[1] Elderly individuals who have been successful economically but whose main socialization took place in another culture (and thus upon whom the American acculturative process has less impact), as well as those who are left behind in the mobility process, become the chief reservoirs from which Orthodoxy must draw its followers.[2]

In addition to its rate, the impact of mobility depends on: (1) the type of culture characteristic of the dominant group and (2) the nature of the minority's own traditional system. If the culture of the minority has strong similarities with the one held by the dominant group, the original system may be less disvalued; the operation of the acculturation process will not suddenly upset the original system. However, should the culture gulf be wide, it will be increasingly difficult to bridge the chasm being expanded by the social mobility. Since narrowing must take place chiefly by means of a modification of the minority group's culture, changes in their traditions will have to be profound. It may not be possible to maintain the fiction that the changes are "natural" (i.e., that they are compatible with the tradition). Minority-group members may recognize the claim of tradition at the same time that they feel the impossibility of adherence to it. In this situation they tend to abdicate their claim to orthodoxy and use a new designation to describe themselves.

The traditional Jewish system is deviant in Western civilization to the extent that the Christian heritage forms one of the basic cultural influences. Leaving the problem of *Weltanschauung* aside and confining ourselves to the more narrow field of religion, we find that in addition to doctrinal distinctions between Christianity and Judaism, important divergencies exist in the area of religious *practices*.[3] Although it originated in the same culture area as did Judaism, Christianity—by its very desire to differentiate itself from the Hebrew religion—made any number of important changes in the field of ritual. Furthermore, in Europe it became "Westernized." While the Jews lived in the West for centuries, they continued to elaborate and observe their Eastern traditions. All this is not to deny that some cultural interchange *did* take place between the two groups, and that the Jewish system underwent some degree of metamorphosis.

In order to illustrate the problem, let us take one of the most obvious symbols of Jewish "Easternness": the segregation of the sexes during worship. According to tradition, women must be confined to a separate part of the synagogue which is curtained off or somehow separated from the main section occupied by the males. Women have no role in the performance of the rituals. While the male is required to observe a multitude of commandments and prohibitions, the formal religious obligations of the woman are only three in number:[4] following the female ritual purifications, lighting the Sabbath candles, and *hallah*.* This eastern pattern was acceptable in the *shtetl*, the small town in Eastern Europe whose population consisted of a relatively high proportion of Jews. In such areas the non-Jews were divided into three groups: a mass of peasants, a small number of government officials, and a sprinkling of aristocrats. Characteristically, there was no Christian middle class.[5]

One additional example will be helpful. The Jewish community has traditionally constituted a "sacred society." Under such circumstances the distinction between sacred and secular is nonexistent. Accordingly, in addition to ritual, religious custom, and morals, the Jewish legal system seeks to regulate behavior in areas

---

* That portion of the dough of the Sabbath loaf which is dedicated to the Lord.

which to the Western mind are of secular concern only. They include "personal" matters like the fiber content of clothing and the type of food and beverages consumed, as well as "social" matters like the method of payment of employees.

The position of the spiritual leader in such a sacred society is unique. His power derives not from priestly functions as in the Western tradition, but rather from his mastery of the intricacies of the sacred code and his ability to make the system viable by dealing with novel situations through the use of established canons of interpretation. Similarly, the ideal layman also deviates from Western standards. The pious Jew is not an individual necessarily engrossed in prayer and contemplation who proceeds to develop "inwardness," or even someone who devotes himself to the performance of good works. It is rather he who is punctilious in his observance of the code and who has mastered it so perfectly that he understands the reasoning behind each commandment and prohibition. Since the study of the sacred system is so highly esteemed, the religious virtuoso is not the saint but the *scholar*. It is a matter of individual preference whether or not the scholar chooses to exercise the rabbinical office, to make his living by some other means, or to be supported by family or patrons.

These particular features of the Jewish system were already under attack in late nineteenth-century Eastern Europe. Their incongruity even in a chiefly peasant, only semi-secularized Roman Catholic or Russian Orthodox milieu was apparent to some. Brought to a secular, industrial environment, dissolution of the integrity of the system was a foregone conclusion. Warner and Srole note that:

> Judaism . . . is a unitary system of legislation sanctified and revealed by God. Transgression of the minutest edict is a sin and offense to God. The moment that one edict is questioned, the authority of the entire system is challenged.[6]

A need consequently arises for a new system which will mediate the crisis brought about when social mobility produces high acculturation. It must reduce the incongruity between a *Western, Protestant, secular* environment and the *Eastern, Orthodox, legalistic* Jewish system. Reorganization may proceed in two directions: (1) Continuation, reinvigoration, or reformulation of *selected* elements in the system which fulfill certain continuing needs and which do not conflict seriously with American norms. (2) The growth of *new* functions both within the old institutional framework as well as outside of it. These are in the nature of compensatory mechanisms filling the void which has resulted from the undermining of the previous system.

The resulting cultural system is no longer a truly sacred one, for it now consists of a number of folkways allowing for considerable deviation. It may be thought of as a subculture whose flexible patterns offer a variety of ways of being "Jewish." Many difficult problems arise in the process of the transition from the "unitary system of legislation sanctified and revealed by God," to the new subcultural system. Their existence is manifested by conflicts which take place between the first and the second generations, by institutional disequilibrium, and by what may be called "religious disorganization." Conservatism, we may assume, is one of the resultants of the organization-disorganization-reorganization cycle.

DESIRE FOR SURVIVAL

In addition to the rate of social mobility and the character of the traditional system, several conditions are required before an adjustment of the Conservative type can be set in motion. The first is the desire for survival: group members must feel that although acculturation is acceptable, *assimilation* should be prevented.

It was once thought that each ethnic group would—in the space of a few decades—leave their "ghetto" and fuse into the melting pot. Sociologists conceded that groups which came here fairly late, against whom discrimination was practiced, or whose original culture was strikingly different from the dominant one, might be more cohesive than others. But assimilation was considered inevitable. At present it is becoming increasingly evident that ethnicity still remains a significant basis of social stratification. For example, an investigation in New Haven, Connecticut, discloses that Swedes and Danes—who came here earlier than many other groups and whose culture was not strikingly deviant —still constitute recognizable entities in that city.[7] Does this result from prejudice, from rejection by the dominant group?[8] Is it traceable to the influence of ethnic survivalists who are strongly attached to the old culture and who preserve the sub-community by influencing marginal individuals to remain loyal? Is it that the content of the original culture, once it is adapted to American conditions, retains a degree of attractiveness? Or is it because ethnic solidarity now serves a new purpose: protection from *anomie*—the atomization and disorganization characteristic of present-day society which results in a loss of the feeling of social solidarity?

This last suggestion is a particularly intriguing one since the problem of *anomie* exists for all peoples who live in a society characterized by mobility, by the segregation of kinship, occupation, and leisure-time roles, by shifting norms, and by clashing social systems. One of the structures which compensates for this characteristic feature of modern life is the voluntary association. These groups help to create for the individual additional primary and secondary relationships. Viewing such bonds as a "defense" against *anomie*, it is apparent that they can be elaborated on various levels: class ends, shared life experiences, similar play interests, or *common descent*. While the present-day ethnic is no longer in need of a therapeutic instrument to reduce the trauma resulting from encountering radically new norms and values (as was the case with his father or grandfather), he *is* in need of meaningful social relationships. Participation in the affairs of his ethnic group may be a convenient way of meeting this requirement. The "defense against *anomie*" theory may well help to explain why some of the sub-communities preserve a degree of integration in spite of the participants having shed many old-world culture patterns.[9]

Rejection, the influence of the survivalists, the adapted culture, and the *anomie* problem are undoubtedly all factors which operate to retard—although perhaps only temporarily—the assimilation of ethnics. With the amount of knowledge which we have at our disposal, it is difficult to decide just how much weight should be assigned to each of these forces, as well as to others detailed below. Whatever the situation in other groups, it will be conceded that Jews have shown themselves *particularly* desirous of retaining some form of group identity.[10] Marden has gone so far as to state that "The prospects for Jews in American society appear different from those of any other minority . . ."[11] for he doubts whether the other groups will be able to persist indefinitely. Marden explains that while Jews have been subject to much acculturation, this process has not led to the further step of assimilation:

> The acculturation of Jews, however, presents some striking differences to that of other immigrant groups. In many ways the Jewish group became more rapidly and successfully adjusted to life in America than the other immigrant groups. This has been true with reference to economic success, participation in civic life, and educational achievement.
>
> . . . increasing acculturation has not led to complete assimilation, nor are there any indications . . . that it will ever do so. The Jewish community within the larger gentile community, modernized and adaptive as much of its cultural content is, still remains distinct.[12]

A full explanation of this almost unique desire for survival will not be attempted here. Some of the causes have already been cited. In addition there is the fact that Jews still possess a feeling of superiority, although more in the moral and intellectual realms now than in the area of spiritual affairs. While the feeling of superiority is a factor which has received comparatively little attention from students of the problem, it is of crucial importance because it operates to retard assimilation. Leaving the group becomes a psychological threat: such a move is viewed not as an advancement but as cutting oneself off from a claim to superiority.[13] However explained, the "will to live" serves to encourage the making of experiments, like Conservatism, which aim to discover a *modus vivendi* for the Jewish community.

THE ETHNIC CHURCH AND RELIGION AS A VEHICLE

Judaism constitutes an *ethnic church*:[14] a fellowship whose members are differentiated from those belonging to other denominations by virtue of their special *descent* as well as by their doctrines or practices.[15] In America the uniqueness of this type of church is its articulation of ethnicity and religiosity in a multi-ethnic society where ethnic groups are essentially minority groups, i.e., subordinate to a majority group presumed to be non-ethnic. In addition to Jews and others, this type of body is found in the three divisions of Christianity: the Protestant, Roman

Catholic, and Eastern Orthodox Churches. To illustrate for the Protestant group, special Lutheran bodies and synods exist for the Danes, Finns, Germans, Hungarians, Icelanders, Norwegians, Slovaks, Swedes, and others. Special nationality parishes have been established in the United States for Roman Catholics who come from Armenia, Croatia, Italy, Poland, Portugal, the Ukraine, and many other places.[16]

These groups are first of all *churches*, for like all religious organizations they seek to provide " . . . a way of facing the problems of ultimate and unavoidable frustration, of 'evil', and the generalized problem of meaning in some non-empirical sense, of finding some ultimate why."[17] But concurrently they have an additional task: the preservation of a particular sub-culture or ethnic group. Note that the language used in sermons, liturgy, or hymns may be the one spoken in the homeland; that certain rites and holidays are observed which are celebrated only by members of the special ethnic group; and that celebrations commemorate events unique to the history of the group.[18] The ethnic church commonly makes special educational arrangements designed to teach its youth those special loyalties necessary for group survival. This frequently includes some training in the language of the homeland. Understandably, the ethnic church appears to be a highly sectarian institution to those who do not possess loyalty to a sub-culture. H. Richard Niebuhr, for example, has complained that:

> . . . many an immigrant church became more a racial and cultural than a religious institution in the New World. Its parochial schools were fostered not only that the children might receive instruction in religion but also that they might learn the mother-tongue and with it the attitudes and social ideals of the old homeland. In many a Sunday School German or Swedish readers were the only textbooks; in many a pulpit the duty of loyalty to the old language was almost as frequent a theme as the duty of loyalty to the old faith. So the churches of the immigrants often found a new and additional reason for their separate existence. They now represented racial sectarianism. . . . They became competitive conflict societies, intent upon maintaining their distinction from other groups, no matter how closely these might be akin to them in doctrine, polity and piety.[19]

Leaving aside consideration of the polemical tone of his statement, Niebuhr is correct in suggesting that these churches have become an important mechanism for the preservation of ethnicity. Religion easily recommended itself for this role. The church was one of the few institutions of the original culture capable of re-establishment in the new land. Also, since the ethnic church is the counterpart of non-ethnic institutions of the same order, it would automatically receive identical formal recognition, although of course its status position may not be on the same level. Further-more, while ethnic separatism is not very highly valued in our culture, religious distinctiveness is allowable—even esteemed in a way because it is "American." Given the attraction of national culture patterns which have slowly but surely impressed them-selves upon the ethnic, group distinctiveness could be preserved —even if emptied of much of its content—under the banner of religion. Thus, because of the challenge to group survival, eth-nicity has tended to retreat and to reappear in a very different form.

In summary, the forces working toward the continuation of the special function of the ethnic church converge from the fol-lowing two directions: (1) From the dynamic of the institution itself. Since the future of the church generally hinges on the persistence of the ethnic group, it must promote ethnic group solidarity in order to survive. (2) From ethnics who—whether consciously or not—realize that religion is an acceptable method of group differentiation, that church functions may include much more than the dissemination of the word of God. Such individ-uals see suprasocial differences as legitimating the perpetuation of divisions in the social structure. While it is true that in some cases group persistence has been in outright ethnic form, in other instances the main index to continuing ethnicity is to be found in the survival of churches whose membership is relatively ho-mogeneous. Most of the group are still descended from individ-uals who come from the same homeland. American ethnic groups are tending to change their outward appearances. They can preserve themselves as religious groups.

On the whole, Jews in the United States choose to be regarded as members of a religious denomination. However, the various groups in the community who have arrived at this consensus are differently motivated. There are, of course, those who feel (as well as act) that religion *is* the prime expression of Judaism. The religious designation is, therefore, expressive of their true ideo-logical preferences. Another segment of the community has wider Jewish interests than simply religion (or even possess other Jewish interests which serve to replace religion), but they feel nonetheless that—given American traditions—*religion must become the main expression of Jewish identification as well as the guarantor of Jewish ethnic survival.* At the very least, they would contend that the designation of the Jewish group as constituting a denomination is a highly convenient fiction which it is wise to cultivate. Lastly, there are those whose feelings of Jewish identification are weak or conflicted, and whose survivalistic urges are consequently questionable. Nevertheless, because of public relations considerations, they feel that it is essential that Jews stress the religious designation. The middle group seems to be the predominant one at present. While few Jews—particularly those in the middle group—could succeed in verbalizing their feelings as we have set them down, there is ample evidence available pointing to the existence of these trends.[20]

It is significant that although overall Jewish identification has remained at a high level (and while synagogue affiliation appears to be greater than previously), Jews today hardly seem very observant of religious practices. Their day-to-day religious behavior is readily apparent from data gathered in a poll conducted by the National Opinion Research Center during 1945. This survey reveals that only 6% of those who identify themselves as Catholic state that they seldom or never attend religious services, 19% of the Protestants make this statement, but no less than 32% of the Jews are found in this category. Of the Catholics, 69% attend religious services once a week or more, 36% of the Protestants do likewise, but a mere 9% of the Jews attend. Worshipping at least once a month are 81% of the Catholics, 62% of the Protestants and only 24% of the Jews.[21] It would seem then that many wish to identify themselves as being members of a religious group while at the same time they lack much religious interest. Because of such a trend, one student of Jewish problems speaks of the ". . . paradox of the concentration of Diaspora survivalism on religious channels in the face of increasing weakening of religion."[22] Although the fundamental tie in the Jewish community continues to be on the level of common ethnicity, many apparently share Mordecai M. Kaplan's viewpoint that ". . . [the synagogue] is the only institution that can define our aims to a world that will otherwise be at a loss to understand why we persist in retaining our corporate individuality."[23]

All of this results in the strengthening of the religious structure in spite of increasing secularization. As we noted, reinforcement comes from different directions. The ethnic survivalists concentrate upon religion as the most satisfactory means of Jewish identification, and the more marginal group seizes upon it as a protective device which will help to raise status, draw allies to the Jewish cause, and in the long run serve to decrease the virulence of anti-Semitism. Both are forced into "making good" on the stereotype by according some support to religious causes. Whatever their real feelings, their very desire to project the stereotype means that they have to concede a responsibility for supporting religious institutions. Additionally, the stereotype—once it is successfully established—reacts back on the Jew himself. Whether because of impressions conveyed by Jews, or because of factors which operate independently of minority-generated pressures, Gentiles may begin to convey that they consider the Jewish group as just another religious denomination. At this juncture, the Jew may find himself propelled into fulfilling the image projected by the Gentile. Although he himself may not actually believe the stereotype to be wholly valid, he feels that he must act like the type of "good Jew" which the Gentile imagines —the Jew who is loyal to his rabbi, interested in his synagogue.

Such developments do not prepare the ground for any kind of true religious revival. Attendance at services may not even grow very substantially. However, religious institutions will receive increasing financial support and community esteem, particularly if they offer a program which includes non-religious activities and is strongly oriented toward ethnic values. We can assume that Conservatism resulted in part from the feeling that the Orthodox synagogue was inadequate to meet the demands of the environment—that ethnic solidarity would have to be perpetuated chiefly under religious auspices and that consequently a new type of institution was required.

CONGREGATIONALISM

The final general factor involved in the growth of Conservatism is the type of religious organization, or *polity*, found in the Jewish group. Religious institutions vary from those characterized by the highly centralized episcopal type of structure to those organized in the congregational form where local bodies retain much of their autonomy. Largely because of the conditions of Diaspora living, Jews in the United States are extremely congregational—they stress the independence and self-sufficiency of the local synagogue. As one student of religion has stated: "Within the local [Jewish] congregation there is full independence. There are no synods, assemblies, or hierarchies of leaders to control anything whatsoever in the synagogue."[24] The directors of each congregation determine their own ritual; ethnic bonds make it well-nigh impossible to read any group out of the fold regardless of its deviant behavior.

What is the importance of this in connection with the growth of Conservatism? It is conceivable that the movement would never have started if a different type of polity existed. Had Judaism been organized along episcopalian lines, dissent might have been driven underground, instead of eventuating in the establishment of new kinds of synagogues. But one could object by saying that the demand for change was too vigorous to stifle. If this were true, the strife that would accompany the split from Orthodoxy would result in a far different type of Conservative movement. Ideological clarification and organizational centralization, both of which—as we shall see—are decidedly absent in Conservatism, commonly result during the initial period in the growth of movements when their opposition to the *status quo* is most marked. In a situation like the Jewish one where over-all organization and authority is so amorphous, deviant types of congregations can hardly be said to be in "revolt" against the system; they have merely effected a compromise adjustment which does not threaten the *status quo* in the ordinary sense.

Although congregationalism promotes differentiation, it is far from being wholly dysfunctional in its consequences. Differentiation permits the retention of over-all loyalties to the group and to the religion at the same time that it promotes the fragmentalization of tradition. In addition to such general perspectives, it is significant to note that extreme congregationalism works toward the simplification of our analysis. Making allowance for certain types of rigidities, it is apparent that the form which the local congregation takes is generally an excellent index to the needs and feelings of the community, or at least that segment of the group which is active in a particular synagogue. Of course, since the congregation is unrelated to any larger entity except by the unstructured bonds of ethnicity, its board of directors is free—if it so wishes—to preserve the *status quo* by conducting its activities along time-honored lines and thereby disregard the defections of the synagogue's more mobile and acculturated periphery. But any clique which is dissatisfied is free to establish its own synagogue.

Among Jewry every congregation must appeal for community support and is entirely on its own resources. In contrast, even the congregationally-inclined Protestant denominations extend help to local units, and frequently subsidize needy congregations for considerable periods of time. They may have available loan funds to assist in the building of churches, and they also frequently possess a network of field offices which help in the organization and counseling of local congregations. Special provisions may be made by denominational agencies to keep alive church units which could not exist but for outside aid.

While Jewish philanthropy is renowned, in the main it has not entered the field of religion except to endow rabbinical seminaries and other educational enterprises. Thus the congregation is not an object of philanthropy of a city and nation-wide character.[25] It is conceived of as a neighborhood enterprise; its constituency take upon themselves the complete obligation for maintenance when they organize on a formal level. If it is a popular and growing synagogue it has apparently gauged the state of public opinion and is expertly serving the needs of its constituency. The Jewish institutional structure presents few blocks to free congregational development or decay.

NOTES

1. For an excellent illustration of the disintegrative effects of social mobility in a Norwegian Lutheran church, see W. Lloyd Warner, *Democracy in Jonesville* (New York: Harper & Brothers, 1949), esp. pp. 176–77.
2. However, there now exists a small group of synagogues (the majority of which are located in New York City) whose leaders are younger, somewhat acculturated, and generally middle class individuals who are determined to remain Orthodox. This is the "Young Israel" movement, a group which has set up its own congregations in response to the fact that the typical Orthodox synagogue is an institution administered for

and by a closed group of elders. Young Israel synagogues are characterized by greater decorum than is typical of most Orthodox houses of worship, by the use of English, by the avoidance of certain administrative practices characteristic of the immigrant and East European synagogue, and by an institutional youth work program. See Milton Richman, "A Descriptive Analysis of a Local Orthodox Jewish Synagogue" (Unpublished Master's thesis, New School for Social Research, 1943), and Young Israel, *President's Report, 1950–51* (New York: National Council of Young Israel, n.d.).

3. For our purpose it is necessary to emphasize dissimilarities rather than similarities. By so doing we do not mean to deny that many parallels or resemblances may exist. Actually, if one looks closely, it becomes clear that certain constellations of Jewish *attitudes* (if not practices) are highly modern and Western.

On the "foreignness" of Jewish practices, note the comments by Robert M. MacIver, in his *Report on the Jewish Community Relations Agencies* (New York: National Community Relations Advisory Council, 1951), pp. 33–34, 47. It is important to note that some Near Eastern Christians continued with "Easternness," but characteristically they have lived in their native lands until very recent times.

4. However, since many of the laws regulate the preparation of food, as well as other aspects of homemaking, the occupational role of woman means that for all practical purposes it is she—and not her husband—who must see to the observance of many commandments other than simply the three "womanly" ones.

5. For a description of *shtetl* life, see Mark Zborowski and Elizabeth Herzog, *Life Is With People* (New York: International Universities Press, 1952).

6. W. Lloyd Warner and Leo Srole, *Social Systems of American Ethnic Groups* (New Haven: Yale University Press, 1945), p. 204.

7. See Mhyra S. Minnis, "Cleavage in Women's Organizations: A Reflection of the Social Structure of a City," *American Sociological Review,* XVIII (1953), 47–53.

8. Note Arnold and Caroline Rose, *America Divided* (New York: Alfred A. Knopf, Inc., 1948), pp. 178–82. These writers stress rejection as the causative factor for minority group identification.

9. Earlier theorists had equated ethnic group identification with cultural deviation. As a consequence the tendency to discard old-world traits was taken as an index of assimilation: cultural assimilation meant group assimilation. The possibility that social differentiation might continue in spite of a high rate of acculturation was neglected. Robert E. Park, for example, considered the problem almost completely from the standpoint of the social processes working to destroy the integrity of immigrant communities. He and others saw ethnic persistence as an imbalance or temporary stage which would be righted as the operation of social processes inevitably levelled these groups. See Robert E. Park and Herbert A. Miller, *Old World Traits Transplanted* (New York: Harper & Brothers, 1921), pp. 303–08, as well as a more recent statement

by Maurice R. Davie, "Our Vanishing Minorities," *One America*, ed. by F. J. Brown and J. S. Roucek (third ed., New York: Prentice-Hall, Inc., 1952), pp. 545–57. For a contrasting view, see Peter A. Munch, "Social Adjustment among Wisconsin Norwegians," *American Sociological Review*, XIV (1949), 780–87.

10. Cf. Louis Wirth, "Education for Survival: The Jews," *American Journal of Sociology*, XLVIII (1942–43), 682–91. For a significant development in the Yankee City Jewish community which illustrates the operation of the desire for survival, see Warner and Srole, *op. cit.*, pp. 205–17.

11. Charles F. Marden, *Minorities in American Society* (New York: American Book Co., 1952), p. 427.

12. *Ibid.*, pp. 415–16. Note that our treatment of American Jewry as constituting an *ethnic* group follows that of many present-day sociologists. In addition to Marden, see R. A. Schermerhorn, *These Our People* (Boston: D. C. Heath & Co., 1949), and Warner and Srole, *op. cit.* This designation should be taken as an approximation. We do not deny the possibility that Jews can also be studied with profit by the employment of a special category necessitated by the presence of certain features unique to the group, e.g., their intermarriage taboo and consequent endogamy.

13. I am grateful to Mark Zborowski for pointing up this factor in the course of discussions conducted about another piece of research. It is hoped that it will be fully documented and developed in a future publication.

14. In order that the Negroes may be included, some prefer the term "minority church" instead of "ethnic church." See Stanley H. Chapman, "New Haven Churches" (Unpublished Ph.D. dissertation, Dept. of Sociology, Yale University, 1942). Chyz and Lewis, on the other hand, use the term "nationality church." See Y. J. Chyz and Read Lewis, "Agencies Organized by Nationality Groups in the United States," *The Annals*, CCLXII (March, 1949), 149–53. For an analysis of some of the main distinguishing marks of the ethnic church, see Ch. I of *CJSA*.

15. Of course in the broadest sense all denominations, in contrast with sects, are descent groups. Furthermore, by distinguishing between "ethnic" and "non-ethnic" churches we mean only to imply that the non-ethnic churches represent the dominant group. Thus ultimately they are also "ethnic," and possess ethnic functions.

The classic statement of the relationship between *religio* and *ethnos* is Emile Durkheim's, *The Elementary Forms of the Religious Life*, trans. Joseph Ward Swain (Glencoe: The Free Press, 1947). Aside from the functionalists, interesting contemporary examples of the problem can be found in a historical treatment such as Salo W. Baron, *Modern Nationalism and Religion* (New York: Harper & Brothers, 1947). Another significant application is made by Werner Cahnman, "Religion and Nationality," *American Journal of Sociology*, XLIX (1943–44), 524–29.

16. Some Lutheran churches, it should be noted, exhibit ambivalence about

their ethnicity and would prefer to be identified as non-ethnic churches. See Erich C. Knorr, "The Adjustment of the Lutheran Church to Social Change in the Modern World" (Unpublished Ph.D. dissertation, Dept. of Sociology, University of Washington, 1946). On the other hand, the Jewish group may well constitute the "ideal type" in the ethnic church category. If one wishes to remain a Jew, except in certain special cases the only church to which he may belong is the Jewish one. Thus in Judaism *religion* and *ethnicity* are perfectly articulated. The following case cited by Baron illustrates the process: "The first Czechoslovak census of 1921 [revealed] that eleven residents of Prague and hundreds more throughout the country registered as belonging to the Jewish 'nationality' and the Roman Catholic 'religion'. . . . Six other Prague Jewish 'nationals' stated that they professed Protestantism or Greek Orthodoxy. The Zionists [the group which tended to de-emphasize religion by their very stress on ethnicity and who, as nationalists, might be expected to welcome everyone who was of Jewish descent] had long received with open arms Jews having no religious affiliation, but they drew the line in the case of converts to another faith." (Baron, *op. cit.*, p. 241). For a detailed analysis of Jewry as an "ideal type," see *CJSA*, pp. 27–34.

17. Robin M. Williams, Jr., *American Society* (New York: Alfred A. Knopf, Inc., 1951), p. 307. See also J. O. Hertzler, "Religious Institutions," *The Annals*, CCLVI (March, 1948), 1–13.

18. See Chyz and Lewis, *op. cit.* When an international church is resistant to special ethnic purposes, or favors one ethnic group as over against another, schisms may result. This has been the case with the Catholic Church in the United States, and may be illustrated by the relationship between the Church and the Polish-American group. While the Catholic Church in Poland had been very sympathetic to nationalistic aspirations, the Poles found that here it was controlled by the Irish. This group favored a policy of de-Polonization and discriminated against Polish priests in the making of clerical appointments above the parish level. Hence starting in 1904 we find the growth of a secessionist movement under the name of the "Polish National Independent Catholic Church."

19. H. R. Niebuhr, *The Social Sources of Denominationalism* (New York: Henry Holt & Co., 1929), pp. 223–24. Cf. Robert M. MacIver and Charles H. Page, *Society* (New York: Rinehart & Co., 1949), p. 493.

20. They will be documented in a forthcoming publication by the author and others of a study of the attitudes of some two hundred Jewish families residing in a middle-sized Eastern city.

21. *Opinion News*, V, 13 (December 25, 1945). Cf. Havemann and West, *op. cit.*, pp. 105–07. Some would doubt whether attendance at services is a valid criterion of religiosity for the Jewish group. They would hold that the home is as important as the synagogue as a *locus* of religious observance. Even if this approach were a correct one, these figures would still be highly significant.

22. Abraham G. Duker, *Outline of Comprehensive Introductory Adult Jewish Studies* (New York: American Jewish Congress) p. 25. Some significant interpretations of trends in Jewish communal life can be found in H. B. Grinstein, "Communal and Social Aspects of American Jewish History," *Publications of the American Jewish Historical Society*, XXXIX (1949–50), 267–82.

23. M. M. Kaplan in *Jewish Communal Register*, 1917–18 (New York: Kehillah of New York City, 1918), p. 122. While Kaplan stresses the factor of Jewish ethnicity in his writings, at the same time he generally compares Jews to Catholics and Protestants (see, for example, *The Reconstructionist*, XVI, 15 [December 1, 1950], 29). In addition, note Samuel Margoshes in R.A., *Proceedings*, X (1947) 261–62.

That the synagogue-centered forces in the Jewish community appeal for support on the basis of their actual or potential contribution toward bettering group relations can be gathered from the documents quoted by Rabbi Ahron Opher in *American Jewish Year Book*, XLVIII (1946–47), 133–35. As a non-Jew, MacIver's general agreement with Opher's viewpoint is particularly significant (see MacIver, *op. cit.*, passim).

24. F. S. Mead, *Handbook of Denominations in the United States* (Nashville: Abingdon-Cokesbury Press, 1951), p. 103.

25. These conclusions need to be qualified by the realization that since the end of World War II, some Jewish religious groups *have* opened field offices which assist local congregations, and that in recent years a few subsidies to congregations have been granted due to certain special circumstances. See Union of American Hebrew Congregations, *Seventy-fourth–Seventy-sixth Annual Reports* (New York: Union of American Hebrew Congregations, 1950), pp. 27, 29, 64, 256; and Young Israel, *op. cit.*

STENCE OF TRADITION:
Y IN AMERICA

It is commonly believed that Jews constitute a homogeneous group. True, there are many characteristics that they share: heritage, history, tradition, experience, and religion. At the same time, they also differ from each other. Among them are groups that speak different languages, are products of different cultures, and have different attitudes and values to which they subscribe with lesser or greater intensity and zeal.

This diversity is an extraordinary phenomenon that aids in Jewish self-preservation.[1] Diversity among Jews becomes evident as one notices the various existing religious ideologies. This diversity is particularly obvious among those who maintain and preserve traditional Jewish practices with stubborn perseverance despite the continuous Americanization process to which Jews have been exposed. Jewish life in the United States has been a continuous process of adjustment toward Americanization. Attempts to revise Jewish ritual practices and laws have mainly concentrated on bringing about a new system of religious expression that would be meaningful to the native-born American Jews.

Observers of American Judaism have mostly written about those phases of Jewish life that have been American in purpose and thought. For years non-Orthodox Jews were more articulate and they spoke in the name of Judaism. Prominent non-Orthodox Jews participated in many civic and political activities. Those Jews *ipso facto* represented the Jews before the non-Jewish world. Orthodoxy has been neglected in the literature because it did not smoothly follow a pattern of Americanization, its adherents had great difficulty in making themselves understood, it was ineffective in transmitting the culture and values to the next

Original for this volume. This study was partially supported by the Central University Research Fund, University of New Hampshire.

generation, it created an image that was mainly Eastern European in philosophy and behavior, and it was poorly organized. Until very recently Orthodox Jews were thought of as immigrants who failed to Americanize and yet continuously fed members into the Conservative and Reform camps. As it is often said, "Orthodox Jews are the fathers, Conservative and Reform are the sons."

The term Orthodoxy was applied to Jews for the first time in 1807 by the president of the Paris Sanhedrin,[2] Abraham Furtade. Later, with the advancement of Reform Judaism, "Orthodoxy" was used in a derogatory sense to differentiate between liberal Jews and Jews who were considered "backward" and filled with "affected piety."[3] Consequently, those to whom the term "Orthodox" was applied and who adhered to traditional practices resented the use of this term. In the past proponents of Orthodoxy considered Judaism to be universalistic and to include all Jews regardless of their religious participation. For them there is only one type of Judaism—the tradition that has been transmitted from generation to generation. Samson Rafael Hirsch, the outstanding leader of Orthodoxy in Germany of the nineteenth century said, ". . . Judaism does not recognize any variance. It knows of no mosaic, prophetic or rabbinic, and of no Orthodox or progressive Judaism. It either is Judaism or is not."[4]

Whatever the origin of the term and the attitudes associated with it, in contemporary Jewish life "Orthodox" refers to Jewish groups with specific patterns of belief and institutionalized behavior. Their ideology is a fundamentalistic one within the framework of a Judaic theological system. Their whole conception of the essence of Judaism is in marked contrast to those branches of Judaism that advocate a liberal viewpoint and progressive reform. Within this broad fundamentalistic framework Orthodox Jews have a common identity, however greatly they may vary in intensity, emotional involvement, personal religiosity, and commitment.

The years following World War II saw a resurgence of Orthodox Judaism and it became more visible and articulate. It was the first time in American history that second and third generation Jewish Americans followed the social and religious patterns of their parents. It was the first time that an emerging youth turned back to a way of life that their parents and grandparents had left with shame and disgust.

THE SEPHARDIM

The earliest Jewish immigrants to America were Orthodox. They were the Sephardim—Jews of Spanish and Portuguese origin who came from the Netherlands, England, and European colonies of Central and South America. The earliest Jewish settlers wanted to reestablish in the new land the same kind of life and societal norms that they had left in the old country.

The first twenty-three settlers arrived in New Amsterdam in 1654.[5] In 1656 these Spanish and Portuguese Jews obtained a piece of land for a cemetery. Although at the time they were not permitted to worship in a public synagogue, these settlers practiced their traditional religious ritual on an individual basis. They observed the Sabbath, as is indicated in a document which states, "in June 1658 two cases were brought in the municipal court against Jacob Bar Simson. He did not appear in his own defense, but no default was entered against him as the court recognized that he had been summoned on his Sabbath."[6] There are further indications that the early Jewish settlers observed traditional Jewish practices. It is cited in the writings of Benjamin Franklin that in 1723 he was employed by a printer named Samuel Keimer, whom he described as a man who "wore the long beard, and kept the Jewish Sabbath with great strictness."[7] Years later the Sephardim established synagogues in New Amsterdam (Shearith Israel, 1730); Savannah (Mikveh Israel, 1735); Charlestown (Beth Elohim, 1750); Newport (Jeshuat Israel, 1768); Philadelphia (Mikveh Israel, 1782) in which they maintained the traditional Hebrew services. Members of synagogues were expected to observe the traditional law. It has been reported:

> . . . at a meeting of the trustees of the Congregation Mikve Israel of Philadelphia, held on Sunday, the 17th of September, 1782, Mr. Jonas Philips, who occupied the chair, stated that he was informed by Mordecai M. Mordecai [that] Ezekiel Levy, contrary to our laws, had shaved on a Sabbath at Baltimore. A discussion then arose as to summoning the accused. The majority decided affirmatively, and Mr. Levy, one of the original signers of the document, who had recommended the rearing of a permanent synagogue and had continued to be a member in good standing, was made to appear.[8]

While in these synagogues the traditional ritual was practiced, many of the Sephardic Jews soon became Americanized and integrated into the larger community. "The more wealthy and influential of them were apparently accepted into the communal life of the Gentile upper class of the day. Considerable inter-marriage appears to have taken place, which led eventually to the absorption of the intermarried Jew . . ."[9]

ASHKENAZIM—REFORMED JUDAISM

In the early eighteenth century the Sephardim were followed by the Ashkenazim—Central European Jews who came from the various German states and who spoke German or Yiddish and pronounced Hebrew differently from the Sephardim. It was not essential for the Ashkenazim to form new synagogues. Since the Sephardim were the upper class, the Ashkenazim "were only too glad to join the established synagogues and thus become accul-turated Sephardim."[10] While most of the Ashkenazim who fol-lowed in the nineteenth century subscribed to traditional Jewish practices, there were among them political liberals and religious reformers. They did not long remain satisfied with the traditional Sephardic practices. They contended that the religious services of the synagogue were "long and unattractive . . . the decorum was bad. No discourse was delivered . . . and . . . no instruc-tion was offered to the congregation."[11] In 1825 in Charlestown twelve members of the congregation Beth Elohim broke away and organized the Reformed Society of Israelites.

In New York German Jews also established traditional syna-gogues (Benei Jeshurun 1830, Anshei Hased 1841, Shar Hasho-mayim 1842, Rodeph Shalom 1845). In 1843, however, religious reformers formed an organization called *Cultus Verein*, in or-der, "(1) to win for Jews a position of greater respect among their fellow citizens, (2) to enable Jews to worship with greater dignity, and (3) to attach to themselves the rising generation."[12] Two years later this organization, consisting of thirty-three members, established a congregation Emanu-El, which later be-came the famous synagogue on Fifth Avenue. In the beginning years the prayers were in Hebrew and the sermons were given in German. It was not until 1879 that the use of German was dropped completely.[13]

In 1873 Isaac M. Wise organized the traditional synagogues that had become Reformed and the newly organized Reformed synagogues into the Union of American Hebrew Congregations. Two years later this organization founded the Hebrew Union College for the training of American Reform rabbis. Reform Judaism repudiated the belief of the coming of a personal Messiah, renounced the authority of the rabbinical code, abolished the observance of the second day of the Jewish holidays, recognized women's equality in religion, introduced sermons in English, mixed choirs, the organ, the uncovering of heads during worship, and confirmation services for boys and girls.[14]

ASHKENAZIM, HASIDIM, AND CONSERVATIVE JUDAISM

The German Jews were followed by immigrants from Eastern Europe. By the 1870s and 1880s the German Jews were well organized, had established social work agencies, and were attempting to Americanize the Jews from Eastern Europe. Unlike the German Jews, Eastern European Jews did not generally join the established German synagogues. In fact the social chasm between the two groups based on cultural, social, and religious factors was extremely pronounced.

At this time a great transformation took place in Jewish life in America.

> Between 1880 and 1920, American Jewry was completely transformed. In 1880, they numbered about 250,000, approximately one half of one percent of the total population. . . . In 1920 about 3,500,000 of the 105,000,000 inhabitants of the United States were Jews—nearly 3½ percent of the population. Moreover, in 1880 the relatively small number of Jews blended with the American environment. They were members of the respectable middle-class, not too concentrated in any particular locality, and at home in the language and mores of the country. However, during the last two decades, and especially after the turn of the century, as the flood of East European immigration continued, the mass of American Jewry became conspicuous as an immigrant element. In several large cities, they lived huddled together in "ghettoes," spoke their own tongue, and perpetuated customs and ideas which appeared alien to many of their co-religionists. . . .[15]

Jews from Poland and Russia established hundreds of congregations and houses of worship most of them located on the Lower East Side of New York. According to one estimate there were 300 congregations established by Russian Jews at the turn of the century on the Lower East Side.[16]

Jews coming from small primary communities were suddenly exposed to a world where the old community control did not exist. Persons who were not satisfied with the congregation's rules or the leadership of one synagogue left and organized another congregation. New synagogues and small worship houses opened on the smallest provocations, irritations, or dissatisfactions. For example, in 1865 a group of people withdrew from the first Russian congregation and formed their own because the rabbi opposed the appointment of a particular *shochet*, a ritual slaughterer.[17]

Individuals resigned from their synagogues not only for dissatisfaction or internal politics, but also for many other reasons. People from the same European community or from the same section of a country formed their own synagogues. In these synagogues and prayerhouses they established the same religious customs and rituals as were practiced in the European communities. Persons who were able to read the "finer prints of Hebrew," although ignorant in Jewish law, became the leaders in all matters of religion. Some meager knowledge of Jewish law and a personal involvement in religious practices were prerequisites to becoming a religious adviser. In these hundreds of synagogues there was no uniformity in the observance of the ritual; there were no standards, no rules, and no clear definitions. The synagogues were established by individuals on an individual basis and the ultimate authority was in the hands of the membership. In these loosely organized houses of worship was laid the groundwork of American Jewish Orthodoxy. It emerged and grew unfettered. It did not provide a systematic arrangement for a structured and disciplined religious institution.

Out of these poorly organized congregations and a subdivided Eastern European Orthodoxy, Conservative Judaism came into being. Orthodoxy was not able to establish a community control to hold its constituents. As soon as the immigrants became Americanized they moved out of their Orthodox environment. They were neither ready nor able to join Reform Judaism, in which Protestant form of worship was highly valued, Hebrew was minimized, national sentiment was overemphasized, services were often held on Sundays, and the dietary law was characterized as "Kitchen Judaism." Eastern European Jews needed a religious expression that was rooted in the American scene, but not too far from the *shtetl*.

In the 1880s there were Reform rabbis who were dissatisfied with the extreme steps of their organization. They particularly opposed the Reform Pittsburgh Platform that stated, "We consider ourselves no longer a nation but a religious community and therefore expect neither a return to Palestine . . . nor the restoration of any of the laws concerning a Jewish state." Thus in 1887 the Jewish Theological Seminary of America was organized. The goals of the seminary were to establish and maintain a Jewish Theological Seminary for the training of rabbis and teachers, and other related purposes that might become appropriate.[18]

The purpose of Conservative Judaism was not to establish a new denomination, but to modify Orthodoxy and to bring it into consonance with patterns of American life. In fact the first president of the Jewish Theological Seminary wanted to name it, "Orthodox Seminary." The second president in 1913 organized the United Synagogue of America with the intention of uniting American Jewry. However, during the administration of the Seminary's third president, Cyrus Adler (1863–1940), the Conservative ideology became a movement and a third denomination within Judaism. In the words of Adler, "The Reform movement was showing a constantly increasing tendency to break away from Jewish history and tradition and base itself upon what it chose to call prophetic Judaism. The Orthodox party was growing more self-conscious and exhibiting the tendency to revert to the abnormal attitudes of Eastern Europe."[19]

Mordecai M. Kaplan expressed dissatisfaction with the lack of philosophy in Conservative Judaism and "devised the term 'Reconstructionism' to characterize his outlook and around it built an organization for the propagation of his ideas. The Reconstructionist Foundation is not quite a movement but it has been a force which has profoundly affected thinking within the Conservative movement . . ."[20] The Reconstructionists consider that Jewish religion has been subject to the laws and limitations of the human mind and spirit. Obedience to traditional practices and negative sanction in case of disobedience can no longer be expected to exist in the modern world. Reconstruction is not a separate entity. Basically it offers a well-articulated and clear picture of the Conservative position. In fact a great many of Kaplan's ideas and proposals have been incorporated into the mainstream of the philosophy of the Conservative movement and are no longer associated with Kaplan.

AMERICAN JEWISH ORTHODOXY

The first attempt to establish a United Orthodoxy was made in 1879, but no meeting was ever held. In 1886 a convention was held by the leaders of fifteen leading Orthodox congregations at which it was decided to organize The Association of the American Hebrew Congregations.

In the same year the Union of Orthodox Rabbis of the United States and Canada was organized. Its members consisted of rabbis who received their training and ordination in Europe. One of the major undertakings of this rabbinical organization was the supervision and enforcement of *kashrut*, the dietary law requirements in ritual slaughtering and food processing. The additional cost of *kosher* food was already looked upon with disfavor by the Orthodox consumers. The involvement of *kashrut* supervision by the many European rabbis caused even greater dissatisfaction with religion and Orthodoxy.

Despite some efforts to unify Orthodoxy, it never became amalgamated into one body. Orthodoxy remained divided organizationally, philosophically, and ideologically. Today Orthodoxy in America falls into four basic categories. The differences are based mainly upon religious observance and commitment to traditional Judaism. Religious involvement is basically manifested by the individual's selection of the type of Jewish education for his children, observance of the four fundamental rituals (i.e., Sabbath, dietary laws, ritual bath, and synagogue affiliation), and subscription to the authority of the traditional Jewish law.

Basic Categories

In contemporary America the Orthodox Jews' conception of Judaism, their relationship with other Jews, and the meaning of the world around them depend mainly upon their intensive subscription to fundamentalistic ideologies. At one extreme are those

Orthodox Jews who are basically Western in thought and behavior and to whom religion under normal circumstances may be incidental, secondary, or subordinate. At the other extreme are those who are far removed from a secularistic Western world and to whom religion is paramount in determining every conceivable behavior.

Members in Orthodox Synagogues.   These Orthodox Jews' main identification with American Jewish Orthodoxy is through synagogue affiliation. These people, in contrast to those who belong to Reform and Conservative synagogues, consider themselves and are classified by their associates as "Orthodox." Yet they do not hold a clear conceptual framework of theology or ideology of Orthodoxy that distinguishes them from other branches of Judaism. Their affiliation may be based on economic considerations,[21] proximity of the synagogue to their home, the availability of a synagogue,[22] or long family ties with a particular congregation. Some of the members do not want to leave a synagogue, but wish to change *its* affiliation to Conservative.

Subscribers to Orthodox Ideology.   This group includes those Orthodox Jews who, in addition to being members of an Orthodox synagogue, accept Orthodox ideology and responsibility in principle, although they have had no extensive religious training. While only partially conforming to religious practices, they excuse their failure to fulfill religious requirements by saying that they "cannot help themselves, because they live in a country where strict religious practices are difficult."

Members of this group consider themselves *Neo-Orthodox* or *Modern Orthodox* with a secular outlook on life. Their interests are primarily worldly and cultural rather than exclusively oriented toward the synagogue. Within the reach of their social and educational levels, like mere "members," they freely participate in activities offered by the non-Jewish community. They place greater emphasis upon the social and secular than the religious attainments of their children. While insisting on belonging to Orthodox synagogues, they make a clear distinction between the activities within the synagogue and activities outside. Religious law is not the focal point that regulates the political, social, and secular activities of the members of this group.

Despite their secular orientation, however, and in contrast to

Reform and Conservative Jews, members of this group consider themselves "traditionalist . . . hoping for some synthesis of Western thought with Jewish ancestral heritage."[23] Consequently their leaders freely interact with other non-Orthodox Jewish groups. Their rabbis hold membership in the New York Board of Rabbis, their congregations may be affiliated with the Synagogue Council of America and other organizations composed of non-Orthodox Jews. They openly advocate a "more progressive Orthodox outlook [since] Judaism never required an ostrich-like indifference to currents of thought that prevailed in the world about."[24]

Observers of the Torah and Commandments. This category includes Orthodox Jews who adhere in *principle* and *practice* to the prescribed religious behavior. This group may or may not be externally identified as Jews. They do not necessarily wear beards or sidelocks by which they would be recognized as "Orthodox." Their affiliation with religious bodies is an integral part of their way of life. Socially they associate almost exclusively with Jews of similar backgrounds and convictions, but there is no limitation to the extent of their association with others in business or professional affairs.

The members of this group tend to identify themselves by specific terms in order to distinguish themselves from non-observant Orthodox groups. They call themselves *Haredim* (literally, "God-fearing"), or *Shomrei Mitzvot* (literally, "Observers of the Commandments"), or *B'nai Torah* (literally, "sons of the Torah" or "men learned in Jewish ritual").

Usually they have had extensive religious training, having studied Jewish religious law and the meaning of ritual observances and have thereby developed positive attitudes toward strict religious observance. Their religious education has been a preparation solely for learning to behave as an observant Jew. They consider their religious training necessary for religious observance and maintain that only those Jews who have carefully studied religious law and understand the basic meaning of the ritual can observe Jewish religious practices in detail as described in the *Shulchan Aruch*, the Code of Jewish Law.

Members of this group insist that a Jew must find solutions to the problems of everyday life through the Torah, and that Judaism demands a full-time religious involvement. The more militant among them claim that there is basically but one type of Jew, the Torah Jews; and but one type of Judaism, Orthodox Judaism. They make great efforts to maintain their social and religious identity and consider the Torah and the prescription of Jewish tradition as it has come down through the ages to be the all important element in life.

Absolutists or Obgehitene Yiden.   These so-called ultra-Orthodox Jews conform strictly not only to the minute religious practices, but are also most meticulous and zealous in their observance. They observe all the commandments and precepts with the greatest care. They wear beards and special traditional clothing for the purpose of identifying themselves as Jewish; and thereby reinforce their isolation so they "may refrain from any possible sin" that might result from contact with others.

Members of this group are deeply imbued with their religious commitment. Religious ideology is strongly and inseparably interlocked with the traditional interpretation of Jewish laws and practices. In fact they fail to recognize that the religious expression of the Reform and Conservative Jews is still within the framework of Judaism. They pity Jews who do not practice traditional Judaism and deplore those who are seeking a more liberal interpretation of the traditional law.

This group includes the Hasidim.[25] They are not only externally identified and identifiable as Jews, but their external appearance serves as a symbolic criterion for social stratification. For example, the members of Class I, which is the highest in social rank, are identified by the following: *bord* and *payas*, the beard and sidelocks, which are never cut or shaved; *biber* hat, large-brimmed hat made out of beaver; *kapote*, a long overcoat, usually black, worn instead of a jacket; *shtreimel*, a fur hat made out of sable; *bekecher*, a long Hasidic coat made of silk or silky material in which the pockets are in the back; *schich* and *zochen*, slipper-like shoes and white knee socks into which the breeches are folded.[26]

Hasidim rigorously oppose any form of acculturation. Resistance to Americanization is so strong that a "sociological wall" separates this group from any activities that might encroach on its cultural stability. Even their economic activities are carried on in such a manner that they are conducive to an Hasidic way of life. The family, religious organization, social stratification, religious leadership, and all other phases of life are oriented toward the preservation of group norms, and only those patterns of behavior that reflect Hasidic values and attitudes are permitted. To them most individuals who do not belong to Hasidic groups do not meet the standards of *Yiddishkeit*, Jewish traditional principles. In fact the slightest innovation is perceived as a dangerous threat to the group's traditional way of life. For example, a member of the group complained about "modernism" among Hasidim by saying, "Just imagine how far we have gone, when our children are actively curling their sidelocks in order to have a handsome appearance."[27]

Religious Separatism

One of the major factors in the persistence of tradition is separatism. Those Jews who are more deeply involved in their religious behavior than their brethren tend to isolate themselves not only from the non-Jewish community, but also from less religiously involved Jews. There is a strong tendency among the "members" and "subscribers" to synthesize the secular values of society and religion and seek a satisfactory social relationship between Orthodox and non-Orthodox Jews. The "observers" and the "absolutists" advocate the establishment of a pronounced demarcation line between observant and non-observant Jews. Ultra-Orthodox Jews do not enter a Conservative synagogue, which does not have a "separation wall" between the men and women. Rabbis of this group refuse to officiate at a wedding ceremony with a Conservative or Reform rabbi.

Among rabbis this separatism is no longer voluntary—it has become an institutionalized pattern. Heads of ultra-Orthodox rabbinical schools issued in 1955 a "rabbinic decree" prohibiting Orthodox rabbis from holding membership in any rabbinical organization to which Conservative and Reform rabbis belong. Similarly the chief rabbi of Jerusalem issued an official prohibition in 1956 against teaching or studying in non-Orthodox rabbinical seminaries.

Prohibition against holding membership in non-Orthodox associations is based on the group's fear of assimilation—the recognition of non-Orthodox rabbis in religious decisions and policy making could gradually reduce Orthodox and non-Orthodox differences to the point that they would no longer be regarded as socially significant. A strong demarcation line is upheld in order to maintain the group's distinctiveness.

The demarcation between observant and non-observant Jews is even more pronounced among the Hasidim. The monthly bulletin of a Hasidic congregation denounces those congregations that display a Jewish flag in the synagogue. The denunciation in part reads, "The display of Israeli flags near the holy ark symbolizes atheism and the denial of the existence of God and the holiness of the *Torah*."[28]

Many ultra-Orthodox Jews consider the establishment of the State of Israel a threat to the traditional authority of the Jewish religious laws. Israel, as a national state, has policies and laws that are not based upon the *Shulchan Aruch*,[29] the code of Jewish Law. The new Jewish state and the majority of its inhabitants are not religiously observant—certainly not in an ultra-Orthodox sense. The educational system and the social institutions of Israel are based on secular concepts and not on religious principles. This presents a tremendous problem to the ultra-Orthodox, who still consider religious laws the major bonds and guiding principles for all Jews. Inasmuch as Israel and its leadership may have a strong influence on the religious behavior of the Jew, Israel may become the official spokesman of world Jewry even in matters of religion. To avoid this ultra-Orthodoxy dissociates Zionism and Israel from religion and considers the Israeli flag a "symbol of atheism and the denial of the existence of God."

Such groups isolate themselves from those who do not subscribe to the same principles. They develop homogeneity through their insistence on and enforcement of their values and attitudes. They exclude all those who do not adhere to the prescribed norms. Thus their circle shrinks and a strong line marks the group's distinctiveness. And the more intensive the religious involvement of these groups becomes, the more they try to maintain their distinctiveness and isolation.

The Educational Systems

Another vehicle to preserve tradition is religious education. Educational systems transmit the traditional culture and socialize the children in uniquely Jewish behavior. In a multigroup society even religious expressions have taken diversified forms and methods. In America each religious congregation has autonomy in directing and controlling its own affairs. Within Orthodoxy, too, there are many opposing values and observance patterns. In education, however, Orthodoxy is approaching a more systematic uniformity in religious values and observances.

In larger Jewish communities throughout the country great efforts are being made to establish the so-called Day Schools in which secular and religious subjects are given equal emphasis. Similar schools were established in Germany and Russia before World War II. In both Europe and America the purpose of the school is to combat assimilation. The major function of the Day School is to reinforce:

> Jewish distinctiveness through special emphasis on five basic aims: (1) to cultivate goodness and piety; (2) to keep alive Jewish brotherhood and fraternity; (3) to ascribe to the Torah divine revelation; (4) to maintain a feeling and sentiment of the Diaspora and consequently longing for redemption; and (5) to maintain an attachment to Israel.[30]

Orthodox religious education has taken a direction never before known in America. Schools teaching intensive religious observance have increased twentyfold in the last ten to fifteen years. According to the National Society for Hebrew Day Schools' Directory in the United States there were 17 day schools in 1935, 200 in 1956, 266 in 1962, and 303 in 1964. The 1964 enrollment in Day Schools has been established at approximately 61,000 of which 42,000 were said to be in New York City.[31]

Orthodox leadership believes that graduates of these schools will be the true participants in traditional Judaism. Although it was found that the religious observance of the graduates of these schools was not always necessarily "up to the standards of the religious observance taught by the school in which they studied, they were deeply committed to Jewish life and Jewish culture."[32]

There are four distinct educational systems, which are based upon levels of age, religious instruction, and religious observance. Within each educational system there is much variation in the intensity of religious instruction and practices. In the less religiously intense schools the major emphasis is on the Hebrew language, while in the highly intense schools the major emphasis is on ritual behavior.

Yeshiva Ketana. The "All-Day" school is attended by children at the primary age level. There are two departments, Hebrew and

English, or "sacred and secular" studies. The days are also divided into two sections; in the morning Hebrew classes are held and in the afternoon classes for English or secular studies are conducted. The child remains "all-day" in a religious atmosphere and environment.

Most of the day schools are coeducational, but stricter ones are not. Indeed in the most ultra-Orthodox Day Schools boys and girls are separated from kindergarten on. Religious standards, too, vary from school to school. Whereas most schools emphasize religious observance with a liberal outlook upon life, others insist upon a most rigid pattern of observance. Because this essay concentrates on the persistence of tradition in American Jewish Orthodoxy illustration will be drawn from the most traditional schools.

A translation of a copy of the regulations of an ultra-Orthodox Day School for girls, which parents must sign prior to registration, may illustrate some of the means through which tradition is maintained. The document reads as follows:

> With the aid of God.
>
> A COPY OF THE REGULATIONS OF THE . . . SCHOOL
>
> 1. Children from such homes in which mothers wear their own hair [i.e. whose head is not covered ritually] or whose parents go to movies or theaters or similar places are not accepted in . . . school.
>
> 2. Children who go to movies, theaters or public libraries, or read books from public libraries are not accepted in . . . school.
>
> 3. Children must conform to the rules of propriety and must wear long stockings and may not wear transparent or translucent clothing.
>
> 4. The children are not allowed to paint their nails or use lipstick.
>
> 5. The parents must pay 11 months' tuition; the same applies for kindergarten children.
>
> 6. The fathers must participate in school-sponsored parties and dinners which are conducted for the benefit of the school.
>
> 7. The parents must buy their meat, poultry, and provisions from the butcher who is under the supervision of our honored, holy rabbi, may he live long and happily, so that through the profits, the school may be financially supported.
>
> 8. The parents must see to it that the children are under strict supervision and control.
>
> 9. If a child does not comply with one of the above rules

the parents will be firmly warned to correct the error. If after warning, the child still does not observe the rules, she will be expelled from the school and the parents will be held responsible.[33]

Yeshiva Gedolah. This school system on the secondary level is attended by boys between the ages of thirteen and twenty-two. Originally these schools had the primary function of preparing students for the rabbinate, but such is no longer the case. The main stress of the school is to train and produce *observant Jews* who will follow the traditional patterns within the prescription of the Jewish law.

The basic philosophy of a Yeshiva Gedolah is described by a headmaster of such a school as follows:

> We are trying to prepare American young men to enter the world by equipping them with a religious knowledge and religious appreciation. We hope that regardless of their occupation they will become religious leaders in communities in which they settle because of their education and background. The Yeshiva Gedolah produces individuals who live by religion and whose actions are guided by our religious code. We hope that when they leave the Yeshiva, wherever they may be, they will continue to lead a religious way of life, and that they will be guarded and guided by Jewish tradition, Jewish life and religious principles.[34]

Students thus receive rigorous training, which is devoid of all possible contacts that may have a negative effect upon their religious convictions.

With regard to the curriculum of a Yeshiva Gedolah, its English program is similar to those of public high schools. It covers the seventeen units required for college entrance. The Hebrew program, however, has a strong religious orientation. The curriculum covers first and foremost Talmud, the Torah or the Five Books of Moses, Jewish law and history, the Prophets and Holy Writing, and Hebrew.

In addition to its standard curriculum the Yeshiva Gedolah tries to create a subculture with a set of social values. The transmission of these values is not done through teaching alone; many powerful social forces are also operating. There is a hierarchical social status arrangement among the student body. The two major criteria for upward mobility among students are seniority and the intensity of religious behavior. The new student soon finds out that conformity to the existing norms of the school is most important to his prestige and social acceptance.

As of 1961 there were 69 Yeshiva Gedolah schools on the junior and high school levels, 32 of which were located outside of greater New York. In 1964 there were 83 secondary schools of which 43 were located outside New York.[35] As stated earlier, the major aims of these schools are to prepare students not as religious "functionaries" but as *observing* Jews. Orthodox leaders claim that traditional Judaism in America can be preserved only through those individuals who are undergoing a Yeshiva-type education and by those who are closely associated with them.

Mesifta.   The third type of educational institution is the rabbinical school, in which, after the completion of their studies, students may receive *semicha,* or rabbinical ordination. Not all students working toward this degree intend to enter the rabbinate. Some may enter occupations related to the rabbinate, such as Hebrew teaching or religious supervision. Others may prefer to remain just "learned *baalei batim,*" lay members of a community.

There is a great diversity between the philosophies of the various rabbinical schools with regard to their students' academic education beyond high school. Out of the twelve rabbinical schools, those with modern orientation (constituency of "members" and "subscribers") demand that their graduates have college degrees and encourage their ordained men to continue with their secular training beyond the bachelor's level. The leaders of these schools claim that it has become necessary for the modern Orthodox rabbi to be educationally and intellectually equipped to meet his members on a higher level, not only in religious matters, but in secular ones as well.

Other rabbinical schools with a more traditional orientation (constituency of "observers") do not encourage, but only tolerate students' pursuing an academic education. Even this tolerance depends upon the individual student and circumstances. In some cases students are allowed to go to college only because the school faculty prefers that they go to college with their permission rather than without. In some other cases only those students are allowed to go to college who have displayed enough "God fearingness" so that college may not hurt their personal involvement in religion.

Yet the *Mesifta* schools with the most strict traditional orientation (constituency of "enthusiasts") strenuously oppose secular education beyond high school. It seems that the basic objections of religious authorities against college education are of great significance. Religious authorities do not want to cast an aura of sanctity over academic or secular institutions lest the legitimacy of their authority be jeopardized. They do not want to facilitate the individual's continuous adjustment to his secular world, which would limit the influence of religion upon him. And they do not want to sanction some of the secular social norms of the college which might place traditional and religious behavior in jeopardy.

Kolel. The study colony is basically a learning establishment on a postgraduate level for married students. Most colonies are associated with a *Mesifta* and after marriage students may enter the colony to continue their studies. These colonies are established to give dedicated students an opportunity in their early marital state to further their Talmudic studies without worries and financial difficulties. They are partially or fully supported by the *Kolel*, and receive a stipend according to their personal needs.

As of 1964 out of the twelve *Mesifta* rabbinical schools there were eight study colonies in America with approximately 215 married students. These students live with their wives and children in private dwellings and are fully integrated into the program of the school. It is estimated that 60 per cent of these students are American born.

An average student stays in the *Kolel* for about four to six years. He may then become an instructor, a headmaster, or a dean in a *Yeshiva*, rabbinical school or a *Mesifta*, but seldom does he become a practicing rabbi with a pulpit in a synagogue. Many of these students, however, after their intensive Talmudic training participate in Orthodox Jewish life even though they enter non-religious occupations.

The emphasis on higher religious education and training in religious practices for the laymen seems to be some indication of the intensification of religiosity in American Jewish Orthodoxy. Today there are many congregations in which these learned laymen, many of whom are qualified rabbis (but not functionaries), play an important role. Thus the newly established system of education is a major contributing factor to the persistence of Jewish tradition. Those who are involved in intensive religious study acquire full knowledge of appropriate religious behavior. In their various communities they become the models or proto-types of religious behavior for those who are less knowledgeable and less observant. These people in turn, who are still ultra-Orthodox in behavior, become the models for others who are still less observant than they. And so in a hierarchical order they influence the larger circle of their contacts.

Orthodox leaders claim that the lack of religious participation is not so much caused by changing conditions (although they are closely related) as by great "am-ha-aretz-ness," illiteracy in Jewish law and custom. Hence the Orthodox learning establishments help the children and the young adults to acquire the attitudes, values, knowledge, and motivation for the preservation of tradition. They try to minimize the access of nonreligious groups to and their influence on the individual. They encourage personal interaction within the group that subscribes to similar values. And most important they reduce the susceptibility to outside community pressure by training learned *baalei batim*, full-fledged participating members of the community, who have always constituted the core of traditional Jewish life.

Religious Rituals

It must be recognized that the practice of religious ritual depends upon religious identification and intensity of commitment. An Orthodox Jew is required to observe all that is prescribed in religious law, but in practice different emphases are placed upon their observance. There are four basic forms of religious behavior that constitute the main criteria for Jewish Orthodoxy. These four include: Sabbath observance; *kashrut*, traditional dietary observance; *mikva*, ritual bath; and synagogue affiliation.

Sabbath observance. This has become one of the most important indices of personal religiosity for Jewish Orthodoxy. Expressed not only by attending the synagogue service and spending the day leisurely and not partaking in work and business, it also involves a highly specialized compliance with religious law.

Appropriate observance of the Sabbath is specifically required in religious law, but religious authorities interpret the proper forms that this observance shall take. Some interpretations of the term "appropriate" go far beyond the specific law. Those following such interpretations constitute ultra-Orthodoxy and are the chief upholders of Jewish Orthodox traditions. For example, [36] in 1959 the Union of Orthodox Rabbis of the United States and Canada prohibited observant Jews from supporting Yiddish newspapers that published on the Sabbath.[37]

In addition to such extreme rabbinical injunctions and warnings, Sabbath observance is strongly pressed and demanded in all areas of community life. The merchandise of Sabbath-observing bakers is sought after in many communities in the United States. Proprietors of many types indicate their trustworthiness in matters of religion by observing the Sabbath. Many grocery stores, barber shops, gasoline stations, and clothiers have signs in the window which read, "Sabbath observer." Thus in certain neighborhoods the observance of the Sabbath is an economic advantage as well as a religious necessity.

Kashrut. Historically, supervision of *kosher* food was in the hands of the local rabbis. The local rabbi's judgment in religious matters was beyond question and was considered a sanction and a guarantee for *kashrut.* Although to a limited extent this is still the case, many circumstances have changed the role of the local rabbi with regard to his supervision of *kosher* food. First, Jews have moved into communities that did not have a rabbi. Second, the modern rabbi places less emphasis upon supervision of food. Third, *kosher* food products have been imported from outside communities, which has lessened the demand for the supervision of *kosher* food by local rabbis.

These and other conditions in American life made necessary the establishment of an organization to provide a uniformity of *kashrut* or a systematic rabbinical sanctioning and supervision of the production of *kosher* food on a national scale. The Union of Orthodox Jewish Congregations of America, in cooperation with the Rabbinical Council of America, established a Department of Kashrut to coordinate and direct the activities of the supervising rabbis in various food industries and to sanction food and other related products for Jewish consumption.

The great expansion of supervision and certification of food and its allied products in America may not necessarily be an indication of greater religious involvement. It may be due to modern marketing techniques and to the popularization through advertising of *kosher* food among non-Jewish consumers. It is quite possible that *kosher* consumption today is more a demand for a particular type or quality of food. *Kosher* food is not necessarily purchased by observant Jews alone. Nonobservant Jews purchase *kosher* food as a form of identification with Jewish culture, or they may eat *kosher* food simply because they have become accustomed to it.

On the other hand, the expansion of supervision and certification of *kosher* food products may very well be an indication of religious intensification as evidenced by religious adjustment to modern technology of food processing in America. Modern food processing was not known to Jews in Europe. New methods of producing food invited certain doubts in the minds of *kosher* food consumers and it became necessary to provide rabbinic sanction for doubtful items. Because of the complexities involved in today's food production and the possible inclusion of non-*kosher* ingredients such as emulsifiers or stabilizers, there is a need for a "religious guarantee" for certain food items. This is provided by the Union of Orthodox Jewish Congregations and is claimed to be a public service.

The requirements of personal observance and religious commitment narrows the circle of observant Jews. Those Jews continue to identify and associate with those whose requirements in *kashrut* are similar. In addition, insistence upon dietary observance with an intensity of commitment that leads to greater and greater demands for the strict observance of the dietary requirements is another major factor in the persistence of tradition.

Mikvah. Another basic criterion for Jewish Orthodoxy is the observance of the ritual bath by the women. *Mikvah* literally means "gathering"; specifically it means the "gathering of waters." Traditionally it refers to a ritual bath built according to rabbinic specifications. The initial source of the water must be natural and not drawn by vessel. Its source must be either a natural spring, rain, or water obtained from natural ice. Other water may be added once the minimal amount of the *mikvah* requirements have been met. The basic law is derived from Leviticus 18:19 that deals with the prohibition against intercourse during the wife's monthly period and requires subsequent to the latter a ritual cleansing in a *mikvah*.

The observance of the *mikvah* was always considered one of the basic rituals in Jewish life. Jewish law still requires that no

Jews shall reside in places where there is no *mikvah*. It is permitted to sell a synagogue in order to build a *mikvah*. According to Jewish law when a community has insufficient means with which to provide a synagogue, a Torah, and a *mikvah*, the last takes precedence over the other two. A synagogue or a Torah scroll may even be sold to provide funds for the *mikvah*.[38]

The Spero Foundation of New York periodically publishes a booklet called *Jewish Family Life, the Duty of the Woman*. It lists in the United States, as of 1963, 161 *mikvahs* in 39 states and 124 communities. (In addition it gives the names and addresses of all the known ritual baths in the world.)[39] Many new ritual baths have been built in communities throughout the United States in recent years. There were many ritual baths before, owned and operated by private bathowners. Many were set up in established Turkish and Russian baths. Today *mikvah* associations are established on a community level among those interested and participating in the ritual and they are independent of any commercial establishment. A board of trustees heads the organization and there is a dues paying membership. The baths are tended by women who are familiar with the necessary ritual and can be trusted to carry it out.

Again participation in these activities of establishing and building the new ritual baths and attending and observing the associated ritual narrows the circle of Jewish Orthodoxy to the point that only participants are considered truly Orthodox. Among these Orthodox Jews the ties are strong and the cohesiveness of the community is maintained. A truly Orthodox couple may travel to any community in which there is a ritual bath, call the person who is in charge of it, and tell him that the bath is required and without any further introduction a tie is established. There seems to be a specific language of communication based on common familiarity with religious Orthodoxy and similar styles of life. The observance of the ritual bath is truly a most effective factor in the perpetuation of tradition.

Synagogue affiliation.   Another area of Orthodox Jewish identification is affiliation with religious congregations. An Orthodox house of worship is defined as a permanent place specifically designated for public worship by at least ten adult Jews. Because Orthodox synagogues are not required to affiliate with a national organization, it is difficult to establish the number of Orthodox houses of worship in America. However, the leaders of the Union of Orthodox Jewish Congregations estimate the number of Orthodox synagogues in America to be approximately 3,000.

A variety of types of houses of worship must be distinguished in order to understand the functions and affiliations of contemporary Orthodoxy. A synagogue is a building that has been specifically designed or built as a sanctuary. It is externally and internally identifiable as a house of worship, and is formally associated with a religious congregation. It has an elected board of trustees and a number of officers. The organization engages a rabbi and perhaps one or more other religious functionaries such as a cantor, a *shamos*, or sexton. Membership ranges from about 75 to 500 families.

The *Bet Hamidrash* is a place either built or remodeled for religious learning and used for regular public worship. Most of these are associated with religious schools. A *Bet Hamidrash* is not organized as a religious congregation but is usually maintained by supporters of the school. It does not have a rabbi but one of the rabbinical instructors in the school may function as such during public worship.

The *Stibl* is a house or a room that has been remodeled into a house of worship. There are four types:

1. The *Stibl* that is formally organized by a religious congregation with voting members. It employs a rabbi in order to attain a congregational status and a possibility for growth through popular appeal in the larger community. This type of *Stibl* may be the beginning of an established synagogue if the neighborhood in which it is located continues to attract Orthodox Jews.

2. A *Stibl* loosely organized by a religious congregation that has fewer organizational characteristics and does not employ a rabbi. It relies upon the religious training of its members, some of whom may be learned in Talmud and are qualified to perform in matters of religion.

3. A *Stibl* that is not organized by a congregation but is owned by a rabbi. Its earnings are those of the rabbi. He maintains the place and owns the building and everything in it. All social transactions are on a personal basis between individuals and the rabbi.

4. A *Stibl* loosely organized by a congregation named for an Hasidic rebbe. It is so named because its constituents identify themselves as followers of the rebbe or as having the type of worship of that specific rebbe.

The *Minyen* is not a place necessarily designated or constructed for public worship. It is temporarily set up so that a minimum of ten adult Jews can meet for religious services. For example, in New York many religious Jews who live in apartment houses do not use the elevator on the Sabbath. Consequently they maintain a *minyen* in an apartment on one of the central floors of the building. There are other such arrangements on a daily basis as well. This type of religious worship may go on for years on a temporary basis or it may develop into a *Stibl*. It has neither religious functionary nor a corporate body, but usually a person volunteers to take charge of the services.

A truly Orthodox synagogue must have a *mechitzah*, separation wall, to keep men and women apart during religious services. According to all Orthodox authorities, synagogues must have this separation wall for, without one, it has no sanctity as a house of worship.

There is great diversity in the qualifications necessary for membership in various Orthodox synagogues. In some synagogues one only needs to be a Jew. In Hasidic synagogues one must pledge that he will not have television or radio in his household. Whereas in some synagogues only the officers must be Sabbath observers, in others all members must be beyond question or doubt in their personal religious commitment. Orthodox Jews seek affiliation with synagogues in which the members are of similar backgrounds and ideology and subscribe to similar religious requirements and behavior. The degree of one's religious commitment can be indicated by the synagogue in which one holds membership. For example, when two Orthodox Jews meet and try to find out each other's level of Orthodoxy, one will inquire, "In what *shul* do you *daven?*" or "In what synagogue do you pray?" Membership in a particular house of worship will be indicative of the values, attitudes, and general range of one's religious observance.

The obligation and commitment to observe the religious rituals places upon the truly Orthodox Jew not only social but physical limitations as well. Under normal circumstances Orthodox Jews will not live in communities where they could endanger the possibility of observing their religious rituals. Orthodox Jews must take occupation where they can observe the Sabbath, must live in communities where *kosher* food is accessible or available, must live where there is a *mikvah*, must live where there is an

Orthodox synagogue that subscribes to traditional practices, and must live where there is a religious day school.

For these reasons and for the fact that religious and social norms are enforced better within a community whose members adhere to similar values, Orthodox Jews in America live mainly in communities where either a *mikvah* or a religious day school or both are available. Obtaining *kosher* meat is no longer a grave problem because it can be imported from New York. In communities where there is a greater Orthodox concentration the insistence on having and maintaining traditional facilities is strong. Consequently new facilities are established to fulfill expanding religious needs.

There are Orthodox communities in about 39 states and in 146 cities. The truly Orthodox, however, concentrate in relatively few cities. In addition to greater New York, including Brooklyn, Manhattan, Queens, and Long Island, the truly Orthodox are gaining religious strength in Baltimore, Boston, Chicago, Cleveland, Detroit, Los Angeles, Philadelphia, and the Spring Valley-Monsey region of New York. It is, however, most difficult to establish the actual number of Orthodox Jews in America. All estimates available are highly inadequate, and range from 675,889[40] to 3.5 million.[41]

The Halacha—Fountainhead of Authority

Perhaps one of the most important single principles associated with the persistence of tradition is continuous submission to the strong authority of the *halacha*.[42] *Halacha* in Jewish life is what may be called in Talcott Parsons' terms the "fountainhead of authority beyond which there is no appeal."[43] It is that authoritative compilation of Jewish law, which is the " 'correct doctrine' [and which] is assumed not to be dependent on any human will, but to be infallibly specific and definite, with a clearly authorized human agency for its implementation."[44]

Throughout history Jews who have valued the continuity of traditional Jewish life have regarded the *halacha* as the authoritative prescription for everyday behavior and the guiding principle of life in general. Social changes, community conditions, internal pressures, and the utilization of new inventions and technology have had to be sanctioned through the application of *halacha* by the religious authorities of the time.

Today as Orthodox Jews become more exposed to a non-Jewish culture the consultation of *halacha* seems to occupy a more prominent place. For example, college students, members of Yavneh, an Orthodox student organization, explained that all their secular activities are in line with *halacha*. When these young men were asked in an interview to discuss their dating habits, they explained that according to *halacha* one must get married, and in American society it is through dating that a man finds a woman for marriage. Dating is not only permissible, they said, but actually it constitutes a quasi-religious activity that may lead them to an even greater religious end, marriage. The question is not to what extent this is the case, nor to what extent they are molding their lives to *halacha* or *halacha* to life. The point is that these Orthodox students with a Yeshiva background deem it necessary to justify their behavior according to *halacha*.

Halachik involvement on a more sophisticated level can be seen in the activities of the Association of Orthodox Jewish Scientists. In 1948 a number of young Orthodox Jews engaged in the physical and biological sciences formed an organization called the Association of Orthodox Jewish Scientists. The organization as of 1962 had approximately 330 members in chapters in various American cities and in England. The main function of the organization is:

> to promote the orientation of science within the framework of Orthodox Jewish tradition; to obtain and spread information relating to the interaction between the traditional way of life (*halachah*) and scientific developments; to interest and assist Orthodox Jewish youth in the study of science.[45]

A brief analysis of the orientation of this group is necessary in order to understand the intensity of its religious commitment, on the one hand, and its scientific pursuits and interests, on the other. The policy of the organization in promoting science within the framework of Orthodox Jewish tradition is not only to attempt to prevent the interference of science with religious observance. On the contrary they consider science an instrument through which religion can be understood. An Orthodox Jewish scientist writes:

> Science [is] a tool for the study and development of *halacha*. It has long been recognized that many *halachic* problems require for their solution, and at times even for their useful formulation, a considerable degree of specialized scientific or

> technical knowledge . . . the value of science to the *hala-khist* goes considerably beyond its use as an aid in understanding the cases which *halakhah* treats. . . . When the *halakhist* attempts to formulate *halakhic* principles by generalizing from existing precedents, or to decide new cases by applying established principles, he runs a serious risk of basing his generalizations and decisions on superficial resemblances between the precedents and/or the new cases if he does not have a proper understanding of certain scientific fundamentals.[46]

The leadership of the organization expresses a desire to be of great service to *halachik* authorities and considers it a duty to aid rabbis in making religious decisions. In addition to a medical-dental committee whose responsibility is to make doctors aware of the existence of and the possible solution to many religious problems that arise in the course of medical practice, the organization has established a *Halacha* and Science Committee, offering a consultation service to rabbis in connection with traditional religious questions requiring scientific knowledge relating to *halacha*.

In addition to showing that science and Orthodoxy are not necessarily contradictory, the group also aims to offset the impact of secularism among Orthodox youth. Even religious leaders who openly oppose college training for Yeshiva boys recognize the great difficulty in holding back the more worldly from college. Since Orthodoxy did not stop youth from entering colleges, it joins them at the campuses. The Association of Orthodox Jewish Scientists appeals to the Orthodox youth not to be blinded by the great glamour science holds today, but to "synthesize" science with religion.

In the past when the Talmudic student left Torah learning and entered the universities there was no one there to make this appeal. Consequently he abandoned his religious practices as he acquired academic knowledge. Today Orthodox scientists attempt to offset the great secular influence and to draw a strong relationship between *halacha*, traditional religious practices, and scientific knowledge.

It can be seen that even in contrasting spheres, such as science and religion, *halacha* is the authority by which behavior of the religious Jew must be guided and justified. Fundamental to the acceptance of *halacha* is the position of the *posek*, which complements, supports, and reinforces it.

The *posek*, interpreter of *halacha*, is the renowned Torah scholar, held in high esteem and honor. He enjoys international fame. His decisions on religious matters are subject for conversation, study, and controversy in religious communities throughout the world. He is respected and recognized, even if not followed by all, as "The Torah Authority of Our Time." As an expression of reverence, homage is paid to him after his death. For example, the funeral of Rabbi Aaron Kotler, an outstanding Talmudic authority, who died on November 29, 1962, was attended by 25,000 people on the Lower East Side of New York.

The *halacha* and the *posek* constantly reinforce each other. The *halacha* remains authoritative because the interpreter uses it as the basis for his interpretation. On the other hand the interpreter remains in an authoritative position because the *halacha* reinforces his decisions. The continuous consultation of the *halacha* and seeking answers on *halachik* principles as to what is "religiously appropriate," is in fact a major aspect of the persistence of tradition. The *halacha* is sought for permission and endorsement; it is studied for recommendations; it is searched for approval; it is asked for advice; it is consulted for suggestions; it is begged for sanctions and license. It is the basis to which the religious Jew can relate his everyday life and from which he can draw meaning and an orderly schema in an otherwise confusing social system.

THE FUTURE OF AMERICAN ORTHODOXY

Some of the underlying social and religious factors that contribute to the maintenance of a seemingly strong ethnic tradition have been described. Religious separatism enables the group to develop as a more or less homogeneous unit, reinforces its isolation, and narrows the circle of the group to those adhering to traditional observance. The educational system socializes the children to accept traditional values and to conform to the traditionally prescribed behavior. Ritual, the exercise of religion, provides a quality of sacredness and reinforces attitudes and values. The *halacha*, supported and sustained by the *posek*, is the religious Jew's guide in all his adjustment processes in a continuously changing social system.

The increasing intensity of religious observance in recent years has narrowed Orthodox Jews into their own camp. A strong division is emerging between observant and nonobservant Jews. It is highly probable that the term "Orthodox" as a designation for religious Jews may lose its meaning. The term may only indicate local or national organizational affiliation. The major consideration in one's identification with Judaism will be to what extent does one follow traditional Jewish practices. Distinctions between one Jew and another will not be based so much on ideology, theology, and faith as on behavior. The question will be *what* and *how much* does one do in terms of being Jewish? Activities that are not related to Jewishness cannot distinguish one Jew from another. Only activities that are fully Jewish, such as the observance of the major rituals, will distinguish one Jew from another.

It does not seem that in a democratic society, in the United States, Jews will be completely separated from each other. There will always be many areas of common interest (i.e., Israel, charities, social welfare, anti-Semitism, etc.). However, with regard to marriage, social and religious interaction will take place only among those whose subscription to religious patterns are similar. There will be closer ties between Conservative and Reform Judaism on philosophical, ideological, and behavioral levels. There will be closer ties between Conservative and nonobservant Orthodox Jews. These groups will try to change the religious rites, rituals, philosophy, and ideology of Judaism in order to bring them in concert with the American culture.

The "ultra," or the "truly Orthodox," groups who isolate themselves from the larger community and thereby maintain a "world of their own" are less likely to imitate the manners and customs of the larger society. Those groups that adhere and practice the traditional ritual and whose life is fully absorbed in being Jewish are less likely to become indifferent to religion. These groups among the Orthodox Jews will continue to regard themselves as struggling for existence in a "foreign land" and a "foreign culture." In their struggle for survival they will resort to their *own* groups and fellow members, their *own* organizations and institutions, for comfort and encouragement.

It is not difficult to predict that Jews and Judaism will survive as they have throughout the ages. True, many will leave and become assimilated. Many will change their patterns of living so that their religious practices will no longer resemble traditional

Judaism. Jews of the "ghetto" and those who keep close contact with them will provide the continuity linking the past to the future.

NOTES

1. Elias Canetti, *Crowds and Power* (New York: Viking, 1962), p. 178.
2. In 1807 Napoleon appointed a Jewish religious court, consisting of 71 members, of rabbis and laymen, to consider questions of relationship between Jews and the state. See Sidney B. Hoenig, *The Great Sanhedrin* (1953).
3. Herman Schwab, *The History of Orthodox Jewry in Germany* (London: The Mitre Press, 1950), p. 9.
4. Quoted in Samson Rafael Hirsch, *Die Religion im Bunde mit dem Fortschritt, Von einem Schwarzen* (Frankfurt am Main, 1854).
5. David and Tamar DeSola Pool, *An Old Faith in the New World* (New York: Columbia University Press, 1966), p. 3.
6. *Ibid.*, p. 32.
7. John Bach MacMaster Series, "Benjamin Franklin—American Men of Letters" in Henry Samuel Morais, *The Jews of Philadelphia* (Philadelphia: The Levytype Co., 1895), p. 11.
8. "Sabato Morais, Mikve Israel Congregation of Philadelphia," *Publications of the American Jewish Historical Society*, 1893, Vol. 1, pp. 13–24.
9. Milton M. Gordon, *Assimilation in American Life* (New York: Oxford University Press, 1964), p. 183.
10. E. Digby Baltzell, *Philadelphia Gentleman* (New York: Free Press, 1958), p. 276.
11. Samuel S. Cohen, "Reform Judaism in America," in Theodore Freedman and Robert Gordis, eds., *Jewish Life in America* (New York: Horizon Press, 1955), pp. 75–76.
12. *Ibid.*
13. *Ibid.*
14. David Philipson, "Reform Judaism," *The Jewish Encyclopedia* (New York: Macmillan, 1907), Vol. 10, pp. 358–359.
15. Oscar I. Janowsky, *The Jewish Welfare Board Survey* (New York: Dial Press, 1948), p. 239.
16. J. D. Eisenstein, "The Beth Hamedrash Hagadol," *The History of the First Russian American Jewish Congregation*, publications of the American Jewish Historical Society.
17. Eisenstein, *op. cit.*
18. Mordecai Waxman, *Tradition and Change—The Development of Conservative Judaism* (New York: Burning Bush Press, 1958), p. 8.
19. Cyrus Adler, "The Standpoint of the Seminary," in Waxman, *op. cit.*, p. 181.
20. Waxman, *op. cit.*, p. 211.

21. Membership dues in Orthodox synagogues are usually less than in Conservative and Reform congregations.

22. In some communities only Orthodox synagogues are found.

23. Emmanuel Rackman, "American Orthodoxy—Retrospect and Prospect," *Judaism*, Vol. 3 (Fall 1954), pp. 1–8.

24. *Ibid.*

25. Hasidism is a pietistic movement that originated in the eighteenth century among the Jews of Eastern Europe. The founder of the movement was Israel Baal Shem Tov who emphasized zeal, prayerful devotion, and humility as a religious expression. The disciples of Baal Shem Tov and their children, grandchildren, and great grandchildren, the *Tzadik-im* (righteous) or *Rebbes* (masters of rabbis) became leaders of Hasidic communities throughout Eastern Europe. Some of these *Rebbes* came to the United States after World War II and established Hasidic congregations and communities. See Solomon Poll, *The Hasidic Community of Williamsburg* (New York: Free Press, 1962).

26. *Ibid.*, pp. 66–68.

27. From the files on informant UL9, data collected for a work in progress on American Jewish Orthodoxy.

28. *Mitteilung*, Congregation . . . No. 3, 1965. Translated from Yiddish.

29. The *Shulchan Aruch* is the compendium of Jewish Rabbinic Law by Joseph be Ephraim Caro (1488–1575), the greatest Talmudic authority of the sixteenth century. It has been considered ever since the most authoritative code of Jewish Law.

30. Elijahu Kitov, "Chinuch Goals for the Yeshiva Ketana," *Hamenahel*, National Conference of Yeshiva Principals, New York, 1962, pp. 3–4.

31. *Torah Umesorah*, National Society for Hebrew Day Schools Directory, 1965.

32. George Pollak, "The Graduates of Hebrew Day Schools," unpublished Ph.D. dissertation, Western Reserve University, 1961.

33. From the original document, translated from Yiddish.

34. From an interview with the headmaster of Yeshiva . . .

35. See National Society for Hebrew Day Schools Directory. It must be noted again that not all of these schools are of the caliber described in the text.

36. The examples given are somewhat far removed from the ordinary observances of the Sabbath. They, however, illustrate the extreme conception of the involvement of religious ritual.

37. *Der Yid*, September 18, 1959.

38. Naftali Zevi, *Meshiv Davar*, Berlin, p. 145.

39. Sidney B. Hoenig, *Jewish Family Life, the Duty of the Woman*, 9th rev. ed. (New York, 1963), pp. 65–76.

40. *American Jewish Yearbook*, 1965.

41. Leaders of the Union of Orthodox Jewish Congregations in America.

42. "The formularization and standardization of Halacha became the chief activity of Jewish study, and probably before the fall of the Temple there was in existence a body of Halachat covering the whole field of

the Oral Law." See Valentine's *Jewish Encyclopedia*, A. son and A. N. Silverman, eds. (London: Shapiro, Valent. pany, 1938), p. 262. See also Z. H. Chajes, *The Students' Gu. the Talmud* (New York: Philip Feldheim, Inc., 1960), p. 4.

43. Talcott Parsons, *Essays in Sociological Theory* (New York Press, 1958), p. 376.
44. *Ibid.*
45. From the Constitution of the Association of Orthodox Jewish Scientists.
46. Azriel Rosenfeld, "Halacha and Science—Areas of Interaction," *Intercom*, Vol. 4:2 (October 1961), p. 3.

ISH RELIGIOUS UNITY:

RDECAI M. KAPLAN

SEYMOUR SIEGEL

THE THEME of this symposium is somewhat difficult to define. My own—awkward—working title, arrived at after much deliberation, was finally formulated as: "What Are the Foundations for the Future Religious Unity of the People of Israel?" Let me explain what I mean.

All of us are, in one way or another, and to one degree or another, committed to the people of Israel and to the faith of the people of Israel. All of us feel a very strong commitment of love and of obligation to both. Out of this commitment to the people and to the faith of Israel—leaving the definition of these terms, for the time being, as flexible as possible—arises for all of us, in many different ways, a very strong desire to advance the unity of the people of Israel in and outside of the State of Israel. This is so for a number of reasons, the most obvious one being that we hope in that way better to be able to perform our tasks in history and before the Holy One, blessed be He. To put it simply, I think that the theme of our discussion this afternoon is—*ata echad v'shimcha echad, umi ke'amcha yisrael goi echad ba'aretz*— "Thou art One and Thy name is One, and who is like unto Thy people Israel, a singular people on earth."

Now, obviously, the unity of the people of Israel is, at the present moment, not a factual reality. Nor is it a reality theologically, religiously, organizationally, politically, geographically, and in any number of other ways. It is a goal. (I ought to emphasize perhaps, at this early stage of the proceedings, that however we may eventually come to define "the unity of Israel," that

Reprinted by permission of the authors and the publisher from *Judaism*, 15 (Spring 1966), pp. 133–150. Introductory remarks by Steven S. Schwarzchild. Copyright 1966 by the American Jewish Congress.

phrase means to none of us anything even distantly similar to the *uniformity* of Israel or the *homogeneity* of the people or of the faith.)

In view of such considerations, another way of posing our question would be to ask: With respect to the unity of Israel, how do we get from where we are to where we want to go? How do we get from our present divisions and divisiveness, and often even acrimony, to some kind of eventual serviceable Jewish unity? What resources do we possess, religious resources especially, that we may utilize in order to achieve our goal?

In connection with this, let me say, too, that all of us hope and expect that our discussion this afternoon will stress all the positive factors that we can possibly find, and all the positive programs that we can possibly put forward—though we understand, of course, that a certain amount of candid self and mutual criticism is unavoidable. We hope, however, that such criticism will be kept within the larger frame of reference of the positive goals which we want to pursue. . . .

We have therefore asked four men, from divergent institutional and organizational, as well as personal and ideological, backgrounds, to discuss the problem at hand. All are personal friends and close associates. All have shared many significant and even path-setting Jewish experiences, and all are, in one way or another, significant on the Jewish scene. I think we shall promptly discover that they even share some operative and very effective theological orientations with one another. . . .

IRVING GREENBERG

The question, "Can there be one religious Judaism in America?" makes sense only on certain levels of discourse. On the institutional level, every law of organization and bureaucratic systems and the loyalty of their participants suggests that it is a futile or premature question. To the extent that there are people willing to overcome existing lines, they are, for the most part, people who do not care. A unity based on such a consideration would be spurious. It would be a reprise of the old saw about interfaith dinners: a Jew who does not believe in Judaism meets a Christian who does not believe in Christianity and they find that they have much in common.

Furthermore, the denominational lines are not without pragmatic value. Jews who would never sit through an Orthodox service may find that the Conservative synagogue gives them the type of participation which they desire. A Jew who wishes to marry a divorced woman who has no *get* [a bill of divorcement] or a non-Jewess who does not wish to convert may find a Reform rabbi who will perform the ceremony. Thus he will identify his marriage and home as Jewish although he otherwise would not have done this. If, then, there are real advantages in institutional pluralism, the question of unity must be posed on a different level altogether.

Let me also, for brevity's sake, state the other major assumption which informs my paper. Jewish survival, and unity, merely on a biological level is probably both useless and hopeless. The historical fact of the rapid universalization of culture and the disappearance of ethnic groups and the sociological fact of American culture's high receptivity to the persistence of religious communities and its low tolerance for ethnicism coincide with the central theological affirmation of the tradition: "The Lord did not set His love upon you, nor choose you, because ye were more in number than any people . . ." (*Deut.* 7:7). We were chosen not for our numbers or success or brains and, certainly not, for our power but rather, as God's singled out people. And these are the only people who survived the "Long Trek" of Jewish history. "But ye that cleave unto the Lord your God are alive every one of you this day" (*Deut.* 4:4). This recognition is growing among Conservative and Reform ideologists as well. If anything, the tradition is more "modern" and "liberal" in that it places a greater premium on the secular Jew's mere existence—for there can be no Judaism without Jews. It therefore sees in the secular Jew, *qua* Jew, a value and a statement. Even though the Jew may be in flight from his calling as a Jew, he testifies—if only in fierce rejection of certain values rather than in affirmation of his own tradition. What then is the good that asks us to seek for religious unity?

We are the generation of Job. Shattering experience has piled so closely upon shattering experience that we have been unable to respond. Three watershed experiences of Jewish history have rolled over us—the completion of the Westernization of Jewry, the European Holocaust, and the rebirth of the State of Israel. The first experience—Westernization—created the denominational, ideological and institutional lines which divide Jewry. It is a measure of our hard-heartedness and routinization as well as of the fundamental numbness which has clutched at us from such devastating blows that the Holocaust has not undone these lines. Surely the implications of Holocaust have shattered every conventional position in the Jewish community from left to right and demonstrated, by and in affliction, that we are deeply united in faith and destiny.

The experience of building—the unbelievable fact of Israel reborn—has equally overtaxed our capacity to understand and respond. With the exception of such secular Messianists as Ben-Gurion (who comes close to converting the fruits of this redemption into another idolatry), the entire community has seen the experience through the eyes of convention. Religious and nonreligious Jews alike have comprehended the event in purely naturalistic terms—thus tacitly denying that the redeeming hand of God in history (the awareness which has animated living Jewry since Abraham) is still operating.

No preceding generation lived through experiences fractionally as powerful as these without releasing powerful Messianic movements. The recognition that the surface of reality was breaking up released a vast yearning for deliverance from a world whose normal set presupposes the indefinite persistence, if not dominance, of evil, division and disharmony. Our own policy reflects the extent to which contemporary culture has gotten us to enter totally into it. We play roles wholly circumscribed within its universe of discourse so that the tyranny of its thought categories and institutional alignments has repressed our hopes for redemption.

After such experiences in the past, Jews proclaimed that the *status quo* of evil and the failures of man and society was not as enduring or as unassailable as it tricked men into thinking. It is true that this yearning often led to surrender to false Messiahs and facile solutions. But it may be that those Jews were more rational and perceptive than we are. For they were wrong for the right reasons and we are right for the wrong reasons—to wit, routine, the tyranny of modern categories and sheer lack of feeling. And we have persisted, despite the fact that our bankruptcy increasingly stares us in the face.

Nevertheless, we are seeing now the first signs of thaw. There is an unmistakable beginning of ferment in all groups—what the classical tradition would call a *hirur t'shuva*—a hesitation and a weighing of the possibility of turning from the present path so that we may live. This very symposium is laughable unless we consider this question through the eyes of a yearning for redemption rather than the categories of institutional realities. The historical experiences of our generation which have burned themselves deep into the psyche of every Jew now come to the surface. They animate the dream which haunts us today. In this spirit, I would like to suggest some things that all of us, and Orthodoxy in particular, can do to bring closer the possibility of ultimate unity. We must keep in mind, however, that this is a unity which, on one level, already exists. It is the unavoidable implication of the impact of the Holocaust and the policies under which it was carried out on the one hand and the anticipation of redemption which Israel raises on the other. Our task is to buy time for these implications to permeate the community and to speed the process.

There are two immediate crises which must be surmounted to keep open the door of ultimate unity and they should be mentioned first.

One is the problem of marriage and divorce. Some time ago, out of rejection of Halachah [the part of Jewish literature which deals with religious ethical, civil, and criminal law] and with little evaluation of the specific results that would follow in this area, the Reform rabbinate (almost in its entirety) and the Conservative rabbinate (in substantial part) and many secular Jews gave up *gittin* and conversion procedures which could be acquiesced in by Jews who take Halachah seriously. Now the rising divorce and remarriage, intermarriage and assimilation rates are creating the real possibility that Halachically loyal Jews will be unable to intermarry with this segment of the Jewish people. Aside from the psychic and religious wounds that such a situation will open, this will condemn the bulk of the Jews to eventual assimilation. And they will undoubtedly take a number of committed Jews with them, for love rules paramount in our society. These people are not so committed that they will restrict their marriages. The further alienation which their Halachically pariah status will induce, as well as the removal of the influence of more committed Jews, clearly suggests that many, if not most, will be lost. Yet in all three religious groups there are few or no serious attempts to deal with the issue. Orthodox Jews, often in insulting manner, appeal to non-Halachic rabbis to observe the law. I have heard such rabbis, in turn, ridicule the whole outdated machinery.

The only step that can buy time is a massive effort that would override institutional concerns out of a spirit of desperate concern to save what can be saved. The non-Halachically observant elements should ask themselves whether they are prepared to push procedures which they do not fully subscribe to for the sake of making future unity and Jewish intermarriage possible. The Halachic elements for their part have to extend themselves to make these procedures acceptable. This means exploring the full range of the Halachah to eliminate situations like *agunot* [permanent "widowhood" as in the case of a missing husband], husbands who abuse their superior rights in the *get* process, brothers who take advantage of *chalitza* [religious ceremony by which obligation to marry brother's childless widow is annulled], etc. The very Beth Dins [rabbinical courts] available in Orthodox circles are all generally culturally and aesthetically offensive to non-Orthodox Jews. Nor are there sufficient reliable, legal and financially reasonable Beth Dins available. A joint fund should be raised to underwrite the availability of proper and acceptable Beth Dins. The Halachic Jews must train men who can perform these procedures in intellectually and culturally appealing terms. Perhaps a ceremony in which the referring rabbi can participate should be created. In this way he will not be stopped from urging his people to use these procedures by the fact that he knows he will be "humiliated" by the attitude and exclusion of the Halachists. True, the Halachists risk "legitimating" a rabbi and a position which destroys theirs. But the others equally extend themselves by involving themselves in a process which otherwise they would not respect. The risk on both sides is dictated by the overriding demands of *knesset yisrael* [the Jewish community].

The second crisis grows out of the emergence of new leadership and trends within denominations. All three groups are on the brink of a shift in leadership. The old leadership was a generation of the desert—either too rooted in European or previous models or too impressed with Americanism, or both. In Orthodoxy, the traditionalist group, in recent years has emerged—aggressively assertive, Americanized, or, at least, much less impressed with Americanism. Their economic and social advances have made them more willing to be unequivocal and unyielding. In Con-

servatism, the young Turks are no longer "guilty Orthodox."
They are recruited from American cultural homes, frequently
homes with little or no ancestral Jewishness. The feeling of
obligation or awe for the "old tradition" or for those who seem
to uphold the "full tradition" is absent or even offensive to them.
In Reform there is both a critical rethinking and an even more
thoughtless and aggressive affirmation of secular liberalism in the
younger generation. It may well be that the new leaderships will
be more communicative and that we will see the end of gastronomic and sentimental Judaisms and all their ilk. It may well be
that the new leadership will be more radical and searching in its
formulations. This is all to the good. Surely the current nostalgia
which is the cement of the American Jewish community will
hardly stand a generation or two more of the corrosive acids of
modernity, college, etc. Nevertheless, the fact is that significant
institutional restraints have been lifted. The result may well be an
attempt at *Gleichschaltung* [equalization], with each group's
leadership attempting to eliminate the inconsistencies and concessions of the past. The net result will be an increased partisanship
and even bitterness which will be unwilling to make *ad hoc*
concessions.

Rabbi Soloveitchik once pointed out that Sodom and Gomor-
rah were destroyed, according to *midrash* [commentary on the
biblical texts], after they appointed Lot as a judge of the city.
The question is: Why should such evil cities be destroyed only
when they finally elected an honest judge? His answer was that
the laws had always been crooked and vicious. The one saving
grace was that the judges were corrupt and could be bribed not
to execute the law. When an honest and inflexible judge was put
in, the resultant evil required the destruction of the cities. We
face the prospect of honest judges who will carry out the logic of
the denominational positions, missing perhaps the deeper logic of
this historical moment. It will take extraordinary restraint and
emotional sensitivity for the new leadership not to act out the
logic of its position and to exercise a certain patience in the face
of the fact that history has proven more elusive than any of the
formulas we have applied to it. Unless this vision of unity remains
vivid, there will be too many justifiable occasions for further
splintering. It behooves all who live in light of our generation's
experiences to bind together, to keep communication lines open,

and to resist the righteousness of institutions, no matter how justified it may appear.

Finally, I should like to say what I think Orthodoxy can do to make possible a future unity. Orthodoxy must change its identity from a fundamentalism to a religion, from preserving Judaism to affirming it and its sovereignty in modern culture. In short, it must go through the modern experience. I am not speaking of *kulot,* or of dismantling the law. Still less am I calling for uncritical acceptance of the categories of modern thought..If anything, there is a need for more *mitzvot* [virtuous deeds]. There is a need for the renewal of the process of imbuing the contemporary experience with religious import by applying religious values and practices to all areas of secular life. But this can only be done when Orthodoxy actually works through, in depth, the modern experience so that it speaks to this generation and in it. There is not a single affirmation or *mitzva* [commandment] that it must *a priori* surrender. If men remain open and ready to hear, the voice of God may speak from anywhere. But it must be crystal clear that such affirmations do not proceed from being in a cultural backwater or because Orthodoxy does not yet recognize the problems which have been raised.

It is true that there is an enormous risk in undergoing such a process. Too often, those who have gone through the process thus far have been so enthralled by the experience that they excessively swallowed the categories of the world which we live in. The great tension in Jewish religious history has been between the demand of the eternal and the claims of the temporal for concretization within the world as it exists. He who goes too far toward the pole of eternity becomes irrelevant; he who enters totally into the immediate world accepts experiences and values which later Jews have lived to regret. Had all the Jews accepted the claims of the temporal we might have been lost long ago. In the dialectic of these two calls in the modern era, all the positions taken, thus far, should be seen as first statements. In response to the modern claim, Orthodoxy said: not an inch. Others said: we accept the sovereignty of your categories. The real issue now is: Can there be a more subtle and refined exploration of what within the Tradition speaks and how it speaks in this generation? Among the Orthodox, this exploration will grow out of the conviction that all this is divine rather than simply historical experience or something in tune with the great insights of man. Nevertheless, there is no way of escaping the detailed, painstaking scholarship and the leaps of religious intuition and experience which alone can create a viable Tradition. Understandably, this will take generations. Until then, Orthodoxy will be crippled in its participation in serious ecumenical dialogue. It is not that we have no need to speak in the interim. But until all three groups rethink earnestly and rebuild from within, we cannot have an ultimate substantive unity.

The current divisions of Jewry loom very large. In the past there have been similar experiences of such deep-rooted divisions and we can learn from them. One thing I learn is that from the point of view of the committed Jew, it may be too early to strive for excessive unity at this point. In the past, as now, there were occasions when the bulk of Jews had so assimilated to the culture of their time that to all practical purposes they were residual Jews. It was only a matter of time until the implications of what they had accepted were spelled out and they disappeared. Therefore, I think, the consensus we are striving for will not have to be somewhere in the middle of the current Jewish community. The harsh and real fact is that the bulk of Jews who today see themselves as Jews in America are terminal Jews. They are living off the residue of sentiment, loyalty, and nostalgia which is totally vulnerable to the increasing inroads of contemporary culture. It is obvious that the group that will survive will be drawn mostly from the committed. Orthodoxy has no monopoly of this group, but I believe it will be a much higher percentage than it is in the present community. Nor do I speak of this disappearance with pride or expectation. Rather, I speak with all the shattered soul of a Jew who, having lost six million Jews in his own time, sees the coming loss of millions more. But this means that all talk of unity must work on the assumption that those who are seriously committed, who are willing to explore the vocation of the Jew as the people called by God, who take the Covenant and its implications for Halachah seriously will provide the nucleus of the future reunified people. Such a unity could be made possible only by a genuine *t'shuvah*—by a willingness to rethink fundamentals and even explore the unthinkable. If Herman Kahn has prescribed thinking the unthinkable for post-thermonuclear survival, we can do no less for Jewish survival. Perhaps the only thing that can sustain us in such an enterprise would be the promise, reported by the Rambam: "Israel ultimately will turn." To live by this promise is to muster the courage to explore all these areas. There will be no facile solutions. Undoubtedly, many of the current answers will be found historically premature or stillborn. Still we may hope that our generation of Job will be worthy of taking the first step on this path and will thus fulfill the prophecy that "on the day the Temple was destroyed, the Messiah was born."

JAKOB J. PETUCHOWSKI

The somewhat cumbersome title of the topic which I have been asked to discuss contains words like "future," "religious," and "unity." It thereby betrays the truly "Messianic" character of the topic. The advantage of this long-range vision is that it obviates the necessity of taking into consideration the somewhat less-than-promising aspects of the contemporary scene and its *institutional* involvements. It would be unrealistic, in this pre-Messianic age, to cherish dreams of a real "institutional" unity. Of course, it is just barely possible that true "religious unity" could, even before the Coming of the Messiah, transcend the deeply entrenched institutional divisions. To that possibility we ought to give some thought.

A second disclaimer with which I must begin is related to the first. I have been asked by the editor of *Judaism* to be one of the four speakers in this symposium. Seeing that my three colleagues on this panel have been chosen from the ranks of Orthodoxy, Conservatism, and Reconstructionism respectively, it would stand to reason that I "represent" Reform. To a certain extent, I hope that I do. I am sure that *some* Reform Jews would associate themselves with my position. But I am equally sure that others would quite emphatically dissociate themselves from it. By the same token, I do not want to be held responsible for any statement ever made by *a* Reform Jew.

Finally, a third disclaimer. There is a tendency in modern Jewish life to cast the net of one's definitions as wide as possible, so that the greatest number of Jews might be accounted for. There is the Zionist-nationalist definition, which makes no demands in terms of religious creed and observance. There is the Reconstructionist definition which foregoes belief in a Personal God and in the Election of Israel. Of course, there is also the

Halachic definition, which regards him as a Jew who was either born of a Jewish mother or converted to Judaism by the accepted rites of conversion. None of those definitions, it seems to me, do justice to the realities of modern Jewish life. We must, I believe, recognize that life in America presents us with opportunities and with challenges never faced by us before. "Jewishness" as a matter of ethnic and cultural heritage may be no more lasting in this climate than the ethnic and cultural heritage of Norway, Sweden, and Ireland. I personally cannot see, for example, how the ethnic-cultural definition of "Jewishness" can realistically be placed in the way of a contemplated intermarriage. Nor does the Halachic definition, in and by itself, fit the contemporary scene completely. In America, at any rate, mere Jewish descent does not yet automatically assure Jewish posterity. And not only in America. The picture is not too different in the State of Israel, either. Halachically, no doubt, Mr. Uri Avneri, M.K. and his fellow-Canaanites are Jews. But will they continue to be Jews once peace with the Arabs is made, and intermarriage will be as much of a problem in the State of Israel as it is here? The Halachic definition may have been fully adequate to Ghetto existence. It does not reckon with the "free society" in which the "vanishing Jew" is a distinct possibility. All of which by way of a disclaimer.

It is in the nature of an attempt to define "the foundations of the future religious unity of Israel" that one is tempted to seek the lowest common denominator; and, in a secular age, the lowest common denominator is liable to be found in a realm other than that of religious affirmation. But, seeing that my task here is to speak about the future *religious* unity of Israel, I feel free to leave the "vanishing Jew" to his own fate. I shall confine my remarks to the destiny of those who have consciously chosen to identify themselves as Jews *religiously*. Fully aware of the distinct possibility that numbers of us are going to "vanish," both here and in the State of Israel, I want to speak of those who are imbued with—what Caesar Seligmann so aptly called—*Der Wille zum Judentum*, the "will to Judaism."

"The will is everything," wrote Seligmann. "First our fathers had to will to maintain Judaism, before Judaism could maintain itself. It is true, one says that Judaism has preserved the Jews, that religion, faith, idea are the indestructible element. But have religion and idea also preserved those who did not wish to be preserved—the Ten Tribes, the Hellenists, and the apostates of all centuries? What would have become of Judaism without the will of our fathers and mothers?" (*Geschichte der Jüdischen Reformbewegung*, 1922, p. 19).

Now that we have narrowed our purview to those who have the "will to Judaism," we are still faced with the greatest variety in the manifestations of that will—both in belief and in practice. A hundred years ago or so, there were some nicely worked out positions: Reform, Orthodoxy, and Conservatism. Today, it does not really work out that way any more. The specific "denominational" affiliation of the American Jew is no longer any guarantee of his theological commitment, or of the degree of his religious observance. And so, here we are, groping in darkness and confusion, relying as best we can on yesterday's guides. What do we conscious religious Jews have in common? To what kind of greater unity may we yet aspire?

One of the most encouraging answers to those questions has recently been given by Eliezer Berkovits, in the magazine *Tradition*. Writes Berkovits:

> The *Ikkarim* (principles) that should determine ideological divisions in Israel should be so formulated as to leave the gates wide open for communication with the broadest possible sections of *Kelal Yisrael*. We suggest that the recognition of three principles is sufficient to become the foundation of ideological unity. They are the belief in a personal God, in *Torah min hashamayim* (that the Torah was revealed by God to Israel) and *Torah shebe'al peh*, the inseparable connection between the Written Torah and the Oral tradition. Jews who acknowledge these principles, even though they may disagree with each other in matters of interpretation, should be looked upon as belonging to the same ideological grouping. Once the basic principles are affirmed, differences in interpretation should not be permitted to become dividing walls between Jew and Jew.
>
> (*Tradition*, Vol. VII, No. 2, Summer 1965, p. 80.)

To all of this I can only say, "Amen and Amen!" In the essentials which Berkovits has singled out, he has, I believe, laid the foundations of the future religious unity of Israel. There is little I could add by way of improving on his formulation. Perhaps I would have liked him to be a little more specific in spelling out the difference between what he calls "principle" and what he calls "interpretation." If, for example, *Torah min hashamayim*, as a "principle," permits of the kind of interpretation which Louis Jacobs gives to it, then it is a "principle" which I can and do accept. (I would even allow the "mechanical" view of Revelation as *a* possible and legitimate "interpretation" of that "principle.") But if the "principle" itself is meant to commit us to fundamentalism—as the London *beth din* means it to commit us—then, of course, the "principle" itself could not be one of the foundations of a future religious unity. Again, if the centrality of *Torah shebe'al peh* can legitimately be understood in the way in which Zacharias Frankel understood it, it would be a suitable "foundation." But if the "principle" itself is meant to commit us to the position of a Samson Raphael Hirsch, then, obviously, it could not serve as a foundation of religious unity. In short, I do believe, with Eliezer Berkovits, that the future religious unity of Israel demands an affirmation of the Personal God, of Revelation, and of the centrality of the Tradition.

It does, however, demand also something more. It demands the recognition of a consciously and sincerely voiced "will to Judaism" as a basis for religious unity—quite apart from any specific degree of religious practice which may go with it. By this I mean that we must all agree to evaluate Judaism qualitatively, rather than quantitatively. I do not think that the variations in religious observance are going to vanish. They might even increase. The old Halachic way of life has broken down together with the environment in which it held sway. At least, it has broken down for very many Jews today—including some of the most devoted. And the new Halachah has not yet come into existence. Today we have, what Franz Rosenzweig called, the common landscape within which we are all working at our own individual roads, and no longer the common road on which we walked together until the period of the Emancipation. Only blindness could make us deny that—however we might choose to evaluate that phenomenon. Under the circumstances, there will always be a *marbeh*, the Jew who observes a maximum of the 613 *mitzvot*, just as there will always be a *mam'it*, a minimalist in observance. What I would consider one of the important foundations of religious unity is the willingness, on the part of all of us, to concede—in a sense of far wider sweep than that implied in B. *Berachoth* 17a— that *echad hamarbeh ve'echad hamam'it ubilevad sheyechaven libbo lashamayim*, "there is no difference whether one observes much or little, as long as one's heart is directed towards God." *If* there is acceptance of the principle of *Torah min hashamayim*, and *if* there is observance at all, and *if* the heart is directed towards God, then let God alone be the judge—and not the fellow-Jew—as to who is the better Jew. Let us get away from the quantitative evaluation of Jewish living. Let us not simply assume that the Jew who waits six hours between meat and milk is *ipso facto* a "better" Jew than the one who waits only three hours—or even than the one who does not wait at all. Far be it from me to suggest to the Orthodox that they reduce their religious requirements. On the contrary, I happen to be a proponent of more religious observance even within Reform Judaism. But let those be matters of personal decision, in the category of *ben adam lamakom*. So long as some of us set themselves up as judges who judge their fellow-Jew's Judaism quantitatively, it would be foolish even to dream about religious unity.

I realize, of course, that, in asking my Orthodox brethren to forego the quantitative yardstick in matters of personal religious observance, I am making a very heavy demand. I am asking more of them than the Reformers did a hundred years ago when they wanted to abolish the *yekum purkan* [refers to two Aramaic prayers, "May Salvation . . . be granted"]. But, to be fair, I am going to make very heavy demands of others as well. While I reject quantitative evaluations when it comes to the individual and his observance, I cannot see how we can manage without a quantitative yardstick when it comes to the constitution of the Holy Community as a whole. The field of Jewish education is one such area. Here, good intentions are not enough. Standards— of the highest order—will have to be accepted by all. A Jewish education which spends eight years in transmitting the knowledge of the 22 consonants of the Hebrew alphabet *is* inferior to a Jewish education which, in the same number of years, manages to expose Jewish children to the text of the Mishnah [the text of the Oral Law].

And then there is the complicated area of Jewish marriage and divorce law. It is inconceivable to me how we could have religious unity and, at the same time, create a state of affairs where Jews are no longer able to marry within their own ranks. I am not referring to the ridiculous statement recently released by the Orthodox ecclesiastical authorities of England which denies valid *kiddushin* [ceremonial validation of marriage] to any and all marriages performed in Reform synagogues—much as I might personally relish the thought that, for almost twenty years, I myself have been living in sin. But I am concerned about those instances where marriages have been "solemnized" in defiance of the Halachah, and in which the validity of *kiddushin* may legitimately be questioned—not to mention the hardships imposed on their innocent offspring. If the future religious unity of Israel is to include Reform Jews as well, then Reform Judaism will have to find a more positive approach to traditional marriage and divorce law, and to the traditional procedures of admitting proselytes.

This demand made of the Reformers is, I suppose, as heavy a demand as the one I made of the Orthodox when I asked them to give up the quantitative yardstick in measuring Jewish piety. But, then, any discussion about a "future religious unity" would, of necessity, have to involve some give-and-take. Moreover, before our Reform Jews can come to terms with marriage and divorce Halachah, some work will have to be done in this area by the Orthodox themselves. They will have to show the same courage in our day that Rabbenu Gershom [who introduced monogamy into Ashkenazic Judaism] showed in his; and the changed position of woman in our society—to mention but one aspect—will have to be reckoned with in a Halachic reformulation of marriage and divorce law.

Both groups, therefore (and I do not want to exclude the Conservatives, either), will have to do some hard re-thinking. And this is a very crucial area. If we cannot come to an agreement here, it would be futile to strive for more exalted theological agreements. While the "will to Judaism" is the prerequisite, Jewish family life is the locale. Any further "foundations" will have to be established on those bases.

SEYMOUR SIEGEL

It has been frequently charged that Jewish thought imitates Christianity. This charge must be revised in the light of what is transpiring in the Jewish community. Ecumenism is the order of the day in Christendom. In Judaism, however, whatever mutual goodwill had existed, is fading away. The reasons for this are well known to this distinguished audience. What Shakespeare said of

Cleopatra can be applied to the American Jewish community as well as to world Jewry: "Age cannot wither her, nor custom stale her infinite variety."

The situation was all too well expressed by one of my professors who, in an essay on humor in the Talmud, noted that the most humorous statement in Rabbinic literature is: *Talmidei chachamim marbim shalom ba'olam*—"The disciples of the wise increase peace in the world."

However, we cannot continue to tolerate the deterioration of Jewish unity. We had better get busy rethinking our position to see whether we can find a basis upon which to build—for no other reason than that bickering and disunity will make us even more boring than we might already be. As the late Hayim Greenberg once wrote: "I do not now wish to step on anyone's corns. It is not desirable to discuss the difference between Orthodox, Conservative and Reform Jews, and their respective merits or shortcomings. But there is one danger which they must all eschew—the danger of tedium. When Satan wishes to undermine religious life, he afflicts it with a yawn."

An answer to the problem of how to achieve Jewish religious unity might be gained by looking to the past. If we cannot find an answer, we might at least find an approach toward a solution. In certain epochs—the Biblical period and especially the period of the Second Commonwealth—Judaism was characterized by great diversity. There were many groups differing from each other in theology and in practice. Yet somehow they managed to live together. But this toleration of diversity was not absolute. Some groups did not remain part of the Jewish community. An interesting historical and theological question is: By what principle were Christians excluded from the Jewish community while the schools of Hillel and Shammai, for all their serious disagreements about fundamental problems, remained part of the same people?

Professor Judah Goldin, in an essay which was published in *A Reader's Guide to the Great Religions*, writes as follows:

> When we seek to discover what is normative about these centuries, we must recognize that all the sources are a record of particular teachings striving to become normative; all represent the ambition of particular groups to have the whole of Israel adopt their particular emphases. And so long as they

were vigorously arguing with each other, Judaism was in process toward final formulation. One might say it was feeling its way toward definitiveness. What made the teachings of some one or other group not normative was the withdrawal of the particular group from the common argument, from this resolution to press its point of view on the folk as a whole where the folk as a whole was located. Issuing polemical statements from a reservation to which one had retired and where one had adopted a particular routine for privileged initiates is already an expression of giving up, of disengagement, and a sign of having become tangential. Whatever else Talmudism was, it was the determination of its exponents to engage themselves with what was daily happening as a whole and to engage that society with the terms of the Rabbis' debates and values.

According to Professor Goldin, therefore, only those groups which remained in the community, arguing their point of view with opponents, were able to create normative Judaism. Those groups which withdrew from the common dialogue and the common concern were doomed to separate themselves from Judaism, and had no part in the formation of the common world-outlook.

Professor Max Kadushin has suggested another tool, or handle, by means of which to understand the toleration of diversity in Rabbinic Judaism, whilst maintaining an overarching unity. He attributes this to the fact that "Rabbinic Judaism based itself upon value-concepts which are not only undefined but non-definable." The value-concepts have a dual role. Since they are non-definable, they can be flexible and can, therefore, respond to, and express, the *differentia* of human personalities. At the same time the value-term does convey an idea of the concept which it represents and this generalized idea is common to all the members of the group. Concepts such as Torah, Israel, Messiah unite the people. They stand for their common commitment. Variety, however, is possible because there is room for diverse interpretations of these concepts, both in life and in teaching. Thus there is unity and diversity.

The medieval age is looked upon as the time when dogmatic formulations of Jewish belief put Judaism into a theological straitjacket. Professor Julius Guttman, however, in a celebrated lecture on the "Principles of Judaism" pointed out that the formulation of dogma by Maimonides and others was undertaken not in order to create a catechism. Rather the function of the "Principles" was to set the limits of interpretation:

> Why did that generation [of the Middle Ages] find it necessary to establish Judaism upon a foundation of articulated principles? . . . Even in the Middle Ages there were deep and serious religious differences in Jewry. On the one hand, popular beliefs, that were basically divergent from Judaism, had an intense hold on the masses, and, on the other, challenging philosophic views entered the Jewish world, not necessarily in the same manner as has happened in our time, but no less distant from the biblical-talmudic faith. It therefore became necessary to mark the boundaries beyond which one could not go in discussing Judaism. In setting up lists of principles, such a boundary line was achieved . . . The establishment of principles, fundamentals, or dogmas serves to limit the apparently limitless freedom of interpretation.

Medieval Judaism was based on the notion that the Torah was to be interpreted. The dogmas set the limit beyond which interpretation could not go. A wide area was left to the interpreter. He could roam about to his heart's content—unless, or until, he crossed the boundaries set by the whole of the tradition.

Therefore, what emerges from this brief consideration of the problem in an historical perspective is that the two processes of conservation and interpretation were at work. Conservation saves the Tradition from whim; interpretation (or *midrash*) saves it from arterial sclerosis. Both conservation and commentary must be at work simultaneously. One without the other is empty and meaningless.

The contemporary situation is, of course, different in several crucial respects from that which obtained in Talmudic and medieval times. Yet it is instructive to use past solutions as guidelines in our own time. What unites the religious wings of Judaism are the determination to remain in the fray and to carry on the dialogue one with the other, and also common loyalty to a series of common value-concepts, action-concepts—such as the existence of God, the acceptance of Torah as a guide to Jewish living, the recognition of the special vocation of the people of Israel as it is expressed through the covenant, and the expectation of Messianic fulfillment. There will be different interpretations of these concepts. The different groups will coalesce around the varying interpretations. But, there can be an overarching unity

based on the commonality of the commitment to the concept-
experiences.

Is there a limit to the kind of interpretation which can be
allowed? In other words, do we need to formulate a new dog-
matism? In general, the naming of the concept-terms themselves,
as Professor Kadushin maintains, sets some limit to the interpretation. Though we are told that in 1984 people will be convinced
that "peace is war," it is hard to believe that a concept such as
God will be interpreted to yield the idea of atheism. There is yet
another factor at work in the limitation of interpretation, and
that is the consensus of the religiously committed Jews. This is
what Solomon Schechter had in mind in his famous idea of
"catholic Israel." Somehow and in some way the judgment of the
adherents of Judaism is rendered upon interpretations which do
violence to the whole.

To effectuate this unity based on common commitment and
diversity flowing from differing interpretations, one other condition is necessary. Each group tries to foster its own interpretations of the concepts of Judaism. But, it must honor and respect
those who differ. The reason for the indispensability of this attitude is not only liberalism and good will. It also has a theological
foundation. Professor Heschel has suggested that we differentiate
between "theology" and "depth-theology." The latter refers to
the experience of faith, the deep stirrings of the soul when it
encounters the Divine. The term "theology" refers to the formulations and descriptions of these "depth" experiences. The formulations are always much less than that which they describe.
Therefore, to insist on the absoluteness and exclusiveness of the
formulations, to be dogmatic about articulated principle, is to
betray the religious experience itself. Thus, there is always a
tentativeness about our dogmatics—though they are necessary
for self-clarification and communication. We can also profit from
that which Professor Tillich has pointed out concerning the
function of doubt in religion. Doubt is part of faith. Faith is the
finite being grasped by the infinite. The finite cannot exhaust the
infinite. Therefore, what we say is never enough, and doubt is
part of religion. We need not only the courage to believe, but
also the courage to doubt and to believe in spite of doubt. Rav
Kook once said: *Tzrichim l'havin, shegam miperudei hadeyot
yotzeit tova klalit*—"We must understand, that also from differences of opinion a general good can result." An attitude such as

that expressed recently in a much quoted article about Orthodox Judaism: "Orthodoxy perceives itself as the only legitimate bearer of the Jewish tradition. To Orthodoxy, this tradition is expressed almost exclusively in its religious form."—must be eschewed. If Orthodoxy continues to perceive itself as the only legitimate bearer of the Jewish tradition, then this symposium is in vain.

Therefore, we must affirm the notion that although we have differing interpretations of the imperatives of Judaism, we respect and honor those who see them in another light. It was Franz Rosenzweig who pointed out that "truth" is a noun only for God. For us it is an adverb. We live truthfully, authentically.

Is one religious Judaism possible? We can affirm one Judaism united by concept-experiences expressed in the ancient phrases of Jewish faith—God, Israel, Torah, Messiah. One exclusive interpretation of these concepts is neither desirable nor possible. There must be overarching unity, mutual reverence and respect, cooperative enterprises and hopes. This kind of one-ness must be achieved not at the expense of the right to formulate and understand in the light of experience and understanding.

What I have been saying is expressed by the Rabbis in their comment on the verse in *Kohelet* [book of Ecclesiastes]: "The words of the wise are like goads, and as nails fastened by the masters of the assemblies, which are given from one shepherd" (12:11).

> The teachers of the Law are those who are gathered together, who sit in groups and busy themselves in the Torah. Some say "clean" and others say "unclean"; some prohibit and others permit, some disqualify and others qualify. Perhaps a man will say, "How can I learn Torah now?" Therefore the verse says, "They were given from one shepherd." One God has given them, one Providential Being has said them. As it is said, "for the Lord has said *all* these things." Therefore make your ears like a funnel and achieve an understanding heart to listen both to the words of those who declare unclean, and to those who declare clean, those who say permitted and those who say prohibited, those who qualify and those who disqualify.

Unity based on concept-experience and ancient faith, but which includes freedom of interpretation—this, I believe is the basis for the future religious unity of Israel.

MORDECAI M. KAPLAN

Talmidei chachamim marbim shalom ba'olam. The increase of peace and unity is the highest ethical assignment to those who speak in the name of religion. Rabbi Hanina, the author of that saying, had a *static* conception of unity. To him, unity had to be based on uniformity. He would have regarded diversity as not only irreligious, but also as incompatible with peace. However, since democracy has come to be recognized as an ethical aspect of human relations, the duty of interpreting *shalom* as implying unity without uniformity must henceforth be the ethical principle by which those in a position of leadership should try to govern themselves. I am, indeed, glad to have heard from our chairman that the purpose of this discussion was to try to find a way in which we can have unity without uniformity. It is to that purpose that I shall address myself.

The problem of Jewish unity, not as outwardly motivated by the hostility of non-Jews, but as inwardly motivated by Jewish religion, is now on the agenda of Jewish life. Since a religion gives purpose and meaning to the existence of those who profess it, the problem of Jewish unity is to identify that element in the life of all Jews throughout the world which gives purpose and meaning to their existence as Jews. By purpose, we understand a common goal. By meaning, we understand common motivation, implementation and desirable consequences. A religion, any religion, is authentic to the extent that its purpose is the advancement of universal welfare and peace. In that respect the Jewish religion is unqualifiedly universal. Its purpose, however, is not to have all non-Jews adopt Judaism, though those who adopt it out of conviction are more than welcome.

What is Judaism? In a discussion of this kind each of us starts from different conceptions of the basic terms we use. Each of us understands something different by religion, by Judaism, by the idea of God, by the idea of person, and so on. To make myself understood, I wish to make clear at once that to me Judaism—or that which has united all the generations of the Jewish people—is more than a religion. It is an evolving religious civilization. As a *civilization*, it is the life of an ongoing people, with a land, a history, a language, a culture, with laws and morals. As a *religious* civilization, all of its foregoing elements are related to the one God, King of the Universe. As an *evolving* religious civilization, all of its elements, including the conception of God, have undergone and are undergoing change. Hence the only *locus* of Jewish unity can be the Jewish people, since the latter is the only *continuum* amid the changes due to environmental and cultural differences.

Judaism's purpose, however, is not to have all non-Jews adopt Judaism. We cannot expect non-Jews to adopt our Jewish civilization. Jewish religion is an *indigenous* religion, an outgrowth of the history of the life and experiences and the hopes of a people. It is not based on dogmas. Dogmas tended to become prominent in Jewish religion at a time when Judaism had to define itself in relation to Christianity. The Jewish religion fostered Jewish unity by highlighting within Judaism, as an indigenous religious civilization, the *sancta*, i.e., the extraordinary events of the Jewish people, its spiritual heroes, its sacred writings, its sacred language, Hebrew, its holy land, its ethical ordinances, its just laws, and its holy days. These *sancta* have created among Jews a feeling of fellowship and a consciousness of kind to the point of reciprocal responsibility. Not only are *kol yisrael chaverim*, but *kol yisrael arevim zeh ba zeh*. This is what it means to be a Jew, to have the feeling of mutual responsibility as a Jew for all Jews in the world, for their well-being, their happiness, their fulfillment. If we have that in common, we have Jewish unity. And, in the light of what has been said by Professors Petuchowski and Siegel, the matter of *interpretation* cannot, in the modern climate of opinion, possibly be expected to be uniformly dogmatic in character.

The *sancta* have sustained the Jewish people throughout the centuries of dispersion, persecution and statelessness. These *sancta* have become all the more indispensable now that the Jewish people is broken up into four or five denominations, and that the State of Israel is liable to create an impassable gulf between the Jews in Israel and those outside the State of Israel. What dogmas are expected to do for other religions, *sancta* do for the Jewish religion. Jewish religion, in being indigenous, possesses the advantage of being able to undergo considerable change in its beliefs and in the reinterpretation of the *sancta*, without jeopardizing its identity, its unity, and its continuity.

Jewish religion has already passed through 1) an unreflective, 2) a metaphysically rational, and 3) a mystically rational stage, and is now on the point of entering 4) a functionally rational stage. This fact is integral to the history of our people and its religion. Can we say that our idea of God is the same as what we find in the Bible? When we read in the Torah that God hardened Pharaoh's heart, can we take that in the sense in which it was understood by our ancestors? Can we subscribe to the idea of the physical world and of its creation as portrayed in the first chapter of *Genesis?* And yet, because the Torah is our holy of holies we must find in that first chapter of *Genesis* a common purpose. The meaning varies with time, but the purpose is the same: that there is one God, and that only by reflecting the "image of God" can man transcend the beast. That purpose is compatible with the most radical conception of human nature and of the cosmos.

The consummation, however, of this latest stage in Judaism and the Jewish religion depends not upon theological uniformity, but upon the reconstitution of the Jewish people throughout the world as one people with its hub in the Jewish community, not in the State of Israel. Such reconstitution would have, for world Jewry, the significance of a renewal of its Covenant with God. The time has come when we Jews must have some duly authorized body formulate our status in the world as a people, with an evolving religious civilization, dedicated to the permanent values which are inherent in our tradition. That would lead to our reinstatement by the rest of the world as a *de jure* people, and contribute to our dignity and self-respect, without which mere unity is of little worth.

HUMANISTIC JUDAISM AND THE "GOD IS DEAD" THEOLOGY

SHERWIN T. WINE

I. THE ECLIPSE OF "GOD LANGUAGE"

A LIBERAL CATHOLIC recently said to me that the most disastrous thing that happened at the Vatican Council was when the Council voted to translate the Mass into the language of the country. For the educated Catholic, when the Mass was in Latin and he wasn't fully aware of what was going on, it was tolerable. Now that it was translated into English it was *in*tolerable.

About one hundred years ago, among Jews, there arose a proposal called "The Reform Movement" which began with the idea that if you took all the nice Jewish prayers, adjusted them in little ways ideologically and translated them into English, then, all of a sudden, Jews who weren't praying any more would come back to prayer. The authors of the movement forgot something. When the prayers were in Hebrew, and most of the Jews didn't understand them, the prayers were tolerable. When they were translated into English they became *in*tolerable.

Of course, this defines the whole problem of Jewish life today. The problem is the crisis of belief that pervades not only the Jewish world but the Christian world as well. The crisis of belief is important because what you believe is crucial. I have often run across many liberals who tell me it doesn't make any difference what one believes. Such an assertion is, of course, foolish. If I believe that Negroes are inferior, it determines my attitude on civil rights. If I believe the earth is flat, it determines the way I travel. Belief is crucial.

The Jewish crisis is aggravated by the problem of belief and the failure of liberal Judaism to deal with it. The Reform Move-

From *Religious Humanism*, 1 (Winter 1967), pp. 17–21, and 1 (Spring 1967), pp. 37–40. By permission of the publisher and the author.

ment, unfortunately, was concerned mainly with the problems of Jewish emancipation. Since the Jews had been in the ghetto and the Jews had certain customs, practices and ceremonies that were bizarre in Western culture, there was a deliberate attempt to adjust the Jew to the emancipated society, and this adjustment usually occurred in a Protestant society. Therefore, the *sancta* of this society; namely, the Bible, God, the Psalms, etc., were retained, and those practices that Protestant society found bizarre were discarded. Many of the old customs, the ceremonies, and the reliance on the Talmud, vanished. Reform was an adjustment to assimilation.

But today we are told by *Time* magazine that Jews are "in." It is fashionable to be Jewish. This fashionableness of Jewishness is highlighted by the absence of another factor that prompted Jewish survival—something called "anti-Semitism." There are anti-Semites around. But the power of anti-Semitism has declined, and with this decline much of the strong urge for the maintenance of Jewish identity is fading.

Another important factor that highlights the crisis is the death of "guilt-feelings-twisting." Let me explain it. You are a grandmother raised in the Old World. You have a child who has a child, and the grandchild is going to be thirteen years old and ready for Bar Mitzvah. Your child could really care less about the tradition and so you call your daughter up. You say to her, "Look, I'm only your mother. I'm only your mother, so why should you be concerned with me. So I'll go to an early grave. Don't be concerned. Don't be concerned over the fact that millions of Jews are dying for the thing you won't even have your kid Bar Mitzvah'd for!"

Most of my early exposure to religion in Detroit, where I was raised, was on the basis of guilt feelings. If one discussed the Shema, the so-called Creedal Statement: "Hear, O Israel, the Lord our God, the Lord is One," the Rabbi would never bother to demonstrate the intrinsic truth of the statement. He would rather point out how many people died to preserve it. It's pretty much like trying to prove the vitality of Christianity or its relevance by demonstrating how many Christians were swallowed by lions. In many cases "guilt-feelings-twisting" is probably one of the most powerful forces for the maintenance of denominational identity. For the Jews who have suffered a great deal, it is very important.

But even grandmothers and grandfathers die and the generation that was doing the twisting is dying out and therefore, although the massive bar mitzvah factory which in many cases maintains synagogues and temples is not coming to a halt (it still continues), in the next ten, fifteen or twenty years dramatic changes will occur.

But the most important factor that reveals the crisis of belief and makes it stand out is the fact that today over eighty per cent of young Jewish people are going to college. In the university the forces that are molding their minds and the way they think are totally different from the forces that molded the minds of their grandparents. Their entire belief framework has been altered. Now, in order to understand the Birmingham Temple [Birmingham, Michigan], in order to understand what we have done under what we call "Humanistic Judaism," we have to understand something that has defined your mind and mine. The factor is what I call the "University Religion." There is a religion, a commitment that pervades the whole mood of a university. If you ask the students who attend what the religion is, they cannot tell you directly. But, if you articulate its principles, they will recognize them. In fact, these principles are the basic tenets of the religion of a large number of people who are both unaffiliated and affiliated with liberal churches. Even the "God Is Dead" Movement in Protestantism cannot be understood without reference to this University Religion.

The first principle which I think is absolutely crucial is something that I call "secularization," which is much talked about in the "God Is Dead" Movement and certainly among liberal religionists. A famous sociologist by the name of Émile Durkheim once gave this definition of religion:

> A religion is a unified system of beliefs and practices relative to sacred things, that is to say, things set apart and forbidden. Beliefs and practices which unite into one single moral community, called a church, all those who adhere to them. Religion, therefore, presupposes classification of all things into two classes of opposed groups—profane and sacred.

Durkheim, of course, was seconded by Rudolph Otto, who found in "the sacred" the basic category of religion.

Now, no one who goes to a university can for long retain what I call the category of "the sacred." One of the basic principles of a university or college is something we call "free inquiry." Free inquiry simply means that there is no idea, no value, no notion, no hypothesis, no theory that is beyond proving, questioning or measuring. Sacredness means untouchability and taboo. It implies that there is no option of rejection, while free inquiry demands with regard to any value or idea that there is the option of rejection.

Harvey Cox in *The Secular City* expresses this very well. This is what he has to say:

> Both tribal man and secular man see the world from a particular social and historical point of view. But modern secular man knows it and tribal secular man did not. Therein lies the crucial difference. Awareness that his own point of view is relative and conditioned has become for secular man an inescapable component of that point of view. His consciousness has been relativised. He knows not only his language, his customs, his clothing style, but also his values and his very way of perceiving reality are conditioned by his personal biography and the history of his group. In our time the Copernican Revolution has reached out to incorporate everything into its sweep—all things are relative and profane.

Thomas Altizer, to some degree, is saying the same thing. When he says, "God is dead," he means that in the modern age the whole category of the sacred, the taboo and the untouchable is dead. He puts it this way:

> Confronted as we are by a new and revolutionary moment of history, we can accept our destiny only by acknowledging the loss of all our traditional images. No sacred images whatsoever are present upon our horizon. The original form of Jesus has disappeared and is no longer sacred. Transcendence has been swallowed up by immanence. No heaven can appear above the infinite stretches of a purely exterior spaciality, and no grace can appear within the isolated subjectivity of a momentary consciousness. May we hope the time has at last arrived when the Christian faith can transcend the language of images. Is the moment at hand when Christianity can fulfill its heritage of a Torah that forbids all images?

It is here, of course, that Altizer expresses what he considers to be the unique contribution of Protestantism. "The Catholics," he says, "have become the Protestants of today in the sense they have embraced the Bible, translated the liturgy and all that. If Protestants are going to be different they are going to have to take the Protestant principle to its extreme." The Protestant principle at its extreme is the rejection of all idols and all images. That means that Protestants may smash statues, break stained glass and destroy all the accoutrements of the old church. They may even deny that God can be expressed in almost any form in the visible space-time world. But then they cannot keep a person like Jesus or a book like the Bible free from the same challenge. In our profane age the sacred is gone and the Protestant principle of challenge to idolatry has incorporated both Jesus and the Bible. There is nothing sacred on the horizon. All is secular. This is the secular and profane age. There is neither taboo nor untouchable.

A man called Gabriel Vahanian proceeds to endorse the same thing, but he has a complaint against Altizer. Altizer, in his mystic manner, at most makes a sacred principle out of the so-called "Protestant challenge." Perhaps he best expresses the secular age. This is what Vahanian says:

> It was bad enough to inherit a God-based concept which had lost all concrete meaning. It is incomparably worse to attenuate and in fact deny the death of God by sublimating it into a newfangled Savior concept. To argue that a historical fact totally and exclusively lays claim to my whole existence like the death of God amounts to making into a new absolute an idol hailed at the front door with all the red carpet treatment, while God is whisked out through the back door. If atheism is made sacred it's just as bad as theism as sacred. Indeed which position is more radical? Simply to hold the death of God as the cultural event that definitely seals the transition from the Christian to the post-Christian Era, or to turn it into some Savior premise to recognize that Godlessness is today a valid alternative to faith in God. Precisely because it denies not only God but any other kind of sacred universal hypothesis including itself.

So nothing is "sacred." Perhaps the anti-idolatry principle expressed in what the Jews refer to as the second of the Ten Commandments, taken to its logical conclusion and absorbed in the Protestant principle, has resulted in what we call "secularization." This secularization, this profane world without the category of sacredness is a real part of the Jewish world as it is now of the Protestant world and the Christian world in general.

The second and very important principle in the university religion which to a large extent dominates the minds of the young

Jews today is empiricism. Traditional Jewish truth-searching was author-centered like traditional Christianity and Islam. There are certain authority figures: Moses, Isaiah, Ezekiel, Jeremiah. The process of determining the validity of statements, informational or evaluative, is to establish that the chain of authority you have in your possession to prove the statement is valid, because it can be traced back to the same authority figure in the past. An empiricist may have his saints. He may love Freud, idolize Einstein and perhaps worship Bertrand Russell. Nevertheless, the true empiricist could care less about who made the assertion. The truth of a statement is dependent upon the evidence presented by controlled investigation. This procedure has certain implications for Judaism with which young Jews struggle.

1. With an empirical point of view there can be no forever and ever answers about the world. The next moment something may happen that will force one to re-adjust one's whole belief framework.

2. One must be temporarily strong enough to accept uncertainty because with regard to most statements about the origin of man all one can say really is, "I don't know."

But empiricism has a further implication, the implication of meaningfulness, and perhaps this is the common problem that is attacking both Jews and Protestants today.

I frequently talk to Jewish university students and I ask them how they feel about theology. The general reaction is not "I like," or "I don't like," but, generally, "I could care less." This sums up most reactions to contemporary religious discussions. As you very well know, every statement has two problems. One is the problem of truth and the other is the problem of meaning. If I say, "goo goo, true or false?" your reaction mostly is, first of all, "I'd love to tell you whether it's true or false, but first tell what does 'goo goo' mean?"

When the fundamentalist speaks of God, there is never really any problem. You know what he is talking about. He generally is using "God" in the ordinary sense of the word and is referring to some kind of invisible celestial father figure who created the world, issues orders, rewards and punishes, etc. I never have any problem with fundamentalists. I know what they are talking about and I generally know what they are saying is false.

My theological problems are generally with liberal theologians. I rarely understand what they are talking about. Their obscurity is the result of an old dilemma. Over 2000 years ago in Greece rational men had ceased to believe in the existence of celestial father figures. They were left with two alternatives. Either they could say, "No, I don't believe in 'God' as the word is ordinarily used." Or they could say (perhaps unconsciously), "I can't bear to give up the word 'God.' Therefore, I will find something or other in the universe I can use the word to refer to." The net result is that theology for the past two millennia has been a dreary attempt to save a word.

Their way to try to save the word "God" is generally to find some reference that is transempirical. Here empirical evidence is held to be irrelevant and thus "God" is saved. The sophisticated believer denies that God is a person in time and space (although that kind of God is meaningful; if I know there is somebody around watching me, I would be an idiot to ignore it).

"But, no, God is never something so primitive! Only Philistines, idiots, insensitive boors, people who have no real understanding would ever have that kind of conception!" "God is," said Philo, "ultimate reality." "God," said Thomas Aquinas, "is necessary existence." Real *isness*, not the phoney kind of *isness*. "God," said Paul Tillich, in his more profound moments, "is the ground of being."

Why do most university students on hearing these statements say, "I could care less!" The problem is they don't know what to do with the information they are receiving, since they are receiving no information.

One of my favorite stories was composed by John Wisdom and quoted by Antony Flew. In this story, Wisdom demonstrates how the person desperately trying to save the word "God," inch by inch, removes him from any kind of meaningful test. "Let us begin," says Flew, "with a parable. It is the parable developed from a tale told by John Wisdom in his haunting and revealing article, "God."

> Once upon a time two explorers came upon a clearing in the jungle. In the clearing were growing many flowers and many weeds. One explorer said, "Some gardener must tend this plot." The other disagreed. "There is no gardener." So they pitched their tent and set a watch. No gardener was seen. "But perhaps he is an Invisible Gardener," said one. So they set up a barbed wire fence, they electrified it, they patrolled it with bloodhounds, but no shrieks suggested that any intruder had ever received a shock; no movement of the wire

ever betrayed an invisible climber. The bloodhounds never gave cry, but still the believer is not convinced: "There is a gardener, invisible, intangible, insensible to electric shock, a gardener who has no scent and makes no sound, a gardener who comes chiefly to look after the garden in which he lives." At last the skeptic despairs. "But what remains of your original assertion? Just how does what you call an invisible, intangible, eternally elusive gardener differ from an imaginary gardener? Or even no gardener at all?"

This, of course, is called by Flew the "principle of non-falsifiability." If the same evidence can demonstrate both the truth and falsity of a statement, then what meaning—what real meaning—does it have? Or, if I can conceive of no circumstance that could possibly demonstrate the falsity of the statement, then what difference does the statement make in terms of any experience which I may have? This, by the way, is reflected in the statement of the mystic Thomas Altizer, who recognizes that in our modern day and age statements about the transcendent are simply impossible. He puts it this way: "We Christians are called upon to be loyal only to Christ, only to the incarnate Word who has appeared in our flesh and therefore we should already have been prepared for the appearance of Christ without God. We know that Christ is present in the concrete actuality of our history. We must confess that God has died and this is the path to the fully profane moment of our time. But we cannot meet our time if we remain bound to a God who no longer appears in time and space." Which is saying reality for our age is defined in terms of space-time, in terms of experience and sense data. If you talk about a God that makes no difference in terms of this experience, then in a sense you are talking about nothing at all.

The man who was most influenced by the linguistic analysts who have reached these conclusions is a man called Paul Van Buren, who expresses in "The Secular Meaning of the Gospel" perhaps the crucial issues that one finds to be true when one talks to Jewish young people of university education. "We can no longer share the faith of a man who thought that his God lived in a tree and that his God would die if the tree were burned down. Or who conceded the weakness of a God who did not respond to calls for help from the dangers of nature or man. We should say he was mistaken, but his religious assertions were understandable. An assertion of qualified literal theism, on the other hand, is meaningless and the moral exasperation of Flew's skeptical explorer is not to be dismissed lightly by those who claim to serve the truth.

"Flew raises the question of orthodoxy. What is orthodoxy in this era when many sincere Christians do not know what to do with the word 'God.' Or can use it only in a way entirely different from the orthodox usage during the early centuries of Christianity? Today we cannot even understand the Nietzschean cry that God is dead for if it were so, how could we know? If we don't know what the statement, 'God exists,' means, then how can we possibly either say God is alive or God is dead? No, the problem now is that the *word* 'God' is dead."

One can go through an entire university education without ever needing to cite God-statements or use God-language other than studying the history of religion, because no statement about God today is relevant to any real kind of empirical investigation. Theology is verbal frosting and Van Buren's analysis most likely is right. The word "God" is dead.

Some liberal theologians attempt to use the word "God" to refer to something that is not transcendent. Why not take the word "God" in a naturalistic way and have it refer to something in the natural world in space-time? The problem then is to convince people to do that. The reason it is hard to do is expressed very well by Sidney Hook, who, in an article in *Commentary* called "Modern Knowledge and the Idea of God," put it this way:

> The great problem which Humanism as a religion must face is not so much the validity of its conception of God, but how to justify its use of the term God. The defense can be made briefly. All large terms in human discourse are historically variable in meaning, or actually ambiguous in use; atom substance, experience, reason, love, even man. Also this variation of meaning. Each term stands for a family of meanings which resemble one another, but are nevertheless not completely consonant. Consequently it is argued that if the same complex of attitudes are manifested in the use of the term God, which designates not a thing or a person, but our highest ethical commitment, no legitimate objection can be raised, providing of course, we make it clear that the new use or meaning is different from the old.
>
> The criticism could be made just as briefly. The new use always invites confusion with the old use and there is, after all, such a thing as the ethics of words. By taking over the word God as the religious Humanists do, the waters of

thought, feeling and faith are muddied; the issues blurred; the word itself becomes the object of interest and not what it signifies.

What Hook is saying, I think, is valid. One cannot take an ordinary English word which is a *person* word in English, involving all kinds of sentences historically such as "God loves," "God knows," "God sees," "God hears," and by individual fiat turn it into a *thing* word, an *it* word referring to feelings and emotions or impersonal forces up there. To do so is neither ethical nor does it work.

The third and final principle of the University Religion is what is called Humanism. Man in a primitive society cannot regard himself as separable from the environment in which he lives. Later on he finds it difficult to consider himself separable from his creator-father. Therefore, for the theist, traditionally speaking, since he is inseparable from his father as the child is almost from the mother, only God can be the author of value. But Humanism draws from a heightened sense of individuality for the human being. This heightened sense of individuality has progressed over the past seven or eight centuries to the point where now man views himself as the author of value. Even if there were a God, or a series of Gods, and they were issuing all kinds of orders, modern man would still have the right to evaluate them. If there is a knock on my door, and if I open the door and there stands Jehovah who says, "Sherwin, I am very dissatisfied with your behavior and the particular statements you've been saying about me. Quite frankly I have a purpose for you in life. I want you to pick up and go to the North Country, Northern Canada, and teach the Eskimos how to read English." Then I may say, "Well, I'm delighted to receive instruction and I certainly respect you (you're one of my favorite deities) but quite frankly I think your instructions are all wet." Since a deity is just another authority figure the person receiving the instructions can still turn to the deity, the transcendent, whatever it is, and say: "Is what you are asking me to do consistent with my sense of values?"

There are two kinds of values. One we call ultimate or final values, and I suppose they are not empirically discovered in the sense that there is an empirical procedure. There is also a kind of basic intuition in each of us that discovers for himself, or for the person involved, the intrinsic value of a particular experience. Extrinsic values for the Humanist are empirically arrived at.

Brushing my teeth is good for preserving the health of my teeth. Eating is good for maintaining survival. These goods can be empirically determined. But ultimate values, final values, can only in a sense be determined intuitively and, therefore, each man in his own particular situation, by his own particular intuition, has to find by virtue of his experience what those experiences are that are self-validating, and intrinsically valuable.

II. HUMANISM AND JUDAISM

Secularization, empiricism and humanism, in the sense that I have discussed them, molded to a large degree the minds of the young people that I encounter. If I am going to present any kind of significant message for their lives to the Jews that I work with, I have got to talk within this framework. I do not do this opportunistically because I want to save them for religious organizations or for Jewish identity (and therefore I mold myself to their particular situation), but rather I do this because I, as a person, have been shaped by the same forces and the same education. This is the present agony of the rabbinate and of the Protestant ministry and perhaps now, incipiently, of the Catholic priesthood. The agony of a Jeremiah was not God language or finding some meaningful way to use the word; it was carrying out the instructions of God. For the rabbis I know, in most cases, the great agony is rather how to save God language for themselves, and that can be a considerable agony.

Therefore, what we have done in the Birmingham Temple together (rabbi and congregation) is related to a condition we share. Several years ago eight families and I got together in suburban Detroit. In a sense we shared a dissatisfaction with the existing Jewish religious situation. We really were not sure, initially, that organized religion was the best way to solve the problem. Nor did we have any fixed notion or fixed statement or limit in terms of the philosophy of the group. All we started out with, in a sense, was secularization—which meant total free inquiry to explore the question of meaning, of purpose, of value in life, and also to explore the meaning, the value and the purpose of Jewish identity.

The conclusions we arrived at are the results of the forces I outlined to you. The program of our Temple, what we call

"Humanistic Judaism," is a result of the conditioning of our general environment and not a running away from our past. Many traditionalists accuse us of running away from our past, and my reply is always: "What is my past?" My past is indeed Jewishness, but my past is also the whole training of western culture and civilization in which I have been reared. That is my past too and I cannot ignore it.

Humanistic Judaism, as expressed in the Birmingham Temple, is based on the following procedures:

1. Religion, historically, has been concerned with meaning in life. That is, a discovery and an expression of what is regarded as ultimately or intrinsically valuable. Now this is not what I call a uniquely defining characteristic of religion. Perhaps sacredness is. Certainly a search for meaning is shared by other kinds of groups in society. One of the assumptions in this search for meaning is the following: There is no one set of intrinsic values which we as human beings all share. In fact, a religious organization, if it exists, must be based on certain shared values and commitments. A variety of religious organizations can arise in the future even among Humanists through the fact that different Humanists may discern different intrinsic values and order them differently. A Humanist like Maslow may find in a mystic experience a self-validating experience. Another may find in the act of compassion something intrinsically valuable. Both, however, may share both values but order them differently. I could conceive of a religious organization based on emphasizing the self-validating nature of the mystic experience, and another which is primarily concerned with compassion as expressed in social action. Therefore, there can be the variety within the framework of Humanism that exists among individuals. Moreover, there may be no permanent set of intrinsic values for any individual. They may alter as one grows older or changes.

2. The expression of this search for meaning, even though we call it "religion," must be secularized. There must be the removal of a notion of sacredness. Initially in the history of the Birmingham Temple we used the words "sacred" and "holy" extensively. We used them in the sense of respect. But our experience indicated that the words have overtones of untouchability and taboo. Perhaps as we develop we may find substitutes (our Ritual Committee today is considering discarding the category of sacredness

and holiness because it stands in the way of the open-mindedness, the prevention of idolatry, that is so important to us).

In the 1930's a Jewish Humanist movement began which was headed by a Conservative Rabbi called Mordecai Kaplan. The name of that movement is Reconstructionism (there are now five or six congregations of Reconstructionists throughout the United States). The movement's headquarters is in New York. Mordecai Kaplan affirms himself a Humanist, but he has said very clearly that in Jewish life religion is defined by certain *sancta;* he certainly follows Durkheim's definition. The *sancta* are not necessarily ideas about the world, but they may be customs, ceremonies and words. One of the basic *sancta* of Judaism, he affirms, is the word "God"; it is taboo and, in a sense, untouchable. The Jew may not reject it; if he is a naturalist he must struggle, even though unsuccessfully, to re-define it. Dr. Kaplan believes he has re-defined the word "God" successfully as the sum total of all the forces in the universe that work for man's salvation. Try substituting that in any ordinary Hebrew prayer for the word "God" and see what you get!

Humanistic Judaism, as we view it, has no *sancta*. It has no words, no idea, no world view, no values, that do not have the option for us of rejection. Even Jewish survival is not a *sanctum*. One of the problems, by the way, in carrying on any kind of intelligent discussion in Jewish groups is that there is a sort of understood *sanctum* present—which is that you may never, never question the sacred quality of the survival of the group. I do not know whether Unitarians ever ask the question whether a Unitarian church is essential, or whether the organization, by virtue of its vested interests, becomes a *sanctum*, a non-rejectable item which you must save regardless. "Jewish survival," once it becomes that, inhibits intelligent discussion. There is no group in this world that is from the secular point of view free from the option of rejection.

3. We accept, as part of Humanistic Judaism, empiricism as the only valid method for the discovery of informational truth. We recognize that in the case of ultimate values each individual's intuition operates uniquely. In the case of extrinsic values empiricism operates. The procedure implies that, though each of us has strong conclusions, there cannot be in our congregation any official view of man or the universe.

Jewish texts which are a primary concern in ordinary Judaism are of secondary concern to us. Traditionally it was believed that the Bible contained unique information for man that could not be acquired anywhere else. Therefore, the Bible was of primary significance. But if one is an empiricist any statement about man or the universe must have its verification demonstrated by appealing to the evidence, not by appealing to some authoritative book of the past. Therefore, Jewish historical texts have for us an historic interest. They are in many cases confirmatory, not primary. This situation, by the way, is one of the agonies of the modern liberal rabbinate. When you know that today in the twentieth century there are psychologists and philosophers who say much more clearly what you believe than some struggling prophet or seer in the past, why should you prefer the prophet or seer of the past to the person who speaks more explicitly in the present?

4. We are committed to finding a meaningful language for the expression of our shared values. We reject God language as a meaningful way in which to express humanistic ideas. We refuse to sit around day after day struggling, trying to say words that are not salvageable. Therefore, we are saying that our position is ignostic. A theist, as you know, says: There is a God, what you are saying is meaningful and it is true. An atheist says: Your statement is meaningful and it is false. An agnostic says: Your statement is meaningful and I wish I knew whether it is true or false. An ignostic says: I'd love to use your language if only I understood what you were talking about. We refuse to attempt to formulate naturalistic redefinitions because we think that instead of clarifying the situation, as Sidney Hook says, they muddy the waters by dragging in a whole host of historical associations that cannot be dismissed.

5. Jews in America have always been threatened by a cultural label. In fact, the most liberal Jews have always preferred to think of the Jews as purely a religious denomination so that, if they want to get out of being Jewish, all they have to do is say: "I no longer believe in the Torah." We know the reality of Jewishness is not that at all. If Mr. Cohn becomes a Buddhist monk, he simply becomes a Jewish Buddhist. That's the way people use the word "Jew" in ordinary English and I cannot take ordinary English words and make them mean what they do not

mean because they bother me emotionally. Perhaps as Jews grow more secure they can relax with their label.

If Judaism is defined as a set of fixed ideas about God, man, the Torah, etc., then the overwhelming majority of young Jews today would simply not be Jewish. Or, the overwhelming majority of Jews in the State of Israel who are religiously unaffiliated would simply not be Jewish or part of what we call "Judaism." Mordecai Kaplan defined Judaism as a civilization or as a culture; this is a rather good definition, because it emphasizes what we call the ethnic and cultural aspect of Jewishness. As Hellenism is the total historic culture of the Greek people, Judaism, in a sense, is the total historic culture of the Jewish people.

There are many secular Jews who seek to define Judaism not in terms of God, or even in terms of ethnicity, but in terms of what they call Jewish values. I often ask these people: "Name me one value that is uniquely Jewish. Love of family? Love of education? It is true they are Jewish values, but they are certainly not uniquely Jewish. And it would be presumptuous for any group to go around saying that they are. If you cannot define your group by what is uniquely yours then there is no definition."

Reform Judaism sought to define Jewish uniqueness in an odd way. In the days when Unitarians were mainly theists, orthodox rabbis said to Reform theologians: "You are nothing but a bunch of Unitarians—you believe in God and the moral law. Who doesn't?" Reform's answer was to say: "The unique doctrine of Judaism is the mission of the Jew; Jews have been chosen to be moral missionaries to the world." I once said to a rabbi who endorsed this doctrine, "How do you feel about getting up in a pulpit and saying either 'I am a moral example,' or 'I am going to be one'?" People who claim to be moral "missionaries" have ceased to be moral examples because what makes the person a moral example is not being conscious of the fact that he is one; and for any group to go around saying that we have been chosen to be preachers of morality is a kind of hideous presumption which can only be the result of the lack of a sense of humor (and that Jews are not supposed to have).

The act of defining the uniqueness of the religions of the "God Is Dead" Movement is also a problem. If you throw away the traditional Christian theology, then you are left with Jesus, the man, and therefore there has to be something unique about Jesus that differentiates him from any other person. Van Buren tried to say that Jesus is the embodiment—the unique embodiment—of the free man, the man who challenges, if you will, the *sancta* and *sacra* of society. But is Jesus the only example or the best example of that challenge? Some try to make Jesus the example of a radical love, a suffering love. Is Jesus the only and best example of that? Unless there is a unique ethical characteristic that Jesus had but that nobody else had already demonstrated, there is no real or unique defining characteristic of Christianity. Unless, perhaps, one treats Christianity merely as an aesthetic and cultural option.

We affirm that Judaism is a cultural and aesthetic option and within that option there can be a whole host of different intellectual commitments. One may ask: Why Jewish poetry? Why not have a kind of smorgasbord—Hanukkah in December, Buddha's birthday in the spring, etc. Why not a whole series! Why stick to one! Our reality is the following (and I speak of the Jewish situation now): Jewish identity is a *social* reality. Part of the problem of many Jews who believe humanistically and joined humanistic congregations that were non-Jewish, was their inability by this action to deal with their Jewish identity. Many were able to, and still can, function within the Ethical Culture movement or within the Unitarian church. But it is true that there are also many Jews who have to deal with the reality of a Jewish identity which is not purely voluntary. It is a social identity. Therefore, we start out with a negative position: we *are* Jewish. This leads us to a positive one: we will therefore look at Jewish poetry, Jewish aesthetics, Jewish customs and ceremonies and see how within the reality of our Jewish identity we can use them.

Lastly, we affirm that Judaism assumes a secondary role. The search for meaning in terms of the congregation is primary, and the welfare of the individual is primary. We also accept the cultural primacy of the English-speaking culture. Most discussions about Jewish survival are unrealistic because most speakers start out by saying that Judaism or Jewish commitment must be primary. Therefore, they are not talking about the reality of Jewish life in America. Ironically, Jewish identity will survive only if it becomes secondary, because if it is treated as primary, then there will be no feasible program. All programs will end in frustration.

So, in Birmingham Temple we accept certain realities:

1) There is no guarantee of Jewish survival. 2) Organized religion is for some Jews but not for everyone. 3) Even non-Jewish Humanistic organizations are for some Jews, but not for all. 4) We want to create a Jewish organization that will first of all provide group support in the search for meaning, and second —by virtue of the reality of our Jewish identity—provide, through the aesthetics of Judaism, a suitable poetry. 5) Lastly, as a congregation, on the belief level, we have almost nothing in common with the ultra-orthodox Jew. What we do share with him is a cultural past, a sense of identity which is a social reality, that we cannot ignore. But we share with all Humanists a "common religion," a common ideology. In a sense, we have two identities, and our Humanist identity is primary. Therefore, as a congregation, as a group, we want to work and co-operate, if we can, with all other Humanists in an attempt to find meaning for man and society through the framework of this ideology.

IS RELIGION NECESSARY?

KENNETH STERN

MOST PEOPLE, when they are asked to explain what it means to be called a "Jew," tend to mention a number of different characteristics. As commonly conceived, a Jew is taken to be a person who (a) has certain religious beliefs, (b) belongs to a certain ethnic group by birth, and (c) has what Webster's calls a "sense of community" with a particular cultural and historical tradition. Of course, such characterizations are quite nebulous. For instance, it is not clear what religious beliefs are involved, nor how strongly they should be held. Neither is it clear just what constitutes belonging to an ethnic group. Is belonging a matter of birth, or is it, as Nathan Glazer suggests, a matter of "feeling" that one belongs? Again, what sort of tradition is meant—ritual observances, linguistic patterns, food preferences, or modes of living?

Even if such looseness in the concept of "being a Jew" is accepted, it would still be important to add that a person could properly be called a Jew even if he did not meet all three of these conditions, so long as he met one or two of them. Thus I should argue that a person (like me) might very well feel a sense of community with other Jews, but be an agnostic or an atheist and *still* be a Jew. For me, having religious beliefs is not a *necessary* condition for being a Jew; it is not even a very important condition. I would add that if any condition is important, although not essential, it would be the third, the sense of community. (This point will be of some significance in the latter part of this article.)

There are many persons who would disagree. They would say that a man must subscribe to the religious tenets of Judaism to be a Jew. In doing so, I think they would be smuggling in a value judgment, one which would be more readily accepted for being covert and not overt. Rather than clearly stating, "We ought not

Original for this volume.

to count anyone a Jew unless he has religious beliefs of a certain sort," which would naturally provoke the response, "And why not," they say the same thing in a nonvaluative idiom: "A Jew is a man who holds certain religious beliefs."* In this way the impression is that they are asserting a matter of fact, when they are doing no such thing. It is an old rhetorical dodge to induce others to accept certain values by getting them to accept a particular phraseology as a statement of fact. (One philosopher, Charles Stevenson of the University of Michigan, calls such a device "persuasive definition.")

If a *new* use of the word is suggested, then it should be made explicitly as a valuative judgment, and reasons should be given for adopting this new use. The fact is that what distinguishes the word "Jew" from the words "Catholic" or "Moslem" is the necessary presence of religious belief. A necessary condition for being a Catholic or a Protestant or a Mohammedan is that such persons confess to having some religious beliefs. Catholicism and Mohammedanism are quintessentially religions; Judaism is not, no matter how some would like to insist that it is.†

It seems to me that such insistence on religious beliefs tends to alienate many Jewish college teachers from the Jewish community. Nonacademic members of the Jewish community, members of synagogues, and Jewish organizations often complain about the estrangement between them and Jewish academics. Part of the reason for such estrangement is certainly that a good many of the Jewish members of the academic community have come to the conclusion that not only is religion irrelevant, but also that it is irrational. Academics are usually committed to the world of ideas, which must be submitted to close critical scrutiny before they are accorded belief. Their commitment as searchers for truth is to an "ethic of belief." The prime postulate is that "it is wrong always, everywhere, and for anyone, to believe anything upon insufficient evidence." This was written by W. K. Clifford, who in his famous essay, "The Ethics of Belief,"‡ also wrote:

* The tipoff would be if they said, "A *real* Jew . . ." or "A *true* Jew . . ."

† Of course, if we consider the word "Jew" etymologically, then "Jew" does connote a religious believer. But etymology does not give the "real" meaning of the word. The "real" meaning is the meaning it has as it is presently used.

‡ This was the first part of a three part essay originally printed in *Contemporary Review* (January 1877) and reprinted in W. K. Clifford, *Lectures and Essays* (1879).

> Every time we let ourselves believe for unworthy reasons, we weaken our powers of self-control, of doubting, of judicially and fairly weighing evidence. . . . if I let myself believe anything on insufficient evidence, there may be no great harm done by mere belief; it may be true after all, or I may never have occasion to exhibit it in outward acts. But I cannot help doing this great wrong to Man, that I make myself credulous. The danger to society is not merely that it should believe wrong things, though that is great enough; but that it should become credulous, and lose the habit of testing things and inquiring into them; for then it must sink back into savagery. The harm which is done by credulity in a man is not confined to the fostering of a credulous character in others, and consequent support of false beliefs. Habitual want of care about what I believe leads to the habitual want of care in others about the truth of what is told me. Men speak the truth to one another when each reveres the truth in his own mind; but how shall my friend revere the truth in my mind when I am myself careless about it, when I believe things because I want to believe them, and because they are comforting and pleasant.

Most academics would, I think, accept Clifford's words as the credo of the researcher, and, to put it mildly, they are uneasy in association with those who find comfort in the myths of the prescientific age.

What about "faith"? To have faith is to have a commitment to believe something. But it is always in order to ask whether the commitment is itself rational, to ask for reasons for the commitment. We should not be deceived by the slogan, "I believe on faith," with its implication that faith itself is a reason for believing. To say, "I believe on faith," is not to give a reason, it is to confess to not having any reasons. You cannot confess to not having any grounds for your belief and at the same time claim to have a ground and call it "faith." In the words of John Locke, "I find every sect, as far as reason will help them, make use of it gladly: and where it fails them, they cry out, 'It is a matter of faith, and above reason.'" There are many "faiths," each claiming to be the true one. Why accept one rather than another? A man who makes a commitment ought to be able to produce reasons for it, and if he cannot, he ought not to pretend that he can. I can do no better here than to quote Antony Flew, who in his book, *God and Philosophy* (New York: Harcourt, Brace & World, 1967, pp. 159–60), wrote that a man who claims a religious belief, should give:

reasons . . . for having a faith, and for making it this one; or reasons for believing that there are authorities on the crucial issues, and that these are they. Failure to produce any presentable apologetic even of this sort amounts to the confession that there is no good reason whatsoever for believing what you believe. This may very well be a true confession. But a recognition that this is indeed the case can scarcely consist with proselytizing fervour . . . there are extremely important practical consequences (of this) which are, it seems, very rarely drawn; and which would, surely, be unwelcome to active and enthusiastic believers. Campaigns for proselytization must become . . . perfectly preposterous if there not only is, but if it is also admitted that there is no good reason to believe the doctrines preached. Again—and this is in many countries a matter of urgent and sensitive political concern—if matters of faith have not the sort of claim to constitute knowledge or even reasonable guesses, then the religious indoctrination of children is immediately exposed as a moral outrage. . . . if, however rightly you concede that there are no sufficient reasons for holding that the doctrines of your faith are even probably true—much less known to be true—then you surely have no business teaching anyone that these doctrines are in fact true. It is one thing to teach as religious knowledge facts about what religious people believe: quite another to teach those beliefs as if they were themselves religious knowledge.

Much of what Flew says about faith may seem irrelevant to Judaism, for Jews have never been great proselytizers. But what he says about education and religious indoctrination seems exceedingly relevant. It is true that a great many Jews who insist that children receive a "Jewish education" also hold that such education should be presented from an historical rather than a religious viewpoint. However, I suggest that except in rare cases what they want their children to receive and what their children actually get are two very different things. In most Orthodox and Conservative religious schools, religious beliefs are taught as though they were some species of empirical truth for which we had good evidence. Certainly it must be admitted that what is taught is based on faith alone. The Reform movement seems little different. If one doubts what I say here, it is supported by *The New York Times* (June 21, 1967) which reported that at a meeting in Los Angeles last spring, "Spiritual leaders of *Reform* [italics added] Judaism formulated a set of guidelines to cope with what they describe as the 'increasing alienation' of Jewish college students from organized Jewish cultural and spiritual life." The article quotes a Rabbi Jospe as saying that when a Jewish student is thrust into a university atmosphere he is exposed to the challenge of new ideas. The student "frequently feels that one cannot be 'religious' and 'intelligent' at the same time." It would appear that Rabbi Jospe's method of coping with this (as he sees it) problem, is to indoctrinate such students to be impervious to any unsettling ideas. He recommends that "activities and classes for the study of Jewish thought and life be extended into the years before confirmation and graduation from high school. He [Rabbi Jospe] emphasized that these activities culminate in a program that addresses itself specifically to the graduating high school seniors to introduce them to the most important intellectual challenges to their faith that they would encounter in the university."

I wonder whether it would be possible for Rabbi Jospe, in a nonfervent moment, to consider seriously that this feeling that religion and intelligence are incompatible might actually reflect something real. As a college teacher, I find it curious and abhorrent that someone might regard the new ideas to which college students must be introduced as a kind of dangerous bacilli against which he must be immunized in advance. It is, of course, possible to discuss religion and faith rationally, but dispassionate investigation of ideas and indoctrination of ideas are worlds apart. However, I doubt that religionists are able to discuss religion rationally. There are reasons that would make it difficult—after all, they have an axe to grind. Moreover, if one looks at discussions by rabbis about religious questions, one finds a paucity of rational discourse.

An illustration is found in the August 1966 issue of *Commentary*, which featured a symposium on "The State of Jewish Belief." The participants in the symposium were rabbis of various Jewish denominations. A number of questions were posed, ranging from whether they believed that the Torah was a "divine revelation" to their opinions concerning the recent "Death of God" movement in Protestant theology. What immediately struck me about the replies was a naïveté in most of them and a dogmatic tone in nearly all of them. The conductor of the symposium, Milton Himmelfarb, commented, "In general, there is far less theological ferment than among Christians, and there are few new ideas about Judaism." Inasmuch as all of the respondents were rabbis, it was not to have been expected that they would raise questions concerning the rationality of religion itself, although Protestant theologians have. But I should have expected fewer diatribes against nonbelieving Jews. One of the participants attacked the "Secular Humanist" as adhering to an ethic that is derived from man or society. Consequently, such an ethic must remain forever "relativistic." Secular ethics, he continues, possess neither universal nor absolute validity. For example, Nazi criminals were correct when they pleaded that they acted in accordance with the laws of their state.

The foregoing argument is a tissue of confusion. Many nonreligious philosophers have proposed nonreligiously based ethics for which they have claimed "universal and absolute validity." In any case, why must any ethic be "universal and absolute"? The fact that the Nazis acted in accordance with the legal system of Germany is irrelevant to whether they acted rightly. The rabbi confuses legal obligation with moral obligation. Finally, the rabbi confounds questions of origin with questions of justification. From the fact that morality has a human *origin* it in no way follows that morality cannot have a justification. If morality has, as clearly it does, an important function in society, indeed, if society as such is inconceivable without morality, then this would seem sufficient justification. God need not come into it at all.

On the other hand, it is a moot point whether or not religion has any function. It would seem to me silly to propose that morality requires *religious* backing when it is clearly religion itself that requires justification. Accepting that morality has a vital function for society does not answer the question, which morality is the "right" one? Nazi society did have a morality, but since the society itself was evil, so was the morality. But it is not religion that tells us that. After all, throughout the centuries men have used religion to defend very different moral beliefs, some nearly as abhorrent as those included in Nazism. Ethical injunctions, whether or not religious, are usually formulated in the most nebulous and ambiguous terms, and have always provided men with a rationalization for what they wanted to do anyway. Enjoining a stormtrooper not to slaughter Jews because God had told us that murdering human beings was evil would have done no good if he believed that Jews were not human beings.

The rabbi ought to have asked himself the same question that Plato asked in his *Euthyphro* and that was discussed at length by medieval philosophers. Is an action right (or wrong) *because*

God says it is, or does God say of an action that it is right (or wrong) because it *is* right (or wrong)? If God is a good God then he will, of course, tell us that an action which is right is indeed right and that an action which is wrong is indeed wrong. That is quite different from saying that it is simply the fact that God says of an action that it is right, or that it is wrong, that makes it right or wrong. The second view holds that right and wrong are relative to the whims of God. This implies that if God were to say of an act of murder that it was right, it would be right.

Here the rabbi might object that since God is all powerful he could at pleasure make an action right or wrong, and since we know that God is good, we could trust him to choose correctly. But that would be wrong for at least two reasons. First, it is not clear what it means to say that God could make murder right, no matter how powerful he is. Whether murder is right or wrong seems to be independent of the will of any being. St. Thomas Aquinas once pointed out that to say that God was all-powerful was to say that God could do anything *that could be done*. It is not to say that he can do anything, even those things *that cannot be done*. He cannot, for example, make a triangle that has four sides. That is not something that can be done, so not even God can do it. In the same way, even God cannot make a wrong act right, for that is not something that can be done. Second, to say that God is a good God presupposes some standard of goodness and evil that is independent of what God says or does not say. A God who told us murder was all right, or torture was all right, could not be called a good God. For if we insisted that he was good even if he commanded us to do what was *evil*, what would we mean when we said he was good?

These questions demand an answer. Anyone who tells us that only religiously based ethics can have validity and does not address himself to such questions and try to answer them is not being serious. At the very least, he must be judged naïve. It is not as if these questions are new; they have been debated down through the centuries. I looked in vain through the symposium for any suggestion that those symposiasts who pontificated about the relation between ethics and religion were even acquainted with such issues.

Still another symposiast tells us that we need religion because "Scientific Knowledge is not the *only* true knowledge" and that the "scientific method precludes from the very start any consideration of the factors of purpose and value." It is difficult to know where to begin here. What sort of knowledge is "true knowledge"? Is there "false knowledge"? Does science ignore purpose and value? If the rabbi thinks so let him read John Dewey. Is it the business of science to preach to us which goals we should seek? Ought not our values be up to us as rational and responsible human beings? Perhaps what is most distasteful in what this rabbi says is in his implicit argument. Science excludes purpose and value. But since we need purpose and value, it must lie outside of science. It should be asked whether it necessarily follows that because we need something that science (allegedly) cannot provide and that human beings cannot provide for themselves, religion will provide for us with these things? How often is this line of argument met in religious apologetics? Its frequency seems to me to support Freud's analysis of religion as an exercise in wish fulfillment. Freud seems to be telling us that religion is the consequence of all that is childish in human beings. And surely, there is no behavior more childish than to insist that what you wish for must be true, that what you need will be provided. Freud somewhere tells us that the world is not a nursery. Does religion contend that it is?

Most Jewish college teachers respect ideas, no matter how fervently held, when those who hold them are not only passionate, but also aware of the difficulties contained in the ideas and are aware of their obligation to provide some reply to these difficulties. The chasm between the Jewish academic and the ordinary member of a Jewish religious community is a consequence of the disinclination of the leaders of Jewish religionists to discuss their ideas, or even to be aware of any difficulties contained in them. It is a paradox that Judaism, which has so profound a *secular* connection with education and learning, is in its religious aspects so backward, unlike modern Protestantism or even Catholicism. There seems to be a terror of anti-intellectualism in modern Jewry.

I have already suggested, to adapt a well-known advertising slogan, "You don't have to be religious to be Jewish." But there is a related question that needs asking. If an individual Jew need not be religious and wants to remain a Jew, can he? Can Jewish identity survive without religion? In other words, can Judaism as a group phenomenon survive the passing of religious belief? If religious belief is discarded, it may well be argued that what eventually will happen is what eventually did happen to other ethnic groups, such as the Italians and the Irish—slow but sure assimilation and the consequent loss of identity. According to this argument religious belief of some kind is the psychological foundation of Jewish identity and community. Even if religion is not requisite for the *individual* Jew, it is necessary for the maintenance of the group. Only as long as there is a Jewish ethnic group can the individual, although not religious, retain his Jewish identity.

This poses a disturbing ethical problem. If the sociopsychological hypothesis is right, then the only way the nonbelieving Jew can maintain his identity is by identifying himself with the Jewish community whose identity exists *through* religious belief. The nonbelieving Jew then takes, but does not give. He disparages religion as false, but profits from the religious beliefs of others. Is he not a parasite? A freeloader? This is the sort of ethical dilemma that is most closely identified with Kantian morality. It was Kant who pointed out that the evil of a liar's behavior, for example, is that a liar could not lie unless other men were honest. If no one were honest, then he could not get himself believed, which is the only way a successful lie is possible. In the same way, unless there are believing Jews, there will be no Jewish community; and if there is no Jewish community, then the unbelieving Jew cannot maintain a Jewish identity. Therefore, the unbelieving Jew must will that there be believing Jews. But is this not immoral? Can someone morally expect others to believe what he thinks it is wrong for himself to believe?

I find it difficult to answer this question and, indeed, what I shall say will not really be an answer. I see no way to *untie* the knot, I can only cut through it. But first let me point out that the problem only arises if we accept the view that religious belief is necessary for the maintenance of the Jewish community. This is an empirical thesis that may well be false. In any event, being a philosopher and not a social psychologist, I am incompetent to judge its truth. Let us suppose then that it is true, what then? The Jewish nonbeliever who wants to maintain his ethnic identity is confronted with this disturbing ethical dilemma. My disbelieving Jewishness seems to depend on others' believing Jewishness. Should I therefore believe what I do not believe to be true? Even if that could be morally defended, it would seem to be psychologically impossible. I cannot hold a belief that I believe in my heart is untrue. No one can, and no one should. It is surely a betrayal of one's self, one's intellect, even to try. I am therefore forced to conclude that the nonbelieving Jew must, if some sociologists are right, contemplate the possibility that Jewish identity will vanish and still not lift a finger to prevent this. Let me admit at the same time to a profound sense of regret and sorrow when I contemplate this prospect. What I am not sure about, however, is *whether my feelings are rational.*

Spinoza, the greatest of all philosophers who were also Jewish (and who was excommunicated from Judaism for the heresy of denying the existence of a personal, human-like God), held that regret, an enervating emotion, was never rational, for it was always about the inevitable. To regret is to cry over spilt milk, or over milk that must in the scheme of things be spilt. Spinoza also argued that we can undermine and perhaps even eliminate weakening and fruitless emotions, such as regret, by understanding that what has happened, or what will happen, must *be*, and by trying to understand, in terms of its causes, why we feel that regret. Understanding our feelings by understanding their causal antecedents, and so bringing reason to bear upon them, will help remove their pang and their sting, and in so doing we will be released from their bondage (what he called Human Bondage). Many centuries later, Freud argued along identical lines.

Let me apply the advice of these two great thinkers to myself. I know that I have been raised in a certain tradition that has deep emotional associations. Certain lilts of the voice fill me with warmth and certain Yiddish expressions come readily to my mind to express my feelings. I find Jewish jokes particularly amusing and I "understand" them. Many sorts of food (how important is the connection of Jewishness and food!) give me a Proustian relation to the past and to the world about me. Much of this I connect with my grandparents, now nearly twenty years dead. These feelings and this tradition are deeply related to them and their love as well as to my parents and other members of my family. My entrance into the academic world has in no way weakened these feelings. It seems clear to me that my regret over the loss of Jewishness is closely connected with the deep sorrows and fears that I have concerning the loss of those who protected, nurtured, and loved me as a child. To see these emotions as originating in my childhood, to understand them as in some sense childish is not to denigrate them, but it is to understand them and, through them, more of myself. Moreover, it is to see that they are connected with the recognition that one must grow up and take his place in the world as an adult. I have already mentioned Freud's profoundly wry saying, "The world is not a nursery," but it is difficult in various degrees for people to recognize this truth, for it is difficult to grow up. In this way, I understand my regret.

Let me say in conclusion that I recognize that along with the prospective demise of Jewishness, there will be a concomitant loss of values, or, at least, things I hold valuable. Most of these will be aesthetic. On the other hand, perhaps an important good will arise out of this loss. Perhaps the demise of Judaism will be the first in the demise of all the racial and national separateness that has caused the world so much havoc throughout its history. If this is the price, the loss of Jewish community, shall anyone say it is not worth paying?

Jews
and
Politics

AMERICAN POLITICAL THEORY AND THE POLITICAL NOTIONS OF AMERICAN JEWS: CONVERGENCES AND CONTRADICTIONS

DANIEL J. ELAZAR

INTRODUCTION

ACCOMPANYING THE REVIVAL of Jewish political life in the past two centuries there has been a growing concern among Jewish scholars and laymen alike with the relationships of Jews as individuals and of Jewish communities to political matters. To date, much of this concern has been with the manner in which Jews have acquired political rights as individuals in their various countries of residence and as a community in the land of Israel. Secondarily, there has been a concern among Jews with questions of ideology, particularly with the ideologies of the Left.[1]

With the virtual conclusion of the struggle for political rights and the decline in importance of nineteenth-century ideologies since the Second World War, new problems present themselves for consideration, among them the relationships between the political attitudes and behaviour of Jews and those of their fellow citizens in the various countries of the Diaspora and the connexions between Jews living in different countries with differing political patterns. These new questions are closely related to the larger study of political culture which has begun to concern political scientists in general and which should interest students of contemporary Jewry as well.[2] This article represents an attempt to explore some of these new questions concerning the

Reprinted by permission of the author, Professor Moshe Davis for the conference at which this essay was originally presented, and the editors from *The Jewish Journal of Sociology*, 9 (June 1967), pp. 5–24.

Jews and politics in order to begin the examination of the problem of political culture within the world Jewish community.

The immediate question posed here is related to a larger underlying theme, a problem of great significance for the study of contemporary Jewry—and for the determination of the character of world Jewry in the future. Given the integration of Jews as individual citizens into their respective countries of residence and their loss of any separate political or corporate status as members of a separate community, is there anything markedly distinctive about their political ideas or attitudes to distinguish them from their fellow non-Jewish citizens and unite them with other Jews elsewhere regardless of citizenship? If there are such ideas or attitudes, what produces or has produced them? Is their origin distinctively Jewish in any way or do they stem from other sources? Do they relate in any way to the classical Jewish political ideas found in the Bible and the Talmud? Indeed, are there such things as 'distinctively Jewish' political ideas or attitudes, or, at the very least, political ideas and attitudes with a distinctively close relationship to the Jewish world view? Can any distinctively Jewish political ideas or attitudes be maintained in an environment that is not Jewish, where there are no significant Jewish political institutions affecting the general Jewish population? And, one might add conversely, are such ideas or attitudes maintained even when there is a Jewish environment and Jewish political institutions?

These questions are not easy ones to answer. They pose serious problems for the investigator, problems of temporal change over millennia and problems of 'national character', to mention only two of the most difficult ones. Here we will hardly do more than raise these questions and outline the manner in which they manifest themselves in one situation, and in a preliminary way. The effort is made with incomplete—even inadequate—data simply in order to begin the study.

The American case is the 'hard case' when it comes to trying to answer any of the above questions. The Jews are, in all probability, better and more completely integrated into American society and political life than in any other diaspora country, now or in the past. Moreover, American political theory draws more heavily upon classical Jewish sources than that of any other nation (perhaps including Israel), and American values and aspirations generally coincide with Jewish ones in significant ways.[3] If any positive answers to the questions can be discovered in the American case, we may believe that there are good grounds for discovering positive ones in other cases as well.

This essay will concentrate on the exploration of those political notions common to American Jews and their relationship to the classical political ideas of the United States. The exploration here is necessarily quite limited, not only for lack of space and data, but also because any full explanation would be dependent upon a number of questions of first importance relating to the study of society and Jewish history that are not even stated here.

Before beginning the analysis, we need to understand several of its limitations.

(1) Unless otherwise indicated, the American Jews referred to in these pages are those who have come to the United States since 1881 from eastern Europe, and their descendants. The Jews of this group form the bulk (over 80 per cent) of the American Jewish community.[4] Consequently, their attitudes dominate American Jewish life. This is not to minimize the degree to which the earlier waves of Jewish immigration (the Sephardi-western European and German-central European elements) and their descendants have shared the same ideas or contributed to American Jewish life. In fact, the most notable Jewish contributions to American public affairs have been made by the descendants of those earlier waves but, with few exceptions, the contributions were made by individuals whose impact on the ideas of American Jewry came as a consequence of their public recognition but who themselves reflected ideas acquired from a predominantly non-Jewish environment. There will be specific reference to these earlier immigrants where their influence has been relevant.

(2) Furthermore, this study considers American Jewry in the aggregate, disregarding the obvious differences that can be found among them. Consequently, the discussion of American Jewish political notions is couched in the most general terms. No significant effort is made to draw lines of distinction between the notions of different Jews or Jewish groups. Limitations of space demand this approach, and lack of sufficient data as to the nature of the difference reinforces it. Of course, generalization at the level presented here is inevitably over-simplification. Moreover,

generalizations of the type presented here tend to lead to questions of 'national character' always difficult to resolve by empirical study.

(3) The discussion of American political ideas is similarly couched in the most general terms. It represents an effort to present the basic or mainstream political ideas shared most widely by the American people and is based on my continuous study of these ideas over the past decade in an effort to extract those basic to the American political system.[5] Except where specified, the discussion here ignores the nuances of change in those ideas over time. Unless qualified, the reference to 'American political ideas' is invariably to the classic ideas of the American political tradition formulated and expressed in the first century of American independence. Twentieth-century modifications of these ideas are specified within the body of the paper where necessary.

(4) The summary statement of classical Jewish political ideas is also presented here in general terms without corroborating evidence, for lack of space. It represents my present assessment of the political ideas expressed explicitly and implicitly in the Bible and the Talmud as developed through a preliminary (and continuing) exploration of the basic Jewish texts for their political implications.[6]

(5) 'Political ideas', in the sense used here, refers primarily to conceptions of the political process and secondarily to the purposes of politics. Thus we shall be less concerned with abstract conceptions of social justice than with notions about the best political order for the achievement of justice.

I

The thesis presented here is a simple one. Though classical American political thought owes much to classical Jewish political ideas, the most that can be said of the great majority of the Jewish immigrants (who came to America with little political knowledge or concern) is that their Jewish heritage predisposed them to be perhaps tangentially receptive to the fundamental American political ideas. Moreover, those politically conscious Jews who came with formed political ideas espoused notions substantially different from those either of the United States or of classical Judaism, based as they were on continental notions of elitist democracy and socialism. Finally, such political ideas as were brought from Europe by Jews of all persuasions and levels of political interest had been developed in response to the political experiences of Europe in the eighteenth and nineteenth centuries, particularly those produced by the French Revolution; experiences which ran in paths quite different from those of America. Consequently, the immigrant Jews and their descendants have had to adapt themselves to American political ideas, either as a matter of desire or simply out of necessity. That process of adaptation is still going on. Its successful completion may have the paradoxical effect of bringing American Jews closer to classical Jewish political ideas (albeit unknowingly) than at any time in the past seventeen centuries while, at the same time, breaking down previously shared political attitudes that have linked Jewries in the United States and in other countries in a common frame of reference.

Classical American political ideas are derived in part from the liberal 'natural right' tradition developed as part of the scientific revolution that ushered in the modern age in the seventeenth century and the Enlightenment that gave the modern age its intellectual tone in the eighteenth.[7] They are derived to an equal or greater extent from the English and American interpretations of Biblical (or, in their terms, Old Testament) political ideas, particularly those of the Torah and the Former Prophets, in the same centuries.[8] Both streams came together in the formation of the United States. The former was dominant among the new nation's intellectuals of the squirarchy and the liberal professions, particularly in the middle states and the South, and the latter was dominant among the nation's intellectuals of the church and the academy, particularly in New England and the West; but both were shared to some degree by all elements involved in the development of America from the Revolutionary era until the Civil War.

For our purposes, we may identify four key idea complexes that have shaped American politics.

(1) *Tradition* (*as opposed to Ideology*). This is the sense that there exists an American tradition supported by a general consensus of all Americans within which American politics is con-

ducted. It is to this tradition, rather than to any ideology (or ideologies), that Americans turn to justify current political interests or notions, even though crypto-ideologies may exist on the American scene from time to time. In practical terms, this reliance on tradition allows Americans to be pragmatic in their approach to specific political problems, at least up to the boundaries of the tradition itself. It also discourages the advance formulation of grand programmes.[9]

(2) *Agrarianism (as opposed to Urbanity)*. American political values look to the vision of a commonwealth that supports and encourages the agrarian virtues of individual self-reliance and family solidarity within the framework of a co-operative community and the agrarian ideals of classlessness (or minimal class distinctions), religiosity, and ownership of private property by those somehow involved in its use. Qualities of urbanity, sophistication, and cosmopolitanism (despite their undeniable attractiveness) have been rendered secondary to the agrarian virtues where the American public has consciously faced crucial choices over the years. In practical political terms, this has meant that Americans have preferred to keep the role of government as limited as possible but as active as necessary in any given age to maximize the possibilities of individual freedom, opportunity, and choice, and to help maintain life styles that reflect agrarian values.[10]

(3) *Federalism (as opposed to Centralism)*. Federalism is the fundamental principle governing the structure and process of government in the United States. The federal idea of individuals and communities linked by a constitution or covenant under the rule of law in such a way that each member of the covenanting community retains his (or its) ultimate integrity and a measure of power under the covenant law, with its consequent political implications of power dispersed among many centres rather than concentrated (even theoretically) in one, is a principle which has been maintained in the face of many pressures over the years. In practical applications of this principle, Americans have sought to maximize local control where government has had to act, within the framework of national consensus, and to maintain a separation of powers between the federal government, the states, and the local governments, even as all these separate centres of power are expected to co-operate with one another in partnership.[11]

(4) *Messianism (as opposed to Fatalism)*. American politics is animated by a messianic vision of the meaning of America and of the role the United States is destined to play in the improvement of humanity. This messianism is based on the notion that Americans have their own covenant with the Almighty to do good works. It stresses the unique character of America and its institutions, but it also encourages Americans to take an optimistic attitude regarding the possibilities for significant improvement in mankind as a whole. Thus it is politically incumbent upon Americans to use politics for such improvements at home and abroad as appear to be possible at any given time.[12]

These four elements have their roots, wholly or in part, in the political ideas of the Bible. The ancient Israelite tribal confederacy was bound together by the unique tradition of Sinai and the covenant which demanded that the Jews maintain a civil society based on agrarian virtues in order to serve as witnesses to the ultimate achievement of a messianic order of world-wide scope.[13] The Jews who came to the United States were not only unacquainted with the non-Biblical sources of the American political tradition but, despite the infusion into their lives of Biblically-rooted values, were further removed from a political understanding of the Bible than their non-Jewish hosts whose school civics texts until recently cited Biblical sources to justify fundamental American political ideas.[14]

II

Because of the circumstances of Jewish life in Europe, the overwhelming majority of the Jews arriving in America came from highly apolitical backgrounds; and nowhere were they more apolitical than in eastern Europe. In no country in Europe had the Jews had a share in the government, either because they were excluded as Jews or simply because they came from countries where only the inner circle of the aristocracy participated in politics. However, most of the Jewish immigrants from western and central Europe came after their countries of origin had felt something of the impact of modern republicanism. Eastern European Jews did not have even that experience. While their communities had a substantial measure of internal autonomy, by the nineteenth century Jewish self-government had become little more than the narrow legal construction of the Codes by rabbinical authorities or had degenerated into a form of oligarchic rule in which the rabbis and the rich shared power.[15] In the wake of the European revolutionary eruptions of the eighteenth and nineteenth centuries, some Jews had managed to acquire a limited political education—limited in the sense that it was primarily revolutionary, concerned with tearing down old regimes, but extraordinarily naïve about the problems of erecting new ones or maintaining a post-revolutionary political order. Most of their brethren, however, had to acquire political knowledge along with political experience after arriving in the United States.

Since the French Revolution (and its subsequent 'heirs') gave most Jews their first opportunity to participate in politics after some seventeen centuries of exile from the political realm, the Jews became and remained partisans of that revolution, persisting in their partisanship to our own day.[16] When the Jews began their great migration to the United States at the end of the nineteenth century, they brought modifications of European revolutionary ideas with them in various guises (ranging from Jacobin liberalism to Marxism). While the American experience softened most of the more radical expressions of those ideas, they remained a strong influence even among many of the more assimilated and prosperous Jews.[17]

If the idea complexes behind the political notions of the Jewish immigrants were to be fitted into a four-point framework analogous to that set forth above for their American counterparts, one might find that over the years tradition had been abandoned as a source of political ideas and replaced by ideology, particularly the ideologies of the left. The agrarian virtues and ideas had been replaced by a kind of urban liberalism based, on one hand, on the great socio-economic differences between groups and, on the other, on an elimination of political distinctions between individuals. In place of federal notions, expecting the diffusion of power among many centres in civil society, there was a general expectation that government, good or bad, would necessarily be monarchical, at least in the original Greek sense of centring attention on a single head of state as the primary political decision-maker, perhaps within some constitutional framework. This notion persisted even among the revolutionaries. Finally, though the messianic idea had persisted among the immigrants, it was completely secularized and redirected to this-worldly economic advancement (individual or collective), even losing the political elements of the older, religiously-inspired vision.[18]

Important manifestations of these idea complexes can be seen reflected in the political ideas of subsequent generations of American Jews.[18] Normally quite sophisticated in worldly matters, even those highly attuned to questions of political ideology have retained a curious lack of sophistication in matters of political organization, structure, and policy. In practical terms, this has meant that the Jews have reacted to the institutions of government, the forces of politics, and the development of issues in ways different from those characteristic of the American people as a whole.

In the beginning, relatively few Jews understood the structure of the American federal system—something which requires a certain amount of political sophistication—and even today relatively few appreciate it on its own terms. Since an understanding of the system has required some sense of local (meaning, in this case, state) involvement as well as national concern, this may be partly accounted for by the Jews' lack of attachment to particular states, even where they have developed ties to certain large cities.[19] More significantly, the immediate past experiences of the Jewish people did not prepare them to appreciate the subtleties of a political system based on the diffusion of power among several centres and placing maximum emphasis on local control.

In the first place, Jews have been used to focusing attention on the single political leader, be he benevolent or malevolent, as the source of all significant political decisions, because in the Old World their communities existed on the sufferance of, and were beholden to, king or emperor.[20] Coming to the United States, they transferred this attention to the President. Thus *siddurim* published in the United States by Jews of east European ancestry merely substitute a prayer for the President and Vice-President while completely ignoring such important elements of American Government as the Congress or the States which, strictly speaking, should receive equal mention in such prayers.[21] Coming to America, they and their descendants have persisted in looking to the national government as the source of all good.

The founders of the United States sought to strengthen the liberties and political rights of all individuals through a system of limited, locally-centred government whose scope of activity was hedged in by a federal system designed to keep power diffused among a number of centres. The pattern is still considered to be the ideal one by most Americans. Even as subsequent generations have modified that pattern in substance, they have sought (with considerable success) to preserve its spirit.[22] The Jews of Europe, on the other hand, found locally-centred government rooted in the communitarian values of the *ancien régime* a barrier to their enfranchisement as citizens because it reflected the quasi-feudalism of pre-revolutionary days. They supported the French Revolution's assault upon those institutions in the name of collectivism and centralized government based on Jacobin notions of democratic consent via the 'general will' rather than via influence from many local sources.[23]

Government, to most American Jews, has tended to be a matter of law and law enforcement rather than politics. Nowhere is this more evident than in the characteristic channelling of active Jewish political participation through the courts. As a community, American Jewry has left its mark on American government in the courtrooms rather than the legislatures or the bureaucracies. The great figures of Jewish origin in American politics have tended to be jurists more often than not. Moreover, Jewish organizations with American political missions, such as the American Jewish Congress and the Anti-Defamation League, have conducted the greater share of their political activities in the courts. While the nature of the issues which interest them is influential in directing them to the courts, the tendency to literalness in viewing the law also leads them to reject political solutions with their built-in demands for compromise based on broad interpretation of the statutes and constitutions.[24] Lying behind these phenomena is a conception of politics-as-law no doubt traceable to the character of Jewish self-government in Europe, where the notion that men could make laws through the political process was unknown. Law came from God and Torah and such changes in the law as were made came from quasi-judicial proceedings dominated by rabbinical judges who claimed to be no more than interpreters of the law.[25] Mainstream American notions, on the other hand, have always held law to be a matter of legislation. Even the Constitution, whatever its ultimate connexion with 'higher law', is viewed as a humanly willed document subject to change through the legislative process. Hence politics is of the essence even under a highly law-oriented system.[26]

Finally, the Jewish immigrants, with their strong penchant for the left, included among their number a considerable leavening of people seeking radical changes in the established order. Unlike most American reformers, they did not start with the view that the political system in which they were located was basically good and that the changes required revolved around a restoration of the proper balance of power within it.[27] While the socialists, anarchists, and communists of various shades remained a minority among the immigrants, they did much to set the political tone in the new Jewish communities. They edited the Yiddish periodicals, dominated the speakers' platforms, and organized the first Jewish-dominated political action groups.[28] As part of this sympathy for those interested in radically changing the world, American Jews have had a penchant for messianic internationalism not only working for greater American involvement in world affairs, but often seeming to place greater faith in such international organizations as the United Nations than in the representative institutions of the United States.[29]

In several ways, the political notions brought from abroad were strengthened by the experiences of the new immigrants and the political interests generated thereby. The first and foremost political interest of the Jews was to become fully accepted as members of the American body politic.[30] In spite of the bias towards equal acceptance within the American political tradition, the Jews, like other immigrant groups outside the Anglo-Saxon or Nordic cultures, encountered some immediate hostility, usually in the form of social and economic discrimination. Thus the Jews had to engage in a struggle for acceptance which, though it was child's play as compared to the European experience, served nevertheless to reinforce European political notions. Even in America, the liberals and the left had the most appeal for the new immigrants and offered them the greatest degree of acceptance; so the Jews, like the others, went left or stayed with the liberals. Then, too, the first direct and continuing contacts between the Jews and government came over questions of church-state relations. At least at the local level, American governments were concerned with questions of social morality in the Biblical spirit, though with an obviously Christian orientation. Sunday 'blue laws' seemed to prevent Jews from making a livelihood while observing their Sabbath; public schools where Bible reading and recitation of the Lord's Prayer were common inflicted Christian beliefs on Jewish children; radical prohibitionists among the Protestant fundamentalists threatened the Jewish ceremonial use of wine. In response to these challenges, the Jews adopted a militant secularist position also akin to that embraced by the European left, and began a battle (which still continues) for removal of those 'offensive' signs of their minority status.[31] Thus the Jews were to be found in the paradoxical position of opposing essentially Jewish ideas as to the religious purposes of civil society in order to attain equal rights as individuals.

The way in which all these factors made their appearance (or the way in which the appearance was perceived) tended to persuade Jews to turn to the federal government for relief, encouraging a version of the European notion that centralization equals democracy. While, in actuality, the non-centralized character of American politics aided the Jews by increasing the value of their votes in key states such as New York, Pennsylvania, and Illinois, the Jews saw national figures—invariably presidents such as the two Roosevelts, Wilson, and Truman—as their champions. They accepted state and local political rewards as their due and coveted national political recognition; then transferred their sympathies to the national government without appreciating that it was their local strength that qualified them for consideration in national councils.[32] Moreover, in church-state questions, the possibility of successfully appealing to the United States Supreme Court had an important impact on Jewish attitudes. The Court, which had the additional attraction of being a place where politicking was carried on through the law in a manner familiar to the Jews from their own European experiences and one which they were able to master from the start, has responded favourably to most of the Jews' secularizing demands, thus reinforcing the notion that the federal government is more friendly to 'democracy' (as the Jews define it) and that law is preferable to politics as a means of gaining democratic goals.

Finally, the fact that most Jews were first exposed to local politics in its worst form in the United States—in the big cities dominated by the crudest forms of city bossism—also turned them towards Washington. The moralistically-inclined Jews settled in the nation's biggest cities when those cities were morally at their nadir. They were not happy with the ward politics they saw around them, and, in rejecting them, rejected local government as a democratic instrument generally.[33]

By holding the ideas they did, the Jews did not stand outside the broad spectrum of legitimate American political ideas so much as they stood along its outer limits. In each specific case, they could find company with other groups safely ensconced within American society, but in no case did they stand close to the mainstream.

In one sense, the Jews fitted into a certain pattern of American politics immediately. The Jews' attachment to reform was not only based on perceptions of self-interest, but also reflected the fundamental moral concern which is part and parcel of the Jewish attitude towards politics. Here, too, the evidence available is less than systematic or comprehensive, but its overall thrust is clear. Politics, even to the Jews who came to America from an unpolitical environment, was considered to be a matter of morality, a device for achieving justice and establishing the good commonwealth. The overwhelming majority of Jewish immigrants could not conceive of politics as a business or a means for personal economic advancement, nor would they accept instructions from any authority or institution (religious or political) as to the casting of their votes. In this respect, the Jews demonstrated from the first that they shared the same political culture as the old line Yankees, what I have called elsewhere the moralistic political culture.[34] In the United States, this moralistic political culture is one of the nation's three basic political subcultures (the other two being the individualistic and the traditionalistic). These political subcultures reflect differences in political attitudes and outlook that cut across such factors as the date of immigration to American shores, tying together long established ethnic groups and those more recently arrived with common bonds.[35] The moralistic political culture is clearly the most respectable of the three in the United States but, at the local level, it is confined to a minority of the population. The attachment of both the Jews and the heirs of the Puritan tradition to the moralistic political culture is not simply a coincidence. In both cases, the view that politics is a tool to achieve moral ends (rather than simply a means for material advancement or the maintenance of traditional ways of life) comes from the same Biblical source. For the Jews, this provided an *entrée* into the American political system at a level appropriate to their interests and background.

III

Whatever the contradictions between American political ideas and Jewish political notions born out of circumstance, they did not affect the political involvement of the Jews as citizens and voters, perhaps because they did not reflect differences in underlying values. For, despite the apolitical background of the Jewish immigrants to America, no group became involved in the exercise of the rights of American citizens more rapidly than the Jews. The Jews who came to the New World were not peasants like so many of the other immigrants; the great majority were literate and began to follow politics with almost religious zeal because they sensed that political participation was one important way to become Americanized, while it was also good in and of itself in the light of their larger values. As soon as possible, Jews became citizens and voters in the New World, and, having acquired the right to vote, they continued to make use of it in proportions far in excess of the national average and even in excess of the average in comparable socio-economic groups.[36]

The Jews were involved in politics as progressives or liberals from the first.[37] This, indeed, was true of the earlier Jewish immigrant groups as well. The predominantly Sephardi or Sephardicized Jewish community of the late eighteenth century strongly embraced the American revolutionary cause and then, after the establishment of the United States, became staunch—and in some cases prominent—Jeffersonian Democrats. Jews also followed Andrew Jackson and his persuasion a generation later. Fuchs claims that Jewish ties to the Democratic Party reached their peak in the administration of Martin Van Buren, Jackson's heir to the presidency. The decline of Jewish attachment to that party reflected a general shift of the progressives to the Republican Party. It is very likely that a majority of the German Jews became Republicans from the first. Coming at the time when the struggle over Negro slavery was reaching its peak, their generally anti-slavery sympathies led them into the newly organized G.O.P.

With the emergence of the conflict over laissez-faire in the last years of the nineteenth century, a majority of the Jews again chose the progressive side. Most of the members of the established Jewish community sympathized with the progressives, even if they stood on the right wing of the reform movement. Among the new immigrants there were many socialists who attempted, at first, to transfer their Old World ideas to the American scene. In time, most of them became supporters of Franklin D. Roosevelt, the New Deal, and the Democratic Party. The bulk of the new immigrants ultimately arrived at the same position, though not via socialism. As early as 1900, the Jews of New York City voted solidly for William Jennings Bryan, the Democratic candidate for President, despite his erstwhile associations with the supposed nativism of the greater West. The next year, the Jewish voters of that city were instrumental in electing a reform administration, joining with the uptown 'blue bloods' in a fusion movement.[38]

From the 1890s until the early 1930s, when both the Democratic and the Republican parties contained active conservative and progressive or liberal wings which struggled within each party for control, the Jews voted independently, choosing candidates for their personal stands rather than following one party or the other consistently. Thus the Jewish vote went for both Bryan, the Democrat, and Theodore Roosevelt, the Republican, on the basis of their progressivism without regard to their party differences. As the progressive-liberal coalition won greater power in the Democratic party and the conservatives increased their hold on the G.O.P., the Jews moved towards the former.[39]

By the 1930s, American Jews had given their full commitment to the Democratic Party, which not only offered a prospective solution to the problems of the depression, but also offered eastern European Jews the kind of political recognition previously accorded only to Sephardi and German Jews.[40] This commitment to the Democratic Party has persisted, but less today for ethnic reasons so much as for reasons of ideology. The Jews of the 1960s vote Democratic because they are liberals in the way their fathers voted Democratic because they were Jewish.[41]

In any case, the commitment of the Jewish voters to liberal candidates and causes has been consistent and overwhelming. Such statistics on the matter as are available show that from 75 to over 90 per cent of the Jewish voters have supported the Democratic ticket in national elections in the last generation. And, in every case, this support has included Jews from economic levels that among non-Jews have continued to vote Republican.[42]

Whatever their early difficulties, the history of the Jews in the United States has been one of unparalleled success in expressing their basic socio-political instincts as a function of their securing full membership in a predominantly non-Jewish society. The facts of that success are well-known and need not be documented here. The reasons for that success are somewhat more conjectural, but even they are reasonably familiar.[43] I would suggest that three reasons of first importance should be accepted, at least one of which is directly related to the points made in the previous section.

(1) American society has traditionally been an open society that has valued some measure of pluralism. It has no ruling group with a widely accepted prior claim to Americanism, and it came into being with no established feudal institutions to militate against full integration of non-Christians into 'the American way of life.'

(2) America has had a dynamic society with a continually growing economy offering new opportunities in every generation. The nation has never been forced to redivide the same economic pie, but has been able to give new groups a share in an economy that is ever-expanding. Moreover, those (like the Jews) who have been able to contribute significantly to the nation's growth, have been especially welcome to share in the growing economic pie.

(3) The basic values, both positive and negative, of the American and Jewish civilizations are quite similar, encouraging a measure of convergence and identification not present in other civilizations that have been hosts to Jews. That is to say, the great moral values of American society are directly related to the great moral values of Jewish tradition and, indeed, are taken predominantly from that tradition as it is expressed in the Bible. At the same time, various negations of those values, particularly those which have gained popularity in the twentieth century, are found in large measure among Jews (one might even say that they are typically Jewish negations) often in exaggerated form. Frequently Jews are in the forefront of those who seek to justify these negations intellectually and morally.

Successful Jewish integration into American society has been coupled with great successes in the economic and intellectual realms. In the former, the Jews as a group have achieved the highest level of material prosperity of any single ethnic group in the country while at the same time making important contributions to the American economy as a whole. In the latter realm, individual Jews have, in recent years, become the nation's pace-setters.

In politics and governmental service, however, the Jewish record has been distinctly mixed. In the political realm, Jews participate as individuals everywhere, holding every office except the very highest in the land, and even that office is no longer considered unattainable. Yet, unlike members of other immigrant groups such as the Irish and Italians, few Jews sought to advance themselves through politics, preferring to follow business, professional, and intellectual pursuits for economic and social advancement. Thus, despite a measure of Jewish activity in numbers out of proportion to their three per cent or less of the total population, Jews have not been nearly as visible in public life as in other fields. Take, for example, the employment pattern of Jews in Detroit in 1935. Less than one per cent of the gainfully occupied Jews in that city were engaged in the public service, including female secretaries and clerks in public offices. Whereas, the Jews constituted 5.9 per cent of the gainfully employed in all industries, they constituted only 1.7 per cent of those in the public service—less, if women are excluded.[44] In a survey of 234 cities, conducted between 1948 and 1951, John P. Dean found that 'the participation of Jews in politics or in public office appears to be relatively limited, compared for instance, with that of Irish, Italian or other immigrant descended groups'; that 'participation is somewhat greater in appointive offices . . .'; and that 'the most common type is the appointment of lawyers to positions such as assistant district attorney, civil service commissioner, or housing commissioner'.[45]

Until very recently, even those Jews who later became political leaders all entered public life after having made careers elsewhere. Moreover, the Jews of the last migration and their descendants have been distinctly under-represented as a group among those Jews who have been leaders in political affairs. The Sephardi Jews with their prior background in Western societies (even though they never constituted more than a few thousand souls) produced numerous men who entered public affairs as early as the seventeenth century; and they continued to do so for three centuries. The German Jews, within one generation of their arrival in significant numbers, contributed political figures who were able to compete in national politics. Eastern European

Jewry is only now beginning to produce men of recognized importance, after three generations.[46]

The Jews have expressed their political concern in other ways, however, primarily through voluntary service in the cause of radicalism or reform. In the early years, this involved activity in specialized or fringe organizations. Then Jews became active as amateurs or volunteers in mainstream political groups, with increasing success in recent years. This volunteering spirit persists today, most recently in the civil rights movement in the South, where the number of Jews may exceed 50 per cent of the white participants, and the Peace Corps, where the Jews are reported to compose 60 per cent of the volunteers.[47]

IV

Looking at the relationship between the political notions of the American Jews and the political ideas of America generally over time, one sees that there has been a general tendency for the bulk of American Jews gradually to Americanize their political notions, but with an interesting and important cleavage in their manner of doing so. The general Jewish population has done so uncritically, simply as part of their overall assimilation into American life. The Jewish intellectuals, on the other hand, have either fought that Americanization or have sought to alter the American political ideas themselves. While this distinction has had interesting consequences for the United States as a whole, its Jewish significance is limited and will not be discussed here.

What is important is the way in which the Americanization of the Jews accompanied a leftward shift in the political notions of the American majority as well, as a result of the pressures of twentieth century war, depression, and technology. In sum, while the American Jews today resemble the American majority in their overt political behaviour more than ever before, the Jews reached their present political position by turning from an even more leftist one (either socialist or strongly inclined towards the left), while the American majority has turned towards an acceptance of the welfare state, with considerable reluctance, from an earlier limited or anti-government position. The difference in their respective directions of evolution reflects a difference in immediate political ideas and is also a reflection of different social experiences.

In reality, despite the uniqueness of the Jewish experience in America, one sees marked similarities between their support of the liberal left (or left-liberals) and the general tendency of Jews the world over to support the same groups in their respective countries since the French Revolution. These common attitudes appeared and were grounded in the Jews' immediate political experiences all over the western world in the century following emancipation. To the extent that the liberal-left has been an agent for the achievement of greater social justice, the favourable attitudes have been reinforced by Jewish tradition (there is some evidence that this reinforcement was direct wherever the two streams came into contact); but the simple sociological fact of Jewish interest in emancipation and equal rights and the promotion of that interest by the left is sufficient to explain this leaning leftward by a people noted in other respects for its conservatism.

What of the relationship between contemporary Jewish political ideas and classical Jewish political thought? I believe that there is such a thing as classical Jewish political thought even though, in the course of so many centuries of absence from political life in the normal sense, the Jews have virtually forgotten its existence even when it speaks out to them from the pages of their sacred texts, particularly the Bible and the Talmud. The contents of classical Jewish political thought cannot be set forth in any detail here. Basically, the political thought of the sacred texts looks to two things: (1) government by and through a covenant system, and (2) politics as a form of moral action. From the first, flow several principles of political organization, and from the second, several principles of political purpose, all of which (and their various applications) were discussed either directly or through illustration in the Bible and the Talmud. Using the terminology of today's political science, we may say that the first leads to ideas of constitutionalism, limited and republican government, and dispersal of power among different centres (both public and private) in a manner reminiscent of federalism or derivatives of the federal principle. The second leads to notions of the activist state with overtones of public regulation of individual enterprise on behalf of the common good and for the protection of individuals as well. A summary of the prophetic vision of the ideal commonwealth as presented in the Book of Joshua reveals all of this clearly. There, in the course of an idealized description of the Israelite conquest of Canaan, the author presents a vision of a tribal federation (1) operating under a Divine constitution with (2) a national government led by (3) a strong charismatic leader who is the servant of God (not a sovereign in his own right) and is thus bound by the constitution to obey its terms and to consult with (4) the national assembly which is representative of the tribes and embracing (5) tribal and local governments structured along republican lines under the national constitution; a social order in which every man sits under his own vine and fig tree, where his rights are protected by law, and in which he joins with the authorities to protect the rights of his neighbours.[48]

Reading the statement presented here in its simplicity, we might conclude that classical Jewish political thought is virtually identical with the American political tradition. Though, in a broad sense, there are clear similarities, there are certain points of equally clear contradiction between the two, and there are others in which unresolved problems could indicate potential points of disagreement. Classical Jewish political thought, for example, starts from the premise that the truth is given to man by God and that properly qualified authorities must protect that truth by suppressing certain kinds of error. There is certainly an element containing this view within the American political tradition, but American liberalism does not accept it and the liberal view has been dominant. On another level, the American notion that every man is free to choose his religion and his citizenship cannot easily be squared with the Jewish notion of national and religious inheritance. Of course, there are also great differences in the level of sophistication of the political institutions developed out of the two systems.

Nevertheless, the convergence between the two systems is remarkable, especially if we consider the great gulf in time and space that separates their points of origin. This convergence can be explained historically, but for our purposes here it is sufficient to recognize its existence, particularly in the light of the considerable contradiction between the political notions brought to America by the Jews and the ideas of the American political tradition.

Today, American Jews are edging away from the political

notions of their immediate ancestors. In some cases the change is almost a caricature of assimilation, as when Jews in Texas become supporters of the radical right like their non-Jewish neighbours, and Jewish doctors back Barry Goldwater because they fear the possibility of socialized medicine (or, conversely, when Jewish intellectuals advocate legalization of various abnormal sexual practices in the name of liberalism and freedom). In most cases, however, the change is one of newly found interest in commitment to a political tradition now unreservedly theirs.

The decline of the issues of the French Revolution in contemporary politics has given most American Jews a chance to relate to the very different political ideals of America. Curiously enough, in doing this, they may be returning—albeit unconsciously—to political ideas more closely related to those endorsed in the classical Jewish sources (the Bible and the Talmud), such as federalism, communitarianism, and republican government within a democratic context—the very ideas which the Americans initially derived in large measure from Biblical sources.

NOTES

1. A good general summary of the political concerns of Jews from the mid-sixteenth to the mid-twentieth century can be found in Howard M. Sachar, *The Course of Modern Jewish History*, New York, 1958.
2. Political culture has been defined by Gabriel A. Almond as the 'particular pattern of orientation to political action' in which groups or political systems are embedded. See his 'Comparative Political Systems' in *The Journal of Politics*, Vol. 18, 1956, pp. 391–409.
3. Much has been written on this convergence, generally in the way of Jewish apologetics. Despite the slight disrepute which may adhere to the subject because of that, the convergence remains substantial. See, for example, Will Herberg, *Protestant-Catholic-Jew*, rev. edn., Garden City, N.Y., 1960.
4. In the absence of accurate statistics on the composition of the American Jewish population, the figure is an estimate and probably a low one. See Nathan Goldberg, 'Jewish Population in America', *Jewish Review*, Jan.–Dec. 1948, and 'The Jewish Population in the United States', *The Jewish People: Past and Present*, New York, 1948, Vol. II.
5. See Daniel J. Elazar, 'The United States Political System' (mimeo., 1964) for a summary statement of those basic ideas.
6. Unfortunately little has been done to isolate the political ideas of the classical Jewish texts. Before our own time, Jews were barely concerned

with things political within the Jewish community, and most contemporary writing on the subject has taken the form of apologetics, seeking to show that Judaism and democracy (variously defined) are cut from the same cloth. Characteristic of the latter type is the essay by Milton R. Konvitz, 'Judaism and the Democratic Ideal' in Louis Finkelstein, ed., *The Jews: Their History, Culture, and Religion*, Philadelphia, 1949, Vol. II, pp. 1430–51. For more systematic efforts to isolate these ideas, see Harold Fisch, *Jerusalem and Albion*, New York, 1964; Robert Gordis, *The Root and the Branch*, Chicago, 1962; and Hans Kohn, *The Idea of Nationalism*, New York, 1944, chap. II. Yehezkel Kaufmann discusses the political ideas of ancient Israel in *The Religion of Israel*, Chicago, 1962.

7. See Ralph Henry Gabriel, *The Course of American Democratic Thought*, New York, 1940, and David W. Minar, *Ideas and Politics: The American Experience*, Homewood, Ill., 1964.

8. Discussions of the influence of Biblical ideas with particular reference to England can be found in Edwyn R. Bevan and Charles Singer, eds., *The Legacy of Israel*, London, 1927, particularly the essays by Smith, Box, Isaacs, Selbie, and Roth. For their influence in the United States, see Joseph Gaer and Ben Siegel, *The Puritan Heritage: America's Roots in the Bible*, New York, 1964; Perry Miller, *The New England Mind*, New York, 1939, particularly 'The Seventeenth Century'; and Oscar S. Straus, *The Origin of the Republican Form of Government in the United States of America*, New York, 1926.

9. For a discussion of this, see Daniel Boorstin, *The Genius of American Politics*, Chicago, 1953.

10. For a discussion of agrarianism as a persistent influence in the United States, see Henry Bamford Parkes, *The American Experience*, New York, 1947, and Anselm Strauss, *Images of the American City*, New York, 1961, especially chap. 10.

11. See 'Federalism', *The International Encyclopedia of the Social Sciences*, New York, and Elazar, *op. cit.*

12. See, for example, David Noble, *Historians Against History*, Minneapolis, 1965, and also President Lyndon B. Johnson's inaugural address.

13. For a survey of the Biblical discussion of these four elements, see John Bright, *A History of Israel*, Philadelphia, 1959, particularly chapter 4, and Kaufmann, *op. cit.*

14. See Ruth Miller Elson, *Guardians of Tradition: American Schoolbooks of the Nineteenth Century*, Lincoln, Nebraska, 1964, for a biased but thorough account of the contents of the school texts. By the same token, the politicization of the Jews once they came to the United States led them to begin to see the political elements in the Bible. See, for example, *Jewish Tidings*, 14 December 1886, for an explicit reference in this regard.

15. See Sachar, op. cit., and Salo W. Baron, *The Jewish Community*, Philadelphia, 1942, particularly Vol. II.

16. Sachar, op. cit., and Ismar Elbogen, *A Century of Jewish Life*, Philadel-

phia, 1944, provide the best discussions of the overall Jewish movement to the liberal-left. While studies of Jewish voting behaviour in Europe are few, those that exist confirm this. See, for example, Walter B. Simon, 'The Jewish Vote in Vienna' in *Jewish Social Studies*, XXIII, 1, January 1961.

17. See Sachar, op. cit., Chapter XVI; Lawrence H. Fuchs, *The Political Behavior of American Jews*, Glencoe, Ill., 1956; and Werner Cohn, *Sources of American Jewish Liberalism—A Study of the Political Alignments of American Jews*, unpublished Ph.D. dissertation, New School for Social Research, 1956.

18. See Baron, op. cit., Elbogen, op. cit., and Sachar, op. cit., particularly chaps. V, VI, XIII, and XIV, for a survey of the development and functioning of these idea complexes, particularly in European Jewry. Ben Halpern presents a discussion of the ideological roots of American Jewish attitudes to Judaism in *The American Jew: A Zionist Analysis*, New York, 1956.

19. Unfortunately, research to this effect is hard to come by. The sense of the situation becomes apparent, however, when one examines the standard sociological studies of American Jewry. See, for example, Marshall Sklare, ed., *The Jews: Social Patterns of an American Group*, Glencoe, Ill., 1958. Perhaps more impressive is the pattern of Jewish historical writing. Focusing on either national or community histories, only the Jews of the transmississippi West have produced histories of the Jews of particular states, as a rule.

20. See Baron, op. cit.; Heinrich Graetz, *History of the Jews*, Philadelphia, 1891, vols. III, IV, and V; or any specialized history of the Jewish communities of medieval Europe, for discussions of this relationship.

21. This is true even in such Americanized *siddurim* as that of the United Synagogue. Contrast the American Sephardi *siddur* which refers to 'the President and Vice President of the United States of America, the Governor, the Lieutenant Governor, and the people of this State represented in Senate and Assembly, and the magistrates of this city'. David de Sola Pool, ed. and trans., *Book of Prayer According to the Custom of the Spanish and Portuguese Jews*, New York: Union of Sephardic Congregations, 1941, p. 204.

22. William Anderson discusses this in *The Nation and the States: Rivals or Partners?*, Minneapolis, 1955.

23. Cohn, op. cit., discusses the antipathy between the Jews and locally centred government.

24. See, for example, the publications of the American Jewish Congress regarding civil rights legislation and court action. I have found some evidence to support this in the responses of my students.

25. See Louis Finkelstein, *Jewish Self-Government in the Middle Ages*, New York, 1964, 2nd ed.

26. See, for example, Herbert Agar, *The Price of Union*, Boston, 1950.

27. The Jewish attitude is discussed in Abraham Menes, 'The Jewish Labor Movement' in *The Jewish People, Past and Present*, New York: YIVO,

1955, Vol. IV. The American attitude is exemplified in Russel B. Nye, *Midwestern Progressive Politics*, East Lansing, Mich., 1951.

28. Menes, op. cit., and Sachar, op. cit., chap. XVI.

29. Lawrence H. Fuchs, 'Sources of Jewish Internationalism and Liberalism' in Sklare, op. cit., pp. 595–613.

30. Anita Libman Lebeson, *Pilgrim People*, New York, 1950, presents a standard view of this overriding purpose and the accepted chronicle of how it was achieved.

31. The so-called 'defence' organizations, beginning with the American Jewish Committee and including the Anti-Defamation League and the American Jewish Congress, have all adopted this posture despite the differences among them on other issues that are judged from the 'conservative-liberal' perspective. The chronicle of their efforts is available in *American Jewish Year Book*, published annually by the American Jewish Committee and the Jewish Publication Society since 1891.

32. Despite the attention they gave their radicals, the Jews did gain power politically when they used their 'muscle' as voters in particular states and localities. Thus the Jews of New York's East Side took a major step forward when they elected Meyer London to represent them in Congress in 1914 (Sachar, op. cit., pp. 324–5). It has been suggested that even the great Brandeis achieved national office only after he developed roots in the Jewish community, and thus filled the political requirements which President Wilson had to accept; cf. Yonathan Shapiro, 'American Jews in Politics: The Case of Louis D. Brandeis' in *American Jewish Historical Quarterly*, LV, 2, December 1965.

33. Nathan Glazer and Daniel Patrick Moynihan discuss this in the case of the largest Jewish community in the United States, in *Beyond the Melting Pot*, Cambridge, Mass., 1963, pp. 137–80. See Charles Bernheimer, ed., *The Russian Jew in the United States*, New York: Young People's Missionary Movement, 1905, for a contemporary discussion of east European Jewish political experiences in the Old World and involvements in the New.

34. Daniel J. Elazar, *American Federalism: A View From the States*, New York, 1966, chap. IV.

35. Briefly, the moralistic political culture views politics primarily as a means to advance the public good; the individualistic political culture accepts politics as a means for individuals to advance themselves economically and socially; and the traditionalistic political culture views politics primarily as a means to support an established social order.

36. Bernheimer, op. cit., Fuchs, op. cit., Glazer and Moynihan, op. cit., and Sachar, op. cit. See also Stuart E. Rosenberg, 'Notes on the Political Attitudes of the *Jewish Tidings*' in *Jewish Social Studies*, XVII, 4, October 1955.

37. The following paragraphs are based on Cohn, op. cit., Fuchs, op. cit., and Lebeson, op. cit.

38. Bernheimer, op. cit., pp. 256–79.

39. Until the New Deal, the Orthodox Yiddish press was generally Repub-

lican, partly in opposition to the dominant Jewish socialists of the lower East Side and partly as a reflection of their predilection for conservatism in politics as well as religion. The German Jews were also predominantly Republicans in this period; see Cohn, op. cit.

40. The New Deal brought the Jewish socialists into Democratic ranks, too. See Cohn, op. cit., and Bernard D. Weinryb, 'The Adaptation of Jewish Labor Groups to American Life' in *Jewish Social Studies*, VIII, 4, October 1946.

41. Recent studies to this effect include Maurice G. Guysenir, 'Jewish Vote in Chicago' in *Jewish Social Studies*, XX, 4, October 1958, and Edgar Litt, 'Status, Ethnicity, and Patterns of Jewish Voting Behavior in Baltimore' in *Jewish Social Studies*, XXII, 3, July 1960.

42. This is not to say that there is absolutely no correlation between economic level and voting behaviour among American Jews. Among those Jews earning in excess of $20,000 annually, there appears to be a clear tendency for nearly a majority of them to vote Republican. See Judith R. Kramer and Seymour Leventman, *Children of the Gilded Ghetto*, New Haven, 1961, which indicates that this was the case for the Jews in Minneapolis in the 1956 presidential election.

43. The recent literature on American socio-religious pluralism discusses this question in some detail. See Herberg, op. cit.

44. Henry J. Meyer, 'The Economic Structure of the Jewish Community in Detroit' in *Jewish Social Studies*, II, 2, April 1940.

45. John P. Dean, 'Patterns of Socialization and Association Between Jews and Non-Jews' in *Jewish Social Studies*, XVII, 3, July 1955.

46. While no overall calculations are available for the nation as a whole, a survey of the names associated with political affairs in the standard histories of American Jewry will confirm this observation. See, for example, the names cited in Lebeson, op. cit. For more specific examples, see the names listed in Louis J. Swichkow and Lloyd P. Gartner, *The History of the Jews of Milwaukee*, Philadelphia, 1963, Appendix 32, 'Milwaukee Jews Who Held Public Office', pp. 514–518. In the Necrology lists of the *American Jewish Year Book*, volumes 62–6, covering the period from 1 July 1959 to 3 December 1964, 26 Jews are listed as having held public office, appointive or elective. One was of Sephardi origin, seven of eastern European birth or parentage, and eighteen were descended from German Jews.

47. The author received this information from confidential sources.

48. Yehezkel Kaufmann makes a case for the classical character of pre-monarchical political ideas in the Jewish tradition. See, for example, his chapter, 'Israel in Canaan', in Leo W. Schwarz, ed., *Great Ages and Ideas of the Jewish People*, New York, 1956, particularly pp. 38–53. See also the sources cited in note 6 above for further discussion of these ideas and their classical character.

JEWISH RADICALISM IN
THE UNITED STATES

LOUIS RUCHAMES

A RECENT HISTORIAN of radicalism has characterized the radical as "a motive force of history."[1] Throughout United States history the radical has been the conscience of each age, the opponent of privilege and injustice, the advocate of justice and equality. It was the radical who created the American Revolution, fought against slavery, denounced wars fought for gain, championed the cause of the destitute immigrant, and identified himself with the inhabitants of the slums and the exploited laborers of factory and farm.

While men of all races, religions, and national groups have contributed to the cause of radicalism, it is the Jewish radical who concerns us here. Jewish radicalism has been the result of historical conditioning and of a cultural and religious response to specific historical situations. The source of early Jewish radicalism and of much of its strength through the ages may be found in Jewish slavery in Egypt more than three millennia ago. The memory of that period and the antislavery attitudes resulting therefrom were deeply ingrained in Jewish religious thought and practice and have had a significant impact even upon nonreligious Jews. On Passover the Jew is enjoined to regard *himself* as having been enslaved in Egypt. And every Sabbath as he recites the blessing over the wine he recalls that the Sabbath was ordained to memorialize the exodus from Egypt as well as the seventh day of creation. The recollection of Egyptian bondage with the concomitant emphasis upon liberty are among the most important facts of Jewish history. In ancient Jewish life these resulted in egalitarian and libertarian emphases in Jewish religious thought and a marked sympathy for the oppressed and enslaved. Ultimately these views were embodied in the Mosaic laws of the Old

Original for this volume.

Testament and in the subsequent teachings of the prophets of Israel.

Hugo Valentin emphasizes that the social legislation of the Old Testament and its prophetic writings indicate "a disposition to radicalism on the part of the Jews." He accepts the view that Moses "was the first to proclaim the rights of man," and notes that while the ancient world almost universally regarded the slave as an animal or chattel, Israel considered him as a human being, though he may have been a heathen. After pointing to such Biblical legislation as the requirement for the owner of a field to leave part of his crop for the poor, the requirement of Sabbath rest for the stranger and the laborer, the cancellation of all debts in the seventh year, and similar laws, he concludes that "it will scarcely appear an exaggeration to describe the ancient Jewish social order as inspired by a unique ethical-religious radicalism."[2]

The impact of Egyptian slavery was reinforced by the dispersion following the Babylonian captivity in 586 B.C. Although many Jews subsequently returned to Palestine, large, flourishing communities remained in Babylonia and other parts of the East. The result of the dispersion was the wandering Jew, a resident yet a foreigner, sometimes a citizen yet often a stranger and a marginal man who lived in two societies and cultures at once and developed an independence of judgment and a refusal to conform to majority opinion, which through the centuries gave rise to the dissenter and intellectual rebel. After the destruction of Judaea by the Romans in the first and second centuries A.D. and the rise of ghettoes and severe persecution during the Middle Ages, there occurred a decline in Jewish social and economic radicalism. The reasons for this are unclear. We find, however, a strong recrudescence of intellectual radicalism, primarily among Jews living in Moslem countries, notably Spain and North Africa, where for many centuries they had much more freedom than among Christians. In these lands they played a vital part in the cultural and scientific renaissance that characterized Moslem life during certain periods of the Middle Ages. Among the most noteworthy were Maimonides and Abraham ibn Ezra. During the latter part of the Middle Ages and the early modern period, we find intellectual radicalism even in Christian countries, notably Italy, where Jews were among the foremost exponents of scientific, rationalistic thought.[3]

It was not until the end of the eighteenth century, however, that Jewish radicalism again flourished. The source of its resurgence was the impact of the French Revolution, which liberated the Jew from the ghettos and gave him social and political equality. It confronted him with the object lesson that his well-being depended upon the triumph of revolutionary forces over the established order. Abram Sachar notes, "In the revolutionary movements the Jews played no unimportant role. Circumstances made them liberal. . . . By training and temperament, too, most of the Jewish leaders opposed the suppression of constitutional and national liberties. . . . They were therefore prominent in every movement which led to the revolutions of 1830 and 1848.[4] Add to this the fact, as Werner Cohn has noted in his study of the sources of American Jewish liberalism, that in the French Revolution Jews were for the first time since ancient days accepted as equals and brothers by non-Jewish revolutionaries, and one can understand the strong attraction that subsequent revolutionary movements had for them.[5]

The French Revolution in great part evoked the earliest radical activities among American Jews.[6] The question of sympathy and support for the French Revolution was one of the issues dividing the conservative Federalists, who feared the French Revolution, from the liberal and radical Jeffersonians or Republicans, who supported it. Lawrence Fuchs suggests that "a confluence of circumstances carried the Jewish community into the Jeffersonian camp almost as one man . . . Jewish support for the Republican cause was virtually monolithic."[7] The "confluence of circumstances" included two factors in addition to the French Revolution. First, Jefferson's identification with the principle of separation of church and state—he had written Virginia's Disestablishment Act and his close friend, James Madison, had introduced the First Amendment. Second, the upper class, aristocratic Federalist party was the party of wealthy merchants, landholders, and speculators, whose members and leaders did not hesitate to express antidemocratic, anti-alien, anti-Negro, and anti-Semitic sentiments in their efforts to remain in power. The Republicans, on the other hand, comprised small businessmen, working farmers and laborers, as well as Southern planters, and defended American Jews from Federalist attacks. The election campaign of 1800, in which Jefferson was elected President, marked the peak of

Federalist anti-Semitic attacks and witnessed the publication of one of the great democratic and radical documents in American history. It was written by Benjamin Nones, a Jewish Revolutionary War veteran and Republican who had come from France to fight in the Revolution. Nones had been attacked in a letter published in a Federalist newspaper in Philadelphia on August 5, 1800, which had expressed contempt for Jews, Negroes, democratic ideals, and the poor. The newspaper refused to print Nones's rejoinder. It ultimately appeared in the *Philadelphia Aurora*, a Republican paper. In it Nones defended his right to be a radical and a Jew, expressed pride in Jewish ideals and Jewish suffering, affirmed his belief in republican as opposed to aristocratic and "kingly" government, and emphasized, "I am a Jew, and if for no other reason, for that reason I am a republican."[8]

The year 1800 marked the high point of Jewish radicalism. It declined noticeably thereafter and remained at a low ebb until a decade before the Civil War. This decline was true of American radicalism generally, with the conspicuous exception of the abolitionist movement. A new chapter in American radicalism began with the rise of antislavery activities under the leadership of William Lloyd Garrison in 1831, but one does not find Jews listed either in the leadership or the membership of the antislavery movement in the 1830s and 1840s. Not a single leader of the Jewish community is known to have raised his voice in opposition to the Mexican War. Not until the 1850s did individual Jews begin taking a public stand against slavery and become activists. Those who did were all immigrants. The best known and most important was Ernestine Rose, the Polish-born daughter of a rabbi, who came to this country by way of England in 1836. A confirmed follower of the English Utopian Socialist, Robert Owen, she soon became a prominent agitator for equal rights for women and for the abolition of slavery.[9]

Between 1853 and 1860 the situation changed somewhat and a number of Jews, primarily German and other European refugees who arrived after the Revolution of 1848, lent their aid to the antislavery movement and other radical causes. August Bondi, a twenty-one-year-old veteran of '48, and two other Jews, Jacob Benjamin and Theodore Weiner, joined John Brown's guerrilla band in Kansas in 1856 and fought in several engagements under his leadership. Rabbi David Einhorn, who occupied a pulpit in Baltimore, Maryland, supported Frémont, the Republican candidate, in 1856 and Lincoln in 1860 and had to flee Baltimore shortly before the Civil War because of his publicly expressed antislavery views. Beginning in 1851 Sigismund Kaufmann, a socialist, abolitionist, and Republican, served as editor of the *Turn-Zeitung*, the national publication of the league of socialist gymnastic societies. There he published the works of various Marxists. Frederick Knefler, a Hungarian '48er, achieved the rank of Brevet Brigadier-General and became the highest ranking Jewish officer in the Union army. Dr. Abraham Jacobi, a friend and sympathizer of Marx and Engels, came to this country from Germany in 1853, continued some Marxist activity, and maintained contact with Marxists until the 1870s (though he was to be remembered as the founder of pediatrics). As a seventeen-year-old in 1857, Fritz Jacobi (unrelated to Abraham) became the first secretary of the then newly formed Communist Club, an office that he held at least until 1859. Isador Bush, a '48er from Vienna, settled in Missouri and became an outstanding antislavery leader there. As captain on the staff of John C. Frémont, Commander of the Western Department of the Union Army, he was discharged with Frémont and his staff when Lincoln rescinded the latter's order of August 30, 1861, emancipating the slaves in Frémont's department. He fought against Missouri's capture by pro-Southern forces, for the abolition of slavery, and for equal political rights for the Negro in Missouri. These people and others helped bring Jews back into the mainstream of American radicalism during the 1850s and 1860s.[10]

There is little to be said about Jewish radicalism during Reconstruction. Morris Marks in New Orleans and Charles S. Kuh in Beaufort, South Carolina, befriended Negroes, and Russian-born S. A. Bierfeld was hanged in Franklin, Tennessee, in 1868 for his pro-Negro activities. During the late 1860s and 1870s individual Jews participated in labor unions, such as the National Labor Union and the Cigar Makers National Union. They also participated in strikes, notably the New York Capmakers' general strike in 1874 (in which, for the first time, hundreds of Jewish workers were active) and the cigarmakers' strike in New York from October 1877 to February 1878 led by Adolph Strasser and Samuel Gompers.

It was in the 1880s, however, that there began the greatest upsurge of Jewish radicalism in the United States. It was to reach its peak during the years 1909 to 1914, gradually declining through the 1920s and reviving once more in the 1930s. The years from 1880 to 1914 were indeed the Golden Age of American Jewish Radicalism. Two characteristics marked this period: first, the transformation of Jewish radicalism from the participation of isolated, individual Jews into a mass movement; and second, the formation of the Jewish labor movement as a distinct entity, yet integrally related to and a vital part of the total American labor movement.

The source of the great changes of the 1880s was a mass influx of Jews into the United States, primarily from Eastern Europe, which resulted in a growth in the Jewish population from 300,000 in 1878 to more than a million in 1900. The immigrants were mainly artisans and workers from the Yiddish-speaking ghettoes of Russia, Poland, and the Balkans. Many of them had participated in the revolutionary movements in those areas and had strong socialistic and trade union biases.[11] They came to this country when the American working class was in deep ferment, the American Federation of Labor in the process of being born, and American socialism about to enter its period of greatest glory. Jewish immigrants pouring into the great urban centers of this country found themselves in rat-infested tenements, working in sweatshops at subsistence wages up to eighteen hours a day, confronted with starvation and eviction from their homes when suddenly unemployed during recurring depressions. They responded as did other workers with vigorous trade union organization and a desperate desire for a more humane and cooperative economic system.

The formation of a separate Jewish labor movement did not preclude the participation of individual Jewish workers in the general American labor movement. Many Jews, unaffiliated with the Jewish labor unions, participated in the Knights of Labor and in unions of cigarmakers, printers, waiters, garment workers, and other local and national unions throughout the country. But it is the Jewish labor movement that represents the most important contribution of American Jewry to the American labor movement.

The motivation for separate Jewish organization was neither religious nor nationalistic, but linguistic. Yiddish was the mother tongue of the masses of East European Jews who constituted the vast majority of Jewish immigrant workers and who, by and large, knew no other language. The idea of separate trade unions based on language was hardly new in the United States. German-and Russian-speaking trade union locals already existed and the formation of Yiddish-speaking unions therefore followed an established precedent. However, while Yiddish did provide the original foundation, ethnic and cultural bonds undoubtedly strengthened the trend toward distinct Jewish unions.

The pioneer Jewish labor organization was the Jewish Workingmen's Union, which was formed in 1885 and existed until the summer of 1887. Though not a trade union, it included hundreds of Jewish workers and played an active part in the Henry George mayoralty campaign of 1886. With its dissolution a number of its former members formed a Yiddish-speaking branch of the Socialist Labor Party in 1887, whose members in turn formed the United Hebrew Trades, "the parent institution of the Jewish labor movement in America."[12]

The new organization defined itself as "a central organization to which all the existing trade unions affiliate, so that they may resist oppression and support each other in the struggle against exploitation." Its purpose was to be achieved "through organization and trade unions on the one hand, and through political struggle on the other." Samuel Gompers, then president of the American Federation of Labor, misinterpreted the purpose of the organization as being religious and cultural and, hence, a divisive force. Yet he did believe it useful as a way station for the assimilation of the Jewish worker into the American labor movement. Consisting originally of only three affiliates, the United Hebrew Trades comprised 22 unions and 6,000 members by March 1890, and by November of the same year its affiliated unions increased to 34.

The growth of the Jewish labor movement was furthered by the early establishment of a Yiddish labor press. The first Yiddish labor and pro-socialist weekly in the United States, *Di Nu Yorker Idishe Folkzeitung*, appeared on June 25, 1886, and for three years, through its publication in Yiddish of various Marxist classics, was instrumental in stimulating the formation of the United Hebrew Trades. Subsequently, the United Hebrew Trades and Jewish members of the Socialist Labor Party supported another weekly, *Die Arbeiter Zeitung*, which appeared in March 1890, remained in existence for twelve years, and helped to strengthen the organization of Jewish workers. A Yiddish anarchist weekly, *Die Freie Arbeiter Shtimme*, appeared in July

1890. However, most important was the *Jewish Daily Forward*, edited by Abraham Cahan, which began publication on April 22, 1897. The *Forward* proved to be the most influential and widely read Yiddish labor newspaper and is still being published.

Despite the support of a fledgling press, the United Hebrew Trades soon lost its momentum and its membership decreased. Ideological conflict between socialists and anarchists had its effect, as did the policy of the Socialist Labor Party. The latter, under the leadership of Daniel DeLeon, a West Indian Jew who was a lecturer at Columbia University, ordered all socialists to withdraw from the AFL and the Knights of Labor and to join the Socialist Trade and Labor Alliance, formed in December 1895. The United Hebrew Trades did join the Alliance; but as the new organization withered through its isolationist and sectarian labor policy, so too did its Jewish affiliates. Given the additional detrimental impact of the depression of 1893–1897, the membership of the United Hebrew Trades dropped disastrously and by November 1897 only five or six unions were left in the organization.

However, the decline soon reversed itself. With the formation of the Socialist Party in July 1901, and the increasing influence of the *Forward* (the party's Yiddish voice), many Jewish socialists broke with DeLeon and helped to form a more realistic and positive trade union policy. The industrial boom during the early years of the new century led to the reactivation of the United Hebrew Trades. By 1907 it had 74 unions and 50,000 members.

Important developments in Jewish radicalism took place with the formation of several national trade unions consisting mostly of Jewish workers. Some of these proved to be weak and lasted but a short while; others had greater staying power. In 1891, for example, at the initiative of the United Hebrew Trades, the United Garment Workers was formed at a convention in New York. Not very effective, the union gave way more than a decade later to the Amalgamated Clothing Workers, which wrote a magnificent record in Jewish labor history. In 1900 the International Ladies Garment Workers Union was formed at a New York convention attended by eleven delegates representing seven local unions with a membership of about two thousand workers. By 1903 it had ten thousand members, half of whom worked outside of New York. Finally, the Jewish capmakers formed the United Cloth Hat and Cap Makers of North America in 1901, with an initial membership of 1,200, and received a charter from the AFL in 1902.

Perhaps the greatest significance of these newly formed unions for the historian of Jewish radicalism is that their leaders and members were essentially socialists. Despite Gompers' public announcement that "socialism is partisan politics and has no place in a trade union or in the American Federation convention," these unions adhered to their principles and insisted on furthering the cause of socialism. The most militantly socialistic ILGWU, for instance, recommended the study of socialism and the socialist movement to its members at its 1903 convention, and at its 1904 convention passed a resolution permitting the study of socialism at future conventions.

Another significant development was the birth of a Jewish workers' mutual aid organization, the Workmen's Circle, in September 1900. Socialist in outlook, the organization grew from 300 members in 1900 to 8,840 in 1906, and 38,866 in 1910. During its first decade it paid out hundreds of thousands of dollars in benefits to its members; helped to further the cause of unionism; educated its members in socialism—until 1920 it pledged them to vote only for socialist candidates; and established Yiddish schools and encouraged every form of intellectual and literary creativity.

Despite great strides forward by Jewish labor at the turn of the century, even greater successes were achieved between 1909 and 1914. These years witnessed an upsurge of labor solidarity and militancy never equaled before or since in American Jewish history. The foundation for this advance was the mass influx of Jews from Eastern Europe during the first decade of the century, which far exceeded the total number of Jewish immigrants who came between 1880 and 1900. The number entering between 1901 and 1910 reached a total of 976,000.

The new immigrants, perhaps even more than in the past, were primarily skilled workers and the vast majority entered American shops and factories. They brought with them new levels of familiarity with labor organizations, greater identification with socialism, and increased militancy. Many possessed experience gained through membership in the illegal Bund, a Jewish labor organization formed in 1897 in Eastern Europe under the name of the General Jewish Labor Federation of Lithuania, Poland, and Russia, which surreptitiously fought for economic and political rights against Czarism and capitalism. Others came after the wave of pogroms that took place in Russia from 1903 to 1906 and after the defeat of the Revolution of 1905. Many had fought against Czarist troops during the street fighting of the 1905 Revolution and perhaps 100,000 of them had participated in Russian strikes during the same year. As early as 1900 newly arrived Russian immigrants formed branches of the Bund in New York and in other cities and workers who were Zionists founded Labor Zionist groups with a socialist organization.

The great mass struggles and victories of 1909–1914 began with the economic recovery in 1909, following the crisis of 1907–1908. While the period was one of intense ferment among workers throughout the country, the militancy among Jewish workers was especially noticeable. Tens of thousands of Jewish workers in cities from New York to Chicago went out on strike for higher wages, a shorter workday, improved sanitary conditions, and union recognition. The United Hebrew Trades in New York grew from 61 constituent unions with 65,000 members in 1910 to 104 unions comprising 250,000 members in 1914. National Jewish trade unions expanded far more rapidly than the labor movement as a whole. Whereas the American Federation of Labor increased in numbers by 28 percent between 1910 and 1913, the garment union showed a 68 percent increase, a rate of growth that surpassed all other labor unions in the country. Between November 1909 and February 1910 about 20,000 women's shirtwaist makers, most of them Jewish women and the remainder Italian, went out on strike in New York and Philadelphia. Despite savage attacks by police and thugs and hundreds of arrests, the strikers remained firm. Their magnificent courage evoked an admiring response, including financial and moral support, from many of the leading citizens of New York. Most firms ultimately capitulated to their demands and Local 25, the Waistmakers' Local of the ILGWU, grew from several hundred at the beginning of 1909 to 10,000 at the end of the strike.

In New York, under the leadership of the New York Joint Board of Cloak and Skirt Makers Unions of the ILGWU, and with the example of the ladies of the Waistmakers' Union as an inspiration, more than 50,000 workers went out on strikes against 1,500 shops. It was during this strike that Louis D. Brandeis appeared as a mediator between employers and workers and gained a sympathy for the aspirations of the Jewish workers that remained with him to the end of his life. The workers won an important victory, decisive improvements in prevailing conditions, and a membership of over 50,000 in New York as compared to 10,000 prior to the beginning of the strike.

One of the great strikes of the period took place in Chicago in 1910 when 40,000 workers, 8,000 of them employed at Hart, Schaffner and Marx's factory, went out on strike. Most of the workers were Jewish, but there were also substantial numbers of Poles, Italians, Lithuanians, and Czechs. Although presumably led by the United Garment Workers of America, Thomas E. Rickert, its conservative president, did everything he could to weaken their efforts by making one agreement after another with the employers behind the workers' backs and the strike was less successful than those in New York. Indeed, the vast majority of workers gained almost nothing for their efforts.

Limitations of space do not permit a description of important strikes by thousands of furriers in New York in 1912, by 15,000 whitegoods workers and 25,000 waist and dress makers in New York in January 1913, and of other strikes in Rochester, Philadelphia, Buffalo, and elsewhere.

The greatest strike of all took place in New York in the men's clothing industry in the winter of 1912–1913. Without any union organization until the fall of 1912, a small local was formed with the assistance of the United Hebrew Trades, strike agitation began, and tens of thousands joined the union in order to be able to vote on the question of a general strike. A vote taken in December 1912 resulted in an overwhelming majority in favor of a strike, which then began on December 30. In a few days 100,000 Jews together with Italian, Polish, Czech, and Lithuanian workers left their jobs. Although the strike was conducted by local union leaders, Rickert again went behind the backs of the workers seeking a settlement. He entered into an agreement with the employers that was forthwith repudiated by the strikers. Finally, in March 1913, the strike was settled with the achievement of a shorter workday, higher wages, and union recognition. Perhaps its most important result was the formation of the Amalgamated Clothing Workers of America under the leadership of Sidney Hillman and Joseph Schlossberg.

The ferment in Jewish trade unionism was equaled by the activity of Jewish political radicalism. The membership of the Socialist Party, in which Jews played a prominent role both in numbers and leadership, grew from less than 25,000 in 1905 to 118,000 in 1912. Yiddish-speaking members of the party, in order to discuss common problems, met in conference from time to time and in 1907 formed a Yiddish Agitation Bureau to work among Yiddish-speaking workers. Ultimately, at the urging of Bundist refugees from Russia, there emerged in 1912 the Jewish Socialist Federation. By 1915 it had about 5,000 members in branches located in 21 states and the District of Columbia and published a weekly newspaper, the *Yiddish Socialist*. Not all socialist Jews belonged to the Federation, which was an autonomous organization within the Socialist Party. Many did not sympathize with what they felt were its sectarian aims. It had neither the support of the *Forward* nor of leaders of the United Hebrew Trades. And many English-speaking Jews who were active in the Socialist Party, some of whom, such as Victor Berger, Meyer London, and Morris Hill-quit, were among its national leaders, had no particular desire to join the Yiddish-speaking Federation.

The organization of the Federation symbolized a change in the nature of the Socialist Party's membership and in the geographical center of its power from the West and Southwest—it was strongest in the mining and agrarian areas of those regions—to the urban areas of the Northeast, especially in New York. The reason for the shift was the strong influx into the party of large numbers of immigrants, principally Jews. Daniel Bell[13] notes that "these new immigrants—again particularly the Jewish group—provided the sinews which sustained the American Socialist Party until 1932." Bell points out, too, that the Jewish unions—the ILGWU, the Amalgamated Clothing Workers, the Furriers, and the Millinery Workers—the vast majority of whose members and leaders were socialists, "became the financial backbone and chief organizational props of the Socialist Party."[14] As a result of the powerful socialist base provided by Jewish immigrants the Social-ist Party was able to elect a Congressman from New York, Meyer London, in 1914. In New York in 1917 Morris Hillquit ran for Mayor on the Socialist Party ticket and received 145,332 votes, 22 percent of the total vote, and carried twelve assembly districts in which there were large numbers of Jews. In the same election ten socialists were elected to the state assembly, seven to the City Board of Aldermen, and one to a judgeship.

. . .

Accompanying the radical economic and political ferment of the last two decades of the nineteenth and the first two decades of the twentieth century, was a Jewish cultural renaissance, especially in Yiddish, strongly radical and primarily secular, which left a permanent legacy of creativity in poetry and prose. The circulation of the *Forward*, which was 52,000 in 1905, reached almost 200,000 in 1916. Under the editorship of Abraham Cahan, it became "not merely the guide, mentor, and organizer of the Jewish trade unions, not only a Socialist educational agency of the first importance, but also, and perhaps preeminently, a powerful cultural and spiritual force among all sections of the Jewish community in New York and near-by centers."[15]

In 1916 there were five Yiddish dailies in New York and three in Chicago. There were dozens of periodicals and newspapers; many were simply trade union organs, yet even these never limited themselves to trade union issues and showed a deep interest in cultural and literary problems. Each important political group usually had its own organ of opinion; the anarchists had their weekly, the *Freie Arbeiter Stimme*, the Jewish Socialist Federation published its *Naye Velt*, and there was the Socialist monthly, the *Zukunft*. All combined economics and politics with a deep cultural interest.

The first Yiddish theater production took place in the 1880s, when a troupe of professional actors brought over from London presented a play by the prominent playwright, Abraham Goldfaden, who is regarded as the father of the Yiddish theater. Morris Schappes notes that the theater as a cultural force "reached more deeply among the immigrant masses than poetry or belletristic prose," and that "by 1887 there were six Yiddish companies performing in New York, and road companies had gone as far as Chicago."[16] The plays ranged from light musical comedies to dramas of profound social significance on such themes as the Homestead steel strike of 1892 and the Dreyfus case. Among the outstanding Yiddish playwrights whose plays expressed social realism and were a force for radicalism were Jacob Gordin, Zalmen Libin, and David Pinski.

Yiddish poetry also expressed the thoughts, the aspirations, and the suffering of the Jewish masses in the United States during that period. It served as a goad to radical action and left a notable literary record of the period. Four proletarian poets were the stars of the Yiddish literary firmament and won renown in world literature as well: Morris Rosenfeld (1862–1923), David Edelstadt (1856–1892), Joseph Bovshover (1872–1915), and Morris Winchevsky (1856–1933).[17]

Of the four, Morris Winchevsky came to be known as the "grandfather of Jewish socialism." He was a Yiddish labor editor in London, where he was already known for his revolutionary songs. In "A Battle Song," his first stanza read as follows:

> *Lift to the breezes our banner of red!*
> *Get into line now, and strike up the band!*
> *Waken the ragged half-living half-dead;*
> *say to them: Brothers, see here's where we stand,*
> *there stands the bloodthirsty foe.*
> *Here marches freedom, and justice, and light;*
> *there lurks oppression, and evil, and night;*
> *brothers, come march with us now!*[18]

Two other writers of that period who made a permanent mark in radical Jewish thought deserve mention. Chaim Zhitlovsky was born in Russia in 1865 and came to this country in 1907 with an established reputation as a brilliant Yiddish writer and thinker. His philosophy of Jewish life sought to combine the two ideologies of Jewish nationalism and socialism on a foundation of Jewish secularism. Dr. Zhitlovsky was a partisan of secular Yiddish schools and helped to found such schools in the United States. Throughout his lifetime Zhitlovsky sought to answer the question posed by the title of an article by him in 1939, "What is Jewish secular culture?" His answer combined Marxism,[19] socialism, nationalism, and secularism with a warm devotion to Jewish identity, Jewish history, and the most progressive elements in Jewish life.

Reuben Brainin was also born in Russia and was a prominent Zionist and writer in Hebrew and Yiddish when he came to this country in 1910. He settled in New York the following year and lived there and in Montreal until his death in 1939. He was a brilliant literary critic who sought to do for modern Jewish literature what Maimonides had done for Medieval Jewish thought—to master all of European literature and to assimilate the best of it to the burgeoning Hebrew and Yiddish literatures of the nineteenth and twentieth centuries. After World War I and the triumph of the Bolshevik Revolution, and especially after

a visit to the Soviet Union in 1927, his political and social preferences turned toward socialism and communism. He was denounced violently by many who condemned him for failing to
recognize the discrimination against Zionism and Hebrew that
existed in the Soviet Union. He wrote increasingly in Yiddish,
primarily for the liberal and radical Yiddish press, and his writings are marked by a deep love of learning, a profound humanism, and a critical spirit.

The entrance of the United States into World War I in April
1917 and the Bolshevik Revolution of November 1917 introduced
two important new elements into Jewish radicalism. First, although the Jewish trade unions, the Workmen's Circle, the
Jewish Socialist Federation, and other Jewish members and leaders of the Socialist Party were antiwar prior to America's declara-
ation and even for a short time afterward, the pressures to support
the war were too great to be resisted. As the months passed
radicals began to capitulate and in August 1917 the pro-war
Jewish Socialist League of America was formed. It in turn
affiliated with the Social Democratic League, consisting of Socialists who had seceded from the Socialist Party after the antiwar
St. Louis convention of April 1917. In May 1918 a national conference of the Jewish Socialist Federation voted to repudiate the
St. Louis convention's antiwar stand and to support the war. The
major Jewish unions, including the Amalgamated, the ILGWU,
the Workmen's Circle, and the United Hebrew Trades, adopted
similar positions, as did the *Forward*. Only a relatively small percentage of the radical Jewish leadership remained opposed to the
war. The division polarized the Jewish labor movement into right
and left wings, which affected Jewish labor and radical history in
subsequent years.

Perhaps the best known Jewish radical of the war and immediate postwar period was Rabbi Judah Leib Magnes (1877–1948),
who had been rabbi of Temple Emanuel and B'nai Jeshurun in
New York. Magnes joined other socialists and pacifists, such as
Eugene Debs, Norman Thomas, Scott Nearing, Oswald Garrison
Villard, and John Haynes Holmes, in opposing the war. He spoke
at public meetings and demonstrations, helped form the Civil
Liberties Bureau in 1918, and a Bureau of Legal Advice for Con-
scientious Objectors. He fought for the release of Debs, Roger

Baldwin, and other antiwar political prisoners. With the outbreak of the Russian Revolution, Magnes' devotion to radicalism deepened. He defended the Revolution at public rallies, denounced the invasion of the Soviet Union by the Allies and White Russians, and was prominent in the effort to ship medical supplies to Soviet Russia. An early defender of Sacco and Vanzetti, he joined in the movement to free them. In 1923, in preparing a volume of his *Wartime Addresses* for publication, he wrote as follows about the addresses:

> Some of them were delivered with troops around the halls and with machine guns in the public square. . . . One would really think that a teacher of religion was expected to be nothing but a fair-weather pacifist. But have spiritual ideals no validity in times of war? Or is the preacher in his pulpit but a jack-in-the-box, bobbing up or down as the strings are pulled by his masters on the political stage and in the established church and in the seats of economic power?[20]

The Bolshevik Revolution impelled the government in Washington to intensify its efforts against all who opposed the war and led to a further weakening of all radical forces. They suffered even more in the postwar campaign of terror against all who expressed any sort of sympathy with Bolshevism or Communism. In the Palmer raids in 1919 and 1920, Attorney General A. Mitchell Palmer and his Special Assistant, J. Edgar Hoover, arrested almost 10,000 "alien radicals," of whom about 300 were ultimately deported. In 1919, testimony before the Senate Committee headed by Senator Overman charged that the Bolsheviks were Jews. Beginning in May 1920, Henry Ford initiated an anti-Semitic campaign linking the Jews with the Bolshevik Revolution, and, during the same year, Congress passed legislation that restricted immigration from Eastern Europe and resulted in a drop in Jewish immigration from 119,036 in 1921 to 49,719 in 1923 and 10,292 in 1925. A number of socialists elected to the New York Assembly in 1920 were denied their seats, as was Victor Berger, elected as a Socialist to Congress from Milwaukee.

To avoid government displeasure some labor and socialist organizations began their own campaigns purging their ranks of Bolshevik sympathizers. The resulting loss of members added to losses occasioned by the overall trend to conservatism during the 1920s in America. The AFL declined from a membership of more than four million in 1920 to a million members in 1923. The

Jewish unions declined similarly, as did the Socialist Party from 108,504 in 1919 to 13,484 in 1921.

If the Bolshevik Revolution led to repressions against radicals and a serious diminution in their numbers during the 1920s, it led also to the formation of the American Communist Party with a strong representation of Jewish workers. In 1922 the first issue of the *Freiheit*, the Yiddish Communist newspaper, appeared under the editorship of Moissaye J. Olgin. With Olgin's death in 1939, the editorship was assumed by Paul Novick, who still continues in that position. Its circulation reached 22,000 in 1925, a number larger than the total Communist Party membership in that year, which amounted to approximately 16,000. (This suggests, of course, that its readers included non-Communists as well as Communists.)

Although the Communist Party remained an inconsequential group until the Depression and the beginning of the New Deal, there is little doubt that Jews played an important part in its early history. Nathan Glazer notes that one "characteristic of the membership of the American Communist Party that differentiated it from almost every other Communist Party in the Western world was that a large proportion of its members were of Jewish origin."[21] This did not mean that the majority of Jews were Communists or Communist Party members, for "whereas the party membership only rose briefly above 50,000, there were in the Thirties and Forties 4,500,000 American Jews."[22] It did mean that "the Jewish group was the largest immigrant group in which the Communists had any important influence—much larger numerically than either the Russian, the Finnish, the Ukranian, the Hungarian, or the South Slavic."[23] Glazer explains this relationship between Jews and the Communist Party by referring to Werner Cohn's discussion of the Jew and modern radicalism.

> But what could the party offer Americans, even if they were immigrants, industrial workers, Jews, Negroes? It could offer them a community, based on a faith in which all were equal. To be a Communist meant to shed the limitations of one's social reality, and to join in a fraternity that transcended the divisions of the world. This was the attraction of Communism to many Jews who no longer thought of themselves in any way as Jewish. And for many, faith remained stronger than interest.[24]

In fact, however, in the twenties Communism had greater attraction for the Russian immigrant than for the native-born American Jew. And this Glazer does not adequately explain. The explanation must take into account the sufferings of Jewish immigrants under the Czar, which caused them to identify with the revolutionaries in Russia. Many, it is true, were Bundists and anti-Communists of various persuasions, but a large number were deeply influenced by the Bolshevik success in overthrowing the Czar, its platform for equality of all races and nations, and its condemnation of anti-Semitism. The exaltation that was felt by so many Jews in Europe and the United States at the victory of the French Revolution in the eighteenth century was repeated with the Bolshevik victory in 1917 and especially affected those Jews who felt most keenly the Czar's overthrow. Their allegiance went to the Communist Party of the United States, which perhaps more than any other organized group identified itself with that Revolution. One may suggest that this allegiance was, perhaps, due less to their desire for a revolutionary reorganization of American society than to their sympathy for the achievements of the Russian Communist Party and the membership of the American party did not increase significantly.

With the onset of the Great Depression there was a renaissance of American and Jewish radicalism. Class consciousness and class struggles grew in intensity. Millions of workers joined unions. The newly formed Congress of Industrial Organizations expressed and further stimulated labor militancy. Both the AFL and the CIO grew rapidly. The CIO alone had almost four million members in 1936 and the combined membership of the AFL and the CIO exceeded eight million in 1940. The Communist Party grew from 14,000 in 1932 to 75,000 in 1938, but its influence was far greater than its membership figures indicate. Sympathizers during the 1930s probably numbered in the hundreds of thousands. Hunger marches and demonstrations by the unemployed were frequently initiated by the Unemployed Councils in which Communists and left-wingers were active and in which the Jews played an important part. During these years Jews played a prominent part in the formation of a left-wing fraternal organization, the International Workers Order. In 1939 its membership exceeded 150,000 and its Jewish section boasted more than 50,000 members.

Among the traditionally Jewish labor unions, the furriers were the most radical and its leaders were most clearly identified with the Communist Party. An organization formed in 1933 to arouse American public opinion against the menace of fascism and Nazism and for the need for collective security was the American League against War and Fascism (its name was changed in 1937 to the American League for Peace and Democracy). Formed by the left, it had large numbers of Jewish members. Strong left-wing student organizations grew, with important Jewish representation and leadership, out of which there emerged in 1935 the American Student Union with almost 200,000 members, and, later, the American Youth Congress. In 1937 the Jewish People's Committee Against Fascism and Anti-Semitism was formed when the American Jewish Congress refused to admit representatives of the Jewish section of the International Workers Order and other Jewish left groups. When war broke out in Spain and the Abraham Lincoln Brigade was formed in 1937, there were hundreds of Jews, perhaps even a thousand, among the 3,000 volunteers who went to Spain. An important source of friendship and admiration for the Soviet Union at this time, among Jews and non-Jews, was its full employment and economic planning, which contrasted with the economic chaos, unemployment, and mass suffering in the capitalist world. Among Jews the greatest source of radical, pro-Communist, and pro-Soviet sympathies was the important role played by the Soviet Union in opposing the expansion of Nazism, its public opposition to anti-Semitism, and its seeming friendliness to Yiddish culture. When the Nazi-Soviet Pact was announced in 1939 these sympathies declined noticeably, only to be revived again with the German invasion of the Soviet Union in 1941.

The cultural renaissance that took place in the thirties, with its strong proletarian and left-wing literary trends, was marked, as Daniel Aaron points out in his essay in this volume, by a "preeminence of Jews." Since Aaron has expatiated upon this aspect of Jewish radicalism there is no need for further comment. However, one point may be made with regard to Jewish radicalism in Yiddish culture. The year 1937 witnessed the organization of the World Yiddish Cultural Alliance, or YKUF, at a convention in Paris in September 1937, in response to a call made by the Yiddish Cultural Front of France. The call urged the formation of a world Yiddish cultural congress to defend modern Yiddish culture against Hitlerism. Although the attendance was predominantly left wing, the Soviet Union failed to send a delegation and the delegation from the United States consisted of both Communists and non-Communist literary figures.

For Yiddish radicalism in the United States, the most important result of the world congress was the formation of an American YKUF organization, which began to issue a monthly literary journal, *Idishe Kultur*, in 1938, and initiated a book publishing venture in 1942. *Idishe Kultur*, which is still being published, gave a vital impetus to Yiddish literary and cultural expression from a leftist, including a Marxist, point of view and added much to the Yiddish-speaking American Jew's understanding and knowledge of Jewish life, literature and ideology. The book publishing enterprise, which is also still in existence, had by 1963 published 174 volumes of poetry and prose. These volumes included the classics of Yiddish literature, the works of outstanding American Yiddish writers, and Soviet Yiddish writers, such as Itsik Feffer and David Bergelson. Both *Idishe Kultur* and the published books represent a vast storehouse of Yiddish thought and creativity on the fundamental problems of Jewish tradition, ideology, and existence.

American radicalism received its final stimulus during World War II. Communists, liberals, and conservatives cooperated on behalf of the war effort in various endeavors, including Russian War Relief. The Jewish Council for Russian War Relief, which included Orthodox, Conservative, and Reform rabbis, as well as outstanding Jewish business leaders, lawyers, labor leaders, Zionists, judges, and others, represented all colors of the political spectrum. Here the radical, who became as respectable as the most conservative businessman, gained an acceptance and popularity that he had never had before and was to lose in great part at the end of the war.

The American Committee of Jewish Writers, Artists and Scientists, formed in 1942 under the chairmanship of Zhitlovsky with Albert Einstein as honorary president, included in its membership outstanding radical and liberal Jewish intellectuals who joined together to promote Jewish culture and unity in the war against Nazism and to express solidarity with the Jews of the Soviet Union. Among its members and leaders were Sholem Asch, Arthur Miller, Marc Chagall, Marc Blitzstein, Howard Fast, Leon Feuchtwanger, Frederick Ewen, William Gropper, Ben Zion Goldberg, Joseph Brainin, Waldo Frank, and many other Jewish notables of the day.

The end of the war and the beginning of the cold war witnessed the onset of government efforts to repress radical activities. Loyalty oaths, investigations of government workers, House and Senate committee anti-Communist hearings, the deepening antiradical and anti-Communist prejudice resulting from the activities of Senator Joseph McCarthy and his committee, the impact of the passage of the McCarran Act, the jailings of radicals who refused to answer questions of investigating committees, the firing of teachers on suspicion of Communist or radical sympathies, the Korean War, and the execution of the Rosenbergs, all played a part in destroying radical activities and radical sentiments among Americans. Jews were no less affected. Radicalism declined among Jews as among the rest of the population.

Perhaps of equal importance in their impact upon radicalism were the revelations by Khrushchev concerning Stalin. For Jews the revelations of the Soviet repressions of Jewish culture, the killings of Jewish authors, Stalin's anti-Semitism, and worst of all the failure of the Soviet leadership to admit the extent of the repressions or to make adequate amends, even to this day, have had a particularly strong effect in diminishing pro-Soviet sympathies, and in a decline generally of radicalism and socialism in the Jewish community.

Among the noteworthy radicals who continued their efforts were Albert Einstein, whose essay "Why Socialism" appeared in the *Monthly Review*—a radical monthly founded in 1950—and who opposed any suppression of freedom of speech and expression. Morris Schappes helped to carry on the radical Jewish tradition through the publication of *Jewish Life*, founded in 1946. This monthly magazine devoted itself to the discussion and interpretation of Jewish life and thought from a left-wing point of view and provided a vehicle for Jewish poetry, short stories, literary criticism, and essays on politics and international affairs. In 1956 *Jewish Life* was renamed *Jewish Currents* and is still being published. Schappes has also distinguished himself as a historian of American Jewish history.[25] His writings bear a deep imprint of Marxism—his introductory essay to the *Documentary History* is probably the first Marxist interpretation of various aspects of early American Jewish history—combined with a strong identification with the Jewish community, especially its secular, Yiddishist, humanist, and working class traditions.

There are many others, too, who are contributing to the maintenance of the Jewish radical tradition. These include Irving Howe, literary critic, teacher, translator of Yiddish, and founder and editor of *Dissent;* Yuri Suhl, writer in Yiddish and English, author of a biography of Ernestine Rose, of two delightful novels of immigrant life in America, *One Foot in America* and *Cowboys on a Wooden Horse,* and of a study of Jewish resistance to Nazism in Europe, *They Fought Back;* Louis Harap, literary critic, author, and an editor of *Jewish Currents;* Aaron Kramer, a sensitive poet in his own right who has translated some of the great Yiddish poets into English; Ben Field, the author; I. F. Stone, the journalist; Rabbi Jacob Weinstein of Chicago, currently president of the Central Conference of American Rabbis, who has applied the prophetic tradition to a lifetime effort of helping the poor and disadvantaged, the Negro, and the worker, and who carries on in the radical tradition in protesting American policy in Vietnam; and Rabbi Abraham Cronbach, a professor of Social Studies at the Hebrew Union College since 1922 who capped a lifetime of service to unpopular causes by championing the cause of Ethel and Julius Rosenberg and delivering the eulogy at their funeral. These and other Jews both secular and religious, have been helping to carry on the radical tradition.

The names that I have mentioned are limited to those Jews whose efforts are related, at least in part, to their Jewish identification and who admittedly have been influenced by Jewish values and ideals. There are many other outstanding radicals who in their writings and other public expressions do not relate their radicalism in any way to Judaism or to their Jewish identity. Their names may be seen on the mastheads of periodicals, such as *Studies on the Left, New Politics, Ramparts, Science and Society, Dissent,* and occasionally in *The Nation* and *The New Republic.* They would, of course, be included in any comprehensive history of Jewish radicalism but do not come within the scope of this essay.

. . .

What is the future of the Jewish radical tradition? The decline in numbers of Jewish radicals has coincided with the decline of the radical movement in general in the United States. The impact of McCarthyism in the 1950s, followed by growing affluence in American society, have played havoc with the entire radical movement. For the Jewish radical tradition the situation may be even more serious. Jewish radicalism in the United States has been the product, in part, of European Jewish immigration that brought over its radical Jewish traditions and, in part, too, especially at the turn of the century, of a militant Jewish working class. With the decline of European Jewish immigration and of the Jewish working class, the sources of Jewish radicalism may be drying up. The embourgeoisment of Jewish workers has been noted by many observers. The sons and grandsons of Jewish workers have left the factories for business, teaching, law, medicine, and other middle class occupations. Although the liberal and radical traditions continue within the Jewish community, and proportionately there seem to be more liberals and radicals among young Jews than among other sections of the population, the hold of the radical tradition appears to be loosening as the years go by and members of the older generation who still harbor the memories of a more radical period pass on.

Yet there may still be a future for Jewish radicalism. Notwithstanding the attraction of success and respectability, a spirit of idealism and devotion to equality and justice continues to exist among those young people today who seek integration and equality for the Negro, strive for freedom of expression, and demonstrate for peace in Vietnam. Indeed, the opposition to the war in Vietnam and resistance to the draft have inspired a resurgent radicalism and idealism among Jewish youth and adults, which may mark a new stage in Jewish devotion to the prophetic striving for peace and justice.

Perhaps the most important task facing Jewish radicals today is a need to study and to absorb the Jewish radical heritage as it has developed through almost three millennia of history. This would include the literature of the Biblical prophets, the great rationalistic-scientific heritage of Maimonides and other Medieval Jewish thinkers, the thought of Spinoza, the contribution of the Haskala or modern Jewish Enlightenment in Russia and Germany, and the history of the Jewish working class movement of modern times with its remarkable literature both in Europe and

the United States. The efforts of present-day radicals are sometimes hidden by a tendency toward anarchistic and individualistic
forms of expression and a search for personal gratification. Some
of this may have little in common with the radicalism of the
earlier generation. Understanding of the Jewish radical past
would give substance and depth to radical striving in the present
and would provide inspiration and guidance to the Jewish radical
facing the problems of the modern world.

NOTES

1. Sidney Lens, *Radicalism in America* (New York, 1966), p. 1.
2. Hugo Valentin, *Antisemitism Historically and Critically Examined*
   (New York, 1936), pp. 236–37.
3. For an excellent survey of the Jewish contribution to creative, independent thought during the later Middle Ages, see George Sarton,
   History of Science (Baltimore, 1931), Vol. II, Parts 1 and 2.
4. Abram Sachar, *A History of the Jews*, 4th ed. (New York, 1953), p. 288.
5. Werner Cohn, *Sources of American Jewish Liberalism—A Study of the
   Political Alignments of American Jews*, unpublished Ph.D. Dissertation,
   New School for Social Research, June 1956, p. 5.
6. It may be argued that the earliest Jewish radical activity in the United
   States was manifested in Jewish participation in the American Revolution. Most noteworthy was the decision of Congregation Shearith Israel,
   under the urging of Gershom Mendes Sexias, leader of the congregation, and Solomon Simson, its president, to leave New York rather than
   live under British occupation. This action was the only one of its kind
   during the Revolution by any religious organization.
7. Lawrence Fuchs, *The Political Behavior of American Jews* (New York,
   1956), p. 26.
8. For the text of the letter, and a detailed explanation of the circumstances of its origin, see Morris U. Schappes, *A Documentary History
   of the Jews in the United States, 1645–1875* (New York, 1950), pp. 92–
   96.
9. For a full length study of Ernestine Rose, see Yuri Suhl, *Ernestine Rose
   and the Battle for Human Rights* (New York, 1959).
10. Morris Schappes, "Jews and the American Labor Movement, 1850–1880,"
    Jewish Life, July 1954, p. 18. This article is one of a series written by
    Schappes, which appeared in *Jewish Life* between February 1954 and
    June 1955, under the general title of *Stories of Three Hundred Years*.
    I am indebted to these articles for much information in the succeeding
    pages of this essay.
11. For a brief yet valuable description of the class structure and revolu-
    tionary activities within the Jewish communities of Russia and Poland,
    see Melech Epstein, *Jewish Labor in U.S.A., 1824–1914* (New York,

1950), pp. 1–17. For the initial reactions of some religious-socialist Jewish immigrants to the American scene, see *ibid.*, pp. 18–32.

12. Will Herberg, "The Jewish Labor Movement in the United States," *Industrial and Labor Relations Review*, Vol. 5 (July 1952), p. 504.

13. "The Background and Development of Marxian Socialism in the United States," in Donald Drew Egbert and Stow Persons, *Socialism and American Life*, Vol. I (Princeton, N.J., 1952), p. 309.

14. *Ibid.*, p. 310.

15. Herberg, *op. cit.*, p. 520.

16. Morris Schappes, *A Pictorial History of the Jews in the United States*, rev. ed. (New York, 1965), p. 139.

17. In 1898, Prof. Leo Weiner, who was then Instructor in Slavic languages at Harvard University, published a volume of Morris Rosenfeld's poems, entitled *Songs of the Ghetto*, in an English prose translation. The monthly periodical edited by Morris Schappes, published first as *Jewish Life* and now as *Jewish Currents*, has placed all students of Jewish literature in its debt by including in its *"Jewish Life" Anthology, 1946–1956* (New York: *Jewish Currents*, 1956), pp. 43–58, an essay on the four poets, entitled "Songs of the Jewish Labor Poets," by Ruth Rubin, accompanied by their selected poems translated by Aaron Kramer. More recently, a volume entitled *Morris Rosenfeld, Selections from his Poetry and Prose*, edited by Itche Goldberg and Max Rosenfeld, was issued in English translation by the *Yiddisher Kultur Farband* (New York, 1964).

18. *"Jewish Life" Anthology, op. cit.*, p. 52.

19. The extent of Zhitlovsky's Marxism is debatable. In a review of a volume of Prof. Salo Baron's essays, Raphael Mahler, a distinguished Jewish historian, denies Baron's contention that Zhitlovsky was a Marxist. "Actually all his life," notes Mahler, "Zhitlovsky was a Social Revolutionary and a conscious volunterist. He was not a Marxist, even though he borrowed from Marxism some of the cornerstones of his doctrine." *American Jewish Historical Quarterly*, Vol. LVI (December 1966), p. 248.

20. Norman Benwich, *For Zion's Sake, A Biography of Judah L. Magnes* (Philadelphia, 1954), p. 103.

21. Nathan Glazer, *Social Basis of American Communism* (New York, 1961), p. 130.

22. *Ibid.*

23. *Ibid.*, p. 135.

24. *Ibid.*, p. 168.

25. He has edited *A Documentary History of the Jews in the United States, 1654–1875* (New York, 1950), with a preface by Joshua Bloch, Librarian and head of the Jewish Section of the New York Public Library, a distinguished scholar as well as a sensitive humanitarian and supporter of unpopular causes. In 1958, there appeared his *Pictorial History of the Jews in the United States* (republished in a new edition in 1965 with a preface by Rabbi David de Sola Pool). He has also edited several volumes of the letters and other writings of Emma Lazarus.

SOME REFLECTIONS ON COMMUNISM AND THE JEWISH WRITER

DANIEL AARON

ALTHOUGH THE PRE-EMINENCE of Jews in the Left movement of the 1930's has long been assumed, the reasons why so large a number of Jewish intellectuals and writers were attracted to Communism have not been extensively studied. Professional anti-semites, of course, continue their lurid 'exposures' of the "International Jewish Communist," but historians and critics have not felt it necessary to comment on the prevalence of Jews in the radical camp;[1] and magazines devoted to Jewish history and culture have understandably hesitated to encourage bigotry and popular misunderstanding by calling attention to the 'Jewishness' of literary protest. The majority of Jews in the Depression decade, after all, were neither Communists nor fellow-travelers, and with few exceptions, the key writers among the literary radicals of the 1920's—the forerunners and mentors of the Left-wing writers in the 'thirties—were not Jews.[2] And even in the 'thirties, most writers, whatever their ethnic origin or religion, were politically 'engaged' in the struggle against economic injustice at home and against Fascism abroad. Nevertheless, the literary historian of the 1930's, while acknowledging that the names of non-Jewish writers and artists are discoverable and important, can scarcely fail to take notice of the high number, if not the preponderance, of Jews in radical literary circles.[3]

How is this heavy proportion of Jewish men of letters in the radical movement to be explained? To be sure they exhibited the same habits of thought that distinguished the intelligentsia every-where—a penchant for radical programs, an impatience with

A version of this essay appeared in *Salmagundi*, I (Fall 1965), pp. 23–36. The editors have kindly permitted publication in this volume.

253

established orthodoxies historically identified (as Nathan Glazer has written) with "oppression, anti-Semitism, restriction." But the appeal of Communism to Jewish intellectuals between the two world wars cannot be adequately explained as a phase of literary intransigence or merely as a response to the menace of Hitler.

Of the vast amount of literature dealing with the Jew in modern times—the analyses of anti-Semitism, the studies of prejudice, the essays on Jewish alienation and Jewish chauvinism and Jewish self-hatred and the like—very little of it bears directly on that question, although passing references to Jewish radicalism are not hard to find. It has been attributed, for example, to the " 'Jewishly' politically conscious" who tried and failed to apply a "product of the political backwardness of Eastern Europe" to the American scene.[4] The novelist, Waldo Frank, implied an explanation in 1919 when he wrote of the Jewish will-to-power (seen in the religion of Jaweh and the myth of the Jews as a chosen people), the Jewish need for mystical abnegation (the thirst for suffering and immolation), and the desire for sensual and mental comfort (evidenced in the Jewish down-to-earth identity with the world).[5] Still another explanation was offered by the novelist and playwright, Mary Austin, in a review of Ludwig Lewisohn's autobiographical *Up Stream*. Lewisohn, she thought, failed to understand the American truism that a man comes into the world with nothing and that he must not interpret personal rebuff as cosmic injury. The attractiveness to Jews "of such economic expedients as Socialism and Communism" she interpreted as a derivative of the belief "that has always had a root in Jerusalem, that the unhappy issues of social living can be cured by a deliberate rationalization of the social organization. From the time that young Lewisohn enters college his interpretation of American life is developed with his mind's eye on the Hand Made Heaven of the born radical."[6]

Yet these and other explanations for the radicalism of Jews, suggestive as some of them are, can hardly be described as conclusive. And no one to my knowledge has tried to arrange the mélange of facts, guesses, theories, and impressions into some kind of systematic presentation.

A good many of the early commentators, it seems, placed considerable emphasis on the Eastern European or Russian context of Jewish radicalism rather than on Jewishness itself. As one writer in 1918 put it: "The Jew has, of course, been always the radical leader. On the other hand there is no conservative so thorough-going—also so numerous—as your middle-class Jew." And then he continued: "The Jewish problem in America has been more largely than one would think the fact of Russia. A problem also of increasing and not quickly assimilated immigration."[7]

Both of these observations have been sustained and amplified by historians, sociologists, and writers. Jewish radicalism in America, it can be plausibly argued, took root in the congested slums of the urban East around the turn of the century, particularly in New York City. Here, in settlement houses, in cafés and restaurants, the Russian-Jewish disciples of Marx, Bakunin, Proudhon, and Nietzsche ("usually intolerant of everything that was not violently modern") brooded over the conspiracy of capital against the working class.[8] Concentrated in the industrial centers and living under the most abnormal conditions, they had little sense of the America beyond their constricted environs. Although intensely intellectual, the ghetto Jews had not much interest in American culture. They might have read "The Raven" or "Hiawatha" in translation—perhaps some Beecher Stowe, Whitman, Mark Twain, Edward Bellamy, Jack London—but they were far more interested in the Russian realists, in Ibsen (whose problem plays apparently had an enormous vogue in the Yiddish theater) and in Knut Hamsun (whose *Hunger* had been translated into Hebrew and Yiddish). Marx and Kropotkin, according to one contemporary, they considered the greatest savants of modern times.[9]

Looked upon with suspicion by the old-stock Americans and returning this suspicion, the ghetto Jew began to take on the characteristics of the "alienated Jew" at the point where he rejected his old traditions and discovered that he was barred from the gentile world he hoped to enter. As Daniel Bell describes the dilemma:

> The young Jew is left helpless, and aware. He is aware of a distance both from Jewish culture from which he came and the Gentile culture into which he cannot or will not enter. He is helpless, for he cannot find his roots in either. Yet out of this tension of understanding and inhibition has been bred a new kind of Jew, the Jew of alienation, a Jew who unconsciously accepts this situation and utilizes his alienation to see, as if with a double set of glasses, each blending their perspective into one, the nature and tragedy of our time.[10]

Notwithstanding this allegedly fruitful consequence of alienation, the early novels and contemporary reports of alienated Jewish intellectuals, throbbing with despair and self-hatred, are unrelievedly painful.

A 1916 account of the Jewish literati in New York describes them as an uncomely group who have developed their minds at the expense of their bodies. Had the Jews discarded the Biblical prohibition against carving and painting the human figure, the author suggests, they might have produced an art to rival the Greeks. Their descendants, residing in New York *circa* 1916 are "a curiously Bohemian group" who haunt the East Side cafés, gossip all day "about shoestrings, or the universe," attack their fellow intellectuals when they aren't attacking the rich, and delight in ferreting out plagiarisms:

> If they make up their minds to be liberal internationalists, they are suddenly reminded by some new phase of anti-semitism that they are Jews. If, on the other hand, they decide to remain distinctively Jewish, they find it difficult to be at all liberal. They must frown down on inter-marriage; must pretend to take interest in Hebrew lore, traditions, holidays, ceremonies, and the like, all of which may be very distasteful to men of their culture.
>
> So they are ever vacillating unhappily from Socialism to Zionism, from Zionism to Anarchism, from Anarchism to Judaism—homeless wanderers even in the realm of the intellect.

The author of this piece, a Jew himself and apparently a most unhappy one, has nothing but contempt for the intellectuals who try to "pass," who want to be considered 'pure Americans' but who can't escape their accent, "who scoff at Judaism but cannot outgrow their early ghetto training. Who sneer (covertly) at their Jewish language, and write wretched English," who make fun of 'causes' while searching for them, who dream of "a snob-paradise, and depend for their living on near-paupers. An ugly lot . . . rank with malice, stupidity, ill-nature, pettiness, and what not . . ."[11]

Their equivalents in the next generation, ostensibly more at home in American society than their parents were, still felt spiritually and intellectually alien, and distrustful of what Veblen called "the community of safe and sane gentiles" to which they vainly sought admittance. It is this group of Jewish intelligentsia who flourished in the 1920's and 1930's or rather the radical branch of it, that I now wish to discuss. The following impressionistic scenario (let us call it "From Communism to *Commentary*"), outlines the progress of the radical Jewish intelligentsia from the late twenties until 1945, the year when the American Jewish Committee founded a magazine to carry forward "our common Jewish cultural and spiritual heritage," and to relate Jewish affairs to American life. A magazine devoted to Jewishness and America could hardly have appealed to Jewish radicals of the thirties, a good many of whom had passed through a Zionist phase before becoming Communists or Fellow-travelers. What changes had evolved in American life to make this possible? My scenario would explain it in some such fashion as this.

II

The New York Jewish intellectuals of the second generation, or those who came to the United States as small children, are literally and figuratively ghettoized, segregated, denied 'community' with old-stock America. They or their parents arrive with memories and legends of pogroms and Czarist oppression together with high expectations about their prospects in democratic America. Some achieve material security in time, and a good many more "Jews without money" (as Mike Gold calls them) do not. The refrain, "a curse on Columbus," becomes a familiar one in novels about Jewish East Side immigrants. But even those who escape from the slums into what a New York City official a few years ago referred to as "gilded ghettoes" fail to penetrate the social barriers erected against them. A prominent Jewish intellectual like Joseph Freeman, whose father became quite well-to-do shortly after World War I, goes to Columbia (instead of CCNY) and presumably makes the leap into the gentile world. Yet in his revealing autobiography, *An American Testament*, he takes care to note whenever he meets a real Anglo-Saxon of revolutionary stock. It seems almost miraculous that he, a foreign-born Jew, should have this remarkable experience. Undoubtedly many of the segregated Jews seldom or never had the chance to become intimate friends with non-Jews of the middle class.

In Communism they find a composite answer to pressing social, psychological, and intellectual needs: (1) a company of associates with whom they can relax and be themselves without fear of social discrimination. ("They really meant 'solidarity forever'," an ex-Communist of Catholic origin has commented, "especially second generation Jews who were cut off from their Yiddish speaking parents and the outside world in general.");[12] (2) the promise of a classless world where Christian and Jew are brothers and in which they might escape from gentile snubs—particularly in the highly stratified and snobbish college and university campuses; (3) a doctrine that appeals to their latent religiosity, to their humanitarianism, and to their rationality, and one that offers a future when the Egyptians will be humbled and the righteous assume their rightful places; (4) a Party that provides opportunities for the Talmudic theoreticians (the lay rabbis contemptuous of business and consecrated to higher speculations) to refine and resolve the ambiguities of the Marxist scriptures; (5) a cause that enables the ambitiously gifted to acquire reputations and power; (6) a movement that offers a cloak of anonymity to people whose origins and background bar them from the gentile community.

And so the Jewish intellectual identified himself with a group that defends the rights of all ethnic minorities in the United States. No one more vehemently upholds the privileges of Negroes or any other suppressed minority or weeps more sincerely for the wrongs of the toiling masses. Because the Jew weeps for himself. His commitment to Communism or socialism is a measure of democratic failure, the response to a cruel exclusiveness. ("Then there was the pain of being Jewish and the hurts suffered in X state," an ex-Communist intellectual observes. "The first community we lived in was very hostile. My reaction was something like 'If I can't belong to any country then I'll belong to no country—therefore nobody should belong to a country,' or 'If I'm merely non-accepted by Gentiles why not join the most different group—give it some meaning rather than just non-acceptance—revel in isolation—so you don't have to wonder about the why of anti-semitism in the first place'.")[13]

In some ways the Depression, like all large-scale disasters, breaks down social barriers. The Jewish intellectual can at least become a participant in the community of misery and suffer with the exclusives. The sporadic flare-ups of organized Anti-Semitism notwithstanding, the New Deal (the "Jew Deal" of the anti-semites) provides opportunities for Jewish professionals, intellectuals, and artists who otherwise might have found no outlet for their talents. Very possibly the New Deal weakens the appeal of Communism for many Jews. What keeps others in the Party, or friendly to it, is the growing menace of German Fascism; the Jew is willy-nilly committed to the support of Fascism's chief enemy. With the establishment of the United Front, Jews can work with the Communist Party without necessarily joining it, and they are more prone to forgive or palliate the dark stories coming out of the USSR, perhaps, than other groups. (I say this while acknowledging that Jews also made up a sizeable proportion of the radical opposition to Stalinist Communism from the very beginning and a decidedly vocal one.) But the Russian-German agreement of 1939 produces a revulsion, and the Jewish intellectual (in anguish or with relief) cuts himself adrift from his very delusive Eden.

The intelligentsia now turns back to America. The war provides them with even more anonymity than the Party, and the soldier's uniform is a much more effective symbol of fellowship than the Party membership card. And the possibilities of 'community' are now greater. In the 'forties and 'fifties, it seems, one can become American by becoming 'religious' like other Americans; the patriotic Jew, the Jew most readily acceptable, is not the deracinated atheist T. S. Eliot objected to but the pious Jew—a naval officer, a baseball player, a pilot, a doctor—who achieves success in the American way and who is respected and welcomed by his gentile neighbors because he is exactly like them in his tastes and aspirations. Herman Wouk is his admiring chronicler, Philip Roth, his sardonic one. No more radical, free-thinking, socialistic, apocalyptic Jews, thank you. The new policy is to become like other Americans—but more so. Thus in 1950, Clement Greenberg can write:

> We do not have to pick our way through the wreckage and poverty of a dying feudal society; we do not live in ethnic enclaves; here bourgeois enlightenment has become a good deal of an official reality, and we are citizens rather than nationals.[14]

III

So much for the preliminary sketch, more descriptive than analytical, but many troublesome questions remain unanswered.

Before the 1890's, American Jews could hardly be said to have played more than a very minor part in radical movements. Co-incidentally, Anti-Semitism was virtually non-existent in the early days of the Republic, if a reviewer in an 1818 issue of *The North American Review* is to be believed. Discussing Maria Edgeworth's *Harrington* (a melodramatic tale of anti-semitism in England), he remarked:

> As it respects this country the lesson might have been spared, for very few among us, who are likely to read Miss Edgeworth's book, can be suspected of supposing Jews and Christians to be different sorts of beings. We know of no social or political privations to which our Jews are subject, and Miss Edgeworth has given us credit for treating them like other people. We think the story is calculated to have an effect rather unfavourable to the Jews of this country, as it tends to single them out as objects of observation, whereas they might otherwise have passed in the crowd without any national distinction.[15]

What prompted the growing hostility to Jews after 1865, a hostility that added an ugly ingredient to American Populism and that took on an even more malevolent character after the influx of Jews from Eastern Europe? To understand these developments, I can think of no better source than Professor John Higham, author of an admirable survey of social discrimination against American Jews between 1830 and 1930.[16]

Higham had been requested by the American Jewish Committee to study the backgrounds of anti-semitism in the United States. "When and why," he was asked, "has discrimination against Jews increased and diminished in America?" To what extent was this discrimination comparable to that experienced by other minorities? Did Jews suffer less discrimination in some parts of the country than in others? If so, why? Did intellectual and political doctrines cause or lessen social discrimination? Professor Higham was not asked to study the prevalence of Jews in twentieth century radical movements, nor does his survey take up the problem, but his findings cast some light on this matter. By playing down (although by no means ignoring) the significance of ideology ("the power of irrational beliefs") in his explanation of anti-Jewish discrimination, and by attributing it primarily to the "actual conflict situation" produced by "a very real" Jewish competition "for status and prestige," he is able to demonstrate with greater accuracy and precision than any other commentator I have read why and when Jews were discriminated against. His survey thus offers at least one clue to the origins, development, and decline of Jewish radicalism.

In brief, Higham's essay may be summarized as follows. Between 1800 and 1830, Jews "occupied a secure, stable, and untrammeled place in American society." Dislike of Jews was not uncommon[17] (the stereotype of the sharp trader, the "Shylock," was already pretty pervasive), but these casual prejudices provoked no social discrimination. Even the immigration of German Jews to America in the 1840's did little to change the picture. In the 1830's, the Jewish population was approximately 15,000 out of a total population of fifteen million. America was still an open pioneer society affording white men "a rough equality of opportunity that few countries have ever equalled."

The decisive change, Higham feels, occurred between 1870 and 1900. In these years, a definite pattern of discrimination took form for the following reasons. By the mid-seventies, the new immigration from Germany and Poland increased the Jewish population to a quarter of a million, one fifth of which was concentrated in New York City. Many Jews, mostly German, had prospered greatly in the free and easy period of the Gilded Age and had become, in the eyes of their gentile neighbors, the most vulgar of parvenus. Higham says that these rich Jews, for the most part uneducated and uncultivated, showed little of that "intellectual drive and distinction" so characteristic of the East European Jews of more recent vintage.

Today we read the waspish and mean-spirited portraits of the parvenu Jew in the novels of Edith Wharton or in the letters of some of the Brahmin worthies as examples of hysterical and irrational prejudice. And so, in a measure, they are. Higham warns us, however, not to "over-emphasize the irrational sources of 'prejudice'" or to ignore its "objective content."[18] Before 1900, he points out, "sober and humane observers repeatedly took note of the core of reality behind the stereotype." Only during the 1930's and after did the scholars and publicists concentrate almost entirely on "ideological unreason" as the cause of Anti-Semitism. (I single out Higham's caveat, because it partly explains, perhaps, the radical Jewish intellectuals' own hostility toward the vulgar Jewish philistine whose unashamed drive for social status struck them as particularly reprehensible.)[19]

The principal discriminators in the post-Civil War years were not the secure patricians (perhaps Higham does not pay sufficient attention to the notable exceptions) but rather the "insecure social climbers" embarrassed by "the crush of applicants" from below. Had class lines been more rigid, as in England, or had the *nouveaux riches* Jews been less zealous in besieging the uncertainly held places of *arriviste* gentiles, presumably (if Higham is right) there would have been less discrimination. He flatly denies Oscar Handlin's and Carey McWilliams' contention that "discrimination grows as reactionary opinion-makers impose undemocratic values on the innocent masses."[20]

In the third period (1900–1917), discrimination against Jews accelerated with the continued influx of immigrants from Eastern Europe. German Jews had become partially assimilated, but the newcomers quickened the resentment against all Jews and raised the barriers against them in schools, resorts, and the professions even higher than they had been before 1900. Between 1897 and 1917, the Jewish population had jumped from one million to over three and a third millions. In New York, Brooklyn, Boston, Minneapolis, and other cities, second generation Jews were breaking out of their enclaves and crowding into areas where they were not welcome. Eager to demonstrate how "American" they had become, many deliberately abandoned their Jewish heritage. But to no avail. The rebuffs they met were all the more painful "because of the social distance they had put between themselves and their immigrant fathers."

The pattern set between 1900 and 1917 continued into the twenties with regional and local variations. Higham demonstrates why social discrimination was always less pervasive in cities and regions where the Jews were early settlers or sparse in numbers. Anti-Semitism was less noticeable in small towns than in cities of 10,000 or over, more noticeable in cities where immigration was of recent origin, and less in cities or areas where Jews joined with other white groups in upholding white supremacy (*viz.*, the South and San Francisco).

In contrast to other minority groups, Jews fared better than some, worse than others. Negroes and Orientals, of course, suffered more severely from discrimination. The Irish and the Germans had their ups and downs, but in general they came to be accepted as they merged into the population at large. But dislike for Jews increased as they improved materially. Higham would ascribe this paradox to the fact that old-stock Americans have not been able to regard the Jew with the patronizing indulgence they have reserved for other ethnic minorities. The Jew has advanced economically more rapidly than other immigrant groups, and his "social expectations" have been consequently higher. Unlike other minorities, content to remain among their kind, relatively slow to aspire to an "equivalent social status" of the old-stock Americans, the Jews' aspirations have been less economic or political than social. "They wanted the full privileges and opportunities of the middle-class society into which, unlike the major immigrant groups, they moved en masse."

It is the social importunity[21] of the Jew, Higham concludes, rather than ideological considerations that have accounted for his hostile reception, and he convincingly demonstrates that the rise of social discrimination against the Jew did not correspond to the waves of ideological agitation. Furthermore, ideological Anti-Semitism flared up in rural areas where the local Jews were generally accepted by the rest of the community. This view, then, might well explain the improved situation of the Jew since the 1930's and the decline of discrimination, since it would follow from his survey that competition "for place and privilege have eased" and that with the end of mass immigration and the assimilation of the third and fourth generation of Jews, they will no longer experience the bitter slights that induced a number of their disenchanted predecessors to espouse the Communist cause.

Higham's analysis, together with the impressions I have gained from talking with a number of Jewish writers once affiliated in some way with the Communist movement, prompt me to make some qualified assertions about the appeal of Communism to the Jewish intelligentsia:

1. The infiltration of Jews into the radical movement coincided with the period in American history when they were barred (or at least felt excluded) from the economic, cultural, and social opportunities available to non-Jewish segments of the population.

2. Although Jewish intellectuals were drawn to the Left because, in some measure, its heterodoxy answered their psychological needs and released dammed up energies and aspirations, the messianic Judaic tradition affected believer and non-believer

alike. A society which promised justice, the elimination of national frontiers, and the brotherhood of man was only a secular blueprint of an old Jewish dream.

3. The native radical tradition did not, at first, evoke their allegiance, first because they were not in touch with it; and second, because American Progressivism, concerned primarily with economic and political equality, had never (as Higham notes) "mounted a vigorous ideological offensive against the barriers of race and nationality."

4. Many Jewish intellectuals had been reared in an environment where Socialism and Marxism were topics of intense interest and where post-Revolutionary Russia had become the symbol of the prejudice-free society in which Jews could play an important and honorable role.

5. As the threat of Fascism mounted, lending support to ideological Anti-Semitism in the United States, Jewish intellectuals naturally gravitated to a movement most vociferously committed to anti-Fascism and to the socialist state which alone seemed able and willing to check Nazi expansion.

6. The Communist Party, in turn, equated capitalism with Anti-Semitism and confused the assault against the Jew-as-radical with the assault against the Jew-as-Jew. The radical Jews were vulnerable on both counts, to be sure, but the Party's revelations of sinister and wide-spread Anti-Semitic plots in the United States had no basis in fact.

7. Jewish writers and artists, for the most part, severed their ties with the USSR and the American Communist Party after they began to comprehend the Soviet regime's brutal and opportunistic policy towards its Jewish nationals.

8. The Jewish intellectual's disenchantment with the Soviets (hastened by the Treason Trials and the Nazi-Soviet pact) happened to coincide with a small but perceptible lessening of discriminatory practices and the opening of opportunities in letters, the arts, and education.

These 'conclusions,' of course, are supposititious and partial. No issue or problem is exclusively 'Jewish,' and the characteristics I have ascribed to Jewish writers and intellectuals apply, in some respects, to their non-Jewish counterparts. The world-wide economic depression suggested radical alternatives to the capitalist order to men of all races and religions. But it seems likely that the Left-Wing Jewish writers in the United States were more consciously or unconsciously motivated by their sense of being outsiders than were the old-stock American radicals, temporarily on the 'outs' with their society, and that the Jewish writer's zeal in espousing Communism or Communist inspired causes was a measure of this deeper alienation. Marxism (usually imperfectly understood) attracted non-Jews as well as Jews, but the Marxian forecast of a splendid future, not Communist tactics or discipline, appealed with special force to talented and ambitious Jewish dissidents.

Close contact with misery, the direct confrontation "with the most devastating examples of the breakdown of capitalism— every day," as one ex-Communist writer recollected, supported the inclination to 'go Left.' "For the first time, it was no longer a matter of rebellion . . . look, I said, 'Marxism is truly an objective statement of objective reality.' "[22] This writer retained his admiration for the goals of Communism and the zeal of idealistic Party workers even after he had become disgusted with the anti-intellectual 'Leather-jacket' proletarian 'snobs' who worshipped all things Russian, employed a barbarous jargon, and did not bother to hide their contempt for the literary Comrades.

Since most of the Left-Wing Jewish writers were not Party members, they were spared the annoyances of Party supervision, but those who signed up as 'intellectuals' ("an intellectual was a white collar worker who couldn't be put in any other category") felt themselves drawn in different directions. Party solidarity, according to one observer then on the inside, carried more than an ideological significance for the Jewish members. ("You don't have to love your brother, but it's more relaxing to be with him than a stranger.") At the same time, writers and intellectuals found the narrow confines of Party life particularly galling and tended to regard themselves and the outside world with greater detachment and irony than single-minded Party zealots did. To remain in the Party and to engage in any kind of creative work demanded a compartmentalizing of thought that was detrimental to both political and artistic activity. The Party preached hate and war to the death against its class enemies. Anyone who wittingly or unwittingly spoke for the capitalist opposition bore the enemy taint; only soft-headed Liberals tried to distinguish the idea from the man.

This was not a palatable creed for serious artists and writers no matter how strongly they felt about social issues, and it disillusioned a good many of them unable to square their political idealism with the illiberalism of the Party. The constant pulling and tugging in opposite directions prompted a former Communist writer (who in later years suspected that Anti-Semitism "must have had something to do with my becoming a Communist") to resign from the Party before the general exodus in 1939. "The price I was paying was the abortion of my talent. . . . I left because I wanted to be a writer."[23] Many others in his situation made the same decision for the same reasons.

Writers left for other reasons as well,[24] but in speculating about Communism's appeal to the Jewish writer and intelligentsia, what the sociologists call the "ecological factors" (more precise than *Zeitgeist* or "social climate") cannot be underestimated. With few exceptions, the Jewish Left-Wing writer's break with Communism became irreparable at that moment in American history when the barriers that had hemmed him in and kept him a 'hyphenate' began to crumble.[25]

NOTES

1. The subject is touched upon in Nathan Glazer, *The Social Basis of American Communism* (N.Y., 1961), and Malech Epstein, *The Jew and Communism* (N.Y., Trade Union Sponsoring Committee, 1959), the latter a history of the Jewish Section of the Communist Party. For an interesting commentary on Glazer's book that pays special attention to "the historic Jewish relationship to the political left," see Lucy S. Dawidowicz's review-essay in the *American Jewish Historical Quarterly*, LIII (Dec., 1963), 192–7. I did not know of this essay, which corroborates some of my conclusions, until after my article had been published.

2. Mr. Joseph Freeman, who challenges "the alleged preponderance of Jews in the U.S. literary Left," mentions Jack London, Lincoln Steffens, Max Eastman, and Floyd Dell among the 'ancestors' of the 1930 writers. However, each of these writers was out of the main stream by 1930, and Mr. Freeman's omission of two names (his own and Michael Gold's) who link the Left movement of the 'twenties with the 'thirties is significant. See "Communism and the American Writer," A Report of the Tenth Newberry Library Conference on American Studies in *The Newberry Library Bulletin*, V (Aug., 1959), pp. 111–114.

3. Waldo Frank, Isidor Schneider, Michael Gold, Henry Potamkin, Henry Roth, Nathanael West, Albert Maltz, Leonard Ehrlich, John Howard Lawson, Michael Blankfort, Lionel Trilling, Matthew Josephson, Philip

Rahv, William Phillips, Irwin Shaw, Muriel Rukeyser, Kenneth Fearing, Edward Dahlberg, Howard Fast, and many others. Almost half of the contributors to *Proletarian Literature in the United States* (N.Y., 1935) are of Jewish origin.

4. Clement Greenberg, "Self-Hatred and Jewish Chauvinism," *Commentary*, X (Nov., 1950), p. 431.

5. Waldo Frank, *Our America* (N.Y., 1919), pp. 78ff.

6. *The Dial*, LXXII (June 1922), pp. 637–8.

7. *The New Republic*, XV (June 15, 1918), p. 209.

8. Van Wyck Brooks, *The Confident Years: 1885–1915* (N.Y., 1952), pp. 122–3.

9. A. A. Roback, "Yiddish Books and Their Readers," *Nation*, CVII (Oct. 12, 1918), pp. 408–12.

10. Daniel Bell, "A Parable of Alienation," *Jewish Frontier* (Nov., 1946), p. 15.

11. *The Pagan*, I (July, 1916), pp. 43–4.

12. Unpublished document in possession of the author. A similar point was made by William Soskin: "The most extreme radicals I know are almost invariably the products of unhappy, orthodox, constricted childhoods, or of extremely vulgar lower middle class homes whence they sought to escape to the most convenient and plausible form of radicalism. Many of them are Jews who have behaved quite in line with Bertrand Russell's description of the type of Jew who, having experienced emotional disruption because of the gentile cries of 'Sheeney!' which did not seem to conform to the glorious condition of the Jewish race he heard about in his Orthodox home, and having too much intelligence to hate all gentiles because of this experience, transfers his hatred to capitalists. And capitalists, being what they are, contribute enough hatefulness to the arrangement to make the Jew's escape to Marxism a plausible affair." "Rhapsodies in Red," *The Forum*, Dec., 1932, pp. 349–50.

13. H. E. Krugman, "The Appeal of Communism to American Middle Class Intellectuals and Trade Unionists," *Public Opinion Quarterly*, XVI (Fall, 1952), p. 339.

14. Greenberg, "Self-Hatred and Jewish Chauvinism," *op. cit.*, p. 431.

15. VI (1818), p. 161.

16. "Social Discrimination Against Jews in America, 1830–1930," *Publications of the American Jewish Historical Society*, XLVII (Sept., 1957), pp. 1–33.

17. Distrust of Jews in early and middle periods of the 19th century and stereotyped notions of Jewish greed, slyness, and materialism were deeply implanted in American folkways. But until the 1870's, anti-Jewish prejudices were primarily religious. Toward the close of the century, anti-Judaism was transformed into Anti-Semitism. As Ruth M. Elson observes, "A religious bias for discrimination offers the possibility for change by conversion, and eventual amalgamation into the national culture. A racial difference, by its very nature, is immutable." See her discussion in *Guardians of Tradition. American Schoolbooks of the Nineteenth Century* (Lincoln, Nebraska, 1964), pp. 81–7.

When, in 1887, the young Frederick Jackson Turner accidentally found himself in the Boston ghetto, it is unlikely that he considered the outlandish Jews swarming in Salem Street suitable material for "eventual amalgamation": "In a moment (he wrote to his sister) I saw what had happened. I was in Jewry, the street consecrated to 'old clothers,' pawnbrokers, and similar followers of Abraham. It was a narrow *alley*, we would say in the west, and was fairly packed with swarthy sons and daughters of the tribe of Israel—such noises, such smells, such sights! Did you ever see a bottle filled first with marbles, then the spaces with buckshot, then smaller shot added until the mass was packed tight? The street was like that bottle, filled with big Jew men—long bearded and carrying a staff as you see in a picture,—and with Jew youths and maidens—some of the latter pretty—as you sometimes see a lily in the green muddy slime,—and the little babies and children filling up all the chinks. At last, after much elbowing, I came upon Old North rising out of this mass of oriental noise and squalor like a haven of rest." F. J. Turner to Ellen Turner, June 30, 1887. Turner Papers, The Huntington Library (quoted with permission of Ray A. Billington).

18. A contemporary English reviewer of Edith Wharton's *The House of Mirth* remarked, however, that the author "had no occasion . . . to obtrude her vulgarly superficial ethnological generalizations in attributing the characteristics of the New York financier, Rosendale (sic)—which were the outcome of *that* occupation in those surroundings—to his racial inheritance." Charles Waldstein. "Social Ideals,—II," *North American Review*, DXCVI (July, 1906), p. 126.

19. Samuel Ornitz, *Haunch, Paunch and Jowl* (N.Y., 1923), Budd Schulberg, *What Makes Sammy Run?* (N.Y., 1941), and Jerome Weidman, *I Can Get It For You Wholesale* (N.Y., 1937) are probably the best known treatments of Jewish parvenus. A lesser known illustration is Edward Dahlberg, "Fantasy in Blue Eyes and Blond Hair," *New Masses*, XI (April 17, 1934), pp. 19–21, a chapter from an unpublished novel, *No Giants Live Here*. Incidentally, this episode is a classic sample of Jewish self-hatred.

20. See Handlin, "The Acquisition of Political and Social Rights by the Jews of the United States," *American Jewish Yearbook*, 1955, pp. 72, 74, and McWilliams, *A Mask For Privilege* (Boston, 1948), pp. 17–21. In "Anti-Semitism in the Gilded Age," *Mississippi Valley Historical Review* (March, 1957), pp. 5–6, Higham criticized both Handlin and Richard Hofstadter for paying too much attention to the "role of ideas" and not enough to "economic forces" in explaining Anti-Semitism during the Populist period.

21. Seen, for example, in the demand for higher education. "I am cutting a faculty meeting," Frederick Jackson Turner wrote in 1922, "which is one of several trying (between ourselves) to deal with the problem of the increasing percentage of Jews in Harvard and the problem they make. Lowell [A. Lawrence Lowell, the President of Harvard] is for courageous and rather drastic treatment; but it is so foreign to the New English ideals of liberalism in race matters, and religious (sic) perhaps,

that he will not find it easy. I am inclined to think that action may be premature; but I don't like the prospects of Harvard a New Jerusalem and Boston already a new Cork. Bad old world and the times out of joint." F. J. Turner to Caroline Mae Turner, May 23, 1922. Turner Papers, The Huntington Library (quoted with permission of Ray A. Billington).

22. Unpublished document in possession of author.

23. Unpublished interview in possession of author.

24. Daniel Aaron, *Writers on the Left: Episodes in American Literary Communism* (N.Y., 1961).

25. See Jules Chametsky, "Notes on the Assimilation of the American-Jewish Writer; Abraham Cahan to Saul Bellow," *Jahrbuch für Amerikastudien*, Band 9, 1964, pp. 173–80; and Daniel Aaron, "The Hyphenate Writer and American Letters," *Smith College Alumnae Quarterly*, July, 1964, pp. 213–17.

JEWS AND CIVIL RIGHTS

MILTON R. KONVITZ

I

A HUNDRED YEARS AGO—in 1867—Emerson cried out to the racist, "You complain that the Negroes are a base class. Who makes and keeps the Jew or the Negro base, who but you, who excludes them from the rights which others enjoy?"[1]

With characteristic sensitivity, Emerson saw, long before others, that the small and comfortable Jewish community in the United States was fast becoming the object of ridicule, prejudice, and hatred. In the 1870s American Jews began to suffer from discrimination—they were so intimidated that they began to discourage further Jewish immigration.[2] As long as the Negro was set apart as a slave, even if the problem of anti-Semitism had been serious, the Jewish struggle for equality and security could have had no intimate link with abolition and Negro emancipation. But Negro emancipation coincided with the rise of anti-Semitism. Its more obvious forms were the exclusion of Jews from resort hotels and resorts generally, from private schools, and from clubs, and the establishment of unfavorable stereotypes superimposed upon the Shylock image.[3] To a keen observer like Emerson, it became apparent that the destinies of Jews and Negroes were linked—*because they were linked in the mind of the racist*. In due course, the leaders of American Jewry came to share Emerson's insight and made the programmatic struggle for Jewish rights a struggle for civil rights generally; for the equal rights of *all* Americans, regardless of race, color, creed, or national origin.

Now, however, a hundred years after Emerson, the situation seems different. In 1960 a Roman Catholic was elected President of the United States. In 1965 the odious immigration laws of the 1920s, based on race and national origins, were repealed. There

Original for this volume.

was now no apparent discrimination against Jews in higher education, employment, housing, politics, or places of public accommodation. American Jews still suffered from the so-called five o'clock shadow—from social exclusion, from discrimination by clubs and some apartment houses; and also from the employment policies of some large banks, large corporations, and some Wall Street law firms.[4] But the residue of prejudice and discrimination has only minor effect on the masses of American Jews; and these practices are no longer brazenly defended in the way that the President of Harvard in 1922 defended a *numerus clausus* for Jewish students.

There are still rabid anti-Semites and neo-Nazis.[5] But even the claim that "American anti-Semitism today is expressed in patterns of discrimination built into many of the basic institutions of our society" must be coupled with the acknowledgment that anti-Semitism in the 1960s was "most apt to be expressed in furtive ways," for the people who practice anti-Semitic discrimination "are usually guilt ridden and defensive."[6]

In fact the Jews have so far outdistanced the Negroes in the struggle for equality that in the 1960s the case of the Negroes was *sui generis*. The problem of prejudice and discrimination had become an almost exclusively Negro problem, which "lacked for others the nagging intensity it had earlier. . . . The Negro was left to suffer alone."[7] By the 1960s, the old racism, by which Jews, Chinese, Japanese, and others were marked as inferior breeds, had given way "to a new belief which recognizes but a single inferior race, the Negro, and but a single impassable line, that created by the color of the black man's skin."[8]

A measure of the change may be found in the fact that a concern with Negro-Jewish relations has in the 1960s attracted far more interest than has the anti-Semitism of the white race. Anglo-Jewish periodicals and Jewish groups in the past barely noticed that American Jews had any reason for interest in Negro attitudes toward Jews; in the 1960s these attitudes seemed to claim insistently for attention and even concern.[9]

II

In the 1960s one often heard Jews ask, "Why haven't the American Negroes done more for themselves? Why do they fight so aggressively for civil rights instead of, like Jews, putting their energies into making a life for themselves? After all, Jews, too, were once slaves, and are not ashamed of the fact, but worked hard, not to erase the memory of slavery but its effects on their character. Can it be that in fact the Negroes are, as the white racists claim, an inferior race?" Many people asked these and similar questions, but with open or secret misgivings, for everyone remembers that only recently the Jew himself had been branded a member of an inferior race—a race not even fit for enslavement but for total extermination.

As one compares Jews and Negroes, significant differences are apparent:

1. The Jews were marked off as a separate group by their religion, but the American principle was to consider religion a strictly personal, private matter, and therefore it was wrong to think of Jews as constituting a separate "race," just as it would be wrong to think this way of Baptists or Methodists or Roman Catholics. There are, of course, religious prejudices, but religious prejudices were considered to be wrong in principle.

But Negroes *are* a race. Their color follows them with their faces and hands. One could be a Jew at home and in the synagogue and an undifferentiated American on the street, but the Negro was everywhere a Negro. Religious liberty, the equal dignity of all religions, and the separation of church and state are basic principles of Americanism; but the principle of racial equality still had to be vindicated. In the "old country" Jews were separate and unequal; in the United States they were never subject, as were the Negroes until 1954, to the constitutional doctrine of "separate but equal." If Jews were separate, it was often by choice, and never by force of laws like the infamous Black Codes and the segregation laws; and constitutionally they were equal, not merely by force of the Fourteenth Amendment of 1868, but also by force of the First Amendment of 1791.

2. If Jews once were slaves, that was in the remote past, well over three thousand years ago; while many American Negroes have heard their grandparents relate incidents from the days when they had been slaves in the South or in border states or in the District of Columbia.

Furthermore, when the Israelites ceased to be slaves in Egypt, they also ceased to be Egyptians and at once started on their forty years of wandering in the desert on their way to the

Promised Land. They never had to face their former masters. And while they knew that they had once been slaves unto Pharaoh in Egypt, they also thought of themselves as God's elect, as His chosen people, with a calling and a destiny marked for them by the God of their fathers with whom He made an everlasting covenant.

Nothing like this happened to American Negroes. They were emancipated, not by God, but by the bloodiest war in American history. There was no Exodus for them from the South—the freedmen continued daily, hourly, to be seen by their former masters.

And their former masters never accepted emancipation except as the result of *force majeure;* they never accepted freedom and equality for members of the Negro race on the moral and emotional level. Even the Christianity of the Southern churches shut out the fact of emancipation. In their relations with the Negroes, white people continued as much as possible to live in a hothouse atmosphere of antebellum values—agrarian, provincial, feudal, caste-ridden, aristocratic, pre-industrial and antidemocratic. It was a system that kept the Negro in a state of peonage or almost total subjection. It also kept the South economically, socially, educationally, and morally backward, so that the South became in some respects America's underdeveloped region—and the Negroes were the most underdeveloped people there.

Nothing remotely comparable happened to the Jews. For centuries they had been kept off the land and locked up in walled cities and towns. The walls of these cities came tumbling down precisely at the time when society was turning to science, technology, industry, and professionalization. The Jews had been conditioned by Christian civilization to think of themselves as an urban, not as an agricultural, people. When they could at long last move about with relative freedom, the Jews were predisposed to enter the fast-growing middle class as business entrepreneurs, members of the professions, and craftsmen (tailors, carpenters, furriers, hat-makers, jewelers, and other callings that had been useful in the ghettoes). Many of their economic undertakings had by their nature the possibility of development, growth, and prosperity: the pushcart merchant could eventually rent a small store, a small store could eventually become an emporium; a small-town lawyer could become a big-city attorney, and he could learn of business opportunities for himself or his clients; a physician could become a great specialist. In any case, there was for the Jews a providential conjunction of psychic preparation and economic opportunity.

The Negro's psychic preparation was for a life of subjection and deprivation. What future could there be for a cotton picker? What else could he ever be? If he or his son showed an inclination to move up on the economic or social ladder, he became an "uppity" Negro who had to be put in "his place."

3. The Jews had not merely religious beliefs, but a religious civilization, that they transported as they moved or were driven from land to land; and often they were far superior in education and morals to their pagan, Christian, or Muslim "hosts."

American Negroes, originally brought in slave ships, came from hundreds of African tribes, and spoke innumerable languages. They had practically nothing in common but their color and their misfortune. The master race put them into a pressure cooker, where they lost all remembrance of their original languages and cultures. Except perhaps at night, around a fire, out of earshot of their white masters, they could not even enjoy the luxury of ancestral memories. In any case, they had no common *shtetl* or "old country" to bring them together into *Landsmann-schaften* or welfare societies, to a *Brisker Shul* or a Warsaw Hebrew Free Loan Society. The American law of slavery refused to recognize even the legitimacy of marriage between slaves or the integrity of the slave's family. Thus, until only a mere century ago everything had been done to kill every trace of the American Negro's original heritage, every memory, claim, or symbol of his human inheritance and standing.

It takes countless generations to build up a culture, but a single "lost generation" can break the chain of transmission and much may be irrevocably lost.

4. Finally, the Israelites in Egypt and in the desert constituted a single mass movement under a single leader, Moses. There were murmurings against him and even rebellions and treasonable acts, but they were effectively punished or suppressed. And Moses was able to keep the erstwhile slaves in the desert until the adults who had been slaves died. It was the next generation, grown into adulthood as free men and women, who were led into the Promised Land.

But the Negroes have had no Moses and no single great mass movement. Negroes, like most other Americans, think and act as individuals and not as members of a race or of a mass movement. The civil rights movement is a latecomer, it is not limited to Negroes, it has no single leader—there is in it considerable dissidence, confusion of tongues, and opposition.

And there is no Promised Land to which the Negroes can be taken. Their greatest need is employment at a time when automation is rapidly reducing their opportunities. The country needs 1,125,000 *new* jobs each year to take care of the newcomers among the employables. This is in addition to jobs needed for the approximately four million unemployed (among whom the rate for Negroes is at least double that for white workers). The Negro is clamoring for blue collar jobs when for the first time in history the economy needs a decrease in the ratio of such workers to white collar and professional workers. These conditions were not made by the Negro. They are like insurmountable mountains in front of him. Steps must be taken to see to it that young Negroes will be educated and trained for the new economic order. The Negro must be willing to take advantage of opportunities, but the availability of the opportunities will depend almost wholly on others.

The contemporary scene looks radically different for the Jew. It is estimated that four out of five Jewish graduates from secondary schools go on to college.[10] In a few years almost every adult Jew in the United States will have a college degree. Relatively few Jews grow up needing an unskilled job. The Jews are a thoroughly urban and an almost wholly educated and trained group. Individual Jews have, of course, career problems, but as a group American Jews have no need to look upon the emerging economic employment patterns with alarm or fear.

III

Thus, from the beginning and for over three hundred years the condition of American Jews has been radically different from that of American Negroes. The constitutional guarantee of religious liberty, of equal dignity and status of all religions, the Jewish proclivity for urban life, the Jewish stress on education, learning, and on mutual assistance as a religious duty—these and other values and experiences have helped the Jews to face and overcome obstacles.

But American Jews also had experiences that were similar to those of the Negroes. They had enemies in common. As we have noted, in the 1870s Jews became the objects of racist and anti-Semitic prejudice and hatred. The Ku Klux Klan harassed Jews as well as Negroes. Nativistic societies, like the Know-Nothings, were against Negroes and also against all "foreign" influences that might affect the "American" way of seeing and doing things. The Jews suffered from discrimination in education, in employment, in housing, in hotels and restaurants, in hospitals, in suburban developments, in the professions, in social relations. They lived in ghettoes near their synagogues, attended neighborhood public schools and after-school religious classes, built their own welfare institutions, and made a living by buying and selling among themselves and patronizing their own professional class.

Significantly, it was not the enemy at home that led the Jews to seek strength from self-organization. In 1859 an Italian-Jewish child, Edgar Mortara, was abducted by Papal officers in Bologna. The case became a *cause célèbre*. It called into being the Alliance Israelite Universelle among Jews of the French Empire, and American Jews, numbering about a hundred thousand, organized the Board of Delegates of American Israelites. It never achieved power, and in 1878 it became the Board of Delegates on Civil and Religious Rights—its new name was significant—of the Union of American Hebrew Congregations (now a Reform, but originally an undifferentiated, national institution).[11]

Then in 1903 the pogrom in Kishinev, Russia, shocked the civilized world. The pogrom left forty-seven dead and ninety-two maimed. By the standards of the mid-century, this would hardly be worth mentioning; but at the beginning of the century people could still react with shock and indignation to acts of brutality. They did not then talk about crimes against humanity—this concept had to wait for the Nuremberg Tribunal of 1945; but they could feel deeply the impact of such crimes. In the United States there were protest meetings and American Jews sent relief funds to aid the stricken community. Then two years later a second massacre occurred in Kishinev. This was only four or five years after the world was stunned by the disclosure that Alfred Dreyfus had been convicted on the basis of forged evidence. The wounds to the Jewish body were raw and painful. American Jews, enjoying relative security and prosperity, decided that the time had come to organize themselves more effectively to help their co-religionists in other parts of the world. Under the leadership of Cyrus Adler, Jacob Schiff, Louis Marshall, Oscar Straus, and Cyrus Sulzberger, the American Jewish Committee was formed in 1906. The organization's charter stated its aims:

> . . . to prevent the infraction of the civil and religious rights of Jews, in any part of the world; to render all lawful assistance and to take appropriate remedial action in the event of threatened or actual invasion or destruction of such rights, or of unfavorable discrimination with respect thereto; to alleviate the consequences of persecution and to afford relief from calamities affecting Jews, wherever they may occur. . . .[12]

There were then in the United States about one million Jews.[13]

The first important concern of the Committee was a problem that dramatically and uniquely compelled its members, and American Jews generally, to see themselves in a double role: as Americans, claiming equal dignity and rights with all other Americans, and as Jews, claiming on behalf of Jews elsewhere equal dignity and rights. They were at one and the same time, Jews, Americans, and members of a people scattered throughout the world, with a deep concern for the security, welfare, and rights of their co-religionists. They thus rejected isolation within the American people and isolation from their own people elsewhere.

Czarist Russia imposed degrading and economically onerous restrictions on its Jewish subjects and also imposed them on American Jews visiting Russia. This discrimination against certain Americans was in violation of a Russo-American treaty of 1832. The Committee called on the United States government to compel Russia to end this violation of the treaty. When governmental representations failed to move Russia, the Committee appealed to the public. In an address in 1911 Louis Marshall formulated the issue in principled terms:

> It is not the Jew who is insulted; it is the American people. And the finding of a proper remedy against this degradation is not a Jewish but an American question. . . . I should deplore the day when there should ever arise a Jewish, a Catholic or a Protestant question in the United States. We can never suffer any question here concerning individual rights but such as relates to the entire American people.[14]

The campaign was successful; at the end of that year the United States abrogated its treaty with Russia. This incident typifies the stance of the Committee, which it has consistently maintained since its founding.

Within the first five years of its existence, however, the Committee saw that it needed to make more explicit its concern with the civil rights of Jews in specific areas. In the decade in which the Committee was formed the Jewish population of the United States was almost doubled by the immigration of nearly a million Jews. Discrimination against Jews, and against all "foreigners"— in immigration laws, in employment, in housing, in social relations, in colleges and professional schools—was becoming flagrant and menacing. The Committee amended its charter in 1911 to clarify its objective "to secure for Jews equality of economic, social and educational opportunity."[15]

From its origin the Committee has worked for the equal rights of Jews by international and national sanctions. In these important respects the Committee set the pattern that was to be followed by other Jewish organizations, such as the Anti-Defamation League of B'nai B'rith, founded in 1913; the American Jewish Congress, which became a permanent body in 1918–1922, and the Jewish Labor Committee, established in 1934. The organizations differ in composition, in methods, and in emphases; but they agree in their concern for civil rights of Jews and in their concern for Jews everywhere in the world. They are interested in the work of the United Nations Commission on Human Rights almost as much as in the work of the United States Congress.

These organizations see themselves as Jewish, but they see themselves also as American. It was inevitable that their concern for civil rights should not be parochial, but would embrace the civil rights of *all* Americans without regard to religion, race, or national origin.

Julius Rosenwald and Louis Marshall, both prominent in the American Jewish Committee, were early members of the Board of Directors of the National Association for the Advancement of Colored People, formed in 1910. The work of Louis Marshall in civil rights and civil liberties has served as an example for other Jewish leaders and their organizations. He worked for the rights of American Indians, on behalf of Japanese-Americans in California, for the rights of Roman Catholics, for Negro suffrage, for the outlawing of the restrictive covenant in housing, for the rights of Socialists and pacifists. He fought against the Ku Klux Klan, against Henry Ford for his anti-Semitism, against censorship, against every curtailment of human liberty or equality. In essentials, the Jewish organizations have followed the model that he set and have worked in his spirit.

IV

The American Jewish Committee in the 1960s had a membership of 26,000, organized into fifty chapters in major cities;[16] but this substantial membership was a recent development. Initially and for many years the Committee consisted of a small group of leading Jews who acted as trustees for their co-religionists. This situation naturally bred dissatisfaction; in 1917–1918 Louis Brandeis, Stephen S. Wise, Julian Mack, Felix Frankfurter, Louis Lipsky, Horace Kallen, and Nathan Straus agitated for the formation of a Jewish parliamentary body that would have a grassroots base.

Another concern of this group of restive young men was the Committee's lack of commitment to the Zionist ideal of a Jewish homeland in Palestine. They felt that at the end of World War I it would be essential for American Jewry to exert influence for the fulfillment of the Balfour Declaration of 1917. Accordingly in 1918 the American Jewish Congress came into existence. Some 335,000 Jews had voted for their representatives to this Congress.[17] Like the Committee in its early years, the Congress was more concerned with the needs of Jews in other parts of the world than with the domestic scene. It sent a delegation to the Versailles Peace Conference to work for the Zionist cause and to win equal rights for European Jews through guarantees in the treaties yet to be made. Toward the end of the following decade, when Hitler began to appear as a menace, the Congress rallied Americans—Jews and non-Jews—to see the evil nature and dangers of Nazism and Fascism.

While the Congress had an interest in fighting against anti-Semitism and for civil rights, it was not until the early 1940s that it entered these fields with commitments and resources. In 1944 it organized its Commission on Community Interrelations, with a staff of sociologists and social psychologists under the direction of Kurt Lewin, famous for his work in group dynamics.[18] Then in 1945 the Congress set up its Commission on Law and Social Action, to "promote the civil and political equality of all minorities in America," to "safeguard American liberties," and to "promote appropriate positive action within the Jewish community" to achieve these ends. Under the direction of Alexander Pekelis, brilliant and energetic legal scholar,[19] the Commission formulated comprehensive programs against racial and religious discrimination in employment, education, and housing, against racial segregation, and against racist and anti-Semitic propaganda. Its program called for promotion of legislation, bringing test cases before courts and administrative agencies, and social action campaigns to effect changes in public policy. The Commission did not limit its efforts to situations involving Jews; wherever there was a significant problem of religious liberty or discrimination, the Commission, alone or with others, undertook the vindication of liberty and equality. Its stance has consistently been an aggressive one in that it did not limit itself to the defense of threatened persons and groups. It constantly sought to push the government on every level toward taking positive steps to fulfill constitutional guarantees of liberty and equal rights.[20]

A notable feature of the Committee, the Congress, and ADL has been their active support of research in the behavioral sciences. Outstanding contributions have been the studies initiated by the Committee in 1944, which resulted in the five volume *Studies in Prejudice*, published in 1950–51. The Committee has initiated research in the relationship of sectarian teaching to intergroup relations.

The Committee, the Congress, and ADL have worked closely with the NAACP, the American Civil Liberties Union, and other groups in litigation and on legislation. In 1950, four years before the Supreme Court's school desegregation decision, a brief filed by the Jewish organizations contended that racial segregation in public education resulted in inequality and that the "separate but equal" doctrine was a fiction that the court should pierce. These organizations told the court that segregation resulted in social, intellectual, physical, and economic inequality, was discriminatory, and when enforced by law was in violation of the Constitution.[21]

They again acted when *Brown* v. *Board of Education of Topeka, Kansas*[22] reached the Supreme Court; the Jewish groups filed briefs that asked the Court to end the "separate but equal" rule. The Jewish agencies, aggressively committed to the principle of legal equality without distinction as to religion or race, had the courage and commitment to fight for this principle when it was generally considered impolitic, inexpedient, and even somehow "subversive" and "un-American" to avow it.

And the Jewish agencies were consistently in the forefront in public agitation to get state legislatures and municipal authorities to adopt or improve civil rights acts or ordinances, with the result that by the time Congress enacted the Civil Rights Act of 1964, there were already thirty-one states with laws forbidding racial discrimination in public accommodations, and twenty-five states with fair employment practices acts.[23]

V

It was natural that the Jewish settlers should seek companionship and a sense of security by joining fraternal orders; besides, as de Tocqueville had observed in 1835, Americans tended to be a nation of joiners. Thus by 1860 there were already five Jewish fraternal orders.[24] Among them, B'nai B'rith, founded in 1843, grew most rapidly. Its members began to project purposes that transcended mere "togetherness," mutual aid, and insurance; by 1868 B'nai B'rith emphasized a program of philanthropy and political action for the protection of Jewish rights in the United States and abroad. Before the end of the century it had established cooperative relations with the Alliance Israelite Universelle, and it intervened against a treaty with Switzerland that discriminated against American Jews.[25] In important respects B'nai B'rith was a forerunner of the American Jewish Committee and of the American Jewish Congress; indeed, when the Committee was formed in 1906, it was apparent to the founders and to B'nai B'rith that their interests overlapped and that there was room for cooperation between the two organizations.[26] In 1913 B'nai B'rith organized its Anti-Defamation League. The League's charter stated that though "the immediate object of the League is to stop . . . the defamation of the Jewish people," the League's "ultimate purpose is to secure justice and fair treatment to all citizens alike and to put an end forever to unjust discrimination against any sect or body of citizens."

It is apparent that all three organizations went through the same stages of development. They began with a concern for Jews who needed help in other parts of the world. They then added the struggle against anti-Semitism in the United States and a concern with winning civil rights for all Americans without regard to creed or race. They are the least parochial of America's civil rights groups. International and transsectarian concerns are built in. And their records show that they have been faithful in pursuing these concerns. ADL, like the other two organizations, also has had an interest in the sponsorship of social research. Its fact-gathering and reporting interests have resulted in many notable volumes,[27] and currently it is sponsoring, at the University of California, a five-year study of the extent and roots of anti-Semitism in the United States.[28]

A danger signal calls to the scene at once, as if in response to a fire alarm, lay and professional troubleshooters from the different Jewish agencies. The need for cooperation has always been apparent. To meet this need, in 1944 the National Community Relations Advisory Council (NCRAC) came into being by resolution of the General Assembly of the Council of Jewish Federations and Welfare Funds. In addition to the Congress and the League, the Council comprises the Jewish Labor Committee, the Jewish War Veterans, the National Council of Jewish Women, and three leading lay religious groups: The Union of American [Reform] Hebrew Congregations, the Union of Orthodox Jewish Congregations, and the United [Conservative] Synagogue of America. Nearly fifty local Jewish community relations councils are also members of NCRAC. Thus the Council is a widely representative organization. It stands solidly and militantly for a civil rights program that embraces all minorities as its beneficiaries, without regard to religion or race.[29]

VI

In its statement submitted to the Large City Budgeting Conference on November 10, 1965, the American Jewish Congress asked for financial support to reestablish its Commission on Community Interrelations because, "There is no more pressing unmet need on the agenda of American Jewry than the issue of Negro-Jewish relations." The 1965 *American Jewish Year Book*, prepared by the American Jewish Committee, contained a summary of events that pointed to anti-Semitism among Negroes. Following the riots in New York City and Rochester, New York, in the summer of 1964, Dr. Martin Luther King, Jr., issued this statement:

> While the outbursts in New York City and Rochester cannot be considered expressions of antisemitism, I am particularly pained to learn that a large percentage of looted stores were owned by our Jewish friends since, as a group, the Jewish citizens of the United States have always stood for freedom, justice, and an end to bigotry. Our Jewish friends have demonstrated their commitment to the principle of tolerance and brotherhood in tangible ways, often at great personal sacrifices.
>
> Can we ever express our appreciation to the rabbis who chose to give moral witness with us in St. Augustine during our recent protest against segregation in that unhappy city? And who will ever forget the sacrifice of two Jewish lives, Andrew Goodman and Michael Schwerner, in Mississippi this last June?
>
> It would be impossible to record the contribution that Jewish people have made toward the Negro's struggle for freedom—it has been so great.
>
> I solemnly pledge to do my utmost to uphold the fair name of the Jews. Not only because we need their friendship, and surely we do, but mainly because bigotry in any form is an affront to us all.[30]

The fact that Dr. King felt it necessary to make this statement is itself some proof of the emergence of Negro-Jewish tensions as a problem for both groups.

A number of reasons for these tensions readily come to mind.

1. The natural resentment felt by Negroes who know that the tenements they occupy probably had previously been apartment houses occupied by Jews, and that many of the churches in which they worship had previously been synagogues. The wearer of hand-me-downs often resents the previous wearer.

2. The fact that Jews have been prominently identified with civil rights work may itself be a cause of resentment. Beneficiaries have been known to feel hostile towards their benefactors. We know that recipients of American foreign aid do not always have a friendly regard for the United States.

3. Jews are often the landlords of slum tenements and owners of the small shops in the Negro ghettoes. Thus the Jews whom the Negroes know are often men whose methods of doing business would hardly recommend them as noble characters.

4. The white race known to many Negroes is often exemplified to him by the Jewish landlord or storekeeper, and thus the hatred of the white race gets to be personified in hatred of the Jew.

5. The Negro has learned of white anti-Semitism. Included in the Negroes' acculturation is the pervasive anti-Semitism, which he "catches" almost as if it were a contagious disease against which he has not been inoculated.

6. The Negro unconsciously resents the Jew who has made good and by implication this success may be seen as a criticism of the Negro who has failed to follow the mandate: "Go, and do thou likewise." That is, the success of the Jew somehow becomes a condemnation of the Negro's failure to emulate him.

7. The Negro in a large city often works for a Jewish employer. The tensions in these relationships can readily become affected by the stereotype of the Jew, which can easily be conveyed to the Negro.[31]

8. At times the Negro worker finds himself adversely affected by a union whose leadership has been Jewish for many years and rightly or wrongly he will interpret his trouble as something due to racial discrimination, which he will then attribute to Jews.[32]

9. In the attempts to end *de facto* segregation in the schools in Northern cities, Negroes have run into misunderstanding or opposition on the part of Jewish parents, who feared that the quality of the education offered their children might be lowered by busing the Jewish child out of his neighborhood school to a school in a Negro ghetto. There was also a Jewish concern that the busing of school children may adversely affect their attendance at Jewish after-school religious classes and this concern was injected into the dispute over busing and integration.[33] It is easy for a distracted, harassed Negro to blame Jews, rather than to blame parents, for aggravating or adding to his problems.

10. There is, too, the competition for political preferment, in which it is now necessary to make room for the Negro, who may sometimes feel that the Jew who is appointed has taken a place that should have gone to a Negro. This situation is another instance of people being naturally led to think in terms of Jew *v.* Negro and Negro *v.* Jew.

11. The Negro is aware that intermarriage with Jews poses, in addition to the racial barrier, also the religious barrier; and he

perhaps suspects that Jews have deeper reluctance than non-Jews to intimate social relations among their young people.

12. In the civil rights movement of the 1960s the non-Jews who identified themselves strongly and courageously with the civil rights struggle often acted as Christian witnesses to their belief in equality. It is estimated that Jews who joined the demonstrations were far larger in number than their relative proportion in the population—perhaps one-third to one-half of the student volunteers in Mississippi in 1964 were Jews, and they were also well represented among the lawyers and physicians who worked there as volunteers.[34] But, as Charles E. Silberman has put it,

> All too often, however, it seems as though Jews who are involved in the racial struggle have no commitment to Judaism, while those who have the commitment to Judaism are rarely involved in the fight for civil rights. There are notable exceptions, of course. . . . But . . . painfully few of the young men and women who went to Mississippi last summer had any understanding that what they were doing was in the least connected with their Jewishness, or with the teaching of Judaism; many would have thought you insane had you suggested that notion. Equally important, the training they received before they went to Mississippi, was provided by the National Council of Churches. No Jewish organization played any role in that training, or in the summer project.[35]

Thus, Jewish students who participated in the demonstrations, and even those who were injured or murdered, marched under the banner of Dr. King's Southern *Christian* Leadership Conference and were trained by the National Council of Churches. They did not identify themselves as Jews and were not known as such. Their contribution to civil rights came as an expression of Christian or American idealism, not as an expression of American Judaism.

In June 1964 sixteen Reform rabbis answered the call of Dr. King and went to St. Augustine, Florida, where they were arrested when they attempted to desegregate a swimming pool; rabbis were among the thousands who participated in the Mississippi Freedom Summer project in 1964, and one of them, Rabbi Arthur J. Lelyveld, of Cleveland, was beaten by segregationists in Hattiesburg; there were rabbis among the demonstrators in Selma

and Birmingham, Alabama; and there were rabbis among the
210,000 Americans who participated in the March on Washington in 1963.[36] But perhaps it was only the rabbis who were seen
and thought of as Jews; the hundreds or perhaps thousands of
other Jews, students and laymen, were assimilated in the great
mass of Christians, both to the eye of the Negro as well as in their
own minds.

13. The Jews of the South—the owners or managers of department stores, drug stores, variety stores, neighborhood stores,
stores on Main Street, owners of small factories or mills, lawyers,
physicians, teachers, professors—were hardly differentiated from
their neighbors in the cities and towns, their fellow members of
the Chamber of Commerce or Kiwanis or Rotary, in attitude
toward the civil rights movement. They were not willing to
stand out and become martyrs. If they broke ranks, they would
be branded as Communists and traitors; if they continued to
practice segregation, they were Jews, and what can you expect of
Jews? In any case, the Jew could not win. They were not blamed
by Negroes on a basis of equality with the non-Jewish merchants
and professional men. More was expected of them—because they
were Jews.

VII

In addressing the Conference on Jewish Social Studies in May
1964, Horace Mann Bond, distinguished Negro educator of Atlanta University, ended his paper by saying:

> And I have frequently reflected, also, that much of the
> sharpest feeling among Negroes about Jews arises from a
> feeling that this man has especially let you down; he, of all
> men, ought to know what it was like; and how it had been;
> but . . . he turns out to be as bad, or even worse, than those
> other white devils.[37]

Perhaps the Negro feels especially hurt when he thinks of the
Jew, because he can say in the words of Zechariah: "I was
wounded in the house of my friends." The Negro expected to be
able to say of the Jews, "Every one with one of his hands
wrought in the work, and with the other hand held a weapon."[38]

The record of American Jews in the struggle for civil rights is
far better than that of any other minority group or denomina-

tion. Still, it is not enough. I do not mean to say that the Negroes are justified in feeling antagonistic toward Jews. In judgment, one should proceed on the principle of judging others leniently and oneself harshly. But the identity of interests between them is bound to predominate over the causes of tensions. More than any other group, the Jews are committed to liberalism and to the struggle against bigotry and racism. Affluence among Jews has not affected their voting pattern—the Jews voted for Kennedy more heavily than did the Irish Catholics.[39] They will continue to support liberal candidates, liberal legislation, liberal causes, their own and other civil rights and civil liberties agencies; for their only chance of survival, as Jews, is in a free, pluralistic society where men, despite their differences, are free and equal.

The same conditions that compel the American Jew to be in the forefront of liberal causes and the struggle for civil rights also compel the American Negro to identify with these struggles. Both the Jew and the Negro must stand together and fight against common enemies. For racism is evil no matter who happens to be selected as the victim. Among Jews and Negroes there is no room for the extremist, for the bigot, for the man who is moved by hatred rather than by a sense of justice and humanity.

It may well be that Negroes generally are aware of the identity of interests which they share with the Jewish community. The five-year study conducted by the University of California Survey Research Center, with the ADL grant,[40] has concluded that the claim of Negro anti-Semitism has been greatly exaggerated. One of the most significant aspects of this study is that it underscores the importance of the scientific method to get the facts in intergroup relations to achieve an understanding of underlying causes of tension. This, as we have seen, has always been one of the objectives of the Jewish civil rights agencies, and is certainly one of their most important and lasting contributions.

NOTES

1. Quoted by William H. Gilman in his Foreword to *Selected Writings of Ralph Waldo Emerson*, Signet Classic (1965), p. xxiv.
2. Joseph L. Blau and Salo W. Baron, eds., *The Jews of the United States 1790–1840, A Documentary History* (1963), Vol. I, p. 5. See also John

Higham, "Social Discrimination Against Jews in America, 1830–1930," *Publics. of American Jewish Hist. Soc.*, Vol. 47, No. 1 (1957), p. 7.

3. Higham, *op. cit.*, pp. 9–13.

4. See D. Baltzell, *The Protestant Establishment* (1965); *Rights*, published by the Anti-Defamation League (ADL), June 1964 and August 1965; Nathan Glazer and Daniel P. Moynihan, *Beyond the Melting Pot* (1963), pp. 147–148, summarizes recent surveys and studies.

5. *Bigotry in Action*, American Jewish Committee (1961), and the annual reports of ADL.

6. Foreword to Benj. R. Epstein and Arnold Forster, *Some of My Best Friends . . .* (1962), an ADL report.

7. Oscar Handlin, *Fire-Bell in the Night* (1964), pp. 48, 50.

8. *Ibid.*, pp. 73–74.

9. *Jewish Social Studies*, January 1965, is devoted to the papers and proceedings of a Conference on Negro-Jewish relations in the United States, by the Conference on Jewish Social Studies. *Conservative Judaism*, published by the Rabbinical Assembly, features a symposium on Jewish-Negro relations in the issue of Summer 1965. *Judaism*, published by the American Jewish Congress, has an article on the subject in the Winter 1965 issue. *Commentary*, published by the American Jewish Committee, has published many articles on the subject, most notably Nathan Glazer, "Negroes and Jews: The New Challenge to Pluralism," in December 1964. See also Shad Polier, "The Jew and the Racial Crisis," *Congress By-Weekly*, September 14, 1964; C. Bezalel Sherman, "In the American Jewish Community," *Jewish Frontier*, July 1964; M. S. Shapiro, "The Negro Revolution—and Jews," *Council Woman*, May 1964; E. Muravchik, "Troubled Allies," *Jewish Life*, March–April 1963; J. L. Teller, "Negro and Jew," *Jewish Frontier*, September 1963; Roy Wilkins, "Jewish-Negro Relations: An Evaluation," *American Judaism*, Spring 1963; James Baldwin, "Negroes Are Anti-Semitic Because They're Anti-White," *New York Times Magazine*, April 1967; Robert Gordis, "Negroes are Anti-Semitic Because They Want a Scapegoat," *New York Times Magazine*, April 1967; Henry Lee Moon, "Of Negroes, Jews and Other Americans," *The Crisis*, NAACP, April 1967; "Symposium on Negro-Jewish Relations in America," *Midstream*, December 1966; B. Z. and May L. Sobel, "Negroes and Jews: Minority Groups in Conflict," *Judaism*, Winter 1966.

10. Alfred Jolpe, "Jewish College Students in the United States," *American Jewish Year Book 1964*, Vol. 65, p. 133. Twenty-seven percent of eligible non-Jews attend college.

11. Jacob R. Marcus, "Background for the History of American Jewry," in Oscar I. Janowsky, ed., *The American Jew: A Reappraisal* (1964), pp. 17–18.

12. *The Pursuit of Equality: A Half Century with the American Jewish Committee* (1957), p. 17. See *Louis Marshall, Champion of Liberty*, Charles Rezinikoff, ed., 2 vols. (1957).

13. Rufus Learsi, *The Jews in America: a History* (1954), p. 201.

14. *The Pursuit of Equality, op. cit.*, pp. 19–20.

15. *Ibid.*, p. 26.
16. *Ibid.*, p. 87.
17. Stephen S. Wise, *Challenging Years* (1949), p. 206.
18. Lewin died in 1947. He wrote *A Dynamic Theory of Personality* (1935), *Resolving Social Conflicts* (1947), and other works.
19. Pekelis died in 1946. See Alexander H. Pekelis, *Law and Social Action*, Milton R. Konvitz, ed. (1950).
20. See mimeographed annual reports of the Congress and of the Commission on Law and Social Action.
21. Brief in *Sweatt v. Painter*, 339 U. S. 629 (1950). See also briefs of the Jewish organizations in *Henderson v. U. S.*, 339 U. S. 816 (1950).
22. *Brown v. Board of Education*, 347 U. S. 483 (1954).
23. See Konvitz and Leskes, *A Century of Civil Rights* (1961), and Konvitz, *Expanding Liberty: Freedom's Gains in Postwar America* (1966).
24. Learsi, *op. cit.*, p. 75.
25. *Ibid.*, pp. 84–85, 89, 132.
26. *Ibid.*, p. 213.
27. For example, Arnold Forster, *A Measure of Freedom* (1950); Ruth G. Weintraub, *How Secure These Rights?* (1949); Benj. R. Epstein and Arnold Forster, *Some of My Best Friends* . . . (1962).
28. *The Chairman's Report*, 1961, by Henry Edw. Schultz, 'pp. 9–10. See: Charles Y. Gloch and Rodney Stark, *Christian Beliefs and Anti-Semitism* (New York: Harper and Row, 1966); and, Charles Y. Glick, Gertrude Selznick, Joe L. Spaeth, *The Apathetic Majority* (New York: Harper and Row, 1966).
29. NCRAC, Plenary Session Report, 1965; NCRAC, *Joint Program Plan for Jewish Community Relations 1965–66;* Bernard H. Trager, *Jewish Community Relations and the NCRAC 1944–1957*, pamphlet of NCRAC, 1957.
30. *American Jewish Year Book 1965*, Vol. 66, Morris Fine and Milton Himmelfarb, eds., p. 188, quoted from the *Southern Israelite* of Atlanta, Ga.
31. See Glazer and Moynihan, *Beyond the Melting Pot*, pp. 72–73.
32. See Herbert Hill, "The Racial Practices of Organized Labor in the Age of Gompers and After," *New Politics*, Vol. IV, No. 2 (1965); see also Glazer and Moynihan, *op. cit.*, p. 178.
33. See *American Jewish Year Book 1965*, p. 180.
34. *American Jewish Year Book 1965*, p. 175.
35. Chas. E. Silberman, "A Jewish View of the Racial Crisis," *Conservative Judaism* (Summer 1965), p. 6.
36. *American Jewish Year Book 1965*, pp. 175–178; *American Jewish Year Book 1964*, p. 18.
37. Horace Mann Bond, "Negro Attitudes Toward Jews," *Jewish Social Studies*, Vol. 27, No. 3 (January 1965), p. 9.
38. Zechariah 13:6; Nehemiah 4:17.
39. Glazer and Moynihan, *op. cit.*, p. 168.
40. *New York Times*, May 26, 1967.

Jews
and
Other
Americans

JEWS AND "THE PROTESTANT ESTABLISHMENT"

E. DIGBY BALTZELL

SEVERAL YEARS AGO an Englishman, visiting America for the first time, remarked to an editor of *Harper's* magazine that nobody had prepared him for his quick discovery that this was not an Anglo-Saxon nation.[1] Although he had long been aware of our multinational, racial and religious origins in the abstract, he simply had not visualized the heterogeneity of our population in general, nor the heterogeneity of the persons of talent and ability in leadership positions. Hollywood, of course, portrays America to people all over the world. Yet the personalities of our screen stars, well-publicized representatives of the American rags-to-riches dream, had done little to dissuade him of our over-all Protestant and Anglo-Saxon ancestry. A brief look at the original names of some of our more famous, pseudo-Anglo-Saxon, Hollywood heroes was indeed a revelation. A sample of the Warner Brothers stable of stars, for instance, included Doris Kapplehoff, Larry Skikne, Bernie Schwartz, Mladen Sekulovich, Marie Tomlinson Krebs, Frances Gumm, and Arthur Gelien; among the famous at 20th Century-Fox were Max Showalter, Virginia Mc-Math, Mitzie Gerber, Balla Wegier, Claudette Chauchoin and Ethel Zimmerman; at MGM were Vito Farinola, Joseph Meibes, Tula Finklea and Spengler Arlington Brough; stars at Columbia included Dianne Laruska, Judy Tuvim, Gwyllyn Ford, Margarita Carmen Cansino, Aldo Da Re and Vincent Zoino; while Zalma Hedrick, Donna Mullenger, Sarah Fulks, Ella Geisman, Issur Danielovitch, Daniel Kaminsky, Dino Crocetti and Joseph Levitch were among the leaders at Paramount.* Just as the original names of these famous stars suggest the ethnic diversity of talent in modern America, so their assumed names attest to the Anglo-Saxon ideal which still persists in our culture. For, in spite of the fact that some forty million immigrants of diverse religious and ethnic origins came to America in the course of the nineteenth and early twentieth centuries, we were a predominantly Anglo-Saxon—Protestant people for almost the first two-thirds of our history. Thus our earliest cultural traditions—in language and literature as well as in our legal, political and religious institutions—were modeled on those of seventeenth- and eighteenth-century England. And, above all, our upper class has always been overwhelmingly Anglo-Saxon and Protestant in both origins and values. The "Sixty Families" or the "Four Hundred," the "Rich and the Well-Born," the "Harvard Man," the "Senator," the "Diplomat," the "Socialite," and the "Man of Distinction in the Executive Suite" are all continuing symbols of this Anglo-American ideal which the Hollywood stars, regardless of their own ethnic origins, have tended to perpetuate. The uncomfortable paradox of American society in the twentieth century is that it has tried to combine the democratic ideal of equality of opportunity in an ethnically diverse society with the persistent and conservative traditions of an Anglo-Saxon caste ideal at the top.

THE IMMIGRANTS' PROGRESS

. . . the WASP upper class remained more or less in control of the American elite throughout the first three decades of this century. This was perhaps inevitable, and, as it served to maintain a continuity of tradition at the level of leadership, it was a healthy thing for society as a whole. In the meantime, however, new ethnic families were gradually establishing themselves on the

---

* The assumed names of the stars, in the order listed above, were as follows: *Warner Brothers:* Doris Day, Lawrence Harvey, Tony Curtis, Karl Malden, Marjorie Main, Judy Garland and Tab Hunter; *20th Century-Fox:* Casey Adams, Ginger Rogers, Mitzi Gaynor, Bella Darvi, Claudette Colbert and Ethel Merman; *MGM:* Vic Damone, John Ericson, Cyd Charisse and Robert Taylor; *Columbia:* Dianne Foster, Judy Holliday, Glenn Ford, Rita Hayworth, Aldo Ray and Vince Edwards; *Paramount:* Kathryn Grayson, Donna Reed, Jane Wyman, June Allyson, Kirk Douglas, Danny Kaye, Dean Martin and Jerry Lewis.

ladder of economic, political and social mobility. By and large this was a three-generational process. The members of the first generation, long used to a subservient and fixed status in the Old Country, clung to their traditional ways, deferred to their "betters," and gradually built up rich ethnic islands in the poorer neighborhoods of our large metropolitan areas. They protected themselves from the strange and often hostile ways of the native Americans by settling along the "Irish Riviera" in South Boston, the "Chinatowns," "Little Italies," or "Ghettos" in New York's Lower East Side and many another booming industrial and commercial city; their language, their patriarchal and familistic mores, and especially their religion, remained that of their . . . ancestors. Economically, they were predominantly unskilled laborers, domestic servants or small entrepreneurs serving the other members of their own communities.

These ethnic islands were, of course, located in the heart of some of the worst slums in the nation, if not in the world. In the Twentieth Congressional District of New York, which sent La Guardia to Congress, some 250,000 people of twenty-seven nationalities, each in its own enclave, were crowded into one square mile. While a vast majority of the foreign-born lived out their lives as best they could, many of their children became delinquents and some of the parents sought an explanation for their suffering in such ideologies as socialism and communism. Thus the Communist Party, although always a minority party with never more than one hundred thousand members throughout the nation, drew a major proportion of its members from foreign-language-speaking groups from the time of its founding in 1919, through the twenties, and into the early thirties. The party had an especial appeal to Finns, to Eastern Europeans who were not devout Catholics, and to Yiddish-speaking Jews.

But leveling ideologies of the socialist variety have never had a wide appeal to the vast majority of ambitious Americans. As the traditional ways to wealth and respectability in business or the professions were more or less monopolized by Protestant Americans of older stock, many of the more talented and ambitious members of minority groups found careers in urban politics, in organized crime, or, for those of the Catholic faith, in the hierarchy of the Church. Of the two largest minority groups, the Irish and the Italian, the former tended to dominate both the Church and the urban political machines which, except in the

City of Philadelphia, were largely responsible for keeping the Democratic Party alive during the years of Republican rule between the Civil War and the New Deal. This dominance of the Church and politics by the Irish may have been one of the factors that led the more overambitious members of the Italian community (the vast majority of whom were solid and law-abiding citizens) into the ranks of organized crime.

The Jewish immigrants and their descendants, a smaller minority than either the Irish or the Italian, followed somewhat different ways to wealth. . . .

While the second and third generations of hyphenated-Americans supplied outstanding leaders in urban politics, the Church and in organized crime, there were at the same time many men who came to the fore in the fields of business, entertainment, and in the arts and sciences. Yet even though they supplied an invigorating talent to the leadership of the nation as a whole, hyphenated-Americans, regardless of occupation or accomplishment, remained more or less isolated from the Protestant establishment. They were too often stereotyped as members of a class of non-Anglo-Saxon immigrants who filled the urban slums of the nation.

But the position of the newer immigrants as a whole was gradually improving. Before the First World War, for example, the center of gravity of the newer immigrants was in the first generation ethnic islands. Between the two wars, however, their sons and grandsons gradually improved their economic positions. As further immigration was cut off in the twenties, by the end of the thirties the center of gravity moved to the second generation. Although the majority were still members of the laboring classes, many had moved up a notch (this was reflected by the increase during the twenties of advertisements for white-collar jobs stating that "no Catholics or Jews need apply"). As this second generation now knew the language, had been educated in the public schools, and had assimilated American values of democracy, self-respect and equal opportunity, they were ready to move into the main stream of American life. And they found support in the Democratic Party, which, in the 1930's, moved out from local machine politics and onto the national stage under the leadership of Franklin D. Roosevelt.

While the New Deal served to bridge the gap between the immigrants and their children and the main stream of American life and leadership, the Second War and the postwar boom hastened the process. By the middle of the 1950's, the descendants of immigrants to the urban slums were increasingly affluent, college educated and members of the great middle class. The center of gravity was now in the third generation.

THE THIRD GENERATION
AND THE TRIPLE MELTING POT

Just what kind of Americans are these members of the third generation? In their attempt to answer this question, social scientists have developed the theory of the "triple melting pot."[2] According to this theory, ethnic and nationality groups are being Americanized, in the third and fourth generation, within three main religious communities—Catholic, Protestant and Jewish. Religious pluralism is replacing the ethnic pluralism of the earlier era. The process is somewhat as follows: prosperity in the expanding postwar economy has allowed large numbers to move out of their traditional ethnic neighborhoods and occupations. This has meant suburban residence, attendance at suburban schools along with older-stock neighbors, and the consequent need for new means of self-identification (especially for children). And this has produced a rapid increase in church and synagogue affiliation. Thus the Jewishness (ethnic) of the urban ghettos, and even in the areas of second settlement like the Bronx or along the upper West Side, is now being translated into the new Judaism of the synagogue-centered suburbia (Nathan Glazer estimates that whereas 75 per cent of the children in the Bronx during the thirties were receiving *no* Jewish training, in the suburbs of the fifties, almost 75 per cent report attendance at Sunday Schools).[3] And similarly, the one suburban Catholic church has replaced the Irish, Polish and Italian churches and institutions which characterized the downtown neighborhoods. In short, the Italian, Polish, Russian or Irish American of the urban, first- and second-generation minorities, has now given way to the Protestant-, Catholic- and Jewish-American sense of self-identity in our postwar suburban era. While the American electorate, for instance, would not elect an obviously Irish American to the White House in 1928, they were apparently less prejudiced about the dangers of a Catholic American being sent there in 1960.

THE JEWISH MELTING POT AND
THE CLASS STRUCTURE

Within each of the three religious communities which make up the triple melting pot there are, of course, several class levels. And mobility within these class systems is one of the major instruments of assimilation. Just as the middle-class Baptist or Methodist is likely to join a suburban Presbyterian church in the course of his rise to a position of elite affluence, and then move on to an Episcopal church in order to assimilate into the upper class, so the Orthodox East European Jew rises out of the ghetto and joins a Conservative synagogue uptown or out in a largely Jewish suburb, and perhaps eventually finds a Reform congregation even more congenial to his tastes as he moves into a predominately German-Jewish upper-class community. In one of the classic novels of Jewish life in America at the turn of the century, Abraham Cahan's *Rise of David Levinsky*, for instance, the hero, just twenty-five years after his arrival in this country, reflects on his participation in this process as follows:

> I was born and reared in the lowest depths of poverty and I arrived in America—in 1885—with four cents in my pocket. I am now worth more than two million dollars and recognized as one of the two or three leading men in the cloak-and-suit trade in the United States. . . .
> Most of the people at my hotel are German-American Jews. I know other Jews of this class. I contribute to their charity institutions. Though an atheist, I belong to one of their synagogues. . . . I am a member of that synagogue chiefly because it is a fashionable synagogue. I often convict myself of currying favor with the German Jews. But then German-American Jews curry favor with Portuguese-American Jews, just as we all curry favor with Gentiles and as American Gentiles curry favor with the aristocracy of Europe.[4]

There are, of course, highly complex class systems within every Catholic community in America, marked by Polish, Italian and Irish parishes, neighborhoods and associations, and led by the Church hierarchy and perhaps a few first families like the Fitzgeralds, Kennedys and Curleys of Boston. Here, however, we will concentrate on the nature of the rather highly organized and rigid class system which developed within the Jewish community after the Civil War. The Jewish class system, in fact, has gone through three historical periods, depending on the size and composition of the Jewish community itself, and on the reactions of the gentile community.[5]

The first Jews in America arrived at New Amsterdam from the Dutch West Indies, in 1654, and a slow flow continued throughout the Colonial period. By the time of our first census, in 1790, some two thousand Jews were spread throughout the colonies. They were mostly merchants who had come from the West Indies and England and consequently were not marked off as a visible community. There were no rabbis in America during this period when, in fact, only five per cent of the population as a whole (in contrast to some 70 per cent today) were church-affiliated. Even where there was a sense of community, as in the Sephardic congregations in Newport or Philadelphia, the small number of Jewish merchants spent most of their time with non-Jews, which fostered intermarriage and assimilation (there was a shortage of Jewish females at this time). This was especially true at the highest levels of society, where Jews were part of the merchant establishment. This, then, was the classic period of aristocratic assimilation, and even today there are leading families within the old-stock and Protestant upper class, some of whose ancestors were prominent Jews during the Colonial period. This process of assimilation continued into the early part of the nineteenth century, when immigration was at a low point because of war and depression in this country and because of the Napoleonic conflicts in Europe.

But immigration picked up after 1820. And an increasing number of Jews came to America during the 1840's and 1850's, along with other immigrants from Germany. Although many of them were considered German rather than Jewish and therefore were assimilated immediately, the American-Jewish community had grown to some 150,000 persons by the time of the Civil War. In contrast to the merchants from the West Indies and England who predominated in the Colonial period, most of the new immigrants from Germany were peddlers seeking opportunities to rise in the world. Fortunately, these pre-Civil War decades were marked by the opening of the West and the rapid growth of small-town America. Thus many Jews became pioneers, first-family founders, and leading citizens in small towns all over the nation, often within one generation of their landing. The integration of the Jews in San Francisco in the years immediately following the discovery of gold in 1849 was more or less characteristic of many other American cities in this second, and predominately German, period of immigration.

Perhaps the most important demographic factors affecting the position of the Jews during this second period was their relatively small number and wide dispersion throughout the land. As of 1880, there were Jewish communities in all states, in 173 towns and cities, with no concentration in any particular part of the country (Jews made up about 3 per cent of the population of New York City in 1880, as against 30 per cent in 1920 and almost 40 per cent today).

These numerous German-Jewish communities centered around the synagogue and the family. Though members were of all classes, they were for the most part middle-class entrepreneurs. Those who became prominent in civic and business affairs formed an elite; they were not barred from belonging to prominent clubs and associations, and many were accepted socially by the best gentile society, some assimilating through marriage. This was especially true before the Civil War, when, for instance, the president of the most prominent men's club in Philadelphia was a member of a Jewish family and head of his synagogue. At the same time, Moses Lazarus—father of Emma, whose poem adorns the Statue of Liberty—was one of the founders of New York's patrician Knickerbocker Club, while Joseph Seligman was a founder of the Union League during the Civil War. Even as late as the 1870's, when young Louis D. Brandeis was welcomed into the best Boston society, Jews still belonged to the best clubs in many cities, and a leading society journal could feature the news of a fashionable "Hebrew Wedding" in New York's Orthodox Thirty-fourth Street Synagogue.[6]

Perhaps the most important feature of this second historical period was the development of an affluent and highly aristocratic German-Jewish upper class.[7] Although the more famous family dynasties such as the Lehmans, Warburgs, Schiffs, Strauses, Loebs, Morgenthaus, Ochses, Sulzbergers, Seligmans and Guggenheims eventually settled in New York, they formed a national upper class composed of small local aristocracies in the larger cities, linked together by intercity marriage alliances. Strict class and religious endogamy was characteristic of this class which was based largely on famous founders who came to America during the forties and fifties and made their fortunes in banking, merchandising and mining. The eminent banking house of Kuhn, Loeb & Company, founded in the middle of the century by Abraham Kuhn and Solomon Loeb, typified the dynastic proclivities of this aristocracy. The senior partner during the freebooting Morgan era, Jacob Schiff, came to America from Frankfurt am Main after the Civil War and married one of Solomon Loeb's daughters; Paul M. Warburg, of a Hamburg banking family, married another daughter; and his brother, Felix Warburg, married Jacob Schiff's daughter. These banking families were also intermarried with the Strauses, who along with the Gimbels and Rosenwalds were among the great mercantile families in the nation. But perhaps the Guggenheims were the most interesting family of them all.

The Family Founder was Meyer Guggenheim, who came to Philadelphia from his native Switzerland in 1847.[8] He began by peddling shoe polish on the streets of the city, then branching out into the lace business, and finally laying the cornerstone of his fortune in mining and smelting. As no dynasty is based on money alone, it was fortunate that his wife bore him eleven children, including eight sons. This second generation, well disciplined by their father's weekly family councils on Friday nights to outline family affairs and instill traditions, carried on the dynasty by enlarging the family businesses to include tin mines in Bolivia, gold mines in Alaska, diamond fields in Africa, copper mines and nitrate fields in Chile and rubber plantations in the Congo. They also married into prominent families within their class and faith, and produced twenty-four children. There was only one divorce, which was forced on the youngest son because he had married someone the family considered unsuitable.

The second Guggenheim generation came to maturity just as the second historical period of the Jewish adjustment to the American environment came to a close. This adjustment, to summarize, included a largely Americanized series of German-Jewish communities, dispersed throughout the nation and headed at the elite level by an intercity aristocratic establishment. As anti-Semitism was only sporadic and idiosyncratic, many individuals still participated at the top levels of gentile society, some being assimilated completely through marriage or conversion and others through membership in exclusive clubs and associations. But all this was changed by the flood tide of immigrants from Eastern Europe who came to America after 1880, when a third period of adjustment began.

This new immigration . . . changed the whole character of American society. It also had a profound influence on the nature of the Jewish community. Just as the Catholic peasant from Italy, Sicily, Poland and Czechoslovakia brought quite different customs, values and traditions to the New World than the earlier, Protestant immigrants from Northern Europe, so the Jews from Russia and Poland were also very different from the Sephardic and German Jews who were already established here as of 1880. It is no wonder that the majority of established citizens, both gentile and Jew, were frankly appalled at this tidal wave of new immigrants, possessed as they were of such alien ways. "One can understand," wrote Nathan Glazer, "the feelings of dismay of the earlier German Jewish immigrants as the Russian Jewish immigration, which had spurted upwards at the beginning of the 1880's, showed no signs of abating, and indeed grew larger. It is as if a man who has built himself a pleasant house and is leading a comfortable existence suddenly finds a horde of impecunious relatives descending upon him."[9]

This horde of impecunious relatives swelled the American-Jewish community to over four million persons by the end of the 1920's, almost 80 per cent of whom were, by this time, of East European origin. But far more than the increased size of the community was involved. First, there was the concentration of East European Jews in our large cities, especially along the Eastern Seaboard. Thus by 1916, a majority of American Jewry were living in the five cities of New York, Philadelphia, Boston, Chicago and Baltimore (while there were 250,000 Jews in all America in 1880, by 1916, 350,000 were living in New York's Lower East Side alone). Moreover, while the majority of German Jews had been middle class and self-employed, the newer immigrants were largely wage workers concentrated in one industry, garment manufacture. This increase in the size and concentrated location of the newer immigrants, as well as their lower-class occupational pattern, was bound to create unfavorable stereotypes and stimulate anti-Semitism.

And these stereotypes which intensified anti-Semitism now applied to the whole Jewish community. Thus the term "kike," first coined by German Jews as a derogatory stereotype applying to the new Russian immigrants, was now used by gentiles when referring to Jews in general, the cultivated and Americanized German as well as the impoverished and alien garment workers on the Lower East Side. This was, of course, a terrible shock to the established Jews, especially the cultivated elite, some of whom became anti-Semitic themselves. For "the outraged 'German' Jew saw, shuffling down the gangplank, himself or his father, stripped of the accessories of respectability," writes Oscar Handlin, a leading contemporary historian of immigration. "This was what he had escaped from, been Americanized away from; he did not like its catching up with him. . . . It was distasteful to incur the ill-feeling of one's fellow citizens on account of these unattractive new Jews; and this unattractiveness, it was frequently pointed out, was 'not so much a matter of religion, but of race and of habits.' "[10]

This new situation might well have precipitated a caste division within the American-Jewish community. For, after all, the differences in "race and habits" as between the newer "Russian" and the older "German" Jews was far greater than the cultural gulf dividing the Americanized German Jews from their gentile neighbors. And indeed there were tendencies toward caste, but the forces of aristocratic assimilation finally won out, and mainly for two reasons. First, increased anti-Semitism among gentiles created new and rigid caste barriers which now excluded all Jews, as well as convinced Christians of Jewish origins, from communal or associational participation in the larger gentile society, especially at the elite level. At the same time, and partly in reaction to new caste barriers raised by the gentiles, a majority of the most influential Jewish leaders within the established upper class, acting on their own ancient traditions of *noblesse oblige*, took the lead in insisting on the rights of Jews to seek refuge in this country, then assisted them in adjusting to their new life here, and eventually assimilated them into all levels of the American-Jewish community. Oscar Handlin describes the values of the leaders of the German-Jewish community at the turn of the century in the following paragraph:

> Of this historic obligation of the rich toward the poor Jews such a man as Jacob Schiff was eminently conscious. Raised in the Frankfurt ghetto and later familiar to the banking circles of Europe, he was a maker of railroad and industrial empires. Riches and power were for him not ends in them-

selves, but means to assist the Jews in performance of a universal mission. He saw himself, the *nogid*, or man of wealth, as a *shtadlan*, or intermediary, between Jews and the rest of the world; and what bound him to Jews everywhere was the conviction "that as Jews we have something precious of high value to mankind in our keeping, that our mission in the world continues, and with it our responsibilities of one for the other." In those words he expressed the sentiments of the successful and powerful men of his generation.[11]

This process of aristocratic assimilation within the Jewish community went through several stages. In the first place, as the nineteenth century came to a close, almost all the charitable resources of the established community went toward aiding the new immigrants from Eastern Europe. And each year the amounts raised and the number of contributors increased. In Philadelphia, for example, the United Hebrew Charities, which raised some $15,000 from about seven hundred contributors in 1870, increased its efforts to raise over $50,000 from more than eight thousand contributors by 1894. These charitable efforts within the established German-Jewish community continued and expanded throughout the early decades of the present century. At the same time, so-called Russian organizations played a larger and larger role in charitable giving, until the two groups, German and Russian, eventually merged. Again taking Philadelphia as an example of a nationwide trend, it was right after the First War that the Federation of Jewish Charities carried on its first combined campaign (over fifty German and Russian agencies cooperated), which set a pattern that has continued down to the present.

The changing patterns of charitable giving, even more so among Jews than among gentiles, are often excellent indexes of change within the elite and the upper-class structures. Thus, while the German-Jewish elite were bearing the main charitable burden at the turn of the century, they were also setting up various caste defenses against the ugliness of the urban melting pot. In much the same way as their gentile peers, they were forming their own exclusive clubs and neighborhoods as well as a series of exclusive summer colonies along the Jersey shore. They also built, in the manner of the Episcopalian gentry, new Reform synagogues, uptown, out in the suburbs and down at the shore. What was happening, in other words, was that both the old-stock gentile and Jewish upper classes, once organized along familistic and communal lines, were now becoming more formal and associational. This was because of the swelling of their ranks as a result of the great expansion of wealth at the turn of the century and the consequent need for formalized institutional ways of assimilating new men and families into the ranks of their respective upper classes. At the same time these exclusive institutions served to protect both upper classes from the rest of the population.

But just as the elite Russian Jews were assimilated into the new and combined charitable organizations after the First World War, so the German upper class gradually let down its caste barriers and admitted leading members of the newer immigrant groups into its ranks. In Philadelphia, the leading Jewish country club as well as the most exclusive men's club in the center of the city were both founded and dominated by old-stock German-Jewish families well into the 1930's. By the end of the Second World War, however, these clubs had absorbed leading members of the new Russian-Jewish elite. And today, although there still remains a certain sense of caste superiority among the elder generation of old-stock Jewish families, the members of the younger generation are tending to blend on the basis of common affinity of culture, manners and wealth, rather than on ethnic origins alone.

At this point, I think, it is appropriate to stress the fact that the strength of the American-Jewish community—its low crime, delinquency and divorce rates, for example, as well as its members' extraordinary accomplishments—is at least partly due to its well-articulated class system which, at the same time, has always been combined with both the aristocratic and opportunitarian ideals of assimilation and mobility.

THE ELITE AND THE MARGINAL MAN

Winston Churchill once said that in any hierarchical situation there is all the difference in the world between the number one man and number two, three, four and the rest. Thus, while most Americans, like David Levinsky, are living and moving up the class hierarchy within each of our larger religious communities, there exists today an important qualitative difference in the nature of social relationships at the very top levels of society. In other words, while there are upper-, middle- and lower-class levels *within the Protestant, Catholic and Jewish communities,* there are Protestants, Catholics and Jews *within the elite.* To put it another way, class tends to replace religion (and even ethnicity and race) as the independent variable in social relationships at the highest levels of our society (see Diagram I).

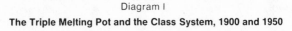

Diagram I

The Triple Melting Pot and the Class System, 1900 and 1950

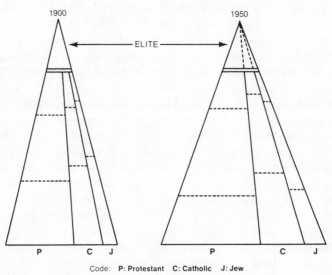

Code: P: Protestant   C: Catholic   J: Jew

And this difference as between the elite and the rest of society is more pronounced in the third, as against the first and second generations. Whereas, for instance, Mayor John Francis Fitzgerald was an "FIF" (First Irish Family) within the Boston Catholic community, his son-in-law became a member of the national elite, both as a multimillionaire businessman and Ambassador to the Court of St. James. While the second generation was still emotionally rooted in a *marginal culture,* the third generation had produced a *marginal man.* This same marginality, as has been shown above, characterized the lives of Baruch, La Guardia and Weinberg, because of their elite positions. While Weinberg, for instance, was very naturally led into such intimate relationships as cruising in Maine with Charles Dickey because of their common elite positions at Goldman-Sachs and J. P. Morgan respectively, the majority of Jewish employees at Goldman-Sachs, even at quite high levels, led their private lives entirely within Jewish communities (and probably had not even met their gentile counterparts at the Morgan firm). And similarly, part of the tragedy of La Guardia's life was that, though he had led a rich and convivial social life among his artistic and professional friends of Italian and Jewish extraction while he was a rising young lawyer in Greenwich Village, when he went to Washington, and later when he became Mayor of New York, he was forced by his functional position of leadership either to lead a social life within the elite or to have no social life at all.

The functional necessity that elite members associate with each other regardless of background or religion (or race, as the complications in the lives of such eminent Americans as Ralph Bunche or Marian Anderson attest to), is paralleled in many other areas of life. In residential patterns, for instance, the lower-class Jew will live within an entirely Jewish neighborhood, the middle-class Jew in a predominately, but not wholly, Jewish suburb, while the elite Jew will more likely be found in an almost predominately gentile neighborhood. In New York City, while elite Jews have lived on the gentile East Side of Central Park for some years now, most of the leaders within the Jewish community will be found on the West Side of the Park. And in the fashionable suburbs, especially in the postwar exurbs, gentiles and Jews live as neighbors within elite class enclaves rather than in religious neighborhoods. One would imagine, for instance, that Jacob Schiff's grandson John Mortimer Schiff, who is married to George F. Baker's granddaughter and lives in the fashionable neighborhood of Oyster Bay, on Long Island, would have most of his primary social relationships with his gentile neighbors and in-laws. Recalling Baruch's experiences with his daughters in an earlier era, one wonders how the patronesses of fashionable dancing classes would handle the Schiff children.

The marginal elite member also has to face the problem of club membership. John Mortimer Schiff, as befitting his residence in Oyster Bay, is a member of the best gentile sporting and golfing clubs out on the Island. In town, however, where he is a senior partner, like his father and grandfather before him, in Kuhn, Loeb & Company and a civic leader of some distinction, he does not belong to any of the more patrician men's clubs—even those which his brother-in-law and Oyster Bay neighbor George F. Baker, Jr., lists in his *Who's Who* biography.

This elite pattern also extends to the socialization of children at school and at college. While public schools are largely neighborhood schools, and thus often ethnically homogeneous, the best private schools cater to a class clientele from all parts of the city and its suburbs, and increasingly tend to include a small nucleus of children from elite Jewish families. The boarding school is, of course, even a more powerful class-assimilating atmosphere for the minority of Jewish youths who go there from wealthy and prominent families. Similarly, the sons of the elite will be living in a far more class-bound atmosphere at Harvard than at the College of the City of New York.

Finally, of course, the class-limited way of life at the top is naturally reflected in the frequency of intermarriages and religious conversions. Thus Baruch, La Guardia and Schiff all married gentiles, as did one of Sidney Weinberg's sons. This pattern was nicely illustrated in the case of the Guggenheims, in the third generation. For while the second generation married into prominent families within their faith and closely knit class, their children not only married gentiles but also established something of a record as far as the frequency of their divorces and remarriages was concerned. This marginal family situation is further complicated by the problem of religious affiliation. Of the members of the Guggenheim family listed in the latest edition of *Who's Who*, none list any religious affiliation, except one, who, in the style of the establishment, lists affiliation in the Episcopal Church (and the Republican Party). Though most elite Jews do not go so far as religious conversion and prefer to live a secular social life outside synagogue or church, one has the definite impression that those who do become Christians prefer the Episcopalian communion, as well as the manners of the communicants, to other Protestant denominations. It is interesting that in Philadelphia, where Quakers tend to be among the city's elite, one often meets Friends of Jewish origins, especially at the more or less one-class suburban meeting houses (while the powerful man of affairs usually converts to the Episcopal ritual, the intellectual convert today—both gentile and Jew—prefers the studied absence of ritual in the Quaker or Unitarian services).

The theory of the triple melting pot, then, must be modified at the elite level in order to take into account the overwhelming factor of class. While in the third generation and at most class levels there is a return to ethnic and religious roots, centered in the suburban synagogue and church, there is a reversal of this trend today at the top levels of national leadership. And the pinch of prejudice will increasingly be felt as more and more non-Anglo-Saxon Protestants rise to this level of society. At the same time, it should be emphasized that this importance of class makes the theory of the persistence of the Anglo-Saxon Ideal—which many sociologists have seen as an important modifying factor in the melting-pot theory—even more important at the elite level than at other social-class levels. This is of course because the nation's leadership is still dominated by members of the WASP upper class, the primary source and carrier of this ideal. The persistence of this ideal and its influence on non-Protestant aspirants to elite status has nowhere been more sensitively expressed than in a recent novel of Jewish life by Myron E. Kaufmann.

While Abraham Cahan's novel, *The Rise of David Levinsky*, painted the classic portrait of an immigrant's rise to affluence within the Jewish community at the turn of the century, Kaufmann's *Remember Me to God*,[12] which Alfred Kazin has called "the most solid and most genuinely created novel of Jewish life in America," is the story of a young Jewish lad, Richard Amsterdam, who goes to Harvard College in the middle of the twentieth century. This pathetic yet touching story of Richard Amsterdam's consuming drive to become a member of the undergraduate establishment of Harvard clubdom includes his inevitable alienation from his highly respectable, suburbanized and Reform-affiliated family; his real and close friendship with Bill Hodge, a Proper Bostonian classmate; his attempted marriage to a rather vacuous debutante; and his moral ambivalence toward his near conversion to Beacon Hill Episcopalianism. His mission in life is outlined in his secret diary, *How to Become a Gentleman— (Handbook)—Anonymous*, in which he catalogues the contrasting Anglo-Saxon ideals of Proper Boston with the middle-class Jewish values he has lived with all of his life, and advocates conversion to the former. He, of course, tries to convert his Jewish friends to his point of view, among them Stuyvesant Gold, a New York intellectual at Harvard who actually has no time for Richard's philo-brahminism. The following excerpt from one of their numerous and lengthy conversations reveals Richard's reverence for the Anglo-American ideal:

> "Stuyvesant," he began leisurely, giving attention to poking his thumb at the glowing tobacco and surrounding ash, which had overflowed a little onto the pipe bowl, "I want you to concentrate on developing a more gentlemanly demeanor, so you won't stick out like a sore thumb. Now, it's not going to be easy, Stuyvesant; let's have that understood. The average Jewish guy isn't 'to the manner born,' so to speak, and he hasn't had it taught in the cradle and the benefit of good schools all his life. Probably his parents never had a chance to go to college, and probably his grandparents were immigrants from eastern Europe. It's going to take a lot of hard, discouraging work to unlearn all these foreign mannerisms and New York mannerisms of yours and set up some new brain patterns so you'll have some polish. Look at me; I've lived around Boston and vicinity all my life and yet I find I'm still learning. I want you to keep an eye on Bill Hodge. You learn what a gentleman is by watching one. And study the guys from Groton and St. Mark's. Their facial expression. How they modulate their voice. It's always clear and distinct and pleasing to the ear. An American should be proud of his language and handle it with respect, because it's the language of Shakespeare." He took a long draw on his pipe, and then watched the smoke curl before him. "And it might be a good idea for you and your father to try and get some hunting in this summer. Go up to the north woods in New York State—I believe you have north woods up there the same as we do in New England. Get yourself a couple of rifles and lumber jackets and those red hunting caps and go up there with your father for a few weeks and shoot game. . . .[13]

Much like Marquand's ironic treatment of the Protestant establishment, Kaufmann's saga of Richard Amsterdam certainly seems overimpressed with the superficial aspects of upper-class life. Yet, to the outsider, perhaps, these may be the very things that do matter. In this connection, for instance, it is of interest that the autobiographies of Alfred E. Smith, James A. Farley and Edward Flynn all emphasize their efforts to be properly dressed. One observes this same pattern among today's college students: on the Main Line, in Philadelphia, one is impressed that the students at Haverford College, an old and venerable Quaker institution, are almost invariably clothed in a most informal, if not downright sloppy, manner, often sporting straggly, adolescent

beards in various stages of growth. A bit further out on the Lancaster Pike, on the other hand, at a newer and rapidly expanding Catholic institution, Villanova University, the students wear coats and neckties, and always appear to be clean-shaven. Similarly, at the University of Pennsylvania in the city, the Jewish fraternities require their brothers to wear coats and neckties, at least in the classroom, while it is often the old-stock Protestants who cultivate the beatnik style. At any rate, young Amsterdam did not take his mission lightly and considered himself a pioneer in the process of assimilation into the American establishment. Thus he tells his real love, a young Jewish girl at Radcliffe, of the seriousness of his mission:

> "Don't you see the significance of what I'm trying to do? Our religion is finally taking its place in this country, and think what it'll mean if I can get up to be a banker and big industrial magnate and run down and advise them in Washington all the time like Mr. Hodge does, and maybe even accept a cabinet post sometime, and at the same time be a Jew that's fully accepted in the inner circles of Boston society. What that will mean for the realization of American democracy, both in terms of my leading those old Yankee families further toward liberalism as a result of my own authority in their different institutions and outfits and everything, and at the same time making them less afraid of minorities by showing them how completely congenial I am. And after I break the ice there'll come Italian guys and colored guys and everything, on any board of directors and in any drawing room. These things are coming, but it's guys like me that push it. I look on it as a mission."[14]

In many ways, young Richard Amsterdam's sometimes pathetic confessions of his mission in life goes to the very heart of the problem of American leadership in the second half of the twentieth century. For, while the social organization of the triple melting pot serves quite effectively in assimilating the descendants of the more recent immigrants into most levels of our pluralistic society, there is, at the same time, constant pressure at the top levels of leadership today, which is increasingly composed of hyphenated-Americans of the third generation, to assimilate *all* talented and powerful men, regardless of their origins or religious convictions, into the main stream of traditional authority by ultimately rewarding them with the dignity, security and family honor implied and nourished by membership in an establishment.

NOTES

1. *Harper's*, March 1955, p. 81.
2. The theory of the triple melting pot in the third generation derives from two main sources: Marcus Lee Hansen, *The Problem of the Third Generation Immigrant.* Rock Island, Ill.: Augustana Historical Society, 1938; and Ruby Jo Reeves Kennedy, "Single or Triple Melting Pot? Intermarriage Trends in New Haven, 1870–1940," *The American Journal of Sociology*, Vol. XLIX, No. 4, January 1944. For a fascinating discussion of this subject, see Will Herberg, *Protestant, Catholic, Jew: An Essay in American Religious Sociology.* New York: Anchor Books, 1960.
3. Nathan Glazer, *American Judaism.* Chicago: University of Chicago Press, 1957.
4. Abraham Cahan, *The Rise of David Levinsky.* New York: Harper & Brothers, 1917, p. 3 and p. 528.
5. Here I am following the historical accounts of American Judaism contained in Nathan Glazer, *op. cit.*, and Oscar Handlin, *Adventure in Freedom: Three Hundred Years of Jewish Life in America.* New York: McGraw-Hill Book Company, Inc., 1954. See also E. Digby Baltzell, *An American Business Aristocracy*, New York: Collier Books, 1962, Chap. 11.
6. For an excellent study of New York's Jews during this period, see Moses Rischin, *The Promised City: New York's Jews, 1870–1914.* Cambridge, Mass.: Harvard University Press, 1962.
7. See Cleveland Amory, *Who Killed Society?* New York: Harper & Brothers, 1960, Chap. VIII.
8. Harvey O'Conner, *The Guggenheims.* New York: Covici-Friede, 1937.
9. Nathan Glazer, "Social Characteristics of American Jews, 1654–1954," *American Jewish Year Book*, Vol. 56. Philadelphia: The Jewish Publication Society of America, 1955, p. 9.
10. Handlin, *op. cit.*, p. 144.
11. *Ibid.*, p. 145.
12. Myron S. Kaufmann, *Remember Me to God.* New York: Signet Books, 1958.
13. *Ibid.*, pp. 112–13.
14. *Ibid.*, p. 180.

THE RISE AND DECLINE OF ANTI-SEMITISM IN AMERICA

DENNIS H. WRONG

To WHAT EXTENT does the striking decline in the prevalence of anti-Semitic beliefs and attitudes in the United States reflect a general decline in all forms of ethnic prejudice? Charles H. Stember, who has conducted a full analysis of all national opinion polls on Jews and anti-Semitism since 1936, writes that "when hostility toward Jews showed an increase in the opinion polls, so did hostility toward other minorities" and he goes on to observe that "this finding throws considerable doubt on the theory that ethnic prejudices necessarily displace one another."[1] He neglects to mention whether the reduction in anti-Semitism has coincided with a general reduction in ethnic prejudice, having confined himself to the formidable task of documenting changing attitudes toward Jews. There is, however, evidence of a general decline in ethnic and racial prejudice and any comprehensive effort to interpret Stember's findings regarding anti-Semitism must begin by taking note of it.

Poll questions on attitudes toward Negroes that were repeated between 1942 and 1963 have also been reviewed by Bettelheim and Janowitz and by Hyman and Sheatsley.[2] They reveal a decline in hostility similar to that reported by Stember in the case of the Jews, although the questions asked are fewer and probe less fully the different dimensions of prejudice. [A] survey was taken in December, 1963, and shows a continuation of the trend toward greater acceptance of Negroes. [It] reveals no substantial evidence of increasing resistance by whites to Negro demands, in spite of signs of such resistance already visible in 1963 and the growing volume of publicity over "white back-

Reprinted by permission from the *European Journal of Sociology*, VI (1965), 311–328.

lash" which was to make civil rights for Negroes an issue in the 1964 Presidential campaign.

Thus the easy assumption that the greater salience of the Negro during the recent period of struggle over racial integration accounts for the decline in anti-Semitism finds no support in the polls. If one considers discriminatory behavior rather than expressed attitudes, a stronger case, though an inferential one, can be made for the view that Negro demands have at the very least distracted attention from the Jews as targets of discrimination. But on the level of attitudes tapped by the polls there can be little doubt that declining prejudice against Jews has been part of a larger trend embracing anti-Negro sentiments as well.

What changes have occurred in American society which have had the effect of reducing ethnic prejudice? It is at least in principle possible that separate and unrelated changes in the relations between majorities and each particular ethnic minority may have modified previously dominant negative images of Jews, Negroes and Orientals. But this is highly improbable. In spite of differences in the location of these groups both regionally and in the social structure, all Americans—majorities and minorities alike—have clearly been affected by changes that have been nation-wide in scope and impact. Moreover, laws and public agencies as well as private organizations striving to improve intergroup relations have adopted policies and issued pronouncements bearing on all forms of ethnic prejudice and discrimination. Finally, much research has shown that prejudiced persons rarely confine their hostility to a single ethnic group. While it is unquestionably useful to know what changes have occurred in the imagery of a particular group and what specific historical events have had an impact on attitudes toward the group in question, an interpretation of a general trend toward ethnic tolerance must search for equally general causes.

1. THE PSYCHODYNAMIC APPROACH

The most comprehensive generalizations about forces in American life promoting and sustaining ethnic prejudice have been advanced by those who have adopted a socio-psychoanalytic approach. This approach has emphasized the psychic roots and functions of prejudice, viewing them as relatively independent of the real attributes of the target of prejudice and of the actual social relationships existing between prejudiced persons and members of the group they despise. From the simple "scapegoating" theory, which has lent itself so readily to popularization in pro-tolerance dramas in the mass media, to the more elaborate technical conceptions of id and superego projectivity and "authoritarian personality", psychological—or, more accurately, psychodynamic—formulations have dominated much of the research and theorizing about prejudice and inter-group relations in the post-war years.[3]

At the same time a good deal of trenchant criticism has been directed against the psychodynamic approach to ethnic relations with its almost exclusive concentration on the subjective dispositions and delusions of the prejudiced. In general, this criticism has converged on the following major points:

First, psychodynamic theories are of little or no help in accounting for changes over time in levels and intensities of prejudice, at least where short-term changes are involved. They cannot supply answers to such questions as "why was there a rise in anti-Semitic sentiment in the United States between 1942 and 1946 and an abrupt decline thereafter?" Psychic mechanisms that are part of the universal repertory of human responses, motivations rooted in the particular character structures of nations and peoples, the proportion of the population possessing personality types prone to ethnic prejudice—none of these psychological conceptions can answer the question "why *now* and not *then?*"; indeed, the first of them cannot even tell us "why *here* and not *there?*" if we wish to compare two different contemporary groups or societies. National character structures and distributions of personality types change too slowly to account for short-run trends in prejudice. The logical canon that one cannot explain a variable by a constant sums up this objection to psychodynamic theories.

Nevertheless, it should be noted that the objection is relevant only to short-run changes in patterns of prejudice. If we wish to account for differences in the general level of prejudice in different societies over long periods of time, we cannot ignore national character. The pervasiveness and persistence of national character differences are impressive, although our lack of anything resembling a sophisticated psychodynamic history of nations and peoples makes it difficult to say just how long the long-run may be in any given case—whether it is a matter of several generations or several centuries. Differences in national character undoubtedly have much to do with the unequal susceptibilities of societies to prejudice. For example, the acute sensitivity to racial differences of the North European, Protestant, Anglo-Saxon and Teutonic peoples clearly has roots in their common character shaped by traditions, family institutions, and histories that they do not share with the peoples of Southern and Eastern Europe.[4] It would, of course, be a gross form of psychodynamic or characterological determinism to attribute the treatment by North Europeans of racially distinct subject peoples solely to their character structure, but character structure may legitimately be regarded as one factor that has influenced their colonial policies and a factor that is usually ignored.

The changes reported by Stember have obviously occurred within too brief a period of time (from the 1930's to the present) for psychodynamic theories by themselves to be of much help in explaining them. One can only agree with the conclusion of Bettelheim and Janowitz that "changes in underlying psychological mechanisms do not account for the decline in hostile attitudes toward Jews and Negroes."[5] Surely, there can have been no sudden decrease in the amount of frustration in American private lives generating free-floating aggression to be mobilized against Jews or Negroes. And surely the proportion of authoritarian personalities in the population cannot have diminished from 1946, when the decline in prejudice began, to the present time, a period that is not even long enough to equal the length of a generation in demographic terms. However, the same objection applies in only slightly lesser degree to sociological theories that see prejudice as declining because of changes in the demographic, socio-economic and educational composition of the population, for, although such theories postulate a trend, it is a trend that moves much too slowly to account for the shifts in prejudice and its manifestations with which we are here concerned.

A second major objection to psychodynamic theories is that they are unable to explain why a particular ethnic group becomes the object of prejudice, nor indeed why ethnic groups should be selected at all out of the infinitude of social objects available for depreciation and victimization.[6] If the choice of the Jews as scapegoat is so arbitrary that bicyclists (as the old anti-Nazi joke had it) or men with striped ties (as *Crossfire*, a post-war pro-tolerance movie, put it) might equally well have been picked, then why indeed have the Jews been chosen so often?

The psychodynamic theorists account for the choice of the object of prejudice by postulating the existence of derogatory "stereotypes" of ethnic groups. These images are transmitted as part of the cultural heritage and thus become available to canalize the free-floating hostilities and anxieties of people who are psychically predisposed to project and externalize their inner conflicts. But any explanation of the origin of these stereotypes lies beyond the scope of psychodynamic theory. Nor can the theory adequately account for changes in the content of the stereotypes of the kind reported by Stember. In effect, stereotypes function as a kind of social or cultural *deus ex machina* for the psychodynamic theorist: they are essential to activate prejudice and to indicate its target but they remain an unexplained "given" as far as the theory itself is concerned.

A third objection to psychodynamic theories, which is essentially a corollary and extension of the second, is that they ignore the actualities of inter-group relations. A minority ethnic group is not simply a figment of the majority's diseased imagination, but consists of real people with real relations to members of the majority group. The relevance of these relations to the attitudes of both groups obviously requires investigation. By concentrating on what exists in the minds of prejudiced members of the majority, the psychodynamic theorist neglects the actual characteristics of the minority and its contacts with the majority.

Sometimes the real qualities of the object of prejudice are treated as irrelevant by the fiat of defining prejudice as *any* negative or hostile attitude toward a group.[7] More often, prejudice is defined as a hostile attitude toward a group about which the prejudiced person holds demonstrably false beliefs that he alleges as reasons for his attitude.[8] But even this more acceptable definition discourages investigation of the possible relevance of actual intergroup relations to particular false beliefs or of social changes that may have falsified beliefs that once were true reflections of an earlier historical situation.[9]

Although his approach derives from a different intellectual tradition, the survey researcher or public opinion analyst shares with the psychodynamic theorist this neglect of the real qualities of the objects about which his subjects voice opinions and express attitudes. The opinion analyst's emphasis on what is in people's minds stems, of course, from a methodological chastity that deters him from going beyond the body of data, collected by survey techniques, that he has assembled. But the result is curiously like that of the more speculative, less "scientific" psychodynamic theorist in stressing the "subjective" at the expense of the real world of events and social relations. Thus public opinion data cannot by themselves, however carefully analyzed, tell us all that we want to know about a topic; they demand further interpretation drawing upon a wider range of evidence.

The inadequacies of a purely subjective approach to prejudice are more obvious today than a decade ago. That whites have long cherished irrational fears and fantasies concerning the Negro, many of them with a strong sexual content, is well-known. But the contemporary racial crisis in the United States clearly arises from conflict between Negro political and social aspirations and white resistance to these aspirations rather than from any increase in sexual anxieties or psychological authoritarianism on the part of the white population. Whites who oppose further collective advance by the Negroes are not necessarily inaccurately informed about Negro living conditions, crime rates or educational disabilities[10], whatever their deeper unconscious attitudes toward Negroes may be. There is, of course, a maddening injustice in white men invoking the very scars of racial discrimination to justify continuation of that discrimination. But this often noted self-fulfilling tendency in racial discrimination is irrational only from the standpoint of man considered collectively as the maker of society and history. The parent who fears that his child's schooling may suffer if the local public school is integrated and the homeowner anxious about property values if Negroes move into his neighborhood are not themselves the creators of the system of discrimination that has branded the Negro with the "mark of oppression" though they may be sustaining it. Nor can their fears be labelled irrational and groundless. They are reacting to a real situation, a "social fact" that is truly "external" to them rather than of their individual making. The tragedy and complexity of the racial crisis lies in the fact that their reactions may perpetuate for others the situation that has evoked them.

The real conflicts of interests that have emerged between Negroes and whites in such areas as school integration and housing raise questions about the surveys showing a general decline in anti-Negro sentiment. It is hard to avoid scepticism that the increasing percentage of respondents since 1942 stating that they had no objection to living next door to Negroes (from only 35% in 1942 to 64% in 1963)[11] provides a real clue as to how these same respondents might behave should they actually confront this situation, or even how they might vote on referenda banning discrimination in housing such as those that were recently defeated in the state of California, Detroit and several other communities. If today we are disposed to doubt whether professions of tolerance in the polls have much relation to acceptance of racial integration in education and housing, in the recent past the reverse situation has often been observed: individuals and communities expressing strong opposition to integration have nevertheless accepted it peacefully when it has been imposed on them by administrative action.[12]

2. THE PROJECTIVE CHARACTER OF ANTI-SEMITISM

What do these contradictory findings about the relation between expressed attitudes toward Negroes and actual behavior in new inter-racial situations suggest about Stember's survey data on anti-Semitic sentiment? If the evidence of growing white resistance to Negro demands is not reflected in surveys, is the decrease in anti-Semitism suggested by the polls equally deceptive? Perhaps, as Ben Halpern suggests,[13] the surveys merely show that anti-Semitic utterances are no longer respectable instead of revealing a real change in underlying attitudes at least potentially relevant to conduct.

It seems likely that the growing ideological disreputability of all forms of ethnic prejudice has collided with a frequently belated awareness by many whites that racial integration will require real sacrifices on their part. The situation is obviously very different where the Jews are concerned. There is no "objective" Jewish problem in America today in the sense in which there is a real Negro problem, or, more accurately, a real problem of Negro-white relations. One sociologist has gone so far as to maintain that the much-studied psychodynamics of prejudice have no relation at all to the social and historical facts of inter-group relations,[14] but he is plainly thinking of Negro-white relations and would be hard put to maintain the same thesis with regard to anti-Semitism, past or present. For just as Jews are a people unlike all others, so is anti-Semitism unlike all other forms of ethnic prejudice. It is no accident that psychodynamic theories of prejudice grew primarily out of the study of anti-Semitism and were always most tentative and least convincing when applied to anti-Negro attitudes as well. It is far more credible that people suffering from definable neurotic disturbances should be attracted by anti-Semitic stereotypes and ideologies than that people expressing anti-Negro attitudes should resemble one another psychologically. Discrimination against the Negro has, after all, long been an established institution in the South and a sanctioned, if unofficial, practice in the North. Anti-Semitism has never had such a status in America nor indeed, except for the Nazi period, in Europe since the emancipation of the Jews.

It is precisely the peculiarly intense, projective character of anti-Semitism in modern Western civilization that has made it appear so mysterious, such an inexplicable "outrage against common sense,"[15] leading some interpreters to declare it an unfathomable mystery forever immune to rational understanding. Their bafflement arises from the enormous disproportion between the actual position of the Jews in modern society and the one imputed to them by anti-Semitic ideology. Any effort to understand anti-Semitism must confront this disproportion and must, therefore, inevitably consider psychodynamic processes in trying to account for it. Such processes are clearly central to the phenomenon.

Yet neither psychodynamic constants nor changes in the objective realities of inter-group relations can by themselves explain the waxing and waning of anti-Semitism in short periods. We need, therefore, to combine an understanding of universal psychic mechanisms with a precise historical account of the events and situations, transitory though they may be, that trigger these mechanisms if we are to understand sudden outbursts of previously latent forms of prejudice. We must show how crisis situations, collective disasters, disturbances in the routine operations of social structures and the temporary physical and social dislocation of large numbers of people activate tendencies to scapegoat, to lust after violence, to assert defensively one's own group identity at the expense of an out-group. The ways in which we go about explaining the sudden emergence of extremist political movements or moods, such as McCarthyism, provide a model.

Stember briefly suggests such an explanation in contending that the tensions and frustrations of the latter years of the war account for the increase in anti-Semitic opinions in the United States at that time.[16] Recalling that the year 1943 witnessed race riots in Los Angeles, Detroit, New York City and several smaller communities, some of which were far more destructive than those of the summer of 1964, I find his suggestion persuasive.

An approach that links psychic mechanisms to specific social situations activating them can also be applied on a more limited scale to common personal situations and crises affecting single individuals rather than large collectivities—the scale of "milieu" as opposed to "social structure" in C. Wright Mills' terms.[17] This is the rationale for the many studies investigating the connection between prejudice and different individual career and social mobility histories, studies that attempt "to relate degrees of social movement to degrees of prejudice".[18] Bettelheim and Janowitz argue, incidentally, that changes in aggregate rates of individual mobility since 1950 are not able to account for the decline in anti-Semitism and ethnic prejudice in general since that date.[19]

Yet although an approach that relates the psychodynamics of prejudice to specific social situations breeding mass insecurities overcomes some of the limitations of purely psychodynamic theories, it still leaves open the question of why one group rather than another becomes the target of prejudice. The Jews must possess some salience and visibility as an ethnic-religious group, or must have done so in the fairly recent past, for anti-Semitism to survive as a possible response to political and social crisis. Anti-Semitism has been the "classic prejudice" of the Western world, but "subjective" or "sham" anti-Semitism, as Eva Reichmann has called it,[20] requires at the very least historical memories of a former "objective" anti-Semitism. If anti-Semitism has generally been weaker in the United States than in Europe, it is largely because historical memories of Jewish/Christian conflicts have been weaker in America and what objective anti-Semitism has existed has been less salient against the background of recurrent immigrant/native-born tensions and the ubiquitous presence throughout American history of non-white races, beginning with the original inhabitants of the continent. By the same token, American anti-Semitism as a mass ideology has been even more shadowy and projective, and its adherents have been even more personally unstable and paranoid, than in Europe.

Eva Reichmann has shown that in modern German history subjective anti-Semitism was prominent in precisely those areas where and periods when there was no significant objective Jewish problem. The Nazis, the final disastrous exploiters of subjective anti-Semitism, made little use of actual tensions between Germans and recent Polish Jewish immigrants in elaborating their demoniacal portrait of the symbolic Jew.[21] The very absence of a Jewish group sharply set apart from its neighbors makes it easier for the ideologue and the demagogue to transform anti-Semitism into a sweeping world-historical doctrine, just as the John Birch Society has been able to construct a total, all-encompassing ideology out of anti-Communism more than a decade after American Communists have lost whatever influence they once possessed in American society.

But the world and the Jews are various and so, therefore, is anti-Semitism, which has existed in a wide variety of different mixtures of subjective and objective forms. Anti-Semitism is certainly the classic case of projective group hatred and Nazism is the prototype of ideological anti-Semitism with its murderous political potentialities. But both have unduly predominated in the psychodynamic interpretations of ethnic prejudice and the balance needs redressing. If the ideological anti-Semitism of the Nazis and the echoes it aroused in this country represent the extreme form of subjective anti-Semitism, social discrimination against *nouveaux riches* Jews by Old American elites, as documented by John Higham,[22] represents the most clear-out form of objective anti-Semitism in American history (excluding earlier anti-immigrant feeling which did not sharply distinguish Jews from other ethnic newcomers). Both of these polar types have become inconsequential in contemporary America. Whatever dispositions to subjective anti-Semitism continue to survive depend upon the continuing salience of the Jews as possible target and victim. Stember's data, as well as much else that has happened since World War II, inevitably raise doubts about this salience. At the same time, the virtually complete acculturation of American Jews has destroyed much of the basis for objective anti-Semitism. *What conceivable blends of psychodynamic disposition, prevailing public images of Jews, and actual traits of the American Jewish population set lower limits to the trend described by Stember or make possible its reversal?* The following somewhat disjointed observations cover what seem to me to be at least some of the relevant considerations in answering this crucial question.

3. THE INSTITUTIONALIZATION OF JUDAISM

It has often been remarked that in America anti-Semitism has never possessed even the shadow of official sanction in a country containing many ethnic and religious minorities and committed both ideologically and out of the pragmatic necessities of democratic politics to equality of opportunity. Not only has this continued to be the case, but since World War II Jews have been, as it were, themselves institutionalized as part of American society. The elevating of Judaism to equal status with Protestantism and Catholicism as the third "official" religious division in American society has largely taken place since the war. Characterizations of our civilization as "Judeo-Christian" have become standard during the same period. The increasing numbers of successful national politicians who are Jewish and the growing practice of accepting Jews along with Catholics as "ticket-balancers" to Protestant candidates for office are also noteworthy. And all this has occurred at a time when the Jews are a declining proportion of the national population and when large numbers of Jews have retained a religious affiliation that has become no more than nominal.

This institutionalization of the Jews has clearly been a policy on the part of powerful elite groups in government at all levels, the political parties, the churches, professional associations and the mass communications industries. Horrified reactions to the Holocaust and awareness of and sympathy with Israel have influenced these elites, however slight, as Stember shows, may have been the apparent response to such recent historical events on the part of the general public.

The new public status accorded Jews seems both to ensure them of continuing visibility in American society and to reduce pressures on individual Jews to abandon their Jewish identities through what used to be called "assimilation". It is, of course, as a religious group that Jews have been recognized. Whatever the obvious advantages of this recognition, it clearly carries with it a risk from the perspective of those who contend, as did Sidney Hook some years ago, that anti-Semitism is a "Christian phenomenon [. . .] endemic to every Christian culture, whose religions made the Jews the eternal villain in the Christian drama of salvation".[23] American society has thus underwritten the survival of the ancient original objective basis of anti-Semitism, or anti-Judaism, as it should properly be called in this connection.

One may doubt whether recent efforts by both Catholics and Protestants to repudiate the doctrine that the Jews were guilty of deicide will have much effect on the laity. The trouble with the view that anti-Semitism is endemic to Christianity, however, is that the contemporary decline in anti-Semitism has occurred at a time when the importance of religious identities has clearly increased in America.[24] American religious identities obviously do not have the same meaning they had in the past and their new significance is not of a kind that challenges the secular, post-Christian nature of our society. Still, religious conflicts between Christians and Jews over such issues as Christmas pageants in the schools are unlikely to disappear and, as the record of one such controversy in Hamden, Connecticut, indicates,[25] they may revive among Christians many of the slumbering stereotypes of anti-Semitism.

Jews are not merely regarded by others as a religious group, but they increasingly so regard themselves. In this respect American Jews appear to have completed a full cycle, returning, with the acculturation of the East European immigrants, to the outlook of the late nineteenth century American Jewish community of largely German origin and Reform persuasion, which saw itself as a marginally differentiated religious grouping within the context of relatively complete acculturation to the larger American society. The point of view that was once called "assimilationism" is no longer advanced as such by many American Jews, perhaps because it no longer seems necessary to talk about something that is actually taking place for so many. Intermarriage and the dropping of even a nominal affiliation with Judaism are probably increasing, although without the name-changing that was so common before World War II.[26] Persons of Jewish origin with names like, say, Goldwater, who have married non-Jews and abandoned all affiliations with Judaism or the Jewish community are likely to become more common. The very decline in anti-Semitism makes such complete but non-defensive assimilation more acceptable by removing the stigma of cowardice from it.

4. THE UPPER-MIDDLE CLASS AND ANTI-SEMITISM

American Jews today for the most part belong to the metropolitan middle class and in large numbers to the upper-middle class. Their collective socio-economic ascent has, as is well-known, been more rapid than that of any other immigrant group. Even before the coming of the East European Jews, the Old American upper and upper-middle classes in many communities resisted the efforts of newly wealthy Jews to gain entrance into clubs, summer resorts, private schools and colleges and residential neighborhoods that had long been their exclusive preserves. Such discrimination, as Max Weber long ago noted, is typical behavior on the part of high-status groups anxious to oppose the claims of sheer wealth to social equality in the name of more intangible values. The stereotype of the Jew as a flashy and vulgar *arriviste* clearly originated in this context. This explains why it does not loom particularly large in the mass images of the Jew reported by Stember and also why certain anti-Semitic opinions and attitudes are more common among upper-income and highly-educated groups, a finding that Stember has more fully documented in a previous work.[27] Since Jews have for so long penetrated the upper levels of the income and occupational hierarchy and are now heavily concentrated there, stereotyping them as *parvenus* has not been without objective foundation and contact with them in intimate, informal situations has often been a real issue for insecure circles of would-be patricians.

Yet the genteel anti-Semitism of upper-class groups and its manifestation in social discrimination have also greatly declined in recent decades. The Jews are now relatively well-established in the upper-middle class while other minority ethnic groups, not to speak of Anglo-Saxon Protestants in the West and Southwest, are more likely to bear the stigmata of the *nouveaux riches*. Anti-Semitism "from above"[28] of this sort, while occasionally becoming an obsession with individuals (e.g. Henry Adams), has never in America been politicized as the basis for a right-wing nationalist movement, as it has in such countries as pre-Nazi Germany, France and contemporary Argentina,[29] although radicals and neo-Marxists, usually misreading the Nazi experience, have often expected this to happen.[30] Genteel anti-Semitism has, in fact, had little connection with ideological anti-Semitism, which in its characteristically American nativist and populist forms has chiefly appealed, as Higham has pointed out, to rural and small-town dwellers who have associated Jews with the hated and feared big city.[31] It is hard to believe that patrician anti-Semitism has much future in America.

True, considerable exclusion of Jews from the private clubs of upper-circle white Anglo-Saxon Protestants remains, as E. Digby Baltzell has recently reminded us,[32] and residential segregation of Jews from non-Jews, though largely by choice, is fairly marked in middle-class suburbs around New York City. Yet the number of Jews employed by large organizations, especially in technical positions, are increasing. So is the participation of Jews in political and civic organizations and some other types of voluntary association organized on a community-wide basis. Despite the surviving barriers to sustained intimate contacts between middle-class Jews and non-Jews, the trend on balance is probably toward more contacts and many of the barriers that remain are upheld by both groups and therefore do not reflect social discrimination practiced by Anglo-Saxons.

Closer contacts both at work and in some areas of community life are likely to create new attitudes toward one another on the part of Jews and non-Jews. Possibly future Jew/non-Jew relations within the upper-middle class will come to resemble those that now prevail in smaller academic, professional and intellectual circles where Jews and non-Jews are brought into close contact, a contact that frequently results in high intermarriage rates.[33] Relations in such circles are by no means free of frictions and covert group animosities which often coexist with a virtual philo-Semitism on the part of some non-Jews and an almost complete abandonment of Jewish identity on the part of some Jews.

The group images formed in such settings more closely reflect the subtle realities of group differences than the standardized imagery of traditional anti-Semitism or the superficial stereotypes of *parvenu* behavior held by socially insecure snobs. Non-Jews are apt to attribute to Jews such traits as intellectuality, political liberalism, intense parental solicitude, a consequent close bond between mothers and sons, the attachment of great importance to extended family ties, a liking for food and physical comforts in general, volubility and emotional expressiveness, fear of violence and ironic humor. These traits are more or less accurately seen as characteristic of Jews and awareness of them clearly requires a degree of intimacy in informal social contexts. They may be evaluated either positively or negatively, either "anti-Semitically" or "philo-Semitically" if these terms are not too strong to be used in this connection.

Jews also see Anglo-Saxon Protestants as possessing distinctive traits having little to do either with formal religious affiliation or with traditional anti-*goyim* stereotypes. Again more or less accurately, they often see "Wasps" (white Anglo-Saxon Protestants) as emotionally reserved, prone to place great value on formally polite manners, often resistant to contemporary fashions and innovations, loyal to institutional attachments, but less so to kin, less permissive in child rearing, and possessing residual traces of asceticism, if not of puritanism. These traits too may be evaluated positively or negatively.

Thus both groups tend to develop new stereotypes of the other as a result of closer contacts between them. The new images, whether favorably or unfavorably evaluated, are far more accurate than the older ones which have long since been historically outdated and subject to the distortions of projective thinking. It is questionable whether such new contacts between Jews and "Wasps" in upper-middle class circles have much relevance to ethnic prejudice in general or anti-Semitism in particular as these have been traditionally understood. They may well, however, open a new chapter in the relations between Jews and non-Jews in America.

5. THE OCCUPATIONAL POSITION OF THE JEWS

What about the far more dangerous anti-Semitism "from below"? If some thinkers have seen anti-Semitism as a permanent ingredient of Christian cultures, others have regarded it as an enduring possibility so long as Jews retain visibility as a result of their concentration in particular occupations and industries.[34]

Certainly, their preponderance in the professions, retail trade, commerce, real estate and the communications and entertainment industries has continued.[35] The dominant image of the Jew as economic man reported by Stember reflects past Jewish over-representation in retail and financial occupations involving, unlike manufacturing, direct contacts with the public, and in such ostentatiously affluent and publicly visible new industries as the movies, although the image has also falsely stereotyped the Jew as prominent in banking. Now most of these occupations, as well as the liberal professions which Jews have entered in large numbers, are among those least likely to be affected by automation. Is it not possible that working-class and white-collar groups threatened by unemployment or occupational downgrading as a result of auto-mation will turn on the Jew, as "doomed classes" have so often done in the past, and provide the mass base for a revival of anti-Semitism?

Several considerations make this, I think, unlikely though by no means impossible. Much social discontent in recent years has been directed against large bureaucratic organizations. Noting the frequency with which the federal government—and in par-ticular such of its agencies as the Supreme Court and the State Department—the big foundations and the Ivy League universities have replaced ethnic groups as the targets of extremist agitation, Richard Hofstadter has half-facetiously commented that stan-dards of hating appear to have risen along with standards of living.[36] Hofstadter's argument is that authoritarian personalities now select new targets in place of formerly maligned ethnic groups. But an alternative explanation that pays greater attention to the grounds on which particular objects of prejudice and scapegoating are picked, would stress the actual involvement of the groups and institutions in question with social changes that have reduced the power and prestige, if not the wealth, of local and regional interest groups. Senator Goldwater obviously has won much support from such groups.

In the past Jews could plausibly be linked to the big city and become scapegoats for the disruptive effects of urbanization[37], but they cannot be similarly associated with bureaucratization and the expanding powers of the federal government. Jews are not especially prominent in the higher ranks of the federal bureaucracy, the foreign service, the defense establishment or the judiciary, nor for that matter, in Big Labor, a more traditional target of rightist agitation. Jews have not typically been "organization men" either in business or in the professions where they have preferred to be independent practitioners rather than salaried experts or administrators in large organizations like hospitals, big law offices, engineering firms and industrial organizations. Nor have they been directly implicated in the introduction of automation, however immune their occupational distribution may render them to its effects. In short, although the psychodynamic potentials that have found an outlet in ethnic prejudice in the past are still with us and social and technical change are producing new frustrations for some groups in the population, it does not seem likely that anti-Semitism will make a comeback and displace the more recent targets of radical right paranoia and conspiracy-mongering, targets readily lending themselves to personalized negative stereotyping as "creeping socialists", "comsymps", or "effete Eastern intellectuals".

6. THE ANTI-SEMITISM OF OTHER MINORITIES

Mention should be made of the anti-Semitism of groups that are themselves minorities and have been victims of prejudice and discrimination. At times the Irish and the Italians, both groups that have risen more slowly than the Jews in American society and have suffered penalties both as Catholics and as foreigners, have been prone to anti-Semitism. But it is Negro anti-Semitism that is more in evidence at the present time. James Baldwin perhaps exaggerated in writing some years ago that "Georgia has the Negro and Harlem has the Jew", but the present antipathy of Negro militants to "white liberals", so many of whom are Jewish, and the appeals to some Negroes of the Black Muslims, who combine the anti-Israeli slogans of the Arab countries with indigenous sources of anti-Semitism, suggest that Negro anti-Semitism is not a passing phenomenon. Some writers have seen it as an outcome of the frequent contacts of Negroes with Jewish retailers on the fringes of the black ghettoes, Jewish housewives in domestic service, Jewish employers in low-wage garment factories, and cohesive Jewish communities in residential areas into which the Negroes are expanding.[38] In all of these situations the Negro confronts the Jew in a subordinate or disadvantaged role. Yet it is unlikely that Negro anti-Semitism is purely objective in character and its subjective sources and functions need further examination.

7. CAMPUS LIBERALISM

In the years of relative prosperity since World War II ethnic tolerance and greater sexual freedom have been virtually the only two durable causes available to middle-class, college-educated youth in rebelling against parental standards. Political radicalism has been (until very recently) in abeyance, atheism no longer carries much emotional charge and avant-garde art and literature have been absorbed by the academy and by conventional cultural entrepreneurs to the point where they have lost their capacity to shock and challenge. Attitudes towards ethnic and racial minorities and towards sexuality have remained live issues, offering young people the chance to define themselves as rebels and bearers of new values.

A few years ago David Riesman complained that his University of Chicago students devoted inordinate energy to combatting minor and residual forms of racial discrimination in and around the campus. Their time would be better spent, he argued, in exposing the petty tyrannies and irrationalities of the academic institution itself instead of supinely submitting to them while fighting more remote evils, a fight in which they did not lack powerful and better-placed allies. Riesman, usually so perceptive on such matters, clearly missed the symbolic significance of ethnic liberalism to contemporary students in an age when so many other causes have been corrupted or have lost their momentum as a result of partial successes. Now that the Negro drive for equality has reached a peak at a time when our economy requires major structural adjustments, Riesman's students of nearly a decade ago no longer seem as quixotic and self-deceived as he then thought them to be.

It is true that ethnic liberalism as a fighting posture often draws upon precisely the same psychodynamic mechanisms of scapegoating, projectivity and compulsive confirmations of identity that have in the past sustained ethnic prejudice itself. As Bettelheim and Janowitz acutely remark: "Fighting against prejudice as a means to buttress one's own threatened identity is an ineffective way to eliminate it in others, because those who are prejudiced feel the self-seeking nature of this pressure".[39] Yet the same psychodynamic causes produce in this instance opposite social and political effects, for the rigid or authoritarian liberal at least contributes to the creation of that minimal consensus on values which is a prerequisite for any effective action to implement equality and freedom.

The negative correlation between age and ethnic tolerance is often attributed to the allegedly greater influence on the young of the official pro-tolerance messages of the mass media in an age when parental authority has been undermined by outside agencies. I doubt that this effect, if indeed it exists, is as important as the need for young people in a rapidly changing and complex society such as our own to identify themselves with distinctive values, values to be sure for which they may claim far greater novelty and radicalism than is justified. True, only a minority of recent college-educated youth define themselves as fighting ethnic liberals and an even smaller minority become involved in picketing, freedom rides and voter registration campaigns in Mississippi. But this minority establishes the dominant atmosphere on the campuses, as the dismal failure of counter-efforts by the Young Americans for Freedom and other *soi-disant* conservative student organizations indicates. With regard to Jews, a kind of philo-Semitism prevails: many non-Jewish liberals who would hesitate at solving the Negro problem in marriage choose Jews as marriage partners, as the rates of inter-marriage in university communities attest.[40] Whatever its causes, it is hard to believe that the ethnic liberalism of the campus is anything but an irreversible development in American life.

8. CONCLUSION

Hopefully, these random observations cast at least some light on the trend shown by Charles Stember's poll tabulations. They also suggest the probable permanence of the decline of anti-Semitism in America, though not its total disappearance. A word of caution, however, is in order, for sociologists have too often found themselves in the position of Hegel's Owl of Minerva—putting forward comprehensive and adequate explanations of a social trend just at the moment when it ceases to exist or is radically reversed by unforeseen historical mutations. Sociological explanations are biased in favor of long-evolving, gradualist processes of social change, of slow structural drifts insensibly modifying the shape of institutions and values, and gently edging people away from their previous moorings at a rate sufficiently measured to allow the sociologist to chart their movement with his own ponderous methods of collecting and assessing evidence. The historian can always chide him for having given insufficient weight to the unforeseen and unforeseeable unique events that set in motion the slowly-developing processes he often mistakenly treats as prime movers. But the historian is able to do this only after the fact; it is not his distinctive obligation to estimate future possibilities and probabilities. The historian is right to chastise the sociologist when the latter presumes to "predict" the future by merely projecting an imperfectly understood trend, but the future is a dimension of time that we already inhabit in the present and we cannot do without guidelines to it.

I shall conclude by confessing that I am unable to foresee what kinds of future historical event might significantly raise the temperature of anti-Semitism in America. An intensified resistance by both white Southerners and Northern city-dwellers to racial desegregation in which blame is assigned to "Jew Communists" as a central ideological tenet, seems at present the most likely possibility. But Stember's data indicate that this has not yet come to pass. Cold War defeats, frustrations in American international relations, economic tensions resulting from automation, and, of course, the ultimate possibility of nuclear war would also create mass insecurities sufficient to unleash all the psychodynamic reactions to panic that have generated anti-Semitism in the past. But we have already experienced in relatively mild form most of these things without anti-Semitism having figured importantly in the responses to them. And I have suggested grounds for doubting that Jews, as distinct from other groups and institutions, are likely to become again the objects of what Hofstadter has called "projective politics". Perhaps the study of the psychodynamics of ethnic prejudice should be redirected and reformulated as the study of collective irrationality in general.

NOTES

1. Charles Herbert Stember, *Jews in the Mind of America* (New York: Basic Books, 1964), p. 233.

2. Bruno Bettelheim and Morris Janowitz, *Social Change and Prejudice* (New York, The Free Press of Glencoe, 1964), pp. 11–14; Herbert Hyman and Paul Sheatsley, Attitudes Towards Desegregation, *Scientific American*, 221 (July, 1964), 16–23.

3. Most of this research and the theories underlying it has been summarized by Gordon W. Allport, *The Nature of Prejudice* (Cambridge, Mass., Addison-Wesley Co., 1954).

4. See the suggestions of Philip Mason, *An Essay on Racial Tension* (London and New York, Royal Institute of International Affairs, 1954), pp. 37–42.

5. Bettelheim and Janowitz, *op. cit.*, p. 80.

6. One of the best criticisms of the scapegoating theory may be found in Hannah Arendt, *The Origins of Totalitarianism* (New York, Harcourt, Brace and Company, 1951), pp. 3–10.

7. See the criticisms of this definition by William Petersen, *The Politics of Population* (Garden City, N.Y., Doubleday, 1964), pp. 238–246.

8. This essentially is Allport's definition, *op. cit.*, p. 10.

9. See Paul Kecskemeti, The Psychological Theory of Prejudice, *Commentary*, 18 (1954), 359–366.

10. See William Lee Miller, Analysis of the 'White Backlash', *The New York Times Magazine* (August 23, 1964), pp. 26, 87–88.

11. Hyman and Sheatsley, *op. cit.*, p. 19.

12. Earl Raab and Seymour Martin Lipset, "The Prejudiced Society", in Earl Raab, ed., *American Race Relations Today* (Garden City, N.Y., Doubleday Anchor Books, 1962), pp. 29–55.

13. Ben Halpern, "The Findings in the Perspective of Jewish History", (New York, 1964), mimeographed for conference on "Jews in the Mind of America", American Jewish Committee, September 13–14, 1964.

14. Arnold M. Rose, "Intergroup Relations vs. Prejudice", *Social Problems*, IV (1956), 173–176.

15. The phrase is Hannah Arendt's, *loc. cit.*

16. Stember, *op. cit.*, p. 138.

17. C. Wright Mills, *The Sociological Imagination* (New York: Oxford University Press, 1959), pp. 8–13.

18. Bettelheim and Janowitz, *op. cit.*, p. 68.

19. *Ibid.*, pp. 25–48.

20. Eva Reichmann, *Hostages to Civilization* (Boston, The Beacon Press, 1951), pp. 37–39.

21. *Ibid.*, pp. 227–235.

22. John Higham, "Social Discrimination Against Jews in America, 1830–1930", *Publication of The American Historical Society*, XLVII (1957), pp. 1–33.

23. Sidney Hook, "Reflections on the Jewish Question", *Partisan Review*, XVI (1949), pp. 471–472.

24. Gerhard Lenski, *The Religious Factor* (Garden City, N.Y., rev. ed., Doubleday, 1963).

25. "Community Conflict: Christmas Observance in the Public Schools", in Earl Raab, editor, *Religious Conflict in America* (Garden City, N.Y., Doubleday, 1964), pp. 198–208.

26. Marshall Sklare, "Intermarriage and the Jewish Future", *Commentary* XXXVII (1964), 46–52.

27. Charles Herbert Stember, *Education and Attitude Change* (New York, Institute of Human Relations Press, 1961).

28. I have borrowed the terms "from above" and "from below" from Kecskemeti, "The Psychological Theory of Prejudice", *op. cit.*

29. For Argentina see Irving Louis Horowitz, "The Jewish Community of Buenos Aires," *Jewish Social Studies*, XIV (1962), 214–220.

30. See Paul Kecskemeti, "Prejudice in the Catastrophic Perspective", *Commentary*, XI (1951), 286–292.

31. Higham, *op. cit.;* also by the same author, "Anti-Semitism in the Gilded Age: A Reinterpretation", *The Mississippi Valley Historical Review*, XLIII (1957), 559–578.

32. E. Digby Baltzell, *The Protestant Establishment: Aristocracy and Caste in America* (New York, Random House, 1964).

33. Sklare, *op. cit.*, pp. 49–51.

34. For example, Werner J. Cahnman, "Socio-economic Causes of Anti-Semitism", *Social Problems*, V (1957), 21–29.

35. Nathan Glazer and Daniel Patrick Moynihan, *Beyond the Melting Pot* (Cambridge, Mass., The M.I.T. Press and Harvard University Press, 1964), pp. 143–155.

36. Richard Hofstadter, "The Pseudo-Conservative Revolt", in Daniel Bell, ed., *The Radical Right* (Garden City, N.Y., Doubleday, 1963), p. 76.

37. Arnold M. Rose, "Anti-Semitism's Root in City Hatred", *Commentary*, VI (1948), pp. 374–378.

38. Glazer and Moynihan, *op. cit.*, pp. 71–73.

39. Bettelheim and Janowitz, *op. cit.*, p. 60.

40. Sklare, *op. cit.*

STRANGERS IN THEIR MIDST: SMALL-TOWN JEWS AND THEIR NEIGHBORS

PETER I. ROSE

FOR MANY YEARS social scientists and historians have been trying to piece together a composite portrait of American Jewry. Owing to their predominant pattern of city residence, research has been focused on the urban dwelling Jews, and the Jews of the United States have been characterized as a metropolitan people. There is, however, a scattered minority of American Jews living in little hamlets and rural villages who do not fully fit this urban image. Such people do not reside in old style ghettoes, in ethnic neighborhoods, or in modern homogeneous suburbs. Unlike their urban coreligionists, they are not members of on-going Jewish communities. They are strangers in alien territory.

Critical examination of Jewish life in the small community would seem to be a logical extension of research in the study of American Judaism and the nature of Jewish-Gentile relations. Yet, while the literature offers a wealth of information about the urban Jew in America, there is a dearth of published material about his "country cousin." And what there is is limited to sketchy life histories, journalistic descriptions, and anecdotal recollections of the experiences of individuals who have lived in, visited, or passed through little villages, appearing in such publications as *Midstream, Commentary*, and *Congress Weekly*.[1]

In an attempt to add to the general literature on Jewish life on the American scene, to assess Jewish-Gentile relations in this neglected setting, and to re-examine the ubiquitous concept of "marginal man," an extensive study of the small-town Jews of

This article is reprinted by permission of the editors of *The Jewish Journal of Sociology*, originally titled "Small-Town Jews and Their Neighbours in The United States," 3 (December 1961), pp. 174–191.

"rural" New York State was conducted.[2] Because the small-town Jew is so often cast in the role of being an ambassador of "his people" to the Gentiles, a parallel study was carried out simultaneously with non-Jewish small-towners also living in upstate New York.

Data were gathered to seek answers to several questions. To what extent do group traditions persist in cases of relative isolation? Does identification wane when unsupported by fellow members of one's own group? How intensive are relationships between the stranger and the world in which he has chosen to live? What kinds of adjustments does he have to make? And, finally, to what extent does interpersonal contact with an isolated minority member influence the stereotypic conceptions and misconceptions held by the majority group members about him?

THE RESEARCH DESIGN

Investigation was confined to one particular area of the country: "rural" New York State. Operationally, "rural communities" and "small-town Jews" were defined as follows:

> Rural communities are those communities with fewer than 10,000 permanent residents, in non-metropolitan counties of New York State, excluding all towns in the Catskill mountain region, in Westchester county, and on Long Island.
> Small-town Jews are persons identifying themselves as being Jewish living in "rural communities" having 10 or fewer Jewish families.

The first of the two studies was an attempt to document and analyze the background, beliefs, and behavior of small-town Jews and to study and record their attitudes relating to the communities where they reside. We were particularly anxious to explore the areas of religiosity, community satisfaction, associations, and patterns of socialization.

Respondents were located through initial contact with twenty individuals who were known to the writer; each lived in a small town in one of twenty different counties. These persons provided the names of all the Jews they knew who fit the criteria established for designating "small-town Jews." These persons, in turn, supplied additional names. This technique provided 180 names in two weeks.

Of the 180 names twenty were randomly selected; and these individuals and their families, together with the original key informants, were personally interviewed in the Spring of 1958. The 160 in the remaining group were mailed detailed questionnaires which asked a number of questions about origins, family life, satisfaction with small-town living, religious beliefs and practices, organizational affiliations, and attitudes about their relative isolation.

In *every* instance—whether in the interview setting or in responding to the survey—respondents were told that research was being conducted on Jews living in small towns and that *their* help was needed to tell *their* story accurately. In no cases did those to be personally interviewed refuse to cooperate; and in the case of the mail survey, 80 percent responded.[3]

The second study was designed to gather information on the impressions and attitudes of small-town community leaders about themselves and their images and attitudes about minority groups. Data were collected on the relationship between generalized prejudices and attitudes toward Jews, Negroes, and "foreigners"; the extent to which isolated Jewish persons might influence stereotypes; and the nature of interpersonal contact and socialization between Gentiles and Jews in rural communities.

The names of community leaders were obtained by writing to the mayor or clerk of each village selected and asking that a form designating 25 statuses of leadership—in business, the professions, in government and politics, in education and social service, and in agriculture—be filled out with the appropriate names and returned.

Twenty towns were included in this second survey. All had fewer than 5,000 residents. Ten towns had from one to three Jewish families; the remaining group had none.

In all, 315 questionnaires which complemented those sent to Jewish participants were mailed. With two follow-up appeals a total of 60 percent were returned.[4]

JEWISH LIFE IN THE RURAL COMMUNITY

Dealers and doctors. Almost to a man the Jews of New York's rural areas are outsiders and not native sons. Most are urban-emigrants who settled in small towns after having spent the early part of their lives in American or European cities. Only 4 percent were born in the communities where they now live. Of the remaining majority half were born in one of the large American metropolitan centers and 12 percent in middle-sized cities in the United States. Thirty percent were born in Europe, many of them refugees from Nazi-dominated Germany and Austria.

How did these urban Jews happen to settle in such hamlets? Two-thirds came for business reasons. These are, in the main, second generation East European immigrants. Many began their careers as traveling salesmen and peddlers who settled down and started a little general store in one of the towns along the circuit. Here they remained and here they prospered.

In addition to these "dealers," the other major group are refugee physicians who fled to America only to find it difficult to establish practices in urban areas. A large number of such doctors were placed in small towns by refugee agencies or professional groups.

Besides these two major groups, there are several lawyers, teachers, insurance brokers, cattle dealers, and farmers to be found within the sample group.

When asked to place themselves into the upper, upper middle, lower middle, or working class, 74 percent marked "upper middle." Only three respondents felt they were "working class": two teachers and one tenant farmer. It was from the ranks of the professional people that the greatest percentage of "upper class" self-ratings came. The high self-evaluation of socio-economic status is reflected in the relatively high incomes of the small-town Jews. In response to the question "Roughly, what was the total income for your family last year?" 30 percent said their income exceeded $20,000, 37 percent gave $10,000–$20,000, 30 percent $5,000–$10,000, and only 3 percent indicated that they made less than $5,000 per annum.

Owing to the large proportion of professional Jews in the sample (36 percent), it is not surprising to find a high level of education. Seventy percent of those questioned hold at least a Bachelor of Arts degree or its European equivalent. The small-town Jews indicated, however, that only 11 percent of their parents had college diplomas and 56 percent said that their parents had gone to the eighth grade or less. As for their own children, nine out of ten parents in the sample indicated that one or more of their children would (or did) obtain at least a college degree.

When asked about their political affiliations 27 percent said they consider themselves Republicans "in most political matters"; 29 percent are Democrats and the rest marked "independent." However, it is interesting to note that a number of "Republicans" wrote in the margin of the questionnaire saying that they were "registered Republicans whose loyalty lies in the Democratic camp."

Finally, respondents were asked the following question: "Basically, do you consider yourself more a rural person or more an urban person?" Two-thirds of the group said "urban."

Once a Jew. . . . Eighty-six percent of the small-town Jews placed themselves in some "Jewish" category: Orthodox, Conservative or Reform. *All* expressed some feeling of religious and/or cultural identity with Judaism. Those who said they did not fit into any of the three categories are not apostates as their response to this particular query might appear to suggest. Rather they tended to qualify their answers with statements like: "I'm a liberal Jew," "My family are ethical Jews," or "We're Jews, that's all."

Three-fourths said they belonged to some religious congregation. At the same time almost all persons said they "rarely" or "never" attend religious services since the synagogue to which they belong is too far away. (Estimates ranged from 15 to 100 miles.)

While they are too isolated to establish some form of Jewish communal existence, many keep traditional observances at home. For example, over half celebrate the Passover holidays, 25 percent never serve bacon or ham, and 15 percent maintain strictly kosher homes importing meat from distant cities. The attempt to maintain the traditions of the faith is found in both the "immigrant" and "refugee" groups. The latter, however, is less likely to display Jewish and Israeli artifacts in the home.

The deep-seated sense of Jewish-identification is evident in the following random excerpts from several interviews:

> I came to this community from New York. There I was raised in a real ghetto. All my friends and associates were Jews. I went to *heder*, to *shul*, etc., like everybody else. This

> was our way of life. Although I wanted to get out of the city and away from the ghetto, I never wanted to forget I was a Jew. This is my fate and I try to live up to it in every way.

Another person phrased it this way:

> Most people like us are city-folk living in rural areas. While our homes are here, our roots are somewhere else. . . . We bring the past with us when we go into upstate communities like this. Part of this past is our religion. We see ourselves as Jews and so does the community. . . .

All told, most small-town Jews maintain some affective connection with their religion even when they leave the geographic boundaries of the urban Jewish community.

A housewife summed up the expressions of many when she said:

> We're not what one might call observant Jews. Yet there are certain traditions we like to keep. We have a *mezuzah* in the doorway and a *menorah* on the mantel. We celebrate some of the holidays like the High Holy Days and Passover. We light the *shabbas* candles and things like that. And, I must say I like a good piece of *gefilte* fish when I can get it. Yet we eat pork, work on Saturday . . . why sometimes I even go to Midnight Mass with my friends.

"Irrespective of whether you follow religious practices or attend synagogue, do you consider yourself a religious person?" Each person answered this question by placing himself somewhere along a continuum of "very religious" to "not religious at all." Five percent considered themselves "very religious," while 62 percent felt that they were "moderately" so. Thirty-six percent said "somewhat religious" and 7 percent said they were "not religious at all."

A strikingly high correlation appeared when one compares the degree to which a person considers himself religious with the extent to which he practices religious observances, and with the nature of affiliation, that is, whether Orthodox, Conservative, or Reform. Taking these three items together we constructed the Religiosity Scale which allowed us to simplify analysis by using this single measure of "traditional" religiousness. Respondents were broken into three groups: high, medium, and low on religiosity.

In communities having several Jewish families the presence of co-religionists tends to reinforce religious identity and to support religious practices. Table 1 graphically illustrates the fact that in towns with more Jews, religiosity is higher among Jewish respondents.

Table 1. Religiosity and the Number of Jews

Religiosity	Number of Jewish Families in Town			
	1	2	3–5	6–10
	%	%	%	%
Low	66	62	59	42
Medium	27	32	26	26
High	7	6	15	32
	100	100	100	100
	(31)	(21)	(44)	(24)

In addition to this demographic factor it was found that religiosity is correlated with several background factors. Those highest in socio-economic status (by self-rating and income) are lowest in religiosity. In relation to occupation, those in the medical arts (mainly of the refugee group) are most apt to be low in this expression of religiousness, while those in agriculture tend to be the highest. This was borne out in the interviews. We spoke to the daughter of an immigrant from Russia, a man who became a cattle-dealer in a small upstate community where he raised his family. She related:

> Our religion was very important to us. We sang Hebrew songs and spoke Yiddish in the house. I couldn't speak English until I first went to school. . . . To my father the family was the core of Jewish life and so we learned about Jews and our religion through discussions at home, through books, through stories. We were always very Jewish.

And a Jewish farmer had this to say:

> It's funny, but though we're really out of touch with Jews we're the ones who try to keep up the traditions. . . . We think of ourselves as more Orthodox than anything. You know, the Gentile farmers around us are pretty religious too. If you can't go to church, then you have to bring religion into the home.

Furthermore, we found that small-town Jews who are low in religiosity are more apt to see themselves as more "urban" than "rural" even though these very people live, most often, in the tiniest hamlets. And those low in religiosity tend to feel Gentile members of the community consider them "different from" rather than "typical of" most Jews while those highly religious stress the reverse; they feel non-Jews think they are typical of Jewish people.

Although respondents were asked the difficult question of telling how they felt others saw them, it seems that they answered mainly in terms of their own self-images. Among those who said they felt they were viewed as "different" the following kinds of reasons were given: "don't conform to stereotypes," "better assimilated," "differ in physical features," "gentler and less crude," "quieter." Most of the adjectives were related to personal demeanor. Moreover, this group felt that Gentiles considered them as "unique" Jews and suggested that they were more likely to be seen as exceptions to commonly held beliefs.

Those who felt they were seen as "typical" tended to give quite opposite reasons; reasons which were related to positive stereotypic images. "I'm wealthy and well-educated," "I still maintain the traditions and practices of Judaism," "have a Jewish name." In other words, these people felt they were viewed as recognizably Jewish, and most expressed the belief that their behavior was, for Gentiles, typical of Jews.

Ambassadors to the Gentiles. Being strangers in a Gentile world, many respondents appear to be more conscious of being Jewish than do their urban cousins who live in the centers of ethnic communities. In one form or other *every* respondent indicated that there are times when he is called upon to represent *the Jews*. Here, as several stated, they are "ambassadors to the *goyim*." Most often this occurs when interfaith functions are held in the community. There the local priest and minister are accompanied by the Jewish merchant to "give balance to the program."

Frequently the Jew serves as a "representative of his people" in less formal settings. He is called upon to give "the Jewish point of view" or to explain why Jews do one thing and not another. When the townsfolk turn to the Jews for information, the respondents related that they often feel a deep sense of responsibility and of inadequacy.

For example, one man told me:

You know, we're curiosities around town. The people always heard about Jews but never met one. Then we appeared. Real live Jews. After some hesitancy they began to ask us all kinds of questions. . . . Often I wished I could answer all of them. . . .

A housewife allowed:

My children have been asked to explain about *Chanukah*, to tell the story of Moses, to explain what the *Mogen David* is. They wanted to know and my kids were the likely ones to ask.

And a merchant had this to say:

"I can't understand it. As kids we learned that the Jews killed Christ. Tell me, [respondent's name]," he says to me, "is it true?" As a Jew, and the only one this guy ever knew personally, I'm supposed to have all the answers.

Friends among neighbors. In small towns Jews find that there are few limitations on formal and informal social participation and interaction. All but 17 percent indicated that they were members of some mixed organization. Over 45 percent said they belonged to professional, business, and social groups. In addition, one-third are members of fraternal orders like the Masons or Elks.

When asked which organization (national or local) gave them the most satisfaction, almost every respondent listed some local (thereby non-Jewish) group. A druggist had this to say:

I think I've been a member of every damn organization in this town. From member of the volunteer firemen to president of the school board. Discrimination? Not in any organizations, that's for sure.

And the owner of a small chain of department stores said:

This is my community. These are my people in many more ways than Jews are. After all, our neighbors are friendly, all the organizations accept us, so we make friends here. This is home. When I join an organization they know they're taking in a Jew but it doesn't make any difference. . . . I've been President of Rotary, on the Chamber of Commerce, a member of the Masonic Lodge, and Secretary of the Rod and Gun Club.

This reflects the attitudes of most people interviewed.

We asked questions about discrimination against Jews. Eighty-seven percent said they could not think of any community organizations they would not wish to join because of antisemitic feeling. In addition, 81 percent said they knew of no discrimination of any kind being practiced in their communities.

However, it is important to note that while most say they personally have not experienced antisemitism, many are of the opinion that they are being exempted from commonly held stereotypes about Jews. Many respondents feel that latent antisemitism exists among some community members, but that Gentiles view *them* as being "different from other Jews." Fortunately we are able to compare these expressions with those of non-Jews. In the second study we found that what the Jews feel as the true pulse of community sentiment is not always the reality of the attitudes of Gentiles.

In predicting what we would find along the lines of socializing between Jews and non-Jews we hypothesized that close proximity to Gentile neighbors and the lack of opportunity to have day-to-day contact with members of a Jewish community would lead to a degree of intimate interfaith socializing unparalleled in larger communities. The majority of persons who were interviewed substantiated this prediction. For example:

> Everyone has close friends. In the city Jewish people tend to cling together. But in the rural village, when you are a minority of one, you associate completely with Gentiles. While it's rare in the city for Jews and Gentiles to be invited to one another's home for informal visiting, this is an everyday occurrence in the little community.

In the small towns Jews are more than participants in formal community functions. In most instances they are an integral part of the social life of their towns. For the adults this includes such activities as parties, trips, dances, bridge clubs, and just plain "dropping in." For the children this often means playing together, going to parties, and frequent instances of dating.

In over 50 percent of all cases small-town Jews designated a Gentile person as their closest friend. Yet, 30 percent said they feel "more comfortable" with Jews than with non-Jews, especially in social situations. Those highest on religiosity, identifying most strongly with traditional Judaism, are most apt to feel this way.

And the next generation. That the strength of identification with Judaism plays a major role in determining patterns of and feelings about informal socializing with Gentiles becomes even clearer when we examine the attitudes of Jewish parents toward their children. Since 90 percent of the respondents are parents, we were able to get reactions to a number of questions; reactions which indicate a firm conviction that Jewish identity should not only be maintained but intensified. Thus, while a high degree of informal interaction is practiced, the small-town Jews, like their urban co-religionists, are anxious for their children to keep the faith and to marry Jews. As a result they send them to Jewish summer camps and, when they are through with high school, encourage them to attend large, metropolitan universities. And, although they themselves are satisfied with rural living, few expect their children to return to the small town after graduation.

Here is the opinion of a retired businessman:

> We've lived here ever since the children—I have three—were born. They grew up among Gentile people. I don't think they ever met another Jew until they were fifteen or sixteen. In no case were they ever discriminated against. My son was captain of the basketball team and played ball for the local Altar Boys Baseball Club. My daughters always went around with local kids and dated boys from school. I can't say I was happy about this, but I didn't try to stop them. Yet, despite a number of crushes on certain fellows, they never got real serious about any of them. . . . When they graduated from high school they all went to college in the city. There they met Jewish people. . . . I'm really happy that my children all married Jews. It's easier that way.

It seems safe to say that the small-town Jew is similar to the city-dwelling Jew to the extent that he wants his children to remain Jews. He is firmly opposed to interfaith marriage. To him this represents either the confrontation of too many social problems or alienation from Judaism: both are considered highly undesirable. Complete assimilation into the Christian community is not the goal of the American Jew. This means giving up a part of himself, a part that sometimes even he cannot explain. Rather, the Jew in New York and "East Podunk" wants to remain a hyphenated American, sharing the "best of both." No better example of this is to be found than in the rural hamlet.

The best of both. Stonequist, Park and others have characterized the Jew as a disturbed marginal man,[5] and eternal stranger[6] unable to reconcile the traditions of his people with the counter-forces of the majority world; "one whom fate has condemned to live in two societies and in two, not merely different, but antagonistic cultures."[7] One might expect to find ample support for such a definition among the small-town Jews who live away from the mainstream of Jewish life. Yet, rather than being on the periphery of two cultures, the ex-urban Jew seems to have internalized the best of each. He is more a part of his community than he is apart from it. He is far more assimilated to the Gentile milieu than his urban cousin. But, as indicated above, he remains a Jew.

While he strongly identifies with fellow Jews—a reference group he can "feel" rather than "touch"—and in many ways expresses a feeling of kinship with his people, he has adapted himself to the folkways of the small town in a variety of ways. He enjoys the advantages of sharing two "cups of life" and, in a word, is bi-cultural. This duality (rather than marginality) causes the majority of respondents to come to agreement with one who stated:

> You see, we feel we have the best of both . . . Judaism with all its tradition, its stress on culture, on learning, on freedom. . . . And the fact that we live in a small town with nice people and good, clean air. . . . We wouldn't trade either for the world.

All told, those who can reconcile the past with the present find that they can share a little of each of their different cultures. Those who find satisfaction in the small community generally seem to agree with one woman who said:

> It's funny. I never thought a city girl like me would like small-town living. But I've changed. I honestly enjoy the lack of sophistication at Home Bureau meetings, the knock-down-drag-out fights at school meetings, the gossip that never escapes anyone. I love the scenery, the simplicity, and the lack of formality here. Sometimes I miss the city. A good play, a concert, a corned beef sandwich! But we get away each year and spend a few days in New York. After about three days I've had enough. I'm ready for home. I want to go back to [name of town].

and with a lawyer originally from New York City:

> I guess having been raised in the city makes you appreciate a community such as this even more than if you were born here. It's just nice not to have to be on the go all the time.

> . . . There was a time when I would have laughed if some-body suggested that I might wind up in the sticks. But here I am and loving every minute of it. People accept you for what you are, not who you are. . . .

Naturally those who gave such enthusiastic testimonials for small-town living were among the most satisfied with their lives in the rural community. Yet only 14 percent of all respondents expressed true dissatisfaction. Two main reasons were most frequently given for disliking the small town. First, there was general dissatisfaction with rural living. "This town is too provincial for me." "Progress is nil. I just wish we could get out." "I'd take the impersonality of the city any day over the gossipy closeness of this burg." The second kind of dissatisfaction related to isolation from other Jews. "Frankly I would be much happier if we could be with Jews more often." "My wife is not happy here. She'd much rather be some place where she can pick up the phone and talk to the girls. We miss Jewish contacts." "If I had it to do over again, I surely wouldn't move out to the sticks. I'd rather be where there are more Jewish people."

Why do they not move out? The answer is provided by a merchant:

> We always plan to leave here for a larger community. My business keeps me here, as it furnishes me with a good income. If I could leave, I would. The small town is too backward for me.

It must be remembered that the dissatisfied residents are deviant cases. The majority of respondents express some degree of satisfaction with their communities. They were either "very satisfied" (50 percent) or "somewhat satisfied" (36 percent).

Satisfaction seems to depend upon whether or not town people are cordial and accepting of strangers. In most cases isolated Jews are, as several interviewees put it, "curiosities and strangers." Generally the burden is on the Jew himself; at least he thinks so. If he accepts the ways of the rural village in which he resides, that is, if he joins the local lodge, contributes to the funds, buys his food and some clothing in town, takes an interest in community affairs, he is "in." According to a storekeeper:

> The secret of a Jew living in a small town—happily—is to assimilate as soon as possible—but, always to remember he's a Jew.

And a doctor said:

> In small rural towns one is accepted for what he is. Religion plays a minor fact in your being accepted. If one is honest and equitable in his dealings with others, you are placed in the forefront of things. . . .

Minority adjustment. The brief description of the findings of our study of Jewish life in the small town are but excerpts from the original report. Yet it is hoped they shed some illumination on the life of the isolated member of one minority group and indicate the role of the ethnic ambassador. From this first study several generalizations are suggested. 1) Those who leave the confines of the ghetto or ethnic community are frequently anxious to seek economic and social betterment, to find acceptance in the new setting without loss of ethnic identity. 2) Once the minority member enters the new "alien" situation, he finds himself in the position of representing his "people" to the community at large. As a stranger his ethnic identity becomes particularly salient to the community and to himself. More often than not, consciousness of minority membership increases when one becomes an isolate. 3) The minority member who lives in the milieu of the majority has infinitely greater opportunity to adapt himself to the folkways of the dominant group than does one who lives in the middle of the ethnic community.

OPINIONS OF COMMUNITY LEADERS

For that part of the research which was designed to tap the attitudes of the majority group we chose to get reactions of community leaders. Such individuals were selected because it was felt that they would have the greatest opportunity to have contact with the widest number of persons in their towns. In addition, being in positions of formal leadership in such small villages (average population 2,500) meant that these same persons would most likely play informal leadership roles as well; they would be the pace-setters for community opinion. It also seemed logical to assume that a higher percentage of community leaders would have closer contact with Jews than rank and file citizens.

Many of the same kind of questions used in the first section of the study were asked of respondents in the second. In addition, a number of items referred directly or indirectly to attitudes about Jews and other minority group members.

Piecing together the varied comments of several different Gentile opinion leaders, all of whom live in one village in central New York State, we have a rough image of "native" small-towners, their attitudes toward the community, general prejudice, and the effects of contact with minority representatives.

> I have lived in this town all my life. . . . I feel that in the small, rural community people are friendly to one another. A common greeting is "Hello Joe" . . . truly a warm feeling, one of belonging. . . . I love it here.

> Well, I'm an American, since before the War of 1812. I guess I feel this makes me a little better. I'm not prejudiced. I just prefer to be with my own kind and I'm sure they'd [Jews, Negroes, and foreigners] prefer to mix together too. . . .

> There are only two Jewish families here and they are highly regarded—one man is a business man. The other is a very fine attorney. No comparison with New York City Jews. They're different. . . .

> I run a store and come into contact with salesmen of different races. I have three Jewish salesmen, all three are good men. There is none of this pushing and trying to sell stuff you don't need like in the city. . . .

The natives. While the small-town Jews are generally outsiders who migrated to the rural community, most of the Gentile respondents were born and raised in their towns or in similar small villages. Only one-fifth of the total group were born in cities and a mere 2 percent were born abroad. Like the Jews, some who came from the outside came for business reasons. But unlike the Jews, most "newcomers" settled down in small towns because of marriage to a community member, because of cheaper housing, or for health reasons.

These people are mainly of old "Yankee" stock with 38 percent claiming that their families—that is, their father's father's family—came to America before 1800. Members of this group tend to call themselves "American," "Scotch-Irish," or "Holland-Dutch" in their self-descriptions. Those whose families immigrated during the nineteenth century are more apt to be of German or Irish descent. The most recent group are most often of Italian origins.

The occupations of those respondents are widely varied, ranging from farmers to bankers, from ministers to mill-hands. Like the Jewish small-towners, most place themselves in the upper middle class. Their average annual family income is, however, half of that of the Jewish respondents, i.e. $7,500. Half of the Gentile participants are self-employed as compared with 80 percent of the Jewish group.

Thirty-nine percent of the Gentiles said thay had a college education or had gone beyond college; 64 percent had at least a high school education. Like the Jews they too have high aspirations for their children. Seventy-six percent of these persons are Protestant (the remainder Catholic); two-thirds are Republicans; and two out of every three see themselves as more "rural" than "urban."

When asked about satisfaction with their communities the most typical response was "This is home." By and large the respondents were highly satisfied with their communities (68 percent) and an additional one-fourth expressed moderate satisfaction. For this group community satisfaction is dependent upon such variables as length of residence, the ties one has to one's home town, and the progressiveness of the community.

When asked for comments a highly satisfied respondent wrote:

> This is a small, rural, closely knit community where newcomers have to make every effort to become an insider. The effort, however, I feel is well worth it. We are not too far from a large city (but far enough to be away from the clatter), our school is excellent and religious relations in this community are excellent. While this town is pretty conservative, I find a great deal of satisfaction in the slow, easy-going pace. I've lived here since I was a boy and wouldn't leave for anything.

For contrast here is the comment of a dissatisfied resident of the *same* community.

> Passivity, complacency and a sheer lack of or neglect of economic intellect in this community has been responsible for the apparent degeneration of atmosphere and attitude in all things related to even a reasonable degree of progress. This, of course, offers nothing of value to the high school generation. It offers nothing to newcomers. All in all, a community

which was once great is slowly but most certainly annihilating itself.

Ethnocentrism and "the good old days." In some instances dissatisfaction with one's town is unrelated to whether the community is a good place to live and work or not; rather it seems to depend upon the image of what the town itself should be (or what it might have been) and what it has become.

Although the lack of change or progress appeared the most significant factor for dissatisfaction with community life, there are some residents who have *become* dissatisfied precisely because changes have occurred. Not the least of these changes is the influx of outsiders to a number of small towns. In almost every village included in our sample there were two or three respondents who longed for the old days, who resented the intrusion of newcomers, who could not accept change as progress.

Several examples serve to illustrate their attitudes:

> I am sure foreign people make a mistake in keeping customs of their own land alive and featured in this country. If this country meets their expectations, they should forget the folklore of Europe, St. Patrick's Day Parades, German Days, and get behind American things. If they can't do this they should be returned to the land they love. This country is supposed to be the world's melting pot. If they won't melt, they should not belong.

> We have a lot of foreigners here. . . . They're all right, keep in their own place, go to their own church. But I must say it isn't really the same any more. This town has a great heritage, it was settled before the Revolution. . . . I don't mean to imply that I am prejudiced or that I dislike foreigners. We all have our place in this great country of ours. I just think it a shame that outsiders like those who live here, have to keep their old ways. It makes it harder for them to be accepted.

These persons were among a small group of respondents (21 percent) who agreed with the following statement: "This country would be better off if there were not so many foreigners here." They were also in agreement with "Religions which preach unwholesome ideas should be suppressed," as were 56 percent of the sample group; and with the statement "Americans must be on guard against the power of the Catholic church," with which one-quarter of all respondents also agreed.

Such attitudes indicate ethnocentric thinking. A Scale of Ethnocentrism based upon responses to the first two questions cited above and one which stated "Some people say that most people can be trusted. Others say you can't be too careful in your dealings with people. How do you feel about it?" was used to assess general prejudice.

A high degree of ethnocentrism is, in most cases, highly correlated with poor paying jobs, low educational attainment, small-town origins, occupations involving working with "things" rather than "people," and "old family" status. If one is ethnocentric, one tends to be more "success-oriented" and less apt to want to be "independent." The highly ethnocentric individual is more likely to indicate a need to belong and express a strong desire to be accepted by others. Those who see themselves as being *upper class* and those who feel they belong to the *working class* are higher in their distaste for outsiders than "middle-class" individuals. Little difference is found between Catholics and Protestants or along political lines.

Does the opportunity to interact with minority members affect the general prejudice expressed by the small-town Gentile? Without a panel study over time it is virtually impossible to answer this query. However, the data do indicate that contact is related to the amount of generalized ethnocentrism one feels, but *only* when this contact is close enough to permit social interaction to accur. As will be noted in Table 2, those who have close association with Jews and Negroes have a much lower degree of ethnocentrism than those who rarely communicate with members of these two groups or have no contact in the community at all.

Attitudes towards Jews and the "exemption mechanism." Prejudice against Jews is more prevalent in the attitudes of the Gentiles (at least among community leaders) than the Jews themselves imagine. Many of the community leaders subscribe to traditional stereotypes about Jews. For instance, 83 percent agree with the statement "Jews tend to be more money-minded than most people"; 80 percent agree that "Jews tend to be shrewder businessmen than most people"; and 77 percent agree that "Jews tend to be more aggressive than most people."

Thus most of the respondents feel that Jews in general possess these "characteristic traits." Whether or not a Jew lives in town is not crucial for changes in stereotyping. Merely buying in a "Jewish store" or visiting a Jewish physician may only perpetuate generalized images of Jews. Many of the small-town Jews in New York State do, in fact, fulfill several of the classic stereotypes; especially for those who never get to know them individually. As a group, they are frequently in business. They are more

Table 2. Ethnocentrism and the Nature of Contact with Jews and Negroes Living in the Community

Degree of Ethnocentrism	Jews			Negroes		
	No Contact*	Impersonal Contact†	Personal Contact‡	No Contact*	Impersonal Contact†	Personal Contact‡
	%	%	%	%	%	%
High	32	33	10	30	50	13
Medium	34	32	36	36	14	31
Low	34	35	54	34	36	56
	100	100	100	100	100	100
	(88)	(46)	(39)	(124)	(14)	(39)

* "No Contact" means that respondents say there are no members of this group living in their community and also includes those who "don't know" whether or not the group is represented in their town.

† "Impersonal Contact" refers to respondents who say they know members of this group but only "to speak to" or someone they "see around."

‡ "Personal Contact" refers to respondents who say they know members of this group who call *them* by their first names, to whom they can say what they really think, or close friends with whom they can discuss confidential matters.

liberal politically. They do tend to possess an urbane demeanor and are thus natural recipients of the traditional suspicions of "city slickers." And their children, being strongly motivated, do tend to do especially well in school. Here there is ample support for the "kernel of truth" hypothesis.

Yet expressions of attitudes and actual behavior are sometimes contradictory. Close examination of the data disclosed the fact that when interaction takes place at an *equal status* level, community leaders, even those with negative images of Jews as a group, tend to accept individual Jews as exceptions to the rule. They see them as being "different."

In general, respondents who have personal and intimate contact with local Jews view their close acquaintances as less clannish, quieter, less flashy, and less radical than they imagine Jews to be. Here are three excerpts of statements appearing on the last page of the mailed questionnaire.

> My experience as to Jewish residents of this community is probably not typical. A high-class, wealthy, cultured, refugee Jewish family came here in 1940 and we have been very close friends ever since then, both professionally and socially. They seem, to me, very different from most Jews.

> Frankly, I'm not too fond of Jews. I've heard too much about how they stick together, how they can chisel you, how they try to get ahead. Yet, here in —— there is a Jewish family who are not at all like this. They are fine, intelligent, honest citizens and very close friends of ours.

> When the —— came to this community everyone was suspicious. We knew what Jews were like and we didn't like what we knew. After a while we found that they were pretty nice folks. We looked at them as a different kind of Jew. They didn't seem the Brooklyn type. Thinking about it now I have the feeling that our children build their image of what a Jew is supposed to be from the contact they have with the children of this Jewish family. Sometimes we have warped ideas about what we think is true. . . .

Repeated *personal* and *informal* contact in the home and around town can serve as a significant factor leading towards the ultimate reduction of prejudice against Jews. Exemption is perhaps an important intermediate step in breaking down predispositions towards minority groups.

One further statement serves to illustrate this proposition:

> When a Jewish family first moved in we wanted them to prove themselves to us. It must have been hard on them but they came through like troopers. They became an important part of the community. They showed us a different kind of Jew. No Shylock. Knowing them for twenty years now when I think of Jews I think of them. I used to think about some mean, hook-nosed character.

Majority reaction. The following generalizations are tentatively offered based upon the study of the community leaders of twenty small towns in New York State: 1) In the small community the minority group member is constantly in direct contact with the majority group. As he gets to know their ways, they cannot help but get to know him. He stands upon the threshold of influencing deep-seated images. He can reinforce such images or aid in the recasting of these by those with whom he interacts. 2) The isolated minority member rarely constitutes a threat to the established order and community members are often willing to accept the individual outsider despite articulated expressions of prejudice. 3) Repeated and intensive contact and personal association often tend to change the mental picture of the isolate from being "different from" to be "typical of" the group he represents. Exemption is viewed as an instrumental step in the ultimate reduction of prejudice.

A FINAL NOTE

On the basis of the two studies reported here, it is logical to predict that increasing interaction with Jewish "representatives," especially those who have spent their early years in the small town, would have a decided effect on changing the overall attitudes of Gentiles toward Jews. A study of the children of small-towners would provide the information needed to test this hypothesis. But any research of this kind would necessarily have to be conducted in the very near future.

As is stated in the summary of the original report:

> Another prediction is, unfortunately perhaps, in order. With the tremendous rate of post-teen out-migration on the part of the offspring of Jews living in rural communities we wonder whether the small-town Jew is, in reality, a disappearing type in the spectrum of American Jewry. Most Jews who settled in small villages did so prior to World War II. Since that time few have chosen to live in such communities. Now the children are grown and rapidly leaving the nest to live in larger centers. Although some children will return to run the business, our studies suggest that small as it now is, the population of American Jews living in small communities will increasingly diminish in the years to come. . . .[8]

NOTES

1. See, for example, Toby Shafter, "The Fleshpots of Maine," *Commentary*, 7 (January–June 1949), 60–67; Earl Raab, "Report from the Farm," *Commentary*, 8 (July–December 1949), 475–479; Harry Golden,

"The Jews of the South," *Congress Weekly*, 31 December 1951; Lee J. Levinger, "The Disappearing Small-Town Jew," *Commentary*, 14 (July–December 1952), 157–163; Louise Laser, "The Only Jewish Family in Town," *Commentary* (December 1959), 489–496; and a letter to the Editor from Gerald M. Phillips, "Jews in Rural America," *Commentary* (February 1960), 163.

2. This research was supported by The Anti-Defamation League of B'nai B'rith, 315 Lexington Avenue, New York City. The original manuscript is entitled *Strangers in Their Midst, A Sociological Study of the Small-Town Jew and His Neighbors*, Cornell University, 1959. The project title was that of the "Cornell Community Studies."

3. Approximately 25 percent of those who did not respond were randomly selected and attempts were made to interview each. Of this group two persons claimed they were no longer Jews and refused. Both were German refugees and had married non-Jews *prior* to their immigration to America. Two persons were deceased. The remaining group all identified themselves as Jews. Four permitted themselves to be interviewed and the information gathered was consistent with that of the less reluctant respondents. One individual refused to be interviewed and expressed the general feeling that such a study could do little to enhance Jewish-Gentile relations.

4. That slightly less than two thirds responded suggests the possibility of a selective bias in the second part of the study. Time and budget did not permit the personal follow-up of non-respondents similar to that in the first study.

5. Everett V. Stonequist, *The Marginal Man: A Study in Personality and Culture Conflict*, New York, 1937; and Robert E. Park, "Human Migration and the Marginal Man," *American Journal of Sociology*, 33 (1928), 881–893.

6. Georg Simmel, "The Stranger," *The Sociology of Georg Simmel*, Kurt H. Wolff, trans., Glencoe, Ill., 1950, 402–408; and Robert E. Park and Ernest W. Burgess, *Introduction to the Science of Sociology*, Chicago, 1921, 286.

7. Park, "Human Migration . . . ," *op. cit.*, 891.

8. Rose, *op. cit.*, 279–280.

IT DID HAPPEN HERE
An Investigation of Political Anti-Semitism: Wayne, New Jersey, 1967

RODNEY STARK / STEPHEN STEINBERG

INTRODUCTION

SCHOOL BOARD ELECTIONS are normally the dullest, least publicized, and most uncontested elections in American politics. Rarely do more than the most dedicated voters appear at the polls. Yet, in February, 1967, such an election in the previously obscure township of Wayne, New Jersey, suddenly attracted nationwide news coverage. A responsible public official had transformed a typical humdrum campaign into the first significant outbreak of overt anti-Semitic electioneering in America for some years.

In the Wayne election, five candidates were running for three vacancies on the school board. Two of the candidates were Jews, one of whom was an incumbent. One week before the election, both Jewish candidates were singled out for attack in a newspaper interview by Newton Miller, school board vice president:

"Most Jewish people are liberals, especially when it comes to spending for education. If Kraus and Mandell are elected . . . and Fred Lafer [a Jewish board member not up for election] is in for two more years, that's a three-to-six vote. It would only take two more votes for a majority, and Wayne would be in real financial trouble.

"Two more votes and we lose what is left of Christ in our Christmas celebrations in our schools. Think of it."

During the last week of the campaign, despite a furor which included his censure by both the school board and the township council, the publication of dozens of sharp protests by officials and clergymen, and coverage by national press and network television, Miller apologized but refused to retract his statement.

Reprinted by permission of the authors and the Anti-Defamation League.

On election day public leaders and officials in Wayne, Jewish and Christian alike, were confident that the injection of prejudice would be overwhelmingly repudiated at the polls. "Open political anti-Semitism simply is no longer tolerated in American life," was the way one observer put it. It seemed a reasonable judgment.

But when the votes were counted the two Jewish candidates had been buried in a landslide as had the proposed school budget. And so this rapidly growing bedroom community of more than 45,000 people, only twenty miles from New York City, raised once more the spectre of political anti-Semitism in America. It couldn't happen here, but it did. Could it happen elsewhere?

The authors, both of whom are participating in the University of California Five-Year Study of Anti-Semitism, immediately went to Wayne to see if there was any clear answer to this question. After talking to leaders, officials, clergymen, teachers, and knocking on doors and interviewing voters, a coherent picture began to emerge. The factors which led to the anti-Jewish voting in Wayne were neither bizarre nor altogether idiosyncratic. Perhaps a similar event could not occur everywhere, but it seems very probable that it could occur in any of the hundreds of American towns that are much like Wayne. This makes the lesson of Wayne extremely important, if future Waynes are to be prevented.

To account for what happened in Wayne, three classes of factors must be isolated, understood, and assembled:

1. The historical and structural strains present in the community;
2. The actual precipitating events;
3. The process by which various sectors of the community came to form conflicting definitions of the situation.

I: SOURCES OF STRAIN

A Legacy of Prejudice

Like many American communities, Wayne's past is marred by bigotry. In the 1920's when the Ku Klux Klan surged beyond the South to a brief nationwide membership, a chapter was located in Wayne. In the 1930's, long before Wayne became a large suburb and while it was still a small country community, a German-

American Bund, complete with Nazi armbands, was operating there. But as elsewhere in America (except for the South) these organized hate groups died out with the advent of World War II.

By the late 1950's America began to experience stirrings of neo-Nazi feelings among scattered groups of young people. On cue, Wayne produced a local instance. In April of 1959, fourteen boys in the local high school were discovered to be involved in what they called "The Nazi Regime of America." A threat against a Jewish teacher prompted an investigation which resulted in the confiscation of Nazi uniforms, swastika flags, armbands, and a revolver.

In the summer of 1965 a cross was burned at a Jewish-owned industrial site. The owner had earlier received abusive phone calls. Three youths confessed these acts. Again in October several threatening phone calls were received at the Jewish temple and "Jews Stink" was soaped on the car of a Jewish resident.

One might expect these incidents to have shocked public sentiments. Instead, they were dismissed as boyish pranks. As a local newspaper commented on the most recent incident: "The use of soap . . . is reminiscent of similar pranks prevalent around Halloween."

The reluctance of the authorities and civic leaders to define these incidents as anti-Semitic reflects their unwillingness to admit the existence of any intergroup tensions in Wayne. It also promoted an insensitivity to prejudice which helps to explain why Wayne residents failed to recognize anti-Semitism when it appeared in their school board election.

Nevertheless, Wayne cannot be explained simply in terms of pre-war bigotry, if only because the Wayne of today is a different town with mostly different citizens. Nor can the acts of prejudice of a few youths be taken as proof that Wayne is an unusually prejudiced town. Such incidents have occurred in many places across the nation, but have not presaged anti-Semitic voting. The Wayne affair requires a more complex explanation.

A Divided Community

In many ways Wayne is a political fiction. The reality behind the name is a conglomeration of a half-dozen distinct residential communities, each committed to its own name. There is not even any real physical unity to Wayne. Several of its communities are separate geographic units set apart by highways that meander through the suburban sprawl called Wayne. There is no downtown. Instead there are several shopping centers, small islands of commerce and parking adrift in a residential sea. Public buildings, schools, and churches are similarly dispersed, standing alone amid houses. Thus, the town lacks any common center and its physical disunity both reflects and sustains the deeper social chasms that divide the community.

Two large sections of Wayne—Packanack Lake and Pine Lake—have been restricted communities, closed to Jews, Negroes, Southern Europeans, and virtually anyone who is not white, Anglo-Saxon and Protestant.

The core of each community is its lake club which functions as country club, community association, swimming, boating and hunting club, youth center, and, finally, as sole arbiter of who may buy a house in the community. Deeds of homes and lots in the area bounding the lakes contained a restrictive covenant stipulating that property could only be conveyed to or occupied by persons who were members of the lake clubs. As private organizations, the clubs escaped the state's anti-discrimination laws; by excluding Jews from their memberships, they also excluded them from their neighborhoods. The result is that thousands of Wayne residents live in areas where Jews are implicitly defined as socially undesirable. In 1966, the Packanack Lake property covenant was struck down by the courts. Consequently, it is doubtful whether Wayne's lake covenant system will be functioning much longer.

Jews are not the only victims of social discrimination. The evidence suggests that Wayne epitomizes American patterns of prejudice. Catholics often are excluded by Protestants. Jews are excluded by both Protestants and Catholics. And Negroes are excluded by all three groups. The result is that some of Wayne's residential areas are drawn largely along religious lines, and that the town has virtually no Negroes (at last report, 36 in a population of 45,000).

This pattern of social segregation is a form of accommodation which prevents open conflict between Christians and Jews. Each group lives in a socially autonomous community, and contact between the two groups is minimal. However, in local elections, one of the few activities that involves the entire community, Jewish candidates were frequently elected. These two facts—the absence of overt clashes between Christians and Jews, and the success of Jewish candidates running for public office—led to a myth that, as an editorial in the local newspaper put it, "Christians and Jews were living in harmony and brotherhood." This myth was accepted by Jews as well as Christians. It was shattered, at least for the Jewish community, by the school board election. As the rabbi confessed in an interview, "I did not fully understand the impact of having two closed communities in Wayne." Clearly, Wayne's segregated communities engender considerable strain, even if it is covert. Recognition of this fact is essential for an understanding of the events surrounding the school board election.

Yet too much should not be made of the divided character of the community. If Wayne is slightly out of the ordinary in the extent and openness of its discrimination in housing and club life, it is not sufficiently unusual to account for the events that occurred.

The Ills of Growth

As are hundreds of other communities on the fringes of metropolitan areas, Wayne is booming.

In 1950 it had 12,000 residents. By 1960 its population was 29,000 and today more than 45,000 people live in Wayne. Although several industries have recently moved large offices to Wayne, the boom is primarily residential. Wayne is basically a bedroom community with more than 90 percent of the employed males working outside the county—primarily in nearby Paterson and in Newark, but a few commute to New York, less than 30 minutes away through the Lincoln Tunnel.

Both the enormous growth (exacerbated by a very high turnover of residents) and the bedroom character of the town have produced a relatively structureless, unintegrated community. Wayne is inhabited by strangers and recent acquaintances.

As a result, public officials and civic leaders—themselves newcomers—are only tenuously linked to the general public. As past studies of suburbia have shown, because leaders lack extensive ties with the grass roots, their power is quite low. Thus, communities such as Wayne are subject to rapid changes of mood and outlook because the stabilizing effects of an influential and established leadership are lacking. This lack of influential leadership proved to be extremely important in Wayne when the public sought to understand and define what was going on in the election campaign.

Rapid growth has produced other strains in Wayne besides disorganization. School enrollment has been increasing by about 800 students a year; the equivalent of one new grade school must be constructed annually to accommodate them. The constantly accelerating costs of education have recently begun to provoke taxpayer resistance. Furthermore, taxes and assessments have also been increasing as new roads, sewers, and public buildings are required to meet the demands of growth. Wayne residents are especially sensitive to these increasing costs of local government because it is not a high income community. In 1960 half of the families earned less than $8,300. The typical taxpayer is a young, lower-white-collar worker, deeply indebted for his house, car, and furniture. Thus increasing taxes and special assessments fall upon families already living at the outer edge of their income.

Compounding this strain between family budgets and the needs of community expansion is a school law that requires the board to submit its budget to the taxpayers for approval annually. This permits direct and easy public intervention into complicated school financing issues, even when they do not require higher taxation. Recently Wayne has been building to a school crisis. Per capita spending on education is presently behind that of neighboring communities, as are teachers' salaries. Because of their need not only to hold their faculty, but to expand it greatly each year, the Wayne School Board proposed sizable pay increases in 1967. Under the Wayne system, teachers' salaries are not merely public. They are publicized and discussed as a voting issue. Some residents expressed disapproval of the fact that top teacher salaries exceeded their own. "Why should they make more than we do when we pay the bills?" one woman said indignantly. Furthermore, facts about the budget have been hard to disseminate in this structureless, nearly leaderless, community. Few residents seemed to have heard that Wayne's educational bills were lower than in similar communities. This lack of effective communication proved fatal when the election crisis occurred.

In God We Trust

The people of Wayne clearly share the prevalent American anxiety over the demise of school prayers and religious teaching in the public schools. A recent national survey showed that more than three out of four Americans approve of Christmas carols and prayers in the public schools. Wayne would be a very odd community if its residents did not share these sentiments.

Wayne's response to court rulings against school prayers was to institute a moment of silent meditation at the beginning of each school day. Urged on by a concerned citizen, the board also installed bronze plaques in each school which read: "In God We Trust." This slogan is also common on bumper stickers in Wayne.

Thus a certain amount of anxiety over the future of religion in the schools also provided a background for what was to come.

The Jewish Influx

Until very recently Wayne was a town virtually without Jews. In 1958 there were about fifteen Jewish families in the community with no temple and no rabbi. Then came a relatively rapid increase. An attractive temple was built, a Reform rabbi was hired, and by 1967 an estimated 850 Jewish families lived in Wayne. Although barred from living in the restricted lake communities, Jews moving to Wayne felt little difficulty in taking up community life in this town of newcomers. They quickly began to participate in civic affairs. By 1967 there were two Jewish members on the nine-member township council. Two of nine members of the school board were also Jews and a third Jew running for the board was considered a likely winner.

Although clearly Jews were not being shunted aside in community-wide public affairs, the influx of Jewish residents had several important consequences. Their presence in increasing numbers helped to activate latent strains in the community. The legacy of bigotry from the past, the fact of lake club discrimination, and the anxiety over religion in the schools now had a relevance that was absent before. With Jews present in sizable numbers the danger of open conflict was real. For those Wayne residents who harbored deep anti-Semitic sentiments, the arrival of a substantial number of Jews may have given new stimulus to their hatred. The subsequent prominence of Jews in civic life must have further exacerbated such resentments.

We have now examined a series of enduring historical and structural sources of strain in relations between Christians and Jews in Wayne. While each played its part in subsequent events, it must be emphasized that these sources of strain hardly produce a unique portrait. A great many American towns could be similarly described. By themselves these factors cannot explain why it happened in Wayne. They were necessary to set the stage for the situational drama which came to pass. But to understand the outbreak of political anti-Semitism it is also necessary to consider several concrete precipitating events.

II: THE PRECIPITATING EVENTS

The Courts Break the Covenant

In retrospect, the first precipitating event of the Wayne affair came in the late Spring of 1966, when the New Jersey courts invalidated restrictive covenants in Packanack Lake, one of the two lake communities. Suit was initiated by two Protestant residents. The case for the plaintiffs revealed the elaborate mechanisms by which the "wrong" people were systematically excluded from either joining the club or buying property in the surrounding area.

The reaction of residents within their lake sanctuaries was strong and fearful. The fear was partly economic. Housing values in these communities are reputed to be considerably above the actual physical worth of the homes. Some portion of this inflation is based on the intangibles of exclusiveness and fashionableness, which are a direct function of the discrimination practiced.

The court action was regarded as a threat to this inflation. This threat was especially acute because it raised more than the spectre of paper devaluation. Local consensus is that the lake community dwellings change hands once every five years. For such transients, changes in the resale prices of homes represent a tangible economic fact.

It is hard to determine whether anxiety over the loss of the covenant influenced the way lake community residents responded to the dispute over anti-Semitism in the school election. That they were fearful and upset by the court decision was reflected in their community newsletters at the time, but these sentiments may have played no direct role in the subsequent voting. Still, it seems reasonable to assume that it did at least make them a bit less willing to oppose anti-Semitism. It seems revealing that while Jack Mandell ran a stronger race in Packanack Lake than in other districts when he was first elected to the school board, he was overwhelmingly rejected by this same district in the most recent election. He was a Jew both times.

Christmas Carols

A slight misunderstanding over Christmas carols in the schools seems to have played only a very minor role in shaping Wayne public opinion, but it perhaps played a major role in prompting Newton Miller's anti-Semitic statement.

Shortly before Christmas the local rabbi met with the Superintendent of Schools to discuss the kinds of Christmas carols appropriate for classroom singing. The fact of their meeting leaked to a local reporter and appeared in the paper giving the impression that there was a dispute going on over Christmas carols. Subsequently, the purpose of the meeting was clarified by the paper and the matter apparently ended.

When questioned later few residents of Wayne recalled that there had been such an event—the circulation of the paper in which the story appeared is not high—and the affair probably had very little impact except among those especially informed about school activities. However, the misunderstanding did appear to disturb Newton Miller at the time. He is reported to have wondered whether there would be any further difficulties over religion in the schools. One can only conjecture whether this event had some effect on him two months later when he drafted his gratuitous and now notorious statement mentioning a Jewish threat to Christ in Christmas.

The School Campaign

Newton Miller was engaged in a typical one-man stand against the rest of the school board over the proposed budget as 1967 began. Furthermore, although more than 100 of Wayne's teachers had threatened resignation this Spring unless their pay was made comparable with that of surrounding communities, Miller demanded substantial cuts in faculty salaries. In his years on the board, the 47-year-old Bell Telephone employee has conducted a personal crusade to slash spending to the bone. For nearly two years he singlehandedly blocked construction of a new high school. He has also conducted an unsuccessful campaign for teacher loyalty oaths. Several years ago, his behavior and statements provoked the school board to censure him.

All other members of the board, and all candidates save one, favored this year's $8½ million budget proposal. Considering Wayne's phenomenal student explosion and the fact that the community spends proportionately less on education than do surrounding towns, this near unanimity suggests, if anything, a modest budget proposal.

Of the five candidates for the three school board vacancies, only Jack McLaughlin opposed the budget. McLaughlin once served on the board, but had been defeated in each of the past two years in efforts to regain his seat. In past elections he had experimented with several different images. This time he was running as a fiscal conservative. But it was hard to tell that he was running at all.

School board and budget elections in Wayne are fought out at dozens of coffee parties held day and night during the weeks before the voting. It is customary for all candidates to appear at each of these coffee hours, in homes throughout the community, and explain their ideas for education in Wayne. In this campaign all went pretty much as usual except that while four of the five candidates regularly attended these meetings, Jack McLaughlin chose to keep out of sight. This tactic drew considerable criticism from the community and earned him ridicule in the local paper. One letter to the editor referred to him as the "phantom candidate."

The campaign for the school budget began in deep trouble. Despite nearly universal support from community leaders, the mood in Wayne was anti-spending and the public disputes between the school and the teachers over pay demands added to voter discontent. But according to experienced officials, who fight a campaign like this at least once a year, the budget was beginning to gather support as the campaign progressed. In the past ten years school budgets have been beaten only once (by a narrow margin in 1965) and it began to seem that once again the budget might pass.

A week before the election, with the budget gaining and the conservative candidate behind, Newton Miller intervened. On Monday evening, February 6, he phoned a local columnist and told her he had some thoughts on the campaign that she might want for the paper. As he began to enunciate his concern about Jewish candidates, the columnist grew uneasy. She asked him if he had his remarks written down. Miller said he did, but not typed. She replied that she would come over and pick them up.

The scene that followed, according to the columnist who is a long-time resident of one of the restricted lake communities, would have caused many men to have second thoughts about making such a statement public. But not Miller. She finally asked him to sign his statement, which he did willingly, and then she took it back to the paper. Tuesday morning she dumped the whole thing on her editor's desk. He immediately recognized the sensational possibilities of the story and Miller's remarks were splashed across page one of the newspaper that afternoon, under the headline: "Miller Warns: Don't Put Mandell, Kraus on Board."

The Reaction

The next day, Wednesday, brought an avalanche of reaction. With one voice, responsible civic and religious leaders deplored Miller's remarks as anti-Semitic, and many called for his immediate resignation. The newspaper filled pages one and two with the denunciations, giving only scant space to a major local blizzard that had brought twelve inches of snow the preceding day. Some typical examples were:

"Mr. Miller has gone off the deep end this time . . . [his statements] are so far off base that they are impossible to give credence to. They are ridiculous and shameless." George Schroeder, president of the school board.

"It's despicable." David Caliri, incumbent school board candidate.

"I deplore this kind of statement. There is no place for an appeal to prejudice." Richard Davis, candidate for the school board.

"These comments are uncalled for." Leonard Pine, Councilman.

"I cannot put into words my reaction to this statement by Newton Miller . . . I am sick over this. I cannot understand bringing religion into this." Andrew Militello, president of the Wayne P.T.A.

Miller, in the face of the potent condemnation that greeted his original statement, tried to call the whole thing misquotation and misunderstanding. Yet, when asked, he reaffirmed the truth of his statements.

By Thursday the national press began to staff the story and the tranquility of the local neighborhoods was interrupted by prowling reporters and television crews. Reactions deploring Miller's remarks began to pour in from farther away, from U.S. Senators Clifford Case and Harrison Williams, and from other political and religious leaders.

That night a dramatic scene unfolded at an emergency school board meeting. Before an emotional crowd of more than 500 townspeople, and the national press corps (while three network television crews filmed the meeting), the school board voted 8 to 1 to "censure Mr. Miller's appeal to bigotry" and called for his resignation. Miller himself cast the lone vote against censure and refused to resign, but rather promised to "serve out my term and do the job I was elected to do for the people of Wayne."

Following the vote, obviously shaken and mystified by the widespread condemnation, Miller rose to deny that he was prejudiced or that his press release had appealed to anti-Semitism. He said he was "truly sorry for the incident," and declared he was prepared to eat "humble crow" [sic]. Yet he refused to retract his original statement. Instead he repeatedly defended it as true, but misinterpreted. To demonstrate his lack of prejudice, he pointed to the fact that he had good friends who were Jews. As evidence he repeatedly referred to his friendship with fellow board member Jack Mandell, one of the two he had attacked in his statement.

Finally, Mandell could endure it no longer. Speaking up for the first time, he turned to Miller, seated next to him, and said quietly, "Newt, you're right. We have been friends. But it grieves me to tell you that you are an anti-Semite and a bigot."

The crowd applauded, while Mrs. Carl Yoder, a board member, wept silently.

Later, Mandell recalled that he had meant to keep silent because he felt that basically anti-Semitism "is a Christian problem," and it was up to the Christians to oppose it. But Miller's performance changed that. "I knew when I spoke that I well may have been jeopardizing my candidacy. But the eyes and ears of the nation were literally upon us and bigger issues were involved. This man had to be told that simply having friendly relations with a few Jews did not exonerate him."

Outside the hall a local history teacher walked a one-man picket line with a placard: "Repudiate Anti-Semitism." A few others circulated a petition asking Governor Richard Hughes to take whatever steps he could to remove Miller from office.

As the meeting broke up, Miller continued to deny that he had meant to cause trouble or to imply anti-Semitism. But he still insisted that his statements were essentially accurate if "correctly understood."

From then on through election night the public outcry increased. The newsmen and TV crews continued to roam the city, and more and more public leaders issued statements decrying bigotry. Wayne had become a seven-day wonder. Each morning residents read new dispatches about their town in the New York as well as local papers and in the evening they watched reports from Wayne on nationwide television news programs.

The town was turning bright red in the glare of press exposure. And it hurt. "My God, they are making a wonderful town sound like Germany, it'll never get its good name back," one resident complained.

The Vote

Condemnations of Miller continued to pour in. In the face of this swift and uniform response by civic and religious leaders, both from Wayne and elsewhere, the outcome of the election seemed certain. As one veteran local observer put it: "Frankly, from the moment I heard about it until the votes were in, I was absolutely certain the Jewish candidates would be elected and that the budget would be a shoo-in. I said to myself, 'Newt has just done the budget the biggest possible favor.' I also thought Miller had committed political suicide. I was sure that you just can't get away with open political anti-Semitism in America anymore." No one, including the Jewish candidates, questioned his logic.

But the voters turned this universal confidence among civic leaders into a shambles. The two Jewish candidates were overwhelmingly defeated, while Jack McLaughlin and two pro-budget candidates were swept in. The school budget lost by a three-to-one margin.

An analysis of the returns makes it clear that the voting singled out the Jews and could not be attributed to a taxpayers' rebellion.

There were apparently three main patterns of voting. A small proportion of voters obviously voted only for the fiscal conservative. But the rest voted for three candidates. A minority cast their ballots for the two Jewish candidates and for David Caliri, a liberal incumbent. A much larger bloc voted for the three non-Jewish candidates: McLaughlin, Davis, and Caliri. Caliri received the most votes because, as one local observer commented, "He was everyone's third man."

How can one be sure that the voting was anti-Jewish? Recall that Jack McLaughlin had not attended the normal campaign functions. His candidacy, which had failed in each of the past two years, was considered a joke before the crisis over anti-Semitism occurred. Yet, he was number two behind Caliri. Richard Davis, the third candidate elected, and also been considered out of the running. He had failed to create any significant public image, though he had favored the school budget. The fact that his own children attended parochial schools created questions in the minds of many voters as to why he wanted to be an overseer of the public school system. This was perhaps another symptom of Wayne's underlying religious prejudice.

Prior to the crisis, the local consensus was that the two Jews and David Caliri were overwhelming favorites. But when the votes were counted it was not even close. The two Jewish candidates trailed the field by a better than two-to-one margin.

Why were the election forecasts of the civic leaders, the candidates, the press, and school officials dead wrong? Were the people of Wayne undeterred, indeed attracted, by open anti-Semitism despite unanimous condemnation by their leaders? Is the veneer of public tolerance so thin that the slightest public provocation releases an uncontrollable backlash? Just what did Wayne voters have in mind when they cast their ballots?

The answers to these questions seem relatively clear, but not simple. They are intimately connected with the complex character of contemporary American attitudes towards Jews and to differences in public conceptions of what anti-Semitism *is*.

III: THE FORMATION OF CONFLICTING DEFINITIONS OF THE SITUATION

The Shades of American Anti-Semitism

Anti-Semitism in contemporary American society bears little resemblance to the classic bigotry of Europe. Our recent empirical studies have shown that only a handful of Americans hold fierce images of a conspiring, subhuman, international Jewry bent on world domination. While about seven percent of Americans do think Hitler was right or partly right in what he did to the Jews, virtually no other Americans will condone actions against Jews such as laws to limit Jewish power. Indeed, few Americans regard Jews as a disproportionately powerful group.

American anti-Semitism is characteristically a matter of shades of grey. Roughly a quarter of the population holds a substantial number of negative stereotypes about Jews as crafty, pushy, greedy, unethical, clannish, and the like. These fall far short of the virulence of the classic European anti-Semitic stereotypes. But they are sufficient for this sector of the populace to know in their hearts that they moderately dislike and distrust Jews. It must be emphasized that their anti-Jewish feelings are not strong enough for them to favor "remedial" laws or actions. They are, however, sufficiently hostile to support some varieties of discrimination.

Such persons can be described as dark grey anti-Semites, in contrast to the black prejudice of hate-mongers such as Gerald L. K. Smith, or the classic European variety of anti-Semitism.

But there is a blander form of anti-Semitism in America, which can be described as light grey. The light grey American anti-Semite holds some of the less noxious beliefs about Jews, but these are not sufficient to cause him to recognize that he dislikes Jews. Perhaps he feels some ambivalence about Jews as a group, but his feelings are not strong enough to intrude in his response to individuals. For such light grey anti-Semites it is actually true that, although they have mild feelings about Jews generally, it is entirely possible for some of their "best friends" to be Jewish. Such persons do not recognize that they are tainted with anti-Semitism because they do not face any internal sense of hostility towards Jews with whom they come in contact. Thus, their sense of innocence goes unchallenged in the day-to-day world.

This distinction between shades of anti-Semitism is crucial for an understanding of the situation in Wayne. Like nearly every American community, Wayne has a small segment of black and dark grey anti-Semites. This is evident from some of the letters that appeared in the local newspaper, as well as from threatening phone calls and similar incidents that occurred during the recent crisis. It is equally clear that many of Wayne's residents are unprejudiced. They hold no invidious attitudes towards Jews as a group, and were willing to take a firm stand against anti-Semitism when it appeared in the election campaign. But if Wayne is at all like other communities in America, the election outcome lay with that substantial number of residents who fall into the light grey area of anti-Semitism. These voters have slightly ambivalent feelings towards Jews as a group, are perhaps even slightly uneasy about the influx of Jews into the community, and will acquiesce when others discriminate against Jews. Yet because their own anti-Semitism is so mild, the contacts they do have with Jews are usually "cordial." As a result they remain unaware of their own prejudice.

The Light Grey Area

In our judgment Newton Miller is unaware of the implications of his beliefs about Jews. In his public life he came into contact with many Jews and evidently dealt amicably with them. It was true when he claimed that Mandell, the Jewish incumbent, was his friend. Mandell publicly acknowledged the friendship and the fact that he and Miller, with their wives, had spent a number of social evenings together. But it was also reported that Miller sometimes made awkward remarks in the presence of his Jewish friends. Thus, like many Americans, Newton Miller was perhaps well-intentioned, but unwitting in his attitudes towards Jews.

Of even greater importance is the fact that what Miller said about Jews in his notorious statement falls into this light grey area of anti-Semitism. It may seem unnecessary to explain here why this is so. However, a great many of Wayne's citizens failed to recognize Miller's remarks as anti-Semitic. In fact, Charles H. Stember, author of two books on anti-Semitism, wrote a letter to the *New York Times* indicating that he could detect nothing anti-Semitic in what Miller said.

First of all, Newton Miller did not charge Jack Mandell and Robert Kraus *directly* as being liberals or big spenders on education. Rather, he said that *because they were Jews* it could be assumed that they were liberals. He ignored the fact that all other board members and all candidates except McLaughlin also favored the proposed budget. Instead, Miller picked out Jewishness, not individual fiscal views, as the key issue. Now it might be the case that a survey would show that Jews in general are more likely than non-Jews to be liberal and favor a high investment in education. Does this reduce Miller's remarks to a simple statement of fact? Hardly. Such a generalization, stated without invidious overtones, might be permissible when the identity of candidates and their personal points-of-view are unknown. But this was not the case, and besides Miller did much more than assert a neutral fact. He further declared, "If Kraus and Mandell are elected . . . and Fred Lafer is in for two more years, that's a three-to-six vote. It would take only two more votes for a majority and Wayne would be in real financial trouble." Thus, not only are Mandell and Kraus deduced to be liberals *because* they are Jews, but Miller seems to argue that *any* five Jews would all vote together to produce financial woes.

Worse yet, according to Miller, these five Jews—whoever they might be—would take Christ out of Christmas in the schools. Miller does not attribute these intentions to specific persons, or even specific Jews, he attributes this threat to *Jews*.

His charges about Christmas do not even have the justification of a distorted truth behind them. Not only does he attribute these intentions to Jews in general, but the charge cannot be given credence both in general and in this particular case. It is reasonable only in the light of an underlying prejudice.

Throughout, Miller suggested that Jews *as such* are not suitable school board members. To warn of Jews in this manner is invidious stereotyping that is only different in virulence, not in kind, from warnings against an international Jewish conspiracy.

However, in the naive perspective of light grey American anti-Semitism, these remarks do not appear to be anti-Semitic at all. The fact that most Americans would not easily perceive the essential prejudice of these charges is one of the keys to what happened in Wayne.

In contrast to Newton Miller, and to the average, mildly prejudiced American, other sectors of our society operate with considerably more sophisticated and sensitive definitions of anti-Semitism. The local columnist who first learned of Miller's statements recognized that the story was sensational. When the local editor, a former New York newspaperman, read the release he also knew immediately that prejudice had been injected into politics. His response was a front-page headline and phone calls to the New York papers and the wire services.

In no newspaper office did anyone need to ponder whether or not Newton Miller was making anti-Semitic charges. Many Wayne residents later criticized the news media for "blowing up" the issue, but when a respected public official begins talking about a Jewish threat in the election, it's news.

Furthermore, no civic, religious, educational, or political leader failed to recognize immediately the open anti-Semitism of the matter. No one defended Newton Miller or his charges; condemnation was universal and strong and swift. Nor did the Jewish community require any coaching to detect the anti-Semitism that had been injected into the election. For them it was clear that again bigotry was threatening Jewish participation in the workings of a democratic society. On the Friday evening before the election 400 members attended services at the local synagogue; the normal turnout is about 100.

Thus leadership, the press, the churches, and the Jews easily arrived at a common definition of the situation: an anti-Semitic incident had occurred and must be opposed.

But for most of Wayne's citizens, as for the average American with his light grey anti-Semitism and his crude notion of what constitutes anti-Semitism, it was *not at all clear* that Newton Miller's charges added up to an anti-Semitic outburst. Rather, they were greatly perplexed about what was going on. What was all the fuss about anyway?

Two Definitions

From the very first, Wayne was separated by two conflicting definitions of the situation: the establishment defined the affair as anti-Semitic, while the bulk of the population could not recognize the anti-Semitism as such.

Beginning with this conflict in initial definition, the course pursued by the establishment led to increasing confusion, incomprehension, and finally to anger and fear among the people. For the tragic fact is that while the statements and acts of censure mounted, indeed became an avalanche, *not a single spokesman effectively explained what was anti-Semitic about Miller's remarks.* Instead, having labelled them as anti-Semitic, most moved on to attack the evils of anti-Semitism, as if Wayne, New Jersey, resembled Nazi Germany. But the people of Wayne could not see what Newton Miller had to do with Nazism. They agreed that anti-Semitism was hideous, but most could not identify anything anti-Semitic in the local controversy.

What then could they see? Mainly they saw an incomprehensible and overwhelming attack on Newton Miller that seemed to lack justification. Although Miller had frequently apologized for causing misunderstanding, because he refused to retract his statements the criticism continued unabated. Unfortunately, the apology, but not the lack of retraction, was widely publicized. Thus, to Wayne citizens the attacks on Miller were not only mysterious, but unrelenting.

"My God," one woman said, echoing the prevalent sentiments of the town, "Newt tried and tried to apologize and they wouldn't accept it. Now I tell you, what do you make of that?"

The local newspaper attributed the following two comments to Wayne teenagers interviewed three days before the election:

> "We've discussed this in class . . . We were upset. We thought the Jewish people should have pardoned Mr. Miller. It's much too blown up."

> "People have said worse things in a campaign. It wasn't the right thing to say but he apologized, what more can he do?"

Another letter to the editor addressed the following to Newton Miller:

> "I would also like to commend you on the public confession and apology you made—to practically the world. I have never yet heard the same apologies offered by any other elected official. You humbled yourself, you admitted any and all mistakes you made—Mr. Miller, we on earth can ask no more of you.
>
> "To err is human—to forgive divine.
>
> "Apparently there are several persons who still want to degrade you, including some of your friends, and political leaders. If this is what is meant by the golden rule then I have nothing but compassion, sorrow and my prayers for them. You have made a mistake, you could have committed murder and been let off easier . . .
>
> "Those who are out to degrade you at this point, if they continue, they are the bigots and should hang their heads in shame."

Still another said in part:

> "All of you who were 'shocked,' refusing his apology, including Mr. Mandell, are nothing more than you accuse him of being . . . Hypocrites. The news media love you all dearly! ! !"

Miller himself complained in all sincerity: "If Jack Mandell had been understanding and extended his hand in the spirit of brotherhood, the Christians of this town would have backed him all the way."

In short, the people of Wayne were dumbfounded by the tidal wave of criticism and nationwide attention that crashed down upon them. They could not see the original cause, so they turned their entire attention to the reaction. It was this that became the issue in Wayne, and it was this that the townspeople ultimately came to define as the unfair attack and the interjection of a religious issue. And it was this that they denounced at the polls.

The *reaction* to anti-Semitism came to be defined in Wayne as the "religious issue," for ironically, many blamed the *Jews* for having injected religious prejudice into the campaign. In interviews with Wayne residents, comments such as the following were common:

> "People around here don't feel that religious issues ought to be raised in politics. That's why they voted that way. Because

the anti-Miller forces tried to put the budget through on a phoney religious issue."

[Note here that by election time the press, the leaders, and the Jews, had come to be referred to in Wayne as the "anti-Miller forces."]

"It was a terrible shame that the Jews caused all this trouble and tried to make it a religious campaign. This is absolutely the first trouble they've caused here in the 8 years I've been here. It was a real shame because it hurt the town so. Why in the world did they do it? Can it really have been worth bringing in all those reporters and ruining the town just to get themselves on the school board? They probably would have been elected if they had just been decent. People really got sore about them trying to stir everything up."

It was through such twisted logic, rooted in incomprehension, that Newton Miller became the embattled underdog. Anti-Semitism never became the issue to the average Wayne voter. For the publicized reactions to Miller failed to educate the people to see that the statements were anti-Semitic. Instead, people could only see public figures and the press of the nation attacking a small-town school board member, and interfering in a local election, ostensibly because of some innocuous statements about Jews *which seemed to be true*. The motives for the attack on Miller remained mysterious. Wayne citizens had to search without effective guidance from their leaders or the press to find a reasonable explanation for what was taking place. Some concluded that the whole thing was a tactic to pass the school budget. Understandably, they thought such tactics were outrageous.

The fact that the majority of Wayne citizens could not recognize Newton Miller's statements as anti-Semitic, and indeed many probably thought they were true, raises another extremely important point about the public denunciations. *No one ever effectively denied the truth of Miller's remarks!*

The Sensitive Nerve

It has become conventional in the battle against bigotry never to dignify the charges of hate merchants by denying them. This is probably the best course when the charges are virulent. On such occasions the mere fact that someone said it identifies him unambiguously and publicly as a bigot. But such tactics are extremely ineffective when the charges fall into the area of light

grey anti-Semitism because a great number of Americans will not recognize such statements as either bigoted or false.

As mentioned earlier, religion in the schools and especially Christmas are very sensitive issues among American Christians. Out of deference to non-Christian children, many, or perhaps most, schools have tried to be somewhat careful in the way Christmas is celebrated and in what carols are sung. So long as a minimum of tact is exercised in these matters, many Jews probably do not regard it as a very important problem. But a certain potential conflict of interests does exist.

However, the fashion in which Newton Miller raised this issue was clearly beyond the bounds of accepted discussion. Clearly he implied that the Jews, like Dr. Seuss' famous Grinch, were out to steal Christmas. This touched an extremely sensitive nerve in the Christian community. Yet the charge was never denied, even though it was false. Neither of the Jews running for the school board reportedly had any objection to the way in which religion was being handled in Wayne schools. But in not dignifying the charge by denying it, they failed to assuage the latent fears that Miller had activated.

"Frankly," Jack Mandell said afterwards, "it never crossed my mind to deny it. Of course I would not vote to discontinue Christmas celebrations in the schools. But Newt's statements were so obviously prejudiced they didn't seem to deserve a denial. My reaction was one of indignation that the issue should have been raised in the first place."

While fears about a Jewish threat to Christmas seemed to have been only a minor sub-theme in Wayne's response to the whole affair, our interviews with citizens revealed that the fears remained unallayed.

"Well, when Newt said that and said 'think about it,' I really did give it some thought. I don't think they'd do that. I would really be against that. I hope they never do it. You don't think they'll try, do you?"

Thus, with the charges undenied, and the anti-Semitic character of Miller's statements undemonstrated, the people of Wayne voted against the "anti-Miller forces" for bringing a plague of "unfair" and damaging press coverage down upon them. If they were initially vulnerable to this misdefinition because most of them were unwittingly mildly anti-Semitic, some may have become more than mildly anti-Semitic now. For they

now "know" that sometimes the Jews do cause "real trouble." And this is part of the tragedy of Wayne: its mild, mannerly, nice anti-Semitism produced a self-fulfilling basis for even more potent prejudice.

It would be a serious mistake, however, to conclude that *all* of the anti-Jewish voting in Wayne was motivated by an inability to comprehend anti-Semitism. Certainly some part of the vote was produced by citizens whose personal anti-Semitism was dark grey or even worse, and who therefore required little encouragement to vote against Jews. Such persons are a common part of the American scene. Recent public opinion polls have revealed that about a fifth of Americans say they would not vote for a Jew for president, regardless of his party or merit. While it could be assumed that less important offices would elicit a smaller anti-Jewish vote, still one would expect to find in Wayne or anywhere else a minority voting against Jews out of prejudice.

Everyone watching the Wayne campaign expected some votes to stem from prejudice. However, these votes by themselves would not have been sufficient to carry the election. Thus it was the unanticipated voting, based on a confused definition of the situation, that proved decisive.

One side effect of the Wayne affair should be reported. The most anti-Semitic elements of the population were unleashed; seemingly Miller's statements suspended the public rules of taste and convention which normally preclude overt anti-Semitism. Thus, Jack Mandell received a number of threatening phone calls. Several incidents of "Jew-baiting" were reported in the schools. A considerable stack of hate mail was received by the Jewish candidates, and a number of explicitly anti-Semitic letters appeared in the local newspaper. For those Americans who do hate Jews, the slightest wavering in the official norms of tolerance seems to provide an irresistible incitement to action. When Newton Miller broke the normative spell he unwittingly caused forces beyond his comprehension to be unleashed.

IV: AFTERMATH

Wayne today resembles a rural Southern community after a major civil rights incident. The residents have retreated behind a barrier of silence and denial. Before the election they had only to bear the publicity produced by the fact that one of their school board members had interjected anti-Semitism into a local election. But now they stand accused before the world as an anti-Semitic community.

In one sense this accusation is true. Clearly, anti-Semitism means unjust disadvantage suffered by Jews merely for being Jews, and does not depend on what is in the minds of those who bring it about. To use an obviously extreme but valid example: the personal motives of Adolph Eichmann, when he had millions of Jews transported to the gas chambers, have no bearing on the anti-Semitic nature of his acts. Nevertheless, it is important to recognize that a great many of Wayne's citizens who voted to exclude Jews from the school board did not really understand the moral significance of their acts. They can truly say they were not consciously voting out of anti-Semitic sentiments because they failed to recognize the anti-Semitic character of the situation. Unfortunately, they *still* fail to comprehend the meaning of what they did and why the outside world regards Wayne as an anti-Semitic town.

Consequently, every effort is being made to erect a quick façade over the newly-rent chasms which separate the community. The school board replaced Newton Miller as vice president with the remaining Jewish member, Fred Lafer. Then they gave Miller a unanimous vote of confidence. The Mayor declared ⸢February 19–26 as Brotherhood Week.

⸢ut for all their good intent, these are acts of public relations, no⸺ ⸺an relations. They ignore the underlying illness: a community ⸺uilt on segregation and discrimination cannot provide a secure base for intergroup harmony.

Behind the facile gestures of conciliation, Wayne remains a divided community. If anything, the divisions are now deeper and are tinged with suspicion and resentment. In both Christian and Jewish communities the grammar now turns on potent "us" and "them" statements.

The wounds are deep and will be slow to heal. Indeed, they may be left untended if once more Wayne refuses to believe that anything anti-Semitic happened. Unlike the cross-burning and other past incidents, this one probably cannot be dismissed as a mere "prank." But most citizens do not want to call it a human relations problem either.

Still, Wayne is not entirely without resources to overcome its legacy of bitterness and prejudice. While the majority of its citizens failed to recognize evil when it appeared, community leaders were virtually unanimous in seeing and opposing it. Both the town council and the school board censured Miller within two days of the publication of his charges. Clearly, Wayne has its share of men of good will and moral rectitude. Indeed, it was Christians, not Jews, who challenged and defeated the Packanack Lake covenant in the courts.

These responsible citizens are not trying to minimize the recent events. Nor are they apathetic about the future. A number of them have vigorously revived their efforts to create a local human relations council. However, they will meet strong resistance from many of Wayne's uncomprehending citizens who simply want to deny that anything unpleasant ever happened, to dismiss it all as press distortion. Indeed, their proposal was immediately challenged by a local newspaper columnist who contended that the creation of a human relations council would erroneously suggest that Wayne has problems with prejudice. [Ed. Note: The township council has since voted 5 to 4 not to establish a human relations council.]

V: WHAT SHOULD HAVE BEEN DONE?

Much of what happened in Wayne was the result of an inability of people to know anti-Semitism when they saw it. As a result they saw Miller as a victim. Had Newton Miller's statement been ignored little might have happened in the election.

However, let no one assume that for this reason it should have been ignored. It would have been utterly foolish to have let the matter pass unprotested. We have moved from a norm of dark grey to light grey anti-Semitism in America precisely because prejudice has been hotly opposed and identified as evil. Thirty years ago polls showed that a substantial number of Americans were attracted to a political candidate who proposed to "do something about the Jews." Today, very few Americans find this attractive.

Had Newton Miller merely been some local citizen with a preoccupation about Jews, he could have, and probably would have, been ignored. But when men holding elective office make such remarks they must be opposed lest prejudice become socially acceptable once more. For progress in human relations depends not upon "peace in our time," but on protest. Indeed, part of the inability of the people of Wayne to detect the anti-Semitism in Miller's statement stems from the fact that past incidents and the open sore of discrimination had not been sufficiently protested. Consequently, the people of Wayne had not previously been forced to ask themselves about prejudice and its implications.

But protest is useless if it does not educate, and when it finally came in Wayne it did not. The leaders who spoke out against Newton Miller were insensitive to the fact that neither the general public nor Miller himself recognized the anti-Semitism in his charges. Thus the reaction assumed that anyone who denied the anti-Semitism in Miller's remarks, including Miller, must in his heart be a bigot. As a result the attack on Miller was both harsh and unenlightening, and the citizens of Wayne were angered rather than educated.

The lesson of Wayne, in our judgment, is that the widely used techniques for opposing prejudice have been made obsolete to some extent by their own past success. Until recently, outbreaks of anti-Semitism in America were virtually always of the black or at least dark grey variety. We have learned to deal effectively with such episodes and it is probably the case that today any public figure who engages in virulent prejudice insures his own immediate ruin. Indeed, had Newton Miller spoken like a true hate merchant the people in Wayne would almost certainly have risen up in wrath against him.

But Miller is not a hate merchant, and the Wayne affair was not an outbreak of virulent anti-Semitism. The methods which in the past have been so effective in opposing virulence, and which have greatly helped to eliminate black and dark grey anti-Semitism from political life, are probably self-defeating when applied to incidents of light grey anti-Semitism.

The response of public spokesmen to Newton Miller was ineffective because it was inappropriate. Instead of an attack upon Miller, the reactions should have tried to inform and educate both Miller and the people of Wayne. It was essential to help people understand why these statements were prejudiced, and why such charges are intolerable in American politics. Newton Miller's outburst could perhaps have been deactivated, and made into an important lesson for the general public, by dispassionate analysis, firm, but not angry. Instead, Miller was inadvertently made into a folk hero through condemnation and outrage.

If a similar situation arises in other towns like Wayne, and if the response is again one of outrage that does not inform, the same tragedy will be re-enacted. Unless we learn from Wayne, it can happen again.

NEGROES AND JEWS: AMERICAN MINORITY GROUPS IN CONFLICT

B. Z. SOBEL / MAY L. SOBEL

SINCE 1960, and increasingly over the last two years, there has been mounting concern among Jews and Jewish leadership, as well as among many Negro leaders, over what is reputed to be an alarming increase in manifestations of anti-Semitism among Negroes. Countless statements in the general press, the Anglo-Jewish press, and in Jewish communal and organizational reports point to the phenomenon with apprehension and not a little surprise. In efforts at meeting the problem, Negro-Jewish dialogues have been launched in several cities, and more can be expected in the future. At least one major conference has been devoted exclusively to the problem, and a spate of articles—some angry, some defensive, and some even attempting solutions—has been published on the subject. Not a single Jewish communal body has failed to include both comment and incipient programs in their organizational schema for combating and containing this disease. The seeming paradox of one minority group not sufficiently loving and casting common cause with another threatened minority group has given rise to anguished questions. "How," it is asked, "can Negroes be prejudiced against Jews when both are the butt of bigots and haters, and both must constantly fight for their rightful place in an only imperfectly open society? Should not Jews and Negroes be natural allies in their common struggle for group security and entrée into the larger society?"

Many Jews and not a few Jewish leaders have viewed the phenomenon of Negro anti-Semitism with a certain resignation and sadness as yet another typical example of what befalls Jews who interject themselves into the mainstream of events *qua* Jews, reaping for their efforts only contempt and calumny. Here the

Reprinted from *Judaism*, 15 (Winter 1966), pp. 3–22, by permission of the authors and the publisher. Copyright 1966 by the American Jewish Congress.

question is combined with a statement like, "After all we've done over the years to further the cause of civil rights in this country, the Negroes repay us by biting the hand—for a long time the *only* hand—that fed them." This has been translated into pressures brought by rank and file against communal leaders to withdraw some of their efforts from the civil-rights field (i.e., Negro rights) and instead to concentrate on purely Jewish problems— "which after all we are supporting you to do." Negro leaders in turn have increasingly expressed resentment over the role of white Jews as leaders in specifically Negro civil-rights groups, questioning not only their supposed usurpation of power but the strength of their very commitment to the end goal. But to raise the question of Negro anti-Semitism does not prove its existence or valence. Is it on the rise or the decline? Is it merely a reflection of our growing tendency to hear and see the Negro, or a by-product of a predictable clash between increasingly competitive social and economic groupings?

I

Most students of the phenomenon of Negro anti-Semitism tend to place its first real expression in the days during and immediately following the First World War, when two factors combined to bring the two groups into closer contact. First of all, this period was marked by a steep increase of Negro migration North and more particularly to the larger urban centers where the Jewish population of the country was and is concentrated. In what is now a classic pattern, Negroes moved into the areas being vacated by Jews, whose flight then increased (becoming a virtual exodus), leaving behind them primarily the older segments of the population and, very importantly, the small businessmen and landlords with whom the Negro community had perforce to deal.

The second factor that bears analysis is to be found in the "unprecedented high wages earned by Negroes during World War I [which resulted in] a number of them [opening] small businesses. This brought the new Negro businessman directly into competition with established Jewish businessmen in Negro communities." According to Chandler Owen, this resulted in tension and led to frustration bearing much the same marks of conflict that has historically involved the Jews. He states: "When Negroes fail to get jobs, they often ascribe their failure to Jewish employers or Jewish stockholders even though in many cases Jews have no connection whatsoever with the stores or factories concerned."[1] In other words, Jews came to play a scapegoating and symbolic-negative role akin to the classic pattern assumed by the phenomenon in the Western world.

Other observers have also noted that the Negro-Jewish problem is intimately related to the dynamics of urban development and contact patterns. But L. D. Reddick introduces an interesting and, we think, highly significant note, when he adds to this assertion the thought that "there is, to be sure, a small body of rhymes in the folklore, which stem from anti-Jewish elements in the Christian tradition." He avers, however, that "aside from their utility as carriers of verbalizations which later may be translated into active opinion these folk-sayings have a limited significance."[2] This, it would appear, is naive and somewhat far from the mark. Once again the pattern followed seems to be along traditional and well-known lines: the Jew as a deicide, or at best an anomalous spectre within the context of sacred history. Reddick further weakens his assertion that Negro anti-Semitism is situational rather than historical when he correctly observes that ". . . Negroes are, also, American and as such have been subjected to the waves of anti-Semitism which have swept over Europe and the Western Hemisphere since the First World War."[3] More to the point is the comment by Richard Wright:

> All of us black people who lived in the neighborhood hated Jews, not because they exploited us, but because we had been taught at home and in Sunday School that Jews were "Christ Killers," with the Jews thus singled out for us, we made them fair game for ridicule . . . to hold an attitude of antagonism or distrust toward Jews was bred in us from childhood; it was not merely racial prejudice, *it was a part of our cultural heritage* (emphasis added).[4]

Given the overwhelming predominance of Protestant fundamentalism within the Negro community, as well as the ambiguous role of the Jew in this tradition, it need not be surprising that a religious basis for Jew-hatred can be said to exist here. The wonder is rather the reluctance of most observers to pay sufficient heed to this factor as a possible causative root. What is true, we believe, is that what might be called the theological factor, while essential in a full explication of the phenomenon of Negro anti-Semitism, has not provided *the* articulate basis, but has rather loomed and hovered in the background—*there but not often verbalized*. Often the same ambivalence noted among white anti-Semites affects the Negro anti-Semite, for, as James Baldwin observes: ". . . They [Negroes] are taught by their preachers that the Jews killed Christ, but Jews in this context mean all those who rejected the light. Then as the Jew became the wandering, persecuted figure, the Negro identifies with him." But Baldwin also explains: "The Negro, facing a Jew, hates, at bottom, not his Jewishness but the color of his skin. It is not the Jewish tradition by which he has been betrayed but the tradition of his native land. But just as a society must have a scapegoat, so hatred must have a symbol. Georgia has the Negro and Harlem has the Jew."⁵ Baldwin, as a youth growing up in Harlem, can remember no Negro who would trust a Jew. Indeed, among the "race men" who populated Harlem street corners in the 'thirties and 'forties there was an abundance of figures like Sufi Abdul Hamid, Arthur Reed, and Ira Kemp, all of whom based their appeal largely on anti-Semitism. They pointed to the existence of Jewish business and Jewish labor-union leaders, ignoring the Greeks, Italians, and Irish who were also much in evidence.⁶ Could it not be that the religious factor was at least an important one in explaining this concentration upon Jews, in explaining its ready acceptance if not its use? In this connection Brian Glanville has suggested that the Jew ". . . is a vulnerable member of the persecuting class, and one admirably adapted for hatred and hostility, first, because he is economically 'there,' secondly, because of the myth of the murder of Christ."⁷

The theological factor expresses itself in an additional and rather strange fashion, and that is a certain suspicion on the part of Negroes going beyond even that of white Christians concerning Jewish exclusivity epitomized in the Jew's reluctance to proselytize. "Why," Cecil Moore asked, "do [Jews] run lock, stock, and barrel when the Negro moves in? The Irish and Italians run too, but at least the Church stays behind and tries to minister to the new population. The only thing the Jews leave behind are the storekeepers and landlords. Why don't you fellows try to convert us?" The immediate assumption on Moore's part and no doubt on the part of the average Negro is that the Jews don't want Negro souls, only their muscle and money. As

Moore put it, "You Jews don't have good p. r.—the R. C. do." Here it becomes possible to see an emergent picture of traditional and classical theological correlates of anti-Semitism operating in the Christian Negro community even further heightened and enhanced by what to others might be one of the Jew's most endearing characteristics—his preference for keeping his religion to himself. To the already sufficiently excluded Negro this is just one more device aimed at keeping him "out."

II

We have suggested two elements of importance in tracing Negro-Jewish relationships: (1) urbanization, with its ecological characteristics of invasion and succession, contact and increased competition; and (2) a basically fundamentalist Christian interpretation of the negative role of the Jew in the divine economy. There is evidence that these internal tensions were played upon by forces external to both groups, such as Nazis and Japanese.

Although it is extremely difficult to isolate or to pinpoint the effects or even the extent of Nazi propaganda efforts among Negroes during and immediately preceding World War II, there does seem to be some evidence that successful efforts were made by the Germans within the Negro community. There was, to be sure, an already prepared if possibly latent matrix for the acceptance and integration of these propaganda ploys, but it is nevertheless difficult to ignore the introduction of these elements as aggravating and focusing items.

In May of 1942 an organization known as the "Peace Movement of Ethiopia" held a meeting in Chicago that was monitored by someone from a leading national Jewish agency and his report notes that Hitler was recorded as being "not really an enemy of the Negroes," and December 7, 1941 was lauded as the day "One billion black people, our colored people, struck for freedom."[8] In studies of the Negro press during 1941 to 1942, this same agency noted its belief that 85% of responsible Negro leaders secretly applauded Japanese victories.[9] By December of 1941 there was, in the urban Negro centers, a growing anti-Semitic movement alleging that the war was a "Jewish war" and that Negroes would be foolish to fight for Jewish landlords and merchants who actively discriminated against and exploited Negroes.[10]

In an effort to overcome Nazi inroads the Anti-Defamation League in the early 'forties put out a seven-page document recounting Jewish individual and communal aid to the Negro. Arthur Spingarn, one of the guiding forces in the NAACP and a Jew, addressed an impressive appeal to Negroes asking them not to be taken in by Nazi propaganda concerning Jews. Joshua Roth Liebman was recruited to perform this role in Boston. Negro publicist Chandler Owens wrote an article in the Chicago *Defender* (which was widely reproduced) entitled "Should the Negro Hate the Jew?" (November, 1941), extolling the Jews and the help they have extended to Negro causes. The article revealingly begins:

> Despite the fact that the Negro is the butt of the Nazi race inferiority program, it is commonplace to hear Negroes say, "Well, Hitler did one good thing; he put these Jews in their place." Indeed the anti-Semitism program has probably been pushed more vigorously among the Negroes than any group in the nation.

In the long run, however, the role played by the Nazis and Japanese was exploitative rather than causative, that is, their propaganda served to focus and verbalize and encapsulate anti-Semitism by hooking onto particular sore points, but it did not create it from the void.

Interestingly—and this becomes evident in some of the materials referred to above—one of these key sore points, then as well as now, is the tendency among Negroes to have looked to the Jews as potential allies who then betrayed this expectation in a variety of real and imaginary ways. Again and again in the relevant literature and documents of the times this expectation (and its frustration) emerges.[11] Kenneth Clark thinks that this "higher expectation" vis-à-vis Jews is a reflection of improved Negro attitudes to Jews, which is on the face of it quite debatable; but as a psychologist Clark certainly knows what the empirical correlates of frustrated Messianism or expectation most often are. As a matter of fact, Clark himself says it is naive to assume that because both Negroes and Jews are oppressed and insecure this will lead to a feeling of kinship between the two. It might very well do the opposite.

One can draw, as Roi Ottley did, an interesting parallel between the failing attempt of abolitionists to get suffragist support for their aims with the Negro expectation of support from the

Jews. Abolitionists falsely saw an intrinsic connection between their struggle and that of the suffragists, which the suffragist did not share; and the same is probably true of the Negro-Jewish hoped-for alliance. Negroes and Jews other than in the broadest sense just do not have the same fight with the "in-groups," and in failing to get this alliance, which is thought to be a "natural," anti-Semitism is doubtlessly stimulated. Clark has observed that the Jews are objectively in a much different situation than the Negro, economically, politically, and socially, so that to compare their ends is factitious.[12] But still the Negro expects and demands more from the Jews. In a study carried out in Detroit in 1944 and following the 1943 race riot in that city, the investigators found that "50% of the Negro youth interviewed believed that Jews treat Negroes better than do non-Jewish whites but 60% said they *expected* [our emphasis] better treatment since Jews know what it is to be persecuted."[13] (It might also be interesting to note at this juncture that 70% of the Jews in the study believed that they had an obligation to treat Negroes well, since they, too, had known persecution. Only 50% of the Jews thought they actually treated the Negro better, however.)[14] On the basis of this evidence we think it is proper to suggest that Negroes and Jews are aware of each other *as Negroes and Jews*, and we cannot be satisfied with the oft-repeated assertion that anti-Jewish sentiments among Negroes are merely reflections of their anti-whiteism.

III

Is anti-Semitism among Negroes qualitatively different from that held by white Gentiles? Preliminary evidence, based on the literature rather than new research, suggests that the phenomenon is qualitatively akin to anti-Semitism as it is practiced and maintained in the white community, with variables such as socio-economic status held constant.[15] If, as we believe, Negro anti-Semitism is *not* new, and if it indeed follows the classic mold of anti-Jewish antipathy as it has unfolded in the Western world, why is there such an increase in concern, both academic and "political," with the phenomenon?

Primarily, the reason for this increased attention is not, we feel, due to any *precipitous* increase in scope or nature, but is rather a function of the fact that for the first time in American history we are seeing and hearing the Negro as a real contender for what is thought to be limited largesse, and as such, a possible threatening force. Anti-Semitism, as we have demonstrated, has existed among Negroes for a long time, probably since they became Christians; but it is only now that we have *begun* to take Negroes seriously, that we have become frightened. This is not to say that only the old tensions exist and these are now being recognized. The old elements of tension remain, and inevitably, as we now listen and see and respond, the thing tends to feed upon itself rather than disappear. For example, many students of the phenomenon have suggested, as a way of getting off the hook, that as the Negro community grows in sophistication and begins more readily to parallel the social and economic structure of the white community, these particular anti-Jewish manifestations will disappear. First, this is unlikely, we feel, because of the continuing theological valence; but in addition we have found an emergent sore point in the growing *competition* between the aspiring middle-class Negro and those immediately above him and thus in his sights, the Jewish middle and lower-middle class. Frazier, Myrdal, and others have already observed that as the Negro professional groups grow it is Jews—at least in the larger urban centers—whom they will have to displace and Jews with whom they will have to contend. Negro doctors and lawyers have for years perceived themselves as being in direct competition with a particular group of whites known as Jews, and this has stimulated tension. Negro small businessmen, unable to muster the kind of credit and the tradition of business acumen and skill required for success in even the most modest of modern enterprises, see Jews (for ecological as well as for psychological reasons) as targets of frustration and displacement.

Nor do the other socio-psychological factors remain constant. In fact it can be argued that, as the Negro attempts to improve his position, anti-Semitism has been and can continue to be strangely and crucially involved in his development.

The Jew is really the only "dislike" the Negro can legitimately feel in common with his white Christian brethren, and just as anti-Negro feeling was part of an immigrant's Americanization, anti-Jewish feeling *can* be viewed as a key to in-group participation. It does indeed offer a real way to identify with the dominant group, and, with a bow in the direction of conflict theory, it may very well help him to gain inner group security. Dubious as might be his other claims to sharing in the general culture, the Negro can join in the use of anti-Semitism as a pretext for the release of aggression as he cannot more readily do with more powerful or accepted groupings.

The fact also that individual Jews have long been active in a variety of civil-rights causes does not have the implied and expected result. Clark takes note of the accusation of "careerism" here, of Jews who, so to speak, make jobs for themselves out of the misery of the Negro masses and their frustrated aspirations. A whole host of Negro leaders, from moderates to militants, have made it plain that the future is theirs and the white usurpers would have to go. It is alleged that these usurpers, many if not most of whom are Jewish, will not be able to go all the way as is required because of their white liberal scruples and divided loyalties. They are as often as not cast out with the cry, "*Jewish* white liberal," rather than the more limited and yet more comprehensive, "white liberal." The Jew is perceived as acting as a hyphenated white, and the new leadership does not hesitate to condemn particular *Jewish* rather than white malfeasance. The classic bent of this "Jewish role" is well understood by Clark who says, after noting the relatively large involvement of Jews in progressive acts, that "the Negroes' interpretation of this has not, however, been altogether favorable. There is sometimes the lurking suspicion that all this is motivated by a desire on the part of the Jew to use him [the Negro] as a shield and reflects a not too well disguised concern about his own status."[16] In other words, the Jew's very liberalism, his altruism, are perceived as a group device, and as such, subject to withdrawal—to say nothing of betrayal.

The Negro civil-rights struggle is beginning a particularly militant and activist phase, and, as is characteristic of such periods, an atmosphere is established wherein "the enemy" or force thought to be in potential or actual opposition is isolated, projected, and encountered. It is, furthermore, characteristic of nascent protest movements to simplify the problem while at the same time attempting to focus fire on a visible object or group, and this for two reasons: (1) to solidify support within the group; and (2) because it may indeed be felt that the enemy has been established.

It is obvious that *all* of white society in greater or lesser measure has been involved in denying equal rights to Negroes and has been guilty of the cruelest oppression and subjugation of dark-skinned peoples in the United States and indeed the world at large. To be sure, the Negro has responded (as has been the case historically with other persecuted minorities) with a largely disguised but nonetheless real hatred and suspicion for the dominant oppressor group, but the category "white," while a satisfactory one (or unsatisfactory, as the case may be) for focusing resentment during a period when protest is unorganized or highly diffused, is no longer satisfactory when a militantly organizational stage is reached or approached.

At this stage the enemy must be made manifest and approachable. A "bill of particulars," as it were, must be leveled and categories reified. In other words, it is no longer entirely sufficient merely to identify whites at large for the pain and indignities inflicted upon the Negro—this category being too slippery and at the same time, paradoxically, perhaps too powerful—so that a movement in the direction of particularization and specificity begins to emerge. It is here that the Jews seem eminently fitted to play their classic role in Western history of a vulnerable absorbent for the strain and shocks of social change.

IV

Bruno Bettelheim reports the following concentration camp incident:

> Once a command of Jewish prisoners was working alongside of some Polish Gentile prisoners. The supervising SS, spying two Jewish prisoners whom he thought to be slacking, ordered them to lie down in the ditch and called on a Polish prisoner, named Strzaska, to bury them alive. Strzaska, frozen in terror and anxiety, refused to obey. At this the SS seized a spade and beat the Pole, who nevertheless still refused to obey. Furiously, the SS now ordered the two Jews to get out of the ditch, Strzaska to get in and the two Jews to bury him. In mortal anxiety, hoping to escape the fate themselves, they shoveled earth into the ditch and onto their fellow prisoner. When only Strzaska's head was barely visible the SS ordered them to stop, and unearth him. Once Strzaska was on his feet, the two Jews were ordered back into the ditch, and this time Strzaska obeyed the renewed command to bury them—possibly because they had not resisted burying him, or perhaps expecting that they too would be spared at the last minute.

But this time there was no reprieve, and when the ditch was filled the SS stamped down the earth that still lay loosely over his victims. Five minutes later he called on two other prisoners to unearth them, but though they worked frantically, it was too late. One was already dead and the other dying, so the SS ordered them both taken to the crematorium.[17]

While this particular incident can be analyzed in various ways, we would like to suggest that we look at it as a parable and seek its moral truth, as it were, by making a transition to current Negro-Jewish developments, with the Negroes taking the role of the Jews in the story, and the Jews that of the Pole. Such a transition might be made as follows: The white community accused the Negroes of evil, and the Jews were welcomed and even invited to the attack upon them and asked to join in the Negroes' burial alive. But the Jews refused (or at least their official voices refused), feeling in part that they as well as the Negroes were prisoners of a sort, and, sometimes in terror and often in anxiety, Jews fought for Negro rights in the courts and in the legislatures. Forces in society were then angered. They raised their spades at the Jews, and suggested to the Negroes that they could more quickly climb out of their ditch if at the same time they would throw dirt at, and try to bury, the Jews. Some Negroes agreed, but other forces operative in the situation protected the Jews.

Here our story stops. Are the Jews going to be willing to bury the Negroes who seemed to be willing to bury them? Or are they different from our once-valiant Pole in the original story? We should remember that there came a point at which there was no turning back—when the burial was final and unredeemable—and that, while on the one hand there were the guilty murdered, on the other was the murderer. Could Strzaska deny his guilt by claiming he was only the prisoner of the SS, or that the Jews who would have buried him had proven that they were not worth the risk of his life? This story points directly to what is perhaps the most important question in this paper: What is the Jewish reaction to the new militancy of the civil-rights struggle as well as to the signs of Negro anti-Semitism? It is a moral dilemma not unlike that of the Pole, for there are many who feel that they are involved in a situation beyond their control, which seems to have an inscrutable and tortured logic of its own, asking for great risk on behalf of a downtrodden people whose "worthiness" has not been accepted.

It should be remembered that the anti-Semitism discussed above is not the only thing the white community, and the Jews as a special part of that community, are seeing for the first time. While it is even possible that Negro anti-Semitism has actually decreased, it is certain that Negroes and Negro reactions are far more *visible* than ever before. This means that Negro leaders and Negro demands are exerting a presence and a pressure radically different from that of five years ago—and in fact, radically different from that of even a year ago.

The historical parallels with the abolition movement of the 1830's and 1840's are significant and suggestive. The change in social climate—the appearance of a new civil-rights ideology—is and was sudden, and the radicalization of that ideology and its leadership is and was rapid and (*popularly*) unexpected. Insignificant achievements, coupled with general societal unrest, economic and political, radicalize leadership, alienate the moderates, and—if the historical parallel continues—can be most dangerous (or likely to reach fruition) if this cause can be welded to other divisive drives, whether sectionally or economically based.

V

Is there a Jewish "backlash"? There is certainly a change in the ascertainable attitudes of Jews, both of the "official" voices and of the layman. We would like to suggest that the voiced attitudes may well have changed far more than the *actual attitudes*, that in some senses there is an apparent rather than a real change.

We think that it is very important that there is current, in the Jewish community, a fund of generalizations about Jewish reactions to the Negro civil-rights struggle which is based upon highly questionable assumptions and faulty data. This accepted analysis is reprinted in Jewish periodicals, in reports to the national agencies, and in the synagogues, both in defense of the community and in the sincere hope of educating and directing future action. It can be broken down as follows:

(1) That Jews and Negroes historically have and objectively should share in a fund of needs and aspirations in the United States.

(2) That Jews have historically helped Negroes far out of proportion to their number in the population.

(3) That by and large Jews feel more sympathy with Negro aspirations than does the rest of the community, and that the Jews recognize that shared fund of aspirations noted above. That Jews have, therefore, indeed joined in the new civil-rights revolution. Stanley Winkelman, in reporting the consensus of the National Community Relations Advisory Council civil-rights workshop, in June of 1963, noted:

> Most Jews have been deeply moved by the passionate determination of Negroes to secure justice and dignity and equality of treatment, and the dramatization of the wrongs and denials imposed on Negroes, evoking echoes of Jewish experience of oppression and discrimination, has aroused and deepened Jewish sympathies.
> Jewish communities appear to have developed a sense of urgency about Negro inequality in direct proportion to the militance with which Negro demands are pressed. This is evidently so both North and South and in communities of various size. The Jewish communities that have moved fastest and farthest in the direction of support of Negro demands are, by and large, in the communities which have witnessed vigorous Negro demands, demonstrations, marches, picketing, boycotts, and other direct action on a major scale.[18]

(4) That while the Jewish community is more supportive of civil-rights extension than is the rest of the white community, there is a wide gulf between the *relatively* radical leadership and the "centrist" laity.

(5) That the generally supportive Jewish reaction can be re-directed to oppose civil-rights extension *only* when there is a threat to other Jewish values: only when educational values seem in danger of being downgraded, or when the fear of violence is introduced, and the value placed upon home and family seems threatened by integrated neighborhoods. There is the general assumption that there is a breaking point, that up until that point most emotions are positive and that only beyond it do we find predominantly negative reactions. It is assumed that the fears which lead to this change in attitude are aroused by threatening Negro actions, such as the violence displayed this past summer.[19]

(6) That in view of these "realities," as well as of the fact that the Negroes have clearly taken the leadership of the civil-rights revolution into their own hands, the Jewish community should, on the one hand, firmly state its willingness to play a role in the revolution, and, on the other, concentrate on stimulating and

supporting individual Jews as individual participants in this American revolution; that much energy should go into self-discipline and self-education.[20]

VI

This then in outline seems to be the most generally accepted picture of current Negro-Jewish relations. We find, however, at this point in our research, that we cannot fully subscribe to these views, and in refuting and restructuring this outline we hope to establish a far different analysis of the dynamics of this interrelationship.

While there are some "academic" questions to be raised as to whether Jews and Negroes do indeed share in a common cause, the question here however is *not* whether there are historical parallels in the sufferings of both people, or mutual needs for opening up American society, but rather whether Jews actually view themselves as prospective partners with Negroes. A study by Bogue and Dizzard unequivocally concluded that "the Jewish respondents . . . display a level of prejudice that very nearly matches that of the native white non-Jewish European population."[21] Jews apparently react, by and large, as white Americans, and regard the Negro as an outsider and an inferior. The interviews in the Bogue study, conducted in Chicago in 1960, rated the Jewish prejudice towards Negroes as the strongest of any prejudice studied, although it was rated only slightly higher than that of native white non-Jews toward Negroes. It must be emphasized that these are the subjective ratings given by the interviewers, who may have been influenced by several factors, including possibly their own higher expectations of Jews as well as a line of questioning that dealt with intermarriage. It should be noted that ethnocentricity and preference for endogamy are not synonymous with prejudice, but it is also true that these factors may and have acted as bulwarks to support prejudice. We have heard the fear expressed, in our interviews in middle-class Jewish neighborhoods, that what Negroes really want is to marry Jews, and that this is why it is so important to keep Negroes out of middle-class, white neighborhoods and schools: "How else can we protect our children?"

There is probably a continuum of reaction we can posit for the

Jewish community. The professional lay leadership and a small percentage of the rabbinical leadership stand at one extreme. They desire legal and social measures in support of integration, and they want the Jewish community visibly to support this position: to give jobs to Negroes, to welcome or at least accept Negroes in their neighborhoods and schools, and to attempt to find ways and means of actually and meaningfully supporting integration.[22] At the other extreme stand the Jewish bigots whose existence is certainly known in the Negro community.

The vast majority of American Jewry lies somewhere in between. We would suggest that there has been major misjudgment as to stance and standing of this largest group. The Jewish community has reacted as a white community both in its prejudice and in its analysis of its commitments. The activist liberal fringe that is not professionally involved with the Jewish community has, by and large, dissociated itself from communal activities and found its voice in secular, non-Jewish organizations.

The top-heavy imbalance of the Jewish record on civil rights is unmistakable. In July, 1963 Rabbi Balfour Brickner, reporting to the National Catholic Conference for Interracial Justice, summarized the activities of Jews in the field. He outlined the total involvement and major programs of the National Community Relations Advisory Council, the Anti-Defamation League, and the American Jewish Congress; he discussed the attempt to organize a rabbinical "task force" to join in civil-rights work; he noted the "house-cleaning" that is the *only* expression of much civil-rights feeling (i.e., the unpoliced attempts on the part of agencies, synagogues, and organizations to deal with non-discriminating firms); he approved of the fundraising for the NAACP and CORE and SNCC, which is one of the communities' stronger expressions of support; and he cited the *single* example of a congregational president joining his rabbi on a picket line, this occurring at Gwynn Oaks in Maryland in July of 1963:

> To my knowledge, this is the first time in modern American Jewish religious life that a rabbi has had such active support. In other instances, boards and social action committees of congregations have given other kinds of support to their rabbis, offering to use congregational funds to pay bail bonds and legal costs incurred as a result of such demonstrations and even to use the legal committee of the congregation to defend the rabbi, but to my knowledge this is the first time that a rabbi has actually been joined on a picket line by one

of his members. It is a significant tell-tale as to how our people felt about what is going on.[23]

Rabbi Brickner felt that this individual act of support was important and that it presaged a more general trend. It is by now clear that this incident was more remarkable as one that stands out from the more general lethargy and/or rejection of such activist involvement. There are active rabbis, and they do have some support, but their numbers are very small, and their meaning for us in this context lies more in what they reflect about the majority.

The Jewish-agency professionals recognize the gulf between their positions on civil rights and those of most of the laity, but we wonder if they correctly estimate its extent. The vastness of the gulf is indicated by the fact that those agencies which have little or no direct contact with constituencies, which are *not* responsible to congregations or organizations, have gone the farthest in their support of new civil-rights measures; they have given of their time and money, directly and indirectly, to specifically Negro activities, ranging from the Philadelphia NCRAC $25,000 overall program of action to the Boston Jewish Community Council loan of extensive film materials to the local freedom schools. The ADL has a constituency, and while its program is extensive and in some ways revolutionary, we have the impression that it is felt that some aspects of it must be underplayed in the Jewish community lest it be castigated for doing work that was not properly its own. This fear is supported by our findings in our preliminary survey, and we are, at this juncture, convinced that the large majority of the Jewish community does not feel a communality of purpose with the Negroes; that if Jews desire civil-rights legislation—and by and large they do—they do not support integration. We would posit the hypothesis that basic Jewish attitudes have not changed; that the majority are not first becoming alienated from integration demands, but rather that these demands were never before made; that the majority never had favored integration; and that what we are hearing is *not* really *a change* in attitude, but is the old attitude being voiced vigorously for the first time in reaction to a new problem.

Beyond this, we must agree that new voices are being heard. Parent and Taxpayer groups (PAT) are unimaginable in the leftist and liberal past of the Jewish community. *Is it,* as is often averred, the Jewish communities' stress upon excellent education for their children that has sparked this particular reaction? An important study of the integration controversy in the Jackson Heights and Corona sections of Queens, in New York City, concludes unqualifiedly that those Jews in the community who were most interested in the education of their children, and in its excellence, favored and fought for integration, while those in the PAT group clearly did *not* evince equal interest in the quality of the education and would oppose integration even if convinced the quality would not fall.[24]

Jewish respondents' comments from several separate studies bear a striking similarity, reflecting among other sentiments a strong fear of intermarriage, of economic short-changing, of violence, and of deviation from the "proper" white approach. Here are a handful of comments which seem to say far more than the statistical analysis of their orientation:

> I believe a Negro should live with his own.

> There are refined and non-refined Negroes; but the ones that I am in contact with are very unclean and the children are wild with no manners whatsoever . . . I have found that the refined ones are in a minority.

> I don't object to them having equal rights as to voting, job opportunity, education, but let the Negroes live among themselves and we'll live among our own kind.

> I feel that the law should enforce equal opportunities in any government supported housing, employment, schools, etc., but do not feel that private individuals should be stripped of their own rights to serve, hire, house those who they choose or not, as their own conscience dictates.

> I feel that the Negro should by his own education, work and ambition "break the chains that bind" him as did other minority groups such as the Jews, the Chinese, the Italians,

> the Irish, etc. However, I do not think that they should demand these things without working for them through education and hard work and ambition.

> . . . as far as citizens rights go the Negro as anybody else should be equal. They have the right to live anywhere, but of course I can move.

You cannot legislate "equal rights." As the saying goes, "you can lead a horse to water, etc." The only way we can ever have a racial or religious justice is to eliminate all present parents and start a new civilization. Possibly in time, thousands of years from now, this problem might be lessened but never resolved. From time beginning man cannot live with man, so how can you legislate this problem? Force will never accomplish what quite subtle pressure can, and force has only raised the ire of neutral and unopionated [sic] persons against the Negro. This plus the usual opinionated "egg heads" has now increased the numbers to work against the Negro.

I feel the Southern Negro needs help from the NAACP. I feel the Northern Negroes are making errors in their marches and de facto desegregation. This makes the Northern Negro more noticeable and disliked.[25]

Many other comments can be seen as reflecting values coming out of minority experiences. Boat-rocking is castigated, and violence abhorred. It is significant in this regard that some Jewish store-owners in the Roxbury section of Boston viewed the Harlem, Brooklyn and Rochester riots as pogroms: they felt this to be a particular vengeance taken out on the Jews. The fact that Jews own most of the businesses in these Negro communities was not directly taken into account, nor were these riots seen as part of a Negro revolution; they were simply the rabble's vengeance on the Jew.

It has been suggested that the Jews have a unique fear and distaste for violence and that this may go far to explain why Negroes move into Jewish neighborhoods where they are not welcomed, and are indeed most often confronted by mass Jewish flight, but where they are not generally subjected to egg- and stone-throwing mobs.

An important New York *Times* poll, attempting to estimate "backlash" in New York City, indicated a surprising spread in the antagonistic group:

> Those whom the key question showed to be critical of the civil rights movement were found, in other answers, to represent all segments of the sample. There were relatively small differences between men and women, among various economic groups, among followers of different religious faiths, and among persons of varying national origins.

Among Protestants, for example, 31% thought the movement was going at the right pace, 19% wanted more speed, and 42% wanted a slowdown. Eight percent were unsure.

Among Jews, 28% said "right pace," 17% "more speed," and 46% said "slow down." Thirteen percent were unsure . . .

A larger percentage of persons in the higher socio-economic categories tended to feel that more speed was needed in the movement, but even among these the majority favored a slowdown.[26]

The *Times* concluded that there definitely is a "backlash": "More than ¼ of those who were interviewed said they had become more opposed to Negro aims during the last few months." But data in the study support the conclusion that the vast majority never favored the civil-rights movement; the new demands as well as the new methods have given them the occasion to express their old opposition to integration. Thus "backlash" should be defined not as a retrenchment of civil-rights support, but rather as a new expression of old integrationist opposition.

These "backlash" statistics indicate that perhaps there is a breaking point, but it is not reached through a conflict in values (as education vs. integration), nor is it true that attitudes prior to that breaking point are generally positive while afterwards they turn negative. Rather, the militancy, the physical immediacy, and moreover the violence of the civil-rights struggle have awakened and activated old sentiments; this has, as it were, opened the floodgates and allowed basic and longstanding prejudices of the white population to flow out. This is the counterpart reaction to the riots whose causes are equally deep-rooted and long-standing.

The leadership of the Jewish community *has* responded to this new phase of Negro militancy and white reaction. It is probable that Jewish leaders in this struggle experienced feelings of violation in their own house when they suddenly found their roles expropriated by Negro militants who often as not do not have the necessary training, ability, responsibility or following to play the roles they have taken over willy-nilly. Some leadership retrenchment is no doubt due to this displacement problem, although it must be noted that many are working very hard to find a viable role in the new situation. Such retrenchment as there has been may be viewed as necessary and reasonable action taken in response to the increasing radicalism of Negro demands. However, the effect of lay pressures should not be discounted.

Irving Greenberg, in a strong indictment of Jewish "concern," draws a rather disturbing picture of the status of Negro acceptance in the Jewish case-work agencies: the Negro is the "stranger" and virtually "does not exist" within the purview of these Jewish agencies. Greenberg reminds us of the Deuteronomic injunction (14:29) ". . . and the *stranger,* and the fatherless and the widow, that are within thy gates, shall come, and shall eat and be satisfied." He answers the oft-given and seemingly persuasive argument that Jewish philanthropy must support Jewish clients by reminding us all of the ethical rather than self-serving import of philanthropy, and he points to the success of the policy of servicing a non-sectarian clientele in the Jewish hospitals. He ruefully notes, and we share his feeling, that "it is ironic that the basis for this decision by the Jewish hospitals is Hippocratic and not Mosaic."[27]

VII

The Jewish relationship to the civil-rights struggle suggests strong and in some ways frightening parallels with the historical role of the Quaker Church in the slavery controversy prior to the Civil War. In the 18th century the Quakers were the outspoken and unequivocal opponents of slavery, cleaning their own house of slave-owners while advocating the end of slavery and the then popular concept of removal and resettlement of free Negroes outside the U.S. They clearly opposed slavery, but they clearly did not, by and large, welcome Negroes into their churches or families. When in the 1830's and 1840's abolitionism became a radical movement, making radical demands upon society, the Quaker Church underwent an internal crisis: it certainly provided a large percentage of the churched leadership in the abolitionist movement, but it just as clearly avoided the North-South split that was to shake the major denominations. The Quaker Church could not move beyond the level of liberalism which had become institutionalized in the 18th century. By 1843, the Quakers had chosen unity in their church *above* entry into the moral battle. They quietly supported freedom, but would not "touch" the radical abolitionists nor even their own Quaker supporters. They withdrew—and there can be little doubt they suffered by their inaction—by their unwillingness to suffer the divisive and bitter struggle that would have divided their own church over slavery, but which might have revitalized the Quaker religious commitment in a very special sense.

The counsels that advise Jews to work as individuals may well be counseling the Jewish community in the direction followed by the Quakers. For when a group loses all vision of a central issue, a binding vision of what the group is and what it is to become, its survival is called into serious question. Especially is this so in complex societies such as our own, where the stimuli, the siren-calls from a variety of diffuse and sometimes contradictory sources ever pose the question: Who am I really? What is my function? Unlike a simpler context where one's affiliation with the group is taken as given, where one does not generally argue with one's specific positioning, the participant within a group in complex environments responding to the freedom of social choice open to him tends to balance his loyalties against a larger canvas of possibilities. Perhaps he sees freedom of choice where it does not in fact exist, but our problem is with what he sees and how he acts or does not act, rather than with objective determinants of possibilities. With the world seemingly open to talent and desire, and with problems confronting man in the abstract rather than a parochial microcosm, why should one choose the more constrained over the all-embracing? If the faith is lost, the ritual dead, authority absent, what is there to lay hold of loyalties?

Jews of the past saw in their lives a mission to live the Torah, to speak to the world of the one true God, and of a latter age to bear the message of prophetic justice and social melioration. There is no comparable central idea for them as a group in the 20th century. One of the possible rallying points for a new social integration might have been found in the secular counterparts of the learned men of yore—the Jewish intellectuals. However, contemporary Judaism has not been able to retain the creative commitment and deeper loyalties of sizeable segments of intelligentsia. These elements have not been able to feel comfortable in making their home in the Jewish community; and while this is equally true for the other religious groups that comprise our society, it seems to have more valence for a people-faith such as the Jews. With respect to the dominant issues and concerns of our time, it appears to this intellectual stratum that Judaism and the Jewish community have little to say today of positive value on the contemporary scene.

It is difficult, to elicit a uniform statement or point of view from all organized segments of the Jewish community on any given issue, with the possible exception of anti-Semitism. But this is really not the major difficulty for those seeking to preserve the survival of the Jewish community, for if it were possible to gain a feeling of consensus, of directiveness on any set of major issues or group ideals, they could still find some basis for solidarity in the presence of a guiding-idea. We have tended to take for granted the liberalism of the Jewish community and its commitment to democratic processes, welfare programs, and, of course, civil rights. This commitment, we believe, is still viable and present. But if we continue to expect the Jews to push harder for civil rights and to support Negro action groups more unstintingly than the other segments of the middle-class white population, we might be disappointed. Jews, to be sure, are still over-represented to a marked extent in militant civil-rights causes and groups—but as individuals rather than as Jews. The organized segments of the community, while sincerely committed to full freedom for the Negro and other subjugated groups, no longer appears to be active enough in this pursuit to be able to participate in an organized way. This cannot be interpreted as Jewish rejection of freedom or equality, but neither can it be seen, as in the past, as a vital and concerted group effort in this direction.

VIII

We have suggested that, contrary to the popular image, most Jews do not and have not desired integration. Negroes tend to react, in part, as "whites" when they react to Jews, exhibiting an historically rooted anti-Semitism; Jews seem to react as "whites" in their reaction to Negroes, fearing and castigating the stranger at the gates. We hide our heads in our own suffocating sand-pile of obfuscation if we in any way assume that inter-relationship to be basically different. The question before the Jewish community now is: What is the proper path to be followed? Should the rabbinical and organizational leadership attempt slowly to educate the Jewish community and get broader support for gradualism? Was not that the Quaker solution, and would it not now be withdrawal rather than moderation? Today there is only one possibility, a difficult choice in a sub-culture so long used to at least two possibilities. There appears to be no way out: community leaders must act as a goad and a rod to prod and push the Jewish community into action. The historic Jewish response has always been: *na'aseh v'nishma* (*Exodus* 24:1)—we will do and then understand. This was the traditional answer to those with doubts, and it must be the present answer, too.

The avenues of approach are both negative and positive. Large-scale work in and with the Negro community must be undertaken, even in the face of a rebuff from the revolutionary Negro leadership, and work in the Jewish community should be intensified even in the face of violent reaction. This could involve the establishment of nurseries, tutoring services, social-work agencies, community centers, and, above all, work to obtain credit, jobs and housing. Efforts must be made to establish the opportunity for interracial experiences for the community, and pressure must be exerted for greater involvement. In addition—and most importantly—all possible pressure, rabbinical and organizational, should be brought to bear on vocal opposition.

Is this a sociologically—grounded answer? Perhaps not, but it is the only answer. There can be little meaningful pressure if it is not widespread. The rabbis who now stand alone are in an extremely vulnerable position. A united leadership might well become alienated from the majority in the community and might well drive a wedge in that community; but there is no second choice, and perhaps there won't be a second chance.

NOTES

1. Chandler Owen, "Should the Negro Hate the Jew?," Chicago *Defender*, p. 9, 11/8/41.
2. L. D. Reddick, "Anti-Semitism among Negroes," *The Negro Quarterly*, Summer 1942, pp. 113–114.
3. *Ibid.*, p. 114: "One woman speaking to a crowd at one of the open air meetings quoted a passage from the Old Testament to show the Hebraic religion's sanction for the charges she was laying at the doorstep of the Jewish merchant: 'Ye shall not eat of anything that dieth of itself. Thou shalt give it unto the stranger that is in thy gates that *he* may eat it; or thou mayest *sell it unto the alien;* for thou art an holy people unto the Lord thy Lord.'" Reddick concludes laconically in noting, "Her listeners seemed to have been impressed" (p. 116).
4. Richard Wright, *Black Boy*, pp. 54–55.

5. *Glenville Jewish Advocate*, May 28, 1964; cited by *AJC Report*, p. 16.

6. Roi Ottley, *New World A-Coming: Inside Black America*, Boston, Houghton Mifflin Co., 1943, pp. 118–121.

7. Brian Glanville, "Paradoxes of Negro and Jewish Attitudes," *Jewish Advocate*, May 28, 1964. Abraham Duker agrees with the theological point: "Anti-Semitism among Negroes stems from the same source as white anti-Semitism, namely, Christian teaching" (New York *Times*, May 4, 1964). In the same piece Negro educator Horace Bond recalls responding as a child to the taunt of a Jewish boy who called him "nigger" with the epithet "Christ Killer," although he avers he doesn't remember where he picked it up.

8. Anti-Defamation League Report from Stan Jacobs, June 4, 1942.

9. *Ibid.*

10. Anti-Defamation League, Inter-City Report, December 5, 1941.

11. Reddick observes that "They [the Negroes] expect more from the Jewish landlord than from landlords in general, for the Jewish people like the Negro people have suffered." *Op. cit.*, p. 16. No less a sophisticated participant than James Baldwin comments that "an understanding is expected of the Jews such as none but the most naive and visionary Negro has ever expected of the American Gentile" (AJC Report, p. 21). He adds, "The Jew, by the nature of his own precarious position, has failed to vindicate this faith." We would correct Mr. Baldwin's comment only to the extent of changing the word "faith," which does not and probably did not exist, to "halting and hopeful expectation," which did and does.

12. *Commentary*, 1964. Clark found as early as 1946 in a study carried out in New York (that is, before the real push for civil rights began), 60% of the Jews held unfavorable stereotypes about Negroes, while 70% of Negroes held them about Jews. Interestingly and as one might have suspected if one were not intent on showing two minority groups in mutual embrace, the Jews held the prevailing notions about Negroes (lazy, brutish, unintelligent, etc.) while the Negroes held those current in the Gentile community about Jews (sharp-dealing, dishonest, smart, etc.).

13. Wolff, Loring, Marsh, *Negro Jewish Relationships*, Wayne State Press, Detroit, 1944, p. 6.

14. *Ibid.*, p. 6.

15. We would question the implication of Clark who holds, "when found in a Negro, anti-Semitism tends to be confused, ambiguous and not directly traceable to organized bigotry. And while there may be some degree of economic jealousy, anti-Semitism in a Negro does not appear to be rooted directly in economic competition" (*Commentary*, 1964). We agree but would point to the fact that this is not the proven root of the white community either, and that the religious and psychological and social factors are more central to the etiology of anti-Semitism, and it is in these areas that the Negro anti-Semite displays a very marked resemblance to his white counterpart.

16. AJC Report, p. 24.

17. Bruno Bettelheim, *The Informed Heart: Autonomy in a Mass Age,* Glencoe, The Free Press, 1963, p. 159.
18. Stanley Winkelman, "Consolidated Report of Workshops on Role of Jewish Community in Meeting the Civil Rights Dilemma," NCRAC, Plenary Session, June 27–30, 1963, mimeo, p. 1.
19. *Ibid.,* p. 2.
20. *Ibid.,* p. 3.
21. Donald J. Bogue and Jan E. Dizzard, "Race, Ethnic Prejudice, and Discrimination as Viewed by Subordinate and Superordinate Groups," Community and Family Study Center, April 16, 1964, p. 7.
22. Cf. Albert Vorspan, "The Negro Victory and the Jewish Failure," *American Judaism,* Vol. XIII, No. 1, pp. 7 ff.
23. Rabbi Balfour Brickner, "A Report of New Jewish Initiatives in the Field of Race," presented before the National Catholic Conference for Interracial Justice, July 27, 1963, mimeo, p. 3.
24. Cf. Kurt Lang and Gladys Engel Lang, Preliminary Draft of Paper presented at A.S.A. Meeting, Montreal, Canada, September, 1964, mimeo, p. 10.
25. These particular statements are all from the B'nai B'rith Woman's Local Area Study in a community outside Boston.
26. New York *Times,* September 21, 1964, p. 26.
27. Irving Greenberg, "Changing Race Relations—Impact on and Implications for Jewish Casework Agencies," for the Regional Committee of the National Conference of Jewish Communal Service, July 31, 1964, mimeo, p. 6.

NEGROES, JEWS, AND MUZHIKS

MILTON HIMMELFARB

CAN ANYTHING still be said about Negro and Jew in the United States that has not already been said—by Fiedler, Glazer, and Podhoretz; by Baldwin, Clark, and Rustin; in conferences, speeches, books, and articles? The relation between American Jew and American Negro has even been examined in the perspective of Israel and Africa. Let us add the perspective of Belorussia and the Ukraine.

European and European-born scholars, like Yves Simon some time ago and Bruno Bettelheim more recently, have shown that the American relation between white and Negro is similar in some ways to the European relation between bourgeois and proletarian before 1939. Like Negroes and whites here, prole- tarians and bourgeois there were two nations. Like Negroes here, proletarians there were exploited, alienated, feared, seen as primi- tive and unclean: George Orwell's shabby-genteel parents used to say, "Workingmen *smell*." In Europe the moral and intellectual elite sided with the workers, here it sides with the Negroes.

All this is clearly true, but I think a better comparison might be with the European peasant, especially before 1914. There are psychosexual reasons, among others, for this: Lady Chatterley's lover was a gamekeeper, the personified principle of opposition to the death-in-life of the factory and double-entry bookkeeping, choosing to be neither bourgeois nor proletarian. In European folklore the depraved noblewoman recruits her lovers from among coachmen, grooms, and goatherds. Their closeness to animals gives them an animal potency, they are stallions; and in their primitiveness and social inferiority she gratifies her taste for lowness, the *nostalgie de la boue*. In the American imagination, of course, the man-stallion is Negro. On the female side, the serf girl was the sexual property of her master and his sons, and so was the

Negro slave girl: Edmund Wilson reads Mrs. Chesnut's *Diary from Dixie* and is reminded of what Tolstoy said about Russia. Like the Negro slaves in America, the muzhik serfs, emancipated at almost the same time, are then perceived as ignorant, improvident, violent, drunken, incontinent—id figures, embodiments of the untamed instincts.

The association of the Jew with the muzhik was older and more intense than that of the Jew with the Negro. With the Negro the association does not go back, essentially, before the memory of men and women still living. For Jews here, the Negro has not been the only Other (though he is most other); and notwithstanding the current Negro talk of the Jewlandlord and Goldberg, proportionately few of us in America deal chiefly with Negroes. By contrast, Jews in numbers had lived and dealt with the Slavic peasantry for the better part of a thousand years—in Poland, the Polish-Lithuanian empire, and finally in the Tsarist Russian Pale of Settlement. Enough time had passed since Khmelnitski led Ukrainian Orthodox peasants in a massacre of the Polish Catholic landowning gentry and their Jewish estate agents and men of business for his name to have become, in the language of our grandparents, a synonym for antiquity. For the Jews of the East European villages and small towns—not the cities, like Warsaw or Odessa—from whom most American Jews are immediately descended, the muzhik was the Other, statistically and psychologically. The muzhik was the Jew's external environment and, more often than not, his livelihood. In the dictionary the Yiddish word for "peasant" is *poyer* (German, *Bauer*), but in fact the Russian or Polish Jew was likely to say *goy*: the muzhik was the consummate Gentile.

When we consider that the history of relations between Jew and muzhik is so old and intense; that muzhik and Negro have been alike, not least in the culture's perception of them; and that even in plural America the Negro is nevertheless most Other— when we consider all this, we may reasonably expect that current Jewish feelings and ways of thinking about Negroes will be affected by older feelings and ways of thinking about muzhiks.

The Jews of the Pale of Settlement thought themselves superior to the muzhiks, feared them, felt guilty about them, pitied them, envied them, and, while distrusting them, wanted to see their lot bettered.

The Jews did not hate the muzhiks. In general, we are poor haters—partly, I suppose, because we have had so many enemies that hatred is pointless. What Jew hates Spain? Of Titus, a traditional Jew will still say, when he has occasion to mention him, "may his name and memory be blotted out" (thus preserving the name and memory), but he does not hate Rome. At most he has a fixed epithet that goes with Rome, "the wicked kingdom." We do not even hate Germany. I still look twice when I see a Volkswagen or Mercedes in the parking lot of a synagogue, and I will make an effort to avoid buying a German article, but I have not taught that to my children, and when they notice what I am doing they regard it as a cute eccentricity; nor can I altogether blame the Israelis for their heavy imports from Germany. If I do not readily work up enthusiasm for Rumania, Hungary, the Ukraine, Lithuania, and Poland, that is not hatred. The emotional relations between Jews and East European Gentiles were asymmetrical. Nothing with the Jews corresponded at all closely to the hatred against us felt—and acted on, murderously—by Rumanians, Hungarians, and the rest.

To return from this digression—I have said that Jews thought themselves superior to muzhiks. On the Jewish scale of values, Jews ranked high and muzhiks low. As between *shabbat* and *hol*, *ruhaniyut* and *gashmiyut*—sabbath and weekday, spirituality-intellectuality and corporeality—the Jews, in their own eyes, stood for the first term of each set, and the muzhiks for the second. Typically, Jews could read and muzhiks could not, and literacy and illiteracy have their distinctive corollaries.

Jews feared muzhiks—for the same reason, basically. The muzhiks were so *physical*, so patently the sons of Esau. Jews remembered that their ancestor Jacob had feared his brother Esau and that only a blind man could be persuaded that the hands of Jacob were the hands of Esau. Muzhiks could kill you—either individually, in a passion or for gain, or collectively, in a pogrom. More than most, Jews have cause for fearing violence.

Jews felt guilty. When a merchant (the word is much too grand) is almost as poor as his very poor customer and when he has the upper hand in such things as simple arithmetic, he is apt to take advantage. He shouldn't, but sometimes he does. The rabbis' insistence on the biblical commandment of just weights and measures and on the sacrilege of violating this commandment in dealings with Gentiles is proof that there were violations. The violators rationalized their conduct: "The muzhik steals me blind, but even when I catch him at it I have to make believe I don't see anything because I'm afraid of him, so the only way I can get my own back is to juggle the figures a little." Or else they took their ability to fool the muzhik as further proof of their cleverness and his stupidity. But they also felt guilty. They knew that what they were doing was not right.

An Israeli joke: Jews from a Polish village have survived Hitler and have established themselves as an egg-and-poultry coopera- tive in Israel. They are grateful to their friend, the peasant elder, for helping to save them from the Nazis, and they are proud of having made themselves into productive, progressive agricultur- ists. As the Zionist song has it, they came to Israel to build and to be built, and they have succeeded. So they pool their money and send a ticket to the old peasant, who eventually comes from Poland to visit them. They show him their modern equipment and methods, and he is impressed. Then they show him how artificial light twenty-four hours a day keeps the hens laying without interruption. He shakes his head and says, "Ah, *Zhidy, Zhidy!* You have no honest Poles to trick any more, so you trick chickens."

Jews pitied the muzhik: he had to bear on his back the weight of the gentry, the bureaucracy, the army, the church, the absolute monarchy. He labored and suffered so that these need not, and so that they could lord it over him. He was a man, by definition created in the image of God, and they had made him less than a man.

Jews envied the muzhik: the other side of revulsion is attrac- tion, even fascination. People under the firm rule of the superego must hanker, whether they know it or not, for instinctual anarchy. As soon as the sovereignty of Torah and the rab- binocracy had been breached, the attraction could express itself: Isaac Babel rides with the Red Cavalry Cossacks, for reasons that Lionel Trilling has finely explained, and the Second and Third Aliyot bring with them to Palestine a Tolstoyan peasant-and-soil romanticism. In I. B. Singer's *The Slave,* when the peasant Wanda becomes the Jewish Sarah, she is more admirable than the homeborn Jewesses. What all modern Jews in Eastern Europe had in common, transcending any difference of formal ideology, was that they valued action, forcefulness, masculinity, and saw the old Judaism as passive, weak, feminine. They liked Esau more than their parents did, and Jacob less. (See Mary Catherine Bateson's analysis of this theme, and of the reconciliation of masculine and feminine in Bialik's poetry, in *Daedalus* for Summer 1966.)

As the Jews did not hate the muzhik, so they did not blame him. They blamed the system, or the authorities—priests, government. I remember the late Hayim Greenberg writing that the ordinary Jew would say, "The peasant is really a good fellow, if he's left alone and if he doesn't get drunk"—exactly what I used to hear at home when my parents spoke of the old country. If only the priests and officials didn't incite the muzhik, if only they cared enough to make him educate his children, if only the social and political system were decent, all would be well, for muzhik and Jew alike.

But Jews believed that the muzhik needed help and guidance and could not be trusted to do things for himself. Without guidance, his childishness, impulsiveness, and propensity to violence would spoil everything. In the 1870's and early 1880's some young Jewish revolutionaries joined the *narodnik* (populist) movement and "went to the people," that is, to the peasant masses. Then came the pogroms. Some Jewish narodniks tried to excuse these as the first stirrings of the revolutionary spirit in a formerly inert mass, but most Jews were strengthened in their conviction that while to do something for the people was just and necessary, to trust them to do it was folly. In the Jacobin formula, the people were to be compelled to be virtuous.

After Hitler and all that the Nazis had done to the Poles, there was a pogrom in the Polish town of Kielce against the handful of Jews who had escaped the crematoria and returned. Most Jews took the pogrom as the signal to leave forever, chiefly for Israel. Those who chose to remain—above all, the polonized and assimilated—were tempted to rely on Stalin and the Red Army to implant virtue in the Poles, and some became agents of the Stalinist Polish Communist police. That suited Stalin and the Stalinists: let the Poles hate the Jews instead, as always.

. . .

Usually, the Jewish distrust of the masses has included a distrust of the leader who comes from the masses, and who is all too likely to share their prejudices and weaknesses, including anti-Semitism. Better by far the patrician liberal, cultured, above plebeian uncouthness. Whether a Jew is modern or traditional, if he has any political theory at all it is apt to be classical: the state must have a monopoly of violence, it should be just, and it should be in the hands of enlightened men. Rule by an establishment can be bad, but in the Jewish experience it is generally less bad than rule by men from the masses, appealing to their emotions.

Raw anti-Semitism is more a plebeian and populist phenomenon than an establishment one. Lueger, the late-19th-century anti-Semitic mayor of Vienna, was the populace's man. Between him and the Jews, protecting them, stood the Emperor Francis Joseph; and the Jews of the Hapsburg empire loved their emperor. Hitler was a kind of tribune of the plebs. (In literature, Céline speaks their rancor, with their voice.) Centuries earlier, in the late Middle Ages and the early modern period, expulsions of the Jews had accompanied the nationalisms and the formation of the national states of Western Europe, in England, France, and Spain; and the impulse for both the nationalisms and the expulsions had come more from the rising new men than from the established old ones. The Spanish Inquisition was populist in its origins, and normally Jews had more to fear from the lower clergy than from the higher.

In the United States, Tom Watson was a Populist, and he helped to lynch Leo Frank. The historians debate whether the Populist movement was really anti-Semitic or only seemed so, but Jews can be forgiven for uneasiness about several things associated with the Populists, including the frenzy aroused by a speech against crucifying mankind upon a cross of gold. For Christians, crucifixion was the Jewish crime; and about the time when Bryan was declaiming, the Tsarist secret police was forging the *Protocols of the Elders of Zion*, according to which there was a gold power out to conquer the world, and that power was Jewish.

McCarthyism was populist and popular. Its target was the establishment—Harvard, the State Department, the Supreme Court, even the Army—and it could be defeated only by the establishment. Civil liberties and the rights of minorities are not characteristically cherished by any populism, which tends toward an intolerant majoritarianism: the Soviet prosecutors of the intellectuals who failed to think wholesome thoughts were able to appeal to popular sentiment. Early in this century American populism won a great victory for democracy, the initiative and the referendum. Today, from coast to coast, these are used with almost invariable success against the civil rights of Negroes. In California, where a large majority voted to put racial discrimination in housing beyond the reach of law, it has been left to the courts, elitist by their nature, to uphold decency against the electorate speaking through the polls. In New York City everybody expects that if the people are allowed to vote on a civilian review board for the police, they will turn it down, and civil libertarians have been hoping that the courts will prevent the people from voting.

On the whole, therefore, we have had some justification for our distrust of populism and men from the people and our preference for the cultivated, liberal, patrician leader. Sometimes, though, we overdo it. We gave and still give to Franklin D. Roosevelt more devotion than he earned, by any cool, political measure of favors done and benefits conferred. But at least Roosevelt was a President, and a great one. What can explain our infatuation with Adlai Stevenson? (I am entitled to ask the question. I voted for him twice.) He was not especially favorable to Jewish causes or interests, nor was he even much of a New Dealer. It was enough for us that he seemed to incarnate all that is enlightened, cultured, and well-bred. (Another good sign: he was obviously no athlete.) To most other Americans, he was not nearly the man Eisenhower was. We were a little tardy in getting to like President Kennedy, because Stevenson was in the way, but when we could perceive Kennedy, too, as enlightened, cultivated, and patrician, we were his—again, a little more than his objective merits or accomplishments warranted.

On the other hand, we have consistently underestimated Truman, and fewer of us voted for him than for any other Democratic Presidential candidate since 1932. Nothing patrician about him. Rather, something folksy-populist, and so a bit disquieting. Twenty years from now, someone may write that we underestimated Johnson, for similar reasons.

. . .

What are the differences between our present attitude toward Negroes and the older attitude toward muzhiks? Negroes are not so exclusively the Other as the muzhiks used to be: Negroes are ten percent or so of the population of America, muzhiks were probably ninety percent in old Eastern Europe. If there had been psychoanalysts in Zhitomir or Grodno, they would have found that the id figures of their Jewish patients' dreams and fantasies were muzhiks, and only muzhiks. Here psychoanalysts no doubt find their Jewish patients dreaming and fantasizing about Negroes, but not only about Negroes. Our society and our culture offer additional possibilities for representing the id.

We also feel less guilty about Negroes, I think. For the sake of argument, let us concede what should not be conceded: to deal with = to exploit. But even of the so-called Goldbergs, even of the Jewlandlords, not all are Jews. Some are actually Negroes. They are called Jewlandlords because they are landlords.

In what way are the two attitudes the same? About Negroes, Jews fear what our grandparents feared about muzhiks, violence. We know in our bones that the civil peace is always fragile, that a habitude of violence is easily established, and that then Jews and people like Jews had better watch out.

In our distaste for violence we differ hardly at all from our grandparents. When they were displeased they did not hit, they acted *broygez* (Yiddish, "offended" or "sulky," from Hebrew *berogez*, "in wrath"): they did not speak to the person who had offended them, they avoided his—often her—company. (In his wife's presence, a man would say to his child, "Tell your mother the soup is cold.") The characteristic response of Jews to an unpleasant situation is still avoidance, flight not fight. If a Jew does not like Negroes moving into his neighborhood, he moves out. He does not band together with his neighbors to burn a cross—of course not—or to throw bricks and bottles. That may be why Jewish neighborhoods turn into Negro neighborhoods fairly easily. It was not where Jews live that Dr. King's marchers for integrated housing needed massive police protection, this past summer in Chicago. It was where Ukrainians, Lithuanians, Poles, and Italians live—the children and grandchildren of muzhiks (and other peasants).

If I were a Negro I would resent a Jew's acting *broygez*, but I would surely prefer it to someone else's violence. Still, that may only prove I am unable to rise above my Jewish thinking. A few years ago the late Malcolm X said on television—publicly, emphatically, to many thousands—that he liked Sheriff Clark of Selma, Alabama, the man with the dogs and the electric prods, better than Jewish liberals and supporters of the civil-rights movement. Malcolm said: Clark is a wolf but the Jewish liberal is a fox, and the wolf is better because with him you know where you are. Now it appears that Malcolm is a great man in his death, and not only among the young generation of Negroes. A university journal has published a rhetorician's effusion about his rhetoric, which purports to demonstrate—*le style c'est l'homme même*—that Malcolm was good and noble and honest, attacking only those people and things that were wicked and base and false. The rhetoric of the wolf and the fox was not mentioned.

As for populism, we like it in Negroes no more than in muzhiks or in white Americans. Once more, it is violence or the aura of violence that worries us, as well as the encouragement to indulge prejudice and dislike of outsiders and the encouragement to suspect and resent elites, whether good or bad. Dr. King and many others have said harsh things about "the power structure," but the non-power structure is usually worse. Most judges are better than most citizens, most mayors than most voters, most union leaders than most of their members, most presidents of chambers of commerce than most businessmen; Goldwater is better than most Goldwater zealots. I do not say intrinsically good, but relatively better. A dozen or so years ago, a close study of American thinking about civil liberties showed that the average chairwoman of a DAR chapter and the average commander of an American Legion post were usually better than their rank and file.

Black power? For what it represents of violence-populism, no. But it also represents something that modern Jewish history knows, favorably, as self-emancipation (Pinsker's auto-emancipation). Emancipated Jews know self-hate, though it seems to be our good fortune now to know less about it at first hand than only a generation ago. We know or knew enough about it for the books on it to be written by Jews, about Jewish examples. (Who can forget the case of Otto Weininger?) In some form, black power has to precede or accompany black self-acceptance and self-esteem. Otherwise, there will be black self-hate.

When Negroes demand better education for their children, it

must be intolerable for them to hear themselves saying that a predominantly Negro school is necessarily an inferior school. Negroes must feel better when they say that white is not better than black, white is only richer than black; with money, Negro schools can be as good as white schools, and better. This may be a myth now, but if so, it is of that species of myth which, by transforming men, transforms itself into reality. Herzl's Jewish state was a myth of the same species—about which he prophesied, truly: "If you will it, this need not be a myth."

Outsiders
Within

THE JEW AS MODERN WRITER

ALFRED KAZIN

EMMA LAZARUS, who wrote those lines inscribed on the base of the Statue of Liberty ("Give me your tired, your poor . . . Your huddled masses, yearning to breathe free"), was the first Jew whom Ralph Waldo Emerson ever met. Emerson's daughter, Ellen, an old Sunday School teacher, noted how astonishing it was "to get at a real unconverted Jew (who had no objections to calling herself one, and talked freely about 'our Church' and 'we Jews'), and to hear how Old Testament sounds to her, and find she has been brought up to keep the Law, and the Feast of the Passover, and the day of Atonement. The interior view was more interesting than I could have imagined. She says her family are outlawed now, they no longer keep the Law but Christian institutions don't interest her either."

Emma Lazarus had been sending Emerson her poems for years; he responded with uncertain praise, for they were excessively literary and understandably raised questions in the mind of so subtle a critic. But although she was not to become a consciously "Jewish" poet until the Russian pogroms aroused her, her being a Jew had certainly distinguished her in the literary world of Victorian America. She was that still exotic figure, that object of Christian curiosity, "the Jew"—and to descendants of the New England Puritans, straight out of their Bible.

Proust was to say that in every Jew "there is a prophet and a bounder." Emma Lazarus was still the "prophet" when she visited Concord. This was in 1876, when Jews in this country were getting known as "bounders." General Grant in a Civil War order had said "Jew" when he meant peddler, but impoverished farmers in the West now said "Jew" when they meant Wall Street financier. New England writers like James Russell Lowell and Henry Adams became obsessed with Jews and "the Jewish question" as soon as there were real Jews on the American scene. The "prophet" figure that literary New England had always known from books had become the "bounder"—and worse, the ragged *shtetl* Jew whom Adams examined with such loathing from a Russian railway car and in New York when he heard him speaking "a weird guttural Yiddish." Henry James, returning to his native downtown streets, announced that "the denizens of the New York Ghetto, heaped as thick as the splinters on the table of a glass-blower, had each, like the fine glass particle, his or her individual share of the whole hard glitter of Israel." The Jew in New York was an instance of alienness, an object to be studied. James would have been astonished to think of a writer coming out of this milieu. And to do him justice, not many immigrant Jews saw themselves as writers in English. Henry Adams's sometime protégé, Bernard Berenson, who had come here from Lithuania, was to find himself only as an art historian in Italy.

William Dean Howells, now a socialist in New York, praised Abraham Cahan's *Yekl, A Tale Of The New York Ghetto*. But Howells was predisposed to Russian literature, Cahan was a "Russian" realist in English, and Howells, like so many Westerners enjoying or soon to enjoy New York's "Europeanness," was also a democratic idealist, naturally friendly to all these new peoples in New York. His friend Mark Twain said that Jews were members of the human race: "that is the worst you can say about them." But this easy Western humor was still very far from the creative equality that Jewish and non-Jewish writers were some day to feel. Mark Twain, like Maxim Gorky in Russia, protested against pogroms and was friendly to Jews; but as late as 1910, when he died, there was no significant type of Jewish writer in this country. The older German-Jewish stock had produced many important scholars and publicists; it was to produce an original in Gertrude Stein. But the positive, creative role of the Jew as modern American, and above all as a modern American writer, was in the first years of this century being prepared not in the universities, not even in journalism, but in the vaudeville theaters, music halls, and burlesque houses where the pent-up eagerness of penniless immigrant youngsters met the raw urban scene on its own terms. It was not George Jean Nathan, Robert

Nathan, or Ludwig Lewisohn, any more than it was Arthur Krock, David Lawrence, Adolph Ochs, or Walter Lippmann who established the Jew in the national consciousness as a distinctly American figure; it was the Marx Brothers, Eddie Cantor, Al Jolson, Fannie Brice, George Gershwin. Jewish clowns, minstrels, songwriters helped to fit the Jew to America, and America to the Jew, with an *élan* that made for future creativity in literature as well as for the mass products of the "entertainment industry."

Proust, with his artist's disengagement from both "prophet" and "bounder"; Henry Adams, with his frivolous hatred of the immigrant ("five hundred thousand Jews in New York eating kosher, and saved from the drowning they deserve"), had never conceived of the Jew as a representative national entertainer. But in the naturalness and ease with which the Jewish vaudevillian put on blackface, used stereotypes, and ground out popular songs, in the avidity with which the public welcomed him, was the Jew's share in the common experience, the Jew's averageness and typicality, that were to make possible the Jew-as-writer in this country. In Western Europe, Jewish "notables" had been a handful—as odd as the occasional prime minister of Italy or Britain; in Eastern Europe, where the Jews were a mass, it was their very numbers that was so disturbing to anti-Semites in office, who even in Soviet Russia were to keep Jews down because the thought of too many Jews being allowed to exercise their talents at once could obviously be viewed as a threat to their own people. As Mikoyan was to say (some years ago) to a Jewish delegation, "We have our own cadres now." But in this country, the very poverty and cultural rawness of the Jewish immigrant masses, the self-assertive egalitarianism of the general temper, and the naturalness with which different peoples could identify with each other in the unique half-way house that was New York (without New York it would no doubt all have been different, but without New York there would have been no immigrant epic, no America), gave individual performers the privilege of representing the popular mind. Never before had so numerous a mass of Jews been free citizens of the country in which they lived, and so close to the national life. And although many a genteel young literatus now analyzing Nathanael West and Saul Bellow shudders at his connection with Potash and Perlmutter, Eddie Cantor and Fannie Brice, it is a fact that this "vulgar culture," proceeding merrily to the irreverent genius of the Marx Brothers (whose best movies were written by S. J. Perelman, the college chum and brother-in-law of Nathanael West), helped to found, as a natural habitat for the Jews in this country, the consciously grotesque style of parody that one finds in Perelman, West, Odets, Bellow, in many Broadway-Hollywood satirists, and even in an occasional literary critic, like Isaac Rosenfeld and Harold Rosenberg, impatient with the judicial tone that comes with the office. The Jewish writer, a late arrival in this country and admittedly of uncertain status, had to find his model in the majority culture, and although this had some depressing consequences in the mass, it was on the whole fortunate, for the sharply independent novelists, poets, and critics to come, that they were influenced more by the language of the street than by the stilted moralism that has always been a trap for the Jewish writer.

But of course the popular culture was invigorating and even liberating so long as it was one of many cultures operating simultaneously on the Jewish writer's mind. Ever since the legal emancipation of the Jews in Western Europe, there had been two principal cultures among the Jews—the orthodox, religious tradition, pursuing its own way often magnificently indifferent to the issues shaking European thought; and the newly secularistic culture of the "Jewish intellectuals," who found in the cause of "progressive humanity," in philosophic rationalism, in socialism, and cultural humanism, their sophisticated equivalent of Judaism. In Western Europe, for the most part, these two cultures no longer irritated each other. But among the Yiddish-speaking Jews of Eastern Europe, "enlightenment" did not appear until late in the 19th century; while in Western Europe the medieval ghettos were a barely tolerated memory, in Russia the Jewish Pale of Settlement, restricting most Jews to certain areas and restricting the intensity of their existence to the *shtetl* and its religious customs, remained a searing memory in the lives of immigrants and their children. The "dark" ages and the "modern" age, the ghetto and the revolutionary movement, persecution and free human development, were conjoined in the Jewish mind. The tension and ardor with which the two cultures of modern Jewry were related, in individual after individual, helps to explain the sudden flowering of painters among Russian Jews in the first years of this century, the extraordinary spiritual energy invested in the idea of socialism, the "twist" that Isaac Babel liked to give his Russian sentences, the general passion for "culture" and "cultural advancement," the revolutionary zeal with which former yeshiva boys turned political commissars spoke of the great new age of man.

Babel wrote of ex-seminarists riding away with the Red Cavalry from their "rotted" Bibles and Talmuds; Chagall's *rebbes* sprouted wings over the thatched roofs of Vitebsk and sang the joys of the flesh. The force of some immense personal transformation could be seen in the conscious energy of Trotsky's public role in the Russian Revolution. These revolutionaries, writers, scientists, painters were the "new men," the first mass secularists in the long religious history of the Jews, yet the zeal with which they engaged themselves to the "historic" task of desacralizing the European tradition often came from the profound history embedded in Judaism itself—it certainly did not come from the experience of Jews with other peoples in Eastern Europe. These "new men" had a vision of history that, as their critics were to tell them, was fanatically all of one piece, obstinately "Jewish" and "intellectual"—a vision in which some subtle purposiveness to history always managed to reassert itself in the face of repeated horrors. But what their critics could not recognize was that this obstinate quest for "meaning" was less a matter of conscious thought than a personal necessity, a requirement of survival, the historic circumstance that reasserted itself in case after case among the Jews, many of whom had good reason to believe that their lives were a triumph over every possible negation, and who, with the modesty of people for whom life itself is understandably the greatest good, found it easy to rejoice in the political and philosophic reasoning that assured them civic respect, civic peace, and the life of the mind.

"Excess of sorrow laughs," wrote Blake in *The Marriage of Heaven and Hell*. "Excess of joy weeps." For Jews in this country, who had triumphed over so much, remembered so much, were in such passionate relations with the two cultures—of religion and "modernity" that many believed in simultaneously—their conscious progress often became something legendary, a drama rooted in the existential fierceness of life lived and barely redeemed every single day. There was an intensity, a closeness to many conflicting emotions, that often seemed unaccountably excessive to other peoples. The need to explain himself to himself, to put his own house in order, was a basic drive behind many a Jewish writer. People to whom existence has often been a consciously fearful matter, who have lived at the crossroads between the cultures and on the threshold between life and death, naturally see existence as tension, issue, and drama, woven out of so many contradictions that only a work of art may appear to *hold* these conflicts, to compose them, to allow the human will some detachment. Surely never in history has a whole people had to endure such a purgation of emotions as took place at the Eichmann trial. It was this that led Harold Rosenberg to show the cruel dramatic necessity behind the trial—the need of the Jews to tell their story, to relive the unbearable, the inadmissible, the inexpressible. The Jew who has lived through the age of Hitler cannot even say, with Eliot, "After such knowledge, what forgiveness?" For he has to live with his knowledge if he is to live at all, and this "knowledge" enforces itself upon him as a fact both atrocious and dramatic, a mockery of the self-righteous Christianity that has always surrounded him, a parody of the Orthodox Judaism that has sought to justify the ways of God to man, a drama founded on the contrast between the victims and all those who remained spectators when the Jews were being slaughtered.

There are experiences so extreme that, after living them, one can do nothing with them *but* put them into words. There are experiences so terrible that one can finally do nothing with them but not forget them. This was already the case with many of the young Jewish writers just out of the city ghettos, who began to emerge in significant numbers only in the early 30's. Looking back on this emergence, one can see that it needed the peculiar crystallization of ancient experiences, then the avidity with which young writers threw themselves on the American scene, to make possible that awareness of the Jew as a new force that one sees in such works of the 30's as Henry Roth's *Call It Sleep*, Michael Gold's *Jews Without Money*, Daniel Fuchs's *Summer in Williamsburg*, Albert Halper's *The Chute*, Odets's *Awake and*

Sing, Meyer Levin's *The Old Bunch,* and even in West's *Miss Lonelyhearts,* whose hero is not named a Jew but who is haunted by the indiscriminate pity that was to mark the heroes of Bernard Malamud and Edward Wallant. In the 20's, several extraordinarily sensitive writers, notably Paul Rosenfeld and Waldo Frank, had emerged out of the older German-Jewish stock; but on the whole, it needed the turbulent mixing of the ghetto and the depression to make possible the wild flurry of strong new novels and plays in the 30's.

Yet the social realists of the 30's were often boxed in, mentally, by the poverty and hopelessness of their upbringing and the bitterness, deprivations, and anti-Semitism of depression America. The extraordinary brevity of so many literary careers in America is a social fact that any account of the Jewish writer in America must contend with as an omen for the future. Although the aborted career is common enough in American writing and was particularly marked among writers of the 30's—many were shipwrecked by the failure of their political hopes, and many crippled as artists by the excessive effort it took to bring out their non-selling books—it is also a fact that writers from the "minorities" have a harder time getting started, and tend, as a group, to fade out more easily, than those writers from the older stocks whose literary culture was less deliberately won and is less self-conscious. A historian of the Negro novel in this country says that most Negroes who have published one book have never published another—and one might well wonder what, until the sudden fame of James Baldwin, would have induced any Negro writer in this country to keep at it except the necessity of telling his own story. Thinking of the family situation portrayed in *Call It Sleep,* one can see why, having written *that* up, to the vast indifference of the public in the 30's, the author should have felt that he was through. The real drama behind most Jewish novels and plays, even when they are topical and revolutionary in feeling, is the contrast between the hysterical tenderness of the Oedipal relation and the "world"; in the beginning there was the Jewish mother and her son, but the son grew up, he went out into the world, he became a writer. That was the beginning of his career, and usually the end of the novel. Jews don't believe in original sin, but they certainly believe in the original love that they once knew in the *shtetl,* in the kitchen, in the Jewish household—and after *that* knowledge, what forgiveness? In this, at least, the sentimental author of *Jews Without Money* parallels the master of childhood in *Call It Sleep*.

What saved Jewish writing in America from its innate provincialism, what enabled it to survive the moral wreckage of the 30's, was the coming of the "intellectuals"—writers like Delmore Schwartz, Saul Bellow, Lionel Trilling, Karl Shapiro, Harold Rosenberg, Isaac Rosenfeld, Lionel Abel, Clement Greenberg, Bernard Malamud, Irving Howe, Philip Rahv, Leslie Fiedler, Robert Warshow, Paul Goodman, Norman Mailer, Philip Roth, William Phillips. It was these and younger writers in their tradition who made possible intellectual reviews like *Partisan Review* and serious, objective, unparochial magazines like *Commentary*— a magazine which has emphasized general issues and regularly included so many writers who are not Jews. *Commentary*, founded in November 1945, was hospitable to this new maturity and sophistication among Jewish writers in America; it established itself on the American scene easily, and with great naturalness, exactly in those years immediately after the war when American Jews began to publish imaginative works and intellectual studies of distinction—*Dangling Man, The Victim, The Middle of the Journey, The Liberal Imagination, Death of a Salesman, The Naked and the Dead, The World is a Wedding, The Lonely Crowd, The Natural, The Adventures of Augie March, The Mirror and the Lamp, The Tradition of the New*.

Even a gifted writer outside this group, Salinger, contemptuous of its ideologies, was an "intellectual" writing about "intellectuals." Even a middlebrow sullenly critical of its preoccupations, Herman Wouk, did it the honor of "exposing" an intellectual in *The Caine Mutiny*. Whether they were novelists or just intellectual pundits at large, what these writers all had in common was the ascendancy of "modern literature," which has been more destructive of bourgeois standards than Marxism, was naturally international-minded, and in a culture bored with middle-class rhetoric, upheld the primacy of intelligence and the freedom of the imagination. The heroes of these "intellectuals" were always Marx, Freud, Trotsky, Eliot, Joyce, Valéry; the "intellectuals" believed in the "great enlighteners," because their greatest freedom was to be enlighteners of all culture themselves, to be the instructors and illuminati of the modern spirit. Unlike so many earlier writers, who had only their hard story to tell, and then departed, the Jewish "intellectuals" who emerged in the 40's found shelter under the wide wings of the "modern movement," and so showed an intellectual spirit that Jews had not always managed in the great world.

Of course the prosperity that began with the war encouraged the new writers to feel that the country was theirs. Immediately after the war, indeed, some of them embraced this new-found land, their America, with an enthusiasm made slightly hysterical by the need to cast off Marxist ideology. Yet this new liveliness could be attributed in the greatest part to the closing up of a time lag, to the sudden eruption of writers whose time had come—and who had often been brought up in old-fashioned ways that impressed the dizzyingly complex new world upon their minds with special vividness.

Sartre says in *Les Mots* of the grandfather who brought him up —"Between the first Russian Revolution and the first World War, fifteen years after Mallarmé's death . . . a man of the 19th century was foisting upon his grandson ideas that had been current under Louis Philippe. . . . Ought I to complain? . . . In our bustling societies, delays sometimes give a head start." Many a Jewish writer has been brought up on his grandfather's ideas, and now engages the last third of the 20th century with special eagerness. Generally speaking, the Jewish intellectuals who since the 40's have exercised so much influence on American culture started very far back. If the young man from the provinces, as Lionel Trilling named him, typifies the encounter with the great world in 19th-century novels, it was significantly the Jewish intellectual who was now to write the key book on Matthew Arnold, the definitive biographies of Henry Adams, Henry James, James Joyce, who was to become the theoretician of action painting, the most resourceful American novelist of the postwar period, the editor of the leading cultural review, the Reichian *enfant terrible* of the universities, the novelist of orgiastic high life in Palm Springs, Las Vegas, Hollywood, and the Waldorf Towers. Often enough, graduates of the old revolutionary movement, with its intellectual ardor, its internationalism, its passion for political complexities, and its taste for action, these Jewish intellectuals combined an American belief in the "tradition of the new" with their own moral tradition and their passion for the Europe of the great thinkers, their driving personal ambition with the knowledge that they were exceptions, "survivors," as Moses Elkanah Herzog said, of the age that had seen their brethren slaughtered like cattle in the abattoirs that the Nazis had made of Eastern Europe. Just as it was Southern writers, with their knowledge of defeat and their instinctive irony, who in the 40's spoke to the chastened American mind, so it is Jewish writers who now represent to many Americans the unreality of their prosperity and the anxiety of their condition. In situations of inestimable complexity, requiring the most "sophisticated" and "expert" "analysis" of the "complex factors," it was often enough Jews, born and pushed to be intellectuals, who became the connoisseurs of the new chaos, the mental elite of the power age. Never was interpretation, explanation, commentary, a vital new *midrash*, so much needed as in the period, starting with the war, when the world was so much compressed and subtilized by the new technological revolution—and never were there so many Jewish intellectuals prepared to do the explaining. The ragged old "prophet" was not much in evidence, and the Jew-as-bounder was not to be thought of, but the age of the intellectuals was in full swing.

All the writers were intellectuals now, the best writers as well as the most conformist—novelists like Saul Bellow and Norman Mailer dealt in the drama of concepts, had heroes who lived by concepts and suffered for them. The world seemed suspended on concepts, and in the mass magazines as in the universities and publishing houses a mass of indistinguishable sophisticates genuflected to the same modern idols and talked the same textbook formulae about Joyce, James, Eliot, Faulkner, Picasso, Stravinsky. The Sunday book supplements were soon all as apocalyptic as a Jewish novelist after a divorce, and one could regularly read footnotes to the absurdity of the human condition, the death of tragedy, and the end of innocence by pseudo-serious minds who imitated Bellow, Mailer, Fiedler, Ginsberg, Goodman as humorlessly as teen-age girls copied hair styles from the magazines.

Definitely, it was now the thing to be Jewish. But in Western universities and small towns many a traditional novelist and professor of English felt out of it, and asked, with varying degrees of self-control, if there was no longer a good novel to be written about the frontier, about Main Street, about the good that was in marriage? Was it possible, these critics wondered aloud, that American life had become so de-regionalized and lacking in local color that the big power units and the big cities had preempted the American scene, along with the supple Jewish intellectuals who were at home with them? Was it possible that Norman Mailer had become the representative American novelist?

It was entirely possible, and certainly the thought would not have astonished Mailer, just as the power of his example for other novelists did not astonish Saul Bellow. Whatever pain this ascendancy might cause to writers who felt out of it because they lived in Montana, or in the wrong part of California, it was a fact that there were now Jewish novelists who, as writers, had mastered the complex resources of the modern novel, who wrote English lovingly, possessively, masterfully, for whom the language and the form, the intelligence of art, had become as natural a way of living as the Law had been to their grandfathers. Literature had indeed become their spiritual world, their essential personal salvation, in a world where all traditional markers were fast disappearing. But in the frothy turbulent "mix" of America in the 60's, with its glut, its power drives, its confusion of values, the Jewish writer found himself so much read, consulted, imitated, that he knew it would not be long before the reaction set in—and in fact the decorous plaint of the "Protestant minority" has been succeeded by crudely suggestive phrases about the "Jewish Establishment," the "O.K. Writers and the Poor Goy," "The Jewish-American Push." Yet it is plainly a certain success that has been resented, not the Jew. And if the Jew has put his distinct mark on modern American writing, it is surely because, in a time when the old bourgeois certainties and humanist illusions have crumbled, the Jew is practiced in what James called "the imagination of disaster," and "does indeed see life as ferocious and sinister." The contemporary literary temper is saturnine, panicky, black in its humor but adroit in shifting the joke onto the shoulders of society. And the Jewish writer, with his natural interest in the social fact, has been particularly quick to show the lunacy and hollowness of so many present symbols of authority. Anxiety hangs like dry electricity in the atmosphere of modern American life, and the stimulus of this anxiety, with all its comic overtones, is the realized subject in the novels of Bruce Jay Friedman, Joseph Heller, Richard Stern, Jeremy Larner, the plays of Jack Gelber and Arthur Kopit. There is real madness to modern governments, modern war, modern moneymaking, advertising, science, and entertainment; this madness has been translated by many Jewish writers into the country they live in, the time that offers them everything but hope. In a time of intoxicating prosperity, it has been natural for the Jewish writer to see how superficial society can be, how pretentious, atrocious, unstable—and comic. This, in a secular age when so many people believe in nothing but society's values, is the significance to literature of the Jewish writer's being a Jew.

THE CONVERSIONS OF THE JEWS

ALLEN GUTTMANN

WHEN THE BUILDERS of Bay Colony likened themselves to the
Israelites of the Old Testament, when they spoke of their settle-
ments at Boston and Salem as a "wilderness Zion," they could not
have known that the Jews of the Diaspora would come, within a
generation, to complicate the metaphor that made America the
promised land. But come they did, only to discover that acceptance in the new world undid them as persecution in the old
had not. Many became Christians. More became converts to the
American Way, to the religion of Americanism.

As early as 1825, Jews in Charleston rejected the Orthodoxy of
Congregation Beth Elohim and organized the Reformed Society
of Israelites. Their statement of principles repudiated rabbinical
interpretations and accepted the laws of Moses only as far, in their
words, "as they can be adapted to the institutions of the Society
in which [we] live and enjoy the blessings of liberty." Their
slogan was simple: "America is our Zion and Washington is our
Jerusalem." Reform Judaism, the intellectual consequence of
Jewish Emancipation, flourished in America under the leadership
of David Einhorn, Kaufmann Kohler, and Isaac Mayer Wise.
The Pittsburgh Platform of 1885, the basic document of Reform
Judaism in America, was a manifesto that might almost have won
the support of William Ellery Channing and Ralph Waldo Emerson: "We recognize in every religion an attempt to grasp the
Infinite One, and in every mode . . . of revelation held sacred in
any religious system the consciousness of the indwelling of God
in man." The Mosaic and rabbinical laws of diet and dress, and
even of morals, were rejected insofar as they did not conform "to
the views and habits of modern civilization."

Reprinted by permission of the author and the publisher from *Wisconsin
Studies in Contemporary Literature*, VI (Summer 1965), 161–176. The paper
was originally presented at the English Institute, Columbia University,
September, 1964.

Even as the Reformers extended the "hand of fellowship to all who cooperate with us in the establishment of the reign of truth and righteousness among men," they must have realized that the "views and habits of modern civilization" are often ignoble. Historians and sociologists—Nathan Glazer, Oscar Handlin, Will Herberg, Moses Rischin, Marshall Sklare—have shown that Jews converted to the Age of Enterprise as well as to the Ideals of Enlightenment. At their best, American Jews have contributed immensely to the institutionalization of liberty, equality, and fraternity. At their worst, American Jews have been late-comers to the "great barbecue" of American capitalism, scramblers after the scraps left by Carnegie and Rockefeller and Vanderbilt, greedy greenhorns of the Gilded Age. Many a reformer of traditional Judaism must have wondered—in the din of the marketplace—if the baggage left behind at Ellis Island wasn't better stuff than the shoddy goods bought and sold in Brookline and in Brownsville. But very few have recanted from their metaphoric conversion to America.

As the words of Emma Lazarus on the Statue of Liberty suggest, the story of Americanization is the first great theme of Jewish literature in the new world. The first great name, after Emma Lazarus herself, is Abraham Cahan, whose novel, *The Rise of David Levinsky*, was published in 1917. When David Levinsky, a pious student of the Talmud, confides in Reb Sender his decision to emigrate, the Rabbi is dismayed: "To America! Lord of the World! But one becomes a Gentile there!" Reb Sender was right. David shears off his earlocks and abandons one by one the 613 commandments by which the pious Jew regulates his life. "If you are a Jew of the type to which I belonged when I came to New York and you attempt to bend your religion to the spirit of your new surroundings, it breaks. It falls to pieces. The very clothes I wore and the very food I ate had a fatal effect on my religious habits." David rises, becomes a millionaire in the garment industry, a freethinker for whom Spencer's Unknowable replaces the Living God of Sinai. His deepest loyalty is to America. David describes a concert where the audience sat apathetically, unmoved by themes from *Aïda* and by Yiddish songs; the national anthem brought the Jews enthusiastically to their feet: "It was as if they were saying: 'We are not persecuted under this flag. At last we have found a home.'" Like Silas Lapham, whom he very much resembles, David remembers the old ways: "I can never forget the days of my misery. I cannot escape from my old self. My past and my present do not comport well. David, the poor lad swinging over a Talmud volume at the Preacher's Synagogue seems to have more in common with my inner identity than David Levinsky, the well-known cloak-manufacturer." Despite nostalgia and regret, there is no return. Abraham Cahan, whose editorship of the *Jewish Daily Forward* made him the foremost figure in Yiddish journalism, wrote his *Meisterwerk* in English.

A generation later, Meyer Levin, in the book that insures him a place in our literary history, chronicled the rise of the second-generation Jews of Chicago's West Side. *The Old Bunch*, published in 1937, moves from 1921 to 1934—the years of *The Jazz Singer* and *Show Boat* and Leopold and Loeb and the Lindbergh Flight and Samuel Insull and Al Capone and the magnificent mid-depression symbol of hope, Chicago's Century of Progress World's Fair. The older generation speaks Yiddish and fears that bobbed hair is the short cut to prostitution. The younger generation leaves the old ways behind as it climbs into the middle class. Doctors, lawyers, dentists, artists, teachers, dry-cleaners, realtors, and part-time bicycle-racers, yes; rabbis and Talmudic scholars, no. *Mitzvot*—God's commandments—are as little regarded as the Volstead Act. Passover becomes a drunken brawl, with paper hats, comic place cards, and a layer cake topped with an effigy of Moses: "Manny picked up a curled streamer that lay near his place and blew noisily. The red crepe paper shot across the table and dropped over Sam's ear . . . The maid brought in an immense, sugar-baked ham." The idealistic lawyer, soon to become a defender of labor-leaders and rent-strikers, rushes in disgust from those who have sold their birthright for a mess of *trefa* (non-kosher food). No one can imagine what bothers him. Isn't he, after all, an atheist?

A generation later, in 1963, Burt Blechman writes of the War of Camp Omongo and charts the erosion of Jewish values in the great out-of-doors. The camp is, of course, run for financial profit and sexual exploration. The boys at the camp are wise in the ways of the Age of Eisenhower: "Nobody believes in God. But you still gotta have a religion." When the camp's rabbi misunderstands his decorative role and begins to speak of Jehovah, the camp's owner drowns him out with a tape-recorded rendition, by the Marine Corps Band, of "The Stars and Stripes Forever." The creed of Camp Omongo is a parody of Sinai's: "All graven images shall be as follows: Gold for 1st; Silver for 2nd; Bronze for 3rd; and Strontium 90 for the rest. . . . Thou shalt kill for God and country on demand. . . . Thou shalt adulterate the water, pollute the land, and poison the air for the sake of our fathers' pride." Burt Blechman, like Philip Roth and Bruce Jay Friedman, seems to disbelieve—and to be appalled by those who disbelieve.

Philip Roth's collection of stories, *Goodbye, Columbus*, appeared in 1960. The Patimkins have risen on kitchen sinks. Business was, during the war-years, phenomenally good. Is not cleanliness more profitable than godliness? Their refrigerators burst with fruit; their trees bear sporting goods. Brenda Patimkin is a paragon of Olympic virtues: she plays tennis, she runs, she rides, she swims. In the pool, she is a long way from the Yiddishe Momma of yesteryear. "I went," says her boy-friend,

> to pull her towards me just as she started fluttering up; my hand hooked on to the front of her suit and the cloth pulled away from her. Her breasts swam towards me like two pink-nosed fish and she let me hold them. Then, in a moment, it was the sun who kissed us both, and we were out of the water, too pleased with each other to smile.

And, as Leonard Baskin laments in a recent symposium, "For every poor and huddled *mikvah* [the ritual bath] there is a ten-hundred of swimming pools." In this suburban world, the past seems passé indeed. In another of Roth's stories, the father who attempts to affirm a heritage he never inherited is shocked to discover what that heritage includes:

> Sunday mornings I have to drive my kid all the way to Scarsdale to learn Bible stories. And you know what she comes up with . . . —that this Abraham in the Bible was going to kill his own kid for a *sacrifice!* You call that religion? I call it sick. Today a guy like that they'd lock him up.

When the hero of the story becomes "a guy like that," he is, indeed, locked up. The suburban Jew, for better and for worse, is far closer to his Gentile neighbors than to the vanished world of the East European *shtetl*.

Theoretically, the ultimate consequence of *acculturation* is *assimilation;*[1] the penultimate step is intermarriage. What prevents the children of nominal Jews from intermarriage with the children of nominal Protestants and Catholics? Very little. Sociologists, who once stated flatly that 5% was the natural limit of the rate of intermarriage, now chart rates three times as high. And higher. Where today, in child-centered America, is the parent who will rend his garments and sit *shiva* for the son who marries a *shiksa*, who will say for his errant son the prayer for the dead? In his very language, the father of Myron Kaufmann's hero, Richard Amsterdam, betrays his inability to stay the course of Americanization: "All these generations, and now I'm the Last of the Mohicans."

Kaufmann's novel, *Remember Me to God* (1957), is one of many commended by sociologists for their insight into the last stages of assimilation. The rabbi of Richard Amsterdam's temple is beloved by his congregation because he *can't* speak Yiddish. Richard himself goes to Harvard, mends his manners, and becomes an unscrupulous aspirant to Hasty Pudding. He scorns a lovely Jewish girl in order to whore after a Jezebel from Beacon Hill. His father, an immigrant who worked himself through law school, is pathetic in his inarticulate efforts to stop his son from intermarriage and conversion to Christianity. No longer aware of the reason of his Jewishness, the father cannot persuade the son to remain a Jew: "I can't explain it. . . . It's sort of as if that word is me. When I hear the word 'Jew,' I know it means me." He is more dignified, even when striking his son and weeping in despair, than Rabbi Budapester, who tells Richard, "It's fun to be a Jew." Budapester borrows from those literary critics who have ignored the Revelation at Mount Sinai in their vision of the Jew as archetypal Victim or Marginal Man; "Jews are Man in the extreme," says Budapester; they "have been at once the most magnificent and the most wretched of peoples, and this is the essence of Man." Richard is unmoved; "I don't want to be anybody's legend. . . . The trouble with you guys is that you want me to act out your fairytale." Rabbi Budapester leaves in a huff— in a Cadillac.

Complications of the subplot prevent Richard Amsterdam's marriage. Paul Shiel, the hero of Neal Oxenhandler's *A Change of Gods* (1962), takes the final steps. Attracted by blonde Candy Martin, he marries her in Florence. He is as free of Jewish traditions as she is of Catholic dogma. But motor-scooter and hotel room are false symbols of mobility and freedom. Families are real. Paul's family is vulgar and oppressive. Candy's grandfather —a philologist—is austere and devout and determined that Paul convert to Catholicism. Paul becomes a communicant, is denounced as an Eichmann and—the plot is complicated—sent to prison. Father and son are consequently reconciled, but the conversion to Christianity is for keeps. Paul has joined the ranks of those who pray on Good Friday, until the Vatican Council shall deem otherwise, for the conversion of the Jews.

There are not, in America, very many Paul Shiels. There are, moreover, Christians who become Jews. Bernard Malamud's assistant and Philip Roth's Libby Herz are fictional characters whose roads to Judaism parallel the improbable paths taken by Marilyn Monroe, Elizabeth Taylor, and Sammy Davis, Jr. As Mordecai Kaplan has insisted since 1934, as Nathan Glazer points out in his excellent history of American Judaism, the real threat to the survival of the Jewish community in America is the pervasive secularism of the modern world. The majority of American Jews are Jews only by the quirks of popular definition.[2] When asked about his heritage, Philip Roth spoke for many:

> I cannot find a true and honest place in the history of believers that begins with Abraham, Isaac, and Jacob on the basis of the heroism of these believers or of their humiliations and anguish. I can connect with them and with their descendants [only] as I apprehend their God. And until such time as I do apprehend him, there will continue to exist between myself and those others who seek his presence, a question, sometimes spoken, sometimes not, which for all the pain and longing it may engender, for all the disappointment and bewilderment it may produce, cannot be swept away by nostalgia or sentimentality or even by a blind and valiant effort of the will: how are you connected to me as another man is not?

American Jews who *have* apprehended the God of Abraham, Isaac, and Jacob have not ignored the threat of assimilation or been blind to the conversion of Jews to secularism. American Jews who have remained true to Torah and Talmud have struggled to win converts, and with some success.

In 1886, only one year after the Reformers' Pittsburgh Platform, Conservative Jews established the Jewish Theological Seminary, the point of departure in the quest for a traditional and historical compromise between Orthodoxy and Reform. The exodus of two million Jews from Eastern Europe saved the Conservative seminary from collapse and enabled the Orthodox to begin, in 1896, the first American Yeshiva, the Rabbi Isaac

Elchanan Theological Seminary, now Yeshiva University. The Gordian rapidity with which secularized Jews severed the bonds that bound them to their tradition brought the leaders of Reform Judaism to Columbus, Ohio, in 1937, in order to restore to their creed the centrality of the Torah and a belief in the peoplehood of Israel. In Horace Kallen's philosophy of cultural pluralism, Jews anxious to avoid assimilation discovered a rationale by which they hoped to be good Americans and yet maintain the ways of their fathers. In the theology of Mordecai Kaplan, Will Herberg, and Abraham Joshua Heschel, many Jews have found a faith relevant to the twentieth century. Although the third and fourth generations continue to drift further and further from any knowledge of historical Judaism, their elders no longer encourage them.

Within the literary world, the campaign to win converts for Judaism has been three-fold: first, the attack on those who defect from or denigrate the Jewish community; second, continued emphasis on the dangers of anti-Semitism; third, an affirmation of the positive aspects of Judaism and of the Jewish community.

In 1937, Meyer Levin's work was, he writes in his auto-biography,

> preached against in the temples and described in some of the Jewish press as a degradation of our people. I received a call from the secretary of the Anti-Defamation League who took me to lunch at one of the downtown Jewish clubs. . . . The general theme was: Why do you young Jewish writers feel impelled to describe your people in this disgusting manner?

More recently, Edward Adler, Jerome Charyn, Babette Deutsch, Leslie Fiedler, Norman Fruchter, Herbert Gold, Irving Howe, Alfred Kazin, Philip Roth, Muriel Rukeyser, L. S. Simckes, and Louis Untermeyer have been denounced as anti-Semitic or abused for their aloofness from the Jewish community. Even Norman Podhoretz, struggling to "do" the modern without un-doing the traditional, has run into difficulty: "Once . . . I nearly caused a riot when I attacked the prosody of a minor Israeli poet by invoking E. E. Cummings as a standard. I was howled down with talk of the blood shed by the six million." A representative chastisement begins as follows: "The renegade Jew in the limbo of lost identity is a sad phenomenon of the West. He is a self-hating, self-created, ectoplasmic figure who, having renounced his origins, realizes from time to time that he has also deprived his own children of a history." The reference to "self-hating" derives from Theodor Lessing's book, *Der Jüdische Selbsthass*, imported into this country by the social psychologist Kurt Lewin. This immensely overworked theory holds that alienated Jews apparently committed to secularism or converted to Christianity are actually driven by self-hate. They seek neurotically to deny what they know to be their true identity. Meyer Levin has, for instance, accused Budd Schulberg of self-hate, written a novel that shows Leopold and Loeb murdering Bobbie Frank because of self-hate, and suggested in his latest novel that converts to Communism are exemplars of self-hate. Preachments against the "self-hate" of Philip Roth have become the missionary's *modus vivendi*. Roth too has been called up and taken to lunch and advised to be more positive. He too has been denounced in the synagogues. Stuart Rosenberg, for example, has noted that Roth is one of those hateful intellectuals who publish in *Commentary*, one of those whose "criticisms, exaggerated by the self-hate of their alienation, cannot serve as an adequate guide to the true condition of the American Jewish community today." Unlike most writers, Roth has braved the fury and answered back:

> The question really is: who is going to address men and women like men and women, and who like children? If there are Jews who have begun to find the stories the novelists tell more provocative and pertinent than the sermons of some of the rabbis, perhaps it is because there are regions of feeling and consciousness in them which cannot be reached by the oratory of self-congratulation and self-pity.

It is the threat of anti-Semitism and the fate of European Jews under Hitler that make understandable the fanaticism of some of the attacks on allegedly "self-hating" young writers. For those who have lived through Auschwitz and Dachau, books that do *not* return us in imagination to the apocalyptic horror of the concentration camps must seem, at times, utterly irrelevant. John Hersey's novel of the Warsaw ghetto seems almost trivial when compared to the facts of history; most of the novels written about anti-Semitism in America seem trivial when compared to John Hersey's book.[3]

If one seeks arguments for the maintenance of the Jewish community, Arthur Miller's *Focus* and Laura Hobson's *Gentleman's Agreement* are worse than trivial. Both novels attempt to demonstrate that Jews and Gentiles are really indistinguishable. Only the name is different. But this argument weakens rather than strengthens the demand that Jews affirm their unique and distinctive faith. Moreover, the tendency of some to rely on anti-Semitism as the *raison d'être* for the community makes quixotic the fifty-year crusade of the Anti-Defamation League. Moreover, as Nathan Glazer notes in his latest book, as Bruce Jay Friedman shows in his novel, *Stern,* as Ivan Gold suggests in his story, "Taub East," the defense against the evil of anti-Semitism can become disproportionately intense in the United States of Arthur Goldberg, Harry Golden, and Barry Goldwater.

The third form of response to the conversion to America is the presentation in literary form of a "positive" view of Judaism and Jewish life. There is, for instance, the case of Charles Angoff, whose multi-volume odyssey of the Polansky family has been hailed, in the Jewish press, as worthy of a Nobel Prize. "Charles Angoff looms head and shoulders above any Jewish writer in America today," says the reviewer in the *Boston Jewish Advocate;* "Angoff arises as a giant of Jewish literature," says the reviewer in the *Chicago Jewish Forum.* There is, for instance, the case of Karl Shapiro, whose poems for, by, and about Jews are a reproach to Joy Davidman, Muriel Rukeyser, Delmore Schwartz, Howard Nemerov, John Hollander, and all others who have forgotten from whence cometh their salvation.

There is, for instance, the case of Herman Wouk, the best-known of writers committed to Judaism. Although *Marjorie Morningstar* is an outraged polemic against assimilation, Wouk begins with an attempt at fairness. The attractions of Central Park West and Columbia University are real. Lobster and shrimp entice. Noel Airman is, despite the withered arm he inherited from Nathaniel Hawthorne, sexually irresistible. Marjorie sleeps with Noel: "There were shocks, ugly uncoverings, pain, incredible humiliation, shock, shock, and it was over." Sexuality without God is a matter of "nasty, squirming, writhing naked bodies." A kindly psychologist helps to restore Marjorie's peace of mind: "Food disciplines are a part of every great religion. Psychologically, they're almost inevitable, and extremely practical." Marjorie abandons Noel to his fate as a TV-writer and turns to a young lawyer who manfully survives the traumatic knowledge of Marjorie's sinful past. Marjorie becomes Mrs. Milton Schwartz,

> a regular synagogue-goer, active in the Jewish organization of the town; apparently that takes up a lot of her time. . . .

> Her husband is active too. . . . The only remarkable thing about Mrs. Schwartz is that she ever hoped to be remarkable, that she ever dreamed of being Marjorie Morningstar.

. . . Sylvia Rothchild borrowed Wouk's formula for *Sunshine and Salt*. The heroine and her husband are suburbanites with only the loosest connection to the Jewish community. Their false Eden is destroyed by the arrival from Brooklyn of the heroine's mother. Mama isn't acculturated. She fears the unnatural darkness of nights in the country. Grass and flowers annoy her. Taken to the kosher markets of a nearby city, Mama sees slums and is nostalgic. Mama brings the urban rabbi home and he nails a *mazuzeh* to the doorpost and demands a list of the lapsed Jews of the suburb. It is hard for the reader to love Mama, but Mama is right. The *goyish* Jews of the suburb discover that the inner sanctum of the Garden Club is closed to them. When Mama dies in a mysterious accident, the Jewish community declares her a martyr. The heroine returns: "I forgot my fierce wish to be myself. I became more involved in the [Jewish] community. . . . I couldn't help myself. Everyone knew I was Celia Abram's daughter."

Samuel Astrachan, Michael Blankfort, Miriam Bruce, Meyer Levin, and Leon Uris are among those who have, since World War II, dramatized conversions to Judaism and to Zionism, but the best of the novels of return remains Ludwig Lewisohn's *The Island Within*, published in 1928. Lewisohn himself came to America at the age of seven and pledged his allegiance to his new home. He taught Sunday School, labored in the Epworth League, and described himself as "an American, a Southerner, and a Christian." He took an MA at Columbia and discovered that Jews, even converted ones, were not hired to teach English literature and that Americans with German names were roughly handled in 1917 and 1918. Lewisohn became convinced that the American dream was an illusion and that survival was possible only in Palestine. The novel is the powerful expression of that conviction. Lewisohn shows that the migration of the Levy family from Lithuania to Germany to America is also a movement from Orthodoxy to the most tenuous kind of secularized attachment. American-born Arthur Levy, thinking the attachment to Judaism has completely vanished, marries the agnostic daughter of a Christian minister. "Couldn't one help to destroy all those remnants of man's barbarous past by living as though they had no real existence, by living in the light of reason?" The answer is an emphatic *No!* Ironically, Arthur Levy, a disciple of Freud, finds himself married to a sexually repressed woman who sublimates her energies into a career as a hack-writer. A distant cousin, Reb Moshe, gradually brings Arthur Levy back to the path he had strayed from. Reading ancestral documents almost a thousand years old, Arthur Levy realizes that Jews are destined to suffer. The Crusaders massacred the Jews of Speyer and Mainz in 1096; Jews die today in pogroms in Elizavetgrad and Kishinev. Arthur divorces his wife and returns to his people.

When Hitler came to power, Lewisohn reminded us that he had warned us. Lewisohn also understood and warned against the only category of conversion to rival in historical importance that of St. Paul—the conversion to Utopia.

> Escape, escape, anything on any irrelevant periphery. Anything but the center, the heart, the blood. Virgin Spain, the Soviet Fatherland. Anything but the real, the attainable, the given, that for which real work can be done in a world of reality and real sacrifices made and real tears shed and real blood; anything but that to which one is called by nature and unperverted instinct and tradition and where one is wanted and needed and where . . . one can give one's whole heart. Any place but home. Any people except one's own. Any God except the God of one's fathers . . . Utopia is the opiate of . . . the Jewish people.

Utopia is the opiate of the Jewish people. . . . Or their truest vocation. When seen in perspective, the commitment to Marxism will be seen as part of a much more important movement of those alienated from the past and dedicated to the future. The history of political radicalism in America from the anarchism of Emma Goldman and Alexander Berkman through the socialism of Victor Berger and Abraham Cahan and Morris Hillquit to the Communism of Herbert Aptheker and Howard Fast and Joseph Freeman and John Gates and Benjamin Gitlow and Mike Gold and Jay Lovestone and Bertram Wolfe—the history of political radicalism in America has very largely been the history of Jews doubly alienated from Judaism and from Christendom, apostates from the Mosaic dispensation and from the gospel according to Adam Smith.

If assimilation means a world of Babbitts tenuously tied to the B'nai B'rith, if assimilation means a transfer of loyalty from the faith of our fathers to that of our neighbors, if assimilation means removal from Brownsville to Miami Beach, if assimilation means a political lemming-drive led by Barry Goldwater, then assimilation is not enough. The task of the writer alienated from traditional Judaism is the secularization of Judaism's historic sense of mission. If the writer departed from the temple is not to lose himself in the lonely crowd, he must labor to bring about the transformation of society. He must create the Zion in which exile can be ended.

For half a century at least, the conversion to Utopia has been a major theme of Jewish writers in America. Israel Zangwill, the English novelist, rewrote *Romeo and Juliet* fifty years before Leonard Bernstein set it to music. David Quixano, the hero of *The Melting Pot*, composes an American symphony, an orchestration of all the ethnic strains of our nation of nations. He and Vera Revenal break through the barriers of hatred that separated them:

> America is God's Crucible, the great Melting-Pot where all the races of Europe are melting and reforming! Here you stand, good folk, think I, when I see them at Ellis Island, here you stand in your fifty groups, with your fifty languages and histories, and your fifty blood hatreds and rivalries. But you won't be long like that, brothers, for these are the fires of God you've come to—these are the fires of God. A fig for your feuds and vendettas! Germans and Frenchmen, Irishmen and Englishmen, Jews and Russians—into the Crucible with you all! God is making the American!

A generation later, Mike Gold's autobiographical sketch of Jews without money ends with an equally millennial vision:

> A man on an East Side soap-box, one night, proclaimed that out of the despair, melancholy and helpless rage of millions, a world movement had been born to abolish poverty. . . . I listened to him. . . . O workers' revolution, you brought hope to me, a lonely suicidal boy. You are the true Messiah. You will destroy the East Side when you come, and build there a garden for the human spirit.

Even Meyer Levin, whose deepest passion was Zionism rather than socialism, wrote in the 'thirties of poverty and injustice, of bribed judges and corrupt doctors and a tendency among policemen routinely to beat anyone suspected of Communism. When the police, on Memorial Day, 1937, killed ten strikers at the Republic Steel Plant in South Chicago, Meyer Levin wrote *Citizens*, a novel still alive with its author's passionate protest against justice denied in Illinois. In the novel, a doctor committed only to his family and his career accidentally witnesses the Memorial Day massacre. He treats the wounded and struggles to keep the police from dragging them from ambulances and hospital beds. He reads the Chicago papers: MOB ATTACKS POLICE, 200 INJURED AS STRIKERS CHARGE, STRIKERS DRUGGED TO ASSAULT POLICE. By the end of the novel, he marches in the procession to pay homage to the dead:

> As the people approached the wreath, the column narrowed to a single file, and passed slowly, one by one they dropped their dark red flowers, like great swollen drops of blood augmenting the spreading dark pool on the ground.

Marxism, as a mass movement, is finished in the United States. It is common among historians to say that the American consensus has always been too strong for the success of a radical movement. It is more correct to say that the progressive transformation of America has vindicated the few who prodded the many to radical reform. Abraham Cahan's decision to vote for FDR was not the betrayal of socialism that it has sometimes been called, nor is Norman Thomas's faint praise for Lyndon Johnson the result of a loss of faith. Although the word "socialism" is political suicide, we *have* crept a long way.

What of those Americans for whom Fabian progress toward social justice is far too slow, for whom the CIA is the sinister symbol of invisible government, for whom the poverty of the "other America" is a national disgrace? It is obvious to all of us that Negroes have now begun to lead the fight for racial equality. It is obvious to readers of *Dissent, The Monthly Review, New America, New Politics* and *Studies on the Left* that many of the most articulate spokesmen for American radicalism are drawn now, as they were a generation ago, from the ranks of men and women alienated from the Jewish community if not from the tradition of the prophets. The movement for Proletarian Literature is an almost forgotten episode in our history; we are waiting, it is said, for Godot rather than for Lefty. But novelists and poets continue to dissent. Saul Bellow, Norman Fruchter, Herbert Gold, Barbara Probst Solomon, and Harvey Swados support socialist journals today as writers on the left supported *New Masses* and *The Partisan Review* thirty years ago. "Socialism," wrote Irving Howe and Lewis Coser, "is the name of our desire."[4]

The strange career of Norman Mailer is one sign of the alienated Jewish intellectual's continued dedication to the radical transformation of society. "The sour truth," writes Mailer, "is that I am imprisoned with a perception which will settle for nothing less than making a revolution in the consciousness of our time." Mailer's quest is for the classless society in which the shits will no longer kill us, for the perfect orgasm that will give us the time of our time. *Barbary Shore* fails as a novel but who has better described what Trotsky meant to American Jews?

> There was a great man who led us, and I read almost every word he had written, and listened with the passion of the novitiate to each message he sent from the magical center in Mexico . . . I lived more intensely in the past than I could ever in the present, until the sight of a policeman on his mount became the Petrograd proletariat crawling to fame between the legs of a Cossack's horde. . . . There never was a revolution to equal it, and never a city more glorious than Petrograd, and for all that period of my life I lived another and braved the ice of winter and the summer flies in Vyborg while across my adopted country of the past, winds of the revolution blew their flame, and all of us suffered hunger while we drank . . . the wine of equality.

Paul Goodman, another Utopian, castigates society's absurdity:

> [Our society] thwarts aptitude and creates stupidity. It corrupts ingenuous patriotism. It corrupts the fine arts. It shackles science. It dampens animal ardor. It discourages the religious convictions of Justification and Vocation, and it dims the sense that there is a Creation. It has no Honor. It has no Community.

No community. The United States today lacks the communal sense of a traditional society, lacks, for instance, the closeness and compassion of the world described by Alfred Kazin in his memoir, *A Walker in the City*. Goodman believes that the community can be re-created by the radical reconstruction of society. His book, *Communitas*, written with his brother Percival, is a blueprint of the new society. His novel, *Making Do*, is the dramatic revelation of the possibility of a reasonable love that transcends barriers of class, nation, religion, race, and sex. The novel contains violence and disappointment as well as love, but Goodman refuses to settle for the world as it is. "No," he concludes, " 'The Lord has yet more light and truth to break forth,' as John Robinson said to the Pilgrims embarking toward America."⁵

Goodman and Mailer are not alone. Herbert Gold's best novel, *The Prospect Before Us*, is the epitaph of a stubborn hotel-keeper who defies the prejudices of white America and rents a room to a Negro girl—and dies for love of her. Harvey Swados' stories and essays document the degradation of factory life and debunk the myth of a happy worker. Clancy Sigal's *Going Away* is perhaps the most minutely thorough criticism of American life since Dos Passos' *USA*. Driving from Los Angeles to New York, Sigal's anonymous hero seeks traces of that lost world of the 'thirties, where *unions* meant sit-down strikes rather than racial discrimination, where *Spain* meant the defense of Madrid rather than another article in *Holiday*. "I really wanted, while I was on the road, to look at America and try to figure out why it wasn't my country any more." Even Henderson the Rain King and Sergius O'Shaughnessy and Moses Herzog are restlessly radical in their refusal to affirm the status quo, in their active quest for a world more attractive.

I am sure—despite the affluence that fills the land with YWHAs—that traditional Judaism will not disappear from America. There will always be those for whom Abraham and Isaac and the Tables of the Law are more important than Danny Kaye and Leon Uris and ledgers in the black. There will always be those for whom the Utopian dream of the brotherhood of man means less than the historical reality of the peoplehood of Israel. I am also sure that these Jews will decline in numbers. They will also, if the descent from Ludwig Lewisohn to Herman Wouk is any indication, decline in literary importance. For the great majority of American Jews, the process of secularization seems certain to continue toward assimilation in a more secular, if not more attractive, America. The Jewish Book Club of the future will have fifty Edna Ferbers to choose from. The Communist Party will search unsuccessfully for a second Michael Gold. If present tendencies continue, Negroes are more likely than Jews disproportionately to fill the ranks of dissent and to imagine in novel and in poem another country better than the one we live in now. Paradoxically, the survival in America of a significant and identifiably *Jewish* literature depends on the unlikely conversion to Judaism of a stiff-necked intractable generation that no longer chooses to be chosen.

NOTES

1. These terms are used throughout as in Milton M. Gordon's book, *Assimilation in American Life* (New York, 1964).

2. For an explanation of this comment, see my article, "Jewish Radicals, Jewish Writers," *American Scholar*, XXXII (Autumn 1963), 563–75.

3. The exception, Saul Bellow's *The Victim*, is a book that suggests that Semite and anti-Semite are essentially the same man.

4. Ironically, dissenters like Irving Howe and Alfred Kazin and Norman Mailer have become highly conscious of their debts to Judaism in the very years that have seen the majority of American Jews covenant themselves under the New Deal and the New Frontier.

5. Bellow's *The Adventures of Augie March* ends with a very similar image: "Why, I am a sort of Columbus of those near-at-hand and believe you can come to them in this immediate *terra incognita* that spreads out in every gaze. I may well be a flop at this line of endeavor. Columbus too thought he was a flop, probably, when they sent him back in chains. Which didn't prove there was no America.

WRITING ABOUT JEWS

PHILIP ROTH

EVER SINCE some of my first stories were published in 1959 in a volume called *Goodbye, Columbus,* my work has been attacked from certain pulpits and in certain periodicals as dangerous, dishonest, and irresponsible. I have read editorials and articles in Jewish community newspapers condemning these stories for ignoring the accomplishments of Jewish life, or, as Rabbi Emanuel Rackman recently told a convention of the Rabbinical Council of America, for creating a "distorted image of the basic values of Orthodox Judaism," and even, he went on, for denying the non-Jewish world the opportunity of appreciating "the overwhelming contributions which Orthodox Jews are making in every avenue of modern endeavor. . . ." Among the letters I receive from readers, there have been a number written by Jews accusing me of being anti-Semitic and "self-hating," or, at the least, tasteless; they argue or imply that the sufferings of the Jews throughout history, culminating in the murder of six million by the Nazis, have made certain criticisms of Jewish life insulting and trivial. Furthermore, it is charged that such criticism as I make of Jews—or apparent criticism—is taken by anti-Semites as justification for their attitudes, as "fuel" for their fires, particularly as it is a Jew himself who seemingly admits to habits and behavior that are not exemplary, or even normal and acceptable. When I speak before Jewish audiences, invariably there have been people who have come up to me afterward to ask, "Why don't you leave us alone? Why don't you write about the Gentiles?"—"Why must you be so critical?"—"Why do you disapprove of us so?"—this last question asked as often with incredulity as with anger; and often when asked by people a good deal older than myself, asked as of an erring child by a loving but misunderstood parent.

It is difficult, if not impossible, to explain to some of the people claiming to have felt my teeth sinking in, that in many instances they haven't been bitten at all. Not always, but frequently, what readers have taken to be my disapproval of the lives lived by Jews seems to have to do more with their own moral perspective than with the one they would ascribe to me: at times they see wickedness where I myself had seen energy or courage or spontaneity; they are ashamed of what I see no reason to be ashamed of, and defensive where there is no cause for defense.

Not only do they seem to me often to have cramped and untenable notions of right and wrong, but looking at fiction as they do—in terms of "approval" and "disapproval" of Jews, "positive" and "negative" attitudes toward Jewish life—they are likely not to see what it is that the story is really about.

To give an example. A story I wrote called "Epstein" tells of a sixty-year-old man who has an adulterous affair with the lady across the street. In the end, Epstein, who is the hero, is caught—caught by his family and caught and struck down by exhaustion, decay, and disappointment, against all of which he had set out to make a final struggle. There are Jewish readers, I know, who cannot figure out why I found it necessary to tell this story about a Jewish man: don't other people commit adultery, too? Why is it the Jew who must be shown cheating?

But there is more to adultery than cheating: for one thing, there is the adulterer himself. For all that some people may experience him as a cheat and nothing else, he usually experiences himself as something more. And generally speaking, what draws most readers and writers to literature is this "something more"—all that is beyond simple moral categorizing. It is not my purpose in writing a story of an adulterous man to make it clear how right we all are if we disapprove of the act and are disappointed in the man. Fiction is not written to affirm the principles and beliefs that everybody seems to hold, nor does it seek to guarantee us of the appropriateness of our feelings. The world of fiction, in fact, frees us from the circumscriptions that the society places upon feeling; one of the greatnesses of the art is that it allows both the writer and the reader to respond to experience in ways not always available in day-to-day conduct; or if they are available, they are not possible, or manageable, or legal, or advisable, or even necessary to the business of living. We may not even know that we have such a range of feelings and responses *until* we have come into contact with the work of fiction. This does not mean that either reader or writer no longer brings any moral judgment to bear upon human action. Rather, we judge at a different level of our being, for not only are we judging with the aid of new feelings, but without the necessity of having to act upon judgment, or even to be judged for our judgment. Ceasing for a while to be upright citizens, we drop into another layer of consciousness. And this dropping, this expansion of moral consciousness, this exploration of moral fantasy, is of considerable value to a man and to society.

I do not care to go at length here into what a good many readers take for granted are the purposes and possibilities of fiction. I do want to make clear, however, to those whose interests may not lead them to speculate much on the subject, a few of the assumptions a writer may hold—assumptions such as lead me to say that I do not write a story to make evident whatever disapproval I may feel for adulterous men. I write a story of a man who is adulterous to reveal the condition of such a man. If the adulterous man is a Jew, then I am revealing the condition of an adulterous man who is a Jew. Why tell that story? Because I seem to be interested in how—and why and when—a man acts counter to what he considers to be his "best self," or what others assume it to be, or would like for it to be. The subject is hardly "mine"; it interested readers and writers for a long time before it became my turn to be engaged by it, too.

One of my readers, a man in Detroit, was himself not too engaged and suggested in a letter to me that he could not figure out why I was. He posed several questions which I believe, in their very brevity, were intended to disarm me. I quote from his letter without his permission.

The first question. "Is it conceivable for a middle-aged man to neglect business and spend all day with a middle-aged woman?" The answer is yes.

Next he asks, "Is it a Jewish trait?" I take it he is referring to adultery and not facetiously to the neglecting of business. The answer is, "Who said it was?" Anna Karenina commits adultery with Vronsky, with consequences more disastrous than those that Epstein brings about. Who thinks to ask, "Is it a Russian trait?" It is a decidedly human possibility. Even though the most famous injunction against it is reported as being issued, for God's own reasons, to the Jews, adultery has been one of the ways by which people of *all* faiths have sought pleasure, or freedom, or vengeance, or power, or love, or humiliation. . . .

The next in the gentleman's series of questions to me is, "Why so much *shmutz?*" Is he asking, why is there dirt in the world? Why is there disappointment? Why is there hardship, ugliness, evil, death? It would be nice to think these were the questions the gentleman had in mind, when he asks, "Why so much *shmutz?*" But all he is really asking is, "Why so much *shmutz* in that story?" This, apparently, is what the story adds up to for him. An old man discovers the fires of lust are still burning in him? *Shmutz!* Disgusting! Who wants to hear that kind of stuff! Struck as he is by nothing but the dirty aspects of Epstein's troubles, the gentleman from Detroit concludes that I am narrow-minded.

So do others. Narrow-mindedness, in fact, was the charge that a New York rabbi, David Seligson, was reported in the New York *Times* recently as having brought against myself and other Jewish writers who, he told his congregation, dedicated themselves "to the exclusive creation of a melancholy parade of caricatures." Rabbi Seligson also disapproved of *Goodbye, Columbus* because I described in it "a Jewish adulterer . . . and a host of other lopsided schizophrenic personalities." Of course, adultery is not a characteristic symptom of schizophrenia, but that the rabbi should see it this way, as a sign of a diseased personality, indicates to me that we have different notions as to what health is. After all, it may be that *life* produces a melancholy middle-aged businessman like Lou Epstein who in Dr. Seligson's eyes looks like another in a parade of caricatures. I myself find Epstein's adultery an unlikely solution to his problems, a pathetic, even a doomed response, and a comic one, too, since it does not even square with the man's own conception of himself and what he wants; but none of this *unlikeliness* leads me to despair of his sanity, or humanity. I suppose it is tantamount to a confession from me of lopsided schizophrenia to admit that the character of Epstein happened to have been conceived with considerable affection and sympathy. As I see it, one of the rabbi's limitations is that he cannot recognize a bear hug when one is being administered right in front of his eyes.

. . .

The *Times* report continues: "The rabbi said he could only 'wonder about' gifted writers, 'Jewish by birth, who can see so little in the tremendous saga of Jewish history.'" But I don't imagine the rabbi "wonders" any more about me than I wonder about him: that wondering business is only the voice of wisdom that is supposed to be making itself heard, always willing to be shown the light, if, of course, there is light to be pointed out; but I can't buy it. Pulpit fair-mindedness only hides the issue—as it does here in the rabbi's conclusion, quoted by the *Times:* "'That they [the Jewish writers in question] must be free to write, we would affirm most vehemently; but that they would know their own people and tradition, we would fervently wish.'"

However, the issue is not knowledge of one's "people." At least, it is not a question of who has more historical data at his fingertips, or is more familiar with Jewish tradition, or which of us observes more customs and rituals. It is even possible, needless to say, to "know" a good deal about tradition, and to misunderstand what it is that tradition signifies. The story of Lou Epstein stands or falls not on how much I "know" about tradition, but on how much I know and understand about Lou Epstein. Where the history of the Jewish people comes down in time and place to become the man whom I called Epstein, that is where my knowledge must be sound. But I get the feeling that Rabbi Seligson wants to rule Lou Epstein *out* of Jewish history. I find him too valuable to forget or dismiss, even if he is something of a *grubber yung* and probably more ignorant of history and tradition than the rabbi believes me to be.

Epstein is pictured not as a learned rabbi, after all, but the owner of a small paper-bag company; his wife is not learned either, and neither is his mistress; consequently, a reader should not expect to find in this story knowledge on my part, or the part of the characters, of the *Sayings of the Fathers;* he has every right to expect that I be close to the truth as to what might conceivably be the attitudes of a Jewish man of Epstein's style and history, toward marriage, family life, divorce, and fornication. The story is called "Epstein" because Epstein, not the Jews, is the subject; where the story is weak I think I know by this time; but the rabbi will never find out until he comes at the thing in terms of what *it* wants to be about rather than what he would like it to be about.

Obviously, though, his interest is not in the portrayal of character; what he wants in my fiction is, in his words, "a balanced portrayal of Jews as we know them." I even suspect that something called "balance" is what the rabbi would advertise as the most significant characteristic of Jewish life; what Jewish history comes down to is that at long last we have in our ranks one of everything. But his assumptions about the art of fiction are what I should like to draw particular attention to. In his sermon Rabbi Seligson says of Myron Kaufmann's *Remember Me to God*, that it can "hardly be said to be recognizable as a Jewish sociological study." But Mr. Kaufmann, as a novelist, probably had no intention of writing a sociological study, or—for this seems more like what the rabbi really yearns for in the way of reading—a nice positive sampling. *Madame Bovary* is hardly recognizable as a sociological study, either, having at its center only a single, dreamy, provincial Frenchwoman, and not one of every other kind of provincial Frenchwoman too; this does not, however, diminish its brilliance as a novel, as an exploration of Madame Bovary herself. Literary works do not take as their subjects characters and events which have impressed a writer primarily by the *frequency* of their appearance. For example, how many Jewish men, as we know them, have come nearly to the brink of plunging a knife into their only son because they believed God had commanded them to? The story of Abraham and Isaac derives its meaning from something other than its being a familiar, recognizable, everyday occurrence. The test of any literary work is not how broad is its range of representation—for all that breadth may be characteristic of a kind of narrative—but the depth with which the writer reveals whatever it may be that he has chosen to represent.

To confuse a "balanced portrayal" with a novel is finally to be led into absurdities. "Dear Fyodor Dostoevsky—All the students in our school, and most of the teachers feel that you have been unfair to us. Do you call Raskolnikov a balanced portrayal of students as we know them? Of Russian students? Of poor students? What about those of us who have never murdered anyone, who do our school work every night?" "Dear Mark Twain—None of the slaves on our plantation has ever run away. We have a perfect record. But what will our owner think when he reads of Nigger Jim?" "Dear Vladimir Nabokov—The girls in our class," and so on. What fiction does, and what the rabbi would like for it to do are two entirely different things. The concerns of fiction, let it be said, are not those of a statistician—or of a public-relations firm. The novelist asks himself, "What do people think?"; the PR man asks, "What *will* people think?" But I believe this is what is actually troubling the rabbi, when he calls for his "balanced portrayal of Jews." What will people think?

Or to be exact: what will the *goyim* think?

II

This was the question raised—and urgently—when another story of mine, "Defender of the Faith," appeared in the *New Yorker* in April 1959. The story is told by Nathan Marx, an Army sergeant just rotated back to Missouri from combat duty in Germany, where the war has ended. As soon as he arrives, he is made First Sergeant in a training company, and immediately is latched on to by a young recruit who tries to use his attachment to the sergeant to receive kindnesses and favors. His attachment, as he sees it, is that they are both Jews. As the story progresses, what the recruit, Sheldon Grossbart, comes to demand are not mere considerations, but privileges to which Marx does not think he is entitled. The story is about one man who uses his own religion, and another's uncertain conscience, for selfish ends; but mostly it is about this other man, the narrator, who because of the ambiguities of being a member of his particular religion, is involved in a taxing, if mistaken, conflict of loyalties.

I don't now, however, and didn't while writing, see Marx's problem as nothing more than "Jewish": confronting the limitations of charity and forgiveness in one's nature—having to draw a line between what is merciful and what is just—trying to distinguish between apparent evil and the real thing, in one's self and others—these are problems for most people, regardless of the level at which they are perceived or dealt with. Yet, though the moral complexities are not exclusively characteristic of the experience of being a Jew, I never for a moment considered that the characters in the story should be anything other than Jews. Someone else might have written a story embodying the same themes, and similar events perhaps, and had at its center Negroes or Irishmen; for me there was no choice. Nor was it a matter of making Grossbart a Jew and Marx a Gentile, or vice versa; telling half the truth would have been much the same here as telling a lie. Most of those jokes beginning, "Two Jews were walking down the street," lose a little of their punch if one of the Jews, or both, are disguised as Englishmen or Republicans. Similarly, to have made any serious alteration in the Jewish factuality of "Defender of the Faith" as it began to fill itself out in my imagination, would have so unsprung the tensions I felt in the story that I would no longer have had left a story that I wanted to tell, or one I believed myself able to.

Some of my critics must wish that this had happened, for in going ahead and writing this story about Jews, what else did I do but confirm an anti-Semitic stereotype? But to me the story confirms something different, if no less painful to its readers. To me Grossbart is not something we can dismiss solely as an anti-Semitic stereotype; he is a Jewish fact. If people of bad intention or weak judgment have converted certain facts of Jewish life into a stereotype of The Jew, that does not mean that such facts are no longer important in our lives, or that they are taboo for the writer of fiction. Literary investigation may even be a way to redeem the facts, to give them the weight and value that they should have in the world, rather than the disproportionate significance they probably have for some misguided or vicious people.

Sheldon Grossbart, the character I imagined as Marx's antagonist, has his seed in fact. He is not meant to represent The Jew, or Jewry, nor does the story indicate that it is the writer's intention that he be so understood by the reader. Grossbart is depicted as a single blundering human being, one with force, self-righteousness, cunning, and on occasion, even a little disarming charm; he is depicted as a man whose lapses of integrity seem to him so necessary to his survival as to convince him that such lapses are actually committed in the name of integrity. He has been able to work out a system whereby his own sense of responsibility can suspend operation, what with the collective guilt of the others having become so immense as to have seriously altered the conditions of trust in the world. He is presented not as the stereotype of The Jew, but as a Jew who acts like the stereotype, offering back to his enemies their vision of him, answering the punishment with the crime. Given the particular kinds of denials, humiliations, and persecutions that the nations have practiced on their Jews, it argues for far too much nobility to deny not only that Jews like Grossbart exist, but to deny that the temptations to Grossbartism exist in many who perhaps have more grace, or will, or are perhaps only more cowed, than the simple frightened soul that I imagined weeping with fear and disappointment at the end of the story. Grossbart is not The Jew; but he is a fact of Jewish experience and well within the range of its moral possibilities.

And so is his adversary, Marx, who is, after all, the story's central character, its consciousness and its voice. He is a man who calls himself a Jew more tentatively than does Grossbart; he is not sure what it means, means for him, for he is not unintelligent or without conscience; he is dutiful, almost to a point of obsession, and confronted by what are represented to him as the needs of another Jew, he does not for a while know what to do. He moves back and forth from feelings of righteousness to feelings of betrayal, and only at the end, when he truly does betray the trust that Grossbart tries to place in him, does he commit what he has hoped to all along: an act he can believe to be honorable.

Marx does not strike me, nor any of the readers I heard from, as unlikely, incredible, "made-up"; the verisimilitude of the characters and their situation was not what was called into question. In fact, an air of convincingness that the story was believed to have, caused a number of people to write to me, and the *New Yorker,* and the Anti-Defamation League, protesting its publication.

Here is one of the letters I received after the story was published:

> Mr. Roth:
> With your one story, "Defender of the Faith," you have done as much harm as all the organized anti-Semitic organizations have done to make people believe that all Jews are cheats, liars, connivers. Your one story makes people—the general public—forget all the great Jews who have lived, all the Jewish boys who served well in the armed services, all the Jews who live honest hard lives the world over. . . .

Here is one received by the *New Yorker:*

> Dear Sir:
> . . . We have discussed this story from every possible angle and we cannot escape the conclusion that it will do

irreparable damage to the Jewish people. We feel that this story presented a distorted picture of the average Jewish soldier and are at a loss to understand why a magazine of your fine reputation should publish such a work which lends fuel to anti-Semitism.

Clichés like "this being Art" will not be acceptable. A reply will be appreciated.

Here is a letter received by the Anti-Defamation League, who out of the pressure of the public response, telephoned to ask if I wanted to talk to them. The strange emphasis of the invitation, I thought, indicated the discomfort they felt at having to pass on— or believing they had to pass on—messages such as this:

Dear———,
What is being done to silence this man? Medieval Jews would have known what to do with him. . . .

The first two letters I quoted were written by Jewish laymen, the last by a rabbi and educator in New York City, a man of prominence in the world of Jewish affairs.

The rabbi was later to communicate directly with me. He did not mention that he had already written the Anti-Defamation League to express regret over the decline of medieval justice, though he was careful to point out at the conclusion of his first letter his reticence in another quarter. I believe I was supposed to take it as an act of mercy: "I have not written to the editorial board of the *New Yorker*," he told me. "I do not want to compound the sin of informing. . . ."

Informing. There was the charge so many of the correspondents had made, even when they did not want to make it openly to me, or to themselves. I had informed on the Jews. I had told the Gentiles what apparently it would otherwise have been possible to keep secret from them: that the perils of human nature afflict the members of our minority. That I had also informed them it was possible for there to be such a Jew as Nathan Marx did not seem to bother anybody; if I said earlier that Marx did not strike my correspondents as unlikely, it is because he didn't strike them at all. He might as well not have been there. Of the letters that I read, only one even mentioned Marx and only to point out that I was no less blameworthy for portraying the Sergeant as "a white

Jew" as he was described by my correspondent, a kind of Jewish Uncle Tom.

But even if Marx were that and only that, a white Jew, and Grossbart only a black one, did it in any way follow that because I had examined the relationship between them—another concern central to the story which drew barely a comment from my correspondents—that I had then advocated that Jews be denationalized, deported, persecuted, murdered? Well, no. Whatever the rabbi may believe privately, he did not indicate to me that he thought I was an anti-Semite. There was a suggestion, however, and a grave one, that I had acted like a fool. "You have earned the gratitude," he wrote, "of all who sustain their anti-Semitism on such conceptions of Jews as ultimately led to the murder of six million in our time."

Despite the sweep there at the end of the sentence, the charge made is actually up at the front: I "earned the gratitude. . . ." But of whom? I would put it less dramatically, but maybe more exactly: of those who are predisposed to misread the story—out of bigotry, ignorance, malice, or even innocence. If I did earn their gratitude, it was because they failed to see, even to look for, what I was talking about. . . . Such conceptions of Jews as anti-Semites hold, then, and as they were able to confirm by misunderstanding my story, are the same, the rabbi goes on to say, as those which "ultimately led to the murder of six million in our time."

"Ultimately"? Is that not a gross simplification of the history of the Jews and the history of Hitler's Germany? People hold serious grudges against one another, vilify one another, deliberately misunderstand one another, and tell lies about one another, but they do not always, as a consequence, *murder* one another, as the Germans murdered the Jews, and as other Europeans allowed the Jews to be murdered, or even helped the slaughter along. Between prejudice and persecution there is usually, in civilized life, a barrier constructed by the individual's convictions and fears, and the community's laws, ideals, and values. What "ultimately" caused this barrier to disappear in Germany cannot be explained only in terms of anti-Semitic misconceptions; surely what must also be understood here is the intolerability of Jewry, on the one hand, and its usefulness, on the other, to the Nazi ideology and dream.

By simplifying the Nazi-Jewish relationship, by making *preju-

dice appear to be the primary cause of annihilation, the rabbi is able to make the consequences of publishing "Defender of the Faith" in the *New Yorker* seem very grave indeed. He doesn't appear to be made at all anxious, however, by the consequences of his own position. For what he is suggesting is that some subjects must not be written about, or brought to public attention, because it is possible for them to be misunderstood by people with weak minds or malicious instincts. Thus he consents to put the malicious and weak-minded in a position of determining the level at which open communication on these subjects will take place. This is not fighting anti-Semitism, but submitting to it: that is, submitting to a restriction of consciousness as well as communication because being conscious and being candid is too risky.

In his letter the rabbi calls my attention to that famous madman who shouts "Fire!" in "a crowded theater." He leaves me to complete the analogy myself: by publishing "Defender of the Faith" in the *New Yorker:* (1) I am shouting; (2) I am shouting "Fire!"; (3) there is no fire; (4) all this is happening in the equivalent of "a crowded theater." The crowded theater: there is the risk. I should agree to sacrifice the freedom that is essential to my vocation, and even to the general well-being of the culture, because—because of what? "The crowded theater" has absolutely no relevance to the situation of the Jew in America today. It is a grandiose delusion. It is not a metaphor describing a cultural condition, but a revelation of the nightmarish visions that must plague people as demoralized as the rabbi appears to be: rows endless, seats packed, lights out, doors too few and too small, panic and hysteria just under the skin. . . . No wonder he says to me finally, "Your story—in Hebrew—in an Israeli magazine or newspaper—would have been judged exclusively from a literary point of view." That is, ship it off to Israel. But please don't tell it here, now.

Why? So that "they" will not commence persecuting Jews again? If the barrier between prejudice and persecution collapsed in Germany, this is hardly reason to contend that no such barrier exists in our country. And if it should ever begin to appear to be crumbling, then we must do what is necessary to strengthen it. But not by putting on a good face; not by refusing to admit to the intricacies and impossibilities of Jewish lives; not by pretending that Jews have existences less in need of, less deserving of, honest attention than the lives of their neighbors; not by making Jews invisible. The solution is not to convince people to like Jews so as not to want to kill them; it is to let them know that they cannot kill them even if they despise them. And how to let them know? Surely repeating over and over to oneself, "It can happen here," does little to prevent "it" from happening. Moreover, ending persecution involves more than stamping out persecutors. It is necessary, too, to unlearn certain responses to them. All the tolerance of persecution that has seeped into the Jewish character—the adaptability, the patience, the resignation, the silence, the self-denial—must be squeezed out, until the only response there is to *any* restriction of liberties is "No, I refuse."

The chances are that there will always be some people who will despise Jews, just so long as they continue to call themselves Jews; and, of course, we must keep an eye on them. But if some Jews are dreaming of a time when they will be accepted by Christians as Christians accept one another—if *this* is why certain Jewish writers should be silent—it may be that they are dreaming of a time that cannot be, and of a condition that does not exist, this side of one's dreams. Perhaps even the Christians don't accept one another as they are imagined to in that world from which Jews may believe themselves excluded solely because they are Jews. Nor are the Christians going to feel toward Jews what one Jew may feel toward another. The upbringing of the alien does not always alert him to the whole range of human connections which exists between the liaisons that arise out of clannishness, and those that arise—or fail to—out of deliberate exclusion. Like those of most men, the lives of Jews no longer take place in a world that is just *landsmen* and enemies. The cry "Watch out for the *goyim!*" at times seems more the expression of an unconscious wish than of a warning: Oh that they were out there, so that we could be together in here! A rumor of persecution, a taste of exile, might even bring with it that old world of feelings and habits—something to replace the new world of social accessibility and moral indifference, the world which tempts all our promiscuous instincts, and where one cannot always figure out what a Jew is that a Christian is not.

Jews are people who are not what anti-Semites say they are. That was once a statement out of which a man might begin to construct an identity for himself; now it does not work so well, for it is difficult to act counter to the ways people expect you to act when fewer and fewer people define you by such expectations. The success of the struggle against the defamation of Jewish character in this country has itself made more pressing the need for a Jewish self-consciousness that is relevant to this time and place, where neither defamation nor persecution are what they were elsewhere in the past. Surely, for those Jews who choose to continue to call themselves Jews, and find reason to do so, there are courses to follow to prevent it from ever being 1933 again that are more direct, reasonable, and dignified than beginning to act as though it already is 1933—*or as though it always is.* But the death of all those Jews seems to have taught my correspondent, a rabbi and a teacher, little more than to be discreet, to be foxy, to say this but not that. It has taught him nothing other than how to remain a victim in a country where he does not have to live like one if he chooses. How pathetic. And what an insult to the dead. Imagine: sitting in New York in the 1960's and piously summoning up "the six million" to justify one's own timidity.

Timidity—and paranoia. It does not occur to the rabbi that there are Gentiles who will read the story intelligently. The only Gentiles the rabbi can imagine looking into the *New Yorker* are those who hate Jews and those who don't know how to read very well. If there are others, they can get along without reading about Jews. For to suggest that one translate one's stories into Hebrew and publish them in Israel, is to say, in effect: "There is nothing in our lives we need to tell the Gentiles about, unless it has to do with how well we manage. Beyond that, it's none of their business. We are important to no one but ourselves, which is as it should be (or better be) anyway." But to indicate that moral crisis is something to be hushed up, is not of course, to take the prophetic line; nor is it a rabbinical point of view that Jewish life is of no significance to the rest of mankind.

Even given his own kinds of goals, however, the rabbi is not very far-sighted or imaginative. What he fails to see is that the stereotype as often arises from ignorance as from malice; deliberately keeping Jews out of the imagination of Gentiles, for fear of the bigots and their stereotyping minds, is really to invite the invention of stereotypical ideas. A book like Ralph Ellison's *Invisible Man*, for instance, seems to me to have helped many whites who are not anti-Negro, but who do hold Negro stereotypes, to surrender simple-minded notions about Negro life. I doubt, however, that Ellison, reporting as he does not just the squalid circumstances Negroes must put up with but certain bestial aspects of his Negro characters as well, has converted one Alabama redneck or one United States Senator over to the cause of desegregation; nor could the novels of James Baldwin cause Governor Wallace to conclude anything more than that Negroes were just as hopeless a lot as he'd always known them to be. As novelists, neither Baldwin nor Ellison are (to quote Mr. Ellison on himself) "cogs in the machinery of civil rights legislation." Just as there are Jews who feel that my books do nothing for the Jewish cause, so there are Negroes, I am led to understand, who feel that Mr. Ellison's work has done little for the Negro cause and probably has harmed it. But that seems to place the Negro cause somewhat outside the cause of truth and justice. That many blind people are still blind, does not mean that Mr. Ellison's book gives off no light. Certainly those of us who are willing to be taught, and who needed to be, have been made by *Invisible Man* less stupid than we were about Negro lives, including those lives that a bigot would point to as affirming his own half-baked, inviolable ideas.

III

But it is the treachery of the bigot that the rabbi appears to be worried about and that he presents to me, to himself, and probably to his congregation, as the major cause for concern. Frankly, I think those are just the old words coming out, when the right buttons are pushed. Can he actually believe that on the basis of my story anyone is going to start a pogrom, or keep a Jew out of medical school, or even call some Jewish schoolchild a kike? The rabbi is entombed in his nightmares and fears; but that is not the whole of it. He is also hiding something. Much of this disapproval of "Defender of the Faith" because of its effect upon Gentiles, seems to me a cover-up for what is really objected to, what is immediately painful—and that is its direct effect upon certain Jews. "You have hurt a lot of people's feelings because you have revealed something they are ashamed of." That is the letter the rabbi did not write, but should have. I would have argued then that there are things of more importance—even to these Jews—than those feelings that have been hurt, but at any rate he would have confronted me with a genuine fact, with something I was actually responsible for, and which my conscience would have had to deal with, as it does.

For the record, all the letters that came in about "Defender of the Faith," and that I saw, were from Jews. Not one of those people whose gratitude the rabbi believes I earned, wrote to say, "Thank you," nor was I invited to address any anti-Semitic organizations. When I did begin to receive speaking invitations, they were from Jewish ladies' groups, Jewish community centers, and from all sorts of Jewish organizations, large and small.

And I think this bothers the rabbi, too. On the one hand, some Jews are hurt by my work; but on the other, some are interested. At the rabbinical convention I mentioned earlier, Rabbi Emanuel Rackman, a professor of political science at Yeshiva University, reported to his colleagues that certain Jewish writers were "assuming the mantle of self-appointed spokesmen and leaders for Judaism." To support this remark he referred to a symposium held in Israel this last June, at which I was present; as far as I know, Rabbi Rackman was not. If he had been there, he would have heard me make it quite clear that I did not want to, did not intend to, and was not able to, speak *for* American Jews; I surely did not deny, and no one questioned the fact, that I spoke *to* them, and hopefully to others as well. The competition that Rabbi Rackman imagines himself to be engaged in hasn't to do with who will presume to lead the Jews; it is really a matter of who, in addressing them, is going to take them more seriously— strange as that may sound—with who is going to see them as something more than part of the mob in a crowded theater, more than helpless and threatened and in need of reassurance that they are as "balanced" as anyone else. The question really is, who is going to address men and women like men and women, and who like children. If there are Jews who have begun to find the stories the novelists tell more provocative and pertinent than the sermons of some of the rabbis, perhaps it is because there are regions of feeling and consciousness in them which cannot be reached by the oratory of self-congratulation and self-pity.

REFLECTIONS ON JEWISH IDENTITY

DANIEL BELL

A PERSISTENT FEAR worried Jews of the early Diasporas and of Hellenistic times: the fear that a child of theirs might grow up to be an *am-haaretz*—a peasant, ignorant of Torah; or, even worse, an *apikoros*—a sophisticated unbeliever who abandons Jewish faith to indulge in rationalistic speculation about the meaning of existence. In either case, the danger felt was that such an individual would not only ignore the commandments and rituals, but that he would, in effect, have lost the sense of his past. Asked, in the classic question of identity, "Who are you?" the *am-haaretz* does not understand; and the *apikoros*, instead of giving the traditional response: "I am the son of my father" (Isaac *ben* Abraham), says: "I am I"—meaning, of course, I stand alone, I come out of myself, and, in choice and action, make myself.

A similar crisis of identity is a hallmark of our own modernity —except that not rationalism, but experience, has replaced faith. For us, sensibility and experience, rather than revealed utterances, tradition, authority, or even reason, have become the sources of understanding and of identity. One stakes out one's position and it is confirmed by others who accept the sign; it is no longer the hand of the father placed upon us—the covenant—that gives confirmation.

Not only the Jew, but all moderns, and particularly the intelligentsia, have made this decision to break with the past. Affecting first revealed religion, and later extended to all tradition and authority, the break has meant that the individual himself becomes the source of all moral judgment. But once experience is the touchstone of truth, then a "built-in" situation develops where alienation from society—which necessarily upholds the established, traditional values—is inescapable. This has meant, in the further fragmentation of society, that individuals have sought kinship with those who share both their sensibility and their experience—that is, with their own generation. The others have had a necessarily different experience. (Here we may see one reason why youth movements, a phenomenon unknown in previous times, are so characteristic a fact of modern life.)

Few of us can escape this mark. This is the way we have been bred. In us, especially the Jews, there has been a hunger for experience. The first generation fled the ghetto or the Pale—the second fled the past itself. For those of us whose parents were immigrants, there was the double barrier of language and culture to confront; and the double urgency of being not only thrust out on one's own, but having to make one's self in the course of discovering the world as home.

Yet no one wholly makes himself; nor is there such a thing as a completely cosmopolitan culture. The need to find parochial ties, to share experiences with those who are like ourselves, is part of the search for identity. There is an old truism that in some ways (biologically) we are like everyone else; in some ways (the idiosyncrasies of personality) like nobody else; and in some other ways still, like somebody else. In the parochial search for those like ourselves, the generation, the common age group, is only one tie. Neighborhood, city, country, vocation, political belief, family—these hold other ties. But prior to all—to begin with—one must come to terms with the past. One cannot wholly escape it. One may reject it, but the very mode of rejection is often conditioned by the past itself. A man is, first, the son of his father. In almost all tribal societies, the patronymic is part of one's name. And the sins of the fathers—in the psychological, if not the legal sense—are apt to be the burdens of the sons as well.

For the Jew, his relation to the past is complicated by the fact that he must come to terms not only with culture and history but with religion as well. For the religious tradition has shaped the others, providing both conscience and the continuity of fate. As an agnostic, one can, in rejecting religion, reject God; one may reject a supernatural or even a transcendental God. But as a Jew, how can one reject the God of Abraham, Isaac, and Jacob—without rejecting oneself? How, then, does a modern Jew continue to identify with the Jewish fate? And if such an identification is made and conditioned largely by experience, by a generational experience at that, what must be the consequences? The initial problem remains the religious one.

. . .

The simplest way of being a Jew is to be Orthodox—at least in ritual, if not always in faith. An esoteric legend ascribes to Maimonides the affirmation that one does not have to believe in God to be a good Jew, one merely has to follow halakhah—obey the law. This is in keeping, in traditional Judaism, with the derogation of the single individual. As the rabbi might say, "Who are *you* to say that you do or do not believe? Does the world exist for *you*?"

But it is in the confrontation with evil that the judging of God arises. In the *kaddish* of Reb Levi Yitzhak of Berditchev, the 18th-century Tsaddik refuses to speak the Sanctification of the Name until he first arraigns God for the suffering of His innocent Jews. And we know the accusation, two centuries later, of the fifteen-year-old boy who, in Auschwitz on Rosh Hashanah, cries, "Why should I bless Him? Because He kept six crematories working night and day, on the Sabbath and holy days?"*

Maimonides, in the *Guide to the Perplexed*, gave the classic answer to this recurrent cry:

> Very often the throngs of the unreasonable will, in their hearts, put forth the claim that there is more evil than good in this world. . . . The cause of this error is that this foolish man and his unreasonable companions in the throng regard the whole universe only from the angle of individual existence. Thus every fool thinks that life is there for his sake alone, and as though nothing existed but him. And so, when anything happens that opposes his wishes, he concludes that the whole universe is evil. But if man would regard the whole universe, and realize what an infinitesimal part he plays in it, the truth would be clear and apparent to him. . . . It is of great advantage that man should recognize the measure of his worth, so that he may not fall into the error of believing that the universe exists only because of him. It is our opinion that the universe exists for the sake of the Creator. . . .

But if life is not present for *me*, if in the design of the universe "Man is like unto a breath," as the Bible puts it, then why fight at all against any injustice or evil? Orthodoxy leads to quietism; suffering is the badge, one accepts it as the mark of fate. One of the more disquieting facts about Jewish behavior in the death camps, as a number of writers have remarked, was the extreme

* From *Night*, a memoir of Auschwitz, by Elie Wiesel.

passivity of the people. We know about the ways in which hunger, fright, privation, can depersonalize an individual. But the fatalism that comes out of the religious tradition violates one's conception of a personal autonomy. A modern man wants to believe that some portion of the universe does exist for him, in the here and now. The Orthodox view of Judaism is too constricted for such a man to feel at home in.

The same pride of self leads to skepticism or rationalism as concerns a supernatural view of the world. To the extent that he must reject religion as superstition, myth, or "absurdity,"* to that extent is the modern Jew's loss of Orthodoxy the victory of philosophy over theology, of reason over faith.

A different mode of Jewish identification lies in accepting the ethical content of Judaism while rejecting the ritual. This has been the path of those who have sought to join the "human" side of faith with the potentialities of science—the path of reform. But if one is too much of a rationalist to accept Orthodoxy, one is too much of an irrationalist to accept the "merely" ethical side of religion. Orthodoxy's view of life may be too fatalistic, but that of ethical Judaism appears to some of us too shallow.

The ethical view is fundamentally syncretistic, drawing on all faiths, for to be valid, an ethical precept must be binding on every man and applicable to all men. Theologically, there is no more justification for a special Jewish ethic than for a Unitarian one, or for Ethical Culture, or for any non-ritualistic creed. The ethical dissolves the parochial, and takes away from individuals that need for the particular identification which singles them out and shapes their community in distinctive terms: terms which make possible a special sense of belonging shared by a group.

Ethical Judaism, in its often superficial rationalism, has taken some disturbing profundities of the Old Testament and trans-

---

* There is, in the esoteric view, the interpretation that Maimonides views God as a necessary "myth" to hold the masses in check. Man, unrestrained, is a *b'hemah*, or animal, who gives way to his instincts and worships cruel gods. Where man regards himself as the measure, then all means, including murder, may be justified to achieve his unrestrained ends. Individual men could live without myth—the premise of stoicism—but the masses could not. Hence the need for the idea of God for the masses. But then is there not equally the question whether Maimonides, in the cunning of reason, may not have fashioned this rationale for private disbelief actually in order to seduce the *apikorsim*—the unbelievers—to public faith?

formed them into glossy moral platitudes. In ethical Judaism, a simplistic idea of human nature has led to the belief that there are few human ills which reason cannot remedy. But beyond that, the view of life represented by ethical Judaism is one of simple good and evil, unaware that a tragic component of choice is the fact that it must always involve some evil—a lesson which has been taught us by recent 20th-century history. As Emil Fackenheim once put it . . . : "In the 20th century, men—all of us—find themselves compelled to commit or condone evil for the sake of preventing an evil believed to be greater. And the tragedy is that we do not know whether the evil we condone will not in the end be greater than the evil we seek to avert—or be identified with it."*

What is left, then, for one who feels himself to be a Jew, emotionally rather than rationally—who has not lost his sense of identification with the Jewish past and wants to understand the nature of that tie? A Jew, we are told by one existentialist thinker (Emil Fackenheim), is "anyone who by his descent is subject to Jewish fate"—the covenant; one who by *fate* is urged to *faith*. The ground here is still faith, though the ground is "absurd," in that the compulsions to belief are beyond one's control, shaped by descent and, therefore, by history. But this is an attempt to defend faith, not fate. Lacking faith, I myself can only "choose" fate. For me, therefore, to be a Jew is to be part of a community woven by memory—the memory whose knots are tied by the *yizkor*, by the continuity that is summed up in the holy words: *Yizkor Elohim nishmas aboh mori:*—"May God remember the name of. . . ."

The *yizkor* is the tie to the dead, the link to the past, the continuity with those who have suffered and, through suffering, have made us witnesses to cruelty and given us the strength of courage over pride. However much, as moderns, we reject the utterances of authority and the injunctions of ritual, the religious link with our fellows is not the search for immortality or other consolatory formulas against the fear of extinction—but is the link of memory and its articulation.

All societies have memorial occasions, a day that commemorates an event of the past, a day of mourning for the dead. A memorial day, a holy day, often becomes, in secular terms, a holiday and an escape from the past. The *yizkor* is different. It is

* Can We Believe in Judaism Religiously?," *Commentary*, December 1948.

recited not just on one day, but on a set of days whose occasions form the wheel of life. For the *yizkor* is said on four days: Passover, Shevuoth, Succoth, and Yom Kippur—the escape from bondage, the giving of the Law, the ingathering of the harvest, and the day of atonement, which is also the day of "at-one-ment."

One lives, therefore, as a Jew, through the meaning of the *yizkor*, through the act of commemoration, through the saying of a common prayer—but singling out in that prayer a specific name of one's own dead. In the *minyan* of my fellows, I am linked to my own parent. In the *yizkor*, through memory, I am identified as a Jew.

If one is a Jew through filio-piety, is such a bond strong enough? Memory has its risks. The sense of the past is often merely the present read into the past. Memory is selective, it screens out the hurts, it throws roseate hues. Remembering what happened in one's lifetime is difficult enough; uncovering the past of history is even more so.

The greatest risk of memory is sentimentality, and Jewish life has paid dearly for its sentimentality. The lachrymose recollections of the *shtetl* (which are still with us) fail to recall its narrowness of mind, its cruelty, especially to school children (to which a whole series of memoirs, such as Solomon Ben Maimon's, testify), and its invidious stratification. In the same vein of nostalgia, there are the glowing reminiscences of the Lower East Side, or Chicago's Maxwell Street—but they omit the frequent coarseness, the pushing, the many other gross features of that life. At its best, this parochial identification exists as a tie of memory through pity; at its worst, it may be the continuity of appetite— the lox, cream cheese, and bagel combinations; or through comedians' jokes.

A different form of filio-piety is in the satisfying of memory, when there is no faith, by "good works." One is a Jew, discharging one's obligations as a Jew, through membership in Jewish organizations. Here lies the second risk, of accommodation. In the *embourgeoisement* of Jewish life in America, the community has become institutionalized around fund raising, and the index of an individual's importance too often is the amount of money he donates to hospitals, defense agencies, philanthropic groups, and the like. The manifest ends are the community functions being served, but frequently the latent end is the personal prestige—*yichus*. This kind of institutional life may even lend itself to historic forms of corruption: of simony, when those who have risen high in Jewish organizations receive their rewards in appointive office in Jewish life; and of indulgences, when leadership is the simple reward of wealth. And in performance of charity as a way of Jewish life, self-satisfaction may take on the face of righteousness. The most sensitive of the Jewish agency professionals, lawyers, and businessmen have often deplored this situation, yet are trapped by the system.

But for the intellectual, the greatest risk of memory is its repression—the past is only allowed to come back in the form of self-hate, shame of one's parents, the caricaturing of Jewish traits (most notably verbal agility), the exaggerated thrust of ambition, the claims to superiority by the mere fact of being a Jew, and all the other modes of aggression that arise from the refusal to accept the tension of being in a minority, and the need to balance the insistent demands of the past with the needs of the present.

Coming to terms with this kind of repression often leads to alienation from Judaism, to the feeling of its insufficiency, even when one has some knowledge of its traditions. The alienated Jew is the Jewish orphan. He comes "out of himself," rather than out of a past. He is homeless. The present is his only reality. Lacking a past, he can have no notion of continuity, or any image of the future. For him there can be no *parousia*, no fulfillment. This has been the signet of Jewish fate, particularly in Central Europe, over the last forty years, and it foreshadowed the fate of a whole generation of intellectuals. As W. H. Auden once said of Kafka, "It was fit and proper that [he] should have been a Jew, for the Jews have for a long time been placed in the position in which we are all now to be, of having no home." The problem is spiritual, not territorial. Israel is no answer. The alienated Jew grew up in *galut*, and the world has been his home. Is it his fault that the world has been inhospitable—rejecting those who refuse to assert a distinctive parochial tie? Yet, in the awareness of his rejection, his life is Jewish, too: he is one of a community of exiles whose common experiences are molded by the common fate—and this becomes his parochial tie.

Finally, in this catalogue of risks, there is the risk of attrition. If, in order to give it meaning, Jewish involvement requires some encounter with tradition, so that one may be able to make choices, then succeeding generations, whose encounters are few and whose memories are hazy, must find themselves with fewer and fewer ties. They are in the most difficult position of all. It is not a question of assimilation, for that is a matter of choice, the choice of severing all ties, and one which is made consciously. Attrition is not chosen—it is a wasting away. There is a word, Jew, but no feeling. And this becomes the most tragic consequence of identification solely through memory.

If identification is an interplay of experience and memory, its shaping elements are in the successive generations themselves. Each generation has its own "entelechy"—its own inherent design, which gives the identification its distinct quality. In these days, generations succeed each other rapidly, and each succeeding one is also longer-lived. The characteristic fact about Jewish life today is the extraordinary palimpsest which the different overlaying generational experiences have become. The different generations can be identified with one or the other of the different forms of response I have described (the five risks of memory) as a rationalization of their own experiences.

The basic shaping element of Jewish life in America has been the immigrant experience—an experience with an inner tension of anxiety and hope. The anxiety was an inevitable consequence of being uprooted and living in a strange land. At times it led, particularly for those who lived away from the large urban centers, to a sense of being "a guest in the house"—which in turn led to a minimizing of Jewish life, subduing an inherent drive and ebullience, temporizing with the neighbors—attitudes that have persisted in smaller Jewish communities in America and that have been repeated for a new mobile class in the suburbs.

For the bulk of Jewish immigrants, particularly those from Eastern Europe, the anxiety was translated into the struggle between fathers and sons. Few generational conflicts have had such an exposed nakedness, such depths of strain as this. The metaphor of Fathers and Sons that one finds in the Russian literature of the 1860's applied to political generations—there the "fathers" left home to go abroad, while the "sons," when they came of age, initiated the radical activity on the land; but both generations were within the boundaries of a common culture. In the American Jewish immigrant experience, it was the sons who left home, and the very boundaries of the culture came into question—the repudiation of the synagogue, the flight from the parents' language, the rejection of their authority, all of it intensified by the fact that both fathers and sons were living in a strange land.

If the immigrant generation was characterized by anxiety, the one after it was shaped by shame and guilt. However, the generational changes cannot be marked into exact historical periods, for generational time is interlinear. Thus the conflict of immigrant fathers and sons that took place before the First World War repeated itself during the depression of the 30's, when the children of those who came at the tail end of the immigrant wave grew up. And these parallels are refracted in the literature. The first immigrant generation found its literary spokesmen in the emotional outpourings of such writers as Sholem Asch and David Pinski, and the response in a Mike Gold or an Isidor Schneider; while the second wave—more wry, disenchanted, the twice-born—found meaning in Isaac Bashevis Singer, in his gothic, bittersweet, explorations of Jewish *shtetl* life, counterpointed to such revelations as Isaac Rosenfeld and Saul Bellow made in their unsentimental, even sardonic narratives of Chicago Jewish life.

Despite overlaying, three major time spans may be demarked. One may say that the first shaping element of the American Jewish experience came to maturity in the years from 1910 to 1930, the second achieved its awareness with the depression and the war, and the third, now coming into its own, emerged in the last decade and this one.

It was in the second of these generations that the rupture with the past was sharpest, the hunger for experience keenest. In its encounter with American life, the generation broke in two: some ran hard (the Sammy Glicks and the Harry Bogens); others, more openly alienated, became radicals. Ironically, both experiences proved to be a mirage. For those who felt that they had caught the world by the tail, using money as salt, the reality proved empty enough: all that was felt, finally, was the appearance of achievement. Those who left home to seek a new community in Marxism, in the expectation that revolutionary activity could be a vehicle for experience, found themselves caught in a net of abstraction and slogans. They had won their intellectual spurs, found places in the academies or in the world of publishing, but they were politically betrayed.

The failure of radicalism together with the death of six million Jews in the Nazi gas chambers brought the generation back. Still, coming to terms with the past proved difficult. For the middle class there was Jewish organizational life; for the intellectuals, theology. But the attractions of both have tended to wither. Those whose status has become tied to Jewish life have remained in the organizational milieux. For the intellectuals who once found meaning in theology (one remembers the intense debates about Simone Weil, Martin Buber, and neo-Orthodoxy in the pages of *Commentary* ten years ago), such problems have worn thin; the discussion has turned to more modish topics as Zen or hipsterism, or it has lapsed, more privately, into political philosophy, art, or humanistic studies.

For many of this generation, the burden of shame and guilt has tended to become less heavy through the catharsis of psychoanalysis and self-awareness, and by the attenuating passage of time. What has remained is a stoic mood, perhaps the only possible response of whoever seeks to resist the innocence of naive hope and the harshness of disillusion. Whether the generation still has a further statement to make remains to be seen.

And for the third generation? If literature is still a mirror of life, one of the most striking things about recent decades has been the disappearance, as a genre, of the *roman fleuve*—the family chronicle. Who today undertakes to write a Forsyte saga or a Pasquier chronicle? The thread of family continuity has indeed been broken. In a recent attempt, André Schwarz-Bart's *The Last of the Just,* the family chronicle (about the ancestors of Ernie Levy) seems contrived and stilted; it is no longer within the range of actual experience; the memory is more literary than real.

This seems to be the fate of the third generation: either memory is fabricated, or there is none at all. In suburbia, one sees the signs of the false parochialism, the thin veneer of identity, which rubs off at the first contact with the world. Many new temples are built, and the children go to Sunday school—because "it is good for them." The fathers have made their accommodation—through their children. Yet it cannot last, for what is unreal to the fathers is doubly so, and hypocritical, to the child; the reckoning is yet to come.

There are no parochial ties and no memories for the children of the intelligentsia. They are driven to be educated (with the British tradition as the exemplar) and to be alienated, but without the moorings of the past that their fathers sailed away from. Just as there is something sorry about individuals who become "counter-revolutionaries" without having been "revolutionaries"—accepting someone else's rancor as one's own—so there is something pathetic about proclaiming one's alienation without having known the world one is rejecting. There is, one is told, a new radicalism among the young; but without a central vision of its own, such radicalism can only be a caricature of the past. The warning from Marx is that the repetition of history is farce.

I write as one of the middle generation, one who has not faith but memory, and who has run some of its risks. I have found no "final" place, for I have no final answers. I was born in *galut* and I accept—now gladly, though once in pain—the double burden and the double pleasure of my self-consciousness, the outward life of an American and the inward secret of the Jew. I walk with this sign as a frontlet between my eyes, and it is as visible to some secret others as their sign is to me.

And yet a disquieting fact remains. If this is an identity shaped by experience, what are the "limits" of my responsibility? The philosopher F. H. Bradley (according to G. R. G. Mure's memoir of him) once remarked late in life that, being so old, he no longer had much recollection of his undergraduate days, and if someone produced evidence of a sin he had committed at that time, he would refuse to accept responsibility for it—a reflection of his doctrine that responsibility rests on the sufficient continuance of personal identity.

How responsible am I for the Jewish past, and therefore for its future? My God—even the one of memory and not of faith—is a jealous God. Do I have to accept the sins of my fathers, and my children those of mine? This is not an academic question, for it confronts us everywhere, and most particularly in "our"—the American's, the Western's, the white man's—relations with peoples who now come forth to assert their own identity. About five years ago, a group of African Negro intellectuals met in Paris, under the sponsorship of the magazine *Présence Africaine,* to debate this very question. How far, some of them asked, can the sins of the fathers be visited upon the children? What these men were saying was that one could *feel* free only after becoming free, only by some overt act of revenge, symbolic or otherwise, against those who had, by deliberately imposing an inferiority complex upon the Negro, robbed him of his identity. And yet the white men alive now were not those who had committed the original sin—though they continued to benefit from it. Should they be responsible for those who did? And, in the accents of the older tribal morality, these Negro intellectuals asserted that responsibility held unto the third and fourth generations—that the act of revenge was not immoral.

All this has been played out before. Orestes, guiltless but guilty, is driven on to carry out the blood revenge by the primitive law of retaliation. And although at the end of the Oresteia a new order of disinterested justice prevails, it is never wholly satisfying, for one feels that though the Furies have been tamed, the personal act, the act created by one's obligation to the past, has now been dissolved as well. In the *Pirke Avot* is the famous saying of Rabbi Tarfon: "It is not thy duty to complete the work, but neither art thou free to desist from it. . . ." Is this the claim which the acceptance of any parochial tie imposes upon us? This is the question raised when one realizes that one does not stand alone, that the past is still present, and that there are responsibilities of participation even when the community of which one is a part is a community woven by the thinning strands of memory.

MARGINALITY AND THE JEWISH INTELLECTUAL

MILTON M. GORDON

EVER SINCE the Jews in Western Civilization began to emerge from the ghettoes of Europe and to confront the values and the social life of the Enlightenment era, they have been faced by choices and have variously executed decisions which have earned them the sociological title of classic "marginal men." The marginal man, so the conceptualization goes,[1] is a person poised on the edge or dividing line of two cultures, fully at home in neither, and therefore on the margins of both. His marginality may be produced by the situation of being the offspring of an interracial marriage when, usually, the two races have different subcultures and subsocieties,[2] or, more applicable to the case at hand, it may stem from new cultural contacts engendered by immigration or social change. While psychological correlates of marginality have been hypothesized as insecurity feelings, nervousness, and hypersensitivity, such hypotheses have never been decisively proven, and some observers have pointed to possible positive traits attendant on marginality such as objectivity, creativity, insight, and self-understanding.[3]

At any rate, the sociological "position" of marginality may be clearly discerned, whatever its psychological consequences. And since the Jew in America has lived, since his initial arrival in colonial times, in a society predominantly Christian and non-Jewish, and under conditions of democratic choice and freedom from official persecution or enforced segregation, much of his adjustment history in the United States has been discussed in terms of the classical kinds of choices which confront the situation of the "marginal man." A large part of this discussion, however, has been rendered less efficacious by a failure to distinguish between the marginality of a man,—a single individual—and the marginal-

Original for this volume.

ity of a group. Individual marginality has already been defined. Group marginality may be said to exist in an assimilative process where all or most members of a minority group *together* face the problem of adjusting the values, behavior patterns, and social relationships into which they have been socialized (or which in the case of the native born second generation exist as parental models), to the values, norms, and social system of the host society. This is a rather different sort of situation from individual marginality, and although in the case of group marginality individuals do face problems of choice, they face them more or less in concert, so to speak, with other individuals who are in the same situation and who, collectively, make up a subsociety that provides a sociological home and source of comfort for the members of the group. In our subsequent discussion, therefore, we shall need to distinguish from time to time these two kinds of marginality, and specify which is more applicable to the subject under discussion.

Group marginality, since it is, virtually by definition, a characteristic to some degree of the minority group undergoing cultural contact, has been present throughout the whole of American Jewish history, although perhaps less so in the present than at any other time because of the massive success of the acculturation process in the United States,[4] and the increasing acceptance of Judaism as one of the three major faiths in America.[5] Instances of individual marginality must be sought in situations of low density, either ecologically, for instance, the case of a few Jewish families living in a small town, or in social space, as when a member of a minority moves up in social class position and finds that none or only a few members of his ethnic group have moved with him. Thus, for instance, W. Lloyd Warner, out of the research done by himself and his associates on ethnic groups in "Yankee City" and "Jonesville," concludes that when members of ethnic minorities move into the upper middle class or higher, they are drawn out of their ethnic group into a position initially of marginality and eventually of incorporation into the class system of the dominant group.[6] This conclusion may well be true for small communities (although, even here it may fail to do justice to the tendency for minority members in a particular small town to band together with families of similar ethnic background in nearby communities, or to attach themselves in part to the organized ethnic communal life in the nearest large city), but it ignores the point that in large cities and metropolitan areas enough other ethnics are also going up the class scale for a "parallel class structure," to use A. B. Hollingshead's phrase, to develop *within* the ethnic group.[7] Thus, Digby Baltzell's study of the general (or Protestant) upper class in Philadelphia in 1940 includes a section on the Jewish upper class that has developed in the City of Brotherly Love, with its own areas of residence, its own synagogues, its own fashionable men's city clubs, and its own country clubs.[8] And Kramer and Leventman, in their later study of Jewish communal life in "North City," a large city in the American Midwest, point to separation in life styles and communal living between the upper portion ("the clubniks") and the lower portion ("the lodgniks") of the class structure within the Jewish community.[9]

Marginality may be factored not only into group and individual subtypes but also by whether the conflicting choices lie in the area of cultural behavior or social structure.[10] If one views modern pluralistic societies as composed of smaller subsocieties, each one made up by the intersection of ethnic group and social class, so that what emerges is a series of "ethclasses"[11] such as "upper lower class white Protestant," "lower middle class white Catholics," or "upper middle class Jews," etc., then the "marginal man" is marginal in social structure to two or more of these subsocieties—that is, he does not confine his primary group relationships and organizational affiliations (if any) to one subsociety but spreads them over at least two, or perhaps neither. He is thus marginal structurally. At the same time, he may be faced with choices in behavior patterns which reflect different values in the ethclass of origin (the minority group) and the ethclass of aspiration (the majority group). This would constitute cultural marginality. While these two processes of marginality and choice probably frequently go together, they may at times exist independently of each other and thus should be conceptually distinguished. The full model may be economically depicted as follows:

Types of Marginality

	Structural	Cultural
Individual		
Group		

With these conceptual tools in hand, we may now begin to examine the American Jewish experience in relation to marginality more closely. Out of this examination the position of the American Jewish intellectual will gradually emerge.

All three migratory streams of Jews who came to America, the trickle of Sephardim and Ashkenazim who came to the colonies and set up institutions under Sephardic dominance, the larger number of Germans who spread westward in the mid-nineteenth century, and the great tide of Eastern Europeans who poured into the United States in the last two decades of the nineteenth century and the first quarter of the twentieth and whose descendants constitute the vast bulk of the Jewish population today—created communities and the institutions of communal life where they settled.[12] Thus while all Jews faced problems of cultural choice, the great majority confronted these problems from the security of a communal structure of their own. This has been true, as we now can see, not only for the immigrant generation, but for succeeding generations as well. Thus we may say that problems of *group marginality* and *cultural marginality* (for the first, and to a considerably lesser extent the second generation) have been the characteristic kinds of marginality faced by the American Jew. To be sure, from the very beginning we hear of individual cases of intermarriage, conversion, and disappearance from Jewish communal rolls, and these phenomena have accompanied the whole history of Jewish life in America. In such instances we know that individual marginality, both of a structural and a cultural nature, has been involved. These have not, however, constituted the dominant process.

Culturally speaking, American values of basically Anglo-Saxon origin, operating through the public school system and mass communications media, have interacted with values stemming from European Jewish life and have largely transmuted the latter into their own image. Thus, not even to mention the triumph of the English language and American clothing styles, Reform Judaism, brought in by some of the German Jewish migrants, and Conservative Judaism, developed by socially mobile Eastern European Jews, greatly modified the Orthodox *shul* of *shtetl* origin in the direction of conformity to American ideals of propriety and decorum in religious worship, and wrought similar changes in the realms of ideology and pious observances.[13] In turn, the United States of America, itself, at first more or less self-consciously a Protestant nation, gradually took on the image of itself as a nation of the three major faiths—Protestant, Catholic, and Jewish.

Degrees in the phenomenon of group marginality of a cultural nature, however, can probably be distinguished between generations. The second generation of Jews faced the problem of reconciling the fact of Yiddish speaking immigrant parents and immigrant cultural values in the home with their English speaking and American oriented way of life eagerly absorbed in the public schools and in the larger society. This was a larger and more tension-producing problem than that more recently and currently faced by the native-born of native parents, even when, in the latter case, social class mobility produced by exposure to a college education, is in the offing.

The role of the Jewish intellectual, then, in relation to the phenomenon of marginality, whether of a cultural or a structural nature, must be seen against the background of general American social structure—which we have already described in terms of an interlocking series of ethclasses, with primary group relationships more or less confined to one's own ethclass, and some secondary group relationships established across class and ethnic lines—and the fact that Jewish communal life has, at least in the larger cities, always been present as a sociological "home" for the vast majority of Jews of whatever generation. Thus those Jews who may have ventured "out" structurally in a tentative sense, attracted by the social institutions of the white Protestant American community, could always retreat to safer, more comfortable sociological territory upon meeting the usual rebuffs. It seems likely that most Jews up until recently never really ventured out in a structural manner to any appreciable extent. Thus was built the American Jewish community with a full array of social institutions, some differentiated from each other by social class, some serving the entire spectrum of social classes. Nor was this process, by any means, simply a Jewish phenomenon. Similar social structures were erected among ethnic groups of Catholic origin, and eventually a pan-Catholic subsociety began to take shape; Negroes and other racial groups developed indigenous institutions under the pressures of discrimination and rigid barriers; and the white Protestants, while assuming that they were simply the Americans, put their own stamp of race and religion on the institutions which they controlled.

It should be remembered, however, that Jews who intermarried with gentiles put themselves in a situation of structural marginality and henceforth faced three basic choices: (1) to identify as a family with the Jewish group; (2) to identify as a family with the white Protestant or white Catholic group; (3) to remain structurally marginal. In the absence of any substantial body of research focussed on this question we do not know how many made which choices or what the respective outcomes were, although in one recent study of the Jews of Washington, D.C., it was found that in 66 percent of the intermarried families who had children living at home, the children were being raised as gentiles.[14] Even in those cases where the family identifies as a unit with one or the other of the three major religious communities through the process of formal religious conversion of one of the partners, the converted partner may obviously still face personal problems of marginality of a psychological nature.

It is against this general background that we must view the situation of the Jewish intellectual.

If the question Who is a Jew? is a difficult one, as many observers have agreed, the question Who is an Intellectual? is difficulty many times compounded. "Few modern terms," writes Lewis Coser in his valuable socio-historical account of the rise of the institutions fostering intellectual life in the modern period, "are as imprecise as the term 'intellectual.' Its very mention is likely to provoke debate about both meaning and evaluation. To many, it stands for qualities deeply distrusted and despised; to others, it connotes excellence aspired to though not often achieved. To some, intellectuals are impractical dreamers who interfere with the serious business of life; to others, they are the 'antennae of the race.' "[15] While Coser in his formal definition reserves the term for those "men of ideas" who take a critical stance toward their society and its values, I prefer to cast the definitional net more widely[16] to include all "people for whom ideas, concepts, literature, music, painting, the dance have intrinsic meaning—are a part of the social-psychological atmosphere which one breathes."[17] As I have put it elsewhere:

> Occupationally, they are characteristically found in the professions, particularly college teaching, research, and the upper reaches of journalism (to a lesser degree, law and medicine), and in the arts, either as creators or performers. If they are

engaged in business, they are likely to be in communications or publishing. Not all persons in each of these occupational categories are intellectuals, and intellectuals will at times be found in other occupations. The academic world of teaching and research, supplemented now by the world of the Foundation, which either carries out or commissions research, is the most salient concentration point of the intellectual life, and this becomes increasingly so as writers, artists, and musicians begin to take on the role of faculty members and "artists in residence," alongside professors of the humanities and the natural and social sciences.[18]

The above occupational discussion, however, implicitly assumes a developmental history—a history of incipient institutions fostering not simply the isolated intellectual but a structured intellectual milieu in which intellectuals could interact with each other and begin to take on the characteristics of a sociological group. The delineation of this history has been Professor Coser's accomplishment in the aforementioned book[19] in which he traces the emergence of institutions fostering the intellectual life from the coffeehouse of eighteenth century London, the French salon, the scientific society, the nineteenth century expansion of the book and periodical market, the rise of the political sect, the appearance of Bohemias and "little magazines" in the early twentieth century, and the more recent explosive growth of the university, the bureaucratically maintained scientific research laboratory, and the foundation.

Before this institutional development has matured, however, the ethnic group member who finds that the possession of intellectual interests constitutes a basic part of his personality structure has three basic choices of sociological response that are represented by the following "ideal types": the passively ethnic intellectual; the actively ethnic intellectual; and the marginally ethnic intellectual. The first type remains within the ethnic group and gratifies his intellectual interests by finding, if he can, other persons of the same ethnic identity who share his concerns. The second type also remains within his ethnic group and "focuses his intellectual interests precisely on his ethnicity. He is the cultural historian of the group, the theologian, the communal leader, the apologist, the scholar of its art, its music and its literature."[20] The third type ignores ethnicity and its boundaries and simply looks for companionship where his ideologies, his politics, his tastes in literature, music and the other arts may lead him. Historically he has been, as his appellation indicates, without question a marginal man.

In the American Jewish experience all three types of intellectual have been present. The passive type is destined to be unsung, but an Abraham Cahan, editor of the *Jewish Daily Forward* and a leading figure in Yiddish journalism until his death in 1951, and a Horace Kallen, Harvard trained social philosopher and principal exponent of the ideology of cultural pluralism, stand in different ways as exemplars of the actively ethnic type. On the other hand, the career of the internationally famous art critic Bernard Berenson, also educated at Harvard around the turn of the century and later to become both expatriate and apostate, illustrates in rather extreme fashion, one type of response to individual structural and cultural marginality.

The basic point is that, with regard to the choices before the marginally ethnic intellectual, for approximately the first forty or fifty years of the twentieth century, intellectual life in America was only minimally structured, and what institutional structure did exist was dominated by white Anglo-Saxon Protestants from the upper portion of the social class hierarchy. College teaching, for example, in consonance with trends carried over from the nineteenth century, was traditionally the province of the white Protestant gentleman, of at least upper middle class origins or orientation. Jewish intellectuals were present in such a setting, but in small numbers and, as it were, on sufferance. Under such conditions, it is the fate of the marginal man when he alights in the institutional setting of his aspiration to be the perennial guest and not really an integrated member of the establishment.

After World War II, however, certain demographic and scientific trends that had been building up prior to that time exploded with great sociological force. These include the great boom in higher education, a phenomenon that meant not only a greatly increased college student body, but a vastly expanded faculty as well; the rise in importance of the professionally trained scientific expert in business and government settings; the development of new industries requiring many employees with advanced degrees in chemistry, physics, and mathematics; the invention of the LP record, thus stimulating the dissemination of classical music on a numerically broad basis; the coming to America of the foreign art film displayed in metropolitan and university centers; the expansion of the market for serious books and periodicals; and many others of an allied nature. Their cumulative effect was to expand greatly the number of people intellectually trained and oriented, and to stimulate the development of institutions that began to give intellectual life in America a sociological format and setting of its own. In other words, there began to be created an intellectual subsociety,[21] the main bastion of which was the world of the academy, but which also included enclaves of people in the various performing arts.

Within this larger subsociety of intellectuals the various smaller groups may have particular concerns, but they tend to share the same communications media and reference groups. *The New York Times*, daily, and even more particularly, the Sunday edition, is the national newspaper of the intellectuals. "More than half the college presidents in the U.S. read the *Times*, and it circulates to virtually every university and college library," writes Roger Kahn in a recent article on that venerable journalistic phenomenon.

> The *Times* is The Paper of The Arts and The Intellectual Community. [sic] It staffs a distinct Cultural Affairs Department, with 40 men and women, and it considers Isaac Stern's purchase of a new Guarnerius as news worth two-thirds of a column on a busy day. Most of its critics are scorned, disliked, patronized, cursed and sometimes faintly cheered. Nonetheless, they are critics of the *Times*. No one else can so powerfully influence the life and death of a play, the reputation of a conductor, the success of a prodigy's debut.[22]

Magazines in the homes of intellectuals, apart from professional journals, tend to be selected from such as *Harper's, The Atlantic Monthly, The New Yorker, The Reporter, Commentary, The Saturday Review, Daedalus, Consumer Reports, The Nation, The New Republic, Partisan Review*, and a few others. Thus, while intellectuals in their status and the ordinary amenities of life-style tend to be upper middle class, they have a particular orientation that is peculiar to them as intellectuals and separates them from other upper middle class members in way of life and social interaction.

In the world or subsociety of the intellectual, ethnicity is not a very relevant issue either in structural or cultural terms.[23] It is in these circles, I would maintain, that considerable primary group interaction takes place across ethnic lines, interfaith marriage is common, and the real melting pot in American life emerges.

While it is not uncommon for such intellectuals to take a nostalgic interest in their particular ethnic background, considerations of religion, national origin, or even race are not the main criteria for choices in dining companions, inter-home visiting, social cliquing, or (race excepted) courtship. Moreover, there is reason to believe that many intellectuals have an awareness of themselves as a distinct group—a group even somewhat alienated from the larger society. Thus Jan Hajda's analysis of survey data on over 2,000 native-born graduate students in twenty-five American universities found that 47 percent defined themselves as intellectuals. This proportion was as high as 53 percent of students in the humanities. About two-thirds of the entire student group gave evidence of a feeling of alienation from the larger society, and Hajda further found that:

> alienation, coupled with intellectual orientation, is generally characteristic of those who expect to stay in the academic world after graduation. . . . The alienated intellectuals among graduate students are persons committed more or less exclusively to the academic community. They are most prone to regard the larger society as anti-intellectual; to have no religious affiliation, or merely formal church membership; to have less intense attachment to their parental families than other students; to have few if any friends from high school days. Their personal career is marked by dissent from religious traditions in which they were reared and by a history of conflict with parental authority. The only non-academic organization that sometimes commands their loyalty is a liberal political movement.[24]

In this newly emerging subsociety of the intellectual, the Jew is no longer a guest. He is, quite to the contrary, a prominent and well-recognized element in its leadership structure and a significantly large and well integrated segment of its rank and file. Creative writers such as Norman Mailer, Saul Bellow, Bernard Malamud, and Philip Roth are at the very crest of the wave of American fiction that surfaced after World War II; literary critics such as Alfred Kazin, Norman Podhoretz, and Theodore Solatoroff assess the world of letters from positions of well-recognized eminence; and social commentators such as David Riesman, Daniel Bell, Lewis Coser, and Max Lerner are household names in those households where serious ideas are seriously discussed. All these men, to my knowledge, are Jews. In fact, the salience (I consciously avoid the word "dominance" here, since it contains connotations that are distinctly not in order) of Jews in American intellectual life occasioned from the writer of a recent semi-serious essay in *The New York Times Magazine* entitled, "Notes on Cult; or, How to Join the Intellectual Establishment," the wry remark, "Rumors to the contrary notwithstanding, you don't have to be Jewish to be an intellectual."[25] And at lesser levels of popular eminence the interlocking worlds of academic life, scientific research, and the creative and performing arts now have such widespread Jewish participation as to make such participation routine and unnoteworthy.

By the foregoing I do not mean to imply that the subsociety of the intellectual is fully developed in all its potential lineaments. Many age-graded organizations and institutional structures present in the standard subsocieties of America are not yet present in the social world of the intellectual, and perhaps many of them, for reasons peculiar to the nature of the intellectual's makeup, never will be. Furthermore, full subsocietal development signifies a degree of self-recognition *as such* (that is, as a subsociety) and recognition by members of other subsocieties that has not yet been achieved, although the dichotomous terms "town and gown" and the separation of social life that the phrase implies carry overtones of such recognition. It is possible that the rudimentary nature of this identificational aspect poses more problems for the children of intellectuals than for their parents, particularly for those families without formal religious affiliation. When little Johnnie, in such a family, comes home and queries, "Daddy, Freddie says he's a Protestant, Susie says she's a Catholic, and Michael says he's a Jew; what am I?" it is unlikely that Daddy can or will settle the matter meaningfully for his son by replying, "Why, Johnnie, you're an intellectual!"

One of the results of the rise of the intellectual subsociety in America is that many intellectuals—perhaps a large majority— become alienated from their ethnic subsocieties of origin. This is not, it should be noted, the same thing as saying that they have become detached from the ongoing functional concerns and processes of American society as a whole. Quite the contrary is the case. There has probably never been a time when American intellectuals have taken such an active part in major party politics, in consultant and high and middle level executive roles in government, and even in the operation of large business concerns, which increasingly draw upon the research skills of highly trained professionals both in production and marketing. But the everyday concerns of the ethnic community and the bustling organizational life that provide the institutional setting for the community's activities function without the participation of those intellectuals who have now found a comfortable milieu elsewhere and for whom the issues and life of ethnic communality are extremely peripheral.[26] For no major ethnic group in America is this problem greater than for the Jews, whose percentage of young people who go on to college and graduate school (and thus become exposed to the existence and attractions of the intellectual subsociety) is extraordinarily high. "One of the first things I discovered," writes Marion K. Sanders in a recent article in *Harper's* reporting on her informal study of Jewish communal life across the nation, "is that Jewish activists worry mightily about the flight of the intellectuals." And her own reception by Jewish communal leaders indicates that this flight is viewed by them more with puzzled hurt than with anger. "I was not prepared," she relates, "to be everywhere welcomed as a prodigal daughter, as a member of the 'Jewish intelligentsia' who had 'come home.' "[27]

The flight of the Jewish intellectual in America from Jewish communal participation and specifically Jewish concerns (I purposefully do not say "flight from Jewish identity"—at least in its minimal form—since I know very few academic Jews who deny that they are Jewish) is by no means complete. *Commentary's* famous symposium on "Jewishness and The Younger Intellectuals," just a few years ago, which overwhelmingly revealed an estrangement on the part of its participants from Jewish communal life and its characteristic issues and ideologies,[28] was followed, perhaps pointedly, in the same year by a symposium in the quarterly journal *Judaism* (published by the American Jewish Congress) in which a group of Jewish intellectuals, drawn largely but not exclusively from the academic world, expressed a constellation of views much closer in feeling and content to the spirit of the symposium title: "My Jewish Affirmation."[29] Moreover, in one town with which I am familiar, a number of Jewish academics drawn largely from the university situated there have together with their families formed a local Jewish community organization that meets periodically to discuss intellectual topics of Jewish and general concern and sponsors an occasional Jewish holiday party that includes the children. Thus it is clear that there are some Jewish academicians who wish to retain some sense of group identity as Jews and some relationship to specific Jewish values either for the benefit of themselves or their children, or both.

The general picture, then, appears to be one in which increasingly large numbers of Jewish intellectuals find themselves drawn by common intellectual and aesthetic interests and by professional activities and concerns into the buildup of the new, intellectual subsociety in America. They seem to find themselves sociologically and psychologically reasonably comfortable there, while a smaller number (which participates in the intellectual subsociety also) has, or searches for, more explicit ties to Jewish communal life and Jewish culture. In either case the problems of marginality for the Jewish intellectual have clearly been considerably reduced. The eventual outcome in communal and identificational terms for later generations of Jewish intellectuals cannot now be forseen and, in part, depends on the general outcome in the development of the total intellectual subsociety. That outcome itself, however, will be shaped in part by whatever efforts, or lack of such, the ethnic subsocieties themselves make to institute an effective dialogue with and contribute to the intellectual subsociety and more especially to their own ethnic members. To date such efforts on the part of the Jewish ethnic community in relation to Jewish intellectuals do not appear to have been either substantial or particularly effective. When a firstrate writer such as Philip Roth is taken to task by some members of the organized Jewish community for his portrayal of Jewish characters in his fiction—a portrayal that many intellectuals, at least, would regard as varied, thoughtful, and conforming to the highest standards of artistic integrity—and when Roth himself rephrases the charge with rueful and elegant irony as, "I had told the Gentiles what apparently it would otherwise have been possible to keep secret from them: that the perils of human nature afflict the members of our minority,"[30] then the gap in basic assumptions and basic thought processes that exists between some parts of ethnic communal life and the intellectual is revealed as clearly and poignantly as it could be by any learned study. It is this gap that needs to be bridged if the no-longer marginal Jewish intellectual is to be able to draw current sustenance from Jewish communal life and culture and, in turn, contribute to the continuing development of his ancestral tradition.

NOTES

1. See Robert E. Park, "Human Migration and the Marginal Man," *American Journal of Sociology*, Vol. 33, No. 6 (May 1928), pp. 881–93; and Everett V. Stonequist, "The Problem of the Marginal Man," *American Journal of Sociology*, Vol. 41, No. 1 (July 1935), pp. 1–12; and *The Marginal Man* (New York: Scribner's, 1937). Later discussions include Arnold W. Green, "A Re-examination of the Marginal Man Concept," *Social Forces*, Vol. 26, No. 2 (December 1947), pp. 167–71; Everett C. Hughes, "Social Change and Status Protest: An Essay on the Marginal Man," *Phylon*, Vol. 10, No. 1 (First Quarter, 1949), pp. 58–65; David Riesman, *Individualism Reconsidered* (New York: Free Press, 1954), pp. 153–78; David I. Golovensky, "The Marginal Man Concept; an Analysis and Critique," *Social Forces*, Vol. 30, No. 3 (March 1952), pp. 333–39; and Aaron Antonovsky, "Toward a Refinement of the 'Marginal Man' Concept," *Social Forces*, Vol. 35, No. 1 (October 1956), pp. 57–62.

2. For a discussion of these concepts, see Milton M. Gordon, *Assimilation in American Life* (New York: Oxford University Press, 1964), pp. 19–59.

3. See Georg Simmel's discussion of "The Stranger," in *The Sociology of Georg Simmel*, Kurt H. Wolf, trans., and ed. (Glencoe, Ill.: The Free Press, 1950), pp. 402–408; and David Riesman, *Individualism Reconsidered* (New York: Free Press, 1954), pp. 153–78.

4. See Gordon, *op. cit., passim.*

5. See Will Herberg, *Protestant-Catholic-Jew* (New York: Doubleday, 1955).

6. W. Lloyd Warner and Leo Srole, *The Social Systems of American Ethnic Groups* (New Haven: Yale University Press, 1945); W. Lloyd Warner and Associates, *Democracy in Jonesville* (New York: Harper, 1949), pp. 168–192.

7. See August B. Hollingshead, "Trends in Social Stratification: A Case Study," *American Sociological Review*, Vol. 17, No. 6 (December 1952), pp. 685–86.

8. E. Digby Baltzell, *Philadelphia Gentlemen* (New York: Free Press, 1958), pp. 273–91.

9. Judith R. Kramer and Seymour Leventman, *Children of the Gilded Ghetto* (New Haven and London: Yale University Press, 1961).

10. This parallels my distinction between cultural assimilation and structural assimilation in the model of "assimilation variables" presented in *Assimilation in American Life*. See, particularly, pp. 70–71.

11. See *Assimilation in American Life*, pp. 51–59.

12. Oscar Handlin, *Adventure in Freedom* (New York: McGraw-Hill, 1954); E. Digby Baltzell, *loc. cit.;* Nathan Glazer, *American Judaism* (Chicago: University of Chicago Press, 1957).

13. Nathan Glazer, *op. cit.;* Marshall Sklare, *Conservative Judaism* (New York: Free Press, 1955).

14. Stanley K. Bigman, *The Jewish Population of Greater Washington in 1956* (Washington, D.C.: The Jewish Community Council of Greater

Washington, May 1957); cited in Albert I. Gordon, *Intermarriage* (Boston: Beacon, 1964), p. 206.

15. Lewis Coser, *Men of Ideas* (New York: Free Press, 1965), vii.

16. There is, I believe, good reason for doing so. Not all people who have the intellect that gives them a serious interest in ideas and the arts and who participate in the intellectual milieu are "critical" of society in Coser's sense.

17. Milton M. Gordon, "Social Class and American Intellectuals," *American Association of University Professors Bulletin*, Vol. 40, No. 4 (Winter 1954–55), pp. 518–19.

18. Milton M. Gordon, *Assimilation in American Life*, pp. 224–25.

19. *Men of Ideas, op. cit.* From a somewhat different point of view the historian Christopher Lasch has also dealt with the rise of "the intellectual as a social type," the subtitle of his *The New Radicalism in America, 1889–1963* (New York: Knopf, 1965).

20. *Assimilation in American Life*, p. 228. See also, "Social Class and American Intellectuals," *op. cit.*, p. 526.

21. See *Assimilation in American Life*, pp. 224–32.

22. Roger Kahn, "The House of Adolph Ochs," *Saturday Evening Post*, October 9, 1965, p. 33.

23. See Charles H. Anderson, *The Intellectual Subsociety: An Empirical Test*, Ph.D. Dissertation, University of Massachusetts, 1966, carried out under the direction of this writer.

24. Jan Hajda, "Alienation and Integration of Student Intellectuals," *American Sociological Review*, Vol. 26, No. 5 (October 1961), pp. 758–77. The quotations are from pages 772 and 775 respectively.

25. Victor S. Navasky, "Notes on Cult; or, How to Join the Intellectual Establishment," *The New York Times Magazine*, March 27, 1966, p. 29.

26. To be sure, the "actively ethnic intellectual" participates in ethnic communality and often in leadership roles. However, it is at least a plausible hypothesis that their number is diminishing and that the pull of the intellectual subsociety becomes increasingly strong for those individuals with intellectual interests and inclinations.

27. Marion K. Sanders, "The Several Worlds of American Jews," *Harper's Magazine* (April 1966), p. 54.

28. "Jewishness and The Younger Intellectuals: A Symposium," *Commentary*, Vol. 31, No. 4 (April 1961), pp. 306–59.

29. "Symposium: My Jewish Affirmation," *Judaism: A Quarterly Journal of Jewish Life and Thought*, Vol. 10, No. 4 (1961), pp. 291–352.

30. Philip Roth, "Writing About Jews," *Commentary*, Vol. 36, No. 6 (December 1963), p. 450.

Epilogue

LESTER DRENTLUSS, A JEWISH BOY FROM BALTIMORE, ATTEMPTS TO MAKE IT THROUGH THE SUMMER OF 1967

CALVIN TRILLIN

ALTHOUGH Lester Drentluss, the mildly promising New York editor, held a party celebrating Israel's military victory and modestly accepted congratulations at the door, he was not someone who had become militantly Jewish only when it became clear that the Israeli armies had crushed the combined might of the Arab world. Lester had detected a fashion for Jewishness in his own world several years before, when Yiddish words began to appear in the conversation of his firm's chief editor, Douglas Drake, a Methodist minister's son from Eau Claire, Wisconsin. "There's no use trying to sell books to the *goyim*," Drake had said one day as he announced his decision to devote 90 percent of the firm's advertising budget to a historical novel based on the saga of the first Jewish frogman.

"But why would he put down his own majority group?" Lester asked later, when he had learned from Drake's secretary, an Irish girl from Queens, that *goyim* means gentiles.

The secretary shrugged. "Everybody's got his own *mishogas*," she said.

Although Lester was Jewish, he felt left out. ("It means 'craziness,'" the secretary added impatiently, anxious to get back to her copy of *Exodus*.) His family had been in Baltimore, Maryland, for five generations, and his parents were so militantly Americanized that he had once been spanked for doing an imitation of Al Jolson in *The Jazz Singer*. Whenever his mother heard anything that sounded as if it might be Yiddish, she immediately said, "Well, I'm sure I don't know what that means"—a habit that was so ingrained that she once blurted out "Well, I'm sure I don't know what that means" after a brother-in-law she suspected of overt Jewishness told her he wanted to keep a bit of gossip "*entre nous.*"

At the first word of Yiddish from Douglas Drake, Lester decided to reappraise his own ethnic situation; Drake was known as a trend-spotter. Soon Lester began to spot some signs of a trend himself—a boom in Jewish novels here, a Jewish Lord Mayor of Dublin there. He noticed an increasing use of Jewish mothers by comedians and of Jewish advisers by politicians. Scotch-Irish professors seemed undisturbed about being included in the category of "Jewish intellectuals." The gentile movie stars who failed to convert to Judaism repented by donating their talents to Bonds for Israel benefits. The subway graffiti had begun to include phrases like "Medea Is a Yenta" and "Kafka Is a Kvetch." Lester's final decision came in February, 1965, while he was reading an article in *Life* magazine about Robert Lowell, the New England poet. "Do I feel left-out in a Jewish age?" Lowell was quoted as saying. "Not at all. Fortunately, I'm one-eighth Jewish myself, which I do feel is a saving grace." Lester decided that the day a Boston Lowell bragged about being Jewish was the day a Baltimore Drentluss ought to let it be known that he was at least eight times as Jewish as Robert Lowell.

That night, he tried out his Jewishness tentatively on Rosemary Higgins, a willowy blonde on whom he had been trying things out tentatively for six months with little success. "I think it's rather ironic that America's Everyman might turn out to be Herzog instead of some *goy,*" he said to Rosemary as they had wine and gefilte fish at the apartment of Lemuel Scroggins, the Southern Populist poet.

"The Jewish sensibility is really rather unique," Rosemary said.

"Thank you very much," Lester said, trying to shrug his shoulders in the manner of Menasha Skulnik. "Nice of you to say so."

Gradually, Lester began to tell self-deprecating stories about the quaintly domineering mother who had raised him on love and chicken soup with kreplach (his mother, in fact, had only tasted kreplach once, at the home of a poor relation, and had taken pains to compliment the hostess on the lightness of her won tons). He published a short literary-quarterly article called "The Schlemiel

as Hero in American Literature." He complained often of heartburn.

Robert Lowell had been right; it was a Jewish world. At work,
Lester's colleagues seemed to take a new interest in his opinions
on which Jewish novel to publish each month. At the fashionable
bagels-and-lox brunches given by Lemuel Scroggins on Sundays,
Lester began to feel more a part of the conversation. Scroggins
phoned to invite him almost every week—usually adding that he
should "bring along that lil' ole blond *shiksa* Rosemary." Lester's
acquaintances began to assume that Rosemary was his to bring
along; she often confided to the girls in the group that the most
exciting men were "Mediterranean types." Lester also suspected
that he was communicating better with Wash Jefferson, the
group's favorite Negro. "Don't think I don't understand your
suffering, Wash," he said to Jefferson just after the Selma march.
"We've all been down that road."

"You sure are a sensitive mother," Jefferson said.

Lester's only problem was his parents, who decided to pay him
a visit when his letters began to take on a disturbingly ethnic
tone. "Well, I'm sure I don't know what that means," his mother
had said after Lester called his gouging landlord a *goniff* while
showing his parents through the apartment. "You certainly didn't
pick up language like that at home, I can tell you that."

Lester's father, who had seemed calmer than his wife at first,
suddenly accused his son of learning Yiddish at Berlitz, an idea
that had actually occurred to Lester at one point before he finally
prevailed upon Douglas Drake's secretary to help him with his
Yiddish during lunch hours.

"I thought you might like to see *Fiddler on the Roof* tonight,"
Lester said, trying to re-establish a friendly atmosphere as he
passed his mother a drink and a plate of cocktail blintzes. "They
say it manages to convey some of the tradition of humor and
suffering that all of us carry from the ghetto."

"What ghetto!" his mother said. She began to cry.

"I'm surprised at you, talking to your mother like that," Mr.
Drentluss said. "Don't the traditions of our people mean anything
to you, Lester—five generations in Baltimore, a law firm full of
gentiles? How can you flout your own heritage?"

"But people change in America," Lester said. "Frankly, Dad,
the old traditions are mostly a lot of *mishogas*."

"I'm sure I don't know what that means," his mother said,

between sobs. "I'm only thankful that your grandparents aren't alive to see this."

For his Israeli Victory Party, Lester had tried to rent Yonah Schimmel's Knishery, and then decided to settle for his own apartment. He and Rosemary arranged a magnificent display of food; Lemuel Scroggins said it looked like "the Great Bar Mitzvah in the Sky."

"*Mazel tov*," Douglas Drake said when he came in. "It's a great day, even though the Ringling Brothers–Barnum & Bailey Tent Fire Disaster of 1944 has erupted in my chest."

"With me it's felt like the Coconut Grove fire since that lunch," Lester said. He and Drake often compared heartburn symptoms, and both were suffering from a huge lunch celebrating Lester's triumph in landing a blockbuster book that every publisher had been after—a first-person account by the only Jewish-American dentist to take part in the Sinai Campaign. Rosemary, clinging to Lester's bicep, told Drake that the company should do a follow-up book on the tradition of ferocity in the Mediterranean fighting man. Lester shrugged.

Just three or four weeks after the Victory Party, during a period when Lester was in the habit of humming "*Havanagilah*" in the elevators, he was surprised and disturbed to read that an officer of the Student Nonviolent Coordinating Committee had made a speech complaining about Zionist aggression and "Jew storekeepers." Two or three Episcopal priests of Lester's acquaintance resigned from SNCC in protest, and some of his Jewish friends endorsed the statement and asked forgiveness. Lester was confused. A few days later, he overheard somebody at a Lemuel Scroggins brunch say that Jewish storekeepers in the ghetto were more at fault for the summer riots than anybody, with the possible exception of Jewish liberals. Lester thought at first that it might have been an isolated incident, but then Douglas Drake, with ominous enthusiasm, asked him to read the manuscript of a black nationalist book called *Can the Jews Atone for Everything on the Day of Atonement?* Moved by the manuscript, Lester phoned Wash Jefferson to apologize.

"I don't blame you," he said to Jefferson.

"Don't blame me for what, man?" Jefferson asked. "Did you get blackballed at one of those clubs I put you up for?"

"I don't blame you for hating me," Lester said.

"I don't hate you, Goldberg," Jefferson said.

"My name is Drentluss."

"You Jews sure are sensitive mothers," Jefferson said.

Lester stopped humming in the elevators. "I don't know what this storekeeper business has to do with you," his mother wrote him when she heard he was depressed. "Your people have been professional men for three generations." Lester was surprised to find himself slightly cheered up by his mother's letter; his relatives were innocent, and he himself could hardly be accused of exploiting the ghetto when he had never been there. A week later, his spirits dropped again when he was not included in a Scroggins brunch honoring some people who had participated in a seminar called "Black Power, the Third World and the Exploiters." Rosemary went, and reported that Lemuel, who had formerly spoken of Negroes as "them poor downtrodden *schwartzas* in Alabama," was beginning to talk about "black people"—whether he was referring to his cleaning lady, Hazel M. Jones, or to Colonel Gamal Abdel Nasser.

One night, late in the summer, Douglas Drake, who no longer seemed to be suffering from heartburn, came to Lester's apartment to drop off a rush manuscript on the agonies of the Palestine refugees. As Drake walked in, Rosemary looked up from a magazine article on the Israeli occupation of Old Jerusalem and asked Lester if he thought it was wise for non-Christians to have control over Christian shrines.

"I don't know much about it," Lester said.

"It's hard to understand why they won't at least give back the West Bank of the Jordan," Drake said. "After all that napalm they dropped on it, it can't be worth much anyway."

"They're a strange people," Lester said. "They surely are." He couldn't understand why Drake seemed to hold him personally responsible for what Jews did in Jordan; his family had been in Baltimore for five generations.

Rosemary looked up from her magazine again. "I think Moshe Dayan might have too much *chutzpah* for his own good," she said.

Drake smiled at Lester knowingly.

Lester looked puzzled. "*Chutzpah?*" he said. "I don't think I know what that means."

About the Contributors

Daniel Aaron is Mary Augusta Jordan Professor of English Language and Literature at Smith College. His many books include *Men of Good Hope* (1951), *America in Crisis* (1952), *The United States*, with Richard Hofstader and W. Miller (1957), *Emerson: A Modern Anthology*, with Alfred Kazin (1959), and *Writers on the Left* (1961).

E. Digby Baltzell is Professor of Sociology at the University of Pennsylvania. His studies of the American class system include *Philadelphia Gentleman* (1958) and *The Protestant Establishment* (1964).

Daniel Bell, Professor of Sociology at Columbia University, is the author of the widely acclaimed *Reforming of General Education* (1966). Among his other books are *Work and Its Discontents* (1956), *The End of Ideology* (1960), and *The Radical Right* (1963).

Zena Smith Blau is Senior Research Associate at the Institute for Juvenile Research in Chicago. She has published widely in academic journals.

Daniel J. Elazar teaches political science at Temple University. He is the author of *The Defeat of Metropolitan Integration* (1961), *The American Partnership* (1962), and *American Federalism: A View from the States* (1966).

Milton M. Gordon is Professor of Sociology at the University of Massachusetts, Amherst, and is the author of *Social Class in American Sociology* (1958) and *Assimilation in American Life* (1964).

Irving Greenberg is Rabbi of the Riverdale Jewish Center in New York City and Associate Professor of History at Yeshiva University.

Allen Guttmann teaches English and American Studies at Amherst College. He is the author of *The Wound in the Heart: America and the Spanish Civil War* (1962) and *The Conservative Tradition in America* (1967).

Milton Himmelfarb is a Contributing Editor to *Commentary Magazine*. Since 1958 he has also been editor of *The American Jewish Yearbook*.

501

Mordecai M. Kaplan is the founder of the Reconstructionist Movement and is author of *Judaism as a Civilization* (1934), *The Future of the American Jew* (1948), *Judaism without Supernaturalism* (1958) and many other studies of Jewish belief and practice. He is currently teaching at the University of Judaism in Los Angeles.

Alfred Kazin holds the chair of Distinguished Professor of Literature at the State University of New York, Stony Brook. He is the author of *On Native Grounds* (1942), *A Walker in the City* (1951), and *Starting Out in the Thirties* (1965) and is editor of books on Fitzgerald and Melville and co-editor of studies of Dreiser and Emerson.

Milton R. Konvitz is Professor of Industrial and Labor Relations and Professor of Law at Cornell University. His many books on civil liberties include *The Alien and the Asiatic in American Law* (1946), *The Constitution and Civil Rights* (1947), *Civil Rights in Immigration* (1953), *The Bill of Rights Reader* (1954), *Fundamental Liberties of a Free People* (1957), *A Century of Civil Rights* (1961), *The First Amendment Freedoms* (1963), and *Expanding Liberties* (1966).

Seymour Leventman teaches sociology at Boston College. With Judith Kramer, he is co-author of *Children of the Gilded Ghetto* (1961).

S. M. Lipset is Professor of Government and of Social Relations at Harvard University and Research Associate in the Center for International Affairs. His books include *Agrarian Socialism* (1950), *Union Democracy* (1956), *Social Mobility in Industrial Society* (1959), *Political Man* (1960), and *The First New Nation* (1963). He is also editor and co-editor of numerous books including *The Berkeley Student Revolt* (1965), *Class, Status and Power* (Revised, 1966), and *Elites in Latin America* (1967).

Jakob J. Petuchowski is Professor of Rabbinics at Hebrew Union College-Jewish Institute of Religion in Cincinnati. Author of *Ever Since Sinai: A Modern View of the Torah* (1961), his most recent work is the *Reform of the Prayer Book: The Liturgy of European Liberal and Reform Judaism* (1968).

Solomon Poll, an ordained rabbi with a Ph.D. from the University of Pennsylvania, teaches sociology at the University of New Hampshire. He is the author of *The Hasidic Community of Williamsburg* (1962).

PETER I. ROSE is Professor and Chairman of the Department of Sociology and Anthropology at Smith College and a member of the Graduate Faculty of the University of Massachusetts, Amherst. His books include *They and We* (1964), *The Study of Society* (1967), *The Subject Is Race* (1968), and *Americans from Africa* (1969). He is currently editing a series of volumes on American ethnic groups.

STUART E. ROSENBERG is Rabbi of the Beth Tzedec Congregation in Toronto, Canada. He is the author of *The Jewish Community in Rochester 1843-1925* (1954), *Man Is Free* (1957), *The Road of Confidence* (1959), *A Time to Speak* (1960), and *America is Different: The Making of the American Jew* (1963).

PHILIP ROTH is one of America's leading novelists. His books include the prize-winning *Goodbye, Columbus* (1959), *Letting Go* (1962), and *When She Was Good* (1967). Mr. Roth has taught at the University of Iowa, Princeton University, the University of Pennsylvania, and the State University of New York, Stony Brook.

LOUIS RUCHAMES is Professor and Chairman of the Department of History at the University of Massachusetts, Boston, and former Adviser to Jewish Students at Amherst and Smith College and the University of Massachusetts, Amherst. Rabbi, sociologist, and historian, he is the author of *Race, Jobs and Politics: The Story of the FEPC* (1953) and editor of *The John Brown Reader* (1959) and *The Abolitionists* (1963).

SEYMOUR SIEGEL, an officer of the Rabbinical Assembly of America, teaches Talmudic Studies at the Jewish Theological Seminary of America in New York City.

MARSHALL SKLARE was, for many years, Director of the Institute of Human Relations, American Jewish Committee. He is now Professor of Sociology at Yeshiva University. His books include *Conservative Judaism* (1955) and *The Jews: Social Patterns of an American Group* (1958). He is presently completing work on a study of Jewish life in America.

B. Z. SOBEL is Assistant Professor of Sociology at Brandeis University. He has published widely on the sociology of Jewish life and on intergroup relations. His articles have appeared in the *Journal for the Scientific Study of Religion, Midstream, Dialogue,* and others.

MAY L. SOBEL teaches history at Boston University. She is a doctoral candidate at Columbia University where she is completing a dissertation on utopianism and religious change.

RODNEY STARK is a Research Sociologist at the University of California, Berkeley. He is co-author, with Charles Y. Glock, of *Religion and Society in Tension* (1965) and of *Christian Beliefs and Anti-Semitism* (1966).

STEPHEN STEINBERG is a Research Sociologist at the University of California, Berkeley. He is currently completing a book with Gertrude J. Selznick on the causes and extent of anti-Semitism in America.

KENNETH STERN teaches philosophy at Smith College. He is a regular contributor to such journals as *Mind, Analysis, The Journal of Philosophy*, and *Philosophical Studies*. He is completing a book on *Philosophy and Common Sense*.

CALVIN TRILLIN is a staff writer for *The New Yorker Magazine* and author of *An Education in Georgia*. His articles and short stories also appear frequently in other magazines.

MELVIN M. TUMIN, Professor of Sociology and Anthropology at Princeton University, is the author and editor of many books on social stratification and intergroup relations. Included among his works are *Caste in a Peasant Society* (1952), *Social Class and Social Change in Puerto Rico* (1960), *Desegregation* (1958), *An Inventory and Evaluation of Research and Theory in Anti-Semitism* (1960), and *Social Stratification: The Forms and Functions of Inequality* (1967).

SHERWIN WINE is Rabbi of the Birmingham Temple in Birmingham, Michigan. He is editor of the new quarterly, *Humanistic Judaism*, and a frequent contributor to journals of religion and philosophy.

DENNIS H. WRONG is Professor of Sociology at New York University. The author of *Population and Society* (Revised, 1967) and co-editor of *Readings in Introductory Sociology* (1967), he is a frequent contributor to *Commentary* and other journals of opinion.

DATE DUE

9/29/69			
OCT 30 1969			
MAY 1 2 1973			
GAYLORD			PRINTED IN U.S.A.